PRAYERS
OF THE BIBLE

PRAYERS
OF THE BIBLE

366 Devotionals to Encourage Your Prayer Life

GORDON J. KEDDIE

Crown & Covenant
PUBLICATIONS

Crown & Covenant Publications
7408 Penn Avenue
Pittsburgh, Pa. 15208
crownandcovenant.com

ISBN: 978-1-943017-11-9
Gift Edition: 978-1-943017-15-7
eBook: 978-1-943017-14-0
Library of Congress Control Number: 2017955863

Printed in the United States of America

To the praying people of the Reformed Presbyterian congregations of State College, Pennsylvania, and Southside Indianapolis, Indiana, in grateful remembrance of their faithfulness and encouragement in thirty years of ministry among them

Foreword

In future generations, should the Lord have tarried, there is little doubt that church historians will be fascinated with our present time. One can imagine a study of American evangelicals in the 21st century, seeking to understand the conduct of Christians at a time when society was collapsing. So many things would commend our churches today! A future historian will marvel at the wealth of Bible study materials, the energy devoted to church planting and evangelism, coupled with a continuing fervor for world missions. How could these Christians have experienced so little cultural influence? But then, turning to the subject of prayer, the historian will place his finger on the telling statistic. While the powers of darkness swirled around the church, were Christians gathering for prayer, calling on the Lord to defend his Word and convert the lost? Did Christians make private prayer a lynchpin of their spirituality? Was there a great movement of the people of God in calling down the power of heaven in a desperate hour? In any sober assessment, the future historian will conclude that the shocking neglect of prayer undermined the efforts of our generation of believers. He will note how the prayer meeting largely disappeared from the life of otherwise devoted congregations, how our prayerlessness marked a fascination with the things of the world and indicated a reliance on our own strength. Written largely over the calamity of our times, surely a studious historian will see the words of the apostle James: "You do not have because you do not ask" (James 4:2).

The crisis of prayer in our present churches sufficiently commends Gordon Keddie's book of devotionals on this topic. What a treasure we find within these pages! Here, a seasoned and zealous pastor records for us a lifetime of reflections on this most valued topic, offering encouragement and guides to the practice of prayer. Married couples who find prayer neglected in their homes may take up this book and find inspiration for a rekindling of the family altar. Pastors, especially, will be greatly helped in the improvement of church prayer meetings. Jehoshaphat, against an earlier assault on the church, summoned God's people for prayer: "all Judah stood before the LORD, with their little ones, their wives, and their children" (2 Chron. 20:13). In answer, God spoke to him words for which we should long: "Do not be afraid and do not be dismayed at this great horde, for the battle is not yours but God's" (2 Chron. 20:15). In *Prayers of the Bible*, Gordon Keddie likewise summons Christians to the throne of grace "that we may receive mercy and find grace to help in time of need" (Heb. 4:16).

Those who are struggling with prayer should turn to the prayers of the Bible as a model and guide. In the Bible, there is no better place for this than the Psalms, which God has given to shape and lead us in prayer. The Psalms are prayers inspired by the Holy Spirit, and it is a useful practice to conclude your morning devotions by praying through one of the Psalms, a habit by which I have been blessed and helped for many years.

Psalm 5 is especially valuable as a general model for prayer. We are not told its circumstances, so it functions as a generic prayer showing how we should approach God, how we can expect to be heard by him, and what we can expect when we pray. A brief consideration of Psalm 5 will commend the devotionals found in this volume.

> First, prayer is coming to God (Ps. 5:1-3). David begins: "Give ear to my words, O LORD; consider my groaning. Give attention to the sound of my cry, my King and my God, for to you do I pray" (Ps. 5:1-2). Here, we are reminded that prayer is not the soul speaking within itself. Prayer has a recipient in God. Many Christians emphasize the value of a prayer partner, yet true prayer always has a partner in the triune God. The Father lovingly receives and encourages his children in prayer (Luke 11:13); the Son intercedes for our prayers by means of his effectual mediation (Rom. 8:34); and "the Spirit helps us in our weakness" (Rom. 8:26). Since prayer is gaining an audience with God for worship, communion, and supplication, let me suggest that the extent of our preparation indicates whether we consider prayer a real encounter with the living God. David compares his praying to the way a priest arranges his sacrifices on the altar in careful accord with God's Word: "in the morning I prepare a sacrifice for you and watch" (Ps. 5:3).

> Second, David sees adoration as the primary matter in prayer (Ps. 5:4-6). "For you are not a God who delights in wickedness; evil may not dwell with you," he begins (Ps. 5:4), going on to exalt the Lord's righteousness against all evil. In a psalm of twelve verses, David does not present a single request until verse 8—more than half of the psalm is coming to God and

worshiping him! Our chief aim in prayer likewise should be to bring glory to God in corporate and personal devotion.

> Third, we notice David's awareness of his own sin as an affront to God's holiness. He shows us that prayer must therefore reckon with sin: "But I, through the abundance of your steadfast love, will enter your house. I will bow down toward your holy temple in the fear of you" (Ps. 5:7). Here, at the center of Psalm 5, David appeals to the covenant mercy of the Lord. Bowing down toward God's temple, he places his faith in the atoning sacrifices offered there for sin, anticipating the great fulfillment in the cross of Christ. Here, we find, is what makes prayer "work"! Not a precise formula of words, not some painful discipline, not many words or an elaborate display before God, but God's faithful covenant love through the blood of Christ is what makes prayer succeed. God answers our prayers not because we get prayer right, but because in his loving mercy he receives and answers the prayers of his people as they trust in the redeeming blood of his Son.

> Fourth, having come to God in adoration and with faith in Christ, prayer involves making bold requests in confidence of God's help (Ps. 5:8-12). David asks the Lord for guidance: "Lead me, O LORD, in your righteousness because of my enemies; make your way straight before me" (Ps. 5:8). He pleads further for God to protect him from enemies: "Make them bear their guilt, O God; let them fall by their own counsels; because of the abundance of their transgressions cast them out, for they have rebelled against you" (Ps. 5:10). Finally, David prays for God's blessing on the righteous: "But let all who take refuge in you rejoice; let them ever sing for joy, and spread your protection over them, that those who love your name may exult in you" (Ps. 5:11). David's concluding confidence, grounded in his knowledge of God and his faithful ways, should inspire us to the value of prayer: "For you bless the righteous, O LORD; you cover him with favor as with a shield" (Ps. 5:12).

In all the ways that David considers prayer in Psalm 5, Christians will receive a great help in the pages of this book. Prayer calls us to know the God before whom we come, and Gordon Keddie's devotions are filled with teaching on the person and work of God in his three Persons. To pray, we must consider sin and ground our hope in Christ, whose ministry and saving blessings sprout in these pages like flowers along the pathway of prayer. To pray we must be bold in making godly requests of the Lord, being confident in the certainty of his loving care and wise provision. Perhaps most valuably, the studies in this book will aid us in preparing for our prayer meetings and prayer lives, following David's example in arranging his appeals before he enters into the Lord's presence.

For many years, I have anticipated each publication from the heart and pen of Gordon Keddie. Having first met him in the pages of his valuable commentaries, I have briefly enjoyed personal correspondence and shared ministry with this friend in ministry. It is my pleasure, then, heartily to commend this volume to readers, confident in the faithfulness, fervor, and wisdom that has animated its production. May our generation be helped and inspired in prayer! For the Lord blesses his people when they pray, granting guidance, protection, and strength to their cause. To him be glory alone!

—Richard D. Phillips
Greenville, South Carolina
August 2017

Preface

These meditations on prayer began to take shape in midweek meetings for prayer in Grace Presbyterian Church (RPCNA), State College, Pennsylvania, where I was the pastor between 1986 and 2004. Like John Bunyan's beginning *The Pilgrim's Progress*, "Neither did I but vacant seasons spend/In this my scribble...."

They grew into their present form in the prayer meeting I started in the Southside Indianapolis Reformed Presbyterian Church, Indiana, where I served as pastor from 2004 until my retirement in 2014. And so, as the illustrious tinker said of his labors,

> For having now my method by the end,
> Still as it pull'd, it came; and so I penned
> It down: until it came at last to be,
> For length and breadth, the bigness which you see.

As a watchword for these latter meetings, we took Jesus's question of his drowsy disciples in the Garden of Gethsemane: "Could you not watch with Me one hour?" (Matt. 26:40). We still meet for one hour, which includes the singing of a psalm, a meditation on a Scripture prayer, followed by the sharing of requests for prayer and at least a half hour of prayer. This volume is one small fruit from these meetings, and it is gratefully dedicated to the praying people of the two congregations in which these brief meditations were shared. They are presented here, as in their original settings, to promote several practical goals:

    ❧ First and foremost, they are designed to be an encouragement to commit to the consistent exercise and enjoyment of prayer as a "means of grace" (see *Westminster Larger Catechism* 195), whether in public worship, family worship, or in the "secret place" (Matt. 6:6). Prayer is the preeminent medium in which we bring the prospects and challenges of the day and of the hour before our Lord and Savior at the "throne of grace" (Heb. 4:16). In a busy world dominated by what Charles Hummel has called "the tyranny of the urgent," this is something we find challenging at the best of times.

- The second goal is to focus upon the Lord through the prayers of the Bible. All the main prayers of Scripture are included here, as are many of the passages that teach us about prayer. There are around six hundred prayers and allusions to prayer in God's Word, so this book is not exhaustive. It does seek, however, to present as full a picture as possible of what the Lord teaches us about prayer in the Bible.
- The third goal is to connect personal devotion and the prayers of the Bible with the Bible's own manual of praise, the five books of what we call the Psalms. Each day includes, for prayer and praise, a portion of a psalm from *The Book of Psalms for Worship*, also published by Crown & Covenant, of Pittsburgh, Pennsylvania. Not every psalm is included, but most are represented, so that, in parallel with the prayers expounded here, you will find a fairly comprehensive presentation of the scope of biblical praise.

Rightly used, each day's entries provide a diet of worship that includes praise, prayer, and the ministry of the Word. These are sent out with the prayer that the Lord would use them to bless his people in homes, families and churches to the glory of his great Name. Or, as Bunyan said of his completed work,

Oh then come hither,
And lay my book, thy head, and heart together.

—Gordon J. Keddie
Greenwood, Indiana
November 2017

Prayers
of the
Bible

GORDON J. KEDDIE

January 1
The First Meeting for Prayer

Calling on the name of the Lord

And as for Seth, to him also a son was born: and he named him Enosh.
Then men began to call on the name of the Lord. — Gen. 4:26

READ GENESIS 4:1–26

Calling on the name of the Lord ought to be the most natural thing for us to do. There is evidence of personal and family worship in the lives of Adam and Eve and their children, Cain and Abel (vv. 3–4). Only after the birth of Adam's grandson Enosh, however, do we have the first record in the Bible of a public meeting for worship and prayer. There were now two growing families serving the Lord—those of Adam and Seth. It appears that they were moved to meet together for praise and prayer. This was when "men began to call on the name of the Lord" (v. 26). What moved them to do this?

Adam and Eve knew that God had created them (Gen. 2:7). "We are all God's offspring," Paul tells the philosophers in Athens (Acts 17:28–29)—but we are not exactly so in the way our first parents were. They knew God created them anew. We know we have had a mother and a father. We also know God made us and that he sustains us. That is why we pray as Jesus taught us, "Give us today our daily bread," and rely upon him for everything else we need (Matt. 6:11). That is why it is our joy to hear God's call to praise him for his blessings, "Oh come, let us worship and bow down; let us kneel before the LORD our Maker" (Ps. 95:6).

Adam and Eve knew that God had saved them from their sin (Gen. 3:15). Believers in Jesus know who saved them and are persuaded that he is able to "keep us from falling" (Jude 24). We therefore continue to pray for grace from the Lord that we would be enabled to live lives that are pleasing to him and are a blessing to ourselves and others. This seems silly to unbelievers, but it is life from above for those who know Jesus as their Savior. "For the message of the cross is foolishness to those who are perishing, but to us who are being saved it is the power of God" (1 Cor. 1:18).

Adam and Eve knew that God was their Lord. We too know that the Lord is king—"head over all things to the church" (Eph. 1:22).

2

There are many dangers in this hostile world and also in our own failings and sins. That is why we pray for God's protection and, most especially, for the salvation of sinners and the advance of his kingdom in people's hearts, in the lives of nations, and in history itself.

Adam and Eve were in covenant with God. God is a covenant God who formed promises for his people from eternity itself (Eph. 1:4), promises he will keep: "Therefore know that the LORD your God, He is God, the faithful God who keeps covenant and mercy for a thousand generations with those who love Him and keep His commandments" (Deut. 7:9). Jesus assures us, his followers, "I am with you always" (Matt. 28:20). How then can we not pray to the God who is our Creator, Savior, King, and Covenant-head? In his Christmas Day broadcast in 1939, with Britain at war, King George VI movingly quoted lines from Minnie Haskins's poem of 1908, "God Knows":

> I said to the man who stood at the Gate of the Year,
> "Give me a light that I may tread safely into the unknown."
> And he replied,
> "Go out into the darkness, and put your hand into the hand of God.
> That shall be to you better than light, and safer than a known way."

At the gate of this year, let us resolve to call upon the name of the Lord together with all who know the Lord Jesus Christ, the Light of the world (John 8:12).

A PRAYER FOR COMMUNION WITH GOD
Sing Psalm 42

THINGS I WILL PRAY FOR TODAY

_____

_____

_____

_____

_____

_____

_____

_____

_____

January 2
Praying for Children

The first recorded prayer

Lord God, what will You give me, seeing I go childless? — Gen. 15:23

READ GENESIS 15:1–6

It is the most normal of aspirations of human beings to want children of their own. Childlessness has historically been thought of as a curse. We want to leave something of ourselves and the fruit of our love in the world when we are gone. We want to be remembered particularly by those to whom we gave life. God has made us to have a sense of the continuity of life in the line of generations. The prayer of the psalmist, "May you see your children's children. Peace be upon Israel!" touches a powerful chord in the human soul (Ps. 128:6).

It speaks volumes of the state of our world that so many regard children as an unwanted inconvenience and that so many governments support this with legislation that permits and promotes the killing of children before they are born! The so-called "right to choose" is no better than a "license to kill." It effectively places the life of an unborn child no higher than a diseased appendix or an ingrown toenail!

Yet it remains true that millions do want to have a family. When they do have children, they are committed to nurturing them and preparing them for their future adult life. People do love children.

Abraham prays for a child (vv. 1–3). Abraham and Sarah were *still childless* some years after God had promised that he would give them descendants who would one day inhabit Canaan (Gen. 12:7). So, after Abraham had declined to take any reward from the spoils of his defeat of the kings who had captured Lot (Gen. 14:23), when God told him in a vision that he — God himself — was his "exceedingly great reward," the future patriarch asked for a child and heir. He wasn't saying that God was not a good enough reward. He was just expressing his heart's desire for a posterity of his own. He feels childlessness as a judgment, not a blessing. Eliezer was presently his heir, but he wanted an heir of his own flesh and blood.

God promptly promises a child (v. 4). What did this promise entail? For one thing, it was tantamount to *life from the dead* for Abraham

4

and Sarah (v. 4). They were at an age when, humanly speaking, they were dead to having children. The new life from Abraham's and Sarah's bodies is effectively a child of resurrection, given by God as a special gift of grace. "Marriage," says the *Westminster Confession of Faith* (WCF) 24.2, "was ordained for the mutual help of husband and wife: for the increase of mankind with a legitimate issue, and of the church with a holy seed." This echoes Malachi 2:15, which says, "He [God] seeks a godly offspring," and so indicates that God means to bring spiritual children to himself from the natural children born to his people.

God also promises life beyond measure. In the end, Abraham would have descendants as uncountable as the stars in the night sky (v. 5). This takes the promise to a higher level because this obviously vastly transcends the natural descendants of Abraham.

This is of course an anticipation of the future church—"the children of Abraham" (Gal. 3:7)—who are saved by grace through faith in Jesus Christ, *the* Seed of Abraham (Gal. 3:16). Abraham *believed God for the promise* (v. 6). This was "accounted to him for righteousness." Paul identifies this as the point at which the Bible's doctrine of justification by faith alone in Christ alone begins to emerge (Gal. 3:6; Rom. 4:13–25). As Abraham believed God, God credited to his account the righteousness that would save him—the righteousness he could not produce by his own best efforts—the perfect righteousness of Christ accounted to him by God's free grace in Christ.

Do we have things to pray about? Then let us believe God for the promises he has given in Scripture for all of his children.

A PRAYER WITH PROMISE FOR A GODLY FAMILY
Sing Psalm 128:3–4

THINGS I WILL PRAY FOR TODAY

5

January 3
Big Problem: Brief Prayer

The shortest prayer

Lord, save me!—Matt. 14:30

READ MATTHEW 14:22-33

It is surely no accident that the shortest prayer in Scripture is about the largest problem in human experience—that of life or death for both time and eternity. After all, people in a desperate situation do not have much time to pray. Besides, says Jesus, it is the "heathen" who "think they will be heard for their many words" (Matt. 6:7). The Lord's brother, James, observes that "the effective fervent prayer of a righteous man avails much" (James 5:16). Length and wordiness cut no ice with the Lord! But pertinence, passion, and personal godliness are all vital components of believing prayer. There are some powerful lessons here for our practice of prayer.

When you are presumptuous in your prayers, you are killing them dead. Peter sees Jesus's miracle—his walking on the water—but his response is to "seek a sign" for himself, rather than worship Jesus as the Son of God (v. 28). Jesus gives him the sign, only for Peter to show by his fear and doubt that he missed the real point. He had presumed to ask Jesus for a miracle out of self-indulgence and not out of any solid desire to exalt the Lord. In the prayers of many Christians there is a lot of what used to be called "cupboard love." We too easily pray for what we want God to do for us so as to make our lives easier and more enjoyable. We presume upon God when we should rather prostrate ourselves before his glory.

A lot of prayers are more like grocery lists than outpourings of hearts in love with God and his Son. It is, of course, always proper to ask God for our needs and those of others. "You do not have because you do not ask," says James (4:2). Paul urges us to be particular in prayer: "Be anxious for nothing, but in everything by prayer and supplication, with thanksgiving, let your requests be made known to God" (Phil. 4:6). Yet, if we leave aside the detailed "prayer requests" that fill up modern prayers even for a moment, we discover that many Christians don't know what to pray! They cannot talk to God about his character, his gospel grace, their

6

sin and need, or their salvation and sanctification! We need a recovery both of the majesty of God and the language of Scripture in our thinking and in our prayers. Above all, the great lesson is about our attitude of prayer. We need to take care to prepare our hearts and concentrate our minds to come to the throne of grace as humble petitioners seeking the help of a Father in heaven, through the beloved Son who is alone the Savior of all who will believe on him (Acts 16:31).

When you feel yourself to be perishing, you had better pray properly. Scripture reminds us, "If I regard iniquity in my heart, the Lord will not hear" (Ps. 66:18). That is surely why Jesus first indulged Peter's desire to walk on water and then left him to sink a little. He meant to expose to Peter's conscience something of his presumption and lack of faith. He meant for him to feel the consequences of his sin. He meant to bring him to "have no confidence in the flesh" (Phil. 3:3), but rather put his trust in the Lord so as not to be put to shame (Ps. 71:1).

The lesson here is to learn to call upon the Lord in the real crises of life. What is of the essence? Surely it is to call upon the Lord along the following lines:

> to pray out of *real need*: Peter saw himself drowning.
> to pray with a *real trust* in Jesus: Peter calls on him as "Lord."
> to pray with *real surrender* to Jesus: Peter cries, "Save me."

When Jesus asks, "O you of little faith, why did you doubt?" he is calling you to act in prayerful confidence and to pray with active confidence, not in yourselves, but in him—your Surety.

A PRAYER FOR DELIVERANCE
Sing Psalm 54

THINGS I WILL PRAY FOR TODAY

_____

_____

_____

_____

_____

_____

January 4
An Encouragement to Pray

Getting answers while still asking

*It shall come to pass that before they call, I will answer, and while they
are still speaking I will hear. — Isa. 65:24*

READ ISAIAH 65:17–25

The vision of the "new heavens" and the "new earth" in Isaiah 65:17–25 is a prophecy of heaven. It sees the blessings of the world to come as also in some measure overlapping the present life of the believer. The elimination of *premature* death in both children and adults (v. 20), does not promise that there will be no more death on earth, any more than it implies that death will continue in heaven. What it does say is that God's promise of life in the gospel is real and substantial both in time and eternity. In other words, the character of new life in Christ in the gospel is also in view. With the Lord's blessing, we will see our homes established, our work made fruitful, and our families flourishing (vv. 21–23). The mention of prayer, in verse 24, clearly anticipates the unhindered fellowship in heaven between God and his people, but it also gives us promises for our present praying that can only encourage us to call on the Lord with the expectancy of blessing.

God has the answer before we offer the prayer (v. 24a). In heaven, we will still be finite creatures bound by time, even if that time is endless. We will speak to the Lord through a succession of thoughts in a procession of moments. We will pray for things to come, even in eternity. But the Lord assures us that he will be answering us, even before we call! It is as if our very thinking the need and framing the prayer will bring the discovery that God's answer is already prepared and its delivery is at the door! Amos expresses a similar idea when he prophesies that "the days are coming…when the plowman will overtake the reaper" (Amos 9:13).

This must also be true in our present experience in this world, because, as Jesus assures us, "Your Father knows the things you have need of before you ask Him" (Matt. 6:8). When Scripture tells us "you do not have, because you do not ask" (James 4:2), God is telling us he has the answer already in place. All we need is faith and prayer.

8

God is also listening, even before we are done praying (v. 24b). That is to say, he is an excellent listener. He is a perfect father. He continues to listen, even when he knows what is coming. When we know what is coming, we tend to switch off. Like a good parent, he knows that his children need to take the time to blurt out what is on their minds and hearts! What grace there is in the Lord, to let us babble on to the limit of our anxieties, and, as he listens, to time the answer that will console the troubled heart and meet the greatest need of the hour!

This, then, is a truth to be believed and applied every day, for every prayer time. We often pray out of great uncertainty, perhaps only half believing that the Lord will hear us, far less answer us. David prays in such a state of mind in Psalm 143:

> Hear my prayer, O LORD, Give ear to my supplications! In Your faithfulness answer me, And in Your righteousness…Answer me speedily, O LORD; My spirit fails! Do not hide Your face from me, Lest I be like those who go down into the pit. Cause me to hear Your lovingkindness in the morning, For in You do I trust; Cause me to know the way in which I should walk, For I lift up my soul to You. (Ps. 143:1, 7–8)

What a comfort and encouragement it is, then, to know we can pray with expectation because the Lord already has in mind both our real need and his perfect answer. What greater encouragement could there be to call upon the Lord in prayer?

A PRAYER FOR GOD'S HEARING
Sing Psalm 143

THINGS I WILL PRAY FOR TODAY

January 5
Let Your Word Come True

The longest prayer (Part 1)

And now I pray, O God of Israel, let Your word come true, which You have spoken to Your servant David my father. — 1 Kings 8:26

READ 1 KINGS 8:22–26

A t thirty-two verses, Solomon's prayer at the dedication of the temple is the longest prayer recorded in the Bible. It begins with adoration and thanksgiving—respectively for who God is and what he has done. He is the one and only God "in heaven above" and "on earth below." And he is the God who keeps "covenant and mercy" with his servants (v. 23). God is truth; his word is truth; his word comes true! From this basic reality, Solomon prays that all God's as yet unfulfilled promises will become living accomplishment in days yet future (v. 26).

God's promise is a covenant promise. He is the "Lord God of Israel." He names his people: "Israel" means literally "prince with God" (v. 23). He binds himself to them, as their guarantor and surety. If this were not the case, we could hardly pray with any conviction. Why would we pray at all, if God were fickle, changeable, and inconsistent with himself? But he assures us that he is the Lord who does not change, and that when we call upon him in faith, he will certainly answer (Mal. 3:6; Ps. 91:15). We call upon a faithful God. After Adam and Eve fell into sin, God covenanted to provide for the "Seed" of the woman to crush the "head" of the serpent (Gen. 3:15). This is rightly called the *Protevangelium*—the first gospel.

Later, the psalmist records a divine declaration pointing to Jesus Christ more explicitly: "I have made a covenant with My chosen, I have sworn to My servant David: 'Your seed I will establish forever, and build up your throne to all generations'" (Ps. 89:3–4). Later still, the writer to the Hebrews sums up the fulfillment of all this after the fact of Jesus's death and resurrection (Heb. 8:7–13). The certainty of God's covenant is nowhere more strongly stated than in Hebrews 6:13–14: "For when God made a promise to Abraham, because He could swear by no one greater, He swore by Himself, saying, 'Surely blessing I will bless you, and multiplying I will multiply you.'" God keeps his word.

God's promise is a gracious promise. He keeps "mercy" for those who live for him "with all their hearts" (v. 23). His grace—pure unmerited favor—saves the believer. And his salvation—ongoing, redeeming nurture—transforms the believer's life. Those who truly love God cannot but feel his love toward them, for "we love Him, for He first loved us" (1 John 4:19). How could we pray at all if we thought that God had no interest in us and no sincerity of a gracious purpose toward us? We call upon the God who loves his people.

God's promise is a sure promise. Solomon records the fact that the completion of the temple is an accomplished promise of God to his father David (v. 24). Why would we pray to a powerless God, who had never once given evidence of following through on a promise? We call upon a God who blesses his people with solid proofs of his ability and determination to keep faith with his promises.

God's promise is a saving promise. The promise of a Davidic king does not fail with the Israelite monarchy, but points to Jesus, the son of David and the Son of God. Jesus makes this clear in Luke 20:21–24 when he comments on David's words in Psalm 110:1: "The LORD said to my Lord, 'Sit at My right hand.'" He points out that David calls the promised Messiah, who is "the Son of David" (Matt. 1:1), his Lord. Christ is the eternal Davidic king who saves his people from their sins. We come to a divine Savior who is "able to save to the uttermost all who come to God through Him" (Heb. 7:25).

A PRAYER FOR GOD'S PROMISES TO BE FULFILLED
Sing Psalm 130

THINGS I WILL PRAY FOR TODAY

January 6
Will God Dwell on the Earth?

The longest prayer (Part 2)

And now I pray, O God of Israel, let Your word come true, which You have spoken to Your servant David my father. —1 Kings 8:26

READ 1 KINGS 8:22–26

Solomon first prays for God's word to come true (vv. 22–26). Without this fulfillment of covenant promise and saving mercy we could have no hope at all (see v. 23). When we do grasp this truth that God's word is coming true, we lay hold on that hope that is the "anchor of the soul" (Heb. 6:19). Consequently, we also increase in the confidence that God is for us, is near us, and will bless us and keep us. Solomon, however, has a nagging thought: Will God, can God, dwell on the earth? Can he come near to us, among us? Having given Israel a temple, thus fulfilling one promise (v. 24), will God then make himself present in that temple? After all, if God is bigger than the "heaven of heavens"—that is, the heaven beyond the heavens that we see with our own eyes—why should he squeeze himself into this tiny temple?

Solomon believes that God is the hearer of prayer. "O You who hear prayer, to You all flesh will come" (Ps. 65:2). Accordingly, he turns to God in prayer and asks that he manifest his presence in the center of the worship of his people (v. 29). He does not have in mind God being present only as a spiritual influence in the hearts and minds of faithful worshipers. He prays that God will be present spatially and with visible glory.

Solomon prays for God's presence with Israel, his covenant people. He claims the promise of Deuteronomy 12:11: "There will be the place where the Lord your God chooses to make His name abide." That place is, of course, the place where sacrifice is to be made for sin, the great temple that has just been built and is now being dedicated to God.

Solomon also prays for God's ear to be attentive to his people's prayers as they are made "toward this place" (v. 30). He expresses the desire that God will be with his people "night and day" without any break (v. 29). Access to God is the whole point.

Solomon's focus is forgiveness. He prays: "Hear in heaven Your

12

dwelling place; and when You hear, forgive" (v. 30). The meaning of the temple itself—of God's coming to humanity and of the sacrifice of animals down through the Old Testament centuries—is forgiveness of sin. Access to God requires atonement for sin and reconciliation to God. Sacrifice bridges the otherwise unbridgeable gap between a holy God and an unholy humanity.

This finds its ultimate fulfillment in Jesus Christ. He is the true temple (John 2:19–21). He is the true atoning Sacrifice, whose blood was once and for all shed to take away the sin of the world (John 1:29). Everything in the tabernacle/temple and its sacrifices and ceremonies points to God's provision of a Savior in the person of Jesus.

> ❧ *Jesus is Immanuel*—"God with us" (Isa. 7:14; Matt. 1:23). In the person of Jesus, "the tabernacle of God is with men" (Rev. 21:3). And God still dwells on the earth in every believer by the Holy Spirit, whom he has sent (John 14:16).
> ❧ *Jesus is our Mediator*, securing what all the blood sacrifices of the temple could only point ahead to: namely, our salvation through his death and resurrection (Rom. 4:25).
> ❧ *Jesus is our heavenly Intercessor*. He ensures our prayers are heard in heaven, God's "dwelling place" (Heb. 7:25; 1 Kings 8:30). In Jesus, Solomon's prayer is answered forever.

Knowing God in Jesus Christ *is* eternal life: "And this is eternal life, that they may know You, the only true God, and Jesus Christ whom You have sent" (John 17:3).

A PRAYER REJOICING IN THE FAITHFULNESS OF GOD
Sing Psalm 139:7–10

THINGS I WILL PRAY FOR TODAY

_____

_____

_____

_____

_____

_____

January 7
Fearing God and Enjoying Life

The longest prayer (Part 3)

...that they may fear You all the days that they live in the land which You gave to our fathers. —1 Kings 8:40

READ 1 KINGS 8:31–40

olomon begins his great prayer with a celebration of the character of God (vv. 23–24). This leads him to pray that God would keep his covenant promise to his people (v. 25–26). This in turn leads naturally to reflection on the need of God's presence with his people and, therefore, to the meaning of the temple in which he chooses to manifest himself (vv. 27–30). Solomon inevitably prays for forgiveness of sin (v. 30), because that is the whole reason for the sacrifices of the temple and the only way for any sinner to be made acceptable to God.

The next step is to pray for personal godliness in God's people (vv. 31–40). Why? It is because a godly life is the obvious implication and purpose of reconciliation to and communion with God. God's people are called to be holy as God is holy (1 Peter 1:16). The fruit of forgiveness of past sin is to be future godliness. When Jesus forgives the woman accused of marital unfaithfulness, he tells her, "Go and sin no more" (John 8:11). Solomon unfolds his argument in four parts, set out as two parallels involving repentance and godliness (A1/B1/B2/A2). Notice the intensifying personal focus:

> A1—*Repentance toward your neighbor (vv. 31–32)*. In private life, are you honest in your dealings with others? God is your witness. If you say one thing and have done the other, then, prays Solomon, may God "hear in heaven, and act and judge."

> B1—*Repentance in national life (vv. 33–34)*. In public life, sin may bring setbacks that call for national repentance and humbling before God.

> B2—*Godliness in national life (vv. 35–36)* can be the occasion of great refreshment from the Lord, from both spiritual and temporal drought.

14

⤳ A2—*Godliness in your heart (vv. 37–40).* The key is your own walk with the Lord. This requires each one knowing "the plague of his own heart" and turning to the Lord for deliverance and for prosperity in daily life.

Notice that this sequence basically takes us from things that happen to us to changes that take place in us. As the Lord deals with both our outward problems and our inward needs we grow in grace. A similar progression can be seen in the New Testament in James 4:1–7:

> Where do wars and fights come from among you? Do they not come from your desires for pleasure that war in your members? You lust and do not have. You murder and covet and cannot obtain. You fight and war. Yet you do not have because you do not ask. You ask and do not receive, because you ask amiss, that you may spend it on your pleasures. Adulterers and adulteresses! Do you not know that friendship with the world is enmity with God? Whoever therefore wants to be a friend of the world makes himself an enemy of God. Or do you think that the Scripture says in vain, "The Spirit who dwells in us yearns jealously"? But He gives more grace. Therefore He says: "God resists the proud, but gives grace to the humble." Therefore submit to God. Resist the devil and he will flee from you.

How then are we to pray? Begin where Solomon ends—the heart-plague of sin must be healed. Then we will in all its richness experience the wonderful paradox of newness of life in Jesus Christ: it is in fearing God that we will truly enjoy life (v. 40).

AN ENCOURAGEMENT TO GODLY FEAR
Sing Psalm 34:11–14

THINGS I WILL PRAY FOR TODAY

January 8
Separated to be God's Inheritance

The longest prayer (Part 4)

For You separated them from among all the peoples of the earth to be their inheritance. — *1 Kings 8:53*

READ 1 KINGS 8:41–53

Solomon's prayer at the dedication of the temple ranges across the whole of Israel's life as a people. The logic of his prayer unfolds in four successive petitions. First is the sovereign grace of the covenant-making God (vv. 23–26). This is followed by the forgiveness of sinners (vv. 27–30). Third is the personal response of believers in their covenant faithfulness in daily life (vv. 31–40). Finally, we arrive at the witness to the world of God's people as those whom he has separated to himself as his inheritance (vv. 41–53). It is a complete prayer aimed at the Lord making his people and his glory complete.

Why has God revealed himself to us? It is to glorify his name in saving us from a fallen world and a lost eternity. Solomon's prayer in effect points us to the gospel that is later revealed in the person and work of the Lord Jesus Christ. Notice the three parts of this last section of the prayer:

> There is grace for the "foreigner" (vv. 41–43). God's salvation is revealed "that all the peoples of the earth may know Your name and fear You, as do Your people Israel" (v. 43). This was a clear indication that the Gentiles would be saved—the very message that so shocked the Jews in Nazareth when Jesus came home and preached to them, and this message led them to try to murder him (Luke 4:24–30). We all want God's grace for ourselves, but we are not so sure some people should be given it.

> There is help for God's people in this world (vv. 44–45). The promise is that the Lord will answer prayer and maintain the "cause"—the essential interests and witness—of his people.

> There is even "compassion" from the otherwise unbelieving world for the repentant people of God. The "cause" of God— that is, his people maintained as his inheritance in the world—is

16

central to human history. Christ is head over all things to the church (Eph. 1:22).

The Lord means to save a vast number of people before this world is done. To this end, the *separateness* of God's people—their love for Jesus Christ, their personal godliness, including their repentance for sin and faith in Christ as their Savior, their humility and service, their prayer and love for people—has a powerful impact on the world.

Christians are called to pray for the world that is alienated from God. As a people separated to God, the disciples of Jesus Christ understand that they are called to be God's instruments in his purpose of grace to draw lost sinners to salvation in Jesus Christ. This shows us the strong missionary heart of all believing prayer. We are certainly to make known to God our requests for ourselves, but this is set in the context of a world of overwhelming spiritual darkness that is always tottering on the very brink of a lost eternity. This is, of course, that God's "inheritance" may grow and glorify God in the land of the living. God's inheritance is redeemed people in this life, as well as the world to come.

Solomon closes his prayer by recalling that the Lord brought Israel out of Egypt. He delivered them from bondage into the liberty of the children of God—so pointing us to the purpose of the gospel of saving grace in Jesus Christ by which men and women are still being saved to be separated to God as his inheritance.

GIVING THANKS FOR A GOOD INHERITANCE
Sing Psalm 16:5–8

THINGS I WILL PRAY FOR TODAY

_____

_____

_____

_____

_____

_____

_____

_____

_____

January 9
Wrong Prayer: Right Answer

A prayer of fraying faith

And Abraham said to God, "Oh, that Ishmael might live before you."
— Gen 17:18

READ GENESIS 17:17–22

The Bible tells us, "Be anxious for nothing." Rather, "in everything by prayer and supplication, with thanksgiving, let your requests be made known to God" (Phil. 4:6). There are two basic requirements here. The first is, of course, a believing attitude, for "without faith it is impossible to please God" (Heb. 11:6). The second requirement is to have some specific goals for praying (see Ps. 37:3–4). Putting it another way, if we are going to pray seriously and truly, we need to know the Lord and we need to know what we want of him.

One thing we do not need to know is God's answer ahead of time. We are too often tempted, if we are honest, to speculate and to try to figure out God's secret will. That is always a fool's errand. God's revealed will, the Bible, ought to be enough. God's secret will is only discovered after the event. Accordingly, what we do need to be certain about in our minds is who God is, how we are to approach him, and what his promises are. We also need to ask ourselves how ready we are to hear his answer, whatever it turns out to be. That is, whether it is a no, a yes, or a "Wait a while." We too often find it especially difficult to take no for an answer. That, however, is exactly the test of living faith that trusts the Lord as opposed to just banking on getting what one wants or believes one needs.

Abraham so wanted every covenant blessing for Ishmael. This was heartfelt and utterly sincere. But it did not come from faith. He had by this time given up on having a son by Sarah. That is why he laughed at the very idea (vv. 17–18). How could Sarah and he have a child in their old age? So, he thought, why not accept Ishmael instead, even if he was the surrogate's son? It was, however, a misguided prayer—the prayer of a fraying faith.

God's answer is both no and yes. But it is not ambiguous or undecided in the slightest, as our yes-and-no answers tend to be. God

18

calls Abraham back to the terms of his covenant promise. No! Ishmael is not the covenant seed. The promise stands and will be fulfilled in the birth of Isaac within a year. Isaac means "he laughs"—a reminder of Abraham's doubting and an affirmation of God's faithful promise (vv. 19, 21). Yes! Ishmael will have a blessing and be a great nation (v. 20), but the covenant line will be through Sarah's son. Abraham prayed for his heart's desire. That was good. He prayed out of a mixture of faith and practical unbelief. That was inevitable, since prayer presupposes our ignorance and also our weakness. The more we feel confused and uncertain, the more we should cry out to God.

Are we ready for the Lord's nos and yeses that we don't expect? God "finished talking" and "went up from Abraham" (v. 22). There was no more room for further prayer, far less debate. It was up to Abraham to take God at his word. Paul has a similar experience with his prayer that his "thorn in the flesh" be removed. He prayed just three times. And the Lord said no, the thorn would stay. But he also said yes to Paul: "My grace is sufficient for you, for My strength is made perfect in weakness" (2 Cor. 12:8–9). God's no is not a rejection, a sad outcome, or a so-called "unanswered prayer." It is the precursor of a more glorious yes that unveils a blessing even greater than the one we asked for. Jesus, says Paul, does "exceedingly abundantly above all that we ask or think, according to the power that works in us" (Eph. 3:20). Let us, like Abraham, pour out our hearts in all our frailty, but let us, with Paul, look to Jesus for the abundant blessing that is above and beyond that frailty.

PRAISE FOR ABUNDANT BLESSING
Sing Psalm 23:4–6

THINGS I WILL PRAY FOR TODAY

January 10
The First Intercessory Prayer

Praying for lost people

Would You also destroy the righteous with the wicked? — Gen. 18:23

READ GENESIS 18:22–33

It is easier to call down fire from heaven on notorious sinners than to love them enough to intercede with the Lord for their salvation. James and John knew what they wanted for the Samaritans who would not welcome Jesus: "Lord, do you want us to command fire to come down from heaven and consume them, just as Elijah did?" (Luke 9:54). Jesus rebuked them sternly and reminded them that "the Son of Man did not come to destroy men's lives but to save them" (Luke 9:56).

When God announces his purpose to destroy Sodom, Abraham's response is not to say, "They've got it coming," but to turn to prayer — the first recorded instance of intercessory prayer in all of Scripture. He "stood still before the Lord" (v. 22). But as we read on, it dawns that his great concern is to save the Sodomites from God's judgment! The Lord, by the way, is the Angel of the Lord in human form, the eternal Son of God and the pre-incarnate Jesus, revealing the will of God to Abraham. Jesus later will say, "Your father Abraham rejoiced to see My day, and he saw it and was glad" (John 8:56).

First he asks God, "Would you also destroy the righteous with the wicked?" (v. 23). It is not that "the righteous" are innocent, but that they are saved people, believers who trust the Lord for their salvation. Would God destroy *his own people* just to mete out punishment to his enemies? Then he argues the Lord down from a minimum of fifty believers to just ten — that is, the equivalent of what would in the future be the one basic synagogue among the Jews. Would God not spare Sodom for the sake of one tiny congregation of believers? "Shall not the Judge of all the earth do right?" (v. 25). The Lord agrees and goes on his way (vv. 32–33).

This surely challenges us to pray for lost people — *for even the most outwardly wicked lost people.* If we have a love for souls, as did Abraham, than we will surely desire to see people saved by the free grace of the Lord Jesus Christ. This is the vital test of our own love for Jesus Christ, because *saving grace* for the notoriously wicked cuts against the grain of human nature and the natural desires we have for justice and even sheer vengeance. Anyone can love his friends.

It also reminds us of the vital role of Christians in relation to whatever temporal blessings a community or a nation may be enjoying. God no doubt spares many a "Sodom" in our world for the sake of even handfuls of believers. Why is there so much evidence of the goodness of God all over the globe, even in countries that are largely godless? The answer is that the Lord has many people across this world (Acts 18:10). It is for their sake that many of the Lord's most determined enemies enjoy his common temporal conserving grace. The irony is that the world that hates Christ and his church is routinely spared divine judgment because of the church and its mission. From eternity, God planned to save sinners. He therefore spares sinners long enough to accomplish his goals for them.

This is our window of opportunity to intercede in prayer that millions who languish in spiritual blindness and rebellion against "the Lord and His Anointed" might be brought by faith to "Kiss the Son" so that they will not "perish in His wrath" (Ps. 2:2, 12). The lost need to be loved by those who, by God's amazing grace (to paraphrase from John Newton's "Amazing Grace"), once were lost and now are found, were blind but now can see. Let us then pray without ceasing for our world that the Lord would bring glory to his name even as he brings grace to the hearts of those who presently most vigorously reject him.

A CALL FOR ALL TO TURN TO THE LORD
Sing Psalm 117

THINGS I WILL PRAY FOR TODAY

January 11
Praying against God's Will

A prayer of faltering faith

Please let me escape there…and my soul shall live. — *Gen. 19:20*

READ GENESIS 19:18–22

Not all the prayers in the Bible are good and exemplary. This is also true of our prayers today. This should shock no one. If our prayers depended on their being unmixed with sin in order to be heard, we would go on whistling in the dark forever. Just as salvation is by grace alone and through faith alone, so is our effectiveness in prayer. It is the "prayer of faith," not of sinless perfection, that will heal the sick and receive forgiveness of sin (James 5:15).

Lot's prayer is a prayer of weak and faltering faith. Even though the Lord grants his request, it stands as a model of how *not* to pray, and is full of instruction for those who want to pray more faithfully. Notice two things in particular:

> Lot says "No" to God (vv. 18–19). The Lord had promised to save him from Sodom, but he insists he cannot "escape to the mountains." God says that if he doesn't, he will be destroyed (Gen. 19:17). Lot thinks that if he does, then the exact opposite will happen: he will be destroyed! He thinks God can save him, but that God's plan for doing so is too much for him.

> Lot accordingly asks for an easier way than God's (v. 20). He would prefer to go to a city that is "near" and "little," and he thinks he'll be safer there. This was Bela (later Zoar), one of the five kingdoms around Sodom (Gen. 14:2). This is closer and more comfortable than a trek into rugged and inhospitable mountains.

God had promised to save Lot in the mountains and was no less capable of saving him there than in any other place. The problem is that Lot is *self-centered* in that he flat out contradicts the Lord; *self-indulgent* in that he wanted God to allow him just a little sin, in staying in the environs of Sodom; and *pragmatic* in that he considered his proposal more "practical" than God's. And how true this is to life! How many Christians

22

play the lottery and pray to win with the promise they will give to the Lord's work from the proceeds? Or date an attractive non-Christian man or woman, with the prayer that God will use them to bring that person to faith before it gets to the point of marriage?

How gracious is our God! He grants Lot's request (vv. 21–22). The "little" city of Bela is spared the destruction that falls upon Sodom, Gomorrah, Admah, and Zeboiim (see Hosea 11:8). Notice that God renames Bela "Zoar," which means "insignificant." This is to say that it is a small mercy—smaller than Lot might have had, had he stepped out in the full obedience of faith. Lost mercies translate into real consequences. Lot lives, but his wife looks back and dies (Gen. 19:26). Lot's daughters sin with their father (Gen. 19:30–35), and this eventually gives rise to Moab and Ammon, two godless nations incorrigibly warring against God's people (Gen. 19:36–38; cf. Zeph. 2:8–9) and now extinct. "Whatever is not from faith is sin" (Rom. 14:23). What does this say to us? Three things:

> - Don't presume upon God's grace by asking him to allow you just a little sin here and there.
> - Don't pray against God's known will for your life, but always trust him for the outcome when it challenges your faith.
> - Don't hanker for "Sodom." Remember Lot and Jesus's call to "Remember Lot's wife" (Luke 17:26–33).

Rather follow the Lord Jesus Christ, who is "able to keep you from falling, and to present you faultless before the presence of his glory with exceeding joy" (Jude 24).

A CONFESSION OF WEAKNESS AND AN AFFIRMATION OF TRUST
Sing Psalm 73:23–24

THINGS I WILL PRAY FOR TODAY

_____

_____

_____

_____

_____

_____

January 12
Praying for Guidance

A prayer in the face of uncertainty

Please give me success this day... — *Gen. 24:12*

READ GENESIS 24:1–14

Abraham had been promised many descendants—enough to make him the father of many nations (Gen. 17:4). So far, he had only Isaac, who was single. Isaac clearly needed a wife if God's promise to Abraham was to be fulfilled. The question was, how to accomplish this? Finding the right spouse is something of a challenge in every time and culture. Abraham decided to send his trusted servant, Eliezer of Damascus (Gen. 15:2; 17:2), to Mesopotamia—modern Iraq—to find a bride for Isaac. What unfolds is a basic blueprint for seeking God's leading. There are three steps and these are of universal application.

The first step is to be sure you are walking in the way of the Lord. Abraham acted on two principles that relate respectively to the people and the land. These are the twin themes of God's covenant and of its fullness in the gospel of Jesus Christ. We who were alienated from God through sin, as Peter says, "were not a people." In Christ, we *"are* now the people of God." We formerly "had not obtained mercy but now have obtained mercy" (1 Peter 2:10). Having become God's people, we have also the promise and possession of a land. In the Old Testament it was Canaan; in the New Testament it is heaven hereafter, and the "holy nation," the church right now. Even if Christians are "strangers and pilgrims" in this sin-wracked world (Heb. 11:13; 1 Peter 2:11), it is still true that "the earth is the LORD's, and all it contains, the world, and those who dwell in it" (Ps. 24:1, NASB). In Christ we are a people and we are not far from home.

This perspective explains why Eliezer was sent out in search of a wife for Isaac, and not Isaac himself. Isaac was not to marry a local Canaanite girl (vv. 3–4). His wife was to be taken from the Shemites (modern Semites) rather than the Canaanites (see Gen. 9:24–26). God's covenant line was drawn from the line of Shem, and none other. Isaac was one of God's people and so must his wife be. Notice also that Isaac is kept from going to Mesopotamia and remains in Canaan (vv. 6–7). This underscored God's promise of the land. Isaac must stay put in God's country and his wife must come to him. One New Testament application of these two themes—the people of God and the land of Promise—is found in the requirement that believers must never be "unequally yoked" in their choice of a spouse, but must only and always marry another believer (2 Cor. 6:14). Practical obedience is the path in which the Lord will bless our uncertain questions with certain answers. God's kingdom advances through covenant families.

The second step is to make sure you pray for the promise of God to be fulfilled. Eliezer faithfully executes his commission. He prays for a girl of the right stock, and of personal winsomeness and quality (vv. 12–14). This is really the first prayer in Scripture that seeks God's guidance in a very specific matter. He also seeks a sign (v. 14)—something warned against in the New Testament, but graciously granted in this case.

The third step is to expect blessing from the Lord (whatever his answer). Eliezer is brightly hopeful—but then, is he not obviously led by the Lord? From verse 15 we know that the answer was already on the way before he was finished praying. Rebekah came out with her pitcher, ready to be revealed as the girl for Isaac! Here is the spirit and expectancy of true prayer: a transparent trust that the blessing is already approaching the intersection with our life. This is true, even if the answer is no because God's alternatives are better than our first choices. It is always true when the answer is yes, because we will see in retrospect that the sovereignty of God was at work leading to the unfolding of his will.

A PRAYER FOR GUIDANCE
Sing Psalm 25:4–5

THINGS I WILL PRAY FOR TODAY

_____

_____

_____

_____

_____

_____

January 13
An Anxious Prayer

A prayer from a bad conscience

I fear him, lest he come and attack me… — *Gen. 32:12*

READ GENESIS 32:9–12

We pray for many reasons. Health, uncertainty, and guidance are probably the dominant concerns in our public prayer requests. Private prayer, however, is more often about fears and anxieties arising from sin and a bad conscience. Do you ever pray for forgiveness of sin? Why so? Is it because you fear not being forgiven? Do you ever pray for that looming difficulty in your life that you have not so far been able to share with anyone else? And is it not fear that you cannot cope with that drives you to seek God's help? Many of our prayers are anxious prayers.

Jacob prays in this passage for two reasons. In the first place, he faces a potentially grave crisis. He cannot go back home and he is afraid to go forward. He can neither fight nor flee. Laban is behind him (Gen. 31:52). Esau is ahead of him and fast approaching with 400 men (Gen. 32:6). He knew himself to be between a rock and a hard place. He faced hard men in hard times, and it made him very worried about his life and his future. Second, Jacob has a bad conscience about his past sin. Twenty years before, he had cheated Esau of his birthright. Esau deserved to lose it, of course, but that doesn't excuse Jacob's chicanery in the matter. It was with good reason that Jacob was afraid of meeting a vengeful brother and of having to face the consequences of his actions (Gen. 27:45). "Conscience doth make cowards of us all," as Shakespeare's Hamlet says.

How Jacob prays also tells a story. He first accepts that he is accountable to the *covenant God* of his forefathers (v. 9a). Second, he records the *commands* God had given (v. 9b). Third, he testifies to God's *blessing* in his life and acknowledges his unworthiness (v. 10). Finally, he appeals to God's *promise* to Abraham, as he asks to be delivered from Esau (vv. 11–12).

Notice how he gives the covenant line and its future as the basis of his pleading. This is a covenantal prayer. It consciously reaches to God's character and promises in his covenant with Abraham. Jacob is bound to the Lord, because the Lord bound himself to Abraham and his seed in the line of the generations of his covenant people. His sins are not seen as isolated from that covenant relationship with God. We often think of sin as abstractions that pop up now and again, almost at random. We even call them "mistakes" or, worse, mere "peccadillos" (literally "mini-sins") and write them off as uncharacteristic lapses. But the fact is that sin is systemic—we are either covenant-keepers or covenant-breakers—and that means we are actually breaking from the Lord when we sin. Sin is not some moment of moral amnesia to be brushed off so we can "move on." It is about our walk with the Lord and our eternal destiny.

How then should we pray? Jacob takes us to Christ, our covenant head, and we plead for our salvation and our immediate needs:

- ⮞ not on the basis of our righteousness, but his perfect righteousness;
- ⮞ not because of our commitment, but his sure promises;
- ⮞ not on account of our sacrifices, but his atoning death on the cross;
- ⮞ not because of our hopes for the future, but his plans for us; and
- ⮞ not because we are so effective as his servants, but because Jesus is the Savior of his people from their sins.

When we are anxious, as Jacob was, we need to lay down our fears before the perfect love that casts out fear (1 John 4:18). We need to do so before the God who loved the world so as to send his Son (John 3:16). And we need to come to the Son who loved us before we loved him (1 John 4:19), and wait upon the Holy Spirit who is able to shed abroad in believing hearts the love of God (Rom. 5:5).

A PRAYER FOR THE FEARFUL
Sing Psalm 64:1–2, 7, 10

THINGS I WILL PRAY FOR TODAY

_____

_____

_____

_____

_____

January 14
Wrestling in Prayer

A persevering prayer

I will not let You go unless You bless me! — Gen. 32:26

READ GENESIS 32:24–32

acob was a worried man, as we noted in yesterday's reading. Esau was coming and Jacob feared that his brother was going to settle old scores by force. This led him to pray what may be regarded as the first *anxious* prayer recorded in Scripture (Gen. 32:9–12). Even as he prepares for his meeting with Esau (Gen. 32:13–21), it is clear that he is anxious. He takes the precaution of sending his people ahead in sections. When a ship is sinking, it's the women and children who are supposed to go first into the lifeboats. Jacob sends the women and children first, not to save their lives, but to save his! The cuteness of the children's faces and the vulnerabilities of the womenfolk were no doubt meant to soften Esau's attitude. These were, after all, his relatives, and they had not stolen his birthright! Jacob was not a fool. He pulled out all the stops in his efforts to soften his offended brother's heart.

Jacob had one more night before he would have to meet Esau. He spent that night alone. All of a sudden in the middle of the night, he is jumped upon by a mysterious stranger whom he eventually realizes is none other than God himself! This is the "Angel of the Lord," the pre-incarnate Son of God! Needless to say, this experience changes Jacob's life in some wonderful ways.

It is God who *initiates* this wrestling bout (vv. 24–25). The common application of the passage is that *we* need to wrestle with God. In fact, the primary truth here is the exact opposite. God starts the fight! He wrestles with Jacob. He reaches out. He persists and prevails. He needs to wrestle with sinners, because we sinners are doing our best to avoid the Lord. He does this precisely because he cares and we usually do not. So the first application is not that *we* need to wrestle with God, but that he is wrestling with us. Most of the time we are just trying to get off the mat altogether and keep him out of our lives! This, then, was an initiative of God's free and sovereign grace arresting a man in need:

‣ *Jacob responds by fighting back (v. 26).* When God says, "Let me go," Jacob refuses and cries out, "I will not let You go unless You bless me!" Jacob could only have said this if he was truly convinced that this midnight mugger could do him some good. Surely he knew this was the Lord. So he perseveres through the night until morning. What a strange encounter! Yet it has a very simple message about our "wrestling" with God. We too easily pray briefly and give up. Or we simply give up and never pray. It is a small wonder that our blessings are often meager and our souls listless and joyless.

‣ *Jacob receives a blessing and happily testifies to his seeing God "face to face" (vv. 27–30).* The Lord changes his name from Jacob, the "Supplanter," to Israel, a "prince with God." Jacob knows who the "Man" (v. 24) is, and he marks this by calling the place "Peniel," which means, literally, "face of God."

‣ *Jacob went on his way to meet Esau (vv. 31–32).* He *limped*—he was reminded of his limitations in a new way. But he moved *forward*—he was not fast but he was going in the right direction. He was not perfectly fit, but he went on in the strength of the Lord. He *aimed* to meet Esau—confronting his fears in dependence on the Lord.

God calls us also to look the real world in the face. So let our prayers be real. Let us look to Jesus and trust him as we confront life's challenges. Let us wrestle in prayer and not let go until he blesses us.

A PRAYER IN A DIFFICULT SITUATION
Sing Psalm 35:1–2

THINGS I WILL PRAY FOR TODAY

January 15
I'm Not Up to This Job!

A prayer of personal inadequacy

O my Lord, I am not eloquent... —Ex. 4:10

READ EXODUS 4:10-17

Christians pray all the time for God to do positive things for them. We ask him to heal our sicknesses—or to save a lost neighbor or loved one. We ask him to fulfill his Scripture promises. Moses's first recorded prayer is, however, the exact opposite! He asks God to *undo* his plan for his life in the immediate future. Moses wants out. He does not see this particular decision of God's to be a positive thing for him. So he starts to negotiate with God. He tells God that he made a mistake in calling him to leave the flocks and go to Egypt (v. 10). After all, he is not very "eloquent." He is "slow of speech." He just is not a good enough speaker to go preach to Pharaoh and the Egyptians. Then he caps it all off by asking God to excuse him and get someone else to do the job to which the Lord has called him (v. 13)! He tries really hard to "dodge the column" without appearing to be ungrateful or disrespectful.

Is this not also true of our lives? Truth to tell, we know a great deal about the Lord's will for our daily lives. It may be as simple as, "Go to work. Listen to the boss. Do the best job you can." And we know that God wants us to be diligent and willing in obeying his will: "And whatever you do in word and deed, do all in the name of the Lord Jesus Christ, giving thanks to God the Father through Him" (Col. 3:17). Yet, like Moses, we just want out, thank you very much! We simply want to be free to do what *we* want to do. We surely identify with Moses. It is sad but true, but we must confess we have often felt the same way about God's will.

Admittedly, there is a unique character to Moses's calling, as compared to ours. We are not, any of us, called to be a little Moses—to expect direct new revelations from God, like voices from the burning bush or thundering from Sinai; or, indeed, to do miracles and bring plagues on whole countries. The role that Moses had as the deliverer of Israel is, of course, already fulfilled in Jesus Christ as our Savior and Lord.

In general terms, however, there are ways in which Moses's experience of God's dealings applies to every modern Christian, whatever his calling may be. They can be stated positively, as follows:

- ⟫ Believe that the Lord is able to equip you to serve him. Our first excuse is invariably, "I just *can't* do that!" The real meaning behind it is "I don't want to do that." It is true that people have different gifts for different callings, but it is equally true that all spiritual gifts essential for effective discipleship are God-given.
- ⟫ Believe that God calls us precisely because he means for us to respond positively. He is not looking for our guidance in his search for disciples. That is why God is angry with Moses in verse 14; help is already on the way and he doesn't need insults from his servants.
- ⟫ Believe that God can enable you to do much more than you could ever imagine yourself doing. See how God provided a staff for Moses with which to do miracles (v. 17). So why borrow trouble on our perceived inadequacies, when we can expect great things from God?

So whether we pray for ourselves or for others, we are called to listen to God's Word for our calling and trust the Lord for enabling strength at every point. "Is anything too hard for the Lord?" (Gen. 18:14). Let us never ask the Lord to "let us off." We will discover, with Moses, that God is able to do "exceedingly abundantly above all that we ask or think, according to the power that works in us" (Eph. 3:20).

PRAISE FOR EMPOWERING GRACE RECEIVED
Sing Psalm 34:4–6

THINGS I WILL PRAY FOR TODAY

January 16
Trouble in the Church

A prayer of an embattled pastor

What shall I do with this people? — Ex. 17:4

READ EXODUS 17:4–7

God's truth is not immediately self-evident to all who hear it. Lack of clarity is not the problem. It is just that sinners take more than a little, or even a lot of, persuading. The Bible goes so far as to say that the truth is quite beyond the unconverted, such is human nature in its godless state (1 Cor. 2:14; cf. Isa. 6:9–10; Matt. 13:13–14).

Even believers who know the transforming grace of Jesus Christ in their hearts—which is none of their doing but a work of God in them—and therefore love the Word of God, realize God's truth comes as a challenge both to the intellect and to faith itself. This is especially a test when trouble hits us personally or strikes the church as a whole. Our mettle is tested and we make some discoveries about our true spiritual state. Our faith is tried. Our spiritual muscles are exercised. Our souls are searched. The Christian life is never a path of roses.

When Israel marched into the wilderness, they encountered a thirsty landscape (Ex. 17:1–3). Both physically and spiritually, they were very low. It was dry, they were thirsty, and they wondered where they were going to find water to drink. On the face of it this is wholly understandable—except that it becomes clear that they were walking by "sight" and not by faith (2 Cor. 5:7).

Moses is frustrated, feels embattled, and is just about beside himself. He cries out to the Lord, "What shall I do with this people?" He sounds like a parent who has to deal with a rebellious child. The problem is more acute, however, as he says, "They are almost ready to stone me." Many of God's prophets have quite literally been stoned to death by the church people of their day (Matt. 23:34; Acts 7:59). Many pastors have paid very dearly for loving their people enough to tell them truths they did not want to hear. Every parent knows what a sulking, complaining child is like when confronted by good old home truths. Dealing with indifferent and complacent church members is bad enough. But when they pick up stones, as they did with Jesus (John 8:59), things become downright lethal. Moses was in peril of his life and he knew it. What are we to do in such situations? God lays out three practical steps for us:

> First of all, hold your course with God (v. 5). Moses, and at least some others, had come this far by faith. Then let them persevere. And let him "go before the people"—that is, to lead them, to confront them, and to be a witness to them. It should be "business as usual" in faithfulness to God, however much the sheep are bleating in their self-inflicted misery.

> In the second place, look to the promise of God (v. 6). God promises to provide water as Moses strikes the rock. Moses believes this, and because he does, he acts upon it by striking the rock. Now it is not his striking the rock that makes the water flow. It is rather the occasion of God's mighty action. It is God's sovereign grace and power that is exercised so as to reward and attest to Moses's faithful obedience. This is how God works, as we believe his promises and claim them in consistent practical obedience.

> In the third place, remember what God did (v. 7). Naming Massah ("Tempted") and Meribah ("Contention") reminds God's people that they doubted God—"Is the Lord among us or not?"

The provision of water that day forever rebuked the practical atheism that led them to doubt the Lord and was designed to arm them against future temptation and contention. Let us rather pray with Moses than prevaricate with doubters.

A PRAYER IN PERIL
Sing Psalm 120:1–2, 7

THINGS I WILL PRAY FOR TODAY

January 17
The Boldest of Prayers

A prayer for delay of God's judgment

Turn from your fierce wrath… —Ex. 32:13

READ EXODUS 32:11–14

od tells Moses on the mountain that the people of God have made an idol of gold. This was the infamous "golden calf." They duly "worshiped it and sacrificed to it" as if it were God (Ex. 32:8). The upshot of this, God tells Moses, is that he will destroy them all and make a new nation from Moses and his descendants (Ex. 32:10)! If you had done as much for Israel as God had, you would have felt the same way—only sooner, as your patience would have worn much thinner more quickly! This moves Moses to pray right away. He prays twice in the immediate aftermath of the golden calf incident: the first time is before he goes to Israel's camp (vv. 11–13), and the second is on the following day, after order has been restored at the cost of some 3,000 lives (Ex. 32:28). Two further prayers issue from this debacle (Ex. 33:12–13, 34:9). It is the first of these, and its immediate outcome, that we want to consider today (vv. 11–14).

Desperate situations inevitably call for desperate interventions. And "desperate" describes Moses's prayer in response to God's impending sentence. He focuses on God's character. He is surely more a deliverer than a destroyer (v. 11). Moses asks, "Why…wrath?" That is, when he had already delivered his people, why *only* wrath? Had God not brought them "out of the land of Egypt with great power and with a mighty hand?" The answer Moses is looking for is obvious, but he adds two arguments in which he successively appeals to God's character and his covenant promise:

> *Argument #1*: Why should the unbelievers have the last laugh (v. 12)? This is just to ask, "What will it look like if God himself cannot even save his own people?" It is an appeal to God's essential character as the God of love and mercy, as well as of justice and power. It is as if Moses says, "What can you say of a God who saves people by mighty miracles only to snuff them out later when they backslide?" It is a good question. We

all know the feeling when a lot of effort goes down the drain because of some mistake later on. "What is the use," Moses is asking, "if it is all to end in the desert?" What boldness, to plead God's own character *against* his declaration of clearly righteous judgment upon apostate Israel!

> *Argument #2*: Why would God compromise his own covenant (v. 13)? "Remember Abraham, Isaac, and Israel, to whom You swore by your own self" and promised a great nation and a land for these descendants. Again, what a bold challenge to the Lord this is! Of course, God wanted to stir up Moses and bring him to claim these promises out of love for the people and for God himself. This was godly audacity on Moses's part, and it stands as a model for prevailing prayer for us all today. God is not afraid of honest questions, and we should not be afraid of asking them of him.

The Lord's answer also stands. He "relented from the harm He said He would do to His people" (v. 14). The glory of this is that the unchanging God—unchanging in his ultimate sovereign will and purpose—tracks us through our changeable ways, especially when by his grace we repent and return to him (see Jer. 18:1–11 for his full explanation). Jonah, you recall, preferred that God's declared judgment fall upon Nineveh—"Yet forty days, and Nineveh shall be overthrown!"—because he suspected God would forgive them if they repented (Jonah 3:4,10). When the Lord spared Nineveh, he taught Jonah (and the rest of us) something about his lovingkindness and about that lack of love for the lost that Jonah had nursed when he sat under his gourd hoping for judgment on the great city. Let us then pray with hearts of compassion for the outpouring of the grace of our Lord Jesus Christ, that it may come to more and more people.

A PRAYER FOR DELIVERANCE FROM JUST JUDGMENT
Sing Psalm 51:14–15

THINGS I WILL PRAY FOR TODAY

_____

_____

_____

_____

January 18
Punish Me Instead of Them

Moses's prayer of self-sacrifice

Blot me out of Your book... — Ex. 32:32

READ EXODUS 32:30–35

f Moses's first prayer after the "golden calf" incident appeals to the righteous character of God, his second prayer appeals from the sinful character of people. Yet, if anything, it most powerfully reveals the character of the sinner who is saved by grace. Moses, the saved sinner, prays to the God who saves by his free grace for apparently hopelessly lost sinners. More than that, Moses expresses his willingness to bear the punishment due to the idolatrous erstwhile people of God! The intimation of Jesus Christ as the once and final substitutionary sacrifice for sin cannot be missed.

Moses confesses the people's sin of idolatry and pleads for their salvation by grace (vv. 31–32a). If this is not possible, he, who is not guilty of this sin, offers his own life in the place of the guilty (v. 32b). What incredible boldness! What love for sinners! Moses identifies with the idolaters and says to the Lord, "Consider me the great idolater and punish me, but let them go." Moses knows very well that he cannot atone for anyone's sins, but he also knows that he is really no better than the rest and is as deserving of judgment, even if his sins are different ones.

The Lord's answer is to forgive while at the same time exacting suitable chastisement. The Lord tells him three things:

- Unrepented — and so unforgiven — sin leads to a lost eternity under the just judgment of a holy God (v. 33). Unrepentant sinners will "be turned into hell, and all the peoples that forget God" (Ps. 9:17). Make no mistake. This is the bottom line of God's Word to man in both law and gospel. A mistake here will be a mistake for eternity. This is hard teaching, but people often choose to have hard hearts against God.

- The "Angel" is understood to be the eternal Son of God before he was enfleshed as the son of Mary. He will lead Moses as he leads the people (v. 34ab). There is a Savior provided and he

36

must be followed. That is the way to life both now and for eternity.

⤳ Actions always have consequences. God does discipline his people (v. 34–35). This took the form of a "plague"; in this case, a kind of illness. It is chastisement, not final judgment for all eternity. It too is part of the work of God's grace toward those whose sins are forgiven.

Do we not have reason to pray with the fervor of a Moses? In Hebrews 4:16 we are commanded to "come boldly to the throne of grace, that we may obtain mercy and find grace to help in time of need." The basis of this is spelled out in verses 14–15: "we have a Great High Priest…Jesus, the Son of God." This Jesus is the same Angel who led Israel forward from what would have been a place of execution, but for his grace, this salvation was undeserved and unmerited. Jesus "passed through the heavens" (Heb. 4:14); that is, from earth to heaven. He died for our sins, rose for our eternity, and "ascended up on high" to take captive our captivity and receive gifts (of salvation) for men (Eph 4:8). Jesus fully identified with our sinfulness, in that he was able to "sympathize with our weaknesses, but was in all points tempted as we are, yet without sin" (Heb. 4:15).

Moses was willing to die for the sake of God's people. So was Paul, who can be viewed in this regard as the second Moses (Rom. 9:3). But, wonderful as their motives were, neither of them, as the hymn-writer Cecil Frances Alexander has said, was "good enough to pay the price of sin." They both knew that very well. Only God could provide the sacrifice, and it is Jesus who alone could "unlock the door of heaven, and let us in." To do this, he gave his life for lost people, to secure forgiveness and eternal life for all who will believe in him. What a Savior! And what an incentive to pray earnestly, as did Moses, in our own idolatrous times!

A PRAYER FOR ALL PEOPLE
Sing Psalm 67:3–4

THINGS I WILL PRAY FOR TODAY

January 19
Face to Face with God

Moses's prayer for the presence of God

Please show me Your glory. — *Ex. 33:18*

READ EXODUS 33:12–23

his is Moses's third prayer after the "golden calf" incident. The first appealed to the holy character of God. The second appealed from the unholy character of people. The third appeals for the daily presence of God with his people. It arises from God's chilling declaration, "I will not go up from your midst, lest I consume you on the way, for you are a stiff-necked people" (Ex. 33:3). God will lead them, but at a distance. Moses understands God's reasons, but it still troubles him. After all, do they not desperately need the presence of the Lord? What could be more lonely and fearful, than living under the constant threat of divine judgment? Moses therefore prays for God's presence with Israel as they march on to the Promised Land. This is in three parts, each followed by the Lord's answer (33:12–13, 15–16, 18).

Moses first settles his own personal relationship to God (vv. 12–13). He recalls God's assurance that he is known "by name" and has "found grace" in God's sight, and asks that this may be his actual experience as God shows him the way. Clearly, if God is not going to be with him, he can have little hope of God consenting to be among his people. God's answer, in verse 14, is instantly affirming and majestic in the simplicity of its grace: "My Presence will go [with you], and I will give you rest." The words "with you" were added by the translators, but the "you" in the Hebrew text is singular and is directed to Moses alone. God will be present with Moses, for sure. It is a chilling singular, because it says that the rest of the people are something else again. It remains to be seen whether God will persevere with them!

Moses then prays for Israel, that God would be with them all and not just with him as an individual (vv. 15–16). Moses essentially repeats his earlier prayer, but substitutes the plural "us" for God's singular "you." You see his discernment and his boldness in this prayer. He wants more than the assurance he as an individual is safe with the Lord.

Accordingly, he launches once more into the covenantal argument, "So we shall be separate, Your people and I, from all the people who are upon the face of the earth." Moses wants an assurance that all of God's people will be God's people indeed! God's answer is to grant the request! He tells us he does so for Moses's sake (v. 17). Moses's mediation is the key. It points us to the need for a Mediator between God and man. Jesus is that one Mediator (1 Tim. 2:5; Heb. 3:1–19; 9:16–24).

Moses now presses the Lord to deliver on his promise! What a bold prayer it is! "Please show me Your glory" (v. 18). And what does God do, but actually, visibly reveal his glorious presence—not all of it, but only what Moses could bear (vv. 19–23). It is a unique and unrepeated manifestation to Moses, but it is proof positive of God's love for his people, then and to this day. All the visible and audible manifestations of God, and his miracles, recorded in Scripture attest to the validity of his message of salvation all the way to Christ and the cross, and on to the promise of his coming again at the end of the age.

Surely we need the nearness of God every day. Do we not pray that he will be with us in our hearts, our thinking, our actions, our circumstances, our challenges, our conversations, our gatherings for worship, our prayer meetings, and, indeed, every aspect of our Christian experience? And does not Jesus promise, "Lo, I am with you always, even to the end of the age" (Matt. 28:20)? And what is Christ to every believer, but "Christ *in you*, the hope of glory" (Col. 1:27)? Let us constantly pray that the Lord will be with us every day, according to his promise, and to the deepening of our walk with him. Oh Lord, please show us your glory!

PRAISE FOR THE LORD'S GLORIOUS PRESENCE
Sing Psalm 102:16–17

THINGS I WILL PRAY FOR TODAY

_____

_____

_____

_____

_____

_____

January 20
Whose People Are These?

Moses's prayer for Israel's acceptance again by God

*If now I have found grace in Your sight, O Lord, let my Lord, I pray,
go among us, even though we are a stiff-necked people; and pardon our
iniquity and our sin, and take us as Your inheritance.* —*Ex. 34:9*

READ EXODUS 34:1-9

As we have seen, Scripture records four prayers of Moses after the "golden calf" incident. The first appeals to the holy character of God (Ex. 32:11–14). The second pleads from the unholy character of people (Ex. 32:31–32). The third begs for the daily presence of God with his people. The fourth prayer (v. 9) intercedes for God's revival and acceptance of the people, in spite of their failings.

The immediate occasion of this fourth prayer is the reissuance of the Ten Commandments (vv. 1–4) and the descent of the Lord in the cloud to reveal his name and his purpose for Israel to Moses (vv. 5–7). This is why Moses "made haste" to worship and pray (v. 8). God had come to him and said, not for the first time (see Ex. 20:6), that he was "keeping mercy for thousands, forgiving iniquity and transgression and sin" (v. 7). In other words, God was again reaching out, inviting repentance and faith, and offering new life to all who would follow him. Moses immediately takes God at his word and claims for Israel the promise of salvation implicit in God's coming to him (v. 9).

Moses's petition provides a beautiful model for any prayer for our acceptance by God. It may be only a one-sentence prayer, but it is packed with the riches of God's grace. It also shows Moses to be a man who understands both the human condition and the character of God. He begins with God's grace, so amply demonstrated in the fact that the Lord had "descended in the cloud and stood with him" and declared himself and revealed both his goodness and severity—and Moses still lives (vv. 5–7)! When Moses says, "If now I have found grace in Your sight, O Lord," he is acknowledging God's goodness to him personally. He is counting his blessings. You can see where he is going—if God can be merciful to him, he can be merciful to the other Israelites! The implicit argument is:

"I am no better than anybody else. I am as undeserving of God's grace as anybody. Grace is grace—unmerited favor. So why not save them too?" Here is the opener for all our prayers for lost loved ones and neighbors.

The body of Moses's prayer is a three-part plea for the Lord to embrace the children of Israel again as his own people. It is a prayer for the reinstatement of the backslidden church, and it remains pointedly relevant to the church in our day:

> First of all, "Let my Lord, I pray, go among us." Don't cast us off. Don't leave us to ourselves. Come among us in grace. Revive us again with your presence. Who can see the lifeless, gospel-less, Christ-less churches of our day and not weep the same prayer? The land is littered with empty church buildings, like so many rotten teeth. Will they be filled, to be useful again? Or extracted to be seen no more? "Will You not revive us again, that Your people may rejoice in You?" (Ps. 85:6).

> Second, "even though we are a stiff-necked people, pardon our iniquity and sin." "Stiff-necked" equals "my way" as opposed to God's way. "Iniquity and sin" is the condition of that rebellion against the Lord. Forgiveness is essential both to reconciliation with God and a new heart to love and serve him as a faithful child to a heavenly father.

> Last, "take us as Your inheritance." Israel had committed spiritual adultery and God was under no obligation to take them back. But Moses prays and God does just that! He renews his covenant with Israel (Ex. 34:10–35) and transforms them (Ex. 35–40). It is a picture of the gospel by which, through faith in Jesus Christ, those "who once were not a people...are now the people of God" (1 Peter 2:10) and have "an inheritance incorruptible and undefiled and that does not fade away" (1 Peter 1:4). "In Him also we have obtained an inheritance" (Eph. 1:11).

PRAYER FOR ACCEPTANCE AGAIN WITH GOD
Sing Psalm 44:20–26

THINGS I WILL PRAY FOR TODAY

_____

_____

_____

41

January 21
Prayer as Benediction

A prayer for the blessing of the church

The Lord bless you and keep you. — *Num. 6:24*

READ NUMBERS 6:22–26

This "Aaronic Benediction" is as much a prayer as a pronouncement of promised blessing. Surely even the slightest wish for God to do good things for others has to be a prayer. After all, we are not the Lord and cannot guarantee his blessing in anyone's life. The beauty of this wonderful benediction is that it is the gift of a pre-answered prayer. It is an invitation to believe the promise it expresses and expect the blessings it pronounces. God is neither a tease nor a maker of empty assurances. He means to do these things for those who love him. And he looks for us to ask, seek, and knock, believing and expecting blessing (Matt. 7:7).

This prayer-blessing is a poem of fifteen Hebrew words. These are arranged in successive sections of three, five, and seven words. Bible scholar Gordon Wenham has pointed out that if you take out the three occurrences of "Lord," you have twelve words left—"no doubt symbolizing the twelve tribes of Israel." This is God's dramatic way of saying that he is their Lord (three times over) and they are his people (all twelve tribes of them). The symbolism encompasses God and his covenant people in the minimum number of words.

The teaching in these fifteen words is a constant, unvarying promise of our redemption by God's sovereign grace. You will notice that the three pairs of expressions run in parallel, each with a statement about what the Lord does for us, and the practical result in us of these actions of God's grace. It looks like this:

What the Lord does for us:	The practical result in us:
(v. 24) Blesses	keeps (protection from harm)
(v. 25) Shines his face	grace (salvation from sin)
(v. 26) Lifts his countenance	peace (assurance of faith)

This corresponds to the work of God the Father, Son, and Holy Spirit as that work is more fully revealed elsewhere in Scripture. The triunity of God may not be explicitly revealed in these verses, but it is discernible in the way our covenant God deals with us as he works in our hearts and lives:

> God the Father purposes from before the creation of the world to save sinners and keep them to be his own covenant people forever (Eph. 1:4–6).
> God the Son purchases the salvation of his people, and they receive their salvation as a gift of grace through saving faith in him as their only Mediator (Matt. 1:21; 1 Tim. 2:5).
> God the Holy Spirit makes dead hearts to live and believe the gospel, and perfects the peace and fellowship of the saints with God (John 3:7–8; 14:26; 15:26; 16:13).

The same blessings are expressed in similar language in Psalm 4:6–8. The psalmist can sleep at night "in peace." Why so? The answer is that the Lord has "put gladness in [his] heart" and made him to "dwell in safety," having "lifted up the light of [His] countenance" upon him. When we pray, we are encouraged to pray to these same ends—for ourselves and others, that they and we may be preserved, purchased, and perfected by the work of God's grace in Christ, through the ministry of the Holy Spirit in our hearts. Then we will experientially discover the wonderful promise of Isaiah 26:3: "You will keep him in perfect peace, whose mind is stayed on You, because he trusts in You."

PRAISE FOR THE PEACE OF GOD
Sing Psalm 4:1, 6–8

THINGS I WILL PRAY FOR TODAY

January 22
Framing Each Day with Prayer

Prayers for daily blessing

So it was, whenever the ark set out, that Moses said, "Rise up, O Lord."
—*Num. 10:35*

READ NUMBERS 10:33–36

After the disaster of "the Golden Calf," the Israelites are revived and reorganized, and press on through Sinai to the Promised Land. God leads them, literally and visibly as "the cloud of the Lord…above them by day" (v. 34), and figuratively and symbolically in the "ark of the covenant" going before them (v. 33). This is the context of the two prayers recorded in our text. Both their context and content said to Israel, "Believe the Lord and follow him each day. Trust him to lead you every step of your way."

Moses's first prayer teaches us to begin each day with the request that the Lord would be our guide and protector throughout our waking hours. "Rise up, O Lord! Let your enemies be scattered, and let those who hate You flee before You" (v. 35). Moses does two things here:

- ❧ He prays that God will, in general, exercise his power to be with his people on their line of march each day.
- ❧ He also prays that God will, in particular, scatter his enemies and ours on any given day.

It is not an accident that David uses these words to open Psalm 68. Jesus applies this very personally when he charges us to "watch and pray" because the threats are real in our daily world. We are facing more than "flesh and blood," for we are constantly challenged by "the spiritual forces of evil" (Matt. 24:42; 26:41; Eph. 6:11–12). Let us pray before we start each day that the Lord will rise up, go before us, and scatter his enemies.

Moses's second prayer teaches us to close each day with prayer for the Lord's abiding presence through the hours of darkness and rest. "Return, O Lord, to the many thousands of Israel" (v. 36). Moses also does two things in this prayer:

⮚ He first prays that God will "return"—or better, "repose"—with his people. That is, that the infinite, eternal, unchanging God will track the finite, time-bound, changeable people of God in the cycles of their daily lives. When we are awake, he is with us, and when we are asleep, he watches over us. "I will lie down and sleep in peace," says the psalmist, "for You alone, O Lord, make me dwell in safety" (Ps. 4:8). "Behold, He who keeps Israel shall neither slumber nor sleep. The Lord is your keeper" (Ps. 121:4).

⮚ The second element is in the words "the many thousands" of Israel. We can sometimes think of God's promise to keep his people in abstract terms. It is as if, like a herd of wildebeest in the African savannah, they come through their wanderings in a mass, but meantime many individuals fall, so to speak, to the lions and the floods along the way. This is not what Moses has in mind, still less the God of all grace. Moses has all of God's covenant people in view, one by one. He wants none to be lost, and all to persevere.

We are called here to frame each day with prayers that God would both rise and repose with us. We want him to keep us in his hands in all we do in daytime and also through the night. These daily cycles parallel life and death. Sleep is a kind of death, is it not? These prayers look to eternal life—life that will never end, death that will never return. Jesus speaks to this when he says of all his believers, "I give them eternal life, and they shall never perish; neither shall anyone snatch them out of My hand" (John 10:28). This is, of course, the glorious doctrine of the perseverance of the saints. Let us then make our "calling and election sure" each day by "looking unto Jesus, the author and finisher of our faith, who for the joy that was set before Him endured the cross, despising the shame, and has sat down at the right hand of the throne of God" (2 Peter 1:10; Heb. 12:2).

A PRAYER FOR A BETTER DAY
Sing Psalm 68:1–3

THINGS I WILL PRAY FOR TODAY

_____

_____

_____

January 23
Please End It All!

The prayer of a weary soul

Please kill me here and now. — *Num. 11:15*

READ NUMBERS 11:11–15

When a great man of God like Moses asks God to kill him on the spot, you know it has to be more because of sheer exhaustion rather than simple unbelief. Moses was worn out. He had to be the moral center of Israel day in and day out. He was the leader, decision-maker, judge, and hearer of everybody's complaints. But he was only a man. Something had to give. He was at the end of his tether. You can surely identify with Moses. We have all sometimes felt like stopping the planet so we can get off. There are times when the burden gets too heavy for us. We can't do it alone (v. 14). It is all too much.

In spite of its gloomy flavor, Moses's request was not suicidal. It did not arise from any lack of trust in God. It was a believing, if despairing, prayer for help. It arose from a sense of his weakness, of a profound tiredness with this sinful world, and a longing for life in the bosom of his heavenly Father. You see something similar in Elijah's prayer during his tough times. He prayed, "It is enough! Now, Lord, take my life, for I am no better than my fathers!"(1 Kings 19:4). Elijah was clearly despairing for his life and, like Moses, in a deep despond about the viability of God's cause in the world. We would say that both Moses and Elijah were looking for an "out." It was all too much. They just wanted some relief—even from what they knew was God's calling—from a calling in which they knew they had been conducting themselves faithfully. Like Elijah after him, Moses was just worn out. This is entirely understandable. Indeed, we marvel that he was able to continue so steadfastly for as long as he did!

What was God's response to this mournful petition? Notice that there were two things the Lord did *not* do. He did not say yes to Moses's prayer. He did not take Moses's life and so relieve him of his calling to lead the people of God. Furthermore, God did not criticize Moses in any way!

The Lord understood with the utmost love and compassion what Moses was going through: "He knows our frame; He remembers that we are dust" (Ps. 103:14).

What the Lord *did* do was to give Moses the help he needed to handle the job effectively. Before the USA entered World War II and Britain was fighting Germany alone, Winston Churchill asked President Roosevelt to "give us the tools, and we will finish the job." What God did was to give Moses the tools for his job. He ordered the appointment of "seventy men of the elders of Israel" whom he endowed with "the Spirit that is upon you" (vv. 16–17). Moses did not have to soldier on without the help he needed to be effective as God's servant. This is an encouragement to us to pray for God to give us the tools we need for our discipleship to the Lord.

Notice also that Israel's complaining was faithless. Unlike Moses, they moaned about God's faithfulness and questioned his wisdom. They wanted meat and hankered after Egypt. The Lord answered them by giving them meat till it came out of their nostrils, and with it an implied rebuke of their faithlessness. Let us pray for what help we need in a believing way. If we must complain, let it be a *believing* complaint that trusts God while honestly laying out the difficulties we are unable to face. It is possible to trust God and complain at the same time. It is all about attitude of heart. David complains about his persecutors: "I pour out my complaint and moan noisily; I declare before Him my trouble" (Ps. 142:2). And almost at once the answer comes: "When my spirit was overwhelmed within me, then You knew my path" (v. 3); and he is led to victory, "For You shall deal bountifully with me" (v. 7).

A BELIEVING COMPLAINT
Sing Psalm 55:1–3

THINGS I WILL PRAY FOR TODAY

January 24
Please Heal Her!

A prayer for comprehensive healing

Please heal her, O God, I pray! — *Num. 12:13*

READ NUMBERS 12:1–13

I t is always good to pray for healing. It is only too easy, however, to stop short and reach no further than the immediate ailment itself. Two vital truths need to be remembered and applied. The first is that illnesses—whether of the body or the mind—ought always to be seen as the first installments of death. And death is the wages of sin (Rom. 6:23a). The second truth is that the healing we need most is that of our relationship to the God who made us. We need that "gift of God" which is "eternal life in Jesus Christ our Lord" (Rom. 6:23b).

What this means is that our illnesses must bring us to God. And our ever-approaching death surely adds urgency for us to do some serious reflection on our relationship to God. We do not, of course, have to see every malady as the result of some particular sin—this is almost always not the case. What we do need to see is that illness and death are the general and universal results for every one of us in this present fallen world. "One event happens to the righteous and the wicked," says Solomon (Eccl. 9:2). We all live surrounded by the uncertainties of the world, and we will all die one day. Every threat to our well-being should lead us to think about the basics of time and eternity. Death and denial are, of course, natural bedfellows. Ultimate questions are inevitably challenging and disturbing. Denial does not convey eternal life, and death is just around the corner and will not go away because you decide not to deal with it.

Miriam's leprosy was a definite judgment of God on a particular and egregious sin. She was jealous of her brother Moses, catty about his non-Hebrew wife, and contemptuous of his position as the mouthpiece of God. The Lord's rebuke is trenchant (Num. 12:6–8). The punishment fits the crime on two counts: she was given white leprous skin for her racist prejudice again dark-skinned Zipporah, and she was silenced in effect by her subsequent expulsion from the camp for claiming to be as much as a spokesman for God as Moses. Our criticisms of other people are often implied criticisms of the Lord. This is obvious in the case of Miriam. We are accountable to God, especially for our treatment of his beloved people.

Moses's prayer for Miriam's healing was essentially a prayer for forgiveness of sin. The need of physical healing is an emblem of our constant need for comprehensive healing from sin in all its forms and effects. God's response to the prayer emphasizes this spiritual aspect. If her father "had but spit in her face," she would have been ceremonially unclean (Lev. 15:8). But the law of the "leper"—by the way, probably not modern leprosy (Hansen's disease) but any number of skin diseases— required seven days outside the camp at the time of cleansing (Lev. 14:1–9). So Miriam was put out of the fellowship of the camp for that week and then restored and healed. The point is that she was chastised, brought to repentance, and restored to fellowship by the grace of God—in answer to Moses's prayer.

There is a vivid New Testament parallel in James 5:15ff., where the Lord's brother tells us that "the prayer of faith will heal the sick, and the Lord will raise him up. And if he has committed sins, he will be forgiven." The apostle John calls us to the heart of what we must always be praying for in the way of healing for lost people: "If we confess our sins, He is faithful and just to forgive us our sins and cleanse us from all unrighteousness" (1 John 1:9). This is the true and permanent healing that every human being desperately needs.

PRAISE FOR THE LORD WHO HEALS
Sing Psalm 103:1–4

THINGS I WILL PRAY FOR TODAY

49

January 25
God's Accountability to Himself

A prayer for mercy consistent with God's own character

And Moses said to the Lord: "Then the Egyptians will hear it, for by Your might You brought these people up from among them."—Num. 14:13

READ NUMBERS 14:11–19 AND
DEUTERONOMY 9:26–29

The accountability of every human being to God is one of the great themes of God's Word. We are answerable to him for "every idle word" (Matt. 12:36), that "each one may receive the things done in the body, whether good or bad" (2 Cor. 5:10). This is a truth that is basic to the preaching of both law and gospel.

When Israel as a whole accepted the report of those spies who had said that conquering Canaan would be too difficult because the inhabitants were too big and too strong (Num. 13:28–33), they decided not to enter the land as God had commanded. God was not at all pleased. He held them accountable and told Moses that he might as well get rid of them all and make a great nation from Moses and his family (Num. 14:11–12).

This moves Moses to prayer. But Moses does not pray as we might expect him to pray—that is, in terms of Israel's accountability to God, acknowledging and confessing sin and seeking his forgiveness and restoring grace. Moses rather prays in terms of *God's accountability to himself*! He pleads the eternal character and past conduct of God and begs him to be merciful to his rebellious people in consistency *with himself*. This is as brilliant as it is bold. Moses appeals along three lines:

> God's glory, honor, and his reputation before the non-believing world is at stake (vv. 13–16). If God kills his people in the wilderness, what will the Egyptians conclude? Why, they will say that God was simply unable to bring them to the land he promised to give them! Who in the big wide world of unbelievers will be impressed by such a performance?

> God's love and mercy toward sinners is also at stake (vv. 17–19, summarizing Ex. 34:6–8). If he finds none to pardon, what will this say of the mercy he promised in the past? A Redeemer who

50

redeems no one can hardly expect to be regarded as "abundant in mercy."

⤳ God's past mighty acts of forgiveness and salvation "from Egypt until now" argue for continuing to save his people from their sins in the present and into the future (v. 19). How can God be less of a Savior today than in the days that are past?

When we pray, we too can claim the very character of God as a basis of our plea. When you think about it, this is just as well because we certainly cannot plead our character or our performance as the basis for being shown mercy! We can never say we deserve to receive love and mercy. Of course we can plead our need. But need does not entitle us to blessing. Need seeks mercy, but mercy is optional with God. He owes us nothing good for anything we have done. Our need is only proof that without forgiveness we will be lost. Our need can only be a call for salvation, and salvation is all of God's free grace—unearned, undeserved, and unmerited.

In believing prayer, we come to the "God of all grace" who has "called us to his eternal glory by Jesus Christ" (1 Peter 5:10). Christ and his death for sin on the cross is the material ground of our plea. We can appeal—just as Moses shows us—to God's perfect consistency with his character and to his free grace, as exemplified in his sending his Son to save "whoever believes in Him" (John 3:16). In pleading Christ alone as our Savior, we are asking God to be merciful to us in his Son as the very revelation of his character as the God of all grace.

PRAISE TO THE EVER-GRACIOUS GOD
Sing Psalm 136:1–3, 23

THINGS I WILL PRAY FOR TODAY

_____

_____

_____

_____

_____

January 26
Praying against Our Enemies

A prayer of justified offense

Do not respect their offering. —Num. 16:15

READ NUMBERS 16

t is not very fashionable these days for any of us to pray for God to be on our side, and still less to pray for his justice upon our tormentors. Of course, if we are not first on the Lord's side, any such prayer would be presumption and even blasphemy against a holy God. So we had better be sure we are on solid ground, standing on the promises of God to be faithful to his word, and blameless in our motivations. Paul's words ought to be our priority here: "Examine yourselves as to whether you are in the faith. Test yourselves. Do you not know yourselves, that Jesus Christ is in you?—unless indeed you are disqualified" (2 Cor. 13:5). The thrust of the question is not merely whether or not you are a believer. It is about the consistency of your life with your professed faith.

Moses and Aaron came under severe criticism from Korah and his Levites and Dathan, Abiram, On, and some of the Reubenites. They basically objected to Moses's leadership and Aaron's priesthood (vv. 1–3). It was a coup d'état in the making. In response to this opposition, Moses "fell on his face" (v. 4). His prayer is not recorded, but he leaves us a good example: when you are under pressure you should pray first, and then argue your case afterward. What we do know is that Moses refers the matter to the Lord for his adjudication on the next day (vv. 5–7), but warns the complainers that they have set themselves in opposition "against the Lord" (vv. 8–11). As we might expect, all this achieves is more abuse and further lying accusations from the rebels (vv. 12–14).

Moses became "very angry" and he prayed forthrightly for the Lord to deal with these people. Moses had done them no wrong (v. 15). There was no reason for him to apologize or, worse, weakly seek some compromise that might placate them. Notice four things in Moses's response:

> He is justifiably offended and righteously angry. This is not fashionable in our own day, but it is proper in God's eyes.

52

> He turns in prayer to the Lord immediately. Prayer is the first resort in a crisis, not the last.
> He prays directly for the overthrow of his enemies. This is not for the faint-hearted but is an encouragement to the upright.
> He appeals to God to judge his innocence of their charges. This is very solemn and requires holy clarity and honesty before God.

The result of Moses's prayer was the destruction of the rebels. In the end, no fewer than 14,000 people perished! If this appears harsh, just remember that the alternative—God giving in to the rebellious—was mass apostasy from God. God has a covenant to keep and a people to save. He is not about to let reprobates overthrow his loving purpose of saving a people to himself. Moses and Aaron know what is coming, and they fall on their faces and pray that the righteous would not suffer because of the wicked among them (v. 22). The Lord's answer is to tell them to put distance between themselves and Korah's faction (v. 26ff.). The judgment duly came upon them, and God's faithful people were spared. It is a foretaste of all judgment to come!

When we are moved to pray for the judgment of wicked people, we had better first see to it that we separate ourselves from their company and their lifestyle. Paul cites Isaiah 52:1 in exhorting us: "Come out from among them and be separate, says the Lord. Do not touch what is unclean, and I will receive you" (2 Cor. 6:17). Then, like Moses, we can cast ourselves with confidence upon the goodness of the Lord, who has promised to deliver us from the hands of our enemies and his, and save us to the uttermost (Heb. 7:25).

PRAYER FOR DELIVERANCE FROM ENEMIES
Sing Psalm 43:1–3

THINGS I WILL PRAY FOR TODAY

January 27
Praying for New Leadership

A prayer for practical help in the mission of the church

Let the Lord…set a man over the congregation. —*Num. 27:15*

READ NUMBERS 27:15–17 AND DEUTERONOMY 3:23–29

Prayer tends, in practice, to be about what comes next. Even when we give thanks for past blessings of God, we have an eye forward to future blessings we desire to see. We pray because we never know what a day will bring forth (Prov. 27:1). Sometimes it is because we think we do know what may happen and are afraid of what the poet Burns called "prospects drear." This kind of "knowledge" of the future—or rather fearful apprehension based on some evidence or the lack of it—has all the more "edge" to it because we are so powerless ourselves to influence these events. And so we pray for wars to cease and killing to stop. We pray to be spared debility and be healed from illness. We pray about whatever catastrophe seems to be looming on the horizon, from global warming to the collapse of the banking system and the stock market. We can pray for anything and everything that brings pleasure or pain into our lives.

As Israel stands on the threshold of Canaan, Moses prays for the opposite reason from what so often motivates our prayers. He prays precisely because he is given to know what a day that was coming very soon would bring forth. The Lord had told him he was soon to die and, in the gentle phraseology of Scripture, "be gathered to [his] people" (Num. 27:13). Impending death ought to concentrate all our minds, even if we do not expect to die any day soon. It surely set Moses to thinking—not about himself, you will notice—about who would lead God's people after he was gone. This was all the more pointed since he was the last of the old generation from Egypt, and he had known for some time that he would never enter the Promised Land (Num. 20:12). A new day was dawning for the work of God's kingdom and that, rightly enough, brought him to seek the Lord in prayer.

Moses prayed for a practical solution. He asked God to raise up a gifted leader, so that upon his death Israel would not be "as sheep which have no shepherd" (vv. 16–17; compare Mark 6:34; 14:27). The illustration from shepherding is apt. Sheep are legendary for their tendency to "go astray" (Isa. 53:6), and this has become the metaphor for man's love affair with sin in all its forms. When the psalmist says "the Lord is my Shepherd" (Ps. 23:1), he is saying he would have been utterly lost without God, but now by faith he has been led into all of his blessings. When Jesus is called "the great Shepherd of the sheep" (Heb. 13:20; compare John 10:2, 11–16; 1 Peter 2:25), the emphasis is upon both his love for his people and his power to save sinners and lead them in "paths of his righteousness" (Ps. 23:3).

The church on earth needs effective godly leadership and God has provided for this by gifting and calling men—pastors, under-shepherds—for the service of his kingdom and people (Eph. 4:7–16). Moses prays for God to choose the right man to lead Israel into the Promised Land. God's answer is to tell Moses to take Joshua, "a man in whom is the Spirit," and invest him with authority to rule God's people (Num. 27:18–20).

Jesus sees a world in which people everywhere are like "sheep having no shepherd" (Matt. 9:36). He is "moved with compassion" and reminds his disciples that there is a harvest to be reaped but "the laborers are few." His practical application for the church then and now is simply, "therefore pray the Lord of the harvest to send out laborers into his harvest" (Matt. 9:37–38). Let us go and do likewise this very day and every day until the Lord's work is done.

A PROMISE OF FRUITFUL SERVICE
Sing Psalm 126:5–6

THINGS I WILL PRAY FOR TODAY

_____

_____

_____

_____

_____

_____

_____

_____

January 28
"No" Is an Answer

A prayer for a privilege previously denied

Let me cross over and see... —Deut. 3:25

READ DEUTERONOMY 3:23-29

Every child knows how difficult it is to take no for an answer. We always want to hear yes. Obviously, we want what we want. So, when Christians talk about "answers to prayer," they usually mean nice positive answers. Scripture does offer the strong prospect of requests being granted (Ps. 21:1; Matt. 6:8; Phil. 4:6). If we want something from the Lord, he urges us to "Ask... Seek...and Knock," with the expectation of blessing (Matt. 7:7). If we ask for what God wants for us, he will give us our "heart's desire," even if we have to be as persistent as Jacob in his wrestling with God, or the widow who importuned the judge until she got justice (Gen. 32:26; Luke 18:3–5).

"No," however, can be as valid an answer as "yes." And the Lord does say no sometimes. For one thing, he rejects sinful prayers: "You ask and do not receive, because you ask amiss, that you may spend it on your pleasures" (James 4:3). To those who outright oppose him, he says, "I will break the pride of your power; I will make your heavens like iron and your earth like bronze" (Lev. 26:19). The sky will not rain and the earth will not yield crops—all of which is to say, "Your prayers will never reach to God's ears!"

God also denies his faithful people at times, even when they ask for good things, simply because he has other, better plans for them. One dramatic example of this is God's denial of David's request to build a permanent temple in Jerusalem (2 Sam. 7:12–13). Moses desperately wanted to enter the Promised Land, but God said no. At Meribah, God told Moses that he would not cross the Jordan, because he had struck the rock twice with his staff, when he had been commanded only to speak to it (Num. 20:1–13). God still gave the water from the rock and no doubt Moses repented of his sin, but the penalty was that he would not enter Canaan. Why could the Lord not let Moses cross the Jordan—just advance that short distance—and give him his heart's desire? Does this seem a cruel and petty punishment? Why not let the old man cross over before he dies? What's the difference?

Well, we must surely believe that God is good and wise in such matters, however puzzling they may seem to us. "The LORD is righteous in all His ways, gracious in all His works" (Ps. 145:17). "He is the Rock, His work is perfect; for all His ways are justice, a God of truth and without injustice; righteous and upright is He" (Deut. 32:4).

We are reminded that sin has practical consequences in this life that are not erased by repentance. Only eternity applies the fullness of salvation to the saved. Moses's behavior at Meribah stands seriously rebuked for the bad example it is. Therefore let none of us think himself wiser than God, even if we seek sincerely to serve him.

Another consideration is that Moses's heritage is to be the leader whom God raised up to bring Israel out of Egypt, while Joshua is unambiguously set apart as the leader who will take God's people into the Land of Promise. You can see God's wisdom, surely, in taking Moses to heaven before crossing Jordan. Heaven is the very place of which Canaan was only a symbol.

God is passing the torch, so to speak, from one leader to another. The work is passing to another, as it always has and always will. Will Moses find himself frustrated in heaven, because in place of Canaan, he has Glory itself and unhindered fellowship with God? Hardly! Indeed, God's no turns out to be the blessing of blessings! And so it always will be for all of God's children. Glory, glory, glory, in Immanuel's Land!

A PROMISE OF GOD'S LOVE
Sing Psalm 91:14–16

THINGS I WILL PRAY FOR TODAY

January 29
Praying for Unsolved Murder

A prayer of community leaders

Do not lay innocent blood to the charge of Your people Israel. — Deut. 21:8

READ DEUTERONOMY 21:1–9

any crimes remain unsolved. Many criminals are never brought to justice in this world. This has several effects upon both the individuals and the communities involved. For one thing, there is a shared sense of being under threat: evil is among us—will it strike again? Then again, there is a tendency for a cloud of suspicion to hang over the community: is someone covering up the crime and protecting the guilty? People whisper, speculate, and point fingers. There ought to be, but frequently is not, a sense of corporate responsibility: Are we under some judgment? Will the Lord withhold blessing if justice is not truly done? And, not least, there is likely to be a challenge to the faith of many. Those who suffered loss will be further grieved by seeing no resolution of their cases. And even believers will question God's goodness and justice, while many who do not believe will find reasons to confirm their rejection of God and his Word, the Bible.

Deuteronomy 21:8 is a "form prayer" for an Old Testament ceremony in which a murder that defies all reasonable hope of being solved is dealt with before God as it impacts community life. Notice four things:

- First of all, a sacrifice is offered in which a heifer is taken and killed by breaking its neck (v. 4). The sin is symbolically laid upon the animal in token of the assurance that God will avenge all evil that is beyond discovery and punishment in this world.
- Then the elders from the closest community to the murder wash their hands over the dead heifer, in recognition of a certain collective responsibility for the failure of justice within their jurisdiction (v. 6). This also represents real compassion and sorrow for the bereaved.
- The elders swear their innocence of the crime (v. 7), thereby clearing themselves before God of any suspicion that the

58

community connived at the crime or may be shielding the guilty—as, alas, many will do for their own flesh and blood.

❧ Finally, the elders pray for the Lord to "provide atonement" for his people and so secure the community from "the guilt of innocent blood" (vv. 8–9). Notice that it is the Lord and not the ritual that alone can forgive sin, and that if hearts are not right with him, no amount of formal sacrifices and muttered forms of prayer will secure God's blessing.

This has practical implications for us as individuals and as a praying community:

❧ We must always be praying for the mercy of God toward those who do not know Christ. All of the atoning sacrifices in the Old Testament point to Jesus as the one and only atonement for sin. "Many sorrows shall be to the wicked; but he who trusts in the LORD, mercy shall surround him" (Ps. 32:10). Pray for the conviction and conversion of sinners, for God "commands all men everywhere to repent" (Acts 17:30).

❧ We must pray for all who are "in high positions" in government (1 Tim. 2:2, ESV), that they would administer justice in the wider community (Mic. 6:8; Rom. 13:1–4). If we would see justice in church and state and families, we must call upon the Lord of Lords to be merciful to us.

❧ We must pray for the church community, that it never wink at sin and cover up anyone's need of personal repentance, faith in Christ, and submission to justice, both divine and human. "For the time has come for judgment to begin at the house of God; and if it begins with us first, what will be the end of those who do not obey the gospel of God?" (1 Peter 4:17).

PRAYER FOR DELIVERANCE FROM ENEMIES
Sing Psalm 26:9–12

THINGS I WILL PRAY FOR TODAY

_____

_____

_____

_____

January 30
Giving God the "First Fruits"

A prayer rejoicing in God's good gifts

My father was a Syrian about to perish... — Deut. 26:5

READ DEUTERONOMY 26:5–15

The offering that occasions this prayer is a portion of the "increase" of "all the produce of the ground" after Israel settles in Canaan (Deut. 26:1–2). This was to be brought to the priest at the Tabernacle every third year, specifically to benefit those who could not easily grow their own food—the Levites, the resident aliens, the orphans, and the widows (v. 12). It was separate from the regular tithes of each year, designed for mercy ministry to those who might go hungry, if no one cared about them. The prayer, then, is an exercise in rejoicing in God's good gifts—gifts plentiful enough to be shared with others as free gifts. It is also a "form prayer" for use with the presentation of the "first fruits" of God's "increase" (vv. 10, 12). Please note that the "form prayers" in Scripture—the Lord's Prayer is the best known of them—were not given to be rattled through mindlessly, as if merely reciting the words makes for a living prayer with an automatic reward. These are to be prayed from the heart and can be used as templates for all sorts of prayers. We are charged to rejoice in this prayer in four ways:

Rejoice in God's salvation (vv. 5–10). What has God done for them? He *multiplied* his covenant people (v. 5). The "father" who was a "Syrian" is Jacob, who was chased to Egypt by the specter of starvation and became a great nation. The Lord was also *merciful* in answering his praying people by delivering them from Egyptian bondage, some 400 years later (vv. 6–8). Third, the Lord *made provision* for his people in "a land flowing with milk and honey" (v. 9). He gave them a new life, as surely as the gospel of Jesus Christ gives new (eternal) life to all who believe in him (John 3:16). The faithful believer therefore joyously declares that he brings "first fruits of the land which you, O Lord, have given me," as an offering of his worshiping soul (v. 10). Our gifts ought to celebrate God's covenant faithfulness and the fulfillment of his gracious promises. Surely every believer can say, "Thus far the Lord has helped us" (1 Sam. 7:12).

60

Rejoice in God's present provision (v. 11). Has he not given us "this day our daily bread" (Matt. 6:11)? Even our meals this very day call us to praise him! The moment we take even these basics of life for granted is when we both deny the character of God as the giver and sustainer of our lives, and fail to see his gifts as entirely the provision of his free and unmerited grace.

Rejoice in ministry to others in need (vv. 12–14). The prayer includes an honest accounting of faithfulness in this special mercy tithe. This is not pride. It is accountability in action. And if we can lie to God when we come to him in prayer, we can lie to anybody about anything. Honesty is essential to prayer and is itself a blessing added to the blessing of the first obedience in tithing.

Rejoice in anticipation of future blessing (v. 15). "Look down… from heaven," says the prophet, "open…the windows of heaven" and "pour…out a blessing" (Mal. 3:10). Let the first fruits be tokens of the later glories of good things to come! As we pray, let us:

> *record* God's grace toward us in the past;
> *reflect* upon God's good gifts to us in the present;
> *resolve* to share his gifts with those in need;
> *rely* upon him for the future; and
> *renew* our commitment to Jesus his Son…

"in whom we have redemption through his blood, the forgiveness of sins, according to the riches of his grace" (Eph. 1:7).

PRAYER REJOICING IN THE LORD
Sing Psalm 9:1–2

THINGS I WILL PRAY FOR TODAY

_____

_____

_____

_____

_____

_____

_____

January 31
Praying with an Ear to Hear

A prayer for God's instruction

What does my Lord say to His servant?—Josh. 5:14

READ JOSHUA 5:13–15

What you listen to, and how much time you devote to that listening, is probably a fair indication of what you think is important. It is remarkable just how little interest many of us show in hearing what God has to say to us. Millions who think themselves Christians never read their Bibles, hardly ever pray, and maybe manage a few annual trips to church—Christmas and Easter and maybe a funeral or a wedding. If you give God a measly five minutes for a daily Bible reading and now and again allow yourself a whopping twenty minutes for a sermon from God's word, you may well be regarded as exhibiting an exemplary commitment! Such is the state of the modern Christian attention span for the things of God!

Joshua knew he needed all the help the Lord could give him. He had led Israel over the river Jordan into the Promised Land. At Gilgal, Israel received the sign of the covenant, celebrated the Passover on the plains of Jericho, and the manna ceased after forty years of God's provision (Josh. 5:1–12). You might say that they were "on their own" in a new way. This surely came home to Joshua when he encountered a man with a sword in his hand. He knew there was fighting ahead for Israel. So he asks the man the obvious question: "Are you for us or for our adversaries?" (v. 13). The man's answer floored Joshua: "No, but as Commander of the army of the Lord I have now come."

Joshua clearly understands the "man" to be God. His response is to offer worship (v. 14). The knowledge that we are in the presence of God should first issue in *worship*—which is praising and adoring him for who he is. It should then continue to will. For Joshua this meant audible word-revelation from the Lord; for us it means the indwelling Holy Spirit speaking in the Scriptures so as to illumine our minds and convince us of his mind and will. Prayer doesn't come any simpler than this, or more profound.

Joshua bows in personal devotion to his Lord. He says, "What does *my Lord* say?" The boy Samuel answered the Lord when he called: "Speak, for Your servant hears" (1 Sam. 3:10). There is submission and love and devotion all rolled into the response of a heart drawn to the Lord. God speaks heart to heart with those he loves, and all to kindle deeper love in them.

Joshua commits himself afresh as a servant of God. He asks, "What does my Lord say to *His servant*?" When we seek God's will we had better be serious about it. This is the trouble with praying that mere form. God warns against this: "These people draw near with their mouths and honor Me with their lips, but have removed their hearts far from Me" (Isa. 29:13). As surely as we remember who God is, we will also not forget who we are, and come to him with transparent souls.

Joshua also surely expected blessing. All we are told is that the Lord told him to take off his sandals because he was on holy ground. This has nothing to do with the ground being what many today misname "the Holy Land." It was rather a reference back to Moses's encounter with God at the burning bush in Sinai (Ex. 3:5). These two meetings both inaugurate new phases in God's redemptive purpose for Israel: the first to deliver Israel from Egypt, and the second to open the way for the conquest of Canaan. A new blessing is at hand whenever the Lord answers the prayer that calls him to speak to his servants. Hear him and he will do us good.

PRAYER FOR MORE OF GOD'S WORD
Sing Psalm 119:11–12

THINGS I WILL PRAY FOR TODAY

_____

_____

_____

_____

_____

_____

_____

_____

_____

February 1
Prayer after a Setback

A prayer for practical help

What will You do for Your great name? —Josh. 7:9

READ JOSHUA 7:6–15

After Oliver Cromwell defeated the Scots at Dunbar in 1650, he declared of them: "They were made by the Lord of Hosts as stubble to the sword." On the other side, Robert Douglas, a prominent Covenanter minister, wrote to King Charles II, blaming him for the defeat because of "the controversy that God hath against you and your family, for which his wrath seems not yet to be turned away." In those days, it was assumed that God's hand was in every event, whether for blessing or curse. Today, it is distinctly unfashionable to interpret setbacks as divine judgments on sin. It is certainly dangerous to speculate on what God is doing in the events of our time. A classic case in Scripture of the pitfalls of such an approach is in the book of Job, where the "comforters" all think Job's tragedies are punishments for secret sins, when in fact he was suffering because he was righteous! God's hand is indeed in everything, but our understanding is distinctly limited and we are well advised to hold our horses on overconfident pronouncements!

The Israelites had taken Jericho, but they fell into bad ways immediately. They "committed a trespass regarding the accursed things" (Josh. 7:1). The next battle was for Ai (pronounced "ay-eye"), which was small and expected to be a pushover. An army of 3,000 men attacked, but after thirty-six casualties they all ran away! Joshua was dismayed and cried out to the Lord for answers. Like all our prayers, this one is a bit of a mixture: It was good that he prayed with *a repentant spirit* ("they put dust on their heads" (v. 6). It was not good that he prayed to *reproach God* for bringing them over Jordan (v. 7). This was self-pity and practical unbelief. It was not good that he *despaired of defeat* by the Canaanites, as if Israel's failure at Ai was irreversible (vv. 8–9). It was not at all good that Joshua did *in prayer* what the 3,000 had done at Ai—that is, run away from God's promise of victory with a plaintive "Then what will you do for your great name?" (v. 9).

64

God's answer tells us what form Joshua's prayer ought to have taken. First, he needed to get off his knees, for self-pitying prayer is not fit to be prayed (v. 10). In any case, it is a substitute for acting in faith on what is known already to be God's will. Second, the reason for the setback was sin involving the theft and retention of heathen objects of worship (v. 11). Third, realize that sin has practical consequences, one of which is the felt withdrawal of God's presence and favor (v. 12). Finally, since you had better repent or you will perish, you must "sanctify" yourselves (vv. 13–15). Joshua acted on all this counsel and the result was the unmasking of Achan and his stash of stolen property!

This suggests important lessons for us when we pray after a setback or a calamity. We can assume God is dealing with us in the events of our lives. We can assume he is completely in charge of these events. We can assume God is good and desires to do his people good. We can ponder the reasons why God might be chastising us, and we can commit to cleansing our hearts before him and seeking his grace to overthrow our present difficulties and restore us to fellowship and effectiveness in our service and discipleship. We are called to keep covenant with Jesus Christ, to pray for his promises to come to fulfillment, to cry out with humbled hearts, and to expect blessing. He is a great Savior. Never doubt him. Always look to him, and you will never be disappointed.

PRAYER FOR DELIVERANCE FROM TROUBLE
Sing Psalm 107:4–7

THINGS I WILL PRAY FOR TODAY

February 2
Asking the Impossible

Praying for a miracle

Sun, stand still over Gibeon. —*Josh. 10:12*

READ JOSHUA 10:1–15

There are many days in our lives that are just too short for all the things we need to do. Even the long Scottish summer nights of my youth, with light till after 10:00 p.m., were never long enough for all the fun we could have! We often groan that there are only twenty-four hours in the day! Joshua led Israel into battle with the "five kings of the Amorites" (v. 5). God told Joshua that he would give him a famous victory (v. 8). The Amorites were duly routed by a surprise attack, a vigorous pursuit, and a hailstorm that killed more Amorites than "the children of Israel killed with the sword" (v. 11). For Joshua, however, the victory was not complete and he was running out of daylight. So gripped was he by the force of God's promise that "not a man of them shall stand before you," that he called upon the sun and moon to "stand still over Gibeon and the Valley of Ajalon" (v. 12).

Joshua was not praying *to* the sun or the moon. He was calling upon God the Creator to give him more time to pursue the enemy, by asking the impossible—that the sun would stand still and the daylight be extended. As to how this happened, we can have no idea. Speculation is useless. The science is impossible. But, after all, that is what makes a miracle a miracle. God made a day like none before or after (v. 14). It is enough to say that it was a unique modification of the natural order, if only for a few hours. It is a vivid reminder that with the Lord all things really are possible (Matt. 19:26). It anticipates the only other day in world history when the light will not fail—the day of Jesus's second coming, which ushers in the new heaven and new earth, where there will be no night whatsoever (Rev. 22:5). On that day, the Lord's enemies will be overthrown and the Lord's people gloriously delivered forever!

We are also reminded that salvation is the work of the Lord. It is not the work of man. What do we pray for as a matter of course?

Surely the content of the Lord's Prayer comes to mind? Can we guarantee the hallowing of God's name, the coming of his kingdom, the doing of his will, our daily bread, the forgiveness of sins, escape from temptation, or deliverance from evil (Matt. 6:9–13)? Can we even get close to accomplishing any of these things? When Jesus speaks of how difficult it is for a rich man to enter the kingdom of God, and says it is as likely as a camel going through the eye of a needle, the disciples gasp and ask, "Who then can be saved?" They grasped that Jesus was telling them that it was impossible for any human being to get to heaven by his own best efforts. But here is where God and the gospel come in. Jesus says, "With man this is impossible, but with God all things are possible" (Matt. 19:23–26).

Believing prayer is, by its very nature, asking God for impossibilities. If we could do it ourselves, why would we pray? We have to have a reason to pray. No doubt many do not pray because they are sure they can go it alone without God. If so, they will be sadly disappointed. Many others will pray in the wrong direction. The Amorites' prayers were dashed down all the way to Beth Horon and Azekah, because nonexistent gods can neither hear nor act for their devotees. Prayer to the wrong "god" is no prayer at all. The God of the Bible is the hearer of prayer (Ps. 65:1). Any old prayer will not do, however, for those who come to him must come truly believing in him (Heb. 11:6). He answers *believing* prayer with all his infinite power and everlasting love. He answers with the love that sent his Son, Jesus, to do what was and still is impossible for us—for us to be saved and to be "kept by the power of God through faith for salvation ready to be revealed in the last time" (1 Peter 1:5).

PRAYER ASCRIBING STRENGTH TO GOD
Sing Psalm 68:34–35

THINGS I WILL PRAY FOR TODAY

_____

_____

_____

_____

_____

_____

February 3
From Puzzled to Persuaded

Praying for answers

If the Lord is with us, why then has all this happened to us?—Judg. 6:12

READ JUDGES 6:11–24

Private prayers are rarely neat and tidy. They are not usually like the public prayers we hear in church or in family worship, which have to be well formed and coherent if they are to lead others meaningfully to the throne of grace. Our secret prayers don't need to be tailored to others, and so they are often conversational, rambling, and ungrammatical. They may simply be "groanings which cannot be uttered" (Rom. 8:26). It is in the secret place that prayer often manifests itself in our experience most movingly. As the poet James Montgomery (1771–1854) puts it:

Prayer is the burden of a sigh;
The falling of a tear;
The upward glancing of an eye,
When none but God is near.
— "Prayer Is the Soul's Sincere Desire," stanza 2

Gideon's prayer is more a quizzical conversation than a considered communication. Gideon is one of that band of blessed and surprised people who have "entertained angels unawares" (Heb. 13:2). Only slowly does it dawn on him that he is speaking to One greater even than an angel. Nevertheless, there is a certain air of prayer in what he says to this Angel of the Lord, and in the end it results in very definite petitions, which God answers gloriously.

The Lord uses a promise of blessing to move Gideon to pray. The Angel of the Lord is actually the eternal Son of God in his pre-incarnate state—the Word who was made flesh in due time (John 1:1, 14). He comes to Gideon, who is threshing wheat in the winepress to hide it from the Midianite raiders who completely dominate Israel during this time. He first hails him as a "mighty man of valor" and assures him "the Lord is with you" (v. 12).

Gideon, however, does not want to be a leader. So he sidesteps the Angel's implication by blaming the absence of God for the sorry state of Israel (v. 13). The Lord repeats the commission in stronger language: "You shall save Israel from the hand of the Midianites. Have not I sent you?" (v. 14). Again, Gideon fobs him off—his clan is the weakest and he is the least of his family (v. 15). A third time, the Lord assures Gideon that he would be with him (v. 16), and a third time, Gideon balks, asking for a miraculous sign confirming his word (v. 17). The chosen sign was an offering that was duly consumed with fire—at which point Gideon knew the Angel was indeed God. He then feared for his life, was assured of God's peace, built an altar, and called it "The Lord is Peace" (vv. 19–24). Gideon gets the final answer to his puzzled and evasive questions!

We often "pray" as Gideon did. We push the Lord away in an effort to evade what we suspect may be his will for our lives. We are confused, don't know quite what we are asking for, and are fearful of consequences. Then the Lord answers with blinding clarity. His answer, as in Gideon's case, is in the opposite direction of our prayer. He answers the prayer we should have prayed, had we greater faith and spiritual discernment. He brings persuasion to our puzzlement, and by his grace sets us on the path of obedience to his will and fruition of his promises. So if we hardly know what to pray for when we turn to prayer, we can look for the Lord to send forth his light and his truth to guide us to where he wants us to be (Ps. 43:3).

PRAYER FOR GUIDANCE
Sing Psalm 86:11–13

THINGS I WILL PRAY FOR TODAY

February 4
Seeking a Sign?

A prayer for a sign from God

Let me test, I pray, just once more with the fleece. — *Judg. 6:39*

READ JUDGES 6:36–40

anging out a fleece" is some people's way of saying they are looking for a sign to confirm the rightness of some proposed action. The original of this is, of course, Gideon's famous fleece. God declares that Gideon is to deliver Israel from the oppression of the Midianites (v. 36). Gideon has already asked, and received, a sign (Judg. 6:17). Now he asks God again to confirm his promise by a miracle. He will lay out a fleece and the miracle will be that dew appears on it even when the ground is dry (v. 37). This duly happens, but it is not enough for Gideon, who has the nerve to ask God to do the reverse and give him a dry fleece on dewy ground! Amazingly, God does what he asks! God gives him no fewer than three signs, and all without a single word (vv. 38–40). How gracious is our God!

Jesus is quite firm that seeking signs is not the right way to confirm God's clearly stated promises. Over the centuries sign-seeking had become something of an obsession among God's people (John 2:18; 1 Cor. 1:22). It is "an evil generation" that keeps asking for signs, says Jesus. They should know that henceforth "no sign" would be given to them, "except the sign of Jonah the prophet." This sign is clearly the resurrection of Jesus himself, so he is the once and for all "sign" (Luke 11:29–32). Has this stopped Christians from looking for signs? Alas, no! Sometimes prayer and mere circumstances are used as if they were fleeces, and the conclusions drawn are invested with all the weight of divine revelation. Christians use language like "The Lord spoke to me," or "God laid it on my heart," as if their inner certainties were invested with a special sanction from heaven.

It is true that God leads us through the unfolding circumstances of his providence and gives inner conviction about his will, as Scripture principle opens up our discernment of his already revealed will. A biblical "sign" was, however, a direct revelatory act of God confirming a special word-revelation already given. Jesus has also said that there will be no signs given after the sign of the resurrection!

Was Gideon right to seek a sign? Surely not! He should have been content with the acceptance of his sacrifice. That was the standard way God affirmed his word in Old Testament times (Judg. 6:17; compare 1 Kings 18). Asking for the fleece signs evidenced doubt and faltering faith, as does all sign-seeking. We are weak, of course, and God understands this—he remembers we are dust (Ps. 103:14). So it was gracious of God to give Gideon his signs. But it was not an endorsement of this method of discovering God's will. There are indeed signs of God's hand at work in all of his creation and providence, but they are common to all humanity. In this sense "the heavens declare his glory" and "day unto day utters speech" (Ps. 19:1–2). Creation is enough to point us to him and leave us without excuse (Rom. 1:20). However, we also need to grasp the once and final revelatory "sign"—namely, that Jesus "was delivered for our offenses and raised for our justification" (Rom. 4:25).

When we pray for guidance, we have no warrant to seek signs, whether fleeces or anything else. Why? Because in Jesus we have the final sign. That is the sign we invoke when we ask him to answer prayer. He is risen. Therefore he is able to answer and is able to carry out his will. He is able to do in us and for us more than we can ask or think (Eph. 3:20), and able to give us peace in believing. We have no need to put him to any tests of his truthfulness (Deut. 6:16).

PRAYER OF CONTENTMENT WITH GOD'S WILL
Sing Psalm 119:33–35

THINGS I WILL PRAY FOR TODAY

February 5
Practical Change

A prayer that evidences sincerity

So they put away the foreign gods from among them and served the Lord. —Judg. 10:16

READ JUDGES 10:10-16

It is never easy for us to change our ways. The famous nostrum of the late Mister Rogers, the American children's TV presenter, is so appealing to us: "I like you just the way you are." That is mostly how people like themselves to be appreciated. God's word is clear, however, that God does not like us just the way we are. No! He wants us to be "holy" (1 Peter 1:16). Christians reared on hymns like "Just as I Am" may object that God wants us to come to Jesus just as we are. "Just as I am without one plea, but that Thy blood was shed for me, and that Thou bid'st me come to Thee. O Lamb of God, I come." When Charlotte Elliot wrote these words, however, she did not mean that we are fine just the way we are, but simply that we must come to Christ without any pretensions, or imagined merit. We come in our need, stripped of pride, self-will, and self-righteousness. We come in order to cast ourselves upon Christ's mercy, so that we can become what he wants us to be—saved sinners, made into new creations in Christ (1 Cor. 5:17).

Notice how the Lord impresses upon backsliding Israel the necessity of radical change. The Israelites have sinned, so God gives them something to think about. In come the Ammonites: out goes their security. After a while, they "get religion"—of a kind. They pray (v. 10), but God only gives them a history lesson and refers to the gods they had been so enthusiastic about until things went bad: "Go and cry out to the gods which you have chosen: let them deliver you in the time of distress" (vv. 11–14). Why is God so hard on them?

The reasons are pretty obvious. He wants them to be honest for a change and face their sins for what they are. He wants them to decide whom they really love—their new-found idols or the living God. He wants them to face the cost of commitment. The Lord lets them "stew in their own juice" for a while. That is tough love at work!

It seems that this concentrates their minds. We cannot read other people's hearts, but we can read the signs. They confess sin. They cast themselves on God's mercy. They throw out their little idols. They come to the Lord for deliverance, to serve him (vv. 15–16a). In this context, the Lord answers their prayers positively. Now notice carefully that even though what they did pointed to the sincerity of repentance, what they said and did could not *merit* their deliverance (Eph. 2:8). God *owed* them nothing, but God could read their hearts and could see that they meant business, especially in the second round of their prayers. Their prayers were confirmed by the practical changes they made in their lives. What the Lord does is to love them to the limit and beyond! He could bear their misery no longer (v. 16b; cf. Isa. 63:9).

Pure love and sovereign grace moved God to save them. He did not save them without first emphasizing their responsibility to cry from their hearts in utter dependence upon his grace and mercy. There can be no appeal to "good works," or "rights," or to "just the way I am." God is not interested in negotiation—still less in excuses. He wants us to flee to Jesus Christ, trusting him for his blood-bought sacrifice for sin on the cross of Calvary. For our prayers, it means praying with an earnest sincerity that is confirmed in lives lived in consistency with God's will and out of love for Jesus our Savior.

PRAYER OF CONVICTION OF SIN
Sing Psalm 69:1–3

THINGS I WILL PRAY FOR TODAY

February 6
Come to Us Again

Praying for more of the Lord

O my Lord, please let the Man of God whom You sent come to us again. —Judg. 13:8

READ JUDGES 13:1–9

anoah and his wife were childless. They surely regarded this with great sadness. When the Angel of the Lord tells them they are to have a son—the future Samson—their excitement is thinly veiled. Manoah immediately prays for a visitation from "the Man of God," whom we know with biblical hindsight, and he clearly suspects at the time, is God himself. Perhaps someone might think he was a little skeptical of his wife's story about the strange visitor and his prophecy of a miracle child, but there is plenty of evidence that he simply and fervently believed her. For all we know, this was an answer to the prayers of many sorrowing years. What emerges is a believing response to the divine visitation.

The Lord's appearance to Manoah's wife implies a desire on his part to be intimately involved in their life as a family. Manoah takes responsibility for their response as a family to God's promise. His prayer is an expression of his leadership in the home. Indeed, husbands and fathers ought to be the ones who conduct family worship in the home and lead the family to the throne of grace. Too many mothers are left to fill the gap left by a husband who shirks his responsibility. Manoah's prayer is simply for *more of the Lord* in their lives: "O my Lord, please let the Man of God whom You sent come to us again and teach us what we shall do for the child who will be born." Three things are clear in this prayer:

- ⟫ Manoah believes God for the promise given to his wife.
- ⟫ He desires the Lord's presence and fellowship in his life.
- ⟫ He acknowledges the need of following God's guidance in the child's upbringing.

These are, in practice, all bare necessities of any believing prayer. Prayer without faith in the Lord is whistling in the dark. Prayer without fellowship with the Lord is speaking to oneself. Prayer without a commitment to the Lord's known will and guidance is no more than empty noise.

The circumstances of this prayer are miraculous and unique. They have to do with God's raising up a deliverer for his people. This event ought to be regarded by us as a milestone on the road to Bethlehem and the Cross—to the birth and death of Jesus Christ, our once and for all Deliverer. Samson is a unique and unrepeatable figure in the unfolding panorama of God's plan of redemption, pointing ahead ultimately to Jesus and the gospel. Without faith, fellowship, and following in and through Jesus Christ, prayer is simply not prayer. It is an exercise in futility and even blasphemy, because it denies the only One who is able to hear prayer and give answers (Ps. 65:1ff.).

For all its uniqueness, Manoah's prayer is ordinary, universal, and applicable to all of us in everyday life. We always need to claim God's promises. We surely desire a deeper walk with the Lord. And don't we want to be taught by God and to grow as his spirit is "poured out upon us from on high" (Isa. 32:15)? Manoah's prayer encourages us to pray for more of the Lord—more love to him, more of his love and nearness to lead us, guide us, and fellowship with us. William Cowper (1731–1800) expressed this so beautifully:

> O for a closer walk with God,
> A calm and heavenly frame,
> A light to shine upon the road
> That leads me to the Lamb!
> —"Walking with God," stanza 1

A PROMISE OF COMMUNION WITH GOD
Sing Psalm 91:1–2, 14–16

THINGS I WILL PRAY FOR TODAY

February 7
Dry as a Bone

A prayer for ordinary needs

Then he became very thirsty: so he cried out to the Lord. —Judg. 15:18

READ JUDGES 15:18–20

"Self-praise is no honor," runs the common English proverb. This has not prevented self-praise from retaining its popularity in our self-centered culture. It is now standard practice for people to lead the clapping in appreciation of themselves and their accomplishments! The victory lap, once frowned on as the indulgence of overweening pride, is now an accepted prize for the winner of a major race. Scripture says, "Let another praise you, and not your own mouth" (Prov. 27:2). Even when God does marvelous things in our lives and uses us in some notable way in his service, we can too easily take the glory for ourselves. It looks as if Samson is doing this when, after killing some Philistines with the jawbone of a donkey, he composes a little victory song. There is no praise to the Lord—just a celebration of himself:

With the jawbone of a donkey,
 heaps upon heaps.
With the jawbone of a donkey
I have slain a thousand men. (Judg. 15:15–16)

Then Samson feels thirsty. The adrenaline of battle and the euphoria of victory had kept his mind off such things. But suddenly, the ordinary human need for water made the slayer of the Philistines feel weak and even helpless. He became very thirsty. Then he turned to God in prayer. Mundane as this may seem to be, it is replete with lessons for us all:

> ☙ We are only human, always human, and sometimes distressingly human! We can deny our humanity, our frailty, and our inevitable death, but it always catches up with us. This ought to humble our pride and self-reliance and rebuke those impulses that lead us away from a self-conscious depending upon the Lord, who, after all, constantly upholds both ourselves and our world by the word of his power (Heb. 1:3).

- We can and must turn to the Lord in the ordinary needs of life, and not only in those challenges that are extraordinary. Thirst for water awakened in Samson a thirst for God, and it is his need of this most ordinary fluid that moves him to further pray that he not now "fall into the hand" of his enemies. "Those that forget to attend God with their praises," writes Matthew Henry in his commentary on this passage, "may perhaps be compelled to attend him with their prayers."
- We have a God who answers believing prayer—in Samson's case, with a miracle as amazing as his earlier deliverance from the Philistines. No need is too "ordinary" for the Lord to meet. Does Jesus not teach us to pray, "Give us today our daily bread"?

This is a standing witness in the Word of God to his faithfulness in the history of Samson. It is clearly given to encourage and embolden us to pray for the most ordinary needs and to expect blessing as we humbly lay these things before the Lord in prayer. You will notice that Samson calls the place where God split the rock to provide his water *En Hakkore*—"Spring of the Caller" (v. 19). This blessing in the past—in providing a well of water for Samson—surely draws us to the fulfillment in Jesus Christ of the prophecy of "a fountain opened to the house of David and to the inhabitants of Jerusalem for sin and for uncleanness" (Zech. 13:1). Jesus is that "fountain of the water of life" (Rev. 21:6) and in him we have the promise of blessings in the future, ordinary and extraordinary, all the way to heaven itself.

PRAISE FOR THE LORD'S DAILY PROVISION
Sing Psalm 146:5-7

THINGS I WILL PRAY FOR TODAY

_____

_____

_____

_____

_____

_____

February 8
Give Me Strength!

The prayer of a feeble believer

O Lord, remember me, I pray! Strengthen me, I pray, just this once.
—Judg. 16:28

READ JUDGES 16:28–31

e naturally think of Samson as the most famous "strong man" in history. Like a great many more ordinary members of the human race, however, he sinned away his strength and in the end—when he would not have been much more than forty years of age—he was an enfeebled man, both in body and spirit. He would have agreed with David's later testimony in Psalm 31:10: "For my life is spent with grief, and my years with sighing; my strength fails because of my iniquity, and my bones waste away." Sin always has consequences and these reach into both body and soul.

Thankfully, this is not the end of the story for either Samson or the psalmist. In the same psalm, David admits, "I said in my haste, 'I am cut off from before Your eyes'; nevertheless you heard the voice of my supplications *when I cried out to You*" (Ps. 31:22, italics added). So it was with Samson, as Matthew Henry notes in his wonderfully pithy way, "That strength which he had lost by sin, he, like a true penitent, recovers by prayer." Prayer is for weak people—or, rather, people who understand their true weakness and the reasons for it, and, not least, the answer to it. Sin and its consequences are not irredeemable, even on this side of heaven.

Notice how Samson prays. He asks for three things. He asks to be *remembered* because he feels forgotten. He asks God to *strengthen* him, because he is a shadow of his former self. He asks this so that he may have *vengeance* for his two eyes. These correspond to the three basic ingredients of any prayer arising from a felt sense of weakness and helplessness:

> The first is *restoration* to a lively and active covenant with God. This is not merely about us calling on God, but is about *the Lord* setting his love upon us afresh. There is a desire that the Lord draw near to us, so that we commune with him in our

hearts. "I want nothing but a further revelation of the beauty of the unknown Son of God," wrote Samuel Rutherford on January 1, 1637.

⟫ The second is the *receiving* of upholding and enabling grace from the Lord, as the equipping necessary to faithful service for him. We are talking about nothing less than a reawakening of the experience of God's power. Paul passionately prayed "that I may know Him and the power of His resurrection, and the fellowship of His sufferings, being conformed to His [Jesus's] death" (Phil. 3:10).

⟫ The third is a *resolving* to act in the future in practical faithfulness to God's cause and kingdom. If Samson looks to be acting too much out of a desire for revenge, it is well to remember that God's perfect will can still be served by the imperfect service of believers as they act in faith, looking to the Lord's honor and glory. The great goal is the vindication of God and his honor and glory in his Son, Jesus Christ.

Do we not, for all our weakness, desire in the end the complete overthrow of the world, the flesh, and the devil? So let us in all our prayers ask the Lord to remember us, strengthen us, and enable our faithfulness to the great goal of his eternal glory and our eternal blessedness in Christ. Jesus has bound the "strong man"—Satan—and it is the grace of the gospel that will "plunder his house" by bringing more and more from darkness to light in Christ Jesus (Mark 3:27).

PRAYER WHEN IN TROUBLE
Sing Psalm 31:9–11

THINGS I WILL PRAY FOR TODAY

February 9
Third Time Right

Prayer that is better late than never

Shall I again draw near for battle? — Judg. 20:23

READ JUDGES 20:23-28

The background to this agonized prayer is one of the most sordid events in biblical history. A mob of Benjamites in Gibeah commit the rape-murder of a Levite's concubine, after he, with brutal callousness, gave her to them to save his own skin, for they really wanted to abuse him. Their perversity is then visited on the poor woman, whom they first rape and then murder. Next day, her former lover divides her corpse and sends a piece to each of the tribes of Israel, calling for the avenging of the atrocity (Judg. 19). In response, Israel mounts a punitive expedition against the tribe of Benjamin. The sides are unequal, but the outnumbered Benjamites twice defeat Israel with large loss of life (22,000 and 18,000). After this rough handling, Israel desperately seeks the Lord's will as to whether they should try for a third time to chastise the defiant Benjamites, who had risen in defense of the depravity of their kith and kin.

What is important to grasp is that up to this point the Israelites either had not sought the Lord's will, or had done so in a most perfunctory manner. They first muster for war without the slightest reference to God. They had simply decided for themselves to punish the men of Gibeah (Judg. 20:11). They then observe the ritual obsequies of national religion (Judg. 20:18). Like the civil religion that lingers on in western secular democracies today, it looks more like a routine request for God to rubber-stamp their agreed policy than any serious inquiry as to his will. God gives them what they want and lets them go down to a horrendous defeat. Obviously chastened by this reverse, they go to God with weeping (v. 23). God again agrees to an attack on the Benjamites, and for a second time they are repulsed with fearful carnage. For a third time they approach the Lord, and for the first time we have solid evidence that they were humbled in heart and broken in spirit before the Lord (v. 26). They weep, they fast all day, they offer sacrifices for sin, and they ask whether they should fight or cease to fight—the first time they seem to be open to being told what they hitherto did not want to hear. God's answer is to send them out to fight, and, for the first time, he promises victory to their arms (v. 28)—and the third time, they gain their victory, albeit with excessive ferocity (Judg. 20:46–47).

What does this teach us? Surely to be careful to understand the revealed will of God *before* we act, and not, as with Israel, only after 40,000 corpses litter the battlefield. We also unquestionably need guidance from the Lord *even when* the situation seems clear and a particular response justified. We also need to recognize that setbacks of all kinds in life are *wake-up calls* to go to the "throne of grace for grace to help in time of need" (Heb. 4:16). Here is a checklist for you:

> Have you ever acted before you prayed?
> Have you ever prayed perfunctorily because you were going to do what you were going to do anyway?
> Have you ever been so desperate that you prayed long and hard, with persistence, patience, reverence, humility of mind, and an expectant trust in the Lord?

Which of these choices were followed by real fruit in your life? Which resulted in real and demonstrable blessing from God? Apply this to your choices for today. It is better to pray later than never, but it is much better to pray early, earnestly, and long before you are put to the test! Depraved injustice needs to be opposed, but unless through prayer the Lord's will is first sought and observed, the effort will inevitably result in false starts and evil fruit. Let us first seek the Lord and get things right the first time!

PRAYER FOR RESCUE
Sing Psalm 6:1–4

THINGS I WILL PRAY FOR TODAY

February 10
Why Us?

Prayer in the wrong direction

O Lord God of Israel, why?—Judg. 21:3

READ JUDGES 21

ivil wars are always relentlessly uncivil. Their ferocity is peculiarly intense. Israel's civil war over the Benjamites' murder of the Levite's concubine was disastrously ruinous, in that it almost resulted in the extinction of the entire tribe of Benjamin. Only six hundred men were left alive when the fighting was over! The Israelites had not only committed genocide, but they had vowed to forbid their daughters to ever marry a Benjamite. They therefore had to find six hundred women from somewhere, if the tribe was to be restarted! This also added up to the Israelites striking a savage blow at the very covenant God had made with them to be his people. They had reason to weep bitterly and cry to God in prayer (vv. 1–2). Sinning against people is sinning against God, and accountability to God entails exposure to the eternal, as well as the temporal, consequences of such wickedness.

Their prayer is basically a self-pitying question: "Why did this happen to us?" There is no evidence they reflected on their sins or seriously sought God's will. Sure, they went to church and prayed. But their answer was to find six hundred marriageable girls elsewhere, through a combination of murder and kidnapping! Did they find that in God's revealed will? Did it come from any application of right biblical principle to their predicament? Of course not! It was no better than brutal pragmatism. It is a wonder of God's grace that he did not obliterate the whole of Israel right there and then! If this is the people's "repentance," it looks, if anything, even worse than their sin! The only comment we have in the text that indicates God's assessment is in the last verse of Judges: "In those days there was no king in Israel; everyone did what was right in his own eyes" (v. 25). God was their king, but they were not listening to him.

"Why?" may be the most common prayer in our world. Pagans pray it. People of all faiths pray it. Even serious Christians pray it. To be sure, asking why something has happened is a legitimate question in itself. But as in Israel's case, it frequently arises from self-pity, continues in the wrong direction, and ends somewhere other than God's clear will. The answer ostensibly sought is often obvious enough but implies guilt that the inquirer denies to admit. Often we ask why not to get a real answer, but to shift the blame to someone or something else. Ultimately, the blame may be shifted to God. Why did he let this happen to me? If he exists and is a loving God, surely he will love me and stop bad things from happening to me—even stop me from doing bad things to myself. Was Israel quietly blaming God for its woes? Maybe yes, maybe no. One thing is sure, the Israelites give little evidence of accepting the blame, and no evidence of a serious desire to know and do God's will.

When we ask God why, we first need to be honest before God. Are we facing the facts? Are we ready to confess sin, or are we determined to shift the blame? Are we serious about knowing God's will? Are we willing to say with Job, "Though He slay me, yet will I trust in Him," even while we honestly argue our case to his face (Job 13:15)? Are we committed to personal holiness in the future? Until we take these steps, one by one, we will never escape from the orbit of the "Why me?" that circles endlessly within us, so often fueled by self-pity and denial. Israel's "why-prayer" was profoundly painful but inherently insincere, and it ended where it began—in a determination to do what was right in its own eyes, rather than God's. This is a warning to us not to make the same mistake, but rather to cry out to the Lord in the humility of a broken spirit and a contrite heart (Ps. 51:17) for his solutions to our perplexities.

PRAYER OF HUMBLED TRUST IN THE LORD
Sing Psalm 38:15–18

THINGS I WILL PRAY FOR TODAY

February 11
A Silent Prayer

A prayer against God's providence

Now Hannah spoke in her heart; only her lips moved, but her voice was not heard. —1 Sam. 1:13

READ 1 SAMUEL 1:6–18

What are God's works of providence? The answer to the *Shorter Catechism* 11 says they are "his most holy, wise, and powerful preserving and governing all his creatures and all their actions." At first sight, this might appear so coldly monolithic that the only godly response would appear to be to bow fatalistically to the inevitability of every event and circumstance that comes along. How could we pray in such a context? Would we not just have to say, with fatalistic resignation, "It is God's will"? Could we ever pray for things to change—*against* the providence of God? Well, Scripture teaches us that we certainly are to pray, and, more than that, that prayer is indeed an instrument of change from the very hand of God! God is in control, but he commands us to pray.

Hannah's prayer for a son is proof positive that God's providence is not fatalism. She is not the first childless person in Scripture to pray for a child (cf. Gen. 15:1–6). She is the first, however, to express outright unwillingness to accept the providence of God. Hannah's problem, twice stated, is that "*the Lord* had closed her womb" (1 Sam. 1:5–6). This fact was wickedly exploited by her rival, Peninnah, and was the root of a consuming misery that blighted every day in Hannah's life. Hannah did not accept all this with serene submission. She wept and could not eat her food (v. 8). She was not happy with her lot in life—God's providence of childlessness—and she hoped this would not be God's last word. She prayed for a son.

Every year Hannah and her husband went to Shiloh to the tabernacle to worship the Lord. This particular visit was to change her life and the life of God's people forever. Her evident unhappiness drew comment from her husband and this appears to have moved her to go to the tabernacle and seek the help of God. She "prayed to the Lord and wept in anguish" (v. 10). It was not a happy prayer full of thanksgiving for her circumstances.

She prayed silently—alone with God, albeit in the bustle of the tabernacle (v. 13). She asked that the Lord remember her in her affliction. She did not reproach God for closing her womb, but she did ask God to give her a child and reverse the painful providence of her childlessness. She promised that the son would be given to serve the Lord all his life as a Nazirite (see Num. 6:1–21). In the end, she had the blessing of Eli, the priest of Shiloh. She was consoled and "went her way and ate and her face was no longer sad" (v. 18).

This has some clear application to our prayer lives:

- We are free—indeed, urged—to bring everything that troubles us to the throne of grace—"for grace to help in time of need" (Heb. 4:16).
- We are also free to pray against known and even longstanding providences of God. The Bible knows no fatalistic acceptance of the *status quo*. Paul ceased to pray for the removal of his "thorn in the flesh" only after direct special revelation that it would stay, and that God's grace would be sufficient for him. We may pray until God answers.
- We are free to invoke God's covenant love and mercy for his people. Is he not "the hearer of prayer"? And is this not why we are to come to him (Ps. 65:1)?
- We are free to promise fresh biblical obedience upon positive answers to prayer: not as bargaining with God, but as a seal of our devotion and commitment to him. Hannah covenanted with God to devote her (Levite) son to the (Levitical) service of God's house, but promised that he be a Nazirite in his devotion as far as she was able to secure it.

God said yes! Let us say, "Hallelujah!"

PRAYER UNDER A DEPRESSING NEED
Sing Psalm 109:21–26

THINGS I WILL PRAY FOR TODAY

February 12
Silent No Longer

A prayer of passionate praise

My heart rejoices in the Lord.—1 Sam. 2:1

READ 1 SAMUEL 2:1–10

here is nothing quite like an answered prayer. Hannah's first prayer was spoken in silence. She prayed for a son. She prayed to be a mother. She begged God to overthrow the hard providence of her childless years (1 Sam. 1:9–11). God does just that, and after Samuel is born, it is no surprise to find her silent no longer! This is pure, passionate, and exultant praise. We can immediately see that it also forms a beautiful model for prayer, as step by step it unfolds the breathings of a thankful, believing heart.

Praise in prayer is always rooted in the joy of salvation. Hannah does two things to start with: she rejoices in the Lord from the depth of her heart, and she also smiles at her enemies (v. 1). These are twin sentiments in believing prayer and they arise in tandem from the fundamental knowledge that God has actually saved her. She can say, "I rejoice in Your salvation," because the blessing of her son has overthrown both her childless condition and the taunts of her rival. In New Testament terms, this means reflecting on what Jesus Christ has done in bringing you to himself. *Step #1 in praising God is to rejoice in one's salvation.*

Praise in prayer celebrates God for who he is. Hannah tells God about himself. Why bother? After all, God knows who he is! But what we say to God about him bears testimony to his true importance in our lives. Too many prayers are all about us and our needs. They leave the distinct impression that God is important more for what he can do for us, rather than who he is in himself. Hannah rehearses four leading aspects of the biblical doctrine of God, precisely because it is the character of God—even more than the gift of her child—that excites her worship and adoration. God is "holy" (perfectly righteous)—and uniquely so (v. 2ab). He is all powerful (omnipotent)—he is the "rock" (v. 2c). He is the God of "knowledge" (omniscient)—therefore there is no place for arrogance (v. 3ab). He is perfectly just—"by Him actions

86

are weighed" (v. 3c). *Step #2 in praising God is to worship him for his intrinsic being and his holy character.*

Praise in prayer recounts God's mighty acts in history and redemption. Hannah mentions three reversals effected by the Lord on a regular basis. He breaks "bows"—i.e., wicked people (1 Sam. 2:4; see Matt. 5:3). He provides for the hungry (v. 5a), and he gives children to the childless (v. 5b). He is able to do this for three basic reasons: he "kills and makes alive" (v. 6); he "makes poor and makes rich" (v. 7); and he "raises the poor from the dust" (v. 8bc). Overarching this is the fact that he is the Creator-God who owns "the pillars of the earth" (v. 8c). *Step #3 in praising God is to count your blessings.*

Praise in prayer looks to what God will do in the future. Hannah speaks prophetically of the Davidic king, who foreshadows Jesus Christ and his Lordship (see Ps. 89:20–21; Luke 22:43). As she prays, she is given a prophetic glimpse of God's coming kingdom and his "anointed" king. This is a promise for all future generations of God's people, for God's "anointed" will "guard the feet of His saints" (v. 9) and "judge the ends of the earth" (v. 10). In the fullness of time, another mother of a special child would pray, "My soul magnifies the Lord, and my spirit has rejoiced in God my Savior. For He has regarded the lowly state of His maidservant; for behold, henceforth all generations will call me blessed. For He who is mighty has done great things for me, and holy is His name" (Luke 1:46–50). *Step #4 in praising God is to expect blessing and claim God's promises in his Son, Jesus Christ.*

PRAYER MAGNIFYING THE LORD
Sing Psalm 34:1–10

THINGS I WILL PRAY FOR TODAY

February 13
Heavens Like Iron

A prayer that deserves to be unheard

He did not answer him that day. —1 Sam. 14:37

READ 1 SAMUEL 14

On the face of it, Saul's prayer looks like the real thing. Saul prayed and God simply chose not to answer on the same day. Who has not waited for answers to his prayer? The context, however, shows this to be an ungodly prayer that the Lord refused to dignify with an answer. God doesn't say "Yes." He doesn't say "No." He just doesn't say! Of course, in his not saying, God registers his displeasure and leaves an implicit warning to Saul—and to anyone else with ears to hear: "It is a fearful thing to fall into the hands of the living God!" (Heb. 10:31). Watch what you say to God and about him.

Why then is Saul's seeking God's will not what it seems to be on the surface? When Saul first responds to Jonathan's attack on the Philistines at Michmash, he calls for the ark and the high priest but then waves them away. He decides he doesn't need God's direction after all! He effectively humiliates God before his people (vv. 18–19).

When he does join the battle, and it is on the way to being won, he makes a vow cursing anyone who eats any food before he, Saul, avenges *himself* on *his* enemies. He does not seek God's will here, either. He just makes a vainglorious vow that is without biblical warrant and is dangerously impractical (v. 24). Several harmful consequences result from this. Jonathan unwittingly transgresses Saul's oath (v. 25ff.). This leads to an angry over-reaction in criticizing his father (v. 29), and it diminishes Israel's victory (vv. 30, 36–37). Later on, it issues in hasty food preparation, so that blood is eaten contrary to God's law (1 Sam. 14:31–35; Lev. 19:26). It exposes Saul's ungodliness in his willingness to kill his own son for violating his silly, vicious, and unlawful vow. Only the resistance of the people spares Jonathan's life (vv. 38–46).

What does this say about Saul's prayer? It tells us it is not a *believing* approach to God. It is rather a case of a man who is ready to *use God* when it suits him, by going through the motions. This tells us that not everything that looks and sounds like a prayer really is true prayer. God's non-answer tells us that there are prayers God will not accept for a moment! Any old prayer is not prayer as God defines it. God looks on the heart. He is not impressed by what looks and sounds like a prayer, however grand and pious the words, when there is not even a spark of a living faith in it. For "without faith it is impossible to please Him, for he who comes to God must believe that He is, and that He is a rewarder of those who diligently seek Him" (Heb. 11:6), and "if I regard iniquity in my heart, the Lord will not hear" (Ps. 66:18).

That is why God let Saul stand and wait for an answer that was not coming. He made Saul's "heavens like iron" and his "earth like bronze" (Lev. 26:19). Whether the Lord says "Yes" or "No" to a believing prayer, his answer is an expression of his love for us. Closed doors are as valuable as open doors, when they are God's will for us. But God's rebuff of unacceptable and unbelieving prayer is a fearful abandonment that leaves us to ourselves, to get what we really want deep down—our own way. Such prayers as Saul's take whatever they can get from God, but on their terms, not his. The Lord will have none of this. He lets the circumstances speak and demonstrates the sinful folly of Saul's behavior. As Saul sowed, so he reaped. The Lord calls us to approach with boldness his throne of grace (Heb. 4:16). He promises answers to the prayer of faith (Matt. 7:7; James 5:16). Believing prayer is what God wants and believing prayer is what God blesses in Jesus Christ our Savior.

AN ACCEPTABLE PRAYER
Sing Psalm 56:1–4

THINGS I WILL PRAY FOR TODAY

February 14
Why Bother?

Praying when the answer seems obvious

He will come down. — *1 Sam. 23:11*

READ 1 SAMUEL 23:10–12

Why bother praying if you are certain you know the answer? David has saved the Israelite town of Keilah from the Philistines, and he is certain that King Saul will soon find out where he is and mount an expedition to arrest him. This is what we would call "a no-brainer." In leaving Keilah to the tender mercies of his nation's enemies, Saul made no effort to fulfill the biblical duty of civil government to protect its own people from their enemies. But faced with a domestic threat to his power, like David, Saul springs into action to preserve his power. Such rulers always find it easier to make war on their own people. David knows this would happen next, but he still seeks God's guidance. Why does he bother? Is God's will not obvious enough in the circumstances?

Saul meanwhile is quite sure that he knows God's will. He is so certain that the Lord has delivered David into his hands, that he sees no need whatsoever to seek his will (1 Sam. 23:7–8). Saul just presumes on God's providence and favor, without showing the slightest evidence of any real reliance on God. This is worse than lip service. David, in contrast, sincerely lays his concern before the Lord (1 Sam. 23:9). In this way, the narrative sets up Saul's dismissive attitude to God as the context for David's care to consult the Lord's guidance. David knows what Saul is up to. Had David acted on this assessment of the obvious, no one would have thought worse of him for not formally consulting God through the high priest's ministrations. Yet he prayed and sought God's will all the same!

The fact remains that David still has a real need for the Lord's guidance. What seems inevitable and obvious to us is not the equivalent of infallible certainty. It is always right to go boldly to the throne of grace *for* grace to help in time of need (Heb. 4:16). It is impossible to waste God's time when going to him in believing prayer. He is the hearer of every prayer of faith (Ps. 65:2). David is a praying man, while Saul is not. Specifically, David needs assurance on two points, even though he is persuaded he is already on the right track. First, will Saul come to Keilah, as David expects? God's answer is yes (v. 11). Second, in that event, will the people of Keilah deliver David to Saul? David surely expects them to do so, if only to save themselves from the same fate as the priests and the people of Nob (1 Sam. 22:17ff.). Again, God's answer is yes (v. 12).

This has some significant implications for the way we approach our personal prayer:

> ⟫ No outcome is so obvious that we will not profit from taking it to the Lord in prayer.
> ⟫ Prayer is not just for extreme situations, but for our daily lives. It is the ordinary private means of grace by which we commune with our Father in heaven, and he with us.
> ⟫ There is no circumstance in which we can cope on our own without the grace of God and the enabling power of the Lord Jesus Christ. And there is no circumstance in which he will leave us to cope alone, provided we ask him to help us.

David understood that he was always dependent on the Lord to preserve his life from Saul and from every other threat in this fallen world. He knew his "times" were in God's hands, but he never took it for granted so as to neglect prayer (Ps. 31:5). We too must look to our Savior in everything, believing that he will answer every prayer of faith with the rich blessings of his grace.

PRAYER FOR DELIVERANCE FROM PERSECUTION
Sing Psalm 143:9–12

THINGS I WILL PRAY FOR TODAY

_____

_____

_____

_____

_____

_____

_____

February 15
What Now?

Praying when friends turn against you

Now David was greatly distressed, for the people spoke of stoning him. — *1 Sam. 30:6*

READ 1 SAMUEL 30:6–8

We expect our "enemies" to give us trouble. When friends turn on us, however, the sense of betrayal and grief is horribly enlarged and intensified. David and his followers live very dangerously when "on the run" from Saul. Yet the Lord preserves them, often in the most amazing ways. Earlier, God had delivered them from Saul on many occasions. Nevertheless, David eventually cracks under the stress of it all and flees to the Philistines (1 Sam. 27:1). This is not his best moment. It also leads to some nasty consequences, the last and worst of which forms the context of the prayer we are considering. After David is released from his entanglement with the Philistine king Achish, he and his men return to Ziklag. They must have been very happy to be going home, spared the necessity of fighting on the Philistine side against their fellow countrymen. Alas, their joy turns to ashes when they discover, after saving Keilah from the Philistines, that the Amalekites have sacked Ziklag and taken captive their families (1 Sam. 30:1–3).

Their various responses are as instructive as they are understandable. They all weep until they have no more capacity for weeping (v. 4). They even, in verse 6, speak of stoning David—an instance of the standard blame-shifting, knee-jerk reaction to disaster. When the football team has a losing season, just blame the coach! David responds in three ways:

> First, David "strengthened himself in the Lord his God" (v. 6). He prayed and meditated about his anxieties over the hostility of his people. David follows his own advice in Psalm 4:1: "Hear me when I call, O God of my righteousness! You have relieved me in my distress; Have mercy on me, and hear my prayer."

> Second, he seeks the Lord's will in the (then) appointed manner (v. 7). He turns from his now-resolved inward upheaval to the

need for God's guidance in the crisis that had overtaken their families.

⤳ Finally, he proposes a course of action and seeks the Lord's will. The Lord answers with the assurance that if he pursues the enemy, he will recover all the captives (v. 8).

The New Testament application is summed up by James: "Is anyone among you suffering? Let him pray" (James 5:13a). When we suffer, our natural inclination is to groan and complain, neither of which solves the problem. The true response of faith is to go swiftly and earnestly from our grief to our God, and resist all temptation to blame somebody or to wallow in endless sorrow and self-pity. If we are to do this, we will have to believe that God is not only there to hear and answer, but is sovereign and also full of grace. David's friends responded—understandably enough—with anger and wanted to take it out on someone who could be held guilty and immediately punished for their woes. David jumped over that tempting entanglement and made straight for God's throne of grace.

Jesus calls us to himself as the one always ready to hear us, and has promised never to leave us but to be with us even to the end of the age. Jesus has faithfully "remembered us in our lowly state, for His mercy endures forever" (Ps. 136:23). Whenever we are cast down and are, as David was, betrayed by our friends, let us pray and expect blessing from the Lord.

PRAYER FOR DELIVERANCE FROM ENEMIES
Sing Psalm 35:24–28

THINGS I WILL PRAY FOR TODAY

_____

_____

_____

_____

_____

_____

_____

_____

February 16
Where Do We Go from Here?

Praying before moving

David said, "Where shall I go up?" And he said, "To Hebron." —2 Sam. 2:1

READ 2 SAMUEL 2:1

Moving is always a difficult thing at the best of times. It is said in our day that the stress of moving house can be a factor in the development of cancer. Whether or not this is true, there is no question that having to pick up and go and live somewhere else is never an easy transition. Throw in taking the reins of power as head of state after a life on the run and the challenges multiply to no end.

After King Saul and his three sons die in the battle at Mt. Gilboa, David knows that his time to become king has arrived. He does not, however, jump the gun and head for whatever passes for the center of government in Israel at that time. In fact, Israel was in chaos. There was no real political center, except maybe Shiloh, assuming the tabernacle still functioned. So David is cautious. His first action is to stay put and seek the Lord's will. Since the legitimate chief priest Abiathar is in his camp, this he can do with some ease and confidence.

David has two simple questions. Should he go up to Judah? And to which city should he go? The answers given through the high priest are "Yes" and "To Hebron." This is not simply a matter of changing jobs and deciding on moving house. We are all used to that and it can be difficult enough. For David, this is nothing less than a step on the road to the right fulfillment of true prophecy. God had promised 500 years before that he would give Israel a king (Deut. 17:15). Saul was the false start. David is the true king of God's choice (1 Sam. 16). So this is a momentous and unique event, not only for David, but for all of God's people and the whole course of world history even to the present day. We also need to remember that the Davidic kingship finds its permanent fulfillment in Jesus Christ, David's greater son, who is also David's Lord (Luke 20:41–44). David stands at a milestone in the history of redemption. He holds his breath and enquires of God.

Our less world-shaking moves are no less to be the subjects of seeking the Lord's will. In James 4:13, the Lord's brother rebukes the businessmen who should have set their moves before the Lord and his will: "You ought to say, 'If the Lord wills, we shall live and do this or that.'" We have no call to go to an earthly priest for chapter and verse revelation as to whether or where we are to go. We also have no warrant to make decisions on the basis of mere feelings or even feelings about some surprising text from Scripture. I was told about someone who was anxious to know where he should move to work and live. He came on Acts 28:12 where Paul tells about landing in Syracuse, and then he just "knew" he had to go to Syracuse—not the one in Sicily, mind you, but the one in New York! Paul only stayed in his Syracuse for three days, but that detail didn't figure in our American's mystical misapplication of Scripture!

What we do have is Jesus, our "great high priest," who answers prayer (Heb. 4:14–16) and who, in the interplay of the Holy Spirit and the Word of God upon our prayerful decision-making, does guide us in the way we should go (Heb. 8:11). We are no more in the dark than David was before he asked the Lord. Indeed we are clearly in the light—because Jesus is the Light of the World and in him we can, must, and will "walk in the light, as He is in the light" (1 John 1:7). Let us pray before all our "moves," however insignificant they may be. God has promised every believer, "I will instruct you and teach you in the way you should go; I will guide you with My eye" (Ps. 32:8).

PRAISE FOR GOD'S GRACE ALONG LIFE'S WAY
Sing Psalm 139:1–8

THINGS I WILL PRAY FOR TODAY

_____

_____

_____

_____

_____

_____

_____

_____

February 17
The Sound of Marching

Praying to the Lord who goes before us

The Lord will go out before you. — 2 Sam. 5:24

READ 2 SAMUEL 5:19–25

rayer worthy of the name presupposes not only that answers exist, but that there is a God who answers and has the power to make his answers stick. Anything less is no better than whistling in the dark. It is like groaning when your back is hurting. Making noise is vaguely comforting but you know it cannot heal anything. It is no more than a powerless wish that the pain would go away! In contrast to this, believing prayer is effectual prayer. The believer comes to God believing that "He *is*, and that He is a rewarder of those who diligently seek Him" (Heb. 11:6, italics added). He comes to the Father through Jesus Christ his Savior (1 Tim. 2:5). Believing prayer presupposes something else, namely that the God who loves his people and who knows what they need before they ask him (Matt. 6:8) is always preparing the way ahead beforehand, so as to answer that prayer. God's answer to David's prayer for guidance in confronting the Philistine invasion makes this marvelously clear by providing a clear sign by which David would know when to strike. Before the Israelite army moves into battle, the Lord will signal that he has already gone into action ahead of them by giving a sound of marching in the tops of mulberry trees! Then David will know for sure that the Lord is going out before him "to strike the camp of the Philistines" (v. 24).

The central fact is that God *is* on the march in human history. He who gave David the sound of marching in the treetops is already going into action ahead of his people. All the time, invisibly and sometimes quietly and sometimes dramatically, God is on the move. He is able and willing to undertake for his people, and for at least three reasons:

➢ He is the *sovereign-God* who is actually and absolutely the "great King over all the earth" (Ps. 47:2, 7). He does his will among the armies of heaven and among the inhabitants of the earth, whether or not they discern it.

96

- He is the *covenant-God* who "keeps Israel" (Ps. 121:4). He loves his people, he watches over them at all times, and he orders their circumstances in his infinite wisdom and everlasting love. Even the bad circumstances will serve a gracious purpose for his people (Rom. 8:28).
- He is the *redeemer-God*, who delivers his people from their enemies, including death, which is the last one, and hell, which is the worst (cf. Ps. 110:7). God loves those who are his and delights in hearing and answering the prayers of the saints. Because of this he sent his Son to save his people from their sins (Matt. 1:21; John 3:16).

When we pray, it is not to inform the Lord of circumstances of which he is unaware. We never need to wake him up, as if he was oblivious to our plight—compare the priests of Baal in 1 Kings 18:26–27. We never need to persuade our Father in heaven of a suitable course of action or get him to change his mind so as to be a better help to us. He is already going on before us—before we pray, even before we know we ought to pray, and long before we act in the obedience of faith. We are the ones that the exercise of prayer is designed to "bring up to speed." And we can come with boldness to the throne of grace precisely because the Lord is ahead of the game...because in Christ we have a Savior who has promised to be with us and never forsake us, every moment of our days.

PRAISE FOR GOD'S GOING BEFORE US
Sing Psalm 44:1–4

THINGS I WILL PRAY FOR TODAY

February 18
Bless This House

Prayer after unusual blessing

With Your blessing let the house of Your servant be blessed forever.
—2 Sam. 7:29

READ 2 SAMUEL 7:18–29

David plans to build a house for God. "See now," he says to himself, "I dwell in a house of cedar, but the ark of God dwells inside tent curtains" (2 Sam. 7:2). Before he even prays, however, God replies through the prophet Nathan. God had never said a word to David about his building a permanent house of worship. God's first concern was to establish David as king of Israel (2 Sam. 7:9–11). He reveals, nonetheless, that he does mean for a such a house to be built, but that this task will fall to David's "seed"— who we know was to be Solomon (2 Sam. 7:12). In other words, God says no to David's dream of building the temple. It was certainly a godly desire, but David had to learn that having a heart to do something for God does not make it the Lord's will. Just as David was not to build his house for God, your dream about serving God in a particular way may not be God's actual plan for your service. We need to know what the Lord wants for us.

God plans to build a house for David! He lays out an amazing covenant. Denied the building of a "house of cedar" for God, David is to be given an everlasting royal "house"! (2 Sam. 7:16) David asked for a building permit and instead receives an eternal covenant for himself and his family—quite a consolation prize! His response is to sit down in the tabernacle he was not allowed to replace, and pray to the Lord who is giving him a kingship for his descendants. He marvels that all the amazing things God has done for him in his life are really a "small thing" when measured against this gift of an everlasting kingdom in the line of his family (vv. 18–19).

When "the world" is "blessed"—according to its own definition of success—the natural impulse is to have a party. When David is promised that God will give a man to sit forever on his throne, he worships

98

God and prays for the promise to be fulfilled in these yet future days that he himself would never see. The body of his prayer is in four parts:

> He praises the sovereign God (vv. 20–22).
> He praises God's covenant faithfulness (vv. 23–24).
> He prays for the glory of God in his works (vv. 25–27).
> He prays for the fruition of covenant promises (vv. 28–29).

It is abundantly clear that David's motive is not any self-aggrandizement or worldly fame, but simply that God's name would be exalted in all the earth. We know from the New Testament that this promise has come to fruition in Lord Jesus Christ, who is exalted a Prince and a Savior to the permanent Davidic throne in heaven and the earth (Acts 5:31). Jesus is the heavenly King who died for our sins and is now risen and exalted as head over all things on behalf of his body, the church (Eph. 1:22–23).

In Christ, believers are God's house—"living stones" being built into a "spiritual house" (1 Peter 2:5). We pray with David for this house to be blessed forever—the church, of course, but also the houses within that house, the families of God's people one by one. "Bless this house, O Lord, we pray. Keep it safe by night and day" goes an old song—but our prayer is not simply for the building we live in, but rather the house that we are, the body of Christ our King. Pray, therefore, for the endless blessing of the house of God.

PRAISE FOR GOD'S HOUSE
Sing Psalm 122

THINGS I WILL PRAY FOR TODAY

February 19
A Father and His Dying Child

Praying with a submissive spirit

David therefore pleaded with God for the child. — 2 Sam. 12:16

READ 2 SAMUEL 12:14–23

There is nothing surprising about a father praying for a sick child. There is, however, something very touching about David praying for his sick child, for the simple reason that God had already revealed to him that this child, born of his sin with Bathsheba, would "surely die" (vv. 14–15). He might have prayed, as many do, out of guilty feelings for the miserable situation from which this all came. We might understand him not praying at all for a child God had said would die. Just descending into a mixture of numbness and anger is a frequent response in those who have given up hope. We know from Psalm 51 that David confessed his sin in this matter, and it is impossible to imagine his sin—and repentance—not figuring largely in his actions that week. At the same time, the indications are that his prayer for the child was driven by nothing other than a profound desire that his young life be spared. He loved that child, pure and simple.

What is remarkable is how David prayed for the child. He "pleaded with God for the child, and…fasted and went in and lay all night on the ground" (v. 16). He did so for a whole week—only rising when the child died! At first glance this might seem to show he was refusing to accept the Lord's revealed will. A closer look, however, shows that David prays with a submissive spirit, while continuing to intercede for his life. He explains his own resolution of this tension: "While the child was alive, I fasted and wept; for I said, 'Who can tell whether the Lord will be gracious to me, that the child may live?' But now he is dead; why should I fast? Can I bring him back again? I shall go to him, but he shall not return to me" (v. 22–23). He understood that, in such matters, the Lord's revealed will often masks a different, secret, and unchangeable decree. You will remember that the people of Nineveh were declared by God to be doomed in forty days' time, but were spared upon their repentance (Jonah 3:4–5). In the famous "potter and the clay" passage, Jeremiah sets

100

out the principles of God's dealings with the nations: "The instant I speak concerning a nation and concerning a kingdom, to pluck up, to pull down, and to destroy it, if that nation against whom I have spoken turns from its evil, I will relent of the disaster that I thought to bring upon it" (Jer. 18:7). Where there is repentance, God shows mercy even in the face of a declared judgment. The prospect of any child's death is an occasion to pray for his life, not a reason to give way to anger or despondency.

The proof of David's submissive spirit is seen in the events following the child's death (vv. 20–23). God said no to his epic prayer, but the first thing he does is wash and dress and go to church! Mourning is so often a mixture of sorrow over our loss and anger that God should have allowed it to happen. David had seven days of the former and none of the latter. After his mourning is over, his life can begin again—and it begins with the worship of God. Notice that the moment of transition from mourning to normal life is when David quietly accepts the reality of death's irreversible character in the context of a believing hope in the Lord. "Can I bring him back again?" he asks. "I shall go to him but he shall not return to me" (v. 23). This is not cold fatalism, but the warm submission of a believer both to present realities and future promises. "I shall go to him" surely has a hint of heaven in it. The life of God's children may be short or long on this earth, but the fullness of that life bursts into flower only in the glory yet to be revealed (Rom. 8:18). Let us live this present life in the light and promise of the life that is to come for all who love the Lord Jesus Christ.

A PRAYER OF UNASHAMED TRUST IN GOD
Sing Psalm 22:1–5

THINGS I WILL PRAY FOR TODAY

_____

_____

_____

_____

_____

_____

_____

February 20
A Most Mysterious Sin

A prayer of confession

Surely I have sinned. — 2 *Sam. 24:17*

READ 2 SAMUEL 24:1–17

David's last recorded sin is perhaps his most mysterious. The gist of it is that the Lord is angry with his backsliding people, Israel. He then "moved" David to count up his potential army—one supposes to expose David's and Israel's proud spirit of self-reliance. First Chronicles 21:1 pinpoints Satan as the prime mover. The problem is not the taking of a census as such. Moses twice counted the people without penalty. In Exodus 30:11–16, however, the Lord required a half-shekel tax on everyone twenty years and older—called "atonement money." This surely stressed the need for humility before the Lord for Israel's prosperity. God's people are a ransomed people, saved and sustained by God's sovereign grace. It must have been a sense of denying this principle that gave David his bad conscience (v. 10). Number crunching in both church and state is too often the occasion of self-centered pride and even contempt for God.

Against their pride, God asserts his sovereignty and seals it with a particular chastisement for Israel and David. David has three choices: three years of famine, three months of war, or three days of plague (see 1 Chron. 21:12). The import of this is, of course, that the numbers so proudly calculated would be reduced! David opts for the short, but sharp penalty—the only one where he can avoid falling into the hands of men and can simply cast himself on the Lord. The plague visits the people with death, although God relents before the time is up (v. 16). David, not knowing that the Lord had stopped the judgment, prays desperately in the face of all the death and misery, confessing himself to be more blameworthy than the people (v. 17). What then does this teach us?

Most obviously, it teaches that personal sin is to be confessed. Sin is to be repented of. If the psalmist can say, "Who can understand his errors? Cleanse me from *secret* faults," then should we not freely admit *known* faults (Ps. 19:12)? Closely related is corporate guilt. We bear a certain responsibility for the sins of the community or nation, whether by active participation or by failing to witness against it. We share these larger problems and should intercede with a repentant acknowledgment of our failures. Notice, too, that the fact that David is a man after God's heart did not immunize him from falling into sin, even in his old age. He needed grace from God all his days, as do we.

Earnest prayer for God's mercy is a standing mandate for us all our days. The fact that God answered David's prayer before he asked it does not make his prayer unnecessary or irrelevant. The reason for this is that the Lord is constantly nurturing our souls in the school of prayer, so as to deepen our relationship with him.

Jesus was "slain from the foundation of the world" (Rev. 13:8), but we are saved later, in time and space. His purposes for our prayers likewise precede our experience of prayer. Should we not, with Ezra, be swift to fall on our knees, spread out our hands to the Lord, and say, "O my God, I am too ashamed and humiliated to lift up my face to You, my God; for our iniquities have risen higher than our heads, and our guilt has grown up to the heavens" (Ezra 9:5–6).

If our sin seems to us to be as mysteriously injurious in its effects on our lives as David's assuredly was, let us pray all the more earnestly. "If we confess our sins, He is faithful and just to forgive us our sins and to cleanse us from all unrighteousness" (1 John 1:9).

AN ENCOURAGEMENT TO SINCERE PRAYER
Sing Psalm 78:34–39

THINGS I WILL PRAY FOR TODAY

February 21
An Understanding Heart

A prayer for wisdom

Give to Your servant an understanding heart.—*1 Kings 3:7*

READ 1 KINGS 3:5–15

f you could have anything in the world, for what would you ask? This is the dream offer for millions, young and old—the game show question with the prize that will solve the problems of my life! And you need little imagination to come up with many of the likely answers. This, in essence, is God's question to Solomon as he starts his reign as king: "Ask, what shall I give you?" (v. 5). God comes to him "by night." His "kindest visits are often in the night," says Matthew Henry, referring to Psalm 17:3. The very question leads us to Jesus injunction, "Ask and it shall be given to you," (Matt. 7:7) and the promise of his grace toward us (John 16:23; 1 John 5:14). Solomon's response to God's invitation is a model of prayer that asks for the right things—the things that will bless our lives on earth and in heaven.

Solomon praises God for his goodness to his father David and to himself as the inheritor of that goodness (v. 6). He counts his blessings and gives the glory to his God. This is the beginning and end of all prayer—the adoration of the "God of all grace" (1 Peter 5:10).

Solomon admits his own frailty and need. He develops this along three lines, all of which are only too familiar to young people venturing out on a life of their own (vv. 7–8):

- There is what we call *pressure*. He has to fill his father's shoes. "You have made your servant king instead of my father David." How can he possibly be equal to this task?
- There is the matter of his *inexperience*. "I am a little child"—Solomon was only twenty. Furthermore, he adds, "I do not know how to go out or come in"—or, as we might say, "I don't have a clue!"
- There is the daunting challenge of *great responsibility*. The kingdom is large—a people "too numerous to be numbered

or counted." Solomon was willing, but clearly grasps the magnitude of the task.

God's servants certainly ought to be modest (Luke 17:10). Some, however, plead this as an "out." Jeremiah begged off his calling as a prophet with the excuse, "Behold, I cannot speak, for I am a youth" (Jer. 1:6). Moses, already an old man, protested, among other things, a lack of eloquence: "I am slow of speech and slow of tongue" (Ex. 3:10). The Lord had none of this. He is able to make us able (cf. 2 Cor. 2:16 and 3:6).

Solomon prays for a wise heart. He asks for "an understanding heart," so that he can "discern between good and evil" and so be able to judge the people of God with effectiveness and righteousness (v. 9). Solomon grasped that wisdom from on high is key to everything else in this life. Small wonder that the Lord is pleased with Solomon (v. 10) and gives him the gift he so desires (v. 12). He rejoiced that the young king had not asked for long life, riches, and success—the perennial obsessions of, alas, even many Christians in our day. James observes, "If any of you lacks wisdom, let him ask of God, who gives to all liberally and without reproach, and it will be given to him" (James 1:5). He later notes, "The wisdom that is from above is first pure, then peaceable, gentle, willing to yield, full of mercy and good fruits, without partiality and without hypocrisy" (James 3:17).

A PRAYER FOR A WISE HEART
Sing Psalm 90:12–17

THINGS I WILL PRAY FOR TODAY

February 22
The Pattern of Our Lives

A prayer of commitment

Let your heart therefore be loyal to the Lord. — *1 Kings 8:61*

READ 1 KINGS 8:54–66

People regularly treat prayer as an optional "extra" in their lives. We may resort to it in moments of desperate crisis or ecstatic joy, when, as Charles Simeon writes, "Our prayers are to be the pattern of our whole lives."Of course, the question then is, "What does prayer as a pattern for life look like?" One answer is found in Solomon's prayers at the dedication of the temple. We have already looked at his main prayer in some detail (1 Kings 8:22–53; see January 5–8), but we must now take a bird's-eye view of the whole event. There are three main components: a prayer of petition (1 Kings 8:22–53) and a prayer of thanksgiving (vv. 54–61), followed by an act of solemn dedication (vv. 62–66).

Petition for specific needs is the focus of Solomon's first prayer (1 Kings 8:22–53). We already examined this in some detail in the January 5–8 devotions. In it, Solomon rests on God's promises (vv. 22–26), relies on God's presence (vv. 27–30), and requests God's particular blessings (vv. 31–51). The specifics asked for are justice in the land (vv. 31–32), redemption from sin's consequences (vv. 33–40), salvation of lost people (vv. 41–43), security for God's people (vv. 44–45), and freedom for hostages (vv. 46–51). The overriding reason for all of these petitions is that God's people are his inheritance and possession (vv. 52–53) and that the whole pattern of their life is formed out of their relationship to him as their Father in heaven. Notice that Solomon prayed in the posture of a humble suppliant—on his knees with his hands "spread up to heaven." Solomon is a king among men, but only just another subject before the Lord.

Thanksgiving for promises fulfilled is the motive of Solomon's second prayer (vv. 54–61). He has several vital concerns. He first gives thanks for mercies received, praising God that "there has not failed one word of all His good promise, which He promised through His servant Moses" (vv. 54–56). Second, he asks God to be with his people so that "He

106

may incline our hearts to Himself, to walk in all His ways" (vv. 57–58). Third, he pleads that his prayers may be remembered constantly by the Lord, to the end that God's people would be sustained and the world know thereby that Israel's Lord is God (vv. 59–60).

Having prayed thus, Solomon exhorts the people to express their gratitude by heart-devotion and practical obedience to God's revealed will (v. 61). All our words will be worse than nothing unless they translate into genuine consecration to God.

Consecration is the goal of Solomon's dedication of the temple (vv. 62–66). The sacrifices he offered may be seen as application of the thrust of the prayers preceding them. Through the blood of the covenant they celebrate their consecration to God their Savior. Consequently, there is joy in the church as the feasting continues (vv. 62–65), and joy in their families when they return to their homes (v. 66). These sacrifices anticipate the death of the Messiah—Jesus who was to come—so when we draw all these threads together, we have a pattern for all of life set before us. We are called to live as praying people who seek the Lord for his sustaining and redeeming grace. We are called to live as thankful people who bless the Lord for all that he has done for we who are his people. And we are called to live as committed people, who serve the Lord with all our "heart… soul…mind…and…strength" (Mark 11:30).

A PROMISE OF HEARTFELT COMMITMENT
Sing Psalm 111:1–10

THINGS I WILL PRAY FOR TODAY

February 23
Intercession for a Rebel

Prayer for a withered hand

Please entreat the favor of the Lord your God, and pray for me, that my hand may be restored to me. —1 Kings 13:6

READ 1 KINGS 13:1–6

"There are no atheists in foxholes," goes a common saying. When bombs are exploding, or financial markets are imploding, very few people are above praying for help in some way or another. One fears that much of this is no better than the Athenian altar inscribed, "TO THE UNKNOWN GOD" (Acts 17:23). Such "prayer" is an exercise in practical unbelief. Jeroboam was neither an atheist, nor a genuine believer. Like many today, he believed in himself and his destiny. He wanted to be a king, so he raised a rebellion and successfully carved out a kingdom for himself. Like almost all the rulers of nations, ancient and modern, he saw a certain usefulness in religion as a way of controlling, or at least distracting, the people. So he set up his own altar in Bethel, to provide an alternative to having to go up to Jerusalem to worship God as the Lord commanded. God did not let this go unchecked.

God sends an unnamed prophet to Bethel with a prophecy against Jeroboam's altar. He presents two predictions. The first is that at some future time a child named Josiah, of the house of David, would arise and destroy the altar and its priests (v. 2; see 2 Kings 23:15–16 for the fulfillment). The second is that a sign would be given immediately in the altar's splitting and its ashes pouring out (v. 3). Jeroboam is furious. This is both a condemnation of and an epitaph for his rebellion and regime. He stretches out his hand to command the prophet's arrest, only to find that his arm has withered in place "so that he could not pull it back to himself" (v. 4). The altar then splits apart "according to the sign which the man of God had given by the word of the Lord" (v. 5). Jeroboam learns the hard way that God is in deadly earnest. He is clearly shaken to the core.

Jeroboam does at least get one thing right. He eats humble pie and asks the prophet to intercede with God for the restoration of his withered hand (v. 6). He does not repent, as his subsequent history clearly shows (1 Kings 13:33–34), but he at least bows to the immediate reality that the prophet is on God's side and that God is real and is seriously dealing with him. He knows he cannot appeal to God directly, but he can ask the prophet to intercede on his behalf. Scripture simply records that "the king's hand was restored to him, and became as before." Like Jeroboam, we are left to draw our own conclusions and make our own responses to this amazing miracle of God's grace.

We know that Jeroboam never turned to the Lord. God was gracious and restored his hand, but even God's most amazing temporal and material blessings cannot regenerate spiritually dead souls. In Jesus's parable, the rich man in hell thinks his brothers will turn from their ways and escape perdition if only Lazarus is sent from heaven to warn them. "But [Abraham] said to him, 'If they do not hear Moses and the prophets, neither will they be persuaded though one rise from the dead'" (Luke 16:31).

Believing in miracles is not the same as believing in Christ as your Savior! In fact, every blessing of God that is unanswered by a living faith from the heart will only harden a heart in rejection of God. It is gospel repentance toward God and faith in the Lord Jesus Christ that is needed (Acts 20:21). Bodies are healed all the time and sinners still give the glory to pills, scalpels, and doctors. God healed Jeroboam and Jeroboam missed the point, which was that he must look to God as his Redeemer and walk in his ways all the days of his life. Every good thing in your life is designed to lead you to the Lord.

PRAYER OF INTERCESSION FOR THE NATIONS OF THE WORLD
Sing Psalm 117

THINGS I WILL PRAY FOR TODAY

_____

_____

_____

_____

_____

_____

_____

_____

February 24
Asking the Impossible

The first prayer in Scripture for a resurrection

O Lord my God, I pray, let this child's soul come back to him.
—1 Kings 17:21

READ 1 KINGS 17:17–24

Personal tragedies are often so overwhelming to our emotional lives, that all potential possibilities of a solution and restitution of joy seem blasted and even inconceivable. The fact is that God does not deliver his people from ever having to face troubles. What was true for the immediate disciples of Jesus also holds true for all of his followers in one way or another. He tells us straight, "These things I have spoken to you, that in Me you may have peace. In the world you will have tribulation; but be of good cheer, I have overcome the world" (John 16:33). He doesn't make our troubles go away. What he does do is deliver us *in* our trials. Faith and trust in him is a kind of deliverance in advance of these tests of life. But when a loved one dies, especially a child as in this case, the shock is invariably strong enough to bring us very quickly to an end of ourselves. So it was with the widow, and so it is bound to be for us when similarly afflicted.

The widow's reaction to her son's death was natural and normal. She was devastated—all the more for the personal and singular nature of the tragedy. In a famine, masses of people share the same privations. In a loss like this, however, the bereaved is virtually alone. Her response is so understandable and so normal for such cases. She casts around for someone to blame.

First, she lays it at Elijah's door as if he has somehow done this to her: "What have I to do with you, O man of God?" (v. 18a). Then she goes to the opposite extreme and blames herself in fearful self-recrimination: "Have you come to bring my sin to remembrance, and to kill my son?" (v. 18b). Isn't this so true to life? We go from blaming others to blaming ourselves, back and forth, without any peace or resolution. We know that she is wrong on both counts, but that is in hindsight. It is never so obvious at the time.

Elijah's response is to pray simply and earnestly for the boy's life. He didn't reproach the woman for anything she had said. He didn't ask God why—the standard resort of a self-pitying attitude that blames God. And he didn't offer any pious advice in the name of giving comfort. Elijah went straight to the real problem and prayed over the corpse, asking for God to resurrect the lad. He acknowledges God's sovereignty (v. 20). He asks for the impossible—the first request in Scripture for a resurrection from the dead (v. 21). God's answer was as simple and direct as the prayer—the boy revived and was restored to his mother (vv. 22–23).

This extreme incident reminds us that all prayer is essentially for the impossible. Why ask the Lord for something we can certainly do for ourselves? We pray only if we trust God for what we know is beyond our resources to meet. We pray believing the Lord will reward us with his answer and his blessings. We pray believing that God is able to do "exceedingly abundantly above all that we ask or think" (Eph. 3:20). We pray believing that God will enable us to glorify him even "in the fires" as we see his grace at work in and through our troubles (Isa. 24:15). With the widow we will rejoice all the more in the promises of "the word of the Lord" (v. 24). "For you were bought at a price; therefore glorify God in your body and in your spirit, which are God's" (1 Cor. 6:20).

A CRY OF THE HELPLESS TO THE LORD WHO HELPS
Sing Psalm 120

THINGS I WILL PRAY FOR TODAY

February 25
Fire from Heaven

A prayer for the honor of God

Hear me, O Lord, hear me, that this people may know that You are the
Lord God, and that You have turned their heart back to You again.
—1 Kings 18:37

READ 1 KINGS 18:30–39

We naturally associate "fire from heaven" with singular judgment from God. James and John—the "sons of thunder"—have this in mind when, after Jesus is rejected by Samaritan villagers, they ask him, "Lord, do you want us to command fire to come down from heaven and consume them, just as Elijah did?" They are referring to the incidents recorded in 2 Kings 1:10ff. Jesus rebukes them, pointing out that he did not come "to destroy men's lives, but to save them" (Luke 9:54–56). Fire does indeed represent judgment. The soldiers sent to seize Elijah perish by the direct judgment of God. On the earlier occasion, when Elijah has his encounter with the priests of Baal, the fire of judgment comes down in a different way—a way that speaks of redemption for God's people.

The essential question posed in this incident is: "Is God the one and only true God, or is Baal the true god?" The proof would be that sacrifices would be made by each party and "the God who answers by fire, He is God" (1 Kings 18:24). The Baalists call on Baal and nothing happens. Now Elijah calls upon the living God. You will notice that Elijah spares no effort to remove any future charge that he is merely tricking the Baalists. He pours on water—enough to drown both the wood and the sacrifice.

Then he calls upon the Lord in a prayer. He appeals to God as the covenant God—the "Lord God of Abraham, Isaac and Israel" (v. 36). This, by the way, is powerfully set to music in Felix Mendelssohn's oratorio *Elijah*. As the God who is in covenant with his people, let him, Elijah pleads, do three things for his people: let him reveal himself, let him vindicate his servant, and let him draw his people back into himself once more (v. 37). Notice that when we are covenanted with God in saving faith, we have personal knowledge of him and hearts that are devoted to him.

112

God answers with the descent of fire. This miraculously consumes the sacrifice (v. 38) and is followed by the people confessing that he is indeed the Lord God (v. 39). Notice that the fire is still representative of *judgment*—but the judgment falls on the *sacrifice*, which is offered in the place of the sins of the people. For this reason, *mercy* flows to God's people, who receive the grace represented in the sacrifice as their substitute.

Christ on the cross is the sacrifice and substitute to whom the animal sacrifices pointed. "The blood of bulls and goats" (Heb. 9:13; 10:4) will never save anyone, but it does point to the "blood of Christ in the everlasting covenant" (Heb. 13:20) that actually cleanses all who believe on him from all their sin. Jesus went through the fires of God's wrath against our sins. He is the accepted sacrifice—consumed by "fire from heaven" (Heb. 13:20)—that he might save sinners from fire that would justly fall upon them outside of trusting Christ as Savior. The proper application is not to pray for "fire from heaven" to consume the wicked. It is rather to pray for the "tongues of fire"—the work of the Holy Spirit from the first Pentecost to our time—to save the lost. Jesus went through the fires of divine judgment so that lost sinners might, through faith in him, be reconciled to God through his blood and not only escape the fires of a lost eternity, but enter into the glory of heaven forever through "the Sun of righteousness who has arisen with healing in His wings"—even Jesus Christ our Savior and Lord (Mal. 4:2).

A PRAYER FOR THE HONOR OF GOD
Sing Psalm 21

THINGS I WILL PRAY FOR TODAY

February 26
Lord, Take Me Away!

Praying for an early death

And he prayed that he might die and said, "It is enough! Now, Lord, take my life, for I am no better than my fathers."—1 Kings 19:4

READ 1 KINGS 19:1–18

The traditional Scottish song "Maiden of Morven" has a hero who has lost his lady-love to a stormy sea. He grieves his loss and the miseries of a hard life: "Blunt my spear, and slack my bow; / Like an empty ghost I go; / Death the only hope I know, / Maiden of Morven." To want to escape the tragedies of life in this world is certainly a common enough thought. The rising tide of suicide in our time bears doleful testimony to the sinking hopes of many. Elijah's prayer shows us that God's people are not immune to such dark sentiments, and God's reply shows us that there is an answer to such seemingly irretrievable gloom.

The prophet Elijah fell into terrible despair and prayed that God would end his life. What makes this so startling is that God had given him a great triumph in the destruction of the priests of Baal and the sending of rain on a parched Israel (1 Kings 18:40–46). But a death threat from one woman, albeit the wicked Jezebel, sent him running for his life and praying for his death! This is not one of Elijah's best moments, but it is so true to life. Success so often leads to a letdown reaction. No sooner do we see wonderful blessing from God, than we are completely unhinged by some discouraging circumstance. For one who trusts in the Lord and has seen his power at work, this is to act as if the living God doesn't exist. Elijah knew better—had he not declared that Baal was the "god" that did not exist (1 Kings 18:27)?—but now, all of a sudden, he acts as if God had never existed. It is unbelieving prayer in the life of a believer.

In the illogical logic of despair, Elijah finds it easier to believe that God can deliver him *from* the world rather than *in* the world. The sounder conclusion would have been to believe God could deliver him from Jezebel—just as he had delivered him from the priests of Baal— because he could deliver him from death itself.

So the prayer for death is not the prayer of faith, but the cry of despair and defeat. Elijah's complaint is twofold:

> ⟐ One is that he is *faithless*: "I am no better than my fathers" (v. 4). He is as much of a failure as they were, so what is the use of going on?

> ⟐ The second is that he is *fruitless*: "I have been very zealous for the Lord.…I alone am left; and they seek to take my life" (vv. 10, 14). I tried, but did the Lord come through for me? Better give up!

The Lord's answer speaks to Elijah's self-pity. First, he speaks with "a still small voice" (v. 13). The Lord is not in the wind, earthquake, or fire, but in the small voice. Meaning? Elijah's ministry is wind, earthquake, and fire—a ministry of judgment—but the *blessing* is in the "small voice"—the whisper of God that breathes life into dead souls (cf. John 3:8—"the wind [*zephyr*] blows where it wishes"). God is not ineffective because wicked rulers persecute his servants.

Next, he says, "I have reserved seven thousand in Israel" (v. 18). Elijah is not alone. There is fruit, even if the remnant is small. Paul planted, Apollos watered, "but God gave the increase" (1 Cor. 3:6). We are not alone and God is at work.

We have no right to throw stones at Elijah for this, but we have the duty to avoid repeating his sinful capitulation to fear and unbelief. If God is God, then we are safe in time or eternity. Let us then pray for life, not death; for engagement (with "the enemy"), not escape; and for faith, not flight. God still had things for Elijah to do—and then he would fly to glory in a chariot of fire.

PRAISE FOR GOD OPENING MY EYES
Sing Psalm 73:13–28

THINGS I WILL PRAY FOR TODAY

February 27
Chariots of Fire

Prayer for eyes to see God's reality

Give to Your servant an understanding heart. — *1 Kings 3:7*

READ 2 KINGS 6:17–23

Real prophets of God can be a real nuisance in the real world. This is, of course, because the truth from God cuts across so much of what is so loftily called "the conventional wisdom" of the day. Modern man lauds what he calls "the human spirit." God declares that "the natural man does not receive the things of the Spirit of God, for they are foolishness to him; nor can he know them, because they are spiritually discerned" (1 Cor. 2:14). Right there, the faithful prophet is not only inevitably on a collision course with the world, but his vulnerability is also exposed because the big battalions seem to be on the world's side most of the time.

In the context of the prophet Elisha's prayer, God's people were painfully aware of their vulnerability. The Syrians were making war on Israel, although God was busy frustrating their campaign by some intelligence supernaturally revealed through the prophet (2 Kings 6:9–12). When the Syrian king discovered that Elisha was in Dothan, he sent his troops to besiege the place. Next day, the prophet's servant looked out, saw the Syrian army and asked Elisha, "Alas, my master! What shall we do?" (2 Kings 6:15).

Get your doctrine straight and your eyes will be opened to God's realities! The prophet's first response is to tell the lad a great truth. Then, over the course of the day he prays three prayers, the answers to which confirm that truth and reveal the true realities of what looks like a hopeless situation.

First, Elisha sets out the *prevailing truth* that "those who are with us are more than those who are with them" (2 Kings 6:16). What are we to draw from it? The answer is exactly what Elisha intended for that fearful lad! This is a *universal truth* to be believed by every child of God! Our God is more powerful that our greatest enemies: "If God be for us, who can be against us?" (Rom. 8:31). Furthermore, all of God's truths are *practical* and are to be acted upon in faith. Elisha tells the boy, "Do not fear" (2 Kings 6:16). We are reminded of God's word in Psalm 46:10: "Be still, and know that I am God; I will be exalted among the nations, I will be exalted in all the earth." Elisha then prays that the young man's eyes would see and understand that truth (vv. 17–23):

> *Prayer #1* asks for the opening of the young man's eyes. The Lord does so and he sees "the mountain full of horses and chariots of fire around Elisha" (v. 17). If we could see the host of heaven, we would be less fearful and more trusting in the Lord. This is the present reality, even though we are not given to see it. Christ is our surety.

> *Prayer #2* is for the closing of the Syrians' eyes (v. 18). This also happens. God hid Elisha from them. We surely do not know how often the Lord shields us from danger by hiding us in plain sight from those who might do us harm.

> *Prayer #3* is for the opening of the eyes of God's enemies. After leading the Syrians to Samaria, their eyes are opened to reveal them in their enemy's capital as prisoners of war (vv. 19–20). Notice that this is not just a victory for Israel, but a triumph of God's grace. The Syrians are fed (see Rom. 12:20) and sent home unharmed to witness to both the power of the Lord and of his grace (vv. 21–23).

The Lord's "chariots of fire" are not all blazing destruction. There is gospel grace at the center of God's purpose. Let us pray for gospel light for our eyes—for believers and unbelievers alike—to welcome the light of Christ Jesus. When we see God's realities with the eyes of our understanding, then we will know we are safe in the arms of the one and only Savior, Jesus Christ, the Son of God.

A PRAYER FOR LIGHT
Sing Psalm 119:17–24

THINGS I WILL PRAY FOR TODAY

February 28
You Are God, You Alone

Praying in the face of the nations' contempt for God

*Now therefore, O LORD our God, I pray, save us from his hand, that all
the kingdoms of the earth may know that You are the LORD God, You
alone.* —2 Kings 19:19

READ 2 KINGS 19:15–19;
2 CHRONICLES 32:20 AND ISAIAH 37:14–20

Scripture strongly warns against mocking God. "Do not be
deceived," says Paul. "God is not mocked; for whatever a
man sows, that he will also reap" (Gal. 6:7). This has not
stopped millions of people from pouring out their disdain
upon the Lord, his truth, and his people. God certainly *is* mocked in our
world! Around 700 BC, the Assyrians under Sennacherib are gobbling up
little kingdoms right and left. In the process, they quite understandably
come to the conclusion that however real the gods of their victims might
be, they look completely powerless to save their own devotees! So, as he
sets siege to Jerusalem, the Rabshakeh confidently announces his master's
mind when he asks the godly king of the Jews, Hezekiah, "Who among
all the gods of the lands has delivered their countries from my hand,
that the Lord should deliver Jerusalem?" (2 Kings 18:35). This question
foreshadows the words of the priests to Jesus as he dies on the cross: "He
trusted in God; let Him deliver Him now if He will have Him; for He
said, 'I am the Son of God'" (Matt. 27:43). It appears to the Assyrians that
their god, Nisroch, is perfectly capable of handling the God of Israel.

Hezekiah prays for deliverance, but not just to save his skin. He
calls on the Lord to answer the blasphemies that "reproach the living God"
as if he is powerless to save his own people (v. 16). His plea is in three parts:

> ⟡ Hezekiah reminds God of his relationship to the world of sinners:
> he is the one and only God the Creator. It will not do for people
> to deny this without accountability and consequences (v. 15).

> ⟡ Hezekiah sets out the threat to God's people and, by implication,
> to God's own relationship to his world (vv. 16–18). The fact is
> that the existence of God's cause and kingdom, in his people,

118

is at stake. Sennacherib reproaches the living God (v. 16); he humbles all the nations (v. 17); and he discredits all the gods of these nations (v. 18). How can the honor of God be upheld if the wicked are not stopped?

⌖ Therefore, Hezekiah petitions God to save Israel from Sennacherib, so that the nations may realize that he is God and he alone (v. 19).

The crucial issue is not the survival of Judah as such, but the visibility and the acknowledgment of God's glory in the world he has made. Hezekiah reasons that, as God saves his people, by humbling the wicked powers of the world, so his sovereignty and glory will be revealed. And so, the Lord delivers Judah by "the angel of the Lord" visiting death on the Assyrian army by night. Later, Sennacherib meets his end in the house of Nisroch at the hands of assassins (2 Kings 20:35–37). *Sic transit gloria mundi!* Thus passes the glory of the world. And in the process, God's glory is held up for all to see, if they have eyes.

When we pray to be delivered from somebody, let us not pray merely for our personal survival and comfort. Let us always also be praying for the heightening of the honor of God among the despisers of the gospel of Jesus Christ. The discomfiture of the Assyrians is not only a warning to those who mock God, but also an invitation to seek the better way—the way of life held out to all who will come to God through Jesus Christ his Son.

A PRAYER FOR GOD TO VINDICATE HIMSELF
Sing Psalm 94

THINGS I WILL PRAY FOR TODAY

February 29
A New Lease on Life

Praying in the face of death

He turned his face toward the wall, and prayed to the Lord.
—2 Kings 20:2

READ 2 KINGS 20:1–11

"As sure as death and taxes!" is what people will say when they ponder something that seems absolutely certain to happen. Taxes touch us every day, of course, and we always live to tell the tale. Death, however, comes to us but once in life and dead men tell no tales. The Bible reminds us that "it is appointed to man to die once, but after this the judgment" (Heb. 9:27). Eternity is a heartbeat away from each one of us. We can be well one day and deathly ill the next. King Hezekiah had seen the goodness of God in the destruction of the Assyrian invaders. His enemy Sennacherib had been assassinated by his own sons. What had been all gloom and doom was now glorious deliverance at the hand of God. But then "in those days"—days filled with blessing—Hezekiah became "sick and was near death"! God even tells him to set his affairs in order (v. 1). We can be forgiven for wondering why the God who saved Israel from national death suddenly lets Israel's godly and eminently useful king become a dying man! On the face of it, it seems a cruel turn of events.

What would you do on receiving such a death sentence? Many people do have to face this question when a doctor tells them they are terminally ill and have only so long to live. This is not uncommon at all. The natural response, as with Hezekiah, is to be devastated. But notice how he expressed this. He does three things: "He turned his face toward the wall," he "prayed to the Lord," and he "wept bitterly" (vv. 2–3). He sought to be alone, so as to approach God's "throne of grace" (Heb. 4:16). He poured out his soul with great intensity before the Lord. What you do *not* see here is anger at God, fear of death, or a spirit of entitlement that expects better than death before age forty (Hezekiah was not an old man). The king goes immediately to the only One who can sustain him in death, as in life. His prayer does not explicitly ask to be spared from death, but that surely is implicit even in his evident submission to God's known will. Humble submission to God is the key. His will be done.

God's answer is to spare Hezekiah and give him fifteen more years. Interestingly, the illness is healed by non-miraculous medical means (v. 7), but confirmed by the distinctly miraculous sign of a ten-point reversal of the sun's shadow on the sundial of Ahaz. The point made is that God can give new life and can do it through ordinary means. The miracle of the shadow on the sundial serves to remind us that behind the prayers of the saints and the provisions of God's providence, there stands the omnipotence of the God who gives life. The "lump of figs" applied to Hezekiah's "boil" effectively saves his life, as do the better-understood medical procedures in our time. The guarantor of the effectiveness of both prayer and means of healing is, however, the God who stands behind the world he has made and "upholds all things by the word of his power" (Heb. 1:3).

We all live our lives in the shadow of death. Fifteen more years is a bonus, but it does not solve the problem of eternity. Hezekiah certainly understood this. Even long life has its limitations. "The days of our lives are seventy years; and if by reason of strength they are eighty years, yet their boast is only labor and sorrow; for it is soon cut off, and we fly away" (Ps. 90:10). Illness or accident or some other bad thing will claim us eventually. Yet it is precisely through the valley of the shadow of death that God's people experience God's "goodness and mercy" all the way to coming to "dwell in the house of the Lord forever" (Ps. 23).

A PRAYER FOR A LONG AND BLESSED LIFE
Sing Psalm 90

THINGS I WILL PRAY FOR TODAY

_____

_____

_____

_____

_____

_____

_____

_____

March 1
A One-Sentence Prayer

A simple prayer for a good life

O that You would bless me indeed, and enlarge my territory, that Your hand would be with me, and that You would keep me from evil, that I may not cause pain. —1 Chron. 4:10

READ 1 CHRONICLES 4:9–10

Prayers do not need to be long in order to be effectual. Jesus berated the Jewish church leaders for their lengthy pretentious prayers (Matt. 23:14). It is a common fault in those who want to impress others with their piety. It takes a simple believer to pray a godly prayer—with earnest conciseness. All we know about Jabez is in 1 Chronicles 4:9–10. He is called "Jabez"—literally "He will cause pain"—because his birth was difficult for his mother. He is "more honorable" than his brothers and he is a praying man—he "called upon the God of Israel." His prayer breathes a fragrant simplicity. It is a single sentence asking for a good life at the hand of his God. Jabez asks for two things:

> "Bless me indeed, and enlarge my territory."
> "Keep me from evil, that I may not cause pain."

The last clause is a play on his name: he who caused pain to his mother at his birth hopes not to cause pain to others in his life. Jabez's abiding desires for his life are material prosperity and practical righteousness.

What are we to make of this simple prayer? Bruce Wilkinson thought there was enough in Jabez's prayer to turn it into a book! He assures us that frequent repetition of Jabez's one-sentence petition will open a world of personal growth and advancement that we will relate "directly to the Jabez prayer." This basically turns it into a New Age mantra promising personal prosperity. His "Jabez Blessing" program is demonstrably less than Christian. Just be sure to repeat the prayer every day! He eventually mentions Jesus, on page seventy-four of his ninety-three pages, but only as a fleeting afterthought. Jesus is not essential in his scheme of things, either to our entrance into God's presence or to "supernatural blessings wherever you go."

Is prayer to be reduced to such naked repetition of a form of words? Even the Lord's Prayer is an outline for our prayers. It is not demonstrably given by Jesus merely for us to recite it back to him. Even Robert Burns, who was a man of the Enlightenment and no friend to evangelical religion, understood the snare and illusion of ritual religious performances. In his wistful evocation of family worship in his poem "The Cotter's Saturday Night," he notes that a lot of praying has "devotion's every grace, except the heart," but that "haply, in some cottage far apart," God "hears, well pleased, the language of the soul." Routinely repetitive and soulless prayers are as dead as they are easy.

Prayer does not truly happen unless we come to the Father through Jesus the Son. He is the only Mediator between God and man (1 Tim. 2:5). Our acceptance with God is grounded on his death on the cross. Old Testament prayer has to be understood in the light of the cross and the New Testament. Prayer cannot be abstracted from Christ. Believing prayer is always to be explicitly offered in Christ's name, because he is our go-between by reason of his atonement for sin. In believing prayer we intersect with his heavenly intercession for us, and so come to the hearer of prayer who loves us for the sake of his Son. Charles Spurgeon, the great Baptist preacher of the nineteenth century, comments on Jabez's prayer with his wonted enthusiasm: "I recommend it as a prayer for each one of you, dear brothers and sisters; one which will be available at all times; a prayer to begin Christian life with, a prayer to end it with, a prayer which would always be appropriate in your joys or in your sorrows. O that you, the God of Israel, the covenant God, would bless me!" All in and through Jesus Christ our Lord, who was crucified for our transgressions and who rose for our justification (Rom. 4:25).

PRAYER FOR THE WORK OF OUR HANDS
Sing Psalm 37

THINGS I WILL PRAY FOR TODAY

_____

_____

_____

_____

_____

March 2
In the Heat of the Battle

Prayer that trusts God for the outcome

They cried out to God in the battle. — *1 Chron. 5:20*

READ 1 CHRONICLES 5:18–20

It is no surprise to learn that Israel's warriors prayed that God would be on their side in battle. Since time immemorial, armies have invoked the help of some god or other. Sad to say, many nations in the Christian era have asked the God and Father of our Lord Jesus Christ to give victory in distinctly wicked causes. Asking God to be on our side is the standard practice of the godless as well as the godly. Crying to God in a tight spot does not prove a man loves the Lord. People who never pray in normal circumstances will often turn to religion when the going gets tough. And God has used such situations to bring many to himself.

What is remarkable in the case of the tribes of Reuben, Gad, and Manasseh is their evident sincerity of heart. We are told about both the motives behind their prayer and the answer that God returned to their petitions. This can only encourage us to cry to the Lord in our times of crisis. How did this work out for Reuben and the other tribes?

For one thing, they acted upon *sound doctrine*. They were persuaded in their hearts that "it is better to trust in the Lord, than to put confidence in princes" (Ps. 118:9). They acknowledged their dependence upon the Lord. They denied any temptation to proud self-reliance. That did not stop them fighting hard, of course. In a later time, they would have understood Oliver Cromwell when he reportedly said to his soldiers, "Trust the Lord and keep your powder dry." Sound theology and intelligent obedience come together in believing prayer that theologically and experientially trusts God for the outcome.

They also rested upon God's *covenant promises*. They were standing on their title from God to the land in Gilead, which had been occupied by the nomadic Hagrites from northeastern Arabia (Num. 32:33). The vital issue is that they combined a genuine trust in the Lord with the claiming of clear Scripture promises. They did not fire off a prayer into the dark, hoping God would favor whatever they had decided to do. It was God's revealed will that moved them. Persuaded of his promises, they claimed them with fervent expectation of blessing.

They were not to be disappointed, for God granted the victory as they had requested. Here we must enter a caution: victory in battle does not prove God's favor is with the victor. It certainly means God's will is for the winner to win—but mere victory, or the mere fact that a prayer is answered, does not prove that God is on the winning side. In this instance, however, God reveals that he has given them the victory precisely because he is on their side: "He heeded their prayer because they put their trust in Him" (v. 20). God is not on the side of all winners, but he is on the side of all who trust him, win or lose. Job can say, "Though He [God] slay me, yet will I trust in Him" (Job 13:15). What does this teach us? That a trusting prayer is a true prayer and will always find God trustworthy. In this case, it led to victory in battle. In other cases, such as David escaping Saul, it involved being delivered from certain death.

Christians are called to look to the Lord, always and in every situation. We are called to trust in Christ our Savior for every outcome, in terms of the fulfillment of his promises. He prays with his people, as their heavenly Intercessor (Rom. 8:26–27, 34; Heb. 7:25), and warns us not to put our trust "in princes, in whom there is no help." Rather, "Happy is he who has the God of Jacob for his help, whose hope is in the Lord his God" (Ps. 146:3–5).

A TRUSTING PRAYER
Sing Psalm 121

THINGS I WILL PRAY FOR TODAY

March 3
Returning a Portion

Giving, and praying afterward

For all things come from You, and of Your own we have given You.
—1 Chron. 29:14b

READ 1 CHRONICLES 29:10–20

Even when God told King David that his son, Solomon, would build the temple, David did not stop working and praying for the successful completion of the project. He had it in his heart to build God's house, but God would not have it because David had been a "man of war" and had "shed blood" (1 Chron. 28:2–3). Having a "heart" for something good and honoring to the Lord is fine, but it is not the same thing as the call of God. God's call always has objective external sourcing—that is, the Word, and, in the case of the gospel ministry, the church. Too many think their subjective internal feelings must be God calling them, but you find none of that in Scripture. The apostles, for example, were all called by Jesus when they had no "heart" at all for what he had in store for them. David accordingly accepts God's decision and bends himself to help Solomon in his calling. He passes on God's previously revealed plans for the temple and its furnishings and encourages him to see the project to completion (28:4–21). Then David recounts how he has collected construction materials and contributed from his own "treasure of gold and silver" (29:1–5). The leaders in Israel then brought their free-will offerings into the "treasury of the house of the Lord" (29:6–8) and "the people rejoiced, for they had offered willingly, because with a loyal heart they had offered willingly to the Lord; and King David also rejoiced greatly" (29:9).

The offerings having been received, David leads the assembly in prayer. He praises God on behalf of the people (vv. 10–20). There are four petitions expressing thankfulness to God:

> ➣ All *glory* is due to God because he is the king, "exalted as head over all" (v. 11). Here is the origin of the long ending of the Lord's Prayer preserved in the Greek text behind the Authorized Version: "Yours, O Lord, is the greatness, the power and the

126

glory." God is sovereign over all things. This is the one and only source of both his provision for us and our confidence in him.

> All *good things* come from the hand of God (v. 12). This is inherent in the holy character of God; "Every good gift and every perfect gift is from above, and comes down from the Father of lights, with whom there is no variation or shadow of turning" (James 1:17).

> All *thanks* are due to the Lord (vv. 13–16). Unbelievers thank themselves, their "lucky stars," and even their equipment (see Hab. 1:16). God's people know where their blessings are coming from and lift up thankful hearts to the Lord who gives them.

> Our *whole heart* should be fixed upon the Lord in uprightness (vv. 17–20). Notice how comprehensive David's prayer is: he gives thanks for himself (v. 17), he prays for the faithfulness of the people of God (v. 18), he asks God to bless his servant Solomon (v. 19), and he calls the people of God to join together in praising the Lord (v. 20). Can we not also give thanks for *ourselves*, pray for *others*, intercede for *God's servants*, and praise God in *public worship*?

Following David's example, we have warrant to pray specifically in thankfulness for the tithes and offerings of God's people in public worship services. Sustaining the Lord's work in our churches may seem more modest than the building of Solomon's temple, but it is no less significant, because in Jesus Christ it is the fulfillment of all that the temple means for the extension of God's kingdom in the hearts of those who are being saved. Let every Christian be a "cheerful giver," for such the "Lord loves" (2 Cor. 9:7; 1 Cor. 16:2), and give thanks for the joy of being part of the work of God's kingdom.

PRAISE WHILE BRINGING OFFERINGS TO GOD
Sing Psalm 96:1–8

THINGS I WILL PRAY FOR TODAY

_____

_____

_____

_____

_____

127

March 4
Do Not Let Man Prevail!

A prayer in the face of powerful enemies

Lord, it is nothing for You to help. — 2 Chron. 14:11

READ 2 CHRONICLES 14:1–15

We do not need to be attacked by a large army to feel desperate. A summons to a tax audit or losing a job or a fire that destroys the house might do as well. We all understand desperation, whatever its source may be. So we can easily identify with Asa, king of Judah, as he contemplates the advance of the Ethiopians up the Valley of Zaphathah. There are moments in life when it seems that it is all over—that there seems to be no way out, no hope of deliverance. Like the "pale Persians" who behold the Tartar horde across the Oxus River in Matthew Arnold's epic poem "Sohrab and Rustum," we can easily imagine that the Jewish soldiers "held their breath with fear" and waited for the inevitable with trembling resignation.

Asa was one of the better men to wear the crown of David. He "did what was good and right in the eyes of the Lord his God" (v. 2). He reformed the church by removing idolatry and other perverse practices, even deposed his grandmother from being "Queen Mother" on account of her wickedness (1 Kings 15:8–15). God prospered his reign. Even so— and perhaps because of this—war came, as enemies cast covetous eyes upon Judah. This is where we discover that Asa was also a man of prayer. There are four facets to his prayer as he watches the enemy approach in overwhelming force:

> ꙮ "Lord, it is nothing for you to help." The numbers imply certain defeat for Judah, but it is no harder for God to gain the victory "whether with many or with those who have no power." Thus Jonathan, years before at Michmash and confronted by many Philistines, "said to the young man who bore his armor, 'Come, let us go over to the garrison of these uncircumcised; it may be that the LORD will work for us. For nothing restrains the LORD from saving by many or by few'" (1 Sam. 14:6). God is able, whatever your senses are telling you.

128

> "Help us, O Lord our God, for we rest in You." Asa gave up all trust in his own resources. He understood in his heart what Jeremiah told the people of Judah centuries later: "Thus says the LORD: 'Cursed is the man who trusts in man and makes flesh his strength, whose heart departs from the LORD" (Jer. 17:5). Perhaps he remembered Asaph's confession, "My flesh and my heart fail; but God is the strength of my heart and my portion forever" (Ps. 73:26). Self-confidence is a snare; "It is better to trust in the LORD than to put confidence in man" (Ps. 118:8).

> "In Your name we go against this multitude." The point here is that there is warrant to fight rather than flee and that warrant is from God. Indeed, his only hope of prevailing is if God gives him victory "against the run of play" (as we say in sporting language).

> "You are our God; do not let man prevail against You!" Asa appeals to God's character and his glory. The destruction of God's people is in effect the humbling of God. Will God let his cause go down to defeat? In all of our intercessory prayers, we are ultimately asking God to be God so that man will never be able to claim that he has prevailed and so rendered God's claims lies and illusions.

It is important to remember that Asa fell into serious sin at the end of his life. After thirty-five years of peace and prosperity—clearly the blessing of God for his faithful rule—Asa made a treaty with the Syrians against Baasha of Israel, for which he was roundly rebuked by God (2 Chron. 16:1–10). He did not take it well. When he falls ill in the last two years of his reign, he "did not seek the Lord, but the physicians" (16:12). Should this not move you to "pray without ceasing"? (1 Thess. 5:17). Will you not heed Jesus when he warns that "because lawlessness will abound, the love of many will grow cold" (Matt 24:12)?

PRAYING FROM DESOLATION TO CONFIDENCE
Sing Psalm 13

THINGS I WILL PRAY FOR TODAY

_____

_____

_____

March 5
Our Eyes Are upon You!

Praying when you don't know what to do

Nor do we know what to do, but our eyes are upon You. —*2 Chron. 20:12*

READ 2 CHRONICLES 20:1–23

Jehoshaphat was one of Judah's good kings. He reigned from 872 to 848 BC and presided over a time of reformation in church and state. His name means "Jehovah has judged," and it can truly be said that he practiced what his name preached. A full account of his life can be found in 2 Chronicles 17:1–20:37 and 1 Kings 22:41–50. The incident occasioned by his famous prayer is an invasion by the nations to the east and south, "beyond the sea"—that is, the Dead Sea (v. 2). These included the descendants of Lot ("Moab" and "Ammon"), those of Esau (Edomites from "Mount Seir"), and others "besides" (probably an Arab tribe, the Meunites; see 2 Chron. 26:7). These were all longstanding enemies of Israel. Like modern Israel, Jehoshaphat's Judah was beset on every side. The situation was as desperate then for the Jews as it is today.

Jehoshaphat took this seriously and turned to prayer and fasting. He was afraid and "set himself to seek the Lord, and proclaimed a fast throughout all Judah" (v. 3). The king's fear of men was completely overwhelmed by his fear of God, so that he turned to the Lord in a confiding spirit of dependence upon his grace. The chapter records the essential elements of the way the matter was handled, and also how it unfolded in God's providential dealings with both Judah and her enemies. Jehoshaphat led God's people in corporate prayer (vv. 5–13). One of the Levites, Jahaziel, prophesied victory without a fight (vv. 14–17). The Levites then led the assembly in the worship of God (vv. 18–19). Finally, we are told that while the people of God sang praises, the enemy defeated themselves (vv. 22–23). Even before Judah could know God had answered their prayers, God had used what we call "the fog of war" to neutralize the danger to his people!

What are we to take from this? That God hears the prayers of his people? Certainly! Is God "able to do exceedingly abundantly above all that we ask or think, according to the power that works in us" (Eph. 3:20)? Yes, he is! But there is a specific "angle" to this incident that suggests something beyond these generalities of answered prayer.

As stated earlier, Jehoshaphat literally means "Jehovah has judged." The amazing result of this incident is that he is given to see a living parable of his name played out before the world. While Jehoshaphat and Judah were praying, the Lord was answering their prayer! Jehovah, in fact, had judged already! Jehoshaphat's own name encapsulates a wonderful reality and promise for God's people. God knows everything before we know anything. He knows what we need before we ask him (Matt. 6:8). Prayer does not change God's will, as much as it locks into his will as it unfolds. May we not think that Jehoshaphat was aware of all this before he prayed? He was not fatalistic. He sought the Lord actively. He went to prayer and fasting. He did not know God's will, but he knew the God who has willed. His own name preached sound theology to his otherwise shaken soul.

When we pray, we also always come to the Lord who already has judged in all that is uncertain to us as we pray. He has not revealed his secret will to us in any of the matters for which we go to the throne of grace. He knows his answer as surely as we know we need an answer. Therefore, expectancy and confidence in the Lord must never be far from us, even as we, like Jehoshaphat, "fear" in the face of discouragement and difficulties. Let us learn from this godly king of Judah. He made a realistic assessment as he sought to discern the times. He was determined to seek the Lord in prayer. He made a practical commitment to fasting to focus his heart and mind. Here is how to face a crisis—looking to the Lord who has already judged.

PRAYING FROM FEAR TO PRAISING WITH JOY
Sing Psalm 64

THINGS I WILL PRAY FOR TODAY

March 6
Atonement and Forgiveness

Praying for forgiveness of sin

May the good Lord provide atonement. — *2 Chron. 30:12*

READ 2 CHRONICLES 30:1–20

ezekiah was twenty-five years old when he ascended the throne of Judah (2 Chron. 29:1). The temple "had been closed for lack of interest." Now, as then, empty houses of worship bear a stark witness to hearts and lives empty of God's saving grace. The young king understood that they must return to the Lord if the rot was to be stopped in church and state. And he wasted no time restoring the worship of God to the heart of national life. He recalled the priests and Levites to reconsecrate themselves to God. They cleansed the disused temple and Hezekiah called the people to worship. "Then Hezekiah and all the people rejoiced that God had prepared the people, since the events took place so suddenly" (2 Chron. 29:36). O that we might see such an outpouring of God's grace in our time!

The next step was to revive the Passover, the Feast of Unleavened Bread (v. 1). Because of the depth of past neglect of God's ordinances, not only was the Passover put back a month—which was allowed by the law in certain circumstances involving unavoidable ceremonial uncleanness (v. 3; cf. Num. 9:9–11)—but its celebration was marred by many worshipers partaking of the Passover meal in a state of uncleanness as defined by Old Testament law (v. 17). Breaches of God's law inevitably invite his disapprobation and even judgment. What is to be done to overthrow the consequences of sin?

Hezekiah turned to the Lord in prayer (vv. 18–19). It might seem to us that breaking Old Testament ceremonial law is a small thing. In fact, it is just like coming to church or receiving communion with a careless and unprepared heart. Scripture tells us to go and be reconciled to the brother who has something against us before we come to worship God (Matt. 5:44). "Let a man examine himself," Paul writes, before he partakes of the Lord's Supper (1 Cor. 11:28). The real issue, you see, is the heart being right with God.

132

Hezekiah therefore prays for three things essential to worship and fellowship with our holy God:

- He asks the "good Lord" to "provide atonement" (v. 18c). He knows that sin must be paid for. God's perfect justice must be perfectly satisfied; otherwise he is not truly righteous and we cannot be truly forgiven. Since we cannot atone for our own sin, God must provide a mediator. Hezekiah therefore prays for a divine Savior, and not merely for forgiveness. He points ahead to Jesus Christ as the true, ultimate, and only mediator who can atone for our sin.

- He pleads this atonement for "everyone who prepares his heart to seek God" (v. 19a). He is not saying that mere "sincerity" merits forgiveness, for God's forgiveness is a gift of grace secured by substitutionary atonement. A person with an unchanged heart, however, can have neither an expectation of mercy nor an experience of genuine forgiveness from the God he continues to reject. Therefore, prepare your heart to seek the Lord.

- He requests that God waive their actual impurity in their Passover observance. This reminds us that we always have impurity in heart and life, even if our sins have been covered by the atonement provided by God. Believers always pray daily for the washing away of the sin that still besets them in thought, word, and deed. Andrew Stewart warns not to be waiting "until you think you have made yourself good enough to come to God." Why? Because, he adds, "That day will never come! Now is the day of salvation when those who are unclean are made acceptable in God's sight because [Jesus] will plead the merits of [his] death upon the cross."

PRAYER FOR FORGIVENESS OF SIN
Sing Psalm 51:1–8

THINGS I WILL PRAY FOR TODAY

March 7
Restoration after Repentance

A prayer of humble repentance

Now when he was in affliction, he implored the Lord his God, and humbled himself greatly before the God of his fathers. —2 Chron. 33:12

READ 2 CHRONICLES 33:1–17

here were few more wicked kings of Judah than Manasseh: "He did evil in the sight of the Lord, according to the abominations of the nations whom the Lord had cast out before the children of Israel" (v. 2). He may be regarded as the archetypal proponent of multifaith worship. He would surely have understood and applauded the religious atmosphere of twenty-first century Europe, which has a place for every heresy imaginable to man, yet rigorously rejects the revealed truth of the inspired Word of God. He rebuilt the high places, raised altars for the Baals, crafted wooden idols, and worshiped the Assyrians' gods, even building altars for them inside the temple. He dabbled with witchcraft and sorcery and was also involved in the worship of Moloch (vv. 1–9)—the "god" Milton described as that "horrid King besmear'd with blood / Of human sacrifice, and parents tears, / Though for the noyse of Drums and Timbrels loud / Their childrens cries unheard, that past through fire / To his grim Idol."

Sin has consequences in human life. The sins of rulers are always paid for by their misruled people, as witnessed by Stalin's Russia and Hitler's Germany. In Manasseh's case, God's judgment meant defeat by the Assyrians and his being bound with fetters and dragged by hooks through his flesh. He reaped as he had sown. "Do not be deceived," says God's Word, "God is not mocked; for whatever a man sows, that he will also reap" (Gal. 6:7). Many, when called to account, will sin more boldly. They cross their fingers, hope for the best, and keep on down the same fatal road. Manasseh, of course, had a more serious check to his career than the setbacks that befall most of us. He was staring death in the face. It looked like his life was over. What he does with this calamity, so clearly related to his rejection of God and his truth, stands to this day as an invitation to self-examination, repentance, and personal reformation. It is also a testimony to the grace of God in transforming this former idolater and apostate.

God is gracious to save and transform sinners who repent and believe upon him. God restored Manasseh to his old throne and to a new life—after he had taken three steps. First, he turned from the idols of his heart and "implored," or sought the face of, "the Lord his God." Second, he "humbled himself greatly," and third, he "prayed to Him." This fully persuaded him that the Lord truly was the living God (vv. 12–13). Is this not how the Lord always works? He calls a sinner to himself, brings him to repentance, and causes him to call upon him in faith, seeking forgiveness, and committing to a new life of obedience.

The fruit of this new relationship with God is practical obedience. He reformed the civil government, repairing the walls of Jerusalem and attending to the defense of the nation (v. 14). He revived the worship of the church by removing idols and heathen altars from the temple, rebuilding the altar of the Lord and reinstituting worship according to the Word of God (vv. 15–16). Even if the "high places" were not removed, at least the people worshiped God there (v. 17). God was again served in church and state. What a powerful reminder this is of God's grace in Jesus Christ. He will never turn away a repentant, believing sinner. He will never allow any he has saved to be plucked from his hand. He continues to draw to himself every day in all of history those who are being saved (John 6:37; 10:28–29; Acts 2:47). Hallelujah! What a Savior!

PRAYING FOR SALVATION'S JOY
Sing Psalm 51:9–15

THINGS I WILL PRAY FOR TODAY

_____

_____

_____

_____

_____

_____

_____

_____

March 8
The Hand of God

Giving thanks for God's sovereignty

Blessed be the Lord God of our fathers, who has put such a thing as this in the king's heart. — *Ezra 7:27*

READ EZRA 7:11–28

When Scripture speaks of "the hand of God" it is to explain the otherwise inexplicable. The mass hysteria of the Philistines over "the ark of God," which they had captured at the battle of Aphek, is attributed to this cause: "They sent therefore and gathered together all the lords of the Philistines and said, 'Send away the ark of the God of Israel, and let it return to its own place, that it may not kill us and our people.' For there was a deathly panic throughout the whole city. The hand of God was very heavy there" (1 Sam. 5:11). God's Word tells us for our encouragement that "the king's heart is in the hand of the Lord, like rivers of water; He turns it wherever He wishes" (Prov. 21:1). The "hand of God" is not always as obvious as we might wish, but it is an article of biblical faith revealed for our encouragement precisely when we are having trouble seeing how God is at work. God is sovereign. Even in the workings of his enemies he accomplishes his will. Those who are spiritually discerning will frequently confirm this in their experience.

Ezra sees God's hand at work in his time and prays accordingly. Judah had ceased to exist as an independent nation in 587 BC. In 458 BC, Ezra led a band of Jewish exiles from Babylon to Jerusalem. Some sixty years before, Zerubbabel had led a first group to rebuild the temple (Ezra 1–6). Ezra's task (recounted in Ezra 7–10) is to rebuild the spiritual vitality of God's people. He has two vital pieces of equipment for the work. The first is his anointing with *heavenly authority* from God. The evidence of this is that he "had prepared his heart to seek the Law of the Lord, and to do it, and to teach statutes and ordinances in Israel" (Ezra 7:10). The second is his letter from the Persian king granting him all the *earthly authority* he needed for his mission (vv. 12–26). God's "hand" works both the inward and the outward equipping Ezra needs to undertake the work

136

God wants him to do in Jerusalem. God "does according to His will in the army of heaven and among the inhabitants of the earth" (Dan. 4:35). Believe it!

What a blessing this was for Ezra and God's people! Even the most powerful ruler, however unbelieving, will in one way or another serve the purposes of God. Notice three things:

➢ *What God did.* He put it "in the king's heart" (v. 27a). You may say the old heathen was just being pragmatic, but the fact is that it was the love of God for his people that moved him to fear the "wrath" of "the God of heaven." Praise God when the government is "God's minister to you for good" (Rom. 13:4), for that is its purpose before God.

➢ *Why God did this.* He meant to "beautify the house of the Lord… in Jerusalem" (v. 27b). Almost incidentally, but very significantly, the king acknowledges the independence of the church in the matter of its own government and growth (vv. 25–26). "Kings shall be your foster fathers" (Isa. 49:23), not the heads of the church, as with the kings of England. Christ is the "only Sovereign, the King of kings and Lord of lords" (1 Tim. 6:15), and the only "head of the body, the church" (Col. 1:18).

➢ *How this blessed his servant (v. 28).* It was all mercy and encouragement to Ezra. He felt the hand of God upon him as he gathered his team—a fellowship of God's best—for the ministry that lay before them. So let us pray that the Lord will lay his hand upon us in all that we do. To those who are his, God's hand is his sovereign grace, undertaking for their empowerment in his service: "Therefore humble yourselves under the mighty hand of God, that He may exalt you in due time" (1 Peter 5:6).

PRAYING IN THANKSGIVING FOR GOD'S GOODNESS
Sing Psalm 76

THINGS I WILL PRAY FOR TODAY

_____

_____

_____

_____

March 9
Traveling Mercies

Praying for safety in travel

So we fasted and entreated our God for this, and He answered our prayer. —Ezra 8:23

READ EZRA 8:21-32

In the jet age, safety in travel is regarded as an invariable norm. I well remember my first airplane flight over four decades ago. I was off to seminary across the pond in the United States. It was six hours, six miles high, at almost six hundred miles per hour. I was a wee bit nervous. Would I arrive safely? As it turned out, the journey was completely uneventful. Travel was not always so in past times. It was invariably fraught with danger. In the days of sail, transatlantic journeys held real risks. Of course, ships still sink, cars still wreck, and planes still crash. Furthermore, although the days of Dick Turpin the highwayman may be gone in England, piracy is alive in the Arabian Sea. Even at home, a wrong turn into a bad neighborhood can too easily end in grief. You still need to be careful out there! In other words, what Christians often call "traveling mercies" are a very real need for everyone who steps out of the house to go anywhere in our time.

Ezra first sought God's help for the trip to Jerusalem. He did not assume it would be smooth sailing. The first thing he did was proclaim a fast (v. 21). He did this for four reasons:

> The first was that they might humble themselves before God. This means, then and now, pausing from everyday things for a definite period to focus without distraction upon the Lord, as those who from the heart acknowledge their dependence upon him and his sovereign and free grace in everything (cf. 1 Peter 5:6).

> The second reason is they might seek a "safe journey" (ESV). The literal reading, "the right way," is not a request for guidance as to the route to be chosen, but for protection along a road well traveled.

> The third reason is that their lives—"us and our little ones"— might be preserved along the way. Think of how many died in

138

the middle passage between the Old World and the New in the days of sail. Or how many left for the mission field, or the trail west to California, and never arrived because they were struck down by disease, starvation, natural hazards, or hostile action.

➣ The fourth motivation is the preservation of their "possessions," which were, after all, the resources they needed for not only the journey, but for their resettlement in Jerusalem. Whether the threat from "the enemy on the road" (v. 22) is deliberate persecution or simply robbery, the prayer is the same. There are plenty of criminals in this world who are only too ready to oppress and steal from law-abiding people if they have the opportunity.

Ezra was concerned to maintain a clear testimony to their trust in the Lord to sustain them. That is why he did not ask the king for a military escort. He had declared, "The hand of our God is upon all those for good who seek Him, but His power and His wrath are against all those who forsake Him" (v. 22). Some might perhaps chide Ezra and suggest it was foolish pride to feel ashamed to ask the king's help. After all, might the king not be God's instrument in preserving God's people from harm? It is true, of course, that we need never be ashamed to use all the proper means for our well-being, but, as Matthew Henry puts it, "when the honour of God is concerned, one would rather expose oneself than do anything to the prejudice of that, which ought to be dearer to us than our lives." Ezra knew that he needed to be seen to trust his God, and that this had to flow from a steadfast trust for the Lord in his heart. This, too, was a unique event in the history of redemption: it was a one-way trip to God's future for his people and a new start after a huge failure. It was a new direction, but to an old and blessed destination—a return to the Lord—from which the people of God would never look back. It was itself a traveling mercy, for the Lord sent them, sustained them, and gave them success.

A PRAYER FOR SECURITY
Sing Psalm 35:1–6

THINGS I WILL PRAY FOR TODAY

_____

_____

_____

March 10
A Peg in His Holy Place

A prayer for the shame of God's people

And now for a little while grace has been shown from the Lord our God...to give us a peg in His holy place. — Ezra 9:8

READ EZRA 9:5-15

It once fell to me to read Ezra's wonderful prayer in a seminary worship service. Afterwards, my apologetics professor, Cornelius Van Til, approached me and drew attention to the words "a peg in His holy place." He quoted the Dutch version—"een nagel...in Zijn heilige plaats"—repeating the words "een nagel" ("a nail"), pointing out that this referred to just one of the many nails that held up the curtain round the tabernacle in Exodus. With tears in his eyes, he added that while we do not deserve even one little nail in God's house, this tiny thing is emblematic of God's abounding love for sinners saved by grace in Jesus Christ. I was struck by the warmth and simplicity of this eminent professor, perhaps best known for his hard-hitting controversial writings. He understood that we are "scarcely saved" and are debtors to the unmerited grace of God in Christ (1 Peter 4:18). When we know ourselves as God knows us, we have every reason to be full of gratitude for his abounding grace!

God's people had a lot to be humble about. No sooner had the exiles returned from Babylon (Ezra 9:32), then it came to light that the people of Israel, and especially their leaders, had been intermarrying with the "peoples of the lands," when they should have been marrying within God's covenant people (Ezra 9:1–2). This sets Ezra to fasting and to prayer at the evening sacrifice. As he prayed, more and more people joined him and "wept very bitterly" (Ezra 10:1). His prayer becomes a confession of national sin. Churches and nations today would do well to cry to God in the same way. Notice its five components:

> *State the problem (v. 6).* This is not confession *of* sin—that comes later—but it is confession *that* sin is the problem between God and Israel. Ezra defines Israel's shame—"our iniquities have risen higher than our heads." The problem is

not political or economic, but hamartiological (from Greek *hamartia*—literally "missing the mark," or sin).

› *Accept the consequences (v. 7)*. It is too easy to explain away national problems by taking the role of victim and shifting the blame from our moral failures to other people and circumstances.

› *Acknowledge God's mercy (vv. 8–9)*. The fact that they are in Jerusalem and coming before the Lord in a rebuilt temple is proof positive that God has been good to them, notwithstanding their failings. The act of prayer itself is an evidence of mercy, for it holds the promise of future blessing. Israel had a new beginning, even if it was marred by sin.

› *Confront particular sins (vv. 10–14)*. Confession of sin in general is as worthless as it is popular. Indeed, it is popular because it costs nothing and requires no change. To say that I sin daily in thought, word, and deed is a mere truism. It is neither conviction of sin nor evidence of repentance. The only sin that can be truly confessed is sin that is defined explicitly and repented of in the details. Israel needed to face its actual sin—in this case marriage to the people of the land—and change its ways.

› *Renew submission to God (v. 15)*. Ezra recognizes that sin has penal consequences and confession does not abolish these. Accordingly, he casts himself on God's mercy and is submissive from his heart to God's will. He implicitly seeks his grace and commits to renewed obedience. Even in the darkest of days, the Lord has given his people "a peg" in his temple—in Christ, who is our temple, sacrifice, and priest, in whom we are called to "hold fast our confession" (John 2:19–21; 1 Cor. 5:7; Heb. 4:14–15). "Let us hold fast the confession of our hope without wavering, for He who promised is faithful" (Heb. 10:23).

PRAYING FOR PERSONAL REVIVAL
Sing Psalm 119:25–32

THINGS I WILL PRAY FOR TODAY

_____

_____

_____

_____

March 11
Dealing with Distress

A prayer for a broken church

We have acted very corruptly against You, and have not kept the commandments, the statutes, nor the ordinances which You commanded Your servant Moses. —Neh. 1:7

READ NEHEMIAH 1:1–11

Nehemiah was deeply distressed over the state of Jerusalem. Jews—exiled in Babylon since the fall of Judah in 587 BC—had returned there, first under Zerubbabel in 537/8 BC and then under Ezra around 458 BC. They had reestablished the city as the center of Jewish life and rebuilt the temple (Ezra 4:5; 24:5). But in 445 BC, after most of a century, they were still in a wretched state—"in great distress and reproach"—in a city with walls that were "broken down" and with gates "burned with fire" (v. 3). Fresh intelligence of this plunged Nehemiah, King Artaxerxes's cup-bearer (v. 11) into a paroxysm of grief. He sat down, wept, mourned, fasted, and prayed for many days (v. 4). He was moved by the low state of the church and cried to "the God of heaven." Should we not be similarly moved as we see the state of much of what calls itself the church today?

This is a prayer for a broken church. As such it comes very close to home for modern Christians and teaches us how to pray for the church today. Nehemiah's prayer unfolds in five distinct steps:

- He first *calls upon* God (v. 5). Notice the focus on the attributes of God as these bear on the needs of the moment. He is the "great and awesome" God, who is omnipotent and therefore able to save his people. He is the "covenant" God, who keeps faith with his eternal plan to save his people. He is the God of "mercy" toward those who love him and obey his commands. He has in himself the power, the purpose, and the perseverance to heal and restore us in our broken state: "Our God is the God of salvation; and to GOD the Lord belong escapes from death" (Ps. 68:20).
- He *appeals for a hearing* from God (v. 6). He comes as a humble suppliant, representing himself and the whole people of God

142

in their desperate need. Notice that he does not merely "say" a prayer. This is a *cri d'coeur*—a cry of the heart—and Nehemiah is pleading for the life and destiny of God's people with every fiber of his being.

> He *confesses sin* against God on behalf of all the people (v. 7). They have "acted very corruptly" against God, and have not kept "the commandments, the statutes, nor the ordinances" given by Moses. The standard and measure of real discipleship is the written Word of God.

> He *pleads the promises* of God (vv. 8–9), alluding to God's Word in Deuteronomy 30:1–5, in which God told Israel he would bring them back from exile, even "the farthest parts under heaven," if they returned to him in the obedience of faith. As their dispersion among the nations is standing proof of their apostasy from God, so their restoration to God's dwelling place is the fruit of repentance and renewal.

> Finally, *he trusts the Lord* for answers and blessings, for all the people and for himself (vv. 10–11). He recalls God's covenant: they are his servants, "redeemed" by his "great power" and "strong hand." He prays that God would hear the prayers of faith and, most practically, prosper his servant in sight of "this man"—his royal master, Artaxerxes, whose cooperation would be vital to his future plans.

Nehemiah did not pray for a few minutes with a list of one-sentence requests. He practically besieged God in prayer from *Kislev* 446 BC to *Nissan* 445 BC—from November/December to March/April (cf. Neh. 1:1–4 with 2:1–2). He prayed, as Paul enjoins us, "without ceasing" (1 Thess. 5:17). He calls us to pray, as David did long before: "Help, Lord, for the godly man ceases!" Also with David, he looks expectantly for the Lord's blessing: "My heart shall rejoice in Your salvation. I will sing to the Lord, for He has dealt bountifully with me" (Ps. 12:1; 13:5–6).

PRAYING FOR HELP
Sing Psalm 12

THINGS I WILL PRAY FOR TODAY

March 12
Arrow Prayers

Praying in a tight spot

Then the king said to me, "What do you request?" So I prayed to the God of heaven. —Neh. 2:4

READ NEHEMIAH 2:1–8

This prayer is at least in one way the opposite of the previous one. Nehemiah had been agonizing and praying for four long months about the state of God's people in Jerusalem. But when the moment came for that prayer to be answered, it occasioned one of the shortest prayers in biblical history. It teaches us that just as surely as unbelievers will not be heard merely for using "many words" (Matt. 6:7), believers will surely be heard, even if their words are ever so few. If we are more often guilty of not taking time to pray, we should be encouraged to know that God will hear prayers that take no time at all! Nehemiah's short prayer has been called an "arrow prayer," to use an expression coined by Augustine of Hippo 1,600 years ago. Here is how we can "pray without ceasing" in those times when we are immersed, even overwhelmed, by the pressures of our work-a-day world and all the responsibilities that go with it.

Nehemiah's sadness was written all over his face. So much so, that his royal master, King Artaxerxes, asked him, "Why is your face sad, since you are not sick? This is nothing but sorrow of heart" (v. 2). Our private burdens have a habit of going public in our demeanor. Nehemiah was put on the spot. His first reaction was fear, but his second was to give an honest answer. He was sad, he said, because of the desolate state of Jerusalem, the city of his "fathers' tombs" (v. 3). What might you have said to one of your subjects from a conquered nation? The king might have said, "Get over it, Nehemiah! Your people lost the war and they got everything they deserved. You Jews seem to think the world owes you a living!" But he didn't. He simply and kindly inquired, "What do you request?" (v. 4).

Nehemiah had no time to go to his room and pray about this in secret and at length (Matt. 6:6). Instead he shot an arrow prayer to the throne of God's grace even as he formed an answer to the question. It is a model worth our cultivating. In a sermon entitled "Pray without Ceasing," C. H. Spurgeon comments on such prayers: "Let short sentences go up to heaven, ay, and we may shoot upwards cries, and single words, such as an 'Ah,' an 'Oh,' an 'O that'; or, without words we may pray in the upward glancing of the eye or the sigh of the heart. He who prays without ceasing uses many little darts and hand-grenades of godly desire, which he casts forth at every available interval.…[T]he sparks will continue to rise up to heaven in the form of brief words, and looks, and desires." Nehemiah prays to the God of heaven and speaks to the king in almost the same breath (v. 5). He simply asks to be sent to Judah in order to rebuild Jerusalem and—wonder of wonders—he is given everything he needs to do the job!

When Jesus says, "Ask…seek, and…knock" (Luke 11:9), his meaning is as simple as that. He doesn't expect us to pray long prayers, still less to wallow in indecision under the cover of pious waiting for some special word from God. Nehemiah's arrow prayer and God's moving of the king's heart in a split second proves that point. There may be things we will have to pray for over a long period of time, but for the most part, the Lord puts the premium on earnest to-the-point praying. Few words will do (Matt. 6:7). Paul prays only three times about his thorn in the flesh. God says no to its removal, but assures him that his grace will be sufficient for his coping with it (2 Cor. 12:7). Being steadfast in prayer (Rom. 12:12) implies both urgency and patience, whether we pray on the run or in the closet.

PRAYING UNDER PRESSURE
Sing Psalm 27

THINGS I WILL PRAY FOR TODAY

_____

_____

_____

_____

_____

_____

_____

_____

March 13
We Are Despised

A prayer for deliverance from reproach

Hear, O our God, for we are despised. —Neh. 4:9

READ NEHEMIAH 4:4–9

It is hardly surprising that the Jews faced opposition in their attempt to rebuild Jerusalem. The descendants of their historic foes—"the Arabs, the Ammonites, and the Ashdodites" (v. 7)—wanted no revival of Israel. Led by Sanballat from Samaria, Tobiah the Ammonite, and Geshem the Arab, they mocked the "feeble Jews" and confidently expected that the new wall of Jerusalem would collapse if "even a fox" jumped up on it (Neh. 4:1–3)! Faithful believers are rarely the most popular people in the world. The reason is obvious enough. The truth of God offends those who reject it. Righteousness is taken as a personal reproach by those who have no interest in God's will for their lives. Persecution is just the logical extension of the denial of God, his Word, his Son, and his salvation. There is no mystery in this. Sinners have bad consciences and the only alternatives to actually turning to the Lord are sinning boldly or redefining sin as good. Opposition to faithfulness to the Lord is endemic to this fallen world. Responding to these realities is always bound to be a challenge. How do you react to ridicule, never mind oppressive threats to life and limb? Nehemiah faces both, but he doesn't fulminate and plot revenge. He doesn't even confront them with their wickedness. He calls upon the Lord. As at every recent crisis point, he prays (Neh. 1:5; 2:4).

Nehemiah first appeals to the compassion of God: "Hear, O our God, for we are despised" (v. 4a). He appeals to the mercy and fellow-feeling of the Lord who loves his own. Recalling God's faithfulness in the past, Isaiah rejoices in his mercy: "For He said, 'Surely they are My people, Children who will not lie.' So He became their Savior. In all their affliction He was afflicted" (Isa. 63:8–9a). He is a *personal* Savior and when we are despised, he understands our pain deeply and keenly. God loves his church and sent his own Son to save her: "For thus says the Lord of

146

hosts: 'He sent Me after glory, to the nations which plunder you; for he who touches you touches the apple of His eye'" (Zech. 2:8).

Nehemiah then appeals to the justice of God. He prays that God would "turn their reproach on their own heads, and give them as plunder to a land of captivity!" (v. 4b). Is this too harsh, and unbecoming the spirit of prayer? Some explain this away by saying it is prophecy, not prayer; or it is Old Testament, not New; or it is only how people talked then; and so on. But must we make excuses for such a forthright prayer? Nehemiah prays in the context of his immediate danger, that God would preserve his people from looming genocide, and, not least, uphold the honor of his own name, cause, and kingdom against outright wickedness. It is not a matter of personal revenge, but of putting a stop to the deadly schemes of men who openly and decisively hate God. Let them reap as they sow and bear the consequences of their sin, as Israel did in her captivity! This is not incompatible with praying for their personal repentance and faith in the Lord. Right now, reversing their present course is what is essential. Will God stop the wickedness and preserve his people? Therefore, pleads Nehemiah, "Do not cover their iniquity, and do not let their sin be blotted out from before You." Don't pass it over and let it go on! Why? Because, "they have provoked You to anger before the builders" (v. 5).

The first fruit of prayer for us is work! The watchword is *ora et labora*—pray and labor—and see God's hand at work in your life! Nehemiah does not sit waiting for God to answer. He sets the people to work on the walls and to stand ready for any attack (vv. 6ff.). The result is that "God had brought their plot to nothing" (v. 15). Therefore, "Let God arise, let His enemies be scattered; let those also who hate Him flee before Him" (Ps. 68:1).

PRAYING FOR DELIVERANCE FROM ENEMIES
Sing Psalm 68

THINGS I WILL PRAY FOR TODAY

_____

_____

_____

_____

_____

_____

March 14
Everybody Say "Amen"

The first response to God's Word to us

Then all the people answered, "Amen, Amen!"—Neh. 8:6

READ NEHEMIAH 8:1–12

mall words often have large implications. We learn yes and no early in life and soon find that when used aright good things follow—and, when used wrongly, quickly get us into trouble! The Hebrew "amen" is also small but very potent. It is a kind of Super-yes. It signals—if it is truly sincere—a large enthusiasm, a deep commitment, and a resolve to follow through in practice. In Scripture it boils down to agreeing with God, completely and without reservation.

A dramatic example of this is in Deuteronomy 27:15–26, where the words "And all the people shall say, 'Amen!'" are repeated twelve times in twelve verses! To say "amen" is to mean business with God in no uncertain manner. It is also to utter a prayer, for every "amen" is said *to* God as well as to ourselves and those around us. "Amen" calls heaven to witness the affirmation we have made and says "Lord, enable me to keep my word to you this day and forevermore."

The returned exiles in Jerusalem gathered in a solemn assembly to hear God's Word. "Ezra the priest" was to read from the "the Book of the Law of Moses" (v. 1). This was a day, remember, in which no one had his own copy of Scripture. Public reading was vitally important because that was where God's people heard God's Word. It surely says something of their hunger for the Word of God that "from morning until midday" they were ready to listen to it being read and taught (v. 3). Their response— outlined below—is most instructive, because it shows the commitment implicit in their corporate "amen":

> They stood up to hear the Word (v. 5). This was a sign of respect for the God of the Word.

> When Ezra prayed—"blessed the Lord, the great God"—they answered, "Amen. Amen!" (v. 6ab).

> As they said "Amen," they did three things with their posture: they lifted up holy hands (v. 6c; Ps. 28:2), they bowed humbled

heads (v. 6d; Ex. 12:27), and they prostrated themselves on the ground (v. 6e; Job 1:20).

>> A series of Levites read the Law and "gave the sense"—that is, they "preached the Word" (vv. 7–8; 2 Tim. 4:2).

>> Many burst into tears, but the leaders told them not to weep and mourn, but to feast together in the joy of the Lord (vv. 9–10).

>> When they really understood the Word, they went home rejoicing (vv. 11–12).

What impact should this have on you today? After all, these are obviously more than casual expostulations that vanish with the wind. Here are some ways in which the lessons of that event apply today.

First of all, it should be clear that your "amen" must be the first prayer by which you respond to God's Word read, explained, and rightly understood. When God's Word is faithfully presented to us, it will not do to shrug our shoulders or say no—still less to dismiss it as offensive or boring, for "God is not mocked" (Gal. 6:7).

Next, your "amen" to God's Word is your first application of practical discipleship. It is a step through the door to implementing your commitment to the truth you have just affirmed. Your agreement with the Lord commands your obedience to his revealed will.

Also, your "amen" with God's people is affirmation of a covenant to worship the Lord together as his family. You cannot say "Amen" to God's Word and stay away from the church and its fellowship as the covenant community.

Finally, your "amen" must be a personal glorying in the cross of our Lord Jesus Christ (Gal. 6:14), for it is in and through Jesus Christ crucified that we are reconciled to God, "For all the promises of God in Him are Yes, and in Him Amen, to the glory of God through us" (2 Cor. 1:20). Jesus is every believer's great amen.

PRAYING WITH PERSONAL COMMITMENT
Sing Psalm 106:41–48

THINGS I WILL PRAY FOR TODAY

March 15
Stand Up and Bless the Lord

A prayer of covenant renewal

And because of all this, we make a sure covenant and write it.—Neh. 9:38

READ NEHEMIAH 9:1–38

We have all made promises we have not kept. Marriage vows, financial agreements, work contracts, and international treaties are almost routinely cast aside. The jails would be empty if all of us kept our covenants with God and man. Such breaches, however small or great they may be, are invariably attended by painful and even irremediable consequences. In human relationships, such breaches are too rarely healed. If we are to keep our commitments, we will need to remind ourselves of them and work intentionally at keeping our promises. This is true of each of us in all our relationships—and it is true of the people of God as a body in their relationship to God and his covenant. The Old Testament church often fell away from the Lord so comprehensively that nothing less than an equally comprehensive covenant renewal was called for. We too often need this call to "stand up and bless the Lord" (v. 5).

God's people had been exiled some seventy years in Babylon for their sins. Over a period of many years they had returned to Israel, first under the leadership of Zerubbabel and then under Ezra, and begun to rebuild Jerusalem. Latterly, Nehemiah was appointed governor by the Persian king and under his leadership the wall of the city was rebuilt. It is at this point that the people were gathered to hear the Law and to express their repentance toward the Lord (vv. 1–4). The Levites led in prayer—a prayer of renewing covenant with God. They called upon the people, "Stand up and bless the Lord your God forever and ever!" (v. 5). Then they led them through a solemn reflection upon all that God had done for them in spite of their repeated falling away from him (vv. 5–31). This culminated in a solemn renewal of their covenant with the God who had been so gracious to them down the centuries: "And because of all this we make a sure covenant and write it: our leaders and our Levites, and our priests seal it" (vv. 32–38).

This prayer of covenant renewal focuses on the attributes of God. He is described successively as follows:

> The *Creator God* who made the heavens and the earth, and therefore commands the worship of his creatures (vv. 5–6).

> The *Covenant God* who promised Abraham and his descendants an inheritance in Canaan (vv. 7–8).

> The *Redeemer God* who delivered them from Egypt and led them through the wilderness (vv. 9–12).

> The *Holy God* who gave them his Law, sustained their lives, and charged them to go into the Promised Land (vv. 13–15).

> The *Gracious God* who, notwithstanding their sinfulness, was "ready to pardon, gracious and merciful" (vv. 16–17).

> The *Faithful God* who sustained them for forty years in the desert and then brought them into possession of the Promised Land (vv. 18–25).

> The *Long-suffering God* who repeatedly chastised them and restored them, and "did not utterly consume them" out of his "great mercy" (vv. 26–31).

The conclusion and response to this review of their checkered past is, appropriately, a prayer of deep contrition. They acknowledge the justice of God in his punishment of their wickedness (vv. 32–37) and covenant themselves afresh to follow the Lord henceforth and for aye. This comes to its true and ultimate fruition in Jesus Christ, the only covenant keeper. Israel failed again and still fails today. We are not saved by our own righteousness but by the perfect righteousness of Christ our covenant head. When we look to him in faith, we keep covenant with him, united to him in his covenant of grace.

PRAYING FOR THE REVIVAL OF GOD'S PEOPLE
Sing Psalm 92

THINGS I WILL PRAY FOR TODAY

March 16
Remember Me!

A prayer for remembrance of good things done

Do not wipe out my good deeds that I have done for the house of my God, and for its services. —Neh. 13:14

READ NEHEMIAH 13:1–31

In an empty church on a weekday, I stood in the pulpit with a discouraged pastor. "I stand here on Sundays," he said, and, pointing to the floor in front of the pulpit, he added, "and I feel my sermons just fall down there." God's servants all want to see fruit in their life's work, but there are times when we wonder how effective we are. Nehemiah knew the feeling. He worked for twelve tough years to reestablish the Jews in Jerusalem. Then he went to Babylon to report to King Artaxerxes (v. 6). While the cat was away, however, the mice came out to play, and the Lord's people reverted to their former wicked ways. Nehemiah returned to find much of his good work undone. He was bitterly grieved (v. 8), but he got back to work and to prayer. Three times he asks the Lord, "Remember me"—each prayer is a wonderful benediction of hope in God's blessing the work of his hands with enduring fruit.

"Remember me, O my God...and do not wipe out my good deeds" (v. 14). With Nehemiah gone, Eliashib the priest clears out a room in the temple used for storing the tithes that provided food for the Levites serving in God's house, and gives it to Tobiah the Ammonite (vv. 4–9; cf. 4:1–8). For their historic hostility to Israel, the Ammonites were banned by God's law from entering the temple (Neh. 13:1–3; Deut. 23:3–4). Furthermore, no storage of tithes meant no food for the Levites, who had to go home to work their fields. Without them, the worship ceased (vv. 10–11). Nehemiah immediately rectifies this by evicting Tobiah, bringing in the tithes, recalling the Levites, and restoring the worship of God (vv. 9–10, 12–13). This surely foreshadows Jesus "cleansing" the temple of the money changers (Matt. 21:12). Well might Nehemiah pray that these good deeds not be "wiped out"! We need more of the like in some churches today.

"Remember me, O my God...and spare me according to...Your mercy" (v. 22). The second problem was the desecration of the Sabbath as the day of rest by treating it as just another day for business and making money. Here too, Nehemiah took resolute action to stop the rot (vv. 15–21). His prayer for God's mercy recognizes that, however faithful our service to God, it is not the ground of our salvation, but its fruit. Nehemiah realizes he is at best an unprofitable servant (Luke 17:10) and as such is saved by the free grace of a merciful God. In him, salvation itself is our rest from sin. The weekly Sabbath points to the risen Christ and the "Sabbath rest for the people of God" that is still to come in eternity (Heb. 4:9, ESV).

"**Remember me, O my God, for good**" **(v. 31).** Finally, Nehemiah deals with the problem of marriage to those who are not the Lord's people. This provision was essential to preserve the existence of the covenant people. It still is vital today that Christians "not be unequally yoked together with unbelievers. For what fellowship has righteousness with lawlessness? And what communion has light with darkness?" (2 Cor. 6:14). Nehemiah's final prayer sums up his longing to "see the goodness of the LORD in the land of the living" (Ps. 27:13).

Whatever our calling in life—whether as parents raising children, as people working in a factory, a school, or an office, whatever we do—we pray with the psalmist: "Let the beauty of the LORD our God be upon us, and establish the work of our hands for us; yes, establish the work of our hands" (Ps. 90:17). And look to the Lord's promise when he said, "Write: 'Blessed are the dead who die in the Lord from now on.' 'Yes,' says the Spirit, 'that they may rest from their labors, and their works follow them'" (Rev. 14:13).

PRAYING IN CONFIDENCE OF GOD'S FAVOR
Sing Psalm 26

THINGS I WILL PRAY FOR TODAY

_____

_____

_____

_____

_____

_____

_____

March 17
Victim or Victor?

A prayer of godly resignation

The Lord has given and the Lord has taken away. —*Job 1:21*

READ JOB 1

"Going postal" is how Americans describe mass murder in the workplace. It started in Edmond, Oklahoma, in 1983, when a disgruntled postal worker killed fourteen coworkers and himself. Such tragic incidents have become almost commonplace today. Adversity so quickly exposes fault lines in human nature. Yet God tells us, "Count it all joy when you fall into various trials, knowing that the testing of your faith produces patience. But let patience have its perfect work, that you may be perfect and complete, lacking nothing" (James 1:2–4). There is another way: that of faith in the living God. But then, that's the rub!

So what do you do when you lose everything? Job is the great example in Scripture of a man whose life was devastated by calamities. He loses his family, his property—and later, his health. His wife tells him, "Curse God and die!" (Job 2:9). And unlike most of humanity, he did not, as they say, "have it coming." He was a good and godly man. But Satan asked to test him. God permits this, albeit within certain limits (Job 1:12; 2:6; cf. Luke 22:31; 1 Cor. 10:13). Does God seem cruel to allow this? But the genius of it is that Job's experience teaches not only Job but also the whole church to this day about life in the real world and God's sustaining grace (Eccl. 9:2; John 16:33).

These lessons are vital to our spiritual growth and ultimate blessing. Not least, they point us to Christ in his uniquely redemptive sufferings and victory. Because, without Christ, we are merely victims, but in him we become victors (Rom. 8:36–37)! Job responds in two ways (vv. 20–22).

He grieves: he "tore his robe and shaved his head" (v. 20a). He is *devastated.* Such sadness, sorrow, and grief are natural and necessary, and not to be denied or suppressed. When faced with loss in this life, we need to face reality and, crucially, "reach toward the eternal kingdom."

154

He worships the Lord (vv. 20b–22). He does not immediately cry, "Why me?" He does not blame God, far less curse him and die.

> *Job believes and trusts the Lord:* When everything else was gone, he turns to God and lifts him up as worthy to be praised. Later he will confess, "Though He slay me, yet will I trust Him" (Job 13:15).

> *Job recognizes the human condition as it really is*: "Naked I came from my mother's womb, and naked shall I return there" (v. 21a). The fact is that "the form of this world is passing away" (1 Cor. 7:31). God owes us nothing and we will leave as naked as we arrived. Even so, as Paul says, "God shall supply all your need according to His riches in glory by Christ Jesus" (Phil. 4:19).

> *Job acknowledges God's sovereignty and ownership*: "The Lord gave and the Lord has taken away" (v. 21b). He accepts that what he has lost was not his own, but the gift of God. Whatever Satan thought he was doing, it is God who has "taken away." The glory of Job's faith and trust is that he is ready to let God take what God has given. Why do we expect to keep everything God gives us, forever (1 Tim. 6:7–9)?

> *Job confesses the goodness of God*: "Blessed be the name of the Lord" (v. 21c). And "in all this Job did not sin nor charge God with wrong" (v. 22). Later he rebukes his wife's bitterness: "Shall we indeed accept good from God, and shall we not accept adversity?" (Job 2:10). Even so, like Paul in 2 Corinthians 6:10, he could say he has "nothing," yet possesses "all things." Let us then learn from Job and turn to Job's Savior. "For thus says the Lord GOD, the Holy One of Israel: 'In returning and rest you shall be saved; In quietness and confidence shall be your strength'" (Isa. 30:15). In Jesus Christ we shall be "more than conquerors" through him who loves us (Rom. 8:37)!

PRAYING IN SERENE DEPENDENCE UPON GOD
Sing Psalm 46

THINGS I WILL PRAY FOR TODAY

March 18
Better Off Dead?

A prayer of agonized despair

O that I might have my request…that it would please God to crush me. —Job 6:8–9

READ JOB 6:1–13

The death of hope is the death of people. In the United States more than 30,000 people take their own lives every year. Three-quarters of a million make the attempt annually. Praying to die may look hopeful in some sense, but it too is the abandonment of hope in this life, albeit dressed up as a kind of virtue. Job's prayer for death is certainly understandable. Eliphaz exposes Job's self-pity (Job 4–5). Job hits back with a defensive wail: his friend does not feel his pain. Of course he doesn't! But Job's indulging in defensive self-justification cannot relieve his pain. He agrees his words have been "rash," but he reckons his agonies entitle him to lash out. He even lashes out at God by complaining: "the terrors of God are arrayed against me" (vv. 3–4). He seems to think his anger will somehow satisfactorily fill the void of helplessness he feels (vv. 5–7). So do many today, but experience teaches that it never solves the problem. Finally, he prays "that it would please God to crush me, that He would loose His hand and cut me off!" (vv. 8–9). This is, quite literally, the prayer request to end all prayer requests. "It is as ill said as almost anything we meet with in all his discourse," observes Matthew Henry, "and is recorded for our admonition, not our imitation."

The loss of the future is what does it for Job. His arguments have crossed many a mind when life has seemed overwhelmed by tragedy:

> *I'd be better off dead!* Job is no suicide—he just wishes God would take him. He offers a pious reason—he'll still be trusting God—and says, "Then I would still have comfort" (v. 10a). He imagines he can trust God for the life to come, when he will not trust him for his present life.

> *I'm being honest and my conscience is clear!* "I would even exult in pain unsparing, for I have not denied the words of the Holy One" (v. 10bc, ESV). This is sheer bravado: he thinks he

can please God in his death wish. This is unbelieving despair masquerading as godliness.

> *What's the use of going on living anyway?* Job asks, "What strength do I have that I should hope?" (vv. 11–13). Which of us has not given up in the face of some challenge? But coming to the end of our strength, which is bound to happen to us many times, is not a ground for giving up, but for trusting the Lord. "I can do all things through Christ who strengthens me," says Paul (Phil. 4:13). Faith looks past the senses and limitations of the flesh.

What is the answer to Job's deadly prayer? Perhaps the first thing to do is to think good thoughts of God. In Psalm 130, the psalmist cries to God "from the depths." But he doesn't stay there, because he looks away from himself to the character of God: "But there is forgiveness with You, that You may be feared" (v. 4). "In our repentance," says Matthew Henry, "we must keep up good thoughts of God." Then ask yourself, "Am I content with Christ alone?" On a Lord's Day evening in March 1699, young Thomas Boston asked himself this question:

In the evening, while I sat musing on what I had been preaching, *viz.* that the soul that has got a true discovery of Christ will be satisfied with him alone, I proposed the question to myself, "Are you content with Christ alone? Would you be satisfied with Christ as your portion, even tho' there were no hell to be saved from?" And my soul answered, "Yes." I asked myself further, "Supposing that, would you be content in him, if you were to lose credit and reputation, and meet with trouble for his sake?" My soul answered, "Yes. Such is my hatred of sin and my love to Christ."

To be alive in Christ is contentment indeed. It is eternal life now and forevermore (Job 19:25).

PRAYING FROM THE DEPTHS OF DISCOURAGEMENT
Sing Psalm 88:1–9a

THINGS I WILL PRAY FOR TODAY

_____

_____

_____

March 19
Let Me Alone!

A prayer that questions God's dealings

Let me alone till I swallow my saliva. —Job 7:19

READ JOB 7:1–21

Suffering without apparent reason is at best insupportable and at worst an outrage. A great deal of the misery in this world is sheer injustice and oppression. The fact is that, aside from the general truth that "all have sinned and come short of the glory of God" and "the wages of sin is death" (Rom. 3:23; 6:23), there is often no discernible connection between personal calamity and personal sin. Job was a sinner by nature, but by God's grace he was a good and godly man—"blameless and upright, and one who feared God and shunned evil" (Job 1:1). Small wonder that he speculates: if his sufferings are not judgment for sin, why have they happened at all?

When Jesus was asked whether those who died in the collapse of a tower were greater sinners than those who did not, he answered, "Unless you repent, you will all likewise perish" (Luke 13:5). The survivors are not less guilty than those who died in that terrible accident. Everyone dies by one means or another. Unless you repent and believe upon Jesus for salvation, you will die the second death in a lost eternity. Suffering can be the most awful mystery.

Job has some serious questions for God:

> *Why is life so hard?* (vv. 1–6). Job has useless days and restless nights (vv. 1–4). He has a wasting body and his fleeting days are unrelieved by any prospect of something better (vv. 5–6). They just grind on—and to what avail?

> *What hope is there for me?* (vv. 7–10). He calls on God as the witness of his short, sad life: "O remember that my life is a breath!" (v. 7a). He confesses he has no hope for a happy life (vv. 7b–10). In the Scottish ballad "Maiden of Morven," the protagonist bemoans the loss of his beloved, who was swept off a rock by massive waves. "Death the only hope I know," he wails in his sorrow. This is the "theology" behind modern

arguments for abortion, euthanasia, and suicide—the idea that death is all that is left in the face of certain afflictions.

> ☙ *What help are you, Lord?* (vv. 11–16). When he looks at what God has done, he sees three things: pain—"the bitterness of my soul" (v. 11); mistreatment—"Am I a sea serpent that you set a guard over me?" (v. 12); and fear—"you scare me with dreams" (vv. 13–14). So he tells God, "Leave me alone, for my days are but a breath."

> ☙ *If I have sinned, why not just forgive me?* (vv. 17–21). Can you not hear the stifled tears in Job's cry to God? He asks, "What is man?"—the same words the psalmist uses in Psalm 8:4, but in the opposite direction from the psalmist. Job is sarcastic. His thrust is to ask what is so great about man, that God should "test him every moment" (v. 18). "How long?" he hisses in his bitterness. "Let me alone till I swallow my saliva" (v. 19).

We all surely identify with Job's questioning of God! He is in intense anguish of both body and soul. He is sorry for himself in all of this. He is angry with God because of a lack of understanding of God's dealings. He is confused. He is sad. He hurts. He cries out. He does not understand the true reasons for his woes. He needs to discover afresh in his heart the love of his Redeemer. His spiritual testing (and ours) teaches us to run to our Savior. These testings will prove the Lord's love against all the malevolence of the world, the flesh, and the devil. Soon Job will confess, "I know that my Redeemer lives, and at the last He will take His stand on the earth. Even after my skin is destroyed, yet from my flesh I shall see God" (Job 19:25–26). This Savior is none other than Jesus Christ, whose own sufferings are our salvation. "Nobody knows the troubles I've seen," goes the old spiritual, "Nobody but Jesus." He saved Job and he will save everyone who trusts in him as Savior. As he was with Job, so shall he be with us, and as we cry to him in our trouble, he will deliver us out of our distresses (Ps. 107:6).

PRAYING FOR DELIVERANCE IN OUR DISTRESSES
Sing Psalm 107

THINGS I WILL PRAY FOR TODAY

_____

_____

March 20
Bridging the Gap

A prayer for mediation between God and man

Nor is there any mediator between us, who may lay his hand on us both. —Job 9:33

READ JOB 9:25–35

aps are the reasons for bridges. Bridges are the "go-betweens" that connect two sides of otherwise inconvenient chasms. In his pain and misery, Job feels separated from God by a gulf he sees no possibility of bridging. God has not only left him, as he sees it, but he has also punished him, and there is no sign of any light at the end of the tunnel. So he asks the question—not as a detached matter of principle, but as a cry of despair—"How can a man be righteous before God?" (Job 9:2). Job acknowledges that God is just. He does not accuse God of wrongdoing. He does not say that he is suffering because God is unjust. The reason for this is that he truly is a believer and a man of God. He believes and knows the Lord to be good. He knows him with a personal and saving faith. He also knows that "no one living is righteous" (Ps. 143:2), and that "all our righteousnesses are as filthy rags" (Isa. 64:6). These two great facts—God's perfect righteousness and man's universal sinfulness—teach him two great practical truths. First, that doing better at being good will never bring anyone to heaven, and second, that only radical renewal of human nature, he knows not how, will accomplish reconciliation of sinners and God.

To Job, the hopelessness of all human attempts to commend ourselves to God backs this up. For one thing, God will not be sweet-talked into letting us sinners off!

The *practical principle* is that, if you try this, you will not "answer Him one time out of a thousand" (Job 9:3). That means you can't argue your way into God's good graces! Saying you are a good person cuts no ice with God.

Then look at the *evidence* (Job 9:4–13). God's wisdom is profound and his power is almighty: "Who has hardened himself against Him and prospered?" (Job 9:4). After all, he is the Creator of heaven and earth—an argument that God will use later to humble and transform Job (Job 9:5–9; cf. 38:2ff.). He is the absolutely sovereign Lord and we, in contrast, are powerless even to see him, still less find fault with him (Job 9:10–12). And he is consistently just: "The allies of the proud lie prostrate before Him" (Job 9:13). This means you can't fight God and win!

It follows that trying to *justify yourself* with God is a fool's errand (Job 9:14–24). Many will compare themselves to others and find themselves decent enough to expect God to wink at their sins. Others are practically Universalists who assume that since God is "in the business of forgiveness"—as I have heard someone say—then they can expect to go to heaven unless they were mass murderers. Scripture says otherwise: "There is none righteous, no, not one" (Rom. 3:10), but self-justifying sinners have an endless capacity to deny the truth about themselves.

Job realizes that the only hope is a "mediator" (vv. 25–35). The gap must be bridged by a third party, so that (human) sin is atoned for and (divine) righteousness is secured for and in the sinner. This is needed because, Job says, man cannot sue God and win acquittal (v. 32). No, we need a go-between "who may lay his hand on us both" in such a way as to save the unholy human being and satisfy the perfect righteousness and justice of the holy God. At this point, Job has no notion as to who this mediator might be. We know in the fullness of the New Testament that he is God's only-begotten Son, "the man Christ Jesus" (1 Tim. 2:5). Christ is divine Mediator, truly God and truly man, who bridges the gap. He bears the sin of sinners for all who will believe on him and his perfect righteousness is accounted to them, and they are reconciled to God: "For He made Him who knew no sin to be sin for us, that we might become the righteousness of God in Him" (2 Cor. 5:21).

PRAYING FOR DELIVERANCE IN OUR DISTRESSES
Sing Psalm 143

THINGS I WILL PRAY FOR TODAY

March 21
Do Not Condemn Me!

A prayer that pleads with God

I will say to God, "Do not condemn me." —Job 10:2

READ JOB 10

eople like to talk about accepting the Lord into their lives. God is assumed to be willing and waiting for whenever we take the notion to accept him. Rarely do you hear someone wonder why God should accept us into his life! "How can God get right with us?" is, however, a vital question. Job thinks about it. In the tenth chapter, he tries to get into God's mind. He as good as says, "I cannot see that God can bring himself to be reconciled to us humans, who fall so far short of him." It is not that he does not understand suffering for sin, but that he does not fathom why God allows a believer, who is faithful and godly in his life, to suffer in the way he was suffering. Everybody tells him he must be experiencing punishment for secret and unrepented sin. Job knows this is not so. He is not sinlessly perfect, but he is saved and seriously faithful. So is he somehow irretrievably under the wrath of God?

Job cries out to God in his pain and confusion. He begs God to tell him what he is doing wrong (vv. 1–7). He asks God why he seems bent on destroying him (vv. 8–12). After all, Job confesses, "You have granted me life and favor, and Your care has preserved my spirit" (v. 12). Job answers his own questions immediately: God has marked his sins and neither forgotten nor forgiven them (vv. 13–17). His conclusion is that he might as well die, as he would surely be better off dead (vv. 18–22). He just feels hopeless. He is drowning in his pain and sees no conceivable escape! This, of course, is what suffering can do, even to a great saint like Job. Providence is always somewhat mysterious and events often defy explanation. The apostle Peter, who was no stranger to being puzzled by providence, came to realize why it was that Christians suffered in a sinful world: "For the time has come for judgment to begin at the house of God; and if it begins with us first, what will be the end of those who do not obey the gospel of God? Now 'If the righteous one is scarcely saved, where

162

will the ungodly and the sinner appear?' Therefore let those who suffer according to the will of God commit their souls to Him in doing good, as to a faithful Creator" (1 Peter 4:17–19). There are sufferings that are the unjust oppressions of the world, not the punishments of our personal sin, and these are, alas, the inevitable tests of faith for those who love the Lord in the midst of a faithless and perverse generation. Job had not yet grasped this, and so he continued to flog himself and excoriate God for afflicting him.

Job knew that he needed a Mediator (Job 9:38). He clearly had no inkling that there was one and that it was through him that he was *already* saved. Derek Thomas is right when he says, "Job needs a mediator, not because he has sinned and is therefore estranged from God. He needs someone who can sympathize with his aches and pains. He needs someone who has stood where Job stood." Job, unwittingly as yet, anticipates the "one Mediator between God and men, the Man Christ Jesus," who would come "in the fullness of the time" (1 Tim. 2:5; Gal. 4:4). In due time, he will grasp something of the fullness and comfort of Christ's saving work (Job 19:25).

There is a Mediator to bridge the gap between a holy God and hopelessly lost sinners. When God accepted Jesus, the one and only Mediator, he accepted all those for whom Jesus died as the sacrifice and atonement for their sin, all those who will believe upon Jesus as their Savior and Lord. And this Mediator Jesus continues to minister in believers' hearts: "For we do not have a High Priest who cannot sympathize with our weaknesses, but was in all points tempted as we are, yet without sin" (Heb. 4:15).

PRAYING FOR DEFERRED COMFORT
Sing Psalm 119:81–88

THINGS I WILL PRAY FOR TODAY

March 22
Of Few Days and Full of Trouble?

A prayer for light on mortality and immortality

All the days of my hard service I will wait, till my change comes.
—Job 14:14

READ JOB 14:1–22

We all know we will die one day, but death is not usually a large part of daily life. That is because, in our experience, people mostly live a long time and are only a relatively short time dying. We may have made a will and planned our funeral, but we usually go to bed expecting to wake up tomorrow. Until and unless we are confronted by death in one form or another—whether by illness, bereavement, violence, warfare, or natural disaster or, not least, solemn reflection upon its inevitability and our eternal destiny—we just get on with living one day at a time. Job, of course, had been confronted with death in a huge way. Yet, even when he says we are "of few days and full of trouble," we have a sense that this is probably not how he thought of his life when all was going well. Our days are limited, to be sure, and troubles do come in life, but the experience of humanity is not uniformly of fewness of days and fullness of troubles. Solomon recognizes this in his famous appeal to the young, "Remember now your Creator in the days of your youth before the difficult days come and the years draw near when you say, 'I have no pleasure in them'" (Eccl. 12:1). Days can be long and troubles few—at least for a season.

Job's lament about our days being "few…and full of trouble," for all the undoubted truth in it, is as much, if not more, the fruit of his despair. He goes on to prove this in a stream of desperate words, all of them mingling a certain degree of truth with a larger degree of practical unbelief: "For there is more hope for a tree, if it is cut down, that it will sprout again," than for a man, who "dies and is laid away; indeed he breathes his last and where is he?" (vv. 7, 10). It is all gloom and doom, and here is the rub: God cannot or will not do anything about it, either! This is pure self-pity. And how we understand it, if we have ever been tested in this life! Despairing thoughts accelerate around the inside of Job's mind, only looking beyond self to throw some reproach in the direction of God. His darkness seems unrelieved.

Even in the gloom there is a glimmer of light. Job is still speaking to God. For all his depressive self-pity, he does not "curse God and die" (Job 2:9). He wonders, "If a man dies, shall he live again?" (v. 14). Yet he is submissive to the Lord: "All the days of my hard service I will wait, till my change comes. You shall call and I will answer You" (vv. 14–15). He is, however, begging for light on the subject. He wants answers and they still elude him. Still, he is willing to wait upon the Lord, even if it is "hard service" (v. 14). His faith is real, and living faith sees the invisible (Heb. 11:1), even if it may seem to the mind shrouded in an impenetrable fog. The day will come when God will give Job more light, such that he will freely confess, "I have heard of You by the hearing of the ear, but now my eye sees You. Therefore I abhor myself and repent in dust and ashes" (Job 42:5–6).

"Happily," writes Herbert Lockyer, "Job's dim light has become a full revelation." How? "Christ has brought life and immortality to light through His Gospel" (2 Tim. 1:10). In Christ who is our life, we have "the hope of glory"—of "an inheritance incorruptible and undefiled and that does not fade away, reserved in heaven" (Col. 1:27; 3:4; 1 Peter 1:4). Job's present doubts would soon give way to an assurance of life after this life (Job 19:25). His faith would persevere. In his living Redeemer, he would prevail over the assaults of Satan (Job 1:12), and the Lord restored his losses with "twice as much as he had before" (Job 42:10). And after that, his days were neither few nor full of trouble!

PRAYING FOR HELP IN DESPONDENCY
Sing Psalm 88:9b–18

THINGS I WILL PRAY FOR TODAY

March 23
Again, Why Bother?

The justification of prayerlessness

What profit do we have if we pray to Him?—Job 21:15b

READ JOB 21:7–15

hy bother?" is the humorist's title for decaffeinated coffee. Why so? Because without caffeine the coffee loses the main reason for our drinking it in the first place—the kick-start that wakes you up in the morning! By the same token, you might ask, "Why bother praying?"—especially if you don't really believe God is there and able to answer. After all, the main justification for doing anything is that it might actually come to something. This is the argument that Job puts into the mouths of people who have no use for prayer. They wave off the very idea, asking, "What profit do we have if we pray to Him?" Rejected as having no practical value, prayer inevitably falls by the wayside.

The deeper reason a person rejects prayer is, of course, out of a desire to be free of God. They say to God, "Depart from us, for we do not desire the knowledge of your ways" (v. 14). If there is such a thing as an atheist prayer, this is it! It certainly expresses the *practical* atheism of all who reject the Bible's God, whatever their religious or Christian credentials may be. The fearful thing is that it is a prayer that God frequently answers with his judicial withdrawal. The godless before the Flood discovered this (Gen. 6:3) and the lost in hell have gotten their wish in being forever deprived of God's presence—though not of his punishment of their sin.

In the context, Job refutes the notion that personal disasters are punishments for personal sin. Wicked people do not demonstrably suffer immediate divine judgment because of their sins. Look at their lives, says Job. Sinners have long and stable lives (vv. 7–8). They live in security (v. 9a), with no sign of God's judgment upon them (v. 9b; cf. vv. 17–26). They have successful careers (v. 10), happy family lives (vv. 11–12), enjoy prosperity, and die easy deaths (v. 13). What they take from all this is that they have no need of God and that there is therefore no profit in praying! They also see no need to thank God for all these blessings. The presence of blessings and the absence of calamities in their lives merely serve to confirm their rejection of God! All of these things are blessings in themselves, but with the predispositions of an unregenerate heart and the consequent determination to keep God at a distance, they inevitably add up to an illusory sense of not needing God at all. The message of God's Word—that we need Job's Redeemer (Job 19:25) and that his gospel ("good news") of salvation is to be found in Jesus Christ—is dismissed as offensive, unnecessary, and unprofitable.

Both personal blessings and calamities will always move believers to prayer. They answer the questions "Who is the Almighty that we should serve Him?" and "What profit do we have if we pray to Him?" (v. 15):

- Our blessings inspire boundless gratitude and our trials lead us to seek the Lord's help. Knowing the Lord, we know that "His compassions fail not" and are "new every morning," and that he has "punished us less than our iniquities deserve" (Lam. 3:22–23; Ezra 9:12–13).

- Our troubles remind us that we live in a fallen world and that we are accountable to God—but they also remind us that he is long-suffering and full of love. They tell us, in the words of an old spiritual, "It's me, it's me, it's me, oh Lord, standing in the need of prayer." This promises future blessing.

- Our blessings ought to send us to God's throne in joy and thanksgiving. Even the most ordinary provisions are actually gifts from our Father in heaven (James 1:17). They are the "profit" of God's goodness to us and are always matched in a believing heart by the profit of coming to him in prayers of thanksgiving. "Why bother?" The answer is, "I will love You, O Lord, my strength" (Ps. 18:1).

PRAISE BORN OF LOVE FOR THE LORD
Sing Psalm 18:1–6

THINGS I WILL PRAY FOR TODAY

_____

_____

_____

_____

March 24
Let Us Reason Together

The prayer that protests too much

I would present my case before Him, and fill my mouth with arguments. —Job 23:4

READ JOB 23:2–7

This is not so much a prayer as a protest. Job's opening words set the tone: "Even today my complaint is bitter; my hand is listless because of my groaning" (v. 2). He has a bone to pick with God. He is desperately unhappy about God's role in his troubles. His friends deepen his disenchantment by basically saying he must somehow deserve his sufferings and should "return to the Almighty" and thus "remove iniquity" far from his tents (Job 22:23). Job, however, is not aware of having turned from God in the first place and sees no necessary connection between his sufferings and any particular sin. He is neither a hypocrite nor an unbeliever. His calamities are mystifying to him. It is not uncommon in our experience to have bad things happen that have no obvious connection to our behavior.

There is a prayer implicit in Job's protest. He wants to dialogue with God: "Oh, that I knew where I might find Him, that I might come to His seat!" (v. 3). Job is certainly eager to come close to God, but it is not to listen, or to wait, or even to petition him. His blood is up for a good argument! His "prayer" is not looking for light from God, but is rather aimed at reasoning with God so as to enlighten him and secure his support in the dispute with his friends!

The true spirit of prayer is lacking when our aim is to persuade God to agree with us. That is what Job is asking for in verses 4–7. It's all about Job talking and God being convinced by his arguments! He declares, "I…will present my case…fill my mouth with arguments…would know the words which He would answer me, and understand what He would say." Then—guess what?—God would not "contend with me," but "take note of me…and I would be delivered forever from my Judge." In other words, Job's irresistible logic will persuade God to vindicate him over against his friends' assertions that he is under God's judgment for some sin.

Oh, the subtle ways we can ungod God and treat him as though we can actually inform and educate him about our true situation! We should rather remember that "God is not a man" (Num. 23:19). He does not need to be enlightened by our arguments.

Prayer itself, as a means of grace, assumes the exact opposite: Namely that it is we humans who need to be enlightened by the Lord on every issue, at every point, and in every detail. The true spirit of prayer is the end of pride and the flowering of humility of mind; it is a willingness to hear what God the Lord will speak. In the end, God teaches Job this lesson. Having been called to account (38:1–39:2), Job humbly replies, "What shall I answer You? I lay my hand over my mouth" (39:3); and he confesses, "Therefore I have uttered what I do not understand" (42:3). When his mouth was stopped, his heart overflowed.

We are, of course, called to reason together with the Lord. "'Come now, and let us reason together,' says the LORD: 'though your sins are like scarlet, they shall be as white as snow; though they are red like crimson, they shall be as wool'" (Isa 1:18). It is, however, the Lord reasoning with us, not us arguing or negotiating with him. We need him to open the eyes of our understanding so that we grasp God's riches for us in his Son (Eph. 1:18ff.). So let us reason with the Lord by praying, "Open my eyes, that I may see wondrous things from Your law" (Ps. 119:18).

PRAYING FOR THE OPENING OF OUR EYES
Sing Psalm 119:17–24

THINGS I WILL PRAY FOR TODAY

March 25
God Breaks His Silence

God's answer to Job's prayers

Then the Lord answered Job out of the whirlwind. — *Job 38:1*

READ JOB 38:1–7; 40:1–7

We all want answers to our prayers, and as soon as possible. Waiting can be a sore test. Indeed, God's silence only conspires to multiply the burden under which we groan, since it seems to indicate that God may be unmoved by our plight or, worse, intent on chastising us further. After all, Scripture teaches us to "come boldly to the throne of grace, that we may obtain mercy and find grace to help in time of need" (Heb. 4:16). Immediate needs look for immediate blessings, whether in the removal of some problem or in the bestowal of some good thing. Prayer can and does encompass the longer-term future, but shorter-term troubles inevitably dominate. Should God's urgency not appear to keep up with ours, we find out rather quickly whether or not we believe that the "testing of our faith produces patience" (James 1:3).

Why is God silent for a time? In Job's case, he began to be silent so as to allow Satan to afflict a godly man. Why? Because Satan had asked, "Does Job fear God for nothing?" (Job 1:9). That is, does Job only follow God when he feels the sunshine of his smile in prosperity and general well-being and it effectively costs him nothing to be his disciple? Is he only a fair-weather friend? Satan is saying, "Let me bring some storms into his life and watch him curse you, God!" (Job 1:11–12). God's silence gives Satan some room to test his claim—and to test Job. What this points out to you and me is that when God is not answering our prayers, he is actually in the process of teaching us a thing or two.

His silence may be *judicial*, as in Psalm 66:18: "If I regard iniquity in my heart, the Lord will not hear" (see Deut. 28:23). His silences are always *didactic*, as in Job's case. At the start, Job "did not sin or charge God with wrong" (1:22), but as the days went by, he did sin with his lips in complaining that God was treating him unjustly (33:12). So God's silence gave room for Job to think about things and ponder his actions.

This is surely why the Lord rarely gives instant answers to many of our prayers. The Lord's silence gives us time to *think* through events and issues. Persuasion is a rational process. It takes time. His silence also *tests* us as to whether we "fear God for nothing"—when it costs us nothing. Satan rattled Job inside and out. God's silence *prepares* us for fresh insight from him. It readies us to receive even more of the knowledge and the grace of God. Finally, the Lord's silence does not last *a moment longer* than he deems necessary for our relief, revival, and restoration. God is good and all things do "work together for good for those who love God" (Rom. 8:28). His grace is even in his silence.

What is God teaching when he speaks? First of all, do not miss the fact that God did answer! This is free grace, in whatever form he speaks (38:1–3). Second, notice the majestic self-revelation of God that rebukes our puny presumption: "Where were you when I laid the foundation of the earth?" (38:4ff.). God preaches a "sermon" that asks "Where were you?" (38:4–40:2) and so completely disarms Job, who, seeing God's glory *and* grace, confesses his sin: "I am vile" and "I lay my hand over my mouth" (40:4a). He offers no excuses. His mouth is empty of "arguments" (23:4)! Job is saying that God is just and the justifier of those who believe in him (cf. Rom. 3:26). Yet God does not explain to Job about Satan's challenge or justify his allowing Satan to test him. He just speaks and reveals his love as the hearer of prayer who saves his suffering servant by his glorious grace.

Do you see what God has done through Job's suffering at Satan's hand? He has taken Job's faith further than it had hitherto advanced, shown him his love beyond all previous experience, and grown his knowledge of salvation more deeply than ever before! Job now knew for sure that his Redeemer lived (19:25)!

PRAYING TO BE READY TO LISTEN WHEN GOD SPEAKS
Sing Psalm 85:8–13

THINGS I WILL PRAY FOR TODAY

_____

_____

_____

_____

_____

_____

March 26
Now I Get It!

The prayer of a humbled heart

Then Job answered the Lord. — Job 42:1

READ JOB 42:1–6

Job's life was shattered. God had given him children, good health, prosperity, a fine reputation, and helpful ministry to others. Job "feared God and shunned evil" (1:1). He lived a happy, godly life. Then Satan challenged God: "Does Job fear God for nothing?" (1:9), i.e., will he still love God when he has nothing? So God permits Satan to test the patriarch, but when Job has nothing left, he still refuses to "curse God and die"! (2:9). He still fears God as a persevering, suffering saint!

Job has unanswered questions. Why is this happening? The so-called "comforters" wrongly insist God is punishing Job for some secret sin. Job rightly protests his innocence, but then he charges God with punishing him unjustly and not answering his prayers. In these things, Job does "sin with his lips" (cf. 2:10). God hears out Job's complaints patiently, but the time comes when he responds. "Would you indeed annul My judgment? Would you condemn Me that you may be justified?" God asks (Job 40:8). This is the heart of the matter, because when we argue with God, we are basically taking to ourselves the government of the world. There is certainly a place for asking God what he is up to. But our complaints are too often outright objections to his will as unfolded in his providence. We are saying in effect that God is sinning against us, and that we not only know better, but are better than he. This is how we justify sitting in judgment upon him! Job needs to be humbled. So do all of us.

Job is disarmed by God's answer. The Lord rebukes Job's presumption firmly but graciously (Job 38–41). Humility is always the first step on the way to blessing. If Job could not handle animals like Leviathan and Behemoth (Job 40:15; 41:1), how could he conceivably handle God? Job is blown away and he knows it. Overwhelmed, he confesses, "I know that You can do everything, and that no purpose of Yours can be withheld

172

from You" (v. 1). Does the power of God's creation not humble you? Did you make the flowers bloom in the spring? Does not God's grace, even more than his power, melt your soul and persuade your mind? Job 42:3–6 beautifully expresses the depth of Job's conviction of and repentance for sin and the sincerity of his faith and love in casting himself upon his Father-God. Notice his swift transition from admitting *ignorance*, to dawning *knowledge*, to confessing *sin*, and finally to expressing *repentance*:

> ⟩ "I have uttered what I did not understand" (v. 3) and
> ⟩ "I have heard of You…but now my eye sees You" (v. 5).

Therefore,

> ⟩ "I abhor myself" (v. 6a) and
> ⟩ "[I] repent in sackcloth and ashes" (v. 6b). Job finally gets it!

Job's humbling actually exalts him. "The depth of his humiliation," writes William Henry Green, "is really the summit of his exaltation in piety, and in the fear and love of God." Green adds, "The faith to which he has now attained, would not only have gained the mastery in this frightful contest, but would have trampled Satan's temptation under foot without a conflict." He needed to be brought down in order to be built up. The Apostle Paul understood this, not only from his conversion experience on the Damascus road (Acts 26:12-18), but in the way the trials of his life in the real world deepened his walk with the Lord. He writes, "Therefore I take pleasure in infirmities, in reproaches, in needs, in persecutions, in distresses, for Christ's sake. For when I am weak, then I am strong" (2 Cor. 12:10). "Humble yourselves, therefore, under the mighty hand of God, that he may exalt you in due time" (1 Peter 5:6). Now, do you get it?

THE PRAISE OF A HUMBLED HEART
Sing Psalm 131

THINGS I WILL PRAY FOR TODAY

_____

_____

_____

_____

_____

_____

March 27
A Ministry of Intercession

Job restored to usefulness

My servant Job shall pray for you. —Job 42:8

READ JOB 42:7-17

ob needed help. His friends, alas, made things worse. They meant well, but their comfort was discomfort. Their answers were more hindrance than help. Job might well have said with the psalmist, "Even my own familiar friend in whom I trusted, who ate my bread, has lifted up his heel against me" (Ps. 41:9). Job got no relief. He was drowning in misguided counsel from his friends, while his own mind boiled over with conflicted, if often insightful, thoughts. But how could he hear God, when everybody, including himself, was talking? The Lord says, "Be still, and know that I am God" (Ps. 46:10), for the simple reason that other noise can only distract us from focusing upon him. If there is to be any solution to our problems, the talking, fretting, self-pitying, complaining, debating, and even receiving counseling all has to stop so we can listen to the voice of God (Ps. 62:1, 5). Only when God shuts him up by speaking to him "out of the whirlwind"—surely itself a parable of Job's state of mind—does Job hear and understand the meaning of what has happened and find his burden lifted. For "the entrance of Your words brings light" (Ps. 119:130). In their intervention—intercession and mediation—his comforters were counterproductive. It took God's intervention to retrieve the situation.

Job's friends need help. They were in trouble with the Lord. Job is commended for speaking "what is right" of God (v. 7). This is amazing, considering his complaining. So how can God say this? The answer is that Job was correct in saying he had not sinned in such a way as to incur God's wrath. God does not punish innocent people. Job had looked to the Lord in faith, believing him for salvation, notwithstanding his struggles and his complaints that God had abandoned him unjustly to his sufferings. Job is therefore justified against his "comforters." Eliphaz, Bildad, and Zophar had meant well, but in fact had not spoken "what is right." This was "folly" and it aroused the Lord's "wrath" (v. 8).

"When words are many, sin is not absent, but he who holds his tongue is wise" (Prov. 10:19).

But why is God so angry? These men cared, and they said many true things. The trouble is that they started from a twisted view of God's justice: namely, that if bad things happen to you, you must be bad. The unintended consequence of this erroneous doctrine was to torture Job by laying false guilt on him, undermining his faith, and promoting a legalistic framework for life that defamed God's name and his free grace. They unwittingly ended up doing the work of the devil! So be careful how you seek to comfort people! Job's "discomforters" were being taught a lesson and had some repenting to do. God tells them to offer sacrifice through Job's priestly mediation. Roles are reversed. Now Job will be their help— "My servant Job shall pray for you" (v. 8). And so they are reconciled to the Lord in connection with Job's ministry of intercession on their behalf.

We all need help. Job, the "servant" who mediates and intercedes, surely points to the Servant of the Lord (Isa. 42:1–4). Job's acting as a mediator surely points to the "one Mediator between God and men, the Man Christ Jesus" (1 Tim. 2:5). Job leads us to Christ, in whom God has provided the Mediator and Intercessor for all the ages. He "is also able to save to the uttermost those who come to God through Him, since He always lives to make intercession for them" (Heb. 7:25). In God's love for Job and his friends, we have a picture of the gospel of Jesus Christ. In Job's intercession for others, we have a reflection of Jesus's mediation and intercession for his people. Job knows even in his darkest moments that his Redeemer lives and intercedes to give eternal life to all who believe upon him as Savior and Lord.

AN INTERCESSORY PRAYER FOR GOD'S PEOPLE
Sing Psalm 20

THINGS I WILL PRAY FOR TODAY

_____

_____

_____

_____

_____

March 28
The One Who Lifts Up My Head

Praying for God's help in the real world

Your blessing is upon Your people. — Psalm 3:8

READ PSALM 3

avid is running for his life (vv. 1–2). His son Absalom has overthrown him and his prospects look decidedly dismal (2 Sam. 15:30). Out of this dark experience comes the first prayer in the book of Psalms, and it is an anguished cry for help. The key word in verses 1–2 is the thrice-used "many." The English Standard Version renders this most clearly: "O LORD, how *many* are my foes! *Many* are rising against me; *many* are saying of my soul, there is no salvation for him in God." When we are under stress, it can seem that everybody is against us. So where do you turn when you feel this way? The focus of the "many" is of course an open contempt for God, confirmed in their minds by the poor state of his professed followers. This tells us right away, if you have a problem, take it to "the throne of grace" (Heb. 4:16).

David cries out in his desperation (vv. 3–4). David might easily conclude that God had deserted him, or was powerless to help. Remember how Job's wife told her husband to "curse God and die" (Job 2:9)? Practical atheism pulls hard on troubled souls. Christians too can be tempted to slight the Lord as if he is far away and doesn't care. This is why Jesus in his sufferings on the cross cries, in (David's) language of prophecy, "Be not far from Me, for trouble is near; for there is none to help"(Ps. 22:11). This experience is echoed in the hard times of many a child of God. David, like faithful Job, cries to God in steadfast faith and is strengthened by the assurance of his protection. His comfort does not come from, as many will say in our day, "feeling better about himself." Of course he *feels* comforted. But it is objective facts that feed his feelings and not his feelings that manufacture supposed or imagined facts. Two solid facts provide grounds for a rising confidence:

⯈ The first is that God *has lifted him up* throughout his life (v. 3). David Dickson sums it up beautifully, "God is a

176

counter-comfort in all calamity, our shield in danger, our glory in shame, the lifter up of our head in dejection." David sees by faith how the good things he has enjoyed have come to him from the Lord, who is his "shield," his "glory," and his deliverer from shame. These are our "Eben-ezers" (stones of helping), which should lead us to say with Samuel, "Thus far the Lord has helped us," and go on with David to trust him still (1 Sam. 7:12).

➢ The second solid fact is that this is attributable to God's *answering prayer*: "I cried to the Lord…and He heard me" (v. 4). This is an objective analysis of his experience in the light of God's promises, not the "if prayer works for you" subjectivism of modern critics of prayer. We believe God for what he has promised, and we are constantly assured by what he actually does.

David rejoices in a celebration of deliverance. He now can sleep and be awoken not by his fears, but because the Lord sustains him with confidence enough to discount the "ten thousands" arrayed against him (vv. 5–6)! "But peace and fearlessness were not enough. He must have victory, otherwise God's declared will would be frustrated,"so he prays with rising expectation—"Arise, Lord; save me, O my God!"—knowing that salvation belongs to him (vv. 7–8). In this, David anticipates the triumph of Jesus Christ, who declares "I looked, but there was no one to help, and I wondered that there was no one to uphold; Therefore My own arm brought salvation for Me; and My own fury, it sustained Me" (Isa. 63:5). Jesus is the One who lifts up the head of every believer and secures their salvation by his own arm!

PRAYING FOR DELIVERANCE FROM ENEMIES
Sing Psalm 3

THINGS I WILL PRAY FOR TODAY

March 29
Stressed Out?

A prayer under extreme stress

You have relieved me in my distress. — *Psalm 4:1*

READ PSALM 4

tress can do strange things. I was preparing to conduct the funeral of a young man who had died suddenly, leaving a wife and eight children. As I knotted my tie, thinking of the grief and loss of the family, my knees literally started to shake. The pity of it all was overwhelming. How could I conduct the service with any composure? The trembling worsened. Then Psalm 4:1 came to mind, in words often sung in worship.

Answer when I call,
O God who justifies.
In my stress You freed me;
Hear in grace my cries.

I prayed it over in my mind with desperate intensity. To my utter amazement, the answer came in a few seconds! The stress lifted and the Lord "made firm the feeble knees" (Isa. 35:3). The service, for all its sorrow, was blessed with "the glorious liberty of the children of God" (Rom. 8:31). The psalmist is "stressed out." Surely you have been at times. His response is to cry to God. Notice the three main components to this godly prayer.

Appeal to God for help (v. 1). David Dickson wrote: "Faith is a good orator, and a good disputer in a strait." He knows that prayer— to truly be prayer—has to arise from a living personal faith in the Lord, for "without faith it is impossible to please Him, for he who comes to God must believe that He is, and that He is a rewarder of those who diligently seek Him" (Heb. 11:6). David heaps up the arguments for God to hear him favorably: he comes to the God who is ready to hear prayer ("Answer when I call," cf. Ps. 65:1); he prays in a righteous cause ("God of my righteousness"); he testifies to having received answers in the past ("You have relieved me in my distress"); and he records that God's grace overcame his unworthiness ("Have mercy on me, and hear my prayer").

Here it is in a nutshell for all our prayers: God hears, God is holy, God has helped in the past, and God is gracious.

Admonish your enemies to repent and turn to God (vv. 2–5). "The most satisfactory revenge which the godly can desire of their persecutors and mockers," Dickson says, "is to have them made converts, to have them recalled from the vanity of their way, and brought to a right understanding of what concerns their salvation." If the Lord has "no pleasure in the death of the wicked, but that the wicked turn from his way and live," then we should rejoice to pray to that end (Ezek. 33:11). It was a failing in the disciples James and John that they wanted fire from heaven to consume the Samaritan village that would not receive Jesus (Luke 9:54). They forgot that it is "through the LORD's mercies we are not consumed, because His compassions fail not" (Lam. 3:22). Surely we desire for the non-Christian the same salvation, by grace through faith in Christ, which we now know but did not deserve ourselves? Yes, you have cause to be angry with folks that do you wrong! God says to you, "Be angry, and do not sin" (Eph. 4:26), look to your own heart, and "put your trust in the Lord."

Acknowledge God's goodness and faithfulness (vv. 6–8). Look, says David to his companions and fellow believers, many say, "Who will show us any good?" Let me tell you what you should be asking for: "Lord, lift up the light of your countenance upon us." Ask for a "gladness" in your heart. And, do you know what? The Lord will give you sleep at night and make you "dwell in safety" all your days! Here is, as Andrew Bonar puts it, "The Godly One's Chief Good."

READY TO LISTEN WHEN GOD SPEAKS
Sing Psalm 4

THINGS I WILL PRAY FOR TODAY

_____

_____

_____

_____

_____

_____

March 30
The Shield of God's Favor

Praying for God's protection through the day

My voice You shall hear in the morning, O Lord. — *Psalm 5:3*

READ PSALM 5

"O! it's nice to get up in the mornin'," goes an old Harry Lauder song, "but it's nicer to lie in your bed." Sometimes it really is difficult to get up and face the day...and not just because it is cold and wintry and work beckons. Real problems can turn our tomorrows into terrors. David prays about his troubles and ponders five considerations that together cover the anxieties on his mind and also serve to be the "strengthening of his hope to be heard."

God's grace enables his people to pray (vv. 1–3). We often assume that anyone can pray a true prayer any time they feel like it. This is clearly not so. It takes God's grace for us to seek him. For, "without faith it is impossible to please Him, for he who comes to God must believe that He is, and that He is a rewarder of those who diligently seek Him" (Heb. 11:6). The psalmist prays out of a lively personal faith. "My King and My God" is a confession of faith from the heart. He seals this with a threefold promise to begin his days with prayer: "My voice you shall hear in the morning....In the morning I will direct it to You...and I will look up" (v. 3). Believing prayer is both a fruit of God's grace and a means of receiving more of his grace.

God's righteousness enables his people to face their enemies (vv. 4–6). This chilling litany of God's just judgments in time and eternity is a warning to the lost. It also encourages hope for deliverance in God's oppressed followers. God's attributes all imply warnings of judgment to come for unbelievers and promises of blessing for believers. The *Shorter Catechism* 4 asks, "What is God?" and answers, "God is a Spirit, infinite, eternal, and unchangeable, in his being, wisdom, power, holiness, justice, goodness, and truth." Each attribute gives the believer hope, but implicitly warns the unbelieving to repent toward God and believe in the Lord Jesus Christ (Acts 20:21).

God's mercy enables his people to worship and serve him (vv. 7–8).

A serious commitment to obeying God's Word is basic to believing prayer. To pray without the intention to worship and serve the Lord in the practical details of daily life is not to pray at all, but to engage in premeditated hypocrisy. In contrast, mercy received in Christ and lived out in step with the Holy Spirit is both the proof and the goal of a heart in tune with God.

God's justice encourages hope of deliverance in his people (vv. 9–10). The psalmist anticipates the fall of godless enemies. There is no vindictive spirit here, but just the prophetic pronouncement of the sad end of determined wickedness and rejection of the living God: Father, Son, and Holy Spirit.

God's favor is a shield to his people in daily life (vv. 11–12). God's people who trust and love him therefore may rejoice. Why? The Lord will surround them with his favor. God's grace that first saved them and moved them to turn to him will be reaffirmed and magnified in a growing experience of his grace in the midst of a daily life often fraught with dangers and pitfalls. As David Dickson said over three centuries ago: "The favour and good will of God toward his own is a strong and glorious defence to them: it is a crowning shield…which circles a man round about and keeps off the dint of the adversary's weapon, even when the pursued believer is not aware." Let us get up every morning and commit every day to the Savior whose favor is our shield whether we are asleep or awake.

PRAYER ABOUT THE DAY AHEAD
Sing Psalm 5

THINGS I WILL PRAY FOR TODAY

March 31
Weary with Groaning

Prayer of a troubled soul

I am weary with my groaning. —Ps. 6:6

READ PSALM 6

ave you ever been "worried sick"? You are a Christian. You love the Lord. You are "walking in the truth" (2 John 4). But, like David in this psalm, you are assailed by troubles of various sorts—he speaks of "workers of iniquity" and "enemies" (vv. 8, 10). And you wonder if this is God punishing you for something you are doing, or not doing, something sinful about yourself you don't understand or haven't grasped. You have a sense that God is angry with *you* and you feel the loss of his favor. It all makes you ill and you just cry out in pain. David's reaction should be help to you. When he feels the absence of the Lord, he chases after him in prayer. He begs him to restore the closeness and favor he feels he has lost. In doing so, he lifts four petitions to the Lord.

"O Lord, do not rebuke me in your anger." In verses 1–3, the psalmist prays for the removal of God's seeming anger, pleading his weakness and discouragement. Remember here that a feeling that God is angry with us does not prove he is really angry. Job's dreadful sufferings severely tested his faith. His friends told him God must be punishing him for some reason. But they were wrong. The truth is that God's love toward him never diminished—something that is hinted at from the outset when the Lord limits Satan's power to harm Job (Job 1:12). Feelings are often misleading. It is natural for us to feel God is angry with us when troubles overwhelm us. But while we may feel or conclude that God is angry, his attitude to us may well be entirely different.

"Oh, save me for Your mercies' sake." In verses 4–5, he asks the Lord to "save" him for his "mercies' sake," pleading the case that only as he survives in the land of the living can he sing praise to the Lord. David is not saying that there is no life after death. He is just saying he wants to go on being a positive witness here on *terra firma*.

"I am weary with my groaning." We all know the feeling. In verses 6–7, the psalmist presents his need and desire for deliverance with a further expression of the depth of his grief and misery. Notice that "though sense feel wrath and see nothing but hot displeasure, yet faith can pierce through clouds and bespeak mercy." God lets us feel he is angry (whether he is or not) so that we may, *by his grace*, rise above our feelings and outward circumstances and, *by faith*, apply to him for mercy. He calls us to "walk by faith, not by sight" (2 Cor. 5:7), "looking unto Jesus" (Heb. 12:2).

"The Lord will receive my prayer." In verses 8–10, he is suddenly filled with the assurance that the Lord has heard the voice of his weeping, such that he predicts the defeat of those who are working to do him harm! In other words, his prayer is effectively answered before it is even concluded! David didn't need to pray too long to get his answer! It is the "fervent"— not the long-winded—"prayer of a righteous man" that is "effective" and "avails much" (James 5:16). Very quickly, even instantaneously, the Lord can change that trembling, grieving soul into a heart full of the joy of the Lord. Are you sorrowful today? Are you a believer in the Lord Jesus Christ as your Savior? If so, will he not send you away rejoicing, even if your circumstances still cast their shadows over your life? These enemies of your body and soul will eventually be swept away, but more immediately you will experience in your heart "peace with God through our Lord Jesus Christ," even "glory in tribulations" and know afresh the "hope that does not disappoint, because the love of God has been poured out in your heart by the Holy Spirit who has been given to us" (Rom. 5:5).

PRAYING IN FAITH UNDER SEVERE DISTRESS
Sing Psalm 6

THINGS I WILL PRAY FOR TODAY

_____

_____

_____

_____

_____

_____

_____

April 1
But I Am Innocent!

A prayer for deliverance from injustice

Judge me, O Lord, according to my righteousness... —*Ps. 7:8*

READ PSALM 7

We are always sinners but are often quite innocent. Innocence is not the same as being sinless before God. It is just being guiltless in particular issues with other people. Innocence is clear when we are the undeserving recipients of injustice—which happens frequently wherever sinners are to be found. Everyone experiences personal injustices, even in the quietest of lives. David clearly faced a threat to his life (vv. 1–2), apparently from "Cush, a Benjamite"—probably a thinly veiled reference to King Saul—and he was overwhelmed by a sense of the injustice of it all. In fact, he had wronged neither "Cush" nor Saul. He was truly innocent. Similar circumstances may have burst into your life. If so, the Lord is showing you through the psalmist how best to respond to such challenges. He suggests three steps:

The first step is to petition for personal deliverance. David prays as one who cannot cope. He truly trusts in God, but notice how he reinforces both his trust and his desperate need by describing the consequences of *not* having the Lord to deliver him: "they [would] tear me like a lion, rending me in pieces" (vv. 1–2). This is so true to life, even in less than life-threatening situations. In our minds we trust the Lord, but we feel terribly helpless and alone. The feeling gnaws at us. We chafe under the unfairness and injustice of it all.

The psalmist makes the case that he is innocent relative to his oppressors by laying his actions before God and inviting his righteous judgment upon himself. Indeed, if his enemy is correct in his (false) charges, "let him trample my life to the earth." The psalmist did not betray or injure the one who was "at peace" with him—that is, who was formerly his friend—and has nothing of which to repent. He can honestly and justifiably call on God to vindicate him and overthrow his enemy (vv. 3–5). When faced by implacable injustice, so can we.

184

The second step is a petition for justice in the earth. The net is now cast wider. David prays that God would arise in "anger" against his enemies and vindicate his servant (vv. 6–8), and that, in bringing "the wickedness of the wicked…to an end," he would "establish the just" (v. 9ab). David also reminds us that God "tests the hearts and minds," for he saves those who are "upright in heart" (vv. 9c–10). To emphasize that it is all of grace (and not our uprightness), he affirms that our "defense is of God."

Why should God do this? He is "a just judge" who is already "angry with the wicked every day" and who has already prepared the means of his judgment (vv. 11–13). In other words, why not sooner rather than later? In any event, the wicked are in tremendous danger if only because wickedness rebounds on itself: "his trouble shall return upon his own head" (vv. 14–16). Or, as we would say, "What goes around comes around." God says, "Do not be deceived, God is not mocked; for whatever a man sows, that he will also reap" (Gal. 6:7).

The final step is a commitment to worship the Lord according to his righteousness (v. 17). You may have noticed that there is no listing of practical measures to be taken: such as, in our terms, going to court, getting a restraining order, moving away, or the like. We know David had to run for his life. The point is that he needed an ultimate solution—both for his own inner peace with God while facing a problem beyond his own resolving and for his outward safety, which in the end came with his exile until his enemy died. He cannot see the solution or even have the slightest idea as to what God will do. But, by faith, he sees the invisible—he has a Savior, and there he is at peace. In Christ, this is every Christian's joy: "Though now you do not see Him, yet believing, you rejoice with joy inexpressible and full of glory" (1 Peter 1:8).

READY TO LISTEN WHEN GOD SPEAKS
Sing Psalm 7:8–13

THINGS I WILL PRAY FOR TODAY

April 2
What Is Man?

A prayer of pure praise for life itself

What is man that Thou are mindful of him?—Ps. 8:4

READ PSALM 8

merson Hall is the philosophy building of Harvard University. Protagoras's famous aphorism "MAN IS THE MEASURE OF ALL THINGS" was to be carved in stone across the front elevation, but President C. W. Eliot supplanted it with Psalm 8:4: "WHAT IS MAN THAT THOU ART MINDFUL OF HIM?" There it remains today—a rebuke to man's oft-proclaimed autonomy from God! The psalmist, as one who bears the image and imprint of his Creator, gives all the glory to the God who gave him his life. His theme is stated in the introduction (v. 1ab) and repeated in his conclusion (v. 9): "O LORD, our Lord, how excellent is Your name in all the earth!" The psalmist presents three arguments in support of this thesis.

The mouths of children respond to the creation with awe for the Creator. God has "set" his glory "above the heavens" (v. 1c). That is, from earth to the heavens themselves there is overwhelming evidence of his glory. Children so often speak "strength" that silences even "the enemy and the avenger" (v. 2). This anticipates a double theme in New Testament teaching. One is that "God has chosen the foolish things of the world to put to shame the wise, and…the weak things of the world to put to shame the things which are mighty" (1 Cor. 1:27). Jesus quotes Psalm 8:2 to make this same point when children hailed his entry into Jerusalem (Matt. 21:15–16). The second is, as Jesus says, "Unless you are converted and become as little children, you will by no means enter the kingdom of heaven" (Matt. 18:3). Do you have a childlike love for the Lord?

The minds of adult believers marvel that God is "mindful of us." After all, when we "consider [God's] heavens," how insignificant we are (vv. 3–4)! Yet God remembers us so as to "visit" us. He cares about us and also cares *for us*. Here the doctrine of divine condescension and the divine practice of the exaltation of the redeemed come together. God has not left us to ourselves! We are not alone in his universe. He has a purpose of grace and salvation for both humanity and creation.

God has given man dominion over the creatures. We are "a little lower than the angels"—that is, near to God (actually his image-bearers)—and "crowned with glory and honor" (v. 5). Being "crowned" in this way implies the possibility of communion with God, something impossible for other non-angelic beings. The poet Robert Burns calls man "the noblest work of God." This truth is a testimony to the God who made us. His is the glory. This is confirmed in man being given "dominion over the works of [God's] hands" (vv. 6–8). Man is appointed the steward of creation, with a mandate to develop the earth and a promise of final victory. Hebrews 2:5–9 applies this to Jesus Christ, who is to be understood, believed in, and trusted as the goal and end of creation. Through his death, we will share in his final triumph. "If we endure, we shall also reign with Him. If we deny Him, He also will deny us" (2 Tim. 2:12). "For He must reign till He has put all enemies under His feet" (1 Cor. 15:25). Jesus himself declares, "All authority has been given to Me in heaven and on earth" (Matt. 28:18). Man's dominion is derived from Christ, and man's stewardship is answerable to Christ. In Christ, God has truly been mindful of us.

Conclusion: mankind's calling is to be mindful of the Lord! The words that begin and end the psalm encapsulate the response of the believing human heart to the life and to the Savior he has given us: "Lord, our Lord, how excellent is Your name in all the earth!" He is "our" Lord, personally, redemptively, and covenantally. He is "excellent," and before the evidence of his majesty in his world we have no excuse for not giving him the glory. This takes us to another abiding, but ignored, Harvard University inscription—her motto since 1692—"*VERITAS* [surrounded by] *Christo et Ecclesiae*"—"Truth [centered in] Christ and Church." Therefore—PRAISE HIM!

PRAISE FOR OUR CREATOR GOD
Sing Psalm 8

THINGS I WILL PRAY FOR TODAY

187

April 3
The Third Side to Every Story

A prayer of praise for God's just judgments

The Lord is known by the judgment He executes... —Ps. 9:16

READ PSALM 9

There are two sides to every story. So goes the common saying. As a caution against listening to only one side in an argument, this is certainly a useful proposition, but it is not the whole story. There is also a *third* side to every story and he is the living God, the God of the Bible. He is not just "the Judge of all the earth" who does "right" *after* the event (Gen. 18:25). He is involved with us all along, in that he has dealings with us throughout our lives. Furthermore, however ignorant of Scripture people may be, the "work of the law" of God is written on every human heart, "their conscience also bearing witness, and between themselves their thoughts accusing or else excusing them" (Rom. 2:15). In other words, in every matter in life, decisions are being made in relation to God and his moral law, whether people accept it or not. God accordingly holds everyone accountable for every decision and action in life. Jesus is crystal clear: "But I say to you that for every idle word men may speak, they will give account of it in the day of judgment" (Matt. 12:36). God is the third party to every story, every day, and for every lifetime. David opens up this truth in Psalm 9 and he praises God for it.

Praise for personal blessings: David thanks God for both his goodness to himself and his righteous judgment of his enemies. Our blessings include not only positive good from the Lord, but also the overthrow of wickedness directed against us, even behind the scenes and beyond our knowledge (vv. 1–4). God works on both fronts to secure his own interests and fulfill his promises to his people.

Praise for the world picture: David blesses God for restraining wickedness among the nations and for his goodness to his people. What is true in the personal experience of the believer is also true on the larger scale of the nations of the world (vv. 5–10). Again notice the three sides to the story of world affairs: the wicked among the nations, who are ultimately

188

destroyed (vv. 5–6); the Lord who reigns, metes out justice, and who is a "refuge for the oppressed" (vv. 7–9); and the believers who will never be forsaken by their steadfast Redeemer-God (v. 10).

Application to all: David *exhorts God's people* to "sing praises to the Lord," who remembers them when he "avenges blood" (vv. 11–12). He *prays for himself*—for God's mercy so that he may testify of God's praise and rejoice in God's salvation (vv. 13–14). He *warns the world*— "the nations"—that sin carries within itself its own inevitable penalties. The "pit," the "net," and the "snare" set for others, become the very things that bring down the wicked. Yet these are also the punishments from the Lord that fit the crimes (vv. 15–16). The somber interjection, "The Lord is known by the judgment he executes," emphasizes again that God is the third side to every story. He is constantly involved and judges justly. The "wicked" and the nations who forget God will go down to death and eternal loss, while the "needy" and the "expectations of the poor" will be neither forgotten nor extinguished (vv. 17–18).

Prayer against evil: David asks the Lord to stop the wicked in their tracks (vv. 19–20). Perhaps we might prefer a more "positive" ending that calls, say, for widespread spiritual revival. But the restraint of evil is a positive desire and the humbling of wicked men and nations is a necessary condition for the peace of God's people. God reminds us that he is the third and decisive side to every story; he is "the LORD our God; His judgments are in all the earth" (Ps. 105:7). The fear of the Lord is the beginning of wisdom. The judgments of the Lord ought to drive us to the love that sent his Son Jesus to seek and save the lost.

PRAISE FOR A HOLY AND JUST GOD
Sing Psalm 9

THINGS I WILL PRAY FOR TODAY

189

April 4
The Godly Man Ceases!

A prayer of discouragement

Help, Lord, for the godly man ceases!—Ps. 12:1

READ PSALM 12

orruption in high places is intensely discouraging. Rot starts at the top and works its way down; "the wicked prowl on every side, when vileness is exalted among the sons of men" (v. 8). One sees it in both religion and politics. So few love the Lord and practice his righteousness. The psalmist cries for help because "the godly man ceases" and "the faithful disappear" (v. 1). The evidence is a culture where the norm is to "speak idly…with flattering lips and double heart." Lying to men and to God is an accepted way of life, even with neighbors (v. 2). The psalmist sees wickedness everywhere he turns and, discouraged, he cries out, "Help, Lord!" Is our culture going anywhere good? People are twittering, flattering, and deceiving themselves to death.

We have plenty of reasons to cry "Help, Lord!" today. And when we do, an amazing thing happens: God begins to answer our prayers before we even say "Amen"! Believing prayer itself is a means of grace. As we pray, God's comforts can and do start to flow and so begin to restore a sense of composure and new confidence. The psalmist mentions three particular comforts he experiences:

> *First is the justice of God (vv. 2–4).* The psalmist is assured he will "cut off all flattering lips." His judgments may not always come quickly enough for us, but they will be no less decisive for any delay. These compulsive liars may protest that they have freedom of speech to deny the Lord and may seem to get away with it (v. 4). But God can wait, for they will find themselves fully accountable to him in his time—even for "every idle word" (Matt. 12:36).

> *Second is the promise of God (vv. 5–6).* His words are "pure… like silver tried in a furnace." He promises he will hear "the oppression of the poor" and "the sighing of the needy," and he will "arise" to "set him in the safety for which he yearns."

But why does the Lord wait and let these terrible things happen? For you, Christian, "the testing of your faith produces patience" (James 1:3). For the unconverted it makes for either the opportunity to repent and be saved (Mark 1:15; Luke 13:3) or to continue to fill up the measure of their sins (1 Thess. 2:16)! Now is the time of God's promise: "Incline your ear, and come to Me. Hear, and your soul shall live" (Isa. 55:3).

> *Third is the* permanence *of God's church (v. 7).* Dark as the days may sometimes be, the godly will not cease from the earth, because God will "preserve them from this generation forever." The church will not go away. The gospel will not cease to be preached. While the world lasts, the Lord will continue to add "to the church daily those who are being saved" (Acts 2:47).

The final word is a plea for realism. If you really grasp that this is a fallen world, there will be fewer surprises to dishearten you. David begins with a cry for the Lord's help, but he ends with the understanding that, wicked as this world is, the Lord is working out his gracious and just purposes. This is true even in the lamentable circumstance in which the highest positions in the land are filled with the lowest kinds of people. As already noted, the rot trickles down from the top, for when "vileness is exalted…the wicked prowl on every side" (v. 8). "Do not put your trust in princes" (Ps. 146:3), for "it is better to trust in the Lord than to put confidence in princes" (Ps. 118:9). But do pray "for kings and all who are in authority, that we may lead a quiet and peaceable life in all godliness and reverence" (1 Tim. 2:2). Let it not be said of you, "the godly man [or woman] ceases"!

PRAISE FOR A GOD WHO WILL PREVAIL
Sing Psalm 12

THINGS I WILL PRAY FOR TODAY

April 5
The True Worshiper

Praying about consistently godly character

Lord, who may abide in Your tabernacle?—Ps. 15:1

READ PSALM 15

o you care about who lives in your house? Surely you do! You decide on who is welcome under your roof and who is not. The psalmist poses a question of God: "Lord, who may abide [live] in your tabernacle [house]?" (v. 1a). He is referring to the tent or "tabernacle" he raised up on Mount Zion—God's "holy hill"—to receive the ark of the covenant when he first brought it to Jerusalem (2 Sam. 6:17). Abiding in God's tabernacle obviously does not mean literally living there. It is a way of speaking about a loving, personal relationship with God. The idea is that the true worshipers of God live in God's house as they live their lives. They belong there. In a very real sense it is their home. We live with the one we love. The Lord, says Moses in another psalm, is "our dwelling place" (Ps. 90:1). This defines the true worshipers of God.

What is the character of those who abide in God's house? David specifies five practical evidences of genuine love for the Lord:

> They are "pure in heart" as in Jesus's beatitude (Matt. 5:8). Each one "walks uprightly, and works righteousness and speaks the truth in his heart" (v. 2). Because they consciously love the truth from their hearts, they strive to practice it by doing good—the result being that they are seen by all as living an upright life (Isa. 38:15).

> They have mastered the tongue. They do not "backbite," slander their neighbors, or join in the unsupported defaming of their friends (v. 3). How easy it is to run down even your friends behind their backs! It takes a love of truth in the heart to maintain integrity in the tongue. James rightly says, "No man can tame the tongue" (James 3:8). The Lord, however, can tame it and make it an instrument of his grace.

> They honor those who reverence the Lord. They know what company to keep. They have no time for "a vile person" (v. 4ab).

192

The fellowship of believers is their natural environment. They love to be with God's people (Mal. 3:16).

> ⯈ They know how to keep their word. The test is, of course, when it costs something to keep a promise; "He swears to his own hurt and does not change" (v. 4c).
> ⯈ They are not devoted to money. They will neither "put out" money at "usury," nor "take a bribe against the innocent" (v. 5ab).

This is all representative of the true character of those who worship and serve the Lord, who are saved by grace, sustained by grace, and sanctified by grace. There is no abstract moralism here—that is, as if you can be "good" without God (see Rom. 3:10ff.). Nor is there the slightest whiff of works-righteousness. This is about the fruit and evidence of a saving knowledge of the God of the Bible.

Are you abiding in God's tabernacle? The psalmist is not only speaking to God, but is addressing his own conscience, when he says, "He who does these things shall never be moved" (v. 5c). Why? Jesus says of his followers, "I give them eternal life, and they shall never perish; neither shall anyone snatch them out of My hand. My Father, who has given them to Me, is greater than all; and no one is able to snatch them out of My Father's hand" (John 10:28–29). The psalmist is committed to being a true worshiper of the living God. He desires unbroken fellowship with his Redeemer. In New Testament terms this is saying to us, Here is the person you are by grace through faith in Jesus Christ your Savior. "For a day in Your courts is better than a thousand. I would rather be a doorkeeper in the house of my God than dwell in the tents of wickedness" (Ps. 84:10).

PRAISE FOR THE GOD WHOSE HOUSE IS OUR HOME
Sing Psalm 84

THINGS I WILL PRAY FOR TODAY

April 6
Pleasures Forevermore

A prayer of resurrection hope

At Your right hand are pleasures forevermore. —Ps. 16:11c

READ PSALM 16

"He's well preserved!" We say this of someone in a healthy old age. It's not an entirely positive thought, because its significance depends on the shadow of inevitable and perhaps imminent demise. In our language, preservation is a static thing. It retards both decay and growth. Fruit preserves are entombed in jars awaiting exhumation and extinction on breakfast tables across the land. Game preserves are managed at essentially fixed levels to provide enjoyment for eco-tourists, but the animals aren't going anywhere. Preservation in this world is about managing an optimal status quo as determined by the experts, so that it keeps on keeping on without much change—for change is the enemy of conservation.

"Preserve me, O God" is the psalmist's prayer. But what does he mean? Is it cradle-to-the-grave security? Good health and a long life? The order of his prayer reveals both the aim and attitude of his heart.

His first step is to turn *to God* (vv. 1–4). This is not mere form but an intensely personal confiding trust in and commitment to his Redeemer: "You are my Lord, my goodness is nothing apart from You." He rejoices in the fellowship of believers—"the saints…the excellent ones" are his "delight." He also grieves for those who worship false gods and who, as a result, face particular "sorrows." He goes to the source. He speaks to God.

His second step is to offer *thanksgiving* to the Lord for present blessings (vv. 5–8). God has given him "a good inheritance" (v. 6); has counseled him, even in the night; and is with him continually so that he will not be moved. You see how he brings in the eternal implications of his inheritance from God? In other words, his prayer to be "preserved" is looking beyond his present life all the way to eternity.

His third step is to rejoice in *resurrection hope* (vv. 9–11). The key is in verse 10: "For you will not leave my soul in Sheol [that is, in death], nor will you allow Your Holy One to see corruption." This "Holy One" cannot be David, for he certainly saw corruption and his body is still not resurrected. So who is God's "Holy One"?

The New Testament provides the answer when it infallibly expounds Psalm 16:8–11 as being fulfilled in and by Jesus the Messiah (Acts 2:25–32; 13:35–39). Jesus is the Holy One who actually conquers death and wins that promised resurrection for us! In Christ, a threefold promise to every believer becomes reality:

> ⟫ Our "heart"/"glory" rejoices ⇒ our "flesh" rests in hope (v. 9);
> ⟫ Our "soul" is not left dead ⇒ our body is not destroyed (v. 10);
> ⟫ Therefore, in Christ we are given a "path," a "presence," and "pleasures" ⇒ which are respectively for us "life" and "joy" and "forever" (v. 11).

When David prays, "Preserve me, O God," he is not thinking merely of the conservation and management of this present life and all its potential and actual blessings, but has in view rather that future life in glory to be secured by God's promised Messiah. David's body would be a thousand years in the grave before the incorruptible Holy One would come and take our flesh, draw death's sting, and deprive the grave of its victory through his death and resurrection. He is the Holy One who was delivered up because of our offenses and was raised because of our justification (Rom. 4:25). And he—the Lord Jesus Christ—and not the best blessings of this life, is the measure of the preservation for which we are to pray with the psalmist. Jesus tells us this himself when he says, "I am the resurrection and the life. He who believes in Me, though he may die, he shall live. And whoever lives and believes in Me shall never die." Then he adds most pointedly, "Do you believe this?" (John 11:25–26). In Christ are "pleasures forevermore"—and also every day right now, even this very morning.

PRAISE FOR THE GOD WHO SAVES ME FOREVER
Sing Psalm 16:5–11

THINGS I WILL PRAY FOR TODAY

_____

_____

_____

_____

_____

April 7
I Shall Be Satisfied

A prayer of confidence in God

I shall be satisfied when I awake in Your likeness. —Ps. 17:15b

READ PSALM 17

Sometimes life's troubles seem overwhelming. We see a tunnel but no light. Our life is, to say the least, unsatisfying. David seems to feel this way as he pens this psalm. Perhaps he is running for his life from King Saul. Whatever besets him, he is struggling and desperate for a way out. He turns to God for help and so bequeaths to us for all time a pattern for prayer that issues in both an empowering confidence in the Lord and the deepest satisfaction of a believing soul.

He expresses his integrity before the Lord. This is startling, because David does not appeal for forgiveness of his sins as the precursor to his deliverance, as for example in Psalm 51. Here, he appeals to his faithfulness and uprightness as the ground of God's favorable answer. He has a "just cause" and asks that God "look on the things that are upright" (vv. 1–2). Has God not tested his heart, tried him, and "found nothing"? He also purposes that his mouth will not transgress, affirms that he has kept from the paths of wickedness (vv. 3–4), and prays to be upheld so that his "footsteps may not slip" (v. 5). David is not sinless, but he is upright and honest before God. When we pray, we cannot expect God to hear us unless we pray out of real integrity or in the attitude of true repentance, for "If I regard iniquity in my heart, the Lord will not hear" (Ps. 66:18).

He explains his need of the Lord. David is confident that the Lord will hear and deliver him (vv. 6–7). He hopes that God will see him as the "apple" of his eye. The apple signifies the pupil of the eye, and the idea here is that as we protect our eyes with the greatest care, then may God likewise protect us from every danger. He prays that God will hide him "under the shadow of [His] wings" (v. 8). The implication is that those who seek his destruction will be thwarted. His need is described in vivid language: "the wicked...oppress" him; "deadly enemies...surround" him; their hearts are hardened and their mouths "speak proudly"; and their "eyes" are set like a lion looking to pounce on its prey (vv. 9–12). Are you so burdened? Then "cast your burden on the LORD, and He shall sustain you; He shall never permit the righteous to be moved" (Ps. 55:22).

He expects satisfaction in the Lord. The "men of the world" oppressing him "have their portion in this life"—in their children and what they leave to them (vv. 13–14). They want to be remembered, but it is all earthbound. In contrast, the psalmist's satisfaction is found in God himself: "As for me, I will see Your face in righteousness" (v. 15a)—that is, not in my own righteousness (cf. Isa. 64:6), but in a righteousness from God. This has to do with "the fruit of new birth." When you have died to your own "tainted" righteousness and turned to receive Jesus as your Savior, you are cleansed from sin *and* clothed in his imputed righteousness. God sees you clothed in the righteousness of his Son. Thus reconciled, we will see his face. *When* does this happen? David says "when I awake"— i.e., come into God's presence at death. How is this satisfaction realized? David says "in Your likeness" (v. 15b). "The soul that loves God," writes John Howe, "opens itself to him, admits his influences and impressions, is easily moulded and wrought to his will, and yields to the transforming power of his appearing glory." Christian, this heavenly satisfaction is in part yours now in Christ believed and followed and will be yours in fullness. For when Jesus "is revealed, we shall be like Him, for we shall see Him as He is" (1 John 3:2). Jesus is the true satisfaction.

PRAISE FOR PERSONAL SATISFACTION IN THE LORD
Sing Psalm 17:13–15

THINGS I WILL PRAY FOR TODAY

April 8
Before the Battle

A prayer of God's people in time of war

Some trust in chariots, and some in horses; but we will remember the name of the Lord our God. —*Ps. 20:7*

READ PSALM 20

When the army of Alfonso VI of Castile arrived at the Tagus in AD 1085, the soldiers hesitated to cross the river in prospect of battle with the Moors. Adelme, the abbot of Chaise-Dieu, then entered the water on his donkey singing Psalm 20:7. The army followed and the Moors were defeated. Leaving aside the question of the justness of that particular war, the invocation of that verse *in a godly cause* was and still is appropriate before combat. A century after David penned Psalm 20, Jehoshaphat offered a similar prayer in the face of invasion by the combined forces of Moab, Ammon, and Edom (2 Chron. 20:5–19).

Psalm 20 is given to God's people to be sung and prayed in all the "times that try men's souls." It sets out four pointers for our prayers:

First, pray before engaging the enemy (vv. 1–5). Here the people pray for the king (David)—but they are implicitly also praying for themselves. And this praying is the first resort of a living faith—not the last, as is too often the case in spiritual trials. Notice how their petitions span everything from the perceived need to the desired solution:

- The *source* of future deliverance is acknowledged: "May the Lord answer you in the day of trouble…the God of Jacob defend you" (v. 1). Lay the trouble before God and "Do not put your trust in princes, nor in a son of man, in whom there is no help" (Ps. 146:3).
- The *covenant faithfulness* of the Lord is confessed: as they go out to battle, they actively trust that God will "help" and "strengthen" them "out of Zion" (v. 2). "Zion" refers to the temple, then newly established by God, and appeals to the covenant God "as the king of his people" who is "as such not only able but bound by covenant to afford them aid." The believer is never forsaken (Deut. 31:8).

198

> The *confiding commitment* of the people of God is professed with "offerings" and "burnt sacrifice" (v. 3; cf. Rom. 12:1).
> A *believing hope* is expressed that God grant the king's "heart's desire" and "fulfill all [his] purpose" (vv. 4–5). Will not our "Father who is in heaven give good things to those who ask Him" (Matt. 7:11)?

Second, rejoice in God's future blessing on account of his Anointed King (v. 6). The plural "we" (God's people) momentarily gives way to the singular "I" (probably a Levite led by the Spirit of God as in 2 Chron. 20:14ff.). Although David is immediately in view, "still the chief reference," writes Andrew Bonar, "is to *David's* Son, our Lord." He is the true and final "anointed" king—literally the "Messiah"/the "Christ."

Third, trust in the strong name of the Lord (vv. 7–8). You can trust in chariots and horses if you like, or Abrams tanks and Apache helicopters. Israel's repeated deliverances from stronger nations confirm that "the king is not saved by his great army" (Ps. 33:16, ESV; cf. 44:5–7). "The LORD is a man of war" (Ex. 15:3). Trust him and watch his enemies fall, while his people rise and stand upright (v. 8).

Fourth, never stop praying for the Lord's salvation (v. 9). The psalm ends with the whole congregation calling for the Lord to save his people, and in the language of prophecy entreating "the King" who is clearly not David, but David's Lord—the Messiah then still to come, but now the crucified and risen Christ, Jesus the Son of God (cf. Matt. 22:43–46). Here, dear Christian, is your daily calling in Jesus your Savior:

Chosen to be soldiers in an alien land:
Chosen, called, and faithful, for our Captain's band;
In the service royal let us not grow cold;
Let us be right loyal, noble, true, and bold.
— "Who Is on the Lord's Side?", Frances R. Havergal, stanza 4

A PRAISE-PRAYER FOR VICTORY IN BATTLE
Sing Psalm 20

THINGS I WILL PRAY FOR TODAY

_____

_____

_____

April 9
Forsaken?

A prayer of one suffering alone

My God, My God, why have You forsaken Me?—Ps. 22:1

READ PSALM 22:1–5

When we are under stress we can feel terribly alone. David elsewhere says, "I looked for someone to take pity, but there was none; and for comforters, but I found none" (Ps. 69:20). This renders the psalmist's cry of dereliction in Psalm 22:1 all the more affecting. It is not just people, but God himself who seems to have deserted him in his troubles. And he doesn't doubt God, for his pleading is that of personal faith: "My God, My God…" He is no atheist staring into the void, or an agnostic vainly hoping there might be someone out there. He truly and fervently loves the Lord. He just feels so alone: "Why are You so far from helping me, and from the words of my groaning?" (v. 1). David is very vocal, day and night, but God is comprehensively silent (v. 2). He has made his "heavens like iron and [his] earth like bronze" (Lev. 26:19). Is there any comfort here for we who love the Lord? God immediately unfolded three great certainties that hold the promise and assurance of his comfort and relief (vv. 3–5).

The first certainty is that God is holy: "But You are holy" (v. 3a). This implies a confidence that God will do all things well and do good to his people. Here is an anticipation of the prophet Micah when he lifts his heart in praise to God during dark days for God's people: "Who is a God like You, pardoning iniquity and passing over the transgression of the remnant of His heritage? He does not retain His anger forever, because He delights in mercy. He will again have compassion on us, and will subdue our iniquities. You will cast all our sins into the depths of the sea" (Mic. 7:18–19). Even if God has not yet answered his prayer, the believer grasps in his heart, as Paul will testify a thousand years on, "I am not ashamed, for I know whom I have believed and am persuaded that He is able to keep what I have committed to Him until that Day" (2 Tim. 1:12). His is the love that will never let us go.

200

The second certainty is that God is praiseworthy: for it is not for nothing that he is "enthroned in the praises of Israel" (v. 3b). God is "great and greatly to be praised" because he is the living God who made the heavens and the earth, not a dumb idol, and he is the one who has revealed himself as the Redeemer of his people (Ps. 48:1; 96:4; 145:3). The implication is that, if he is silent for the moment before my prayers—miserable as it feels to me—there must be good reason for it. It is not unfaithfulness on his part. Here is an echo of Job: "Though He slay me, yet will I trust in Him" (Job 13:15).

The third certainty is that God keeps his promises: "Our fathers trusted in You...and were not ashamed (vv. 4–5). God has acted in history. The collective experience of God's people in the past both praises the integrity of his promises of love and preaches his covenant-faithfulness for the future. The experience of forsakenness in the believing heart is answered by the promise of God, such that we too, like the saints of old, will not be "ashamed" (v. 5). In other words, the sense of being forsaken is not evidence that God has actually forsaken us. It is an artifact of our sorrow and his seeming silence.

Jesus was forsaken on the cross. He too cried, "My God, My God, why have you forsaken Me?" (Matt. 27:46). But he truly was forsaken by God, because his Father was laying on him the sin of sinners. Hence his promise to believers: "I will never leave you nor forsake you....Lo, I am with you always, even to the end of the age" (Matt. 28:20). Because he was forsaken, we are never forsaken, and even the experience of forsakenness is so consistent with God's love that it is designed, not to drive us to despair, but to draw us closer to the Savior who was forsaken, that we might be "found in him" (see Phil. 3:8–9).

PRAISE TO THE ONE WHO WILL NEVER FORSAKE US
Sing Psalm 69:1–13

THINGS I WILL PRAY FOR TODAY

April 10
I Am a Worm

A prayer of deep misery

But I am a worm, and no man; a reproach of men, and despised by the people. —Ps. 22:6

READ PSALM 22:6–8

Charles Haddon Spurgeon calls the words, "I am a worm and no man" a "miracle in language." The reason is that these words point beyond the psalmist's misery to the experience of the Son of God as he suffers as the subject of contempt and ridicule and is humbled to the lowest of the low. Spurgeon adds, "What a contrast between 'I AM' and 'I am a worm'!" "They shoot out the lip, they shake the head saying, 'He trusted in the Lord, let Him rescue Him; let Him deliver Him, since He delights in Him'" (vv. 7b–8). Whatever David suffered—and he endured more than most if not all of us—his trials pale into insignificance before the sufferings of Jesus, the incarnate Son of God. To see the unfolding and fulfillment of Psalm 22:6–8, we need only turn to such passages as Isaiah 53:3: "He is despised and rejected by men, a Man of sorrows and acquainted with grief. And we hid, as it were, our faces from Him; He was despised, and we did not esteem Him"; and Matthew 27:39–40: "And those who passed by blasphemed Him, wagging their heads and saying, 'You who destroy the temple and build it in three days, save Yourself! If You are the Son of God, come down from the cross.'" This psalm cannot stop with David for it finds its fullness in Jesus.

What then is God teaching us here? First of all, we are shown something of the *cost* of gospel salvation. Or more particularly, what salvation cost the Son of God in terms of his humiliation and suffering for sin, and the quality of the love that moved him to give himself as a ransom for sinners like you and me. C. H. Spurgeon asks, "Which shall we wonder at the most, the cruelty of man, or the love of the bleeding Saviour? How can we ever complain of ridicule after this?" When your heart is gripped by the agony of Jesus's bearing of the penalty of our sin, does it not make it easier for you to submit to his Word, to pray, to love others, and to bear reproach yourself? Jesus tells us himself, "A disciple is not above his teacher, nor a servant above his master" (Matt. 10:24).

Second, we are pointed to a deeper grasp of Jesus's *condescension* to be our Savior. Jesus is the perfect image of God, yet he stooped so low—almost lower than men—in order that we might experience the restoration of that image, so fatally marred by sin. He became a "worm"—so to speak—that we who were really lost might "be conformed to the image of His Son, that He might be the firstborn among many brethren" (Rom. 8:29). "He sent from above, He took me; He drew me out of many waters" (Ps. 18:16).

This is all of vital practical importance for the Christian life. We must never become morbid and defeatist about the humiliations we may well suffer for Jesus's sake. The psalmist is not saying that he, or Jesus after him, feels badly about himself. Nor is he suggesting that the more we feel like "worms," then the holier we will be. The psalmist's point is that, as Jesus and his disciples experience being outcasts, they also realize by faith that this is a vehicle and proof of God's blessing. There is no masochistic desire to be reviled and ridiculed, or punished and persecuted, as if pain produces godliness and a more powerful witness. It is just that, in the fellowship of Christ's sufferings, there is also the undergirding consciousness that we are made new creations in the power of Jesus's resurrection (Phil. 3:10). Jesus assures us, "Blessed are you when others revile you and persecute you and utter all kinds of evil against you falsely on my account. Rejoice and be glad, for your reward is great in heaven" (Matt. 5:11–12). He endured being treated like a worm, that we might be made kings and priests to God through his shed blood.

PRAISE TO THE SAVIOR WHO HAS SAVED US
Sing Psalm 18:16–24

THINGS I WILL PRAY FOR TODAY

April 11
You Have Answered Me

A prayer of deep gratitude

You have answered Me. — Ps. 22:21

READ PSALM 22:9–21

he psalmist feels like a worm. The "worm motif" simply says that, to worldly society, he is a piece of dirt. People despise him, no one is listening to him with any sympathy, and there is "none to help" (vv. 6–11). All the external evidence points to this and translates into a dreadful sense of dereliction. We must remember, however, that whatever David is facing in his life, the Holy Spirit gives him words prophetic of the future Messiah as he reflects on his humiliation as he is despised and rejected by men (vv. 6–11; Isa. 53:3). This is Jesus being "obedient to the point of death, even the death of the cross" (Phil. 2:8). In this third section of the prayer that is Psalm 22, the Messiah faces his trials, reflects on encouraging truths and discouraging circumstances, and prays appropriately in response to these, until he is blessed by a glorious answer to his prayers.

I know I am not a worm. God is not visible to the naked eye, but troubles surely are. The evidence of our senses screams at us that we are worms! Like Moses, who only "endured as seeing Him who is invisible" (i.e., by a living faith), Jesus and all who follow him see the truth of God to which unbelief is by nature blind and unreceptive. Messiah declares to his Father in heaven, "You are He who took me out of the womb; You made Me trust while on My mother's breasts.…You have been My God" (vv. 9–10). Through all the palpable pain and deep humiliation he knows the truth: God gave him both life and faith. He is not a worm. Neither are his people.

His prayer — "Be not *far* from Me" — flows from his reaffirmation of faith. To this he attaches two practical arguments: one is "for trouble is *near*," while the other is "for there is *none* to help" (v. 11). When "the help of man is useless," we can only cry to God to "give us help from trouble" (Ps. 60:11). For the godless world, prayer is only a last resort after losing all hope. For the Christian, prayer is the first and continuous resort, because

204

by faith we realize that only God can be our true and ultimate helper. So Christ turns to his Father, and, in the spirit of adoption, we who are his may also (cf. Heb. 5:5–10).

But my sufferings are very real. This section of the psalmist's cry for help employs common Old Testament imagery: "bulls of Bashan," "roaring lion," and "dogs" that surround him paint a lurid picture of his enemies. The effect is to drain him of life and bring him to "the dust of death" (vv. 12–15). At that point, the messianic character of the psalm emerges in a prophecy of Christ's crucifixion. The details are astounding, from the "congregation of the wicked" doing their worst, to the agonies of God's Mediator dying for sinners. Pierced hands and feet, counted bones and staring people (i.e., nakedness), and clothes divided by casting lots all foretell Jesus's atoning death by most of a thousand years (vv. 16–18; cf. Matt. 27:35). Once again, David speaks as a prophet (Acts 2:29–31), and we are pointed to the Savior we need to know personally in "the power of his resurrection, and the fellowship of his sufferings" (Phil. 3:10).

You answer my prayer. Notice that recording his suffering gives way to earnest prayer (vv. 19–21). How he pleads for God's nearness to be his salvation! Again, the vivid images of wild beasts give wings to the consequences of deliverance delayed. The sword of his enemies, who are "dog…lion's mouth…and…wild oxen" personified, threatens, but suddenly in mid-verse God's answer stills his soul: "You have answered me" (v. 21c). Here is one way in which prayer is a means of grace to the Christian. The answer is enjoyed in the soul even before the enemy is observably turned away. Jesus on the cross knows his deliverance before his death and cries, "It is finished!" The believer is assured of God's answer even before he says, "Amen."

PRAISE FOR ANSWERED PRAYER
Sing Psalm 118:1–9

THINGS I WILL PRAY FOR TODAY

April 12
The Wings of Hope

A prayer anticipating certain victory

I will declare Your name to My brethren… —Ps. 22:22

READ PSALM 22:22–31

This wonderful psalm is part prayer and part praise. The psalmist's cry for help (vv. 1–21) gives way to a crescendo of hope (vv. 22–31). "The suppliant now rises on the wings of hope," says James Murphy. Noting the messianic character of the psalm, David Dickson observes, "David's part is but a little shadow, and is swallowed up in Christ's glory, shining in the fruits of his death and resurrection." David, in the language of prophecy, previews the coming of God's kingdom (vv. 22–31) in terms of Christ's resolution to praise God in the church, and his prophecy of the future glory of his kingdom, as it flows from his triumph in and over his death at Calvary.

Christ praises God in the church. Charles H. Spurgeon notes that Jesus here is both preacher and precentor—he preaches the gospel and leads the singing: "I will declare…I will praise You" (v. 22). Declaring God's name "to My brethren" states his theme. Jesus saves sinners and is thereby "the firstborn among *many* brethren" (Rom. 8:29). We are called to praise God in one of his congregations as living, committed members (Ps. 35:18; 89:5; 107:32; 111:1; 149:1). Jesus also tells us to follow his example: "You who fear the Lord, praise Him…glorify Him…fear Him" (v. 23), and we will share his experience of being heard by his Father and ours (v. 24). And Jesus gives us the strong encouragement: "Let your heart live forever" (v. 26). How will we know this life? Jesus tells us: "I am the living bread which came down from heaven. If anyone eats of this bread, he will live forever; and the bread that I shall give is My flesh, which I shall give for the life of the world" (John 6:51). He is our life because he is our Paschal Lamb "slain from the foundation of the world" (Rev. 13:8) and our "feast of choice pieces, a feast of wines on the lees, of fat things full of marrow, of well-refined wines on the lees" (Isa. 25:6).

Christ prophesies the future glory of his kingdom. His kingdom is "not of this world" (John 18:36), but it is in the world and hastening to a completion planned for his second coming. The psalmist's words proclaim the future growth and establishment of his kingly rule. As A. A. Bonar puts it, here is "Messiah bearing the cross and wearing the crown." The language is so absolute in so few words as to beg more detailed definition and explanation. "All the ends of the world...all the families of the nations" and "all the prosperous of the earth" paint a vast canvas—perhaps to us too vague?—of that coming kingdom. It does, however, have reference to the rule of Christ *now* as he continues to accomplish the work of salvation in a world where "all" the people definitely do *not yet* worship and serve him. He prays for what is yet to come in words describing the finished product. This is prayer rising on the wings of hope that simultaneously asks for the blessing and praises God as if it were already given. People from "all the ends of the world" are turning to the Lord and worshiping him (vv. 27–28). Why? Because Christ "rules over the nations" and is saving people from their sins every day. People from all conditions of humanity—rich or poor—will be represented among those who are saved and come to worship him (v. 29). People from all generations past, present, and yet future will bring praise to the Lord (vv. 30–31).

More water will go under the bridge until the Lord comes and the victory is won. But won it will be. And therefore our praying can echo that of Jesus himself—rising on the wings of hope in anticipation of the certain triumph of the Lord Jesus Christ, in whom believers are "more than conquerors through him who loved us" (Rom. 8:37).

PRAISE FOR THE HOPE OF GLORY IN CHRIST
Sing Psalm 22:27–31

THINGS I WILL PRAY FOR TODAY

April 13
The Secret of the Lord

A prayer of confidence in God's mercies

The secret of the LORD is with them who fear Him; and He will show them His covenant.—Ps. 25:14

READ PSALM 25

"Listen, do you want to know a secret?" sang the Beatles in their 1963 hit. Sure we do! We love knowing secrets! Well, God also has his secrets—infinitely more profound and of eternal significance. Some he keeps to himself, but others he shares with us: "The secret things belong to the LORD our God, but those things which are revealed belong to us and to our children forever, that we may do all the words of this law" (Deut. 29:29). Notice, however, that the things which are revealed remain something of a secret to those who don't know the Lord: "The secret of the Lord is with *them who fear Him*," i.e., those to whom he proceeds to "show His covenant" (v. 14). This is because "the natural man does not receive the things of the Spirit of God, for they are foolishness to him; nor can he know them, because they are spiritually discerned" (1 Cor. 2:14). This means in practice that the "secret of the Lord" is hidden in plain sight on the visible, readable pages of the Bible. So it was for the Ethiopian official on the road to Gaza until, through the ministrations of Philip, the Holy Spirit opened his heart (Acts 8:26–40; cf. 16:14). As John Newton and countless Christians have discovered, it takes God's amazing grace to open our eyes to our spiritual blindness and his life-giving light: "Amazing Grace, how sweet the sound, / That saved a wretch like me. / I once was lost but now am found, / Was blind, but now I see."

What then is this "secret of the Lord"? David unfolds this in his three-step prayer—yet another wonderful template for your prayer life. He seeks three practical, personal blessings, which we too must seek:

> A living *relationship* with the Lord (vv. 1–7). "O my God" is not the blasphemous acronym that litters so much conversation today, but the earnest expression of personal devotion flowing from a work of God's grace in the heart. There is confiding

trust (vv. 2–3), desire to be led by and taught of God (vv. 4–5), and seeking and experiencing forgiveness of sin (vv. 6–7).

➢ A deepening *knowledge* of the character of the Lord (vv. 8–15). Because the Lord is "good and upright," he "teaches sinners… guides in justice…pardons iniquity" (vv. 8-11), and communicates his "secret" of covenant love and saving grace to all who look to him (vv. 12–15).

➢ An expectant *commitment* to seeking prayerfully the help of God, both when "desolate and afflicted" and assailed by problems, but also as a way of life in sweet fellowship with the Redeemer of Israel (vv. 16–22). We resort constantly to the promises of the ever-revealed "secret" of the Lord in Christ, his Son and our Savior!

Alan Stevenson (1807–65), renowned Scottish lighthouse builder and uncle of the writer Robert Louis Stevenson (1850–94), lived with a fearfully painful illness that eventually crippled him and shortened his life. He was a serious Christian and also something of a poet. On the flyleaf of the Bible he presented to his son Rob, he points him to the Lord and the "secret" we all need to know:

Read in this blessed Book, my gentle boy;
Learn that thy heart is utterly defiled…
This day five years thou numberest; and I
Write on a bed of anguish. O my son,
Seek thy Creator, in thine early youth;
Value thy soul above the world, and shun
The sinner's way; oh! seek the way of truth.
Oft have we knelt together, gentle boy,
And prayed the Holy Ghost to give us power
To see God reconciled, through Christ, with joy;
Nought else, but Christ brings peace in sorrow's hour.

PRAISE FOR THE SELF-REVEALING SAVIOR
Sing Psalm 25:8–15

THINGS I WILL PRAY FOR TODAY

_____

_____

_____

April 14
Standing in an Even Place

A prayer of love for the house of God

My foot stands in an even place; in the congregation I will bless the Lord. —Ps. 26:12

READ PSALM 26

The grim grandeur of Loch Coruisk in Scotland's Isle of Skye is eerily captured in Walter Scott's description as "that dread lake, with its dark ledge of barren stone." Even getting there by land has a threatening aspect. The rugged seashore path requires the traverse of a great slab of rock, aptly called "The Bad Step," that plunges at a 70-degree angle into the sea. Dangerous on a wet and windy day, it is never for the faint-hearted! It is an apt emblem of human life, for many a "bad step" confronts us—and tempts us—on the way to eternity. That, however, involves more than a challenge here and there, because, short of a saving knowledge of the Lord Jesus Christ, the default human condition *by nature* stands on a "bad step" all the time—an uneven and slippery place under the shadow of God's just judgment. "Surely You [God] set them in slippery places," observes Asaph. "You cast them down to destruction. Oh, how they are brought to desolation, as in a moment! They are utterly consumed with terrors" (Ps. 73:18–19). Yet millions choose to go on their God-denying way, oblivious to, and even contemptuous of, their danger. But there is a way of safety in time and eternity. As we shall see, this is the Lord himself (John 14:6).

Shun uneven places (vv. 1–5). David faced many "bad steps" in his life, some of others' doing, some of his own, and many even life-threatening. Here "the context suggests worship at the tabernacle," for we find him praying about the pitfalls of life. He prays, "Vindicate me, O Lord, for I have walked in my integrity" (v. 1). This almost seems self-righteous, but he is clearly not claiming sinless perfection. It is God's "lovingkindness" that moves him to invite God to examine him in "mind and…heart" about his walking in God's "truth" (vv. 2–3). He testifies to avoiding the vanities of the "idolatrous," the seductions of "hypocrites," the company of "evildoers," and the counsels of "the wicked" (vv. 4–5).

And he prays with his eyes open, trusting the Lord to keep him from slipping, even as he looks where he is putting his feet. This is God's calling and promise for everyone who believes and follows him: "He will not allow your foot to be moved" (Ps. 121:3). Believe it…and walk in God's truth in his enabling grace!

Seek out the "even place" (vv. 6–8). David loves the "habitation of [God's] house" where his "glory dwells." He "entered into the "immediate residence" of God, worshiped him "in the way God himself had appointed," and there "obtained those supplies of grace and peace which his daily necessities required." The "altar" speaks of blood shed for the forgiveness of sins (Heb. 9:22), and points ahead to Christ, in whom "we have redemption through His blood, the forgiveness of sins, according to the riches of His grace" (Eph. 1:7). The "even place" is where the Lord meets his people in worship.

Stand fast in the "even place" (vv. 9–12). This is not secured by *merely* "going to church," but public worship, deeply loved and rightly practiced, is where union and communion with God in Christ is preeminently to be enjoyed as his special means of grace to his covenant people (see Ps. 122). Christ as Savior, God as our Father, and the Holy Spirit as our Comforter are that "even place" from which, says Jesus, "no one is able to snatch [believers] out of My Father's hand" (John 10:29). Then we may know with assurance that "His oath, His covenant, His blood, / Support me in the whelming flood; / When all around my soul gives way, / He then is all my hope and stay." And then we will exult with joy unspeakable and full of glory:

On Christ, the solid Rock, I stand;
All other ground is sinking sand…

PRAISE FOR THE LORD'S ASSURANCE OF MERCY
Sing Psalm 26

THINGS I WILL PRAY FOR TODAY

April 15
Confidence in the Lord

A prayer for godly confidence in the Lord

Wait on the Lord...and he shall strengthen your heart...—Ps. 27:14

READ PSALM 27:1–14

atthew Arnold's epic poem "Sohrab and Rustum" describes the Persian army confidently arrayed at the Oxus River for battle with the invading Tartars. The latter propose resolving their dispute by trial of champions rather than a general battle and call the Persians to nominate their champion—"To fight our champion Sohrab, man to man." Hearing this name, however, "the pale Persians held their breath with fear," their earlier confidence melting away before his sterling reputation. Human self-confidence often works that way: seemingly solid until one inconvenient truth (or error) turns it to jelly. Scripture teaches that a true and abiding confidence requires a work of God in the believer's heart, and Psalm 27 speaks beautifully to this theme. From it, we know that David faces real enemies (vv. 2, 6, 11–12). Will he hold his breath with fear, or will he trust the Lord and go forward in a solid confidence against the enemies of his soul? Here we are taught how to be confident, not in ourselves, but in the Lord:

Affirm your confidence in the Lord (vv. 1–6). David is confident for powerful reasons. The first is that his covenant-God ("LORD") is *personally and experientially* his "light and [his] salvation." When he asks, "Whom shall I fear?" the answer is obvious (v. 1). United to Christ, we need fear no persecution (Matt. 10:28), for "who shall separate us from the love of Christ?" (Rom. 8:35). Second, God had *kept his covenant-promises in the past* with David, through troubles from slander ("eat up my flesh"); to assault ("enemies and foes"); to war itself (vv. 2–3). Third, David has *a desire for fellowship with the Lord*, including anticipation of "behold[ing] the beauty of the Lord" in public worship and the means of grace (v. 4), of preservation in times of trouble (v. 5), and of offering "sacrifices of joy" and "sing[ing] praises to the Lord" for all he will do in his life (v. 6). This does not mean that we will never have troubles—just that through our trials we will discover—and confess with joy—that Jesus is "the Rock that is higher than I" (Ps. 61:2).

Act on your confidence in the Lord by praying (vv. 7–12). And since Jesus is our High Priest, we have "access with confidence" to God's "throne of grace" (Heb. 4:16). Confidence in the Lord will lead us out of ourselves to pray more and not less. The prayer of faith requires faith to pray. It also requests specifics for the obedience of faith to grow to fruition in our lives (Rom. 16:25–26). David offers three confident requests: that he experience God's favor (vv. 7–10); that he enjoy God's guidance (v. 11); and that he be delivered from his enemies (v. 12). All of these are surely what we wish for ourselves.

Apply this doctrine of confidence in the Lord to your practice from heart to hand (vv. 13–14). Verse 1 implies the vital question your heart must answer: "Who is *your* light and salvation?" David says he "would have lost heart" had he not "believed" he "would see the goodness of the Lord in the land of the living" (v. 13). This faith is not some starry-eyed notion that everything will somehow pan out in the end. Still less is it the "cupboard love" of those who will only "believe" if the Lord fills life's pantry with good things. David's is a living, saving faith in his Savior, that he will bless him, whatever his circumstances. How appropriate that this psalm about confidence in the Lord should close with an exhortation to "wait on the Lord" and "be of good courage" in trusting him, and a promise that the Lord "shall strengthen your heart" in your faithfulness (v. 14). In Christ Jesus, we have the glorious assurance that "those who wait on the LORD shall renew their strength; they shall mount up with wings like eagles, they shall run and not be weary, they shall walk and not faint" (Isa. 40:31).

PRAISE TO THE SAVIOR WHO HAS SAVED US
Sing Psalm 27

THINGS I WILL PRAY FOR TODAY

_____

_____

_____

_____

_____

April 16
Our Strength and Shield

A prayer for deliverance from oppressive wickedness

*Save Your people, and bless Your inheritance; shepherd them also, and
bear them up forever. —Ps. 28:9*

READ PSALM 28

njustice nags at the soul. It is the proof and the fruit of
the sinfulness of sin in sinners, and of the curse that the
consequences of sin wreak in this world—a curse confirmed by
the Word of the holy God, who declares that "He is the LORD
our God; His judgments are in all the earth" (Ps. 105:7), and that "when
[His] judgments are in the earth, the inhabitants of the world will learn
righteousness" (Isa. 26:9). Even so, sinners will continually arise to work
their wicked ways and the oppressed will still need to seek relief. David, as
a child of God, turns to his Savior for justice, not as a last resort, but as the
primary, immediate, actual, and ultimate deliverer from evil. In so doing,
he shows us three avenues of prayer as we face injustice in a fallen world.

Pray: seeking the Lord (vv. 1–2). "Prayer" is not a bunch of words
bleated into the blue. Why? No one hears or answers prayer except the
living God. And his Word prescribes the only acceptable way to pray: the
basis of true prayer requires believing that this God is the hearer of prayer,
however simple and rudimentary that conviction may be, for "without
faith it is impossible to please Him, for he who comes to God must believe
that He is, and that He is a rewarder of those who diligently seek Him"
(Heb. 11:6). David knows the Lord personally as "my Rock" (v. 1a), and
prays as one who has a believing "regard for the works of the Lord" and
"the operation of His hands" (v. 5).

> The *reason* for praying in David's case is nothing less than the
> threat of death (v. 1b). The "pit"—like the "bottle dungeon" in
> St. Andrews Castle in Scotland—is a place of no return, unless
> deliverance comes from above. Prayer speaks to the utter
> hopelessness of self-help.

> The *confidence* in our praying comes, not from looking inward
> and conjuring up *self*-confidence, or from external good works

or inward good intentions (cf. Isa. 64:6; Rom. 3:10), but from looking away from ourselves toward God's "holy sanctuary"— i.e., his provision of salvation (v. 2). Here is the Holy Place of the tabernacle, where God is present with Israel and sacrifice is offered for sin, all of which foreshadows the crucified and risen Jesus, to whom believers are united in saving faith: "For we have become partakers of Christ if we hold the beginning of our confidence steadfast to the end" (Heb. 3:14). This confidence is the fruit of free grace in Christ believed, and he tells us to approach him with such boldness every day (Heb. 4:16).

Pray: asking the Lord to deliver us from all dangers, temporal and eternal (vv. 3–5). This involves both the need of God's preserving us from our personal weakness (v. 3), as well as the need for his thwarting those who would do us harm, by bringing them to face the consequences of their disregard for "the works of the Lord" (vv. 4–5).

Pray: blessing the Lord as your strength and shield (vv. 6–9). The Lord answers before the prayer closes. First, the psalmist as an individual is gloriously assured that he is "helped" by him who is his "strength and shield" (vv. 6–7). He switches to the plural, speaks for the whole people of God in the world, and concludes with a crescendo of praise for God's saving his "inheritance" to "shepherd them also and bear them up forever" (vv. 8–9). Here is Christ and his church coming to glory! "Every stream," notes A. A. Bonar, "seems to flow onward to the future day when joy shall no longer be pent up within narrow banks, but have unlimited scope—the people 'saved'—the 'blessing' come—there being no more curse—the heirs arrived at their inheritance, joint-heirs of Him who is 'Heir of all things' [Heb. 1:2]—the Shepherd leading them to living fountains—and reproach all fled away!" Well may you rejoice, dear Christian: "The Lord is my strength and shield; my heart trusted in Him, and I am helped" (v. 7).

PRAISE FOR SALVATION: FULL, FREE, AND FOREVER
Sing Psalm 28

THINGS I WILL PRAY FOR TODAY

215

April 17
God's Goodness to Believers

A prayer of thanksgiving for God's goodness

Oh, how great is Your goodness, which You have laid up for those who fear You... — *Ps. 31:19*

READ PSALM 31

The goodness of God must be a doctrine believed if it is to be an experience enjoyed. This is most keenly tested when bad things happen to us, because it is not obvious that these are evidence of God's goodness in our lives. After all, "His judgments are in all the earth" (Ps. 105:7), and at the time even "all discipline seems painful rather than pleasant" (Heb. 12:11). So the upsets, setbacks, disasters, and tragedies of life—"the same event" that "happens to the righteous and the wicked" (Eccl. 9:2)—cause us distress, not joy, and may tempt us to doubt the goodness of God altogether. We naturally cry out in pain and seek relief and resolution. Again, the Lord shows us the way...

To whom are we to turn in our troubles? Answer: the God who *saves*! David turns to God for deliverance (vv. 1–2), confesses him as his "rock and fortress" (vv. 3–5), and testifies to past mercies from his hand (vv. 6–8). Calvin notes that David "held it as a principle, that the hope which depends upon God cannot possibly be disappointed" and calls us all to act "from a firm persuasion that our safety depends on the power of God." David worked hard at staying alive—running, hiding, fighting, even feigning madness—but he always depended upon the Lord. It is not an accident that he was given to utter words that Jesus would speak upon the cross: "Into Your hand I commit my spirit" (v. 5; Luke 23:46). As David foreshadows Christ trusting his Father, so we are called to aftershadow Christ our Savior, trusting in him as our surety in a world no less challenging in our time.

Why may we have confidence in the face of troubles? Answer: God is the God of *sovereign grace*, who delights in "exercising lovingkindness, judgment, and righteousness in the earth" (Jer. 9:24).

David can claim God's mercy for two basic reasons (vv. 9–13). The first is that God is *in himself* "merciful and gracious, slow to anger, and

216

abounding in mercy" (Ps. 103:8). We are alive "because His compassions fail not" (Lam. 3:22). Even more, we live in "the day of salvation" (2 Cor. 6:2), when "whoever calls on the name of the LORD shall be saved" (Rom. 10:13). This is true for every human being.

The second reason is that God is absolutely sovereign (vv. 14–18). Only because our "times are in [His] hand" do we have a prayer for deliverance (v. 15). "The people of God in every age," writes Murdoch Campbell, "have had the same awareness [as David] of being exposed to constant danger; but 'their life is hid with Christ in God' [Col. 3:3]." God's sovereignty is not cold and distant to us, for he is our "hiding place" (Ps. 32:7; 119:114), and we are his "dove, in the clefts of the rock, in the secret places of the cliff," safe in the Rock of Ages, Jesus his Son (Song 2:14).

What will believers discover even through their troubles? Answer: that God is *good* (vv. 19–24). In all your troubles, child of God, both physical and spiritual, from illnesses to insults, from foolishness and sins to injuries by others, have you not found with the psalmist that God has loved you through them all and been your "rock of refuge" in Christ your Savior? Indeed, it is Jesus who was "cut off from before [his Father's] eyes" (v. 22), but "who, in the days of His flesh, when He had offered up prayers and supplications, with vehement cries and tears to Him who was able to save Him from death, and was heard because of His godly fear..." and "having been perfected," became the author of eternal salvation to all who obey Him" (Heb. 5:7–9). Dear Christian, you are safe in the arms of Jesus! You have found it so thus far, and will so find it in the glory yet to be revealed. Will you now "love the Lord, all you His saints...for the Lord preserves the faithful" (v. 23)? "Oh, how great is Your goodness!" (v. 19).

PRAISE FOR GOD'S GOODNESS IN OUR TROUBLES
Sing Psalm 31:19–24

THINGS I WILL PRAY FOR TODAY

_____

_____

_____

_____

_____

April 18
The Fruit of Forgiveness

A prayer about the joy of forgiveness of sin

Blessed is he whose transgression is forgiven, whose sin is covered.
—Ps. 32:1

READ PSALM 32 AND LUKE 7:36–50

imon the Pharisee did not understand why Jesus allowed a woman who was a "sinner" to wash his feet with tears and anoint them with expensive oil. Jesus turned this into a lesson on forgiveness of sin: "Therefore I say to you, her sins, which are many, are forgiven, for she loved much. But to whom little is forgiven, the same loves little" (Luke 7:47). She loves Jesus "much" because she was forgiven "much," whereas Simon is oblivious to his need of Jesus as his Savior and knows nothing of the forgiveness that moves her actions and causes her to "rejoice with joy inexpressible and full of glory" (1 Peter 1:8).

David understands the impact of true forgiveness. Contrary to some attitudes in our day, his meditation on the subject is not morbid introspection or a clinging to guilt, but a wonderful window on the fruit of forgiveness (cf. Ps. 51:12). Contemplation of the misery from which he has been delivered causes him to rejoice in the blessedness to which he has been brought by God's grace. He understands, as Charles Simeon observes, that "True happiness consists in having our sins forgiven."This is profoundly personal and bears continuing spiritual fruit in those so forgiven:

> *Personal forgiveness* of sin is from the Lord (vv. 1–2). Sin in all its forms—transgression, sin, and iniquity—is not "imputed" (reckoned or accounted) to the saved sinner, and as Paul teaches from these verses as quoted in Romans 4:6–8, God's righteousness is imputed to believers in its place. The practical fruit is a new spirit in which is "no deceit."

> *Personal confession* of sin is made to the Lord (vv. 3–5). David dug in his heels, refusing to confess his sin. So God laid a heavy hand on him and brought him to conviction. He confessed and God forgave him. Hiding sins from God renders seeking forgiveness a sham and is simply a denial of God's justice.

218

- ⸎ *Personal peace* is enjoyed with the Lord (vv. 6–7). Once forgiven, God, as Paul says, "has reconciled in the body of His [Christ's] flesh through death, to present you holy, and blameless, and above reproach in His sight" (Col. 1:21–22). Therefore the "godly shall pray" and the Lord will surround them with "songs of deliverance."
- ⸎ *Personal instruction* is imparted by the Lord (vv. 8–9). The "divine speaker" says "I will guide you with My eye"—the only eye in the universe that sees what is ahead of us! He also warns us against being stubborn as mules! The Lord who forgives also fortifies us for our future fight of faith (1 Tim. 6:12).
- ⸎ *Personal joy* in the Lord's mercy is the abiding privilege and experience of his forgiven people (vv. 10–11). While the lost can only expect "many sorrows," he who "trusts in the Lord, mercy shall surround him." He will "be glad in the Lord and rejoice" and "shout for joy!" Joy is the prevailing and eternal fruit of forgiveness.

Forgiveness is a lifelong experience of God's grace by which he strengthens, grows, and rejoices believers' hearts, even to the coming of "the perfect day" (Prov. 4:18). Salvation is about the forgiveness of the sin of sinners. But we must never forget that Jesus is the most important person ever to be forgiven of sin! On the cross the sinless Son of God died the guiltiest man in history, because the Father "made Him who knew no sin to be sin for us, that we might become the righteousness of God in Him" (2 Cor. 5:21). When we confess our sins, God is faithful and just to forgive us, not because our confession merits forgiveness, but because Jesus, in his death and resurrection, satisfied God's perfect justice and was forgiven as our substitute: "In Him we have redemption through His blood, the forgiveness of sins, according to the riches of His grace" (Eph. 1:7). Therefore "be glad in the Lord and rejoice…and shout for joy."

JOYOUS PRAISE FOR FORGIVENESS OF SIN
Sing Psalm 32:1–7

THINGS I WILL PRAY FOR TODAY

April 19
Hated Without a Cause

A prayer against irreconcilable enemies

Let them not rejoice over me who are wrongfully my enemies...who hate me without a cause. —Ps. 35:19

READ PSALM 35

avid often faced enemies who "hated [him] without a cause" (v. 19). In John 15:25, Jesus tells us that the hatred of the world for himself and his followers is the fulfillment of this verse. This "imprecatory" psalm anticipates in the language of prophecy the New Testament imprecations of Jesus (Mark 11:12–26; Matt. 23:1–36), the apostle (Acts 8:20; 13:10–11), and the martyrs in heaven (Rev. 6:9–10). A. A. Bonar invites us to read it "as the words of the Lord Jesus" pronouncing "the doom of his relentless, impenitent foes." How then are we to pray about those who "without a cause" seek our harm?

The context for the psalmist is not merely being criticized or slandered. He is pursued by people with murderous intentions. Still, there are important lessons for Christians subjected to lesser attacks from God's enemies. Notice how David thoughtfully, methodically, practically, and solemnly sets out his case in his prayer before the Lord. Here is a pattern that we can apply to all of our crisis prayers:

> He opens with *a general plea*, consisting of three requests: (1) that God be his advocate and plead his cause; (2) that God use his power to stop his enemies; and (3) that God give him inward assurance that he is saved (vv. 1–3). All of our prayers must begin with our personal relationship with, and practical resolve to walk with, the Lord.

> He lays out the *particulars of his plea* in two arguments: (1) His enemies *seek his life* (vv. 4–10). Let them be put to shame, brought to confusion, be blown away like chaff, pursued by the angel of the Lord, and caught in their own traps. As the Lord answers his prayer, the psalmist will be "joyful in the Lord" and extol his Name. (2) His enemies *falsely accuse* him (vv. 11–18). They lie, return evil for good, and betray his kindness. As the Lord

hears his prayer and rescues him "from their destructions," he will praise the Lord "among many people." The honor of God, not personal revenge, is the great theme.

> He closes with a *concluding plea* in five distinct requests (vv. 19–28): (1) stop the rejoicing of these enemies (v. 19); (2) Stop their lies and baseless accusations (vv. 20–21); (3) Lord, "awake to my vindication" (vv. 22–24); (4) Lord, put these enemies to shame (vv. 25–26); and (5) let the Lord's people be glad and magnify the Lord's name. Meanwhile, his tongue will speak of his righteousness and praise (vv. 27–28).

How are we to apply this to ourselves? I cannot do better than share a comment of a great Dutch theologian, Wilhelmus a' Brakel (1635–1711). He cautions us to be "on guard that we are not carried away by our own passions, as occurred with the disciples of Christ, who wanted to pray that fire consume the Samaritans who would not receive them (Luke 9:54)." He adds that we "may never pray for someone's eternal perdition, nor for the bodily destruction of someone who is our personal enemy. We may also not do so relative to those who offend God's congregation. If, however, the Lord moves us to pray against those who oppress and persecute the congregation in an extraordinary manner, we may then pray that God would convert them, and if such is not to be the case, that God would punish them so that they would no longer be able to oppress the church. It would thus be apparent that the Lord takes vengeance upon the blood of His church and furthermore that God would be glorified therein." An oft-ignored Bible name of God is "Jehovah-Makkeh"—"the LORD who strikes" (Ezek. 7:9). He who by gospel grace in Christ saves sinners to be his friends also strikes his enemies to preserve his people and his cause and kingdom: "God is still on the throne, and He will remember His own." If you don't know the Lord, go to him now!

PRAISE FOR THE LORD FOR JUST JUDGMENT
Sing Psalm 35:24–28

THINGS I WILL PRAY FOR TODAY

April 20
Make Me to Know My End

A prayer about the shortness of life

Lord, make me to know my end... —Ps. 39:4a

READ PSALM 39

ife will still be short even if we live to be a hundred. In our youth, with life mostly before us, we live as if we are immortal. We also tend to view the old unsympathetically, as if their declining faculties and approaching death is "what old people do" and can cope with easily. Then, when age and infirmity hit us and we realize our lives will be "soon cut off" and we will "fly away" (Ps. 90:10), we perhaps repent of our callousness, or descend into grumbling unhappiness. David is deeply distressed in this psalm, perhaps from opposition, illness, or just weariness. He bottles up his frustration, concerned not to sin with hasty words and be a bad example to both the "wicked" and the "good" (vv. 1–2). But the more he broods, "the fire burn[s]" within him, until he just has to speak up (v. 3; cf. Jer. 20:9). Unlike so many today who endlessly feed their frustration by sharing their complaints with others, David turns to God with a three-part private prayer.

He first prays, "Lord, make me to know my end" (vv. 4–6). This is bold, because it raises two tough issues: facing death, "the last enemy" (1 Cor. 15:26), and pondering our eternal destiny (Heb. 9:27). But the immediate application is to *this life*, because how we handle death and eternity, whether biblical or otherwise, affects every aspect of our thinking and practical living. David asks God to explain his end, days, frailty, etc., emphasizing that "man at his best state is but vapor" and his busy-ness is so much vanity (vv. 4–6; cf. Eccl. 1:2–3, 14). In other words, "What is the use of living?" He doubts it is worth the pain.

His second prayer answers the practical unbelief of his first with repentance and an implicit appeal for help: he hopes in God; he confesses sin; acknowledges that the things that got him down were God's doings; and he admits he needs correction (vv. 7–11). Hard providences are hard to handle, but God's gracious hand is in them.

His third prayer intensifies his plea (vv. 12–13). He is profoundly

222

conscious of disappointing God by doubting his love and sovereignty in the hard experiences that have so worn him down. When he says he is a "stranger" and "sojourner" with God "as all my fathers were," he is not complaining in self-pity, but owning it as a badge of God's covenant love for him and his covenant privilege as a child of God. His final appeal is for forgiveness—"Remove Your gaze from me"—that he might recover usefulness in his service to the Lord, as he says, "before I go away and am no more" in this short life on earth.

Knowing Christ as your Savior is what makes all the difference. Says Andrew Gray,

> The brevity of our lives displays the great love and matchless delight that God has towards sinners. He is longing for the day when all the redeemed of the Lord shall be with Him, to remain with Him forever and ever, to enjoy all delights and all manner of soul pleasures....Many of us may say that we have not received a short lifetime from the Lord, but that we have made a short life unto ourselves; for it is said that wicked men shall not live half their days [Ps. 55:23]. Certainly, these may think their life and appointed time short, whose heaven and joy is ended when their lives are ended. But those who have made use of their lives... to entertain communion and fellowship with God...shall surely rejoice with joy unspeakable and full of glory [1 Peter 1:8]. Now we shall desire to have our eyes failing with looking up, until that day shall come, when our blessed Lord Jesus shall come in the clouds [Mark 13:26ff.]....Let the thoughts of that precious and blessed day comfort your hearts under all your afflictions, and wait with patience for your eternal redemption. Amen.

Amen!

PRAISE ANTICIPATING RESTORED FELLOWSHIP AND FRUITFULNESS
IN THE SERVICE OF GOD
Sing Psalm 39:7–13

THINGS I WILL PRAY FOR TODAY

April 21
Sickness and Salvation

A prayer for healing in body and soul

All who hate me whisper together against me.... "An evil disease,"
they say, "clings to him. And now that he lies down, he will rise up no
more."—Ps. 41:7

READ PSALM 41

he occasion of this psalm," writes Matthew Poole (1624–79), "was manifestly some sore disease or affliction which God had inflicted upon David, and which gave his enemies opportunity to discover their hatred and malice against him." We are so easily seduced by the idea that bad health must be evidence of, and judgment upon, some personal sin—usually in other people! And the converse is the equally seductive notion that health must be a reward for good deeds: thus in *The Sound of Music*, Maria sings, in celebration of her romance with the Captain, "Nothing comes from nothing. Nothing ever could. / Somewhere in my youth or childhood, I must have done something good." Even Jesus's disciples were confused about this. With the man born blind, they ask Jesus, "Rabbi, who sinned, this man or his parents, that he was born blind?" Jesus answers, "Neither this man nor his parents sinned, but that the works of God should be revealed in him" (John 9:2–3). Jesus is, of course, preparing them for the healing miracle he was about to do, but he also implicitly challenges *you*, that if you find yourself suffering illness, you should ask *yourself* what God may be doing in *your* life—and also stop making self-serving judgments about others! The broadest lesson is simply that any response to illness must begin and end with "the God of all grace" (1 Peter 5:10).

The psalmist's prayer has three main focal points:

He begins by affirming the *blessedness from the Lord* of the one who "considers"—i.e., is wisely attentive to—the distress of "the poor" (vv. 1–3). "Poor" here is not narrowly economic, but is a wider wretchedness from many sources. In David's case, it is a combination of serious illness and the threats of his enemies. Those who care personally about "the poor" will themselves be sustained by the Lord from enemies and through illnesses. Although not explicitly stated, it is clear that the character of God as the one who is merciful in himself is the underlying assumption—and application.

He continues with some specific requests (vv. 4–9). He expresses *his need of the Lord's mercy*: "Lord, be merciful to me; Heal my soul, for I have sinned against You" (v. 4). Believers' sins may be forgiven already, but the damage our actual sinning does to others, to ourselves, to our witness, to the church, and to the honor of God means that on this side of heaven we need God's mercy applied continually. He is also concerned with *overturning the damage to his integrity* from his enemies falsely charging his illness to alleged wickedness, and he rightly bristles that, like vultures, they circle around waiting for him to die—under the unmentioned but assumed judgment of God (vv. 6–8). He particularly grieves that he has been *betrayed by his own "familiar friend"* in whom he trusted (v. 9). At the Last Supper Jesus applies this to his betrayal by Judas that very night (Matt. 26:23). "What was true of David's experience," observes Allan Harman, "was fulfilled to an even greater degree in Judas's betrayal of Jesus." Christians may expect similar treatment until the Lord returns on the Great Day.

He concludes by *entrusting himself to the Lord*, who will, he says, "uphold me in my integrity" and "set me before [His] face forever" (vv. 10–12). His sickness does not prove he is a hypocrite under God's judgment. Neither does it prove he is saved. "Many reasons could be mentioned," says Murdoch Campbell, "why the Lord allows these conflicts to enter our lives....[A]ll true Christians discover sooner or later that Satan is bent on their destruction. But those whom God loves shall be kept by His power....'It is in our sorrow that we discover how great is His love.'" In sickness we also are saved.

PRAISE FOR GOD'S LOVE IN ALL OUR TROUBLES
Sing Psalm 41:7–13

THINGS I WILL PRAY FOR TODAY

225

April 22
I Will Remember You

A prayer looking upward to the Father for refreshment

*I will remember You from the land of Jordan, and from the heights of
Hermon, from the Hill Mizar.* — Ps. 42:6

READ PSALM 42

David is thought to have penned this psalm during his flight from Absalom's rebellion. He feels alone, dejected, and bereft of God's presence. He turns to the Lord with an impassioned cry of deep spiritual longing: "As the deer pants for the water brooks, so pants my soul for You, O God" (v. 1). "My tears," he says, "have been my food day and night," and his enemies taunt him (v. 3). His thoughts turn to past blessing, when he went to "the house of God with the voice of joy and praise, with a multitude that kept a pilgrim feast" (v. 4), and he charges himself to "hope in God" in prospect of his help (v. 5). "Happy they who feel this desire," writes Bishop Horne, "and fly to the well of life, that it may be satisfied. 'Blessed are they that thirst after righteousness, for they shall be filled' (Matt. 5:6)." When we feel the Lord's absence in this way, we have good reason to expect blessing.

The sweetest function of that faculty we call memory is to recall the times and seasons in our past life when the Lord dealt with us in grace and refreshed our souls with particular outpourings of his grace. And it is precisely because of his present pain that the psalmist turns in the second part of the prayer to some specific memories from his past: "O my God, my soul is cast down within me; therefore I will remember You from the land of the Jordan, and from the heights of Hermon, from the Hill Mizar" (v. 6). This verse encapsulates the tension in his heart and mind between his dejection and the reality of God's work in his life. These memories are not mere sentiment, as when some childhood scene brings a tear to the eye. Here is the believer fleeing to the Lord in response to remembered blessings. We do not know what the psalmist was thinking of, but we can be sure that "the land of Jordan" recalls Israel's story from Egyptian bondage to the Land of Promise. The heights of Hermon, the highest mountain in Israel, may be a reference to God's might for, and goodness to,

226

his people. The hill Mizar is unknown today. It means "little," so perhaps it led the psalmist to the thought that to the eye of faith even the smallest of God's blessings is really a wonderful treasure in a world under the curse (Gen. 3:17–19). When we grasp, with Jacob, that we are "not worthy of the least of all the mercies and of all the truth" that the Lord has shown us (Gen. 32:10), then, in receiving his mercies and truth, we will surely all the more love the LORD our God with all our heart, soul, strength, and mind, and our neighbor as ourself (Luke 10:27). So also we will "rejoice with joy inexpressible and full of glory" in Jesus our Savior (1 Peter 1:8).

The prayer closes with further wrestling between discouragement and hope (vv. 7–11). This culminates in a repetition of his earlier, hopeful self-rebuke in verse 5, but with two meaningful differences. First, instead of "help of His [God's] countenance," verse 11 has "help of *my* countenance"—indicating that God's help has given light to the psalmist's "clouded and dejected" countenance. Second, he adds "and my God." This reminds us that God is still helping (with "His countenance," as in verse 5), but puts a new emphasis on God's faithful presence. David is answering the question of verse 3, "Where is your God?" He is saying, in effect, "Behold him, he is here. My God is he who dissipates my clouds and animates my hopes." The remembrances of past blessing, which led him to pray for help, have given way to a refreshed sense of the nearness of the Lord as his Redeemer and Friend. May you be similarly helped in your distresses and be enabled to say with the psalmist, "Blessed be the Lord, who daily loads us with benefits, the God of our salvation!" (Ps. 68:19); and "Bless the Lord, O my soul, and forget not all His benefits" (Ps. 103:2).

PRAISE THAT HOPES IN GOD
Sing Psalm 42:6–11

THINGS I WILL PRAY FOR TODAY

April 23
Hope for the Dejected Soul

A prayer for joyous fellowship with God

Why are you cast down, O my soul?...Hope in God; for I shall yet praise Him, the help of my countenance and my God.—Ps. 43:5

READ PSALM 43

The transparent honesty of Scripture in recording the sins of real saints and their experiences of self-doubt and dejection is a testimony to both the stresses of the human condition and the reality of the gospel of saving grace. It is therefore a wonderful encouragement to the flagging spirit of believers battered by adversities of one kind or another. "It has pleased God to suffer many of his most eminent servants to be in trouble," writes Charles Simeon, "and to record their experience for our benefit, that we, when in similar circumstances, may know that we are not walking in an untrodden path, and that we may see how to conduct ourselves aright." It is true that Jesus's "yoke is easy and [His] burden is light" and that in Christian discipleship you will find "rest for your soul" (Matt. 11:29). But the world and our own frailties—and the devil (1 Peter 5:8)—still entail burdens with which we must wrestle. We therefore need those other words of Jesus when he says: "In the world you will have tribulation; but be of good cheer, I have overcome the world" (John 16:33). The psalmist points the way. You will notice that the "cast down soul" theme continues from Psalm 42 into Psalm 43 (see 42:5, 11; 43:5), but the latter has a rising tone and a firmer expectation of blessing. The prayer is in three parts:

A request for deliverance from enemies (vv. 1–3). The psalmist's experience of dejection has three all-too-common features. One is that opposition comes from *within the church* (v. 1). The "ungodly nation" is not some foreign power, but professed covenant people, who are "deceitful and unjust" in turning against the Lord's faithful servants. Opposition from the world we understand (John 16:33), but from God's own people? The second feature of this dejection is a sense that *God has "cast me off"* (v. 2). And because I do believe he is "the God of my strength," I ask why this "oppression of the enemy" is happening to me and why God permits it within his church. The third—and positive—feature is the distinctive *response* in the believer (v. 3). When it seems God has cast him off, the true child of God all the more feels the need for God's "light" and "truth" to give him understanding and to restore him to fellowship. God's "holy hill" (Zion) is the true worshiping church with whom God is present, while the "tabernacle" is the place of accepted sacrifice for sin—pointing to the crucified Christ. Here is where and how a living faith responds to adversity!

A resolve to worship and fellowship with the Lord is the immediate result (v. 4). The "altar of God" was where sacrifice was offered and accepted. Jesus Christ is "our altar" (Heb. 13:10) and believers are united to him in his finished work, as the crucified, risen and ascended Savior. In him, we go to God as our "exceeding joy." You see here how God begins to answer prayer before it is even finished—and before any of the outward causes of distress have been overthrown! The opposition is still there, but the soul is quieted by his grace.

A rebuke of self-pity—"Why are you cast down, O my soul?"—is followed by an affirmation of *hope in the Lord*, whom the psalmist beautifully confesses is "the help of my countenance and my God" (v. 5). We may "hope in God," says Charles Simeon, precisely because "it is God who sends our troubles ("they spring not out of the dust," [Job 5:6]), and he only can remove them." He adds, "We should therefore look unto him, and put our trust in him....he reminds us of his wisdom and power to overrule our trials for good; and exhorts us, when weary and fainting, to wait on him as our all-sufficient Helper [Isa. 40:28–31]." "Therefore," expecting blessing in Christ, "gird up the loins of your mind, be sober, and rest your hope fully upon the grace that is to be brought to you at the revelation of Jesus Christ" (1 Peter 1:13).

PRAISE FOR PERSONAL SATISFACTION IN THE LORD
Sing Psalm 43

THINGS I WILL PRAY FOR TODAY

April 24
Why Do You Sleep, O Lord?

An intensely urgent prayer for God's intervention

Awake! Why do You sleep, O Lord? Arise!—Ps. 44:23

READ PSALM 44

"W here is your God?" is a taunt the world frequently levels against the suffering church (Ps. 42:3, 10; 79:10; Joel 2:17; Mic. 7:10). It is, of course, really directed at the God who, the critic believes, is failing his people because he does not exist. He is mocking God as surely as Elijah mocked the god Baal and his priests when nothing happened in answer to the latter's prayers at Mount Carmel: "And so it was, at noon, that Elijah mocked them and said, 'Cry aloud, for he is a god; either he is meditating, or he is busy, or he is on a journey, or perhaps he is sleeping and must be awakened'" (1 Kings 18:27). The difference is that Elijah's God is the living God, Creator of heaven and earth, whereas Baal and all the other gods in this world have no existence outside the human imagination (Ps. 96:5). When Christians become immersed in troubles, pray earnestly over them, and nothing changes, they sometimes ask, "Where is *my* God?" and charge him with exactly what Elijah leveled at the priests of Baal. When the "slings and arrows of outrageous fortune" are whistling about our ears, we are not always ready to suffer them, even if we think it might be "nobler in the mind" to do so!

With boldness born of extreme distress, the psalmist complains that God has become *Deus absconditus*—the "hidden God," who is effectively absent from the scene and apparently uninterested in the sufferings of his people (vv. 9–16; 23–26). This prayer is timeless. It is a window on the challenges of a world where darkness and light battle for the temporal welfare and eternal destiny of sinners (John 3:19; 8:12; 12:46); it also gives insight into Christian experience under severe testing. This is reflected in the very structure of the prayer, which takes us from remembering past mercies from the Lord (vv. 1–8), through reviewing present miseries (vv. 9–16), and on to requests for future relief and revival (vv. 17–26):

> ⬦ *In the past*, God brought Israel to the Promised Land. The fruit of this is the sure knowledge that *God* has "saved us from our

enemies," and therefore we will "praise [his] name forever." (vv. 7–8). This is not a remote factoid; God's deeds in Scripture history belong to every child of God. God's blessings past point to God's blessings future. We therefore may pray expectantly to "see the goodness of the Lord in the land of the living" (Ps. 27:13).

- *In the present,* circumstances suggest to the psalmist that God has "cast us off" and "put us to shame" (v. 9). These include pillaging the church (v. 10); killing (v. 11a), scattering (v. 11b), and enslaving (v. 12) God's people; and making the church a "byword among the nations" (vv. 13–16). Such hard providences afflict many Christians in our day!

- *For the future,* the psalmist begs the Lord to "awake" and "arise" to redeem them "for [His] mercies' sake." (v. 26). He is grieved, but the bitterness is "corrected by faith." Through the dismay and the pain of these dreadful woes, he testifies that the faithful church—notice the plural throughout verses 17–26—has not broken covenant with the Lord, or turned away from him in heart or actions, even under "the shadow of death" (vv. 17–19). They understand that this is a[n extreme] cost of discipleship: "Yet for Your sake we are killed all day long; we are accounted as sheep for the slaughter" (v. 22).

Paul quoted this as also fulfilled in the experience of the New Testament church, pointing out that none of these privations will separate us from the love of Christ (Rom. 8:36)! The Lord never sleeps or ceases to love his people (Ps. 121; Deut. 31:6; Heb. 13:5). But why his *apparent absence*? Why his *delay* in relieving us from the cruelties of persecution? Many answers can be given, but one that touches our experience is that in our trials we must say with Jacob when he wrestled with Christ at Peniel (Gen. 32:26), "I will not let You go unless You bless me!"

A PRAISE-PRAYER THAT CRIES TO GOD FOR HELP
Sing Psalm 44:13–15

THINGS I WILL PRAY FOR TODAY

_____

_____

_____

231

April 25
The Sacrifices of God

A prayer of repentance to the God of grace

The sacrifices of God are a broken spirit, a broken and a contrite heart—
These, O God, You will not despise.—Ps. 51:17

READ PSALM 51

The sin of David, writes Matthew Henry, "is recorded for warning to all, that he who thinks he stands may take heed lest he fall." He was a believer but he seduced the beautiful Bathsheba, and—so he could marry her and cover up his sin—arranged her husband Uriah's death (2 Sam. 11). Only a brilliant ploy by Nathan the prophet unmasked his self-deception, awakened his conscience, and led him to this humble, yet exalted, prayer of repentance, renewal, and reconciliation to God. The prayer unfolds in five sections: David pleads God's mercy (vv. 1–2); confesses his sins (vv. 3–6); seeks renewed faith and repentance by the work of God's Spirit (vv. 7–12); commits to renewed discipleship (vv. 13–17); and finally petitions God to bless his people, the church (vv. 18–19). Each part is rich enough to fill a book, but two themes stand out: getting right with God and keeping right with God.

Getting right with God is the biggest question for every human being. David, the backslidden believer, is guilty of adultery and murder and, as God's anointed king of God's covenant people, has also perverted his calling and power of office to these ends! There was no forgiveness in the law of Moses for such premeditated sin—and the penalty was death, as it is ultimately for all sin (Rom. 3:23). "But," notes Bishop Horne, "the penitent's first ground for hope of pardon is his own misery, and the divine mercy which rejoices to relieve that misery." David is convicted, and confesses to the Lord, "Against You, You only, have I sinned" (v. 4). This does not mean that he did not sin against Bathsheba, Uriah, the child, the church, and (yes!) also the world (cf. 2 Sam. 12:14). It is because God is the "Judge of all the earth" (Gen. 18:25) to whom *all* sinners will account one day (Rom. 14:11–12). And only God can forgive sin while satisfying his absolute justice. Bishop Horne again: "Every transgression leaves behind it a guilt, and a stain; the account between God and the sinner is crossed by the blood of the great propitiatory sacrifice, which removes the former; and the soul is cleansed by the Holy Spirit, which takes out the latter." David's greater son, Jesus Christ, is that propitiation (Rom. 3:25; 1 John 2:2; 4:10), the *only One* by whom we must be saved (Acts 4:12). And if backslidden believer David must repent and return to the Lord, so must all the unbelievers in the world believe in the Lord, for as Peter says, "Now 'if the righteous one is scarcely saved, where will the ungodly and the sinner appear?'" (1 Peter 4:18 quoting Prov. 11:31). This speaks to our relationship with Christ and trust in him as Savior.

Keeping right with God is the challenge of daily life from here to eternity. People, even some professing Christians, imagine that doing certain "good" things (going to and giving to the church, helping neighbors, reading the Bible, etc.) are "sacrifices" pleasing to God that somehow cancel out their sins. It is a delusion (see Mic. 6:7). For one thing, says Matthew Henry, "The breaking of Christ's body for sin is the only sacrifice of atonement, for no sacrifice but that could take away sin," whereas, "The breaking of our hearts for sin is a sacrifice of acknowledgement, a sacrifice of God, for to him it is offered up; he requires it, he prepares it…and he accepts it." The "sacrifices of God" are "a broken spirit…and a contrite heart" (v. 17). They are the practical fruit of saving faith, not atonement somehow purchasing redemption. Paul shows us the way: "I beseech you therefore, brethren, by the mercies of God, that you present your bodies as a living sacrifice, holy, acceptable to God, which is your reasonable service" (Rom. 12:1). Fresh sin requires fresh repentance, refreshed faith, and a revived heart and spirit energizing a humble walk with God, which is filled with the "sacrifices of God"—plural, persevering, and prevailing.

PRAISE TO THE GOD OF GRACE
Sing Psalm 51

THINGS I WILL PRAY FOR TODAY

April 26
Do You Need Help?

A prayer of the helpless

Behold, God is my helper; the Lord is with those who uphold my life.
—*Ps. 54:4*

READ PSALM 54

Help, I need somebody / Help, not just anybody / Help, you know I need someone, help…" So sang legendary pop-group the Beatles in their 1965 hit song. We often do need help, and a friend in our need is a friend indeed. But such help is limited in time and cannot save us for eternity. David surely felt the need of help. He was on the run from King Saul, and he was hiding in the "wilderness of Ziph." Mind you, he was not alone—he had "about six hundred" men with him (1 Sam. 23:14ff.), but the Ziphites informed on him to Saul (v. 1), who took up the chase with 3,000 men (1 Sam. 26:1ff.). David was in a tight spot! Later in his career, when he was celebrating a victory in battle, he asked the Lord, "Give us help from trouble, for the help of man is useless" (Ps. 108:12). He was all for a strong military, but his watchword in war was, "Some trust in chariots, and some in horses; but we will remember the name of the LORD our God" (Ps. 20:7). With Saul's army combing the hills for him, David earnestly calls on God in prayer, testifying, "God is my helper," and trusting that he will deliver him "out of all trouble" (vv. 4, 7). The prayer unfolds in three practical steps seeking the help of the Lord.

Seek the Lord as your first helper. The key words are "Save me, O God, *by Your name*" (vv. 1–3). This is not mere literary color. It references something profound in God—his character and his track record. This is also true of us, for we all have "a name"—a reputation that tells people about our character and track record. If you have a name for wisdom, people will seek your advice; if for unreliability, people will not trust you. To pray or hope in God's name, says Addison Alexander, "is to trust in the future exercise and exhibition of the same divine perfections which have been exhibited already." There is no trouble you will face that the Lord has not already dealt with in other people's lives, no prayer he has not answered for someone with the same need as you. What is new to us is not

234

new to God. When we invoke his "name," we are asking for "the exercise of those perfections that have been already manifested."Furthermore, in his Son Jesus "we do not have a High Priest who cannot sympathize with our weaknesses, but was in all points tempted as we are, yet without sin" (Heb. 4:15). For this reason, in Christ you can…

Trust the Lord as your just helper (vv. 4–5). He is the Judge with power to act justly in your interest (vv. 1–3). Notice that David's prayer is already answered in his soul, when he says, "God IS my helper" (v. 4a). David Dickson, no stranger to persecution in his native Scotland, observes, "There is more joy in God's felt presence, than grief is felt in trouble." Notice also that God is not our *only* helper, for "the Lord is with those who uphold my life" (v. 4b). And because God is just, we can also say, "He will repay my enemies for their evil" (v. 5). "So we may boldly say: 'The LORD is my helper; I will not fear. What can man do to me?'" (Heb. 13:6 quoting Ps. 27:1; 118:6). You may then…

Praise the Lord as your faithful helper. The psalmist promises to praise the Lord for giving him the certainty of his deliverance (vv. 6–7). The first answer to prayer is often the work of the Holy Spirit, for, as Jesus tells his disciples at the Last Supper, "When the Helper comes, whom I shall send to you from the Father, the Spirit of truth who proceeds from the Father, He will testify of Me.…These things I have spoken to you that you may not stumble" (John 15:26). After Israel defeated the Philistines at Mizpah, "Samuel took a stone…set it up…and called its name Ebenezer [lit., "Stone of Help"], saying, 'Thus far the LORD has helped us'" (1 Sam. 7:12). Do you need help? Then flee to Christ our Ebenezer, who will never cast you out (John 6:37)!

PRAISE FOR THE GOD WHO HELPS THE HELPLESS
Sing Psalm 54

THINGS I WILL PRAY FOR TODAY

235

April 27
O for the Wings of a Dove!

A prayer seeking and finding rest for the soul

Oh, that I had wings like a dove! I would fly away and be at rest.
—Ps. 55:6

READ PSALM 55

One day in April 1927, English boy-soprano Ernest Lough (1911–2000) recorded "O for the Wings of a Dove" and almost overnight became the most famous choirboy in history. His recording went on to sell over a million copies, having caught the imagination of a generation still reeling from the miseries of the 1914–18 War. And who has not wanted to fly away "free as a bird" from his problems in this world? The psalmist is giving voice to his own extensive experience of troubles, but also touches our ordinary lives. And this anticipates, says Bishop Horne, "our blessed Redeemer, on the day of his sufferings, praying earnestly, and repeating his supplications, as in the garden of Gethsemane, at the prospect of the sea of sorrows which was then to overwhelm his agonizing soul" (see Mark 14:33–34). When Jesus prays "let this cup pass," it is his sinless humanity recoiling from these agonies of soul (Matt. 26:39). Andrew Bonar aptly observes that "it is in Jesus, the Man of Sorrows, that the Psalm finds its fullest illustration." Notice how the Lord teaches us to pray in this psalm…

The psalmist sets out three practical steps that give order to his initial desperation: he reacts, reflects, and resolves, all by God's grace.

Reaction (vv. 1–8). David feels the force of the oppression and hatred of "the wicked," and is overwhelmed by "the terrors of death" (see 2 Sam. 15:23, 30). He envies the peaceful dove and longs to fly away from people to the quiet of the desert (vv. 6–8). This stratagem is, of course, an illusion, not a solution. Because Mendelssohn's gorgeous anthem stops at verse 8, it effectively romanticizes world-flight as the answer to worldly woes. But David doesn't stop there, with emotional devastation. He looks away from himself and turns to talk to the Lord about specifics and solutions.

Reflection (vv. 9–15). David prays against the "violence and strife" and "oppression and deceit" that threaten him. There is a twist here: the

236

"deceit" is that his enemy turns out to be a "companion" with whom until recently he shared "sweet counsel" and "walked to the house of God in the throng." Here is the bitterness of betrayal, as per Ahitophel to David (2 Sam. 15:31) and Judas Iscariot to Jesus (Matt. 26:13 quoting Ps. 41:9—"my own familiar friend in whom I trusted, who ate my bread, has lifted up his heel against me"). But also relevant is the awful prospect of God's judgment upon the unrepentant (see Rev. 16:5–6; 18:20). The upshot is that the child of God is not actually alone, even when emotionally overwhelmed. Believers have recourse to the God who loves them and is a "just judge" (Ps. 7:11).

Resolution (vv. 16–23). Flying off to the wilderness is not the answer. Merely "getting away from it all" to a cave in Arabia—or a cabin in the Rockies—is more a counsel of despair than a doorway to a new life. David's destination is pressing onward in a real life of continuing discipleship in dependence upon the Lord. He "will call upon God... pray, and cry aloud" and he will hear his voice. Indeed, the Lord has already "redeemed [his] soul in peace from the battle" that was going against him (vv. 16–18). Here is prayer working as a means of grace to one whom God loves and who loves God. In contrast, the state of the godless is tragic (vv. 19–21). David accordingly (and positively) charges us, "Cast your burden on the Lord, and He shall sustain you." This must be the watchword of your future path. And has not Jesus called us to new life with the assurance, "My yoke is easy and My burden is light" (Matt. 11:30)? Then sing with his saints,

> My soul finds rest in God alone;
> He my salvation is.
> My only Rock, Salvation's fort;
> My refuge most secure.
> —*The Book of Psalms for Worship*, 62A

PRAISE FOR THE TRUSTWORTHY GOD
Sing Psalm 55:16–23

THINGS I WILL PRAY FOR TODAY

April 28
Fears, Tears, and Cheers

A prayer of trembling and trusting

Put my tears into Your bottle. — *Psalm 56:8*

READ PSALM 56

hakespeare's Julius Caesar declares that "Cowards die many times before their deaths. / The valiant never taste of death but once" and reflects, "It seems to me most strange that men should fear, / Seeing that death, a necessary end, / Will come when it will come." Perhaps the historical Caesar was such a fearless fatalist. There are some people who seem quite fearless. They make the rest of us slightly sheepish about our fears, so there is strange comfort in the revelation that a great warrior like David experienced great fear and wept tears over some of his trials. This prayer comes from a time when he was with the Philistines, whence he had fled "for fear of Saul" (1 Sam. 21:10–22:1). When David heard that Achish, the King of Gath, was told he was *the* David who had killed his "tens of thousands" of the Philistines, he became "sore afraid." He had jumped from the frying pan into the fire! This psalm is his prayer from that fearful situation. It unfolds from *fears* to *tears*—and finally to *cheers*...

Fears (vv. 1–4). David is at an end of himself. His enemies aim to swallow him up, every day bringing more pressure, they hound him all day and he is outnumbered (vv. 1–2). Even so, we might ask why believers in the living God, and a notably gifted saint like David, find themselves wrestling so intensely with fear? Augustine (AD 354–430) offers a pithy answer: "*Magnitudinem mali vides, potestatem medici vides*"—"You see the magnitude of the evil; the power of the physician you do not see." How true to our experience! We look at our troubles and take our eyes off God! Natural fears too easily become sinful fears through which we banish God from the picture. What is the remedy? Andrew Bonar answers, "The faith which penetrates the unseen reaches the case." David addresses himself, vertically, to the Lord: "Whenever I am afraid, I will trust in You" (v. 3), and then, horizontally, to friends and enemies alike, "In God I have put my trust; I will not fear. What can flesh do to me?" (v. 4). Central to this commitment is the Word of God, the Scriptures—his trust is in the Lord, "whose word I praise" (v. 4, ESV). The order of praying is:

> ⟩ Look to the Savior in *faith*;
> ⟩ Ask in faith for *deliverance*;
> ⟩ Commit to *trusting* the Lord;
> ⟩ Act in *obedience* to God's Word; and
> ⟩ Anticipate confidently God's *overcoming* the causes of your fear.

Therefore "Do not be afraid of sudden terror...For the LORD will be your confidence, and will keep your foot from being caught" (Prov. 3:25, 26). It is Christ who is invincible, not his enemies.

Tears (vv. 5–11). Troubles are on every side, and conspiracies abound with deadly intent (vv. 5–7). Tears followed the fears, but, says David, "You number my wanderings; put my tears into Your bottle; are they not in Your book?" (v. 8). Robert Hawker (1753–1827) comments, "It is an interesting figure of speech, of bottling their tears: but the sense is, they are remembered. And woe will be to the man that offends one of GOD's little ones on His account. What are now bottles of tears, will be poured out in the end as so many vials of wrath. But, Reader, think how the tears of JESUS have been treasured up, which he shed for the sins of his people." Prayer is a means of grace and God ministers to David as he prays; he is enabled to confess with certainty, "God is for me" (v. 9), and, as he trusts the Lord, he can say, "I will not be afraid. What can man do to me?" (vv. 10–11). His tears are now of joy.

Cheers (vv. 12–13). When the Lord lifts your fears and dries your tears, you can only praise him with holy cheers! After all, our "soul" is "delivered...from death" and our "feet from falling" so that we may "walk" with the Lord in the "light of the living" (cf. Eph. 5:8). Jesus assures us, "Do not fear, little flock, for it is your Father's good pleasure to give you the kingdom" (Luke 12:32). Hallelujah!

PRAISE FOR DELIVERANCE FROM FEAR
Sing Psalm 56:8–13

THINGS I WILL PRAY FOR TODAY

April 29
God's Glory Exalted

A prayer that God will exalt his glory

Be exalted, O God, above the heavens; Let Your glory be above all the earth. —Ps. 57:1

READ PSALM 57

The desire for relief from troubles pervades the Psalms, as it does real life in the real world. As he writes Psalm 57, David is living in a cave in the mountains of Judea, having fled the murderous intentions of a jealous Saul and the perils of fraternizing with the Philistines. As on other occasions, he opens with prayer for mercy. But something new happens—he closes with a proclamation of God's glory! He begins in a cave and ends, as it were, in heaven! And what is so striking on this occasion is the connection between David's parlous situation and his heightened sense of the glory of God. The psalm opens with a prayer for deliverance (vv. 1–6) and closes with praise for deliverance (vv. 7–11). In all of this the psalmist sees something of the heavenly glory of God applied to his soul—that is, of that "inheritance incorruptible and undefiled and that does not fade away, reserved in heaven for you, who are kept by the power of God through faith for salvation ready to be revealed in the last time" (1 Peter 1:5). Notice...

The presence of God's glory is made evident to believers in God's gracious dealings with them (vv. 1–6). "Glory" in common parlance revolves around fame or visible magnificence. Feeling "glory" while skulking in a cave might seem an impossible contradiction, and, to a skeptic, even a strange delusion. But God actually ministers to his people by his Spirit. Prayer is a "means of grace" by which "Christ communicates to his church the benefits of his mediation" (*Larger Catechism* 154). Even when we do not know what to pray for, "the Spirit helps our infirmities, by enabling us to understand both for whom, and what, and how prayer is to be made; and by working and quickening in our hearts (although not in all persons, nor at all times, in the same measure) those apprehensions, affections, and graces which are requisite for the right performance of that duty" (*Larger Catechism* 182). Notice that as David prays for God to be merciful, he

240

trust him, finds refuge in "the shadow of [his] wings (v. 1), and shortly he is able to confide in the Lord as the "God who performs all things for me," who will "send from heaven and save [him]" (vv. 2–3). This is not a merely intellectual transaction—it is God the Holy Spirit convincing us that he is absolutely sovereign, superintends all things by supernatural providential intervention, and saves in the detailed circumstances as they unfold. Of course, he describes how his "soul is among lions" and how helpless he feels (v. 4), but the upshot of this heart-wrestling with the Lord by the Spirit is to cry out, "Be exalted, O God, above the heavens; Let Your glory be above all the earth" (v. 5). The Lord is gloriously saving his skin and his soul from his enemies, and he can see that, try as they will to trap him, they are already falling into their own pit (v. 6)! Now, no fact has changed on the ground as yet. Saul is still coming after him and he is stuck in the cave with his harried band of outcasts. What has changed is his heart-grasp of the Lord's promises.

The perspective of God's glory is being made plain to him—he will live out of the future into the present (vv. 7–11). Experiencing Christ's strength being made perfect in weakness is permanently transformative in the Christian life (2 Cor. 12:9). As long as we fancy we have a bit of strength of our own, whether to resist some sin or perform some good deed, we tend to reserve a bit of glory to ourselves. But when the Lord gives grace, it is enabling of new conviction, devotion, steadfastness of heart (v. 7), and a soul ("my glory," v. 8) that awakens to expanding and ascending sacrifices of praise (v. 9)! We then say with Paul, "For I consider that the sufferings of this present time are not worthy to be compared with the glory which shall be revealed in us" (Rom. 8:18; cf. 1 Peter 4:13). It this glimpse of glory that calls forth the prayer that he exalt himself and his glory above earth and heavens now and forevermore (vv. 10–11)!

PRAISE THAT LIFTS UP GOD'S GLORY
Sing Psalm 57:5–11

THINGS I WILL PRAY FOR TODAY

_____

_____

_____

_____

April 30
Backs to the Wall?

A prayer in the face of seemingly certain death

To You, O my Strength, I will sing praises; for God is my defense, My
God of mercy. — Ps. 59:17

READ PSALM 59

By April 11, 1918, after three weeks of ferocious fighting, the German offensive designed to end the Great War had pushed the British armies back 40 miles on a 50-mile front at the cost of approximately 250,000 casualties on each side. British commander Douglas Haig issued an Order of the Day, in which he said, "With our backs to the wall and believing in the justice of our cause each one of us must fight on to the end." There are times in life when our backs are to the wall and the prospects look grim. This happened to David when King Saul became jealous of him, tried to kill him a couple of times (1 Sam. 18:11), and then, as the psalm's heading puts it, "sent men, and they watched the house in order to kill him" (cf. 1 Sam 19:11ff.). This hit David like a ton of bricks, and in the fifty-ninth psalm he flies to the Lord in prayer, first expressing his shock over this turn of events, and then, by God's grace, experiences the recovery of his confidence in the Lord. It is a word for us all when we feel "our backs to the wall."

Shock (vv. 1–10a). When we are reeling from some unexpected personal calamity, we might say to ourselves, "I feel like my life is over," even though we know it isn't that bad and that God is still on the throne. David's plight is the worst-case scenario. His life is threatened. As to why, well might he wonder, as he would say to Saul in a future day, "The king of Israel has come out to seek a flea, as when one hunts a partridge in the mountains" (1 Sam. 26:20). But he is not a fatalist. He does not say, "God is sovereign. What will happen will happen," and then sit down and do nothing. He gets out the window and heads for the hills (1 Sam. 19:12). And he prays. Notice the logic in the case he presents to the Lord:

> He asks God to deliver him from those who "lie in wait for [his] life" (vv. 1–3a). That is *a call for simple justice* in a context where the civil government is acting in opposition to God's law in his case.

242

- He affirms his *innocence*: "The mighty gather against me, not for my transgression nor for my sin, O Lᴏʀᴅ" (vv. 3b–4a).
- He appeals to God *as Judge*, "Awake to help me, and behold!" (v. 4b)—examine the facts ("behold") and act to help ("Awake").
- He appeals to the Lord as the God of *the covenant* that he would sustain his covenant people against the "wicked transgressors" who dismiss God with a contemptuous "Who hears?" (vv. 5–7).
- He affirms his conviction that God is *sovereign* and will, as he promises, "have all the nations in derision" (v. 8; Ps. 2:4). God's enemies "will in the end become his footstool (Ps. 110:1; 1 Cor. 15:24–25)." This is what will happen if the wicked stick to their guns!
- He confesses his *personal faith* in the Lord as Savior: "O my Strength, I will watch for you, for you, O God, are my fortress. My God in his steadfast love will meet me; God will let me look in triumph on my enemies"(vv. 9–10, ESV).

Recovery (vv. 11–17). Field Marshal Haig did not know that by April 11, 1918, the Germans had already run out of steam. Six months later, their line broken by Haig's armies at Amiens, the war ended. David's back would be to the wall again, many times, but he already knew that God had his back. Now, he has a new assurance of God's grace and a new confidence from the Lord. He prays for his enemies that God, in overthrowing them, would "let them know that God rules in Jacob to the ends of the earth" (v. 13). And whatever will happen, he will praise the Lord: "But I will sing of Your power; yes, I will sing aloud of Your mercy in the morning; for You have been my defense and refuge in the day of my trouble. To You, O my Strength, I will sing praises; for God is my defense, My God of mercy" (vv. 16–17). Jesus assures his disciples, "Lo, I am with you always, even to the end of the age" (Matt. 28:20). Christian friend, Jesus has your back at all times.

PRAISE FOR PERSONAL SATISFACTION IN THE LORD
Sing Psalm 59:13–15

THINGS I WILL PRAY FOR TODAY

May 1
Defeat into Victory

A prayer for the victory of God's cause

Through God we will do valiantly, for it is He who shall tread down our enemies. —*Ps. 60:12*

READ PSALM 60

One of the great memoirs of World War II is *Defeat into Victory* by Field Marshal Sir Willam Slim, recounting the re-conquest of Burma from the Japanese by his British/Indian 14th Army in 1943–45. The campaign it describes follows a pattern often seen in war—and in human experience. First comes the initial shock with its setbacks, followed by slow recovery and protracted struggle, before achieving ultimate victory. Psalm 60 dates from the time of Israel's warfare that culminated in her famous victory in the Valley of Salt (2 Sam. 8:13). This military conflict both echoes and illustrates spiritual warfare of all sorts, for even in physical struggles, "we do not wrestle against flesh and blood, but against principalities, against powers, against the rulers of the darkness of this age, against spiritual hosts of wickedness in the heavenly places" (Eph. 6:12). How Israel prays when faced with enemy armies supplies a standing model for prayer in response to all that wars against both body and soul in a world fraught with opposition to God. The prayer of the psalm is in three parts:

Praying the problem (vv. 1–3). Three kingdoms attack God's people and the latter are not having an easy time of it. When bad things happen, we tend to look for a reason and someone to blame. Too few of us ask whether God might be telling us something about ourselves. Some commentators see the statement "O God, You have cast us off" (v. 1) as a complaint that God is being unjustly hard on them. David, however, appears to accept that God is justifiably "displeased" with them—for unspecified reasons—and is letting them "stew in their own juices" to humble their hearts and concentrate their minds. He doesn't shift the blame in any way, even to the heathen enemies, whose worthiness of divine judgment can be assumed for the usual reasons. When God in his providence shows us "hard things" and makes us "drink the wine of

244

confusion," (v. 3) self-examination and not blame-shifting is the godly response. Israel needed to wake up to her own sin! "Before I was afflicted I went astray, but now I keep Your word" (Ps. 119:67).

Praying the path of hope (vv. 4–8). The hope is in "the banner" God has given to those who fear him, and that banner is God—*Jehovah-nissi*—"the-Lord-is-my-banner" (Ex. 17:15). That banner is to be "displayed because of the truth"—that is, not because of any merit of ours, but because of God's free grace and faithful promises (v. 4). Ultimately it points to Jesus, the "Root of Jesse, Who shall stand as a banner to the people; for the Gentiles shall seek Him, and His resting place shall be glorious" (Isa. 11:10). Then, with the prayer that God save his people (v. 5), David refers to Israel's history in which God divided the land (v. 6), installed his people there (v. 7), and subdued their enemies, who were formidable, but to the Lord were no more than a pot for washing his feet, a slave to pick up his shoes, and a lot of noise (v. 8). Our hope is in the Lord who is the hearer of prayer.

Praying the prospect of victory (vv. 9–12). Prayer is a pathway, not a destination. The psalmist asks: "Who will lead me to Edom?" If Israel is—and if we are—to "move forward into broad, sunlit uplands"of a victorious peace, then two things must happen after prayer: one is that "God give us help from trouble" and that "through God we will do valiantly." And our doing valiantly is at no point independent of God's upholding grace. That was the lesson of Israel's victory at Rephidim, where they fought hard, but prevailed only as Moses's arms were held up by Aaron and Hur, which afterward occasioned Moses's naming the altar of sacrifice "Jehovah-is-my-banner" (Ex. 17:15). So also shall Christ our Banner "tread down our enemies" and turn our defeats into victories by his saving and sovereign grace.

PRAISE REJOICING IN ISRAEL'S RESTORATION
Sing Psalm 60:6–12

THINGS I WILL PRAY FOR TODAY

_____

_____

_____

_____

_____

_____

May 2
Our Only Rock and Shelter

A prayer asking God to lead us to the Savior

When my heart is overwhelmed; lead me to the rock that is higher than I.
—Ps. 61:2

READ PSALM 61

There are more than 2,500 castles in Scotland. My favorite since childhood is the seemingly impregnable Tantallon Castle on a rock with the sea on three sides and landward walls 50 feet high and 12 feet thick. These magnificent ruins, however, bear witness to the ultimate failure of every artifice of earthly security to deliver lasting security. They testify to our yearning for safe places to shield us from the trials of a troubled world—including the distresses of soul and spirit. Since David was king at the time of writing (v. 6), this prayer must be connected with his flight from Absalom (cf. 2 Sam 17:1–4). Whatever security arrangements he had did not stop Absalom's *coup d'etat*. His life was threatened and he knew that he needed a better rock, shelter, and strong tower than any earthly fastness could provide (v. 3).

The psalmist turns to prayer and not only shows us a pattern for our prayers, but also reveals *how the Lord deals with us*—specifically with the believer who is struggling with an "overwhelmed" heart:

> The Lord *draws him to seek a hearing for his prayer.* "The best expedient for a sad soul," writes David Dickson, "is to run to God by prayer for comfort, and to insist earnestly, albeit God should seem not to attend: *hear my cry, O God, attend unto my prayer*" (v. 1). You may be "overwhelmed" in your heart, but you have recourse in the prayer, "Lead me to the rock that is higher than I" (v. 2)—to the Lord who is the "rock of our salvation" (Ps. 95:1; cf. 18:2, 46; 62:2, 6–7; 89:26)—the "Rock" who is Jesus Christ our Savior, if we are his (1 Cor. 10:4)!

> The Lord *enlarges his trust in God* as he prays. He acknowledges what God has been to him up to now—a "shelter" and a "strong tower" (v. 3)—and goes on to declare what he will be to God from now on—a worshiper who "will abide in [God's]

246

tabernacle forever," and a disciple who "will trust in the shelter of [God's] wings" (v. 4). Believing prayer is a means of grace and we grow in grace as we pray.

⊰ The Lord *deepens his assurance of everlasting communion* with God as he prays (vv. 5–7). In this, David is led "to look to one higher than himself, even to Jesus the Rock of his salvation [Ps. 89:19]." These words reach beyond David's life and reign to the Messiah "of [whose] kingdom there shall be no end" (Luke 1:32–33).

⊰ The Lord puts *a new song on his lips*—a song of praise "forever" and practical faithfulness "daily" henceforth (v. 8). The "fervent prayer of a righteous man avails much," says James (5:16)— and nowhere more happily than in the desponding heart that is lifted by the ministry of God's Word and Holy Spirit, even in the course of a single prayer. The Lord is pleased to meet our prayers with his grace.

You don't need to be a famous public figure like David to be overwhelmed in your heart. This fallen world is a vale of tears, and we all are touched by personal setbacks and wrestle with spiritual troubles related to sin in ourselves and in others. The nearness of death can shake us to the core. Those who are "without God in the world" (Eph. 2:12), short of coming to faith in Christ, can only have "a certain fearful expectation of judgment, and fiery indignation which will devour the adversaries [of God]" (Heb. 10:27). Even those who love the Lord "will have tribulation"—but Jesus assures us he has "overcome the world" (John 16:33). Elsewhere David describes his sorrows in words Jesus later applies to his own sufferings in our place, "For my soul is full of troubles, and my life draws near to the grave" (Ps. 88:3; Matt. 26:38a). Our sufferings should lead us to Jesus's own sufferings in our place, to the cross as the atonement for our sin, and to Jesus our Savior and Lord as the Rock "that is higher than I."

PRAISING THE ROCK OF OUR SALVATION
Sing Psalm 61

THINGS I WILL PRAY FOR TODAY

May 3
My Soul, Wait Silently...

Prayerful meditation on confidence in God alone

My soul, wait silently for God alone, for my expectation is from Him.
—Ps. 62:5

READ PSALM 62

hen we are in trouble, our soul chatters to us," writes Tim Keller, "'We *have* to do this, or we won't make it. This *must* happen, or all is lost.' The assumption is that God alone will not be enough—some other circumstance or condition or possession is necessary to be happy and secure." Troubles should drive us to the Lord, rather than to distraction within ourselves. The arm of flesh—to mix metaphors—is a broken reed (Isa. 36:6). David, no doubt from hard experience, knew that frantic self-reliance is spiritual quicksand—the more you flail about, the deeper you sink. He understands what the Lord means when he says, "Cursed is the man who trusts in man and makes flesh his strength, whose heart departs from the LORD" (Jer. 17:5). The Lord has also taught him that the injunction to "be still and know that I am God" is spiritually *and emotionally* the place to be in a crisis (Ps. 46:10), and that it is "in returning and rest [toward 'the Holy One of Israel'] you shall be saved; in quietness and confidence shall be your strength" (Isa. 30:15; cf. 32:17).

The psalmist ponders his theme of silently waiting on God. In the silence of his soul, he talks to himself, to his enemies, to God's people, and finally to God himself. The written record is a model of waiting "silently" upon the Lord. This consists of three equal parts:

- Exercise quiet confidence in the God who saves his own from all the *enemies* that threaten them (vv. 1–4). The assaults, the plots, and the lies of wicked people will eventually be overthrown. Keep calm, trust God, and don't let circumstances drive you to despair. Jesus rules!
- Exercise quiet confidence in the God who *alone* is the refuge for his people (vv. 5–8). Waiting on the Lord is not stoical inaction. It means remaining stable in thought and deed (v. 6),

and it calls you to "pour out your heart" in prayer. This is not pious passivity, but active, godly self-control (Gal. 5:23). It is active discipleship to Jesus, who is the Rock of our salvation, the Rock who is higher than we (1 Cor. 10:4). In him, says David, "I can run against a troop" (Ps. 18:29).

> Exercise quiet confidence in the God who is both *powerful* and *merciful*, and do not trust in the futile schemes to which the godless resort to resolve their problems (vv. 9–12). Here is a stern caution against godless pragmatism. As Solomon reminds us, "Good understanding gains favor, but the way of the unfaithful is hard" (Prov. 13:15). "There is a way that seems right to a man, but its end is the way of death" (Prov. 14:12). Let us then "hope in God" (Ps. 42:11).

Perhaps you notice that Psalm 62 is a prayer without a single petition or thanksgiving? It is still a prayer, however, because the psalmist closes with a direct address to the Lord, "Also to You, O Lord, belongs mercy; for You render to each one according to his work" (v. 12). This implicitly asks us if we *personally* know the Lord as our rock and salvation (v. 6). It implies the question, "What are the consequences of rejecting or neglecting Christ as the sole source and foundation of your happiness and safety?" So asks Murdoch Campbell, who adds, "In answer we quote the Lord's own words: 'And whosoever shall fall on this stone shall be broken; but on whomsoever it shall fall, it will grind him to powder [Matt. 21:44].' Let this therefore, be our prayer; 'Lord, give me the wisdom to say, He only is my rock and my salvation.'" This in turn challenges us to strive to "rest in the LORD, and wait patiently for Him" and "not fret because of him who prospers in his way, because of the man who brings wicked schemes to pass" (Ps. 37:7). Look to Jesus, then, and "wait silently for God alone." And expect blessing in God's faithful promise of sustaining love for you in and through the Son of his love (1 John 4:9).

PRAISE FOR THE REST ONLY GOD CAN GIVE
Sing Psalm 62:1–8

THINGS I WILL PRAY FOR TODAY

_____

_____

_____

May 4
Early Will I Seek You

Prayer for both ends of the day

O God, You are my God; early will I seek You. —Ps. 63:1

READ PSALM 63

avid is in the "wilderness of Judah" after fleeing from Absalom's *coup d'etat* in Jerusalem. He is separated from the "sanctuary" where God is worshiped, but longs to be there (vv. 1–2). He can say, "My soul longs, yes, even faints for the courts of the LORD; my heart and my flesh cry out for the living God" (Ps. 84:2). Many people will say they like to "go to church," but how many "faint" for the worship of God's house? You can say, "I believe in God," but does your heart and flesh cry out for the living God? The pseudo-biblical aphorism, "Blessed is he who expects nothing, for he is never disappointed," is the self-fulfilling prophecy of the churchgoers who are "lukewarm, and neither cold nor hot"—and like the Laodiceans are in danger of being spewed out of God's mouth (Rev. 3:16)! The psalmist's positive encouragement is for all of us to begin and end every day in private extended communion with the Lord.

First thing in the morning, the psalmist seeks communion with God (vv. 1–5). Here we have a beautiful pattern for our personal devotions:

- This can only begin with a *personal relationship*: "my God" is the God who is "in covenant with me." He is my faithful Redeemer and I know him to be such in my heart, even if— perhaps especially when—I am crying out and saying, "with tears, 'Lord, I believe; help my unbelief!'" (Mark 9:24).

- This in turn issues in *prompt devotion*: "early" is the dawn of day (v. 1). We too easily get up in the morning without a serious thought of God, far less a conscious desire for his presence and the satisfaction of spiritual hunger (Ps. 55:17; cf. Prov. 1:28).

- The wilderness, "a dry and thirsty land," reminds David of *previous blessings*. In earlier times of spiritual drought, he says, "I have looked to You in the sanctuary, to see Your power and glory" (v. 2). Past blessings give hope of blessings renewed in time to come.

250

⌐ This in turn can only move the believer to *purposeful praise* (vv. 3–5). How so? Because even banishment from God's sanctuary—where he longs to be—cannot separate David from God! As Paul later says of all Christians, "neither death nor life, nor angels nor principalities nor powers, nor things present nor things to come, nor height nor depth, nor any other created thing, shall be able to separate us from the love of God which is in Christ Jesus our Lord." In Christ, we are "more than conquerors through him that loved us" (Rom. 8:37–39). And this is just at the beginning of the day, when we seek the Lord "early." "Weeping may endure for a night," says the Lord, "but joy comes in the morning" (Ps. 30:5). The psalmist's soul is "satisfied with marrow and fatness" and his mouth praises God "with joyful lips" (v. 5).

Last thing at night, the psalmist rejoices in God's faithfulness (vv. 6–11). He thinks on what has been a day of grace and makes his bed into a place of secret prayer, where, instead of tossing and turning in wakefulness, he closes with the Lord and is strengthened in several amazing ways. Because of going over and over what he had "heard, seen [and] felt of God's word [and] working," his "soul follows close behind" the Lord (vv. 6–8). This also reminds him of the ultimate overthrow of those who would threaten his life (vv. 9–10). And most wonderfully, he is encouraged by the prospect of rejoicing and glorying in the Lord, both for himself, and for all who "swear by Him"—in contrast to the sad fate of the unrepentant enemies of God (v. 11). "What encouragement," says Charles Simeon, "have all to seek after God!…O beloved! Know if you come to God by Christ, you shall never be cast out; and if you commit yourself in faith entirely to Christ, you shall rejoice in him with joy unspeakable, and receive in due time, the great end of your faith, even the salvation of your souls."

PRAISE REJOICING IN FELLOWSHIP WITH THE LORD
Sing Psalm 63

THINGS I WILL PRAY FOR TODAY

_____

_____

_____

May 5
God's Arrows of Victory

A prayer of one who is under attack

But God shall shoot at them with an arrow... —Ps. 64:7

READ PSALM 64

We tend to think that the youthful killer of Goliath was a fearless warrior. David's record is certainly amazing. From childhood scrapes with lions and bears, through warfare for and against Saul, to his many conflicts with Philistines and the like, we are inclined to think he was so "battle-hardened" that he was impervious to the terrors of the battlefield. It has been said that the hero dies once, but the coward a hundred times. Whatever the case, it is certain that both heroes and cowards experience fear. David is a genuinely heroic figure, but he is not ashamed to admit his fear and lay his anxieties before the Lord. In doing so, he provides a pattern for our prayers as we face similar vulnerabilities and share the same desire for relief, by God's grace, from the enemies of our soul. The psalmist takes us from the problem to its solution in four steps.

The threat recorded (v. 1). David's first action in his crisis is to turn to the Lord he loves and cherishes as his Savior. He seeks a hearing for what is on his mind ("my meditation") and his reason for asking ("fear of the enemy"). That includes his enemies themselves, of course, but also involves the potential effect of terror within himself. This was not a theoretical threat. It was an ever-present challenge to his heart, which he could not handle without supernatural help from his heavenly Father. He invariably responded in very practical ways to the needs of the moment—like choosing five smooth stones to sling at Goliath and pretending insanity to escape Achish (1 Sam. 17:40; 21:11–15). But the core is actively depending upon the Lord. His love for the Lord who first loved him takes him to the throne of grace, for grace to help in his times of need (Heb. 4:16).

The threat detailed (vv. 2–6). David goes on to give specific reasons for his dramatic plea. "Workers of iniquity" make "secret plots" against him, "sharpen their tongue like a sword" and "shoot their arrows—bitter words" (vv. 2–3), hoping that no one will see them because they have "perfected a shrewd scheme" (vv. 4–6). Character assassination is their chosen way of "destroying David without soiling their hands with his blood." And you don't have to be famous to be the victim of this species of murder (Matt. 5:22; 1 John 3:15).

The deliverance detailed (vv. 7–9). God, however, can—and David expects will—redress injustice with his arrows of victory, by which justice will be achieved. His arrows are also words—not "bitter," but righteous and "sharper than any two-edged sword" (Heb. 4:12). One edge overthrows the wicked, who will "stumble over their own tongue" (i.e., choke on their words) and "flee away" (vv. 7–8). The other edge cuts the consciences of those who "fear" and see in this "the work of God," having been led to "wisely consider His doing" (v. 9). Righteous reckoning will come sooner or later, and, as Jesus makes so clear, every single sinner will repent—or perish (Luke 5:1–5)!

The deliverance celebrated (v. 10). The application to the godly targets of conspiracy is to "be glad" in anticipation of the Lord's preserving their life and to "trust in Him" and give "glory" to his name. In a world where conspiracies real and imagined perennially terrify people, let us look to the Savior who prevails for his people:

> Fierce may be the conflict, strong may be the foe,
> But the King's own army none can overthrow;
> 'Round His standard ranging, victory is secure,
> For His truth unchanging makes the triumph sure.
> Joyfully enlisting, by Thy grace divine,
> We are on the Lord's side—Savior, we are Thine!

PRAISE FOR ANTICIPATED DELIVERANCE
Sing Psalm 64

THINGS I WILL PRAY FOR TODAY

May 6
Let the Nations Be Glad!

A prayer for the conversion of the nations

Oh, let the nations be glad and sing for joy!—Ps. 67:4

READ PSALM 67

his most exalted of prayers has been described as "perfectly balanced," principally because its seven verses are arranged on a *chiastic*, or crossover, pattern (A1-B1-C1-D-C2-B2-A2), with three parallel thoughts fore and aft of the central masthead prayer of the whole psalm (in v. 4). The logic of it all is that verses 1–3 announce the *prospectus* of the prayer; verse 4 expresses its central *plea*; and verses 5–7 reveal the *promise* hoped for at a time yet future. The very elegance of this presentation serves to emphasize the astounding content of the message, for, notes David Dickson, this song is "a prophetical prayer for a blessing upon the church of the Jews, for the good of the Gentiles and the enlargement of the kingdom of Christ among them." The psalmist's prayer is that the time would hasten when *all the peoples of the world*—not just the Jews—would come to rejoice in the rule of the promised Messiah: "Oh, let the nations be glad and sing for joy! For You shall judge the people righteously, and govern the nations on earth" (v. 4). Here is a glorious example of how to pray today for the nations, peoples, and communities of the world.

The prospectus of the prayer asks God to show mercy to "us"—the Jewish church of the psalmist's day—and that this "salvation" be known "among all nations"—i.e., not just among "us" ethnic Jews, but also among "them," the Gentile nations, who are hitherto "aliens from the commonwealth of Israel" (cf. Eph. 2:12; vv. 1–3). Here in the middle of the Old Testament is a prophecy of the worldwide conversion of the peoples of the world! This prayer is timeless and its prospect of the spread of gospel grace is the great purpose of God for this world all the way to Zephaniah's "great day of the Lord" at the end of history (Zeph. 1:14; cf. Jude 6; Rev. 6:17; 16:14). This is the core meaning of human history—the extension of the kingdom of God's promised anointed Messiah/Christ in days yet future at the time of the writing.

The plea of the prayer is that "the nations be glad and sing for joy." Notice that two very practical reasons are given for this joy. One is that the Lord "shall judge the people righteously," and the other is that he will "govern the nations on earth" (v. 4). Billions of people in the world most certainly do not presently want, far less rejoice in, the rule of God's King: the Lord Jesus Christ. And the more militant unbelievers—especially the political elites, ancient and modern—have a recurrent tendency to "take counsel together, against the LORD and against His Anointed, saying, 'Let us break their bonds in pieces and cast away their cords from us'" (Ps. 2:2–3). But God saves sinners. He overthrows wickedness. The world is not without the evidence of the power of God to salvation in the lives of those who are being saved by grace through faith in the Son of God—or the discomfiture of the erstwhile enemies of God. Christians, we are not on the losing side!

The promise of the prayer (vv. 5–7). "God shall bless us," says the psalmist of God's people in his day. "And all the ends of the earth shall fear Him," he says of the age to come, which has now come in our time and will come in fullness in the Great Day yet future. Meanwhile, our prayers today too often focus on ourselves, our immediate circumstances, and our little circle of friends and acquaintances; the great purpose of God is buried under a mountain of parochial personal preoccupations. But should it not be the most natural thing for we who know the Lord, having experienced his saving grace in Christ, to desire that same saving grace for the lost and unbelieving world around us and beyond us? Surely outreach must be a first priority in prayer, if it is to bear any fruit in practice. Pray then that the nations would be glad and sing for joy in the same Jesus, in whom we rejoice "with joy inexpressible and full of glory" (1 Peter 1:8).

PRAISE FOR THE SAVING OF NATIONS
Sing Psalm 67

THINGS I WILL PRAY FOR TODAY

May 7
Messiah's Broken Heart

A prayer prophetic of Jesus's sufferings for our salvation

Reproach has broken my heart.—Ps. 69:20

READ PSALM 69

he Psalms have been called "the Songs of Jesus," not merely because Jesus sang them, or because, as "the Word...made flesh" he was involved in their inspiration, but because they all point us to Jesus, and some explicitly prophesy his advent. This is the particular glory of Psalm 69. While it records something of David's adversities, the psalm also "touches a depth of sorrow which can only apply to one greater than David, even the eternal Son of God." The New Testament quotes more verses of this psalm than of any other, and these lead us to nothing less than the sufferings of Jesus.

The psalmist offers *importunate prayers* (vv. 1–21). Nowhere in Scripture, excepting Jesus's prayer in Gethsemane (Luke 22:44), are prayers more deeply felt or persistently and passionately pressed. David is brokenhearted over unjust rejection and besieges heaven for relief: "Save me, O God!" (v. 1); "O God, You know my foolishness" (v. 5); "Deliver me out of the mire" (v. 14); "Draw near to my soul, and redeem it....I looked for someone to take pity, but there was none" (vv. 18–20). You can surely identify with David. But there is more here. David prophetically anticipates the broken heart of the sinless, suffering Servant of the Lord. Verse 4 is absolutely true of Jesus's experience: "They hated Me without a cause" (John 15:25). Verse 9a speaks to Jesus's expelling the money-changers from the temple: "Then His disciples remembered that it was written, 'Zeal for Your house has eaten Me up'" (John 2:17). Verse 9b (also vv. 7, 10) anticipate Jesus's general deportment in his self-sacrificial ministry, for "even Christ did not please Himself; but as it is written, 'The reproaches of those who reproached You fell on Me'" (Rom. 15:3). And, not least, verses 20–21 are fulfilled at the cross—alone, uniquely, and exclusively—in the sufferings of Christ as the atoning sacrifice for sin in sinners like you and me (Matt. 27:34, 48; John 19:29). Here is why Jesus prayed as at Gethsemane; why he is a Savior able to save; and why there is a gospel of saving grace both calling all men everywhere to repent and assuring us that whoever calls upon the name of the Lord will be saved!

The psalmist announces *imprecatory predictions* (vv. 22–28). This further prophetic word underscores the urgency of responding in faith to the God of grace. Verses 22–23 are quoted in Romans 11:9–10 to emphasize the danger of rejecting the Lord: "And David says, 'Let their table become a snare and a trap, a stumbling block and a recompense to them. Let their eyes be darkened, so that they do not see, and bow down their back always.'" Verse 24 surfaces in Revelation 16:1: "Then I heard a loud voice from the temple saying to the seven angels, 'Go and pour out the bowls of the wrath of God on the earth.'" Finally, verse 25 specifically applies to the judgment of Judas Iscariot—and by implication all who betray the Lord—"For it is written in the book of Psalms: 'Let his dwelling place be desolate, And let no one live in it'" (Acts 1:20). Judgment is coming to the world of the unrepentant unbeliever!

The psalmist finally exults in *infinite praises* (vv. 29–36). Why? Because while we are great sinners, God's Christ is a great Savior. Jesus bore sins not his own, suffered reproaches due to any and all but himself, and bore brokenhearted the very wrath of God against sin—doing so because God himself loved the world so much as to send his Son to save his people from their sins! This love is as unfathomable as it is underserved: "Greater love has no one than this, than to lay down one's life for his friends" (John 15:13). We are loved more than we know! "Behold what manner of love the Father has bestowed on us, that we should be called children of God!" (1 John 3:1). And shall those who "love His name" (v. 36) not praise their loving Savior who, having suffered in our place, is forever "enthroned in the praises of Israel" (Ps. 22:3)?

PRAISE FOR THE GOD WHO SAVES HIS PEOPLE
Sing Psalm 69:30–36

THINGS I WILL PRAY FOR TODAY

_____

_____

_____

_____

_____

May 8
Make Haste to Help Me!

A desperate prayer for help in a tight corner

Make haste, O God, to deliver me! Make haste to help me, O Lord!
—Ps. 70:1

READ PSALM 70

he seventieth psalm is a standalone version of David's prayer in Psalm 40. In that psalm, he records his thoughts on past deliverances from whatever were the "horrible pit" and "the miry clay" (40:1–12), and follows with a prayer for fresh help in a new tight corner (40:13–17). The latter passage is now reissued with a few verbal adjustments, to provide a prayer suitable to all new crises in all our lives, in all times and seasons. Princeton theologian Addison Alexander suggests we think of Psalm 70 as "a kind of appendix to the sixty-ninth and preface to the seventy-first," presumably because it acts as a bridge between the experience of suffering for the faith described in Psalm 69, and the desire to remain faithful into old age stated in Psalm 71. Realtime, and lifelong, vulnerability is foremost in the psalmist's mind here. The psalm's title is "to bring to remembrance," which calls us to reflect on our past troubles whenever new ones arise and remember how the Lord helped us when we called out to him in these troubled times.

"Make haste, O God, to deliver me!" is the overarching theme. It is a cry of *anguished urgency* (vv. 1–3). Troubles remind us, sometimes most painfully, that we are not actually in control of our lives, even when we feel, humanly speaking, that things are going well and we have everything in hand. David's very life is threatened, so his invoking the active intervention of the Lord is a legitimate act of self-defense: "Let them be ashamed and confounded who seek my life; Let them be turned back and confused who desire my hurt. Let them be turned back because of their shame, who say, 'Aha, aha'" (vv. 2–3). We are free to call upon the Lord in any circumstances that unjustly threaten our well-being, "since it is a righteous thing with God to repay with tribulation those who trouble you, and to give you who are troubled rest with us when the Lord Jesus is revealed from heaven with His mighty angels, in flaming fire taking vengeance on those who do not know God, and on those who do not obey the gospel of our Lord Jesus Christ" (2 Thess. 1:6–8). Psalm 70, like Psalm 69, is an "imprecatory" psalm, in which the Lord assures his people of his justice in their behalf.

This naturally raises a question about the frame of mind we bring with our requests during prayer (vv. 4–5). We are not to come to the throne of grace in a graceless spirit of anger against men or God. However deep the waters we travel through, we come to the God in whom we can—and must and will—rejoice. Notice the three reasons and motivations for this urgent prayer:

> We want *above all* for God to be glorified: "let those who love Your salvation say continually, 'Let God be magnified!'" Believing prayer will issue in rejoicing and gladness in our precious Savior.

> We come acknowledging that we are "poor and needy"—not bitter people who are offended, angry, and, in modern parlance, "demanding our rights." No, we are debtors to mercy in our Lord Jesus Christ.

> We confess personally from the heart to our Redeemer, "You are my help and my deliverer." Jesus assures us that "whatever things you ask in prayer, believing, you will receive" (Matt. 21:22). Believe it!

If you would have God "make haste" to help you, you should always be quick to seek him in prayer. We want God's answers yesterday. Sometimes he does answer immediately, but whether the Lord will "make haste" or teach us to wait patiently for him, let us remember that he is always *applying perfectly* his personal promise, "I will never leave you nor forsake you" (Heb. 13:5).

A SHORT SUNG PRAYER FOR A PRESSING CRISIS
Sing Psalm 70

THINGS I WILL PRAY FOR TODAY

_____

_____

_____

_____

May 9
When the Almond Tree Blossoms

A prayer for the Lord's support in old age

Now also when I am old and grayheaded, O God, do not forsake me.
—Ps. 71:9

READ PSALM 71

Solomon tells the young, "Remember now your Creator in the days of your youth, before the difficult days come, and the years draw near when you say, 'I have no pleasure in them'" (Eccl. 12:1). He then describes these difficulties in a series of wonderfully evocative images, one of which is "when the almond tree blossoms" (12:5). The blossoms come before the leaves and turn the trees spectacularly white, but in a few days they die and the tree returns to dead sticks. Gray hair is no doubt "the splendor of old men" (Prov. 20:29), but it marks the approaching end of this life. And this poses the ultimate questions as to where we are going and what *God* is doing in our lives. The psalmist is likely David in his old age, confined to his bed with hypothermia and confronted with a *coup d'etat* by his son, Adonijah (1 Kings 11ff.). In one sense, this is the same old story of his perennial struggles with his enemies, but here the unique complication is the weakness and weariness of old age. If this has not touched your experience yet, realize that one day, if the Lord spares you, the "almond tree" will blossom for you. Will it be for blessing or for curse? That is the issue.

The psalmist's prayer is yet another model for our response to the pressures we face or will be facing, particularly as we age. The prayer unfolds in five distinct parts, each with its own theme:

> ❧ Prayer seeks *deliverance* from the God who is our hope (vv. 1–4).
> ❧ Prayer confesses *faith* and commits to faithfulness (vv. 5–8).
> ❧ Prayer acknowledges human *weakness in old age* (vv. 9–13).
> ❧ Prayer confides in God's *strength for old age* (vv. 14–18).
> ❧ Praise anticipates God's *reviving grace*—forever (vv. 19–24).

Make this the order for your prayer today, whatever age you may be, and spare some kind thoughts for those known to you who are older.

260

For all its challenges, old age has its consolations—in the Lord. Loneliness is a common burden of the aged. Live long enough and you will outlive loved ones and friends (Ps. 88:18). Godly old folks are all the more concerned to be close to the Lord, for loss of the love and fellowship of the Lord is the most devastating loneliness of all. So David prays, "Do not cast me off in the time of old age…when my strength fails," and again, "Now when I am old and grayheaded, O God do not forsake me" (vv. 9, 18). And as he prays, you will notice how God gives rich encouragements to his soul. He rejoices in God's blessings from past to present: "You have taught me from my youth" and "to this day" he witnesses to God's "wondrous works" (v. 17). He desires that God continue to bless him in the future: "until I declare Your strength to this generation, Your power to everyone who is to come" (v. 18). He exults in the incomparable righteousness and greatness of God: "O God, who is like You?" (v. 19). He accepts that God was sovereign in his "great and severe troubles" (v. 20a), and believes he will also sovereignly revive him again and comfort him "on every side" (vv. 20b–21). And he worships the "Holy One of Israel"—surely a glimpse of Christ—and praises God for answered prayer in the salvation of his soul and the overthrow of his enemies (vv. 22–24).

This brings us back to the almond tree blossom. The almond blossoms in winter and bears fruit the following autumn. It is first to bloom and last to bear fruit. Being "old and grayheaded" has a promise of fruit to come—for those who know the Lord as their Savior. God allowed Jeremiah to see "a branch of an almond tree" and said to him, "You have seen well, for I am ready to perform My word" (Jer. 1:11–12). The almond—blossom and fruit, year after year—is given as a symbol of God's faithfulness. That which marks our passing from this life calls us in Christ to the fruition of the life to come.

PRAISE FOR GOD'S GRACE IN OLD AGE
Sing Psalm 71:9–15

THINGS I WILL PRAY FOR TODAY

May 10
Behind a Frowning Providence

A prayer for the embattled church

O God, why have You cast us off forever? Why does Your anger smoke against the sheep of Your pasture? — Ps. 74:1

READ PSALM 74

The term "providence" is much misunderstood. Some assume that *God's* providence implies that bad things ought not to happen to them. Others, seeing bad things happening, will deny the very existence of God, arguing that a good God could not and would not exercise a providence allowing the evils we see in the world. In their view, a providence that does not provide good things is not provision, but deprivation. *Larger Catechism* 18 offers the biblical corrective to these common misconceptions when it says, "God's works of providence are his most holy, wise, and powerful preserving and governing of all his creatures; ordering them, and all their actions, to his own glory." Yes, God is sovereign over all things, good and bad, in this sin-sick world (Eph. 1:11), and the same things, good and bad, happen to the righteous and the wicked (Eccl. 9:2). However, God is not the author of sin (we humans are), and what he does in his providence is to govern all things so as to preserve *his believing people* through whatever happens to them, good or bad. As a result, all things will in the end work together for their good and nothing will separate them from his love (Rom. 8:28, 38–39). Yes, providence can be hard and, so to speak, frown on us; but on the other hand, God will give the victory to his own people for his own glory and for their inexpressible joy (1 Peter 1:8). This is the message of the two main parts of Psalm 74.

The first part of the psalm is a litany of unrelieved woe (vv. 1–11). The state of the church is so dismal that the psalmist, Asaph, asks God if he has not cast his people off "forever." The sanctuary in Jerusalem and "all the meeting places of God in the land" are devastated (vv. 1–8), the faithful ministry has ceased to function (v. 9), and there is no sign that God will rectify this wretched situation (vv. 10–11). Down through history, faithful remnants have cried to God in circumstances that seem to indicate the death of the church—and that God is judging her for her backslidings. On November 28, 1666, at a place called Rullion Green, 900 persecuted Scots Covenanters faced certain defeat by King Charles II's professional army, and then sang this very prayer: "O God, why hast Thou cast us off? Is it forevermore? Against Thy pasture-sheep why doth Thine anger smoke so sore?" That day indeed brought defeat, and persecution would continue for some twenty-five years! Well might the Lord's people wonder if God had cast them off. But it was not so. And it never will be so, as this prayer now indicates.

The second part of the psalm strikes a brighter note (vv. 12–23). The keynote is Asaph's affirmation, "For God is my King from of old, working salvation in the midst of the earth." He recounts God's sovereignty in history as this touched God's people under various adversities in the past (vv. 13–17)—as if to say to us all, "We experienced many frowning providences before our present disaster, and we eventually saw that God was at work *for us* in all these troubles." Every bit as much, he might have added, as in the balmy days of obvious blessings. This leads to the prayer—confident in tone—that God deliver his beloved people from their enemies, keep his own covenant, plead his own cause, and deal with those who oppose him and oppress his suffering servants (vv. 18–23). The point is that, under discouragements, we must walk by faith and not by sight (2 Cor. 5:7). Let us then remember with the poet William Cowper—who was no stranger to deep discouragement—that we must

> Judge not the Lord by feeble sense,
> But trust Him for His grace;
> Behind a frowning Providence,
> He hides a smiling face.
> —"God Moves in a Mysterious Way"

A PRAISE-PRAYER THAT GOD DEFEND HIS OWN CAUSE
Sing Psalm 74:12–23

THINGS I WILL PRAY FOR TODAY

_____

_____

_____

_____

May 11
Complaint and Consolation

A prayer wrestling with a sense of God's displeasure

And I said, "This is my anguish; But I will remember the years of the right hand of the Most High."—Ps. 77:10

READ PSALM 77

When bad things happen, we naturally wonder why, and all sorts of emotions rush in: depression, anger, self-pity, blame-seeking, and blame-shifting. What marks out the Christian's response is that he cries out to the Lord in his troubles (Ps. 107:4–6). But there is no stiff upper lip, silent resignation in the biblical record of the saints' responses to their predicaments. "Out of the depths I have cried to you, O Lord," is not a cold, stoical announcement of a little local difficulty (Ps. 130:1). This is the normal reaction of the soul to the "day of trouble" (v. 2). And perhaps central to that is an undefined sense of God's displeasure and a question as to what his hand is in these woes. The prayer of this psalm answers this question by opening up the interrelated themes of complaint (vv. 1–9) and consolation (vv. 10–20).

What are we to do with our complaints? The key is in the words "I cried out to God with my voice" (v. 1). Prayer ought to be our first stop. But remember: spoken prayers are not magic spells. The proof of prayer is mostly discovered in patient persistence (Eph. 6:18). Notice how Asaph (the psalmist) has to work at his praying: At first, he has *no comfort* (vv. 2–3). The more he prays, the more intense is his frustration. Consolation seems more remote as his "spirit was overwhelmed." But he doesn't quit! He also has *no sleep* (vv. 4–6). His thoughts rush desperately about the problem, but there is no answer and no "sweet oblivious antidote" to quiet the groaning and confer restful sleep. He feels *alone* (vv. 7–9). Perhaps you wonder if God has abandoned you or perhaps you even question his existence? For Asaph, this is when "his temptation was at its height." He says: "Will the Lord cast off forever...be favorable no more? Has his mercy ceased...His promise failed....Has God forgotten to be gracious... in anger shut up his tender mercies?" Is this not true to real Christian experience? When the Lord is slow to answer, we are quick to despair. But the answer is to keep crying out to the Lord until he settles your heart and mind.

How will we acquire the consolation we seek (vv. 10–20)? You first need to *understand the problem*. When Asaph admits, "This is my anguish" (v. 10a), he accepts reality, without denial or shifting the blame to the Lord! He doesn't wallow in the slough of his despond, but sticks with the bedrock biblical truth about God and his ways. Like Job, he turns from what he sees and feels to his faith about God's truth; "Though He slay me, yet will I trust in Him" (Job 13:15; cf. Hab. 3:17–18; Heb. 11:1). Are you a believer in Jesus? Then consolation begins with trusting your Savior.

Now, and only now, are you in a position to take practical measures to regain your spiritual equilibrium (vv. 10b–20). Asaph looks back on what God has done in his life in the past. We too must do this:

- Remember *God's goodness* to you, "the years of the right hand of the Most High" (v. 10b). Can you recall happy providences, covenant promises fulfilled, answered prayers, and blessings?
- Consider *God's works* (vv. 11–12). "Remember…meditate… talk." The Lord's track record is written in his Word, stamped upon his creation and can be discerned in your life.
- Ponder *God's provision of a Savior* (vv. 13–15). His way is "in the sanctuary," that is, in the provision of atoning sacrifice for sin. He redeems his people by grace. Do you know Jesus as your Savior?
- Celebrate *God Himself* (vv. 16–20). He made and superintends his world, and he shepherds his people through the crises of life. The God who led his people from Egyptian slavery "like a flock by the hand of Moses and Aaron" will bring you through your Red Seas. Like the psalmist, you will rediscover by faith that God's "anger is but for a moment, His favor is for life; weeping may endure for a night, but joy comes in the morning" (Ps. 30:5).

May the Lord so bless you.

PRAISE TO THE GOD WHO DOES US GOOD
Sing Psalm 77:1–10

THINGS I WILL PRAY FOR TODAY

May 12
Where Is Our God?

A prayer for the revival of God's church

Judge me, O Lord, according to my righteousness. — Ps. 79:8

READ PSALM 79

n a sermon entitled "A Christian's Exercise under Desertion," the seventeenth century Scottish preacher Andrew Gray observes that "it is ordinary for God's people to reason from dispensation to relation." He is saying that we tend to define our *relationship* to the Lord on the basis of the "dispensation" or *circumstances* of the moment. When bad things happen to us, we are tempted to wonder if God really loves us, or if he has forgotten us (Isa. 49:14) — or even if he does not exist! At the very least, we reproach him for what seems an injustice. This, says Andrew Bonar, is the "cry of widowed Zion to the Righteous Judge." Psalm 79 shows us how to deal with such circumstances and the temptation to doubt the goodness of God; it offers a four-step remedy.

Step #1 — Face the facts before the Lord (vv. 1–4). The psalm fits with the Egyptian sack of Jerusalem (1 Kings 14:25–26). Thus was the church made a "reproach" and "a scorn and derision" before the watching pagan world. It was a judgment on her spiritual backslidings. You can see this today in the decline of churches that preach "a different gospel," which "pervert[s] the gospel of Christ" (Gal. 1:6–7). This reminds us that the sins of professed believers have often "given great occasion for the enemies of the Lord to blaspheme" (2 Sam. 12:14). If the shoe fits, we need to wear it — and honestly examine ourselves as to whether we are "in the faith" (2 Cor. 13:5).

Step #2 — Accept that God is justified in his judgments (vv. 5–8). The bedrock truth here is that God is just and has his good reasons for everything that he permits to happen in our lives (v. 5). Accepting that, however, does not make bad things good or exempt those who did these bad things from God's justice. It does not make it improper to pray for justice and relief. The Old Testament church brought a lot of trouble upon itself, but the nations who attacked her were not innocent. That they "do not know" God means they consciously and willfully denied him (vv. 6–7). For ourselves, we pray for the Lord to have mercy upon us: "Let your tender mercies come speedily to meet us, for we are brought very low" (v. 8). These were the dying words of the great Puritan John Owen on August 24, 1683. See 1 Peter 4:17–19 for pointed practical application to your soul and your pattern of life.

Step #3 — Seek forgiveness by God's appointed means (vv. 9–12). Cry to the Lord, pleading the glory of his name as a motive for his help (v. 9a). Plead also his provision of atonement for sin, since you cannot earn forgiveness by your best efforts (v. 9b). Plead for his presence and power, that he would preserve those "appointed [by enemies] to die." Why should the godless have successes to boast about and to fortify their hostility to God and his people (vv. 10–12)?

Step #4 — Commit yourself to faithful worship and witness henceforth (v. 13). With this verse, says Bonar, "melody from freed souls bursts upon our ears." The sad, embattled tones of the previous verses are overwhelmed by a powerful anticipation of God's gracious answer to prayer. "We, Your people and sheep of Your pasture" exult in union with the Lord as the covenant God who loves us. That God's people can say "we...will give You thanks forever," testifies to the fact that this prayer is already beginning to be answered in their hearts, even before it is completed! Furthermore, "We will show forth Your praise to all generations" answers the taunting of the godless when they sneer, "Where is your God?" (Ps. 42:3, 10) The Lord is indeed with us — and forever! The psalmist turns full circle. Now he argues from his Savior to his circumstances, instead of the other way round. Where is our God? Jesus assures us, "I am with you always" (Matt. 28:20).

PRAISE IN ANTICIPATION OF REVIVAL
Sing Psalm 79:8–13

THINGS I WILL PRAY FOR TODAY

_____

_____

_____

_____

_____

May 13
Shepherd of Israel

A prayer for restoration and redemption

Give ear, O Shepherd of Israel... — Ps. 80:1

READ PSALM 80

Given the state of the world—and the experience of the church—it is not surprising that fully one-third of the Psalms are described by scholars as "Songs of Lament." The modern Gadarene rush of many churches to set aside biblical morality in favor of what Scripture calls the standards of a "debased mind" (Rom. 1:28) can only move God's people today, with Asaph the psalmist, to lament and appeal that the Lord would revive the visible church in these days. Psalm 80 appeals via a series of questions in which the psalmist boldly asks the Lord if he is not the "Shepherd" of his people, if they are not his "vine," and if therefore he will not then save them.

Question one: "Lord, are you not the 'Shepherd of Israel'?" **(vv. 1–7).** God shepherded his flock in the past (vv. 1–2). Past blessings offer confidence to cry to the Lord for present help. This appeal has three parts: a *plea* for restoration—"Restore us"; the *means* of restoration—"cause Your face to shine"; and the outcome of restoration—"come and save us" (v. 3). The same appeal is made three times—in verses 3, 7 and 19. But God still shepherds his flock *in the present.* For Israel, that involved his withdrawing his blessings, chastising the backsliders, and shaming the church before her enemies (vv. 4–6). This is how the Lord recalls those who "turn from the truth" (Titus 1:13–14), so that they would seek the Lord in prayer that he might cause his face to shine upon them (v. 7). We all should pray daily to this end.

Question two: "Lord, are we not Your 'vine'?" **(vv. 8–16).** Asaph records three truths the church of his day needed to grasp:

> ◇ The church is *the recipient of God's grace* (vv. 8–11). She is "a vine out of Egypt" planted in God's land, with deep roots and boughs that spread from the Mediterranean Sea to the River Euphrates (v. 11). This is the glory of the church expressed in the language of prophecy.

> The church had *backslidden from God's grace* (vv. 12–13). Like a grapevine, the church is planted to bear fruit. God "expected it to bring forth good grapes, but it brought forth wild grapes.… For the vineyard of the Lord of Hosts is the house of Israel.… He looked for justice, but behold oppression; for righteousness, but behold, a cry for help" (Isa. 5:1–7). God's vineyard was a disappointment to him, as Jesus observes in Matthew 21:33ff.

> The church needed a fresh *visitation of God's grace* (vv. 14–16). The psalmist pleads the Lord's sympathetic presence—that he "return…look down…and visit" his vine as the one who owns it and loves it. Surely when he disapproves of our behavior and subjects us to his frowns of rebuke (vv. 15–16), the desire of a believing heart and conscience is to cry, "LORD, lift up the light of Your countenance upon us" (Ps. 4:6).

Question three: "Lord, will you not save us?" (vv. 17–19). How will this happen? The answer is, by "the man of Your right hand…the son of man whom You made strong for Yourself" (v. 17; cf. Ps. 8:4). Andrew Bonar notes that, while these terms are appropriate to "Israel as God's favoured people…the real possessor of the name ['son of man'] is Messiah, God's true Israel." Christ is the Savior. Only Christ! The crucified Christ "who was delivered up for our trespasses and raised for our justification" (Rom. 4:25; cf. 2 Cor. 5:21). Thus revived by God's grace in our hearts, we "will not turn back," and "will call upon [the Lord's] name" (v. 18). The final prayer joyously anticipates the Lord making his face to shine upon us (v. 19). God "is light, and in Him is no darkness at all" (1 John 1:5), and Jesus, the man of his right hand, is the Light of the World, the Great Shepherd of the Sheep, and the true Vine (John 8:12; Heb. 13:20; John 15:1), who is also able "to keep you from stumbling, and to present you faultless before the presence of His glory with great joy" (Jude 24).

A PRAISE-PRAYER FOR THE CHURCH'S REVIVAL
Sing Psalm 80

THINGS I WILL PRAY FOR TODAY

May 14
Conspiracies Confounded

A prayer that conspiracies against God's people be frustrated

Fill their faces with shame, that they may seek Your name, O LORD.
—*Ps. 83:16*

READ PSALM 83

Conspiracies are often treated as thrill rides for the mind —as long as they don't get too serious. Much conspiracy theorizing is silly, but the truth is that terrorists, criminals, and enemies conspire and we would be foolish to ignore the reality that our world abounds in conspiracies. "The kings of the earth rise up…" (Ps. 2:2). Spiritual warfare is waged all around us—even within us (Eph. 6:12). The devil goes looking for victims he may "devour" (1 Peter 5:8). The theme of real conspiratorial threat and how it will be confounded is addressed in this psalm.

See our great danger (vv. 1–8)! The backstory seems to be a war waged by Ammon, Moab, and Edom against Judah in the reign of King Jehoshaphat, c. 850 BC. With the enemy poised to invade, Jehoshaphat proclaims a fast and calls God's people together to seek the Lord (2 Chron. 20:3–4). Asaph, the psalmist, likely penned this prayer for that gathering. He begins, "Do not keep silent, God" (v. 1), implying that Judah's greater peril—than even invasion—is "that God will remain a silent onlooker in this time of danger and distress." "If You are silent to me," says David, "I become like those who go down to the pit" (Ps. 28:1). Judah's enemies are rightly seen as attacking God and his cause (vv. 2–4). They take "crafty counsel," aiming to "cut…off" the covenant people of God (vv. 5–8). Not for the first time, or the last, it is life or death for God's people. You can understand how Christian minorities in many places today must view their situation under persecution.

Strike a blow for justice (vv. 9–15)! The psalmist first appeals to how God helped Israel in the past (vv. 9–12). He defeated the armies of Midian, Sisera, and Jabin, who "became as refuse on the earth." He cut down powerful leaders like Oreb, and Zeeb, and Zebah and Zalmunna (Judg. 7:25; 6:21). God confounded these conspiracies!

He prays that God will likewise bring down his and their enemies in the present (vv. 13–15). "Make them like whirling dust…chaff before the wind…fire [in the] woods…flame [on] the mountains…tempest [and] storm." It is gutsy and realistic. We need not apologize for such an energetic prayer. Did David the shepherd use pepper spray against the lion, or a stun gun against Goliath? "The Lord is a man of war" (Ex. 15:3), and when Jesus comes on the Great Day, will it be with gentle persuasion or *force majeur*? The "lake of fire" is not a luxury home for exiled reprobates (Rev. 20:11–15).

Save us and even our enemies (vv. 16–18)! Here is an Old Testament anticipation of Jesus's teaching, "Love your enemies" (Matt. 5:44). Notice the two goals of the intervention of God that Asaph asks for:

> Goal #1 is that "they may seek Your name, O Lord" (v. 16). The connection is fear and shame, resulting in seeking the Lord. No judgment should be sought from God without a prayer for mercy for the sinners that they might be ashamed and come to the Savior. No one comes to the Lord without a sense of shame.

> Goal #2 is that everybody may know "that You…are the Most High over all the earth" (vv. 17–18). God will be glorified, whether you follow him or flee from him. His *pleasure* is to save sinners to himself! This brings us full circle to the greatest danger of all: the silence of God. Believers pray that the Lord will arise and not be silent, hold his peace, or be still (v. 1). The lost want the opposite: that God would shut up and leave them alone. But the silence of God is a judgment in itself: for God says to those who ignore him and go their own way, "I will break the pride of your power; I will make your heavens like iron and your earth like bronze" (Lev. 26:19). All conspiracies will be confounded. Therefore, cry out to God in and through Christ the Savior. Come to him—and live now and forever!

PRAISE SEEKING THE OVERTHROW OF GOD'S ENEMIES
Sing Psalm 83

THINGS I WILL PRAY FOR TODAY

May 15
Tabernacles of Grace

A prayer rejoicing in the public ordinances of worship

How lovely is Your tabernacle, O LORD of hosts!—Ps. 84:1

READ PSALM 84

You sometimes hear church members saying things like, "I am *thinking* of going to church this Sunday," "I'll be coming to church *more often*," and the ever popular, "The Bible doesn't say we have to go twice on Sunday." Contrast these sayings with the passion of the psalmist when he longs to be in the Lord's house. The idea in verse 1 is, "How loved and lovely is Your dwelling place." This "tabernacle" recalls the "tabernacle…in the wilderness," that portable tent that was a temporary dwelling of God (Acts 7:44). Its holiness, loveliness, and love-worthiness were not in its architecture, materials, or location as such, but in the "holy ordinances" of worship, for, notes Matthew Henry, "the beauty of holiness is spiritual, and their glory is within." The psalmist's prayer teaches us how to view worship and prepare the heart-attitude that honors the Lord and blesses our souls.

Longing for God's house (vv. 1–4). The psalmist isn't "in church." He is far from Jerusalem. His heart and mind turn to the temple, to his desire to be there to worship the Lord. Three fragrant themes absorb his thoughts and form his prayer:

> God's house is where God *promises to be present* (v. 1). True, "the Most High does not dwell in temples made with hands" (Acts 7:48–50), but it is to corporate worship that he promises his presence (see Ex. 25:22). It is no accident that the church of the New Testament begins in the temple, with the Holy Spirit's outpouring (Acts 2).

> God's house is where God *meets with his people* (vv. 2–3). Peter's envy of the birds that nest in the temple precincts announces, "I wish I could be there all the time." The reference to God's "altars" recalls the altars of sacrifice and of incense—the former pointing to Christ's sacrifice in our place, and the latter to Christ's heavenly intercession for us.

272

❧ God's house is *the believer's spiritual home* (v. 4). There we are blessed by the Lord and are moved to praise. Don't you love to worship Jesus? This is our glorious privilege from here to heaven and forever! Indifference surely tells another, darker story?

Loving to go to God's house (vv. 5–7). Our enthusiasms reveal what we really love. Going to church because you "have to" is no evidence of love for the Lord. On the other hand, those "in whose heart are the highways [to Zion]" are blessed in their *resolve* to worship God, for they knows their strength is in the Lord (v. 5, ESV). They are blessed in the *rewards* of faithfulness, which turns dry dusty "Baca" to a "spring" and a place of "pools," i.e., public worship is not a chore, but a joy (v. 6). They are blessed in being *reinforced* "from strength to strength" as active faith brings growth, "grace upon grace" (v. 7a; John 1:16). And they are blessed when they *reach* the church and "each one appears before God in Zion" (v. 7b). Public worship is no mere option on a Sunday morning, but is where Jesus meets us in his means of grace.

Living in God's house (vv. 8–12). The psalmist tells us what this means. He mentions God's hearing of our *prayers* (v. 8); his provision of *a Mediator* (v. 9), who is his "anointed Messiah" in whom "a day" is "better than a thousand in the tents of wickedness" (v. 10); his *promises* of light ("sun") for our darkness, strength ("shield") for our weakness, "grace and glory," and every "good thing" (v. 11); and his *preservation* of those who are trusting in him (v. 12). The point is that this grace in God's Anointed, Jesus Christ, will both last a whole lifetime and prepare us for the glory of the eternal Zion. When Thomas Halyburton (1674–1712) was on his deathbed, he asked for the singing of Psalm 84. Afterwards he said, "I had always a mistuned voice, a bad ear, but which is worst of all, a mistuned heart. But shortly when I join the temple service above, there shall not be, world without end, one string of the affections out of tune." Praise God for the tabernacles of grace!

PRAISE FOR GOD'S GIFT OF PUBLIC WORSHIP
Sing Psalm 84

THINGS I WILL PRAY FOR TODAY

_____

_____

_____

May 16
Unite My Heart

A prayer for a single-minded grasp of the unique God

Teach me Your way, O LORD; I will walk in Your truth; unite my heart to fear Your name. —*Ps. 86:11*

READ PSALM 86

ndecision can be a killer. Elijah asks Israel, "'How long will you falter between two opinions? If the LORD is God, follow Him; but if Baal, follow him.' But the people answered him not a word" (1 Kings 18:21). When the psalmist says, "I hate the doubleminded, but I love Your law," he is expressing the danger of doubt that is a deadly denial of God's Word masquerading as intellectual honesty or superiority (Ps. 119:113–120; cf. Ps. 12:2; James 1:8). We are not told what was troubling David, but whatever the case, the help he seeks involves being singleminded about God's uniqueness (vv. 8–10). This is a prayer for those times when we are assailed by doubts, uncertainties, and confusion. It comes in three parts; two prayers for help, each of seven verses, fore and aft of a central mast to which the psalmist nails the colors of his faith in three verses of singlehearted praise to the God of free and sovereign grace.

All prayer presupposes a felt need of supernatural help (vv. 1–7). David realizes he is "poor and needy," implying his inability to deliver himself (v. 1). He is a believer (v. 2); he has prayed "all day long," seeking joy for his troubled soul (vv. 3–4); and, affirming God's goodness and forgiving character, he prays expectantly for God's mercy in his trials (vv. 5–7). David understands what Jesus teaches us in connection with the Lord's Prayer when he says, "Your Father knows the things you have need of before you ask Him" (Matt. 6:8). Help is at hand, if we will but lift up our souls to our Father in heaven.

Believing prayer comes to the God who is alone able to help us (vv. 8–10). David shows us why we can trust him. God is unique *in himself* as the Creator (v. 8). He really exists. He "made the heavens" (Ps. 96:5). All other gods are idolatrous illusions. God is also unique in his lordship over all nations, and the Savior who will gather in the nations is able to deliver his people (v. 9; Ps. 22:27–28). And God is unique *in his acts in human history* and in our individual experience. It takes spiritual discernment to admit this. It takes love for Christ to experience his grace. "You alone are God" (v. 10) is the conclusion of both revealed truth and Christian experience.

Practical prayer seeks a single-minded grasp of God and his revealed truth (vv. 11–17). There are two main arenas for this prayer:

> ◌ We need to pray about our *inner spiritual life* (vv. 11–13). David makes two requests toward two purposes: "Teach me Your way" so that "I will walk in Your truth"; and "Unite my heart" so that I "fear Your name" (v. 11). Sound doctrine leads to sound practice, and single-mindedness in this makes for unmixed love for the Lord. Before you can walk in the truth cleanly, you need to know the truth clearly. Then, with God's help, you will commit to actions consistent with a life of wholehearted praise (v. 12a); a lifelong celebration of God's great name (v. 12b); and a solid confession of God's free grace in your Savior (v. 13). This is the engine of the triumph of grace in our thinking, and wisdom in our choices, as we strive to walk humbly with our God (Mic. 6:8).

> ◌ We also need to pray about *the outward challenges* to our life (vv. 14–17). Spiritual warfare is real. In the red corner (so to speak), we have the "proud…violent" and godless opponent (v. 14). In the blue corner is the Lord "full of compassion…gracious, longsuffering and abundant in mercy and truth" (v. 15). Prayer is directed to the Lord, "*Turn*…have *mercy*…give *strength*…*save*… show me a *token for good*" (vv. 16–17). The progression is: come to me, strengthen me, save me, and vindicate me. This is where prayer as a means of grace comes into its own, for even before it is finished, we have a real sense that the Lord has already answered: "Lord, You have helped me." This is a prayer for hard times in life. It calls you to Jesus Christ, to a united heart, "casting all your care upon Him, for He cares for you" (1 Peter 5:7).

PRAISE TO THE LORD WHO UNITES MY HEART
Sing Psalm 86:11–17

THINGS I WILL PRAY FOR TODAY

May 17
The Darkness of Blackness

The prayer of one overwhelmed by dark experiences

I have been afflicted and ready to die from my youth; I suffer Your terrors; I am distraught. — Ps. 88:15

READ PSALM 88

lackness Castle is a grim little fortress in Scotland notable for not being ruined after nearly 600 years and for serving as a prison for persecuted Presbyterians in the seventeenth century. Lady Culross wrote to a victim of the time, reminding him that "the darkness of Blackness is not the blackness of darkness"—the latter referring to Jude's description of reprobates as "wandering stars for whom is reserved the blackness of darkness forever" (v. 13). This touches Psalm 88, for the psalmist is going through his own "darkness of Blackness." Many psalms wrestle with troubles and end on a rising note, but only this one begins on a high note and quite literally ends "in darkness" (v. 18)—not, however, the "blackness of darkness" of a lost eternity in hell, but the dark experiences of a believer pointing us to the cross, where Jesus, the man of sorrows, suffered the deepest darkness to save sinners.

We have a window here on how a godly man, drowning in troubles, cries to God for help in his distress. Here is grace for our distress also:

First, he asks the Lord for a *hearing* (vv. 1–9a). He does so as a man of personal faith and persevering prayer: the Lord is the "God of my salvation" (v 1). Alas, this is the high point of his prayer—all that follows is a litany of his terrible troubles, but it shows us how to pray from the heart when our faith is under pressure:

> He cries to God with a *trusting humility* of mind (v. 2). Verses 1–2 are like Psalm 22:1–2, where Jesus cries (from the cross) to his Father, "My God, My God, why have You forsaken Me?"

> He tells how "down" he is with *sorrow of soul* (vv. 3–5). He is "adrift among the dead," a pointer to Jesus facing the cross: "My soul is exceedingly sorrowful, even to death" (cf. Matt. 26:38a).

> He expresses *submission of heart* to God's dealings with him (vv. 6–9a). The key is in verse 7: "Your wrath lies heavy

upon me." This reminds us of Job (Job 13:5) and points to Jesus. "It is the very tone of Gethsemane," says A. A. Bonar. "'Nevertheless, not my will.'"

Second, he asks the Lord for *help* (vv. 9b–12). He testifies to being "steadfast, in spite of sorrows." His posture suggests desperation: "I have stretched out my hands." His petition confirms this and basically says, "Save me—I am like a dead man!" His supporting arguments are simple enough. How will he praise God in this life if he just withers and dies? How will God's "lovingkindness…faithfulness…wonders…and righteousness" be manifested in this world by corpses (vv. 10–12)? The point is that, if I am "dead" in my woes, how can I experience life in my God—and testify to his grace to me (Ps. 119:116)?

Finally, he begs the Lord to *stick with him* (vv. 13–18). In spite of dejection, he has "kept the faith" (vv. 13–14). God has not replied so far, so he feels somewhat rejected, but he clings by faith to God as his Redeemer. His request is that the Lord come into his loneliness of soul and deliver him from his troubles. He speaks of "terrors," of being "distraught," of being submerged in God's "fierce wrath," and of being isolated from friends and loved ones; but he knows God is the key to his trials (vv. 15–18). In all these sorrows, however, he never wavers in trusting the Lord. George Horne (1730–92) is surely right to say, "We hear in this psalm the voice of our suffering Redeemer." Jesus is that suffering Savior by whose stripes all who receive him as Savior will be saved (Isa. 53:5; 1 Peter 2:24). He is the helper for our helplessness.

Abide with me; fast falls the eventide;
The darkness deepens; Lord with me abide;
When other helpers fail, and comforts flee,
Help of the helpless, O abide with me.
—"Abide with Me," Henry Lyte, stanza 1

READY TO LISTEN WHEN GOD SPEAKS
Sing Psalm 88:9b–18

THINGS I WILL PRAY FOR TODAY

May 18
Crown and Covenant

A prayer appealing to God's covenant promise

My covenant I will not break. — Ps. 89:34

READ PSALM 89

The certainty of God's covenant promise to save his people, and his absolute sovereignty over all things, do not mean this world is suddenly turned into heaven. Sin still lives in believing hearts (Rom. 7:23). Trouble still afflicts the just (Amos 5:12). Even if Jesus is our Savior, "sin lies at the door" (Gen. 4:7). We know God keeps his covenant (v. 34), but our circumstances sometimes make it seem as if God's covenant has been abrogated (vv. 38–39)! God is sovereign, but evil exists. This is the gnawing tension the psalmist wrestles with in this prayer. You will notice that he does not trot out a list of bare requests. Instead, he aims to *persuade* God to restore his blessings to his people by appealing to his covenant of grace and his character as "the God of all grace" (1 Peter 5:10). Here is a model for our prayers, particularly when we find ourselves in "deep waters" (Ps. 69:2, 14).

Lord, you are merciful and faithful to save your people (vv. 1–4). His mercies are "established in the very heavens" in the person of the "seed" of David (v. 4) — God's "son" whose "throne" is established "forever" (2 Sam. 7:14–16). He is the promised "seed" of Abraham (Gal. 3:16), Jesus the Mediator between God and man (1 Tim. 2:5), who secures salvation for sinners. Therefore, first remind the Lord of his covenant love and mercy as a reason for showing his mercy to you.

Lord, you are mighty to save your people (vv. 5–18). He is the Lord of incomparable power and glory. We will always "fall short of the glory of God" (Rom. 3:23), but his glory is in heaven (vv. 5–8); on earth (vv. 9–13); seen in his actual mercy and truth (v. 14); and in his redeemed people (vv. 15–18). Therefore, remind the Lord of his glory in creation and redemption as an argument for relieving your distresses.

Lord, you solemnly covenanted to save your people (vv. 19–37). In this covenant, God promises his "holy one" salvation (vv. 19–20); victory over enemies (vv. 21–23); mercy and faithfulness (vv. 24–25);

exaltation as God's "firstborn, the highest of the kings" (vv. 26–27); and a kingship, lasting "as the days of heaven" because he is the "seed" who "shall endure forever" (vv. 28–29). This clearly reaches way beyond David. It is "the covenant between God the Father and the Lord Jesus"—the "counsel of peace" (Zech. 6:13), in terms of which Jesus is the Savior by whom the divine covenant is kept for sure and for all who believe upon him (vv. 30–37). Therefore, remind the Lord of what Jesus has done to secure salvation (Rom. 4:25) and ground your hope in him.

Lord, remember us in our low state (vv. 38–52). The psalmist wonders if God has "renounced" his covenant (cf. vv. 34, 39). The answer is no! But he is teaching us that he will not reward unbelief and expects evidence of living faith in our lives. The psalmist therefore goes on to appeal to the Lord's mercy and love for restoration and redemption here and hereafter (vv. 46–52). Again we are pointed to Christ, for David cannot bear the weight of these prayers and promises. Only Jesus can be our covenant-head and therefore our Savior and Lord. Remember what the man born blind says when he is told Jesus *of Nazareth* is passing by— he cries out, "Jesus, *Son of David*, have mercy on me" (Luke 18:37ff., emphasis added). He knows that the crown of heaven and earth is given to Jesus, and that in him all the promises of his covenant are unbreakable— even "Yes, and in Him Amen, to the glory of God" (2 Cor. 1:20). "Blessed be the Lord forevermore!"

PRAISING GOD FOR HIS COVENANT OF GRACE
Sing Psalm 89:1–6

THINGS I WILL PRAY FOR TODAY

_____

_____

_____

_____

_____

_____

_____

_____

_____

_____

May 19
The Lord Does Not See!

A prayer for the curbing of evil in the earth

"The Lord does not see, nor does the God of Jacob understand." —Ps. 94:7

READ PSALM 94

A decided atheist once said to me, "If I am right and there is no God, it will make no difference to you; but if you are right and there is a God, then I will be in real trouble." The godless have to hope there is no God—or if there is, that "the Lord does not see" (v. 7). Bold sinners will openly mock the Lord and "deny God's government of the world, banter his covenant with his people, and set judgment to come at defiance." But even believers can wonder if God sees what is going on, and ask, "Lord...how long will the wicked triumph? (v. 3). The Lord's seeming inaction tests his faith and leads him to *express the need* to God and *expect an answer* from him.

Express the need to God (vv. 1–11). Notice the three steps here:

- The psalmist begins with *a cry to God* for help (vv. 1–3). "As long as the wicked are getting away with their crimes," notes Eric Lane, "God is hidden from view: he is not seen as Judge of the earth." But God is the judge "to whom vengeance belongs," and his "judgments are in all the earth" all the time (Ps. 105:7). True, there will be weeds (evildoers) and wheat (godly folk) in the world until the last judgment (Matt. 13:30). But because vengeance "belongs to the Lord, it is right to pray that he "shine forth" and "rise up" in his righteousness (v. 1)—albeit according to his timetable.

- He continues with *reasons* supporting the appeal (vv. 4–7). Wickedness works along three lines. People boast of being sinners (v. 4), target God's people and the vulnerable (vv. 5–6); and thumb their noses at God (v. 7). You hear people dare God to strike them with lightning and then cite their "survival" as proof that he is powerless, if he exists at all. It all needs an answer.

- He closes with a *warning* to gainsayers of the consequences of shrugging God off (vv. 8–11). "Get real!" is the thrust—you are out of your mind if you think you can escape God's justice (v. 8). The God who created your ears and eyes, hears and sees you (v. 9). He who gave law to nations, will "correct" them (v. 10a). And the omniscient God knows your "futile" thoughts (vv. 10b–11)! Death and judgment are sure things! But so also is salvation to all who "eagerly wait for Him" (Heb. 9:27–28). The Lord also saves all who trust and follow after him!

Anticipate an answer from God (vv. 12–23). Notice the steps:

◇ God assures us that his justice will be done (vv. 12–15). He knows, loves and blesses his own (v. 12; 2 Tim. 2:19). If he digs a pit for the wicked, he plans rest from "days of adversity" for believers (v. 13). He punishes the wicked, but never casts off his elect people (v. 14) and confirms this in their practical heart-experience of his goodness (v. 15).

◇ God's people will be empowered to be faithful (vv. 16–19). The psalmist recounts his testimony in three salient points: the Lord saved me in the past (v. 17); he answered prayer (v. 18); and he turned my anxieties to rejoicing—rising to a rhapsody of praise, he exults, "Your comforts delight my soul." (v 19).

◇ God's actions call the world to take him seriously (vv. 20–23). God will not cozy up to a "throne of iniquity" [government], "which devises evil by law" [justice-perverting legislation] (v. 20). He will be the "defense" and "rock of...refuge" of his saints (vv. 21–22). All that will be left for the unrepentant and unbelieving will be the fruit of their iniquity—to be cut off from God forever (v. 23). God is warning us—and calls us to repentance and faith in his Savior Son. The Lord sees through all of us all of the time. And this begs the question: "What does he see in you?" A heart of stone? Or a heart for Christ your Savior—even "Christ in you the hope of glory" (Col. 1:27)?

PRAISE TO GOD THE RIGHTEOUS JUDGE
Sing Psalm 94:1–15

THINGS I WILL PRAY FOR TODAY

May 20
The Church that Christ Builds

A prayer of an afflicted man

For the LORD *shall build up Zion; He shall appear in His glory.*
—*Ps. 102:16*

READ PSALM 102

he Jews were exiles in Babylon for approximately 70 years (605–538 BC). Psalm 102 expresses the mourning of the remnant of God's people at a time when the worship of God had all but vanished from the earth. The rebuilding of "Zion" (v. 13) and the restoration of temple worship (v. 21) was the prayer of the exiles. The New Testament, however, identifies this psalm as descriptive of Christ (see Heb. 1:10–12 quoting Ps. 102:25–27), which makes it messianic "in the strict sense."

Alec Motyer aptly asserts, "In Psalm 102 we stand beside our incarnate Lord Jesus, and walk with him through a dark valley into the light of assurance with which the psalm ends." A. A. Bonar sees here "Messiah's complaints and comforts in the days of his humiliation." This prayer unfolds in three steps.

The first (vv. 1–11) is the psalmist's wrenching cry of his felt weakness—"I wither away like grass" (v. 11). The third (vv. 23–28) revisits this theme, but rises to the beautiful conclusion, "The children of Your servants will continue, and their descendants will be established before You" (v. 28). Between these passionate cries of a hurting soul, the psalmist turns from his present need and sorrow, to future revival and joy (vv. 12–22) and treats us to a ringing affirmation of God's glory and grace in the church that God's Messiah is building (see Matt. 16:18).

Second is the building of the church in this world (vv. 12–17). This begins with the fact of the eternal God, whose name will be remembered to "all generations" (v. 12). This truth heralds a new day for the church, when God "will arise and have mercy on Zion" at a "set time" when he will "favor her" (v. 13). This rebuilding (v. 14) will cause the nations and their rulers, respectively, to "fear the name of the Lord" and the manifestation of his glory (vv. 15–16). This is God's answer to "the prayer of the destitute"—the despised, and the "weak things of the world" who flee to the Lord for salvation (v. 17; 1 Cor. 1:27). And this continues as Jesus carries out his Great Commission—"I will build My church" (Matt. 16:18)—until he returns at the end of history. Whatever the difficulties, and even setbacks from time to time, the Lord continues to build his church in the line of the generations of his covenant people. Pray for your church and for mission churches at home and abroad—and see God answer.

The final glory of the church in the world to come (vv. 18–22). The psalmist's prayer looks further ahead than the historical repatriation of the exiled Jews from Babylon to the eschatological expectation of the church. Where is the church going? In the first instance, to embrace "a people yet to be created"—an organization hitherto unseen in the world (v. 18). This is surely fulfilled when "the Gentiles shall come to your [i.e., the faithful Jewish church's] light" (Isa. 60:3) in the era of the "Zion of the Holy One of Israel" (Isa. 60:14; cf. Ps. 116:10ff.), which is the church of Jesus the Messiah in the New Testament era of gospel grace. But it reaches further still, to the salvation of "the prisoner" and those "appointed to death" (in Hebrew, literally "the sons of mortality," vv. 19–20), and on to the final "gathering" of God's people in the heavenly Jerusalem (vv. 21–22). There is a timeless air of expected blessing here, for every generation while the world lasts. This our prayer and also our promise, for Jesus, "as the author of [our] salvation, is able to bring many sons to glory where they shall live in his presence (Heb. 2:10)." Will you pray with holy confidence as Jesus builds his church in our day?

PRAISE FOR THE CHURCH JESUS IS BUILDING
Sing Psalm 102:11–17

THINGS I WILL PRAY FOR TODAY

283

May 21
The Accuser's Danger

A prayer for retributive justice upon God's adversaries

Let my accusers be clothed with shame. —*Ps. 109:29*

READ PSALM 109

od tells us that "it is a fearful thing to fall into the hands of the living God" (Heb. 10:31). Why is this so? Because he also tells us, "All our righteousnesses are like filthy rags; we all fade as a leaf, and our iniquities, like the wind, have taken us away" (Isa. 64:6). The seriousness and urgency of this truth is nowhere more graphically applied than in this most imprecatory of all the psalms. On the face of it, there seems far more "tough" than "love" here, and this, notes Alec Motyer, has led it to be "condemned by commentators as not only lacking but contradicting the spirit of Christ and the Gospel." Motyer calls this "an unthinking reaction," noting that the psalmist expresses *love* for his enemies and *prays* for them (v. 4); lays the problem of their wickedness before God for *his disposition* (as Paul does in Romans 12:19); and never indulges in "vengeful thoughts," which would indeed be "incompatible with the profession of love and the practice of prayer." When he cries for God's justice, he does so with a heavy heart because he knows what that will mean for those who are determined to work their wicked ways (Deut. 19:16–19). And he knows that even God's sternest warnings carry an implicit call of grace for all who have ears to hear (Jer. 18:7–8; cf. Isa. 55:3). The psalm unfolds in three steps that will lead us all as we wrestle through the tension between the wicked injustice of man and the righteous justice of God.

Step #1 sets out *where the suffering believer is coming from* **(vv. 1–5).** He is attacked with "lying" and "words of hatred" and persecuted "without a cause" (v. 3). Being unable to turn matters around, the believer therefore rightly turns to divine justice as his only possible source of relief and redress. He does not seek revenge, but rather asks that God would work his perfect will in the interest of his own glory and the blessing of his believing people—whatever that may be.

Step #2 is an appeal for God to *overthrow the gross injustices* **that occasion the suffering believer's cry for help (vv. 6–20).** All of the imprecations in this long list come down to an appeal to the fundamental principle governing the application of God's righteous justice as stated in the Law: "Then you shall do to him as he thought to have done to his brother; so you shall put away the evil from among you" (Deut. 19:19). David invokes God's doing this in order to put away the evil that he cannot do himself: God's retributive justice—not man's vengeful excess. One example will suffice here: verse 8 ("Let his days be few and another take his office") is declared in Acts 1:20 to be fulfilled in Judas's betrayal of Jesus. Judas's punishment is exactly what he intended for Jesus—a short life and deprivation of his office. Jesus had, of course, foretold Judas's apostasy and fall (John 13:18). *All of this warns every sinner, every accuser, every liar, etc., of his danger*—and, in the context of all Scripture, both tells us we need a Savior and implicitly invites us to flee to him in faith and repentance for salvation.

Step #3 is a petition for God to *effect the fullness of salvation in the suffering believer's life* **(vv. 21–26).** David prays to "the God of [his] praise," whom he will praise with his mouth and "among the multitude"—because the Lord "shall stand at the right hand of the poor, to save him from those who condemn him" (vv. 1, 30–31). The accusers' danger brings David afresh to the saving grace of God, to confess him as his Savior and to reaffirm his desire for deliverance from sin—that of others and of his own—and an unhindered joy of fellowship with his God. Let us look to the Lord and pray with the psalmist, "O my God, I trust in You; Let me not be ashamed; Let not my enemies triumph over me" (Ps. 25:2). He will surely keep his promise to you, child of God. And he will save all who heed his warnings to flee the wrath to come and believe upon "the Lamb of God who takes away the sin of the world" (John 1:29).

PRAISE FOR SALVATION FROM FALSE ACCUSERS
Sing Psalm 109:22–31

THINGS I WILL PRAY FOR TODAY

May 22
I Love the Lord!

A prayer of grateful love

I love the LORD, because He has heard my voice and my supplications.
—Ps. 116:1

READ PSALM 116

This psalm is for every child of God suffering deep trials, encouraging us to lift up our hearts to the Lord we love. From his opening, "I love the Lord," through to his closing, "Praise the Lord!" (v. 19c), we see how the psalmist receives powerful proofs in his soul of God's love for him. And between these two simple, yet profound, affirmations, we are shown both the root (vv. 1–8) and the fruit (vv. 9–19) of the trial and triumph of faith in those who "wait upon the Lord" and discover that the Lord really does "renew their strength" so that they can again "mount up with wings like eagles...run and not be weary...walk and not faint" (Isa. 40:31).

The root of the life of faith is not our love for God within ourselves, but God's love extended to us in his sovereign and saving grace (vv. 1–8). "God is love" and "We love Him because He first loved us" (1 John 4:15–19). Furthermore, when by grace through faith we receive his love and return it, we discover reasons for loving him all the more.

The Lord hears our prayers (vv. 1–4). Our English version begins, "I love the Lord." While this states the general sense of the verse, it diminishes the passion of the Hebrew, which says, "I love, because the Lord..." (v. 1). Love grips the psalmist's soul because the Lord loved him enough in the past to listen to his prayers! Hence his strong conviction: "Therefore I will call upon Him as long as I live" (vv. 1–2). Now he is at "death's door" and cries out in confident hope of a hearing: "O Lord, I implore You, deliver my soul!" (vv. 3–4). Love gives wings to our prayers and stirs our hearts with hope (Rom. 5:5a).

The Lord is merciful to us (vv. 5–7). It is his nature, for he is both "gracious" and "righteous." In him, "righteousness and peace have kissed" (Ps. 85:10). And in his timing, "grace and truth came through Jesus Christ" and accomplished our salvation (John 1:17). This in turn gives us reason to rejoice (v. 6) and cause to quiet our souls, saying, "Return to your rest, O my soul, for the LORD has dealt bountifully with you" (v. 7). He pledges himself to "rest in the Lord" (Ps. 37:7).

The Lord delivers his people and the psalmist's testimony is already that the Lord has kept his "soul from death, [his] eyes from tears, and [his] feet from falling" (v. 8)—now, in time, and hereafter, in eternity (Ps. 73:23–24). O the love of the God who is love!

The fruit in the life of faith is to "walk before the Lord in the land of the living"(vv. 9–19). God later tells us, "As you have therefore received Christ Jesus the Lord, so walk in Him" (Col. 2:6), thus:

> ⋗ The Christian walk begins with personal faith that draws our hearts to trust ourselves to our divine Savior: "I believed, therefore I spoke," whether to profess devotion (v. 9) or confess frailty (vv. 10–11).

> ⋗ The Christian walk deepens with awareness of personal "benefits" from the Lord that move us to "take up the cup of salvation and call upon the name of the LORD" (vv. 12–13).

> ⋗ The Christian walk thrives in purposeful discipleship: "I will pay my vows to the LORD now in the presence of all His people. Precious in the sight of the LORD is the death of His saints" (vv. 14–15).

> ⋗ The Christian walk issues in grateful praise to the Lord he loves (vv. 16–19), and all this in the "glorious liberty of the children of God" (Rom. 8:21). How is your love for the Lord? Jesus says of professed believers in these last days, "because lawlessness will abound, the love of many will grow cold" (Matt. 24:12). If so, will you ask the Lord to (re)light your "candle" (Ps. 18:28, KJV) and refresh the "love of God" that "is shed abroad in our hearts by the Holy Ghost which is given unto us" (Rom. 5:5b)? God's promise in Christ Jesus is, "Love never fails" (1 Cor. 13:8).

PRAISE FOR DELIVERANCE FROM DEATH
Sing Psalm 116:8–19

THINGS I WILL PRAY FOR TODAY

_____

_____

_____

287

May 23
Going Home

The prayer of one who feels so far from home

Woe is me, that I dwell in Meshech, that I dwell among the tents of Kedar. —Ps. 120:1

READ PSALM 120

This psalm is the first of the Songs of Ascent (Psalms 120–134), generally held to have been sung on the ascent to Jerusalem by those going up to worship God and observe the great feasts of the Jewish year. The first—Psalm 120—is the prayer of one who is far from home and in deep distress. The last—Psalm 134— is the praise of rejoicing worshipers who are now home in God's house invoking his blessing upon all his people. Between them are thirteen psalms that speak of the trials and triumphs along life's way. Before John Bunyan coined the phrase, this is "the pilgrim's progress" from the "wilderness of this world" to the city of God—the "Jerusalem above" (Gal. 4:16) of which the earthly Zion is foreshadowing. Psalm 120 is the prayer of a believer under attack, "like a sheep among wolves in his own country," whose "soul longs, yes, even faints for the courts of the Lord," and whose "heart and…flesh cry out for the living God," who alone can deliver him (Ps. 84:2). Here real life meets real faith.

The first step in prayer is to go to the Lord in some measure of a living faith (v. 1). Why? Because "without faith it is impossible to please Him, for he who comes to God must believe that He is, and that He is a rewarder of those who diligently seek Him" (Heb. 11:6), and "whatever is not from faith is sin" (Rom. 14:23). The psalmist does not merely list grievances, pour bitter reproaches upon others, obsess about his sufferings, or wallow in unrelieved self-pity. Still less does he blame God—as many people do. Rather, he remembers that, in the past, while in deep distress, he "cried to the Lord, and He heard me" (v. 1). Perhaps, like the father of a sick child, he "cried…'Lord, I believe; help my unbelief!'" (Mark 9:24). Or like Job, expostulated, "Though He slay me, yet will I trust Him" (Job 13:15). Prayer to God "if he exists" is practical atheism. The psalmist clings to the living God. And so must we

288

in the darkest of our trials, if it is only to "touch the hem of his garment" (Matt. 9:20; 14:36). It is "the prayer of faith" that has the promise of an answer (James 5:15).

The second step is to share your heart's desire with God (vv. 2–4). He is the *covenant* God ("Yahweh") who is committed to each believer, promising to give him "his heart's desire" and not withhold "the request of his lips" (Ps. 21:2). The request here is for deliverance from "lying lips" and "deceitful tongue"—from the culture of deceit that surrounds us and infects us. Obviously, that also begs the question as to the honesty and purity of our own lips and prayer requests. The covenant God is also the righteous God—something the psalmist recognizes when he points to the consequences of bearing false witness: "What shall be given to you, or what shall be done to you, You false tongue? Sharp arrows of the warrior, with coals of the broom tree!" (vv. 3–4). Our heart's desires must be holy before God.

The third step is to reflect on your personal need as it arises from your situation (vv. 5–7). The psalmist rues the time he has lived away from God's people in Meshech and the "tents of Kedar"—places north and south of Israel. When he says, "My soul has dwelt too long with one who hates peace," he is admitting he has been negatively affected by the culture around him. When he says, "Woe is me!" he is saying he needs not just outward physical deliverance, but inward spiritual recovery. He needs to go home to the Lord in every sense. In the modern world, our Meshechs are all around us, and it is Christian churches, families, and fellowship that are oases in the "wilderness of this world" through which we are passing. These all remind us that we are going home to the heavenly Jerusalem and the glory of Immanuel's land to be forever with our Lord and Savior, Jesus Christ.

READY TO LISTEN WHEN GOD SPEAKS
Sing Psalm 120

THINGS I WILL PRAY FOR TODAY

May 24
Joy in God's House

A prayer rejoicing in the church and her worship

I was glad when they said to me, "Let us go into the house of the LORD!"
—Ps. 122:1

READ PSALM 122

Are you glad when people exhort you to go to God's house with them (vv. 1-2)? Matthew Poole notes that the sense of the text is, "It delighteth me much to hear that the people, who had so long lived in the neglect or contempt of God's worship, were now ready and forward in it." When David penned this psalm, the worship of God had been revived and established in Jerusalem, after a long hiatus in which the ark of the covenant—above which God manifested his presence in a cloud of glory—was located in a private house some nine miles west of Jerusalem. Now, the tabernacle tent was installed at the center of Israel's life, signifying a spiritual revival among God's people. Public worship was received as a privilege and anticipated as a rich blessing. Above all, the Lord was once again present with his people to accept their worship and dispense his covenant promises. Israel had stopped wandering and had planted her feet to go into the house of the Lord. There was a new "love for the presence of God and for the fellowship of his people" that echoes down the centuries and calls us today to be "not forsaking the assembling of ourselves together, as is the manner of some, but exhorting one another —and so much the more as [we] see the Day approaching" (Heb. 10:25).

Are you enthusiastic about *being in God's house* **and worshiping him (vv. 3-5)?** The Jews went up to Jerusalem only a few times a year to participate in the three great pilgrimage feasts: Unleavened Bread/Passover, Weeks/Pentecost, and Tabernacles/Booths (Deut. 16:1–17)—and also the "Days" of Trumpets, Atonement, and, much later, Purim. The description of Jerusalem as "compact" and a gathering place for "the tribes of the Lord," secured by the "thrones of the house of David" is a type and foreshadowing of what Paul calls "the Jerusalem above" that is "free" and "which is the mother of us all" (Gal. 4:26). That is the heavenly

Jerusalem, writes A. A. Bonar, "where we shall meet none but friends, our own friends and friends of God—a city where the Lord's testimony is fully opened out, and his name praised—a city at whose gates judgment is truly given, and where 'a King reigneth in righteousness, and princes decree judgment' (Isa. 32:1)." Meantime, in this world we are called, like the Jews of old, to observe the Sabbath day wherever we live, with a "solemn rest" from our labors and a "holy convocation" together (Lev. 23:3). We are to love the services of our churches and enjoy God's means of grace for our rich blessing in time and eternity. "You are worthy, O Lord, to receive glory and honor and power" (Rev. 4:11).

Are you praying for the *peace and prosperity of God's house* **(vv. 6-9)?** "This lovely psalm," observes Murdoch Campbell, "expresses the joy, the prayer, and longings which dwell in the hearts of those who desire a better country and that city which God has prepared for them....[T]hey hoped and believed that in the Jerusalem which is above, they would all meet to go no more out. One great evidence of our being in the way of going to that glorious city is that there is nothing in this world that commands our concern or interest more than the prosperity of God's Zion and of all those who seek its good in every part of the world." The two great motives of this prayer for peace in the church on earth, modeled on the peace of heaven, are love for our "brethren and companions" (before ourselves) and love for the "Lord our God" (above all) whose "house" every true church, every true body of Christ, is (vv. 8–9; 1 Cor. 12:27). We are nowhere called to seek our own way in the church—the root of the strife that too often divides God's people—but rather to seek God's good for his house.

REJOICING TOGETHER AS HAPPY WORSHIPERS
Sing Psalm 122

THINGS I WILL PRAY FOR TODAY

May 25
Looking Upward Day by Day

A prayer for mercy in the face of the world's contempt

Unto You I lift up my eyes, O You who dwell in the heavens. —*Ps. 123:1*

READ PSALM 123

We are more powerfully affected than we know by the influences of the world around us. Even if we are sincerely working to keep ourselves "unspotted from the world" (James 1:27), God enjoins us, "Do not be deceived: evil company corrupts good habits" (1 Cor. 15:33). Why else does Paul exhort Christians, "Do not be conformed to this world, but be transformed by the renewing of your mind, that you may prove what is that good and acceptable and perfect will of God" (Rom. 12:2)? Our hearts are the issue. As Jeremiah reminds us, "The heart is deceitful above all things, and desperately wicked; who can know it?" (Jer. 17:9). And so, says the psalmist to himself, "Set a guard, O Lord, over my mouth; keep watch over the door of my lips. Do not incline my heart to any evil thing, to practice wicked works with men who work iniquity; and do not let me eat of their delicacies" (Ps. 141:3). Psalm 123 recognizes the baleful influence of the ungodly around us, whether in the community or in our work. But, as Alan Harman observes, "Whereas Psalm 120 focuses on God's ability to rescue, this one concentrates on his grace"—his grace sought and received. There are three simple applications here to our own exercise of prayer.

Look up to the Lord: "Unto You I lift up my eyes, O You who dwell in the heavens" (v. 1). Now, if God is everywhere, why does he direct us to lift our eyes to him? In Psalm 121, the pilgrims lift their eyes to *the hills*—the hills of Zion where God dwelt "above the mercy seat" of "the ark of the Testimony" (Ex. 25:22). In Psalm 123, we are to look directly to *heaven*, because it is his preeminent "dwelling place" (1 Kings 8:30, 39, 43, 49). Jesus teaches us to pray, "Our Father in heaven..." (Matt. 6:9). He is "the Majesty on high," who, with Jesus, his mediatorial King at his right hand, is ready to answer the prayers of his people and apply his mercy to their troubles (Heb. 1:3; 8:1). God wants you to look away from yourself, recognize you are no better than a "broken reed" (Isa. 36:6), and seek your help from "the Lord, who made heaven and earth" and "will keep your life" (Ps. 121:2, 7).

Expect blessing from the Lord: "Behold, as the eyes of servants look to the hand of their masters, as the eyes of a maid to the hand of her mistress, so our eyes look to the LORD our God, until He has mercy on us" (v. 2). Matthew Henry points out that the servant looks to the master's "directing...supplying...assisting...protecting...correcting...[and] rewarding hand." Surely that is what every employee worth his salt wants from his superiors. How much more the believer and his Savior God! Notice also his persistence: his "eyes look to the Lord...until He has mercy on us." Pray without ceasing (2 Tim. 1:3)!

Cast your burden on the Lord: "Have mercy on us, O LORD, have mercy on us! For we are exceedingly filled with contempt. Our soul is exceedingly filled with the scorn of those who are at ease, with the contempt of the proud" (vv. 3–4; cf. Ps. 55:22). When the psalmist looks *sideways*, or *inside* himself, he suffers the pain of the scorn and ridicule of those who deny and mock God. This hurts—not just for himself and God's faithful people, but for the besmirched honor of God, and the sad fact that the mockers themselves are hastening to a lost eternity with a laugh and a sneer. Jeremiah echoes this: "I did not sit in the assembly of the mockers, nor did I rejoice; I sat alone because of Your hand, for You have filled me with indignation" (Jer. 15:17). But like the psalmist he will lift his eyes to the Lord (see Jer. 20:7–13). And so must we...

Prayer is the burden of a sigh,
the falling of a tear,
the upward glancing of an eye,
when none but God is near.

PRAISE LOOKING UPWARD TO THE LORD
Sing Psalm 123

THINGS I WILL PRAY FOR TODAY

_____

_____

_____

_____

May 26
Forgiveness Is with You

Prayer from the depths of sin to the heights of salvation

But there is forgiveness with You, that You may be feared. — Ps. 130:4

READ PSALM 130

his short prayer is surely one of the richest passages in all Scripture. Opening with a cry from the depths of a stricken conscience, it swiftly leads to the sobering question: "If You, LORD, should mark iniquities, O Lord, who could stand?" (vv. 1–3). This answers itself. God's holy law stops every mouth and renders us all guilty, "for all have sinned and fall short of the glory of God" (Rom. 3:23). The psalmist is pondering the awful aching void of lostness and alienation from God, which is the natural human condition as confronted by the perfectly righteous justice of God's law. He grasps the fact that there is no salvation either by the "works of the law" (Gal. 2:16), or by the "rags" of his own righteousness (Isa. 64:6). "The wages of sin is death" is not a theory to the reflective hearts and minds of the children of God (Rom. 3:23; 7:22–25). We know in a deeply personal way that "there is none righteous, no, not one" (Rom. 3:10) and understand what God has delivered us from by his wonderful sovereign grace and everlasting love in his Son.

This deliverance is marked by the little word "but," around which the teaching of this psalm pivots (v. 4). While God's law can never forgive the guilty, and his *justice* inevitably requires retribution, the "God of all grace" has exercised his *mercy* in such a way as to both satisfy his justice and "save His people from their sins" (Matt. 1:21). "*But* there is forgiveness with You" reminds us that what *we* bring is our sin. To enjoy forgiveness, we must go to him, because all the grace that forgives is *with him* (i.e. is not apart from him, but in union with him), and "through faith which is in Christ Jesus" (2 Tim. 3:15). The second experiential element in v. 4 is in the words "that You may be feared." It is through the reception of forgiveness — turning to Christ in repentance and faith and continuing with him (Acts 11:23; 20:21) — that we will experience that "fear" of God (which is the positive, loving, and godly reverence that makes for reconciliation with him [Rom. 5:10]), and the joy of worship "in spirit and truth" (John 4:24). No sinner is capable of true worship until and unless he or she has experienced the grace of God in the Christ of the gospel—"in whom we have redemption through His blood, the forgiveness of sins" (Col. 1:14). But, as Allan Harman has noted, "Receiving mercy increases our sense of awe and reverence for God's holy presence." Knowing real forgiveness, by God's grace and through faith in the one and only real Savior, makes all the difference in the world—and hereafter in eternity.

Water is never more refreshing than when the tongue is parched. The psalmist is already a solid believer and this psalm is one of the fifteen Songs of Ascents (Psalms 120–134), which are thought to have been sung by God's people as they went *up* to Jerusalem on their pilgrimages to the temple. He is expressing his elevation of spirit as he goes up to God's house. His soul is lifted up by the refreshed awareness and deepened assurance that God not only can forgive sinners, but has forgiven him by his gracious provision of mercy. This exalted spirit is expressed in verses 5–6, where he compares his enthusiastic waiting upon the Lord with the "impatience of nocturnal watchers for the break of day and that of sufferers for relief, or of convicted sinners for forgiveness." Finally, in verses 7–8, he bursts with joyous earnestness in encouraging us to "hope in the Lord" because "with Him is abundant redemption." Dear friends, Jesus Christ by his death on the cross put the "but" in Psalm 130:4. Without the cross, there could be no "but" at all, and without Jesus there can be no "but" for you and me. *But in Christ Jesus* there is forgiveness, that God may be feared, even redemption from all our iniquities!

PRAISE TO THE GOD WHO FORGIVES SIN
Sing Psalm 130

THINGS I WILL PRAY FOR TODAY

May 27
God's Resting Place Forever

A prayer rejoicing in God's promise to bless his church

For the Lord has chosen Zion; He has desired it for His dwelling place.
This is My resting place forever.—Ps. 132:13–14a

READ PSALM 132

In a cartoon entitled "Overtime," Sam Boyle (1905–2002) portrays a young man in church, psalter in hand, singing the words of Psalm 132:14, where God is saying about Zion, "'Tis my resting place forever; here I'll stay, I'll love it well," but also looking over his shoulder at the clock, which registers 12:10 p.m.—ten minutes over a literal "hour of worship"! The psalm, of course, does not prescribe service length, but it does focus on the foundational issue of God's presence with his worshiping people—and how we ought to respond. Solomon quotes Psalm 138:8–10 in closing his prayer at the temple dedication—"Arise, O Lord, to Your resting place"—whereupon "the glory of the Lord filled the temple" (2 Chron. 6:41–7:2). God came to his resting place—his church! Psalm 132 speaks to this truth by reflecting on *David's promise* to secure a permanent home for God in Israel, and rejoicing in *God's promise* of an everlasting kingdom and its messianic King (v. 17).

David's promise to God invites us to ponder past faithfulness and pray (vv. 1–10)! The psalmist—who may be Solomon—recalls three aspects of his father's faithfulness to the Lord.

David *covenants with God* that he will secure "a dwelling place for the Mighty One of Jacob" (vv. 1–5). Since Sinai, God had manifested his presence as the glory cloud over the ark of the covenant, but this had ceased since the loss of the ark to the Philistines and its subsequent neglect in Israel (1 Sam. 4:10–11; 6:21ff.). God's people lost their center: the presence of God, corporate worship, and covenant community life—somewhat like the Christian who is not a committed worshiper in, and an involved member of, a church today.

David takes *faithful action* by bringing the ark from "the fields of the woods" to Jerusalem (v. 6). He does not stop there: he also calls the church to worship (v. 7). Later he will write, "I was glad when they said to me, 'Let us go into the house of the Lord'" (Ps. 122:1). The challenge remains today: will you say the same—and act on it?

David *prays* for the blessing of God's church. He prays for God's *presence* among his people in their hearts (v. 8); prays for God's *ministers* that they be "clothed with righteousness" and give the saints cause to "shout for joy" (v. 9); and prays for God's *king*—in context, Solomon, as God's "Anointed," and his faithful successors (v. 10). Are these not prayer concerns included in all our prayer meetings?

God's promise to David invites us to plead God's future faithfulness and to rejoice in his promise to bless his church.

God assures David of his *covenant promise* that kings of "the fruit of your body" will sit upon his throne, and if they keep God's covenant, will do so "forevermore" (vv. 11–12; cf. 2 Sam. 7).

God proclaims his *sovereign choice* of Zion as the people with whom he will rest "forever" (vv. 13–18). The temple and the Jewish monarchy are no more, but the promise is not void, for this points ahead to the substance of which it is the foreshadowing—the incarnation of the Lord's Anointed, Jesus Christ, "Immanuel...God with us" (Matt. 1:23). In Christ, God is present with his people whenever and wherever they gather for public worship to this day (Joel 2:27–29; Acts 2:14ff.): "For He Himself has said, 'I will never leave you nor forsake you'" (Heb. 13:5; Deut. 31:6). Will you rejoice in:

- God's *electing grace* in choosing Zion/the church (v. 13)?
- God's *glorious presence* with his believing people (v. 14)?
- God's *provision*, physical and spiritual (vv. 15–16)?
- God's *Messiah*—"My Anointed"/our Jesus (v. 17)? and
- God's *triumph in Christ*, whose "crown shall flourish" (v. 18)?

PRAISE HIM WHO MAKES HIS CHURCH HIS HOME
Sing Psalm 132:13–18

THINGS I WILL PRAY FOR TODAY

May 28
The Exiles' Lament

A prayer reflecting on sorrows, past and future

By the rivers of Babylon, there we sat down, yea, we wept when we remembered Zion. —Ps. 137:1

READ PSALM 137

The 137th Psalm is a powerful evocation of the wrenching realities God's people experienced during the captivity in Babylon. From 586 to 538 BC, godly Jews in Babylon wrestled with the question as to whether God would ever revive his church and kingdom. Their prayer here consists of two distinct heartbroken lamentations: one for the plight of God's church—God's people (vv. 1–6); and the other for the dread prospects for their oppressors—God's enemies (vv. 7–9). This deep sadness tends to be overlooked in the too common approach that sees this psalm as a vengeful call for the annihilation of Edomites and Babylonians, babies and all, and tacitly dismisses it as unworthy of the gospel of Jesus. This is, however, a *lament*, not a vindictive call for judgment without mercy. It is ultimately Jesus grieving for his people and for those who will not repent and be saved.

The parlous state of the church—the people of God in the world—is a recurrent cause for grief in both Scripture and church history (vv. 1–6). The Jews sitting by "the rivers of Babylon" (v. 1) were not indulging some romantic pining for "the good old days," so common among emigrants and exiles in all ages. They were gripped by a theologically informed grief in which their lives as the people of God seemed under judgment. God's covenant promises seem to be suspended, as if the cause of God and truth was vanishing from the earth.

This section is in two parts:

> ❧ The first begins with Babylon, where they wish they weren't (vv. 1–3), and is a song explaining why they cannot sing on account of their sadness. Mockers call for "the songs of Zion"—the psalms—but the voices are silent, the harps hung "upon the willows." God's songs are for joy in genuine heartfelt worship, not for the entertainment of the godless.

298

❧ The second part ends with Jerusalem, where the faithful wish they were (vv. 4–6), and is a testimony to their love for the Lord. They are saying, "LORD, I have loved the habitation of Your house, and the place where Your glory dwells" (Ps. 26:8). Worship pleasing to God, according to his revealed will, and in the place of his appointment, is the desire of their hearts. "Jerusalem" is the joy greater than their "chief joy" and their prayer is for the restoration and revival of the church. In the New Testament era, the church remains the "Jerusalem" in every place in which the "Israel of God" in Jesus Christ worships "in Spirit and in truth" (Gal. 6:16; John 4:24). May our Christian tongues stick to a dry palate if we do not exalt in our singing this "Jerusalem" above all our greatest joys!

The parlous state of the world—the world that denies the Lord and oppresses his church—is recorded in what amounts to a prophecy of the end of those who would destroy God's church (vv. 7–9). Edom and Babylon will reap as they sow—and persisted to sow to the end—and disappear from the face of the earth. And they have long gone. The psalmist is not screaming bitterly for vengeance, but is solemnly and sadly declaring the inevitability of judgment to come for the unrepentant and unbelieving, according to God's revealed canons of righteous justice. The agents of that justice will not be bitter merciless Jews but will be people like themselves who will be happy to do the very things to them that they have done to God's people.

The universal message from God is, "Do not be deceived, God is not mocked; for whatever a man sows, that he will also reap" (Gal. 6:7). But in Christ Jesus salvation is proffered to sinners; as he says, "All that the Father gives Me will come to Me, and the one who comes to Me I will by no means cast out" (John 6:37; cf. Jer. 18:7–11).

SINGING THE LORD'S SONG FAR FROM HOME
Sing Psalm 137

THINGS I WILL PRAY FOR TODAY

_____

_____

_____

May 29
Search Me, O God...

A prayer for a pure heart that rests upon the attributes of God

Search me, O God, and know my heart...and see if there is any wicked way in me, and lead me in the way everlasting. —*Ps. 139:23–24*

READ PSALM 139

The expression "Search me" can vary greatly as to meaning and intention. It can be a simple shrug of inability or disinclination to answer a question, or a protestation of innocence from a charge of stealing. Context makes the difference, so when the psalmist adds "O God," we see him opening his heart to the Lord, asking him to root out sinful thinking and lead him to living his life in abiding fellowship with God—"the way everlasting." He supports this prayer with an *appeal* to the very character of God (vv. 1–18), and follows it up with some powerful *application* to the hearts of all who are ready to listen to what God is saying (vv. 19–24). So intimate and personal is this most searching of prayers that it is no wonder, as Matthew Poole observes, that "this Psalm is esteemed by the Hebrews the most excellent in the whole book." It comes from the soul, and it speaks to the soul.

Appeal is made to the character of God (vv. 1–18). The attributes of God are not to be dismissed as ivory-tower doctrines buried in obscure language, but rather hugged as essential, practical foundations of a close personal walk with the Lord. God's omniscience, omnipresence, and omnipotence are basic to all human experience, both believers and unbelievers. They are life to the former and death to the latter. They can be neglected or denied, but never escaped, either in time or eternity.

God knows it all: omniscient means "all-knowing" (vv. 1–6). In our relating to God, this signifies his complete and comprehensive knowledge of us. He is *inside* our lives: our actions, thoughts, plans, and words (vv. 1–4); and he is the *environment* within the limits of which we live (v. 5). So, the believer confesses "such knowledge is too wonderful for me; it is high, I cannot attain it" (v. 6). We are therefore never alone—and we love this truth, the more we understand and know our Savior God.

God is with us all: omnipresent means "everywhere present"

(vv. 7–12). God is not in a box. He is Spirit, and whether in heaven, death, or in the deepest sea, you cannot, believer, be separated from his presence and his leading and holding you (vv. 7–10). When you are alone in the dark, the Lord sees it "shine as the day" and his eye is upon you in love (vv. 11–12). Is that not a comfort to your soul?

God is over us all: omnipotent means he is all-powerful to fulfill his purposes (vv. 13–18). From conception to birth you were already *you*, written in God's "book" with the days of future life "fashioned...when as yet there were none of them." No wonder God's (revealed) thoughts are "precious" to the believer and are new every morning, for, he says, "When I awake, I am still with You." The Lord who keeps his people neither slumbers nor sleeps (Ps. 121:4). And so we can go to bed saying, "I will both lie down in peace, and sleep; for You alone, O Lord, make me dwell in safety" (Ps. 4:8). What a glorious comfort it is to know personally the Lord who "is able to keep you from stumbling, and to present you faultless before the presence of His glory with exceeding joy" (Jude 24)!

Application is made to the character of man (vv. 19–24). First realize that God holds all the children of Adam *accountable*. Hence the hard but necessary word in verses 19–22 to those who despise God and his holy Law and live for themselves. This forms a dramatic segue to the psalmist's crowning point, which is that God searches and saves people. "Search me, O God, and know my heart" (vv. 23–24), writes A. A. Bonar, "is a prayer that *the omniscient and omnipresent Creator would keep his worshipper forever* on his side." The child of God wants God to search and know his heart, to minister to his anxieties, to cleanse his soul, and to "lead...in the way everlasting." Bonar concludes, "Thus we see that this Psalm is one of joy and happy confidence in God, abounding in views that enlarge the heart and strengthen it." Here we are at home with our heavenly Father.

PRAISE FOR THE SATISFYING NEARNESS OF GOD
Sing Psalm 139:13–18

THINGS I WILL PRAY FOR TODAY

_____

_____

_____

_____

May 30
Terror or Trust?

A prayer for protection from the terrors of evil men

Deliver me, O LORD, from evil men. —Ps. 140:1

READ PSALM 140

errorism" has gripped the world in a big way since 9/11. The English philosopher Francis Bacon (1561–1626) once wrote that "nothing is terrible except fear itself." Many things in life inspire fear, but we surely know from experience that being frantic is always unhelpful, and it can become a self-fulfilling prophecy even when there is no real threat. Fear can kill. David outlines God's way for dealing with fears, whatever their sources, and shows us that trusting in the Lord is basic to taking arms against a sea of troubles. God's standing promise to his people is, "Surely He shall deliver you from the snare of the fowler and from the perilous pestilence" (Ps. 91:3). He assures us, as David Dickson quaintly puts it, that "how wicked soever, how violent soever the enemies of God's children be, God can rescue his servants out of their hands." This deliverance is not automatic but answers to prayers born of a living faith. David's prayer unfolds in four steps:

A request for deliverance (vv. 1–5). David was likely on the run from Saul when he wrote this psalm. Evil and violent men were an ever-present threat to his life and limb. Nothing has changed. The violence, poisonous slanders, and devious entrapment of the modern scene are all here. Such people "exist in all ages," writes Bishop Horne, who also points out that we "cannot pull off our Christian armour for a moment in this world, nor enter into peace and rest, but by a happy death, and a joyful resurrection." We often find ourselves having to look over our shoulder, but God can still deliver his own.

A profession of confidence (vv. 6–8). This depends entirely on a saving knowledge of the Lord: "You are my God...the strength of my salvation." The believer can say, "I know whom I have believed and am persuaded that He is able to keep what I have committed to Him until that Day" (2 Tim. 1:12). The practice of "returning evil for evil" and "reviling for reviling" (1 Peter 3:9) has filled the world with "Hatfields

302

and McCoys" in endless vendettas, from domestic strife to world wars. But the Lord will not allow the spiritual enemies of the Lord's people to frustrate "his counsels for the redemption of his servants." When Joseph's brothers "meant evil" against him, God in the end "meant it for good" (Gen. 50:20). God says of the afflicted believer: "He shall call upon Me, and I will answer him; I will be with him in trouble; I will deliver him and honor him" (Ps. 91:15).

An appeal for vindication (vv. 9–11). God saves some of his enemies and passes others by, but it is always right to pray for the overthrow of wickedness. The vindication of the believer's faithfulness, the relief of God's suffering servants, the preservation of his church, and, not least, the honor and glory of God himself, renders these requests thoroughly justified. Why should the innocent suffer? Let the wicked fall into their own trap! Therefore "Let not a slanderer be established in the earth; let evil hunt the violent man to overthrow him" (v. 11).

An anticipation of blessing (vv. 12–13). The last part of the prayer is effectively the answer to the first three portions. It expresses universal and timeless truth for all God's faithful people. The Lord will stand by the afflicted, the poor, the righteous, and the upright, who will "dwell in [his] presence" (v. 13). John Newton understood what it was for Jesus to take him from terror to trust—and it was and is all of grace:

'Twas grace that taught my heart to fear
And grace my fears relieved.
How precious did that grace appear
The hour I first believed.
—"Amazing Grace," stanza 2

PRAISE IN ANTICIPATION OF GOD'S GRACE
Sing Psalm 140:5–10

THINGS I WILL PRAY FOR TODAY

_____

_____

_____

_____

_____

_____

May 31
The Believer's Legacy

A prayer for a consistently godly life and witness

But my eyes are upon You, O GOD the Lord....Let the wicked fall into their own nets, while I escape safely.—*Ps. 141:8, 10*

READ PSALM 141

Alexander Peden (1626–86), the Scots Covenanter field-preacher, was on his deathbed when he offered parting counsels to the young James Renwick (1662–1688), who had recently embarked on the ministry which would soon make him the last martyr of the "Killing Time" (1680–88). "Auld Sandy" said to him, "Sir, I find you a faithful servant to your Master, go on in a single dependence upon the Lord, and ye will win honestly through and cleanly off the stage, when many others that hold their head high will fall and lie in the mire, and make foul hands and garments." To "win honestly through and cleanly off the stage" aptly describes the desire of David in Psalm 141. It's called "legacy" today—in worldly terms, leaving something good for which to be remembered. For the psalmist, for Peden and Renwick, and for every thoughtful Christian, this is not, however, about looking backward at our reputation after we are gone. It is about knowing Jesus personally as our Savior and enjoying reconciled peace with God through "the blood of His cross" (Col. 1:20); it is about looking forward and upward to the glory and honor of God in himself and in his purposes of grace, and to the day "when His glory is revealed" (1 Peter 4:13), when "generations yet unborn shall praise and magnify the Lord."

The legacy believers are called to aim for consists in an intentional love for and commitment to the Lord. As Paul puts it, "Be watchful, stand firm in the faith, act like men, be strong" (1 Cor. 16:13, ESV). David accordingly prays for exactly what he needs to be able to negotiate the various hurdles that are bound to obstruct his faithfulness to the Lord and bid to knock him off what Jesus calls the "narrow...gate" and the "difficult...way which leads to life" (Matt. 7:14). His prayers set out a pattern for our prayers as we strive to "win honestly through" the storms of spiritual warfare in this world.

‚ First, pray about *your praying* (vv. 1–2). This may sound odd, but it is vital, if you are going to "walk humbly with your God" (Mic. 6:8). God will not hear any old "prayer" that people may utter (Jer. 11:14). Try winning a hearing from your superiors with a disrespectful attitude and abusive language. David "wants his prayer to be accepted by God just as the incense and evening sacrifices are." Second, pray for *wisdom*: for your tongue (v. 3); your heart (v. 4a); your hands (v. 4b–c); and, crucially, your conscience (v. 5a–c). Wisdom reaches beyond understanding and from heart to hand. Without a conscience ready to be accountable and receive rebuke, we will stumble where we might otherwise stand fast. Can you say, "Let the righteous strike me; it shall be a kindness. And let him rebuke me; it shall be as excellent oil; let my head not refuse it"? "Faithful are the wounds of a friend" (Prov. 27:6).

‚ Third, pray against *wickedness* (vv. 5d–7). Even so, indulge the hope that, in time, the wicked will "hear [your] words, for they are sweet." We were all "wicked" until saved by God's gospel grace in Christ. As a trophy of grace, pray for the conversion of those still lost in their sin.

‚ Fourth, pray for *deliverance* (vv. 8–10). The psalmist returns to the danger he faces immediately. In praying that he might "escape safely" the traps set for him by "the workers of iniquity," he affirms that his eyes are upon the Lord in whom he "take[s] refuge." Here is the believer's "legacy" come to fruition: perseverance and deliverance in union with his Savior. With "The Wayfaring Stranger" in the eponymous folksong, he can testify as he approaches eternity: "I'll soon be free from every trial / This form will rest beneath the sod / I'll drop the cross of self-denial / And enter in my home with God / I'm going there to see my Savior / Who shed for me His Precious Blood / I'm just a-going over Jordan / I'm just a-going over home."

PRAISE IN ANTICIPATION OF GOD'S GRACE
Sing Psalm 141:5–10

THINGS I WILL PRAY FOR TODAY

June 1
Bring My Soul out of Prison!

A prayer for one who is at the end of himself

Bring my soul out of prison, that I may praise Your name. —Ps. 142:7

READ PSALM 142; 1 SAMUEL 24

here are times in life when desperation grips the soul. We see no light at the end of the tunnel. We have no solutions and are at an end of ourselves. David is in such a "tight corner." On the run from King Saul, he is trapped in a cave—probably the one in En-gedi where Saul went in "to attend to his needs" and had 3,000 "chosen men" outside (1 Sam. 24:1–7). While David's men saw in this a chance to kill Saul, David discerned a "God-given opportunity to prove his innocence." Killing Saul could only make David a murderer and likely seal his doom at the hands of Saul's men. David's life is hanging by a thread. He decides to sit tight and wait...upon the Lord. And he prays.

Prayer is a gift for every circumstance in life, from thanksgiving to terror and from tragedy to triumph. But it is preeminently a means of God's grace for times of extreme distress: given "that we may obtain mercy and find grace to help in time of need" (Heb. 4:16). This psalm is entitled a *Maschil* in Hebrew—meaning "a teaching poem." It is a carefully considered record of what happened on that day of crisis, designed to draw our hearts and minds to the Lord, teaching us how to pray in our own troubles. David describes why and how he prays. He begins to "cry out" to God, to "make...supplication," to "pour out [his] complaint," and to declare this trouble "before Him" (vv. 1–2).

In this we find four elements of true prayer: (1) an earnest, believing, personal crying out to the living God; (2) a humble seeking for his grace; (3) a full disclosure of what troubles us; and (4) a persistence in bringing it all before him. When "danger...and fear [are] on every side," counsels Bishop Horne, "let us follow the example of David, and that of one greater than David, who, when Jews and Gentiles conspired against him and he was left all alone in the garden and on the cross, gave himself unto prayer (Matt. 26:39)." Like Jesus, we also have a heavenly Father, and in Jesus himself, we have a heavenly Advocate, who "always lives to make intercession" for those he will "save to the uttermost" (Heb. 8:1; 7:25).

David's prayer is a gift to all who will pray under hard times. His prayer sees him addressing God directly: "You knew my path…You are my refuge…[& etc.]" (v. 3, 5). It unfolds in three distinct parts:

- He sets out his predicament while also affirming his faith (vv. 3–4). His spirit is overwhelmed, but God knows what he is going through: the snares set by his enemies, the fewness of friends, the failure of his refuge (Saul was right there in the front door!), and the absence of any who care for his soul. Have you ever felt alone? Jesus certainly did in Gethsemane and at Golgotha—despised and rejected by men—and forsaken by his Father-God in bearing the penalty of our sin.

- He offers his petitions—asking the Lord, whom he confesses to be his "refuge and portion in the land of the living" (v. 5), to do two things: to deliver him, as he says, from "persecutors… stronger than I" (v. 6); and to bring his "soul out of prison, that I may praise Your name" (v. 7ab). This speaks to the spiritual aspects of his trials. The cave is a prison of a kind, as is Saul's hatred and the weariness of running for his life. But doubt and discouragement are also prisons.

- He ponders his prospects of blessing from the Lord: restoration to the fellowship of the righteous because of the Lord's bountiful dealings in his answers to prayer (v. 7cd). Andrew Bonar sees this pointing to Jesus who looks out, "in the confidence of hope, seeing down the vista of the ages, his eye resting on the millions of his saved ones." David teaches us to pray and expect blessing—and all by the grace of his greater Son, our Savior Jesus Christ.

PRAISE TO THE SAVIOR WHO SAVES US
Sing Psalm 142

THINGS I WILL PRAY FOR TODAY

June 2
My Soul Longs for You

Prayer as the voice of faith

I spread out my hands to You; My soul longs for You like a thirsty land.
—*Ps. 143:6*

READ PSALM 143

he richest prayers tend to arise in the most intense experiences, whether of joy or sorrow. This psalm-prayer is one of a number that date from David's time in—and out—of Saul's court, before the final break that sent him into exile (1 Sam. 18–20). Chronologically it falls between Psalms 140 and 141, and experientially it reveals a low point in his confidence relative to these two psalm-prayers. In Psalm 143, he is particularly downcast, deeply feels his vulnerability, and longs in his heart for the reviving presence of God. He is down, on the run for his life, and his faith is shaken and tested. What is he to do? He cries to the Lord "out of the depths" with all the passion of his reeling soul (Ps. 130:1), but also with the conviction that God is his rock and his Redeemer (Ps. 78:35).

This rich prayer unfolds in three sections. First of all, the psalmist *comes humbly* to the Lord, seeking a hearing and casting himself upon the Lord's faithfulness and righteousness (v. 1), pleading dependence upon his unmerited grace, since in his sight "no one living is righteous" (v. 2). He starts where he is meant to continue.

Second, he gives *two reasons* for praying: the first is his persecution by "the enemy" and his resultant distress (vv. 3–4); the second is his encouragement from God's gracious dealings with his people in "the days of old" together with his personal thirst for communion with God—"My soul longs for You like a thirsty land" (vv. 5–6).

Third, he offers nine specific *prayer requests* (vv. 7–12):

- For an answer "speedily," because his "spirit fails" (v. 7a).
- For divine favor, as he fears an imminent physical death (v. 7b).
- For early "lovingkindness," because he trusts the Lord (v. 8a).
- For guidance in "the way" of obedience (v. 8b).
- For deliverance from enemies and for shelter in the Lord (v. 9).

◇ For grace to know God's "will" and walk in holiness (v. 10).

◇ For revival from his otherwise dejected state (v. 11a).

◇ For freeing his soul from the "trouble" of persecution (v. 11b).

◇ For the elimination of "enemies," so he may serve God (v. 12).

What can we learn from this prayer? Bishop Horne observes that "prayer is the voice of faith." David's prayer is more than asking for persecution to stop. It is full of longing for personal communion with his Savior-God. He does not "say" his prayers, nor does he merely reel off a bare list of needs and wants. His prayer is the voice of his personal faith. Paul reminds us that "whatever is not from faith is sin" (Rom. 14:23)— and that applies to prayer that merely mouths a form of words, whether by rote, ritual, or habit. Jesus is clear that "whatever things you ask in prayer, believing, you will receive" (Matt. 21:22). The key is "believing." *Believing* prayers are not "said," they are *experienced* as a means of God's grace! Jesus tells of a Pharisee who thanks God for making him a great guy, superior to people like the tax collector, who, in contrast, "would not so much as raise his eyes to heaven, but beat his breast, saying, 'God, be merciful to me a sinner!'" (Luke 18:9–14). The Pharisee prays a self-satisfied, self-righteous prayer out of his works-righteous "faith." The tax collector cries to God as one who knows he is saved by grace alone—a believing prayer giving voice to his living faith. In the prayers of David and the tax collector, we are led to Jesus, in whom our prayers may be from hearts that are turning in faith, hope, and love to the Lord who loves and saves us (Ps. 62:8). Will you today spread out your hands to the Lord, longing for him like a thirsty land?

PRAISE RESTING IN GOD'S STEADFAST LOVE
Sing Psalm 143:7–12

THINGS I WILL PRAY FOR TODAY

_____

_____

_____

_____

_____

June 3
Happy People?

A prayer anticipating the blessedness of God's people

Happy are the people whose God is the Lord!—Ps. 144:15

READ PSALM 144

David's discouragements while fleeing from King Saul are powerfully described in Psalms 140–143. Psalm 144 is composed after David becomes king (see vv. 2, 10), and God has blessed him with military success and an emerging national peace and prosperity. He still faces enemies, but the gloom has given way to bright vistas of encouragement. His theme is a prayer of praise: "Happy are the people who are in such a state; happy are the people whose God is the Lord!" (v. 15). He is not saying that people in prosperous nations are falsely happy, whereas God's people are truly happy, even if they are relatively poor and oppressed. These "happy" clauses, observes J. A. Alexander, "are not antithetical, but equivalent." God's people rejoice because they are, says James Murphy, "happy in the procuring cause of all blessing, having the Lord for their God." National prosperity is a good thing in itself, but being happy about it in abstraction from knowing and acknowledging God's grace in his Son is only to enjoy the gift while denying the Giver—and so to worship and serve "the creature rather than the Creator" (Rom. 1:25).

David's encouragement blends prayers of thanksgiving and deliverance. This unfolds in five rapid-fire steps to a glorious crescendo of expectancy of God's blessings:

> Thanksgiving for past deliverance and rejoicing in God's unmerited grace in his preserving him and subduing his enemies (vv. 1–4).

> Deliverance from present trials—seeking God's powerful intervention against his and God's enemies (vv. 5–8).

> Thanksgiving promised in anticipation of future deliverance—a "new song" for deliverance from "the deadly sword" (vv. 9–10)

> Deliverance from future trials—anticipating God's future establishment of his people (vv. 11–14).

> Thanksgiving for the future happiness of God's people (v. 15)—

an implicit call for believers to pray in all times to come to the One who is "able to save to the uttermost those who come to God through Him, since He always lives to make intercession for them" (Heb. 7:25).

David's trials lead him to God's triumphs, and here he celebrates answered prayers and the joyous fulfillment of God's promises. This is the true happiness that will never pass away, because it consists in the eternal blessedness of the Lord toward his believing people. In the language of prophecy, we are pointed to David's greater Son and to the "Jerusalem which now is" in him in the New Testament age (Gal. 4:5); we are also pointed to the assurance that even the "the sufferings of this present time"—of which there will always be some (John 16:33)—are truly "not worthy to be compared to the glory which shall be revealed" in those who love the Lord (Rom. 8:18). The great Scottish preacher A. A. Bonar rightly observes that "every member of Christ may take up this Psalm in behalf of his own country and people—yea, in behalf of our common humanity, praying for the day when all earth shall enjoy these blessings, by enjoying Jehovah as their God. It is a prospect that awaits the world when Christ returns." And who will be the happy people in that day? The Lord tells us that it is that "great multitude which no one could number, of all nations, tribes, peoples, and tongues, standing before the throne and before the Lamb, clothed with white robes, with palm branches in their hands, and crying out with a loud voice, saying, 'Salvation belongs to our God who sits on the throne, and to the Lamb!'" (Rev. 7:9–10). Charles Simeon urges us, "Seek after God: seek him as a reconciled God in Christ Jesus: seek him, till he has revealed himself fully to your souls, and enables you to say, 'O God, you are my God.' Then, without fear of contradiction, I will pronounce you happy...and say, in reference to you, 'Happy is the people whose God is the Lord.'"

PRAISE THAT SEEKS ABIDING HAPPINESS
Sing Psalm 144:9–15

THINGS I WILL PRAY FOR TODAY

_____

_____

_____

June 4
Delighting the Lord

Prayer as evaluated by God

The sacrifice of the wicked is an abomination to the Lord, but the prayer of the upright is His delight. — Prov. 15:8

READ PROVERBS 15:8, 29 AND 28:9

here are only three explicit references to prayer in the book of Proverbs. If this surprises you, remember that Proverbs is not a manual for personal piety, but a compendium of practical wisdom for the way we live in our world. This was exemplified in the counsel given by a friend of my youth to his son, when the latter signed up for service on a merchant ship one summer during his college days. The father, a pastor, had served in the British Merchant Navy as a young man and understood its challenges. "Son," he said, "Keep your eyes peeled, your mouth shut, your ears open, and your nose clean; and read the book of Proverbs from end to end and over again and again till you come home."

Prayer is, of course, given to Christians as a means of God's grace in the hurly-burly of life in a fallen world. The paucity of specific references to prayer in the Proverbs should not distract us from the constant and vital exercise of prayer in both seeking and exercising practical wisdom. Each proverbial reference involves a specific contrast between prayers acceptable to God and others that are not.

God delights in the prayers of the upright. This is contrasted with the startling observation that "the sacrifice of the wicked is an abomination to the LORD" (Prov. 15:8a). Any old prayer will not do. To pray, of course, is not in itself a sin. It is "a good duty, but spoiled in the carriage," writes Archbishop Ussher. So all outward show of serving and seeking the Lord, without love for him from the heart, is utter hypocrisy and therefore an abomination to the Lord. On the other hand, "the upright" is one who "truly and unfeignedly gives himself up to God, to be saved in his appointed way—and to serve him with a pure heart and mind." He is not some plaster saint, nor is he sinlessly perfect. But he is "pure" in God's eyes, because he is *in Christ, being united to him by faith.*

312

He is accepted and approved by God, because Jesus's sacrifice is accepted as the atonement for sin. Accordingly, "the prayer of the upright is His delight" (Prov. 15:8b). God loves it when believers come to him in prayer.

God hears the prayers of the righteous. God is not only delighted with believing prayer. He is also always near to his believing *people*: "The LORD is far from the wicked, but He hears the prayer of the righteous" (Prov. 15:29). God is repelled by the "evil heart of unbelief," which drives the unconverted sinner. In the nature of the case, this always leads people to be "departing from the living God," however much they give a show of "religion" (Heb. 3:12). God simply will not draw near to those who draw near to him with their lips, when their hearts are far from him (Isa. 29:13). But those who love Jesus will never go unheard and abandoned by the Lord—however desolate they may feel in a crisis—like the psalmist, they will discover that the Lord is holding them by their right hand (Ps. 73:23).

God blesses those who love his law. On the other hand, "One who turns away his ear from hearing the law, even his prayer is an abomination" (Prov. 28:9). It matters to God what we do with his revealed truth, the Scriptures. Again, our delighting God is the issue. If we love him, we will keep his commandments (John 14:15). And as we love his law, we will know his nearer presence. The "wicked" certainly *should* pray, but ought to pray crying to God for salvation, repenting toward him, and believing in the Lord Jesus Christ. "His desire to seek the Lord," says Charles Bridges, "would be the beginning of *the prayer* that ensures acceptance." God loves it when we pray from a living faith in Jesus.

PRAISE DELIGHTING IN THE LORD
Sing Psalm 116:1–8

THINGS I WILL PRAY FOR TODAY

313

June 5
From Undone to Redone

A prayer of humbled self-knowledge

Woe is me, for I am undone! Because I am a man of unclean lips. — Isa. 6:5

READ ISAIAH 6:1–10

In the book of Isaiah, prayer, praise, and prophecy intermingle almost seamlessly. Formal prayers are very few, but there are plenty pointers as to how, or, more often, how not to pray (Isa. 1:15; 16:12; 29:13). There are some "arrow prayers" that suddenly wing to heaven from the middle of extended prophetic revelation from God. Isaiah's call to be a prophet to Judah is a striking example. The Lord appears to him and before even a word is said, Isaiah shoots off an arrow prayer about how unworthy he is before the Lord! Surely any sense we may have of God's calling us is bound to bring us to cry out to him, whether in hesitation or in enthusiasm. Small wonder, then, that we find Isaiah, on being called to be a prophet, protesting his fitness not merely for the task, but for being permitted to see God! "God is not to be trifled with," comments Derek Thomas. Isaiah knew it and feared for his soul. When God seems to be turning your life upside down, prayer will never be far away, for "it is a fearful thing to fall into the hands of the living God" (Heb. 10:31).

Why did this vision have such an impact on Isaiah? The answer is threefold: it reveals the authority, the holiness, and the awesome power of God (vv. 1–4). Here we find the words of the *Sanctus*, historically associated with the prayer consecrating the bread and wine in the Lord's Supper: "Holy, Holy, Holy, is the Lord of hosts; the whole earth is full of His glory." Charles Simeon observes that the triple "Holy" emphasizes "the holiness of his nature," while the manifestation of the fullness of his glory in creation points to "the wonders of his grace." Isaiah's response is also threefold:

He immediately *confesses* to the Lord his uncleanness because of sin: "Woe is me, for I am undone!" (v. 5a). Luther renders the latter clause *Ich vergehe* — German for "I am dissolved." We might say, "I'm toast!" The Lord's holiness is always going to expose our personal sinfulness and, even more, our incapacity either to atone for our sin, or to eradicate it from our thoughts, words, and deeds. How can he, or we, see God and live?

He already understands that his *cleansing* from sin can only come from a source outside of himself. The Lord answers his prayer by sending an angel, who touches Isaiah's lips with a hot coal [from the altar of incense (Ex. 30:1–10)] and tells him, "Your iniquity is taken away, and your sin purged" (vv. 6–7). The prophet is already a believer; this is for his consolation and his encouragement that he is righteous in God's eyes and can therefore live and speak for him.

He then *commits* to the Lord's calling that he proclaim his word to his people (vv. 8–10). Isaiah was already a prophet, but this confirms and seals his call for the future. He knows his message will be difficult and unpopular, but he responds wholeheartedly—"Here am I! Send me!" And so it begins with words that are later applied to the Jews of Jesus's earthly ministry: "Keep on hearing, but do not understand" (Isa. 6:9–10; John 12:40). Prophets are to speak God's revealed truth to lost humanity's need of a Savior! It isn't an easy job!

What impact must this vision have upon us? John's Gospel reveals that it was Jesus who appeared to Isaiah in this vision: "These things Isaiah said when he saw His glory and spoke of Him" (John 12:41). This is the same Jesus who convicts, cleanses, and calls men and women "out of darkness into His marvelous light" (1 Peter 2:9). This is the same Jesus who calls and sends out his messengers into the world to proclaim the same gospel of his free grace—in Jesus believed as personal Savior and Lord. Here you are! Will you say, "Send me"?

PRAISE AND PRAYER FOR GOD'S LOVINGKINDNESSES
Sing Psalm 119:41–48

THINGS I WILL PRAY FOR TODAY

June 6
The Wells of Salvation

A praise-prayer of the joy of salvation

Therefore with joy you will draw water from the wells of salvation.
—Isa. 12:3

READ ISAIAH 12:1–3

Prayer and praise are two sides of the coin of Christian experience. Isaiah 12 is generally called a hymn, but it is half prayer and half praise combined in a prophetic utterance expounding the joy the Lord's people will have in the promised Messiah. The first half includes the text of a prayer (vv. 1–3), while the latter half is a song of praise (vv. 4–6). The key to understanding the passage is in the words "*in that day* you will say" (vv. 1a, 4a). At one level, "that day" might be seen as any day of deliverance and thus as an encouragement to pray and praise God. The context, however, points to a larger experience of God's grace. It is a day of deliverance by "Immanuel" (Isa. 7:14; 8:8), who is the "Child" born to us (Isa. 9:6–7), and the "Branch" and "Root" from the stem of Jesse upon whom rests the Spirit of the Lord (Isa. 11:1, 10). This identifies "that day" with the New Testament era that dawned with the advent of Christ and his gospel of saving grace!

Comfort for believers. Believers "in that day" will understand how they are reconciled to God: "Oh Lord, I will praise you: though you were angry with me your anger is turned away" (v. 1b). God's anger is turned *away* from us, because it is turned *toward* Jesus Christ! God has made "His soul an offering for sin" (Isa. 53:10). Christ crucified is salvation for whoever believes in him. And the practical fruit is God's comfort. "You comfort me" is the believer's personal testimony to the saving grace he or she experiences in Christ (v. 1c): "Therefore, having been justified by faith, we have peace with God through our Lord Jesus Christ, through whom also we have access by faith into this grace in which we stand, and rejoice in hope of the glory of God" (Rom. 5:1–2). Such soul-comfort is the engine of true prayer and worship.

Trust in the Lord. When you can say with true assurance of faith, "Behold, God is my salvation," then richer experiences of grace will follow. The practical fruit is that you "will trust and not be afraid," you will know him as your "strength and song," and you will freely confess, "He also has become my salvation" (v. 2). The believer begins with the heart-conviction that God "is" his salvation and ends with a stronger heart-conviction that God has "become" his salvation. The more we go to the well of God's grace, the more we will be refreshed with the assurance of his love, and his power to save us.

Joy in your salvation. The prayer is followed with the promise that believers will rejoice to draw from "the wells of salvation" (v. 3). These "wells," says Matthew Henry, are "God's promises revealed, ratified, and given out to us, in his ordinances." That is, the means of grace—the Word of God, the sacraments, and prayer. They are essentially the Word as it proclaims Christ as life-giving Savior. Isaiah 12:3 was quoted annually by the High Priest at the Feast of Tabernacles, when he poured water from the Pool of Siloam on the altar in the temple, thus commemorating God's provision of water for Israel in the desert as a symbol of his redemption. Jesus applies this to himself as the life-giver: "On the last day, that great day of the feast, Jesus stood and cried out, saying, 'If anyone thirsts, let him come to Me and drink. He who believes in Me, as the Scripture has said, out of his heart will flow rivers of living water'" (John 7:37–38). Christ is that inexhaustible well of living water, and he assures us that "whoever drinks of the water that I shall give him will never thirst. But the water that I shall give him will become in him a fountain of water springing up into everlasting life" (John 4:14). Here is the source of eternal joy: new life in Christ.

PRAISE FOR SHOWERS OF BLESSING
Sing Psalm 72:1–8

THINGS I WILL PRAY FOR TODAY

_____

_____

_____

_____

_____

_____

June 7
Wonderful Things

A praise-prayer for God's amazing deeds

You have done wonderful things. — Isa. 25:1

READ ISAIAH 25:1–5

The great paradox of the birth of Jesus Christ is that this baby is God: "Behold, the virgin shall conceive and bear a Son, and shall call His name Immanuel [God with us]" (Isa. 7:14). This helpless baby is one day going to rule the world, for "the government will be upon His shoulder: and His name will be called Wonderful, Counselor, Mighty God, Everlasting Father, Prince of Peace" (Isa. 9:6). For this child to achieve anything at all, he must be God as well as a grown man. He is not revealed to us as a great teacher, a fetching personality, a persuasive preacher, a charismatic figure, or a pretty face that would attract adoring fans. The *government* will be upon his shoulders! He is to be the *Prince* of Peace. In the fullness of time, he is to exercise power!

This puts in perspective the many judgments prophesied by Isaiah. God does not merely rain wrath on the reprobate; he rules with a plan to save and sends a Savior with a plan to rule! Isaiah points us to the gospel of the Messiah/Christ. Centuries on, the apostle Paul testifies, "I am not ashamed of the gospel of Christ, for it is the power of God to salvation for everyone who believes, for the Jew first and also for the Greek" (Rom. 1:16). Isaiah leads us from the judgment of the whole earth in chapter 24 to a prayer of praise to the Lord in chapter 25 for his delivering his people. God's judgments upon his enemies mean deliverance for his friends. And, says Jesus, "You are My friends if you do whatever I command you" (John 15:14).

Isaiah records four ways God blesses his people in their troubles: *God has done "wonderful" things:* things that excite us to praise and prayer (v. 1). In spite of difficult trials, the believer can see God's hand at work in marvelous ways: personal tragedies become unlikely, if painful, occasions for the deepening of faith; the dashing of careful plans opens otherwise unanticipated doors to joy and blessing; and supposedly chance meetings are amazing providences that change life's direction for the better. Jesus meets the woman of Samaria at a well and transforms her life forever (John 4). Every Christian can say that, in becoming a believer, he is "like a turtle on a fencepost." You know he did not get there by himself! Wonderful things happen on the way to salvation.

God has had a wonderful plan from the start: "Your counsels of old are faithfulness and truth" (v. 1). What a comfort to know that God both made his plans for us long ago and that they are faithfulness and truth—that is, he keeps faith with his eternal purpose as he ministers to us in our changeable lives. "Forever, O LORD, Your word is settled in heaven" is surely a phrase to treasure in a time of personal stress (Ps. 119:89).

God destroys wicked nations and brings even "strong people" to "glorify" him (vv. 2–3): From ancient history to modern journalism, we have endless evidence of the humbling of powerful nations and autocratic rulers. Empires never last. God sees to it. How? He "put all things under His [Jesus's] feet, and gave Him to be head over all things to the church" (Eph. 1:22). Jesus rules and "then comes the end, when He delivers the kingdom to God the Father, when He puts an end to all rule and all authority and power" (1 Cor. 15:24). What a relief that will be for those who are alive at his coming!

God has been "a strength to the poor" and to the needy "in his distress" (v. 4): If you are poor and needy, spiritually and physically, and you turn to the Lord and embrace him as your Savior and Lord, he will be to you "a refuge from the storm," and so the "song of the terrible ones will be diminished" (vv. 4–5). His truth shall be your "shield and buckler" (Ps. 91:4). "The Lord has done great things for us," says the psalmist, "and we are glad" (Ps. 126:3). Believe it. Look for it. It is true. Praise him in all your prayers and glorify and enjoy him forever.

PRAISE FOR GOD'S WONDERFUL WORKS
Sing Psalm 111:6–10

THINGS I WILL PRAY FOR TODAY

June 8
"Shalom Shalom"

A praise-prayer rejoicing in true peace of mind

You will keep him in perfect peace, whose mind is stayed on You, because he trusts in You. — Isa. 26:3

READ ISAIAH 26:1–6

Peace of mind can be a will o' the wisp. It comes and goes with the shifting ups and downs of our moods and circumstances. Even when people think they have peace, it can be quite false. God says of Israel's priests that "they have healed the hurt of the daughter of my people slightly, saying, 'Peace, peace; when there is no peace'" (Jer. 8:11). The solemn truth is that "there is no peace for the wicked" (Isa. 48:22; 57:20–21). Isaiah reminds us that if we want true and lasting peace, we must go to the Lord who alone can give it to us. This glorious gift is called "perfect peace" in our English bibles (v. 3a). But the Hebrew reads *shalom shalom*—literally "peace peace." This double *shalom* denotes "uninterrupted continuance forever." Whatever betides, we will know God's peace even in the turmoil of life in a fallen world. Thus Paul prays, "Now may the God of peace Himself sanctify you completely; and may your whole spirit, soul, and body be preserved blameless at the coming of our Lord Jesus Christ" (1 Thess. 5:23). As we grow in his grace, we will also grow into his peace. Notice three aspects of this *shalom* in Isaiah 26:1–6.

A new day has dawned upon this world (v. 1). In the previous chapter, Isaiah records that God promises the ruin of the cities of his people's persecutors (25:2–3). Thus perishes *the city of man*—as witness the now extinct Moab (25:10–12). In contrast to this, we have "a strong city...a righteous nation"—*the city of God* (vv. 1–2). This emerges "in that day" (26:1)—referring ultimately to the era of the Messiah—the age of the new covenant in Christ (Heb. 8:8 quoting Jer. 31:3ff.). We now live "in that day" and are blessed with the fruition of God's promises in Jesus our Savior. There are, and will be, wars and rumors of wars. Nonetheless, we live in an era of blessing. Why? Because, however much the wreckage of human sin litters the globe, the gospel grace of the knowledge of the Lord

320

is covering the earth "as the waters cover the sea" (Isa. 11:9; Hab. 2:14). Isaiah sings his song of salvation—Isaiah 26—in anticipation of "that day" when Christ is revealed.

A new peace is established in God's people (v. 3). This "shalom" is not political peace, but shalom of soul in believers, secured by the Messiah as the sin-bearing, but perfectly righteous, Savior of sinners. So it is, believers in Jesus, that "the peace of God, which surpasses all understanding, will guard your hearts and minds through Christ Jesus" (Phil. 4:7). The two experiential evidences of "the peace of God" are a *mind* "stayed on" the Lord (Isa. 26:3b) and a practical *trust* "in" the Lord (v. 3c). The believer has this peace, observes Charles Simeon, "in relation to his pardon and acceptance with God"; "his perseverance in the divine life"; and also "in relation to everything that may occur on his way to heaven." Jesus assures every believer, "Peace I leave with you, My peace I give to you; not as the world gives do I give to you. Let not your heart be troubled, neither let it be afraid" (John 14:27). Jesus's *shalom* is a foretaste of the eternal *shalom* of heaven itself.

A new portion of God's "everlasting strength" will justify the believer's trust in Christ and secure his eternal safety (vv. 4–6). The Christian's peace will be as everlasting as is the Lord's strength to save his own and bring them to glory. We are *never to be passive* in this matter. To "rest in the Lord" and "wait patiently for Him" is an active obedience (Ps. 37:7). The "will of God, your sanctification" (1 Thess. 4:3ff.) is your striving to be holy, as you are by his grace "enabled more and more to die unto sin, and live unto righteousness" (*Shorter Catechism* 35). May "grace and peace be multiplied to you in the knowledge of God and of Jesus our Lord" (2 Peter 1:2).

PRAISE THAT REJOICES IN PEACE FROM GOD
Sing Psalm 34:11–22

THINGS I WILL PRAY FOR TODAY

June 9
Your Dead Shall Live!

A prayer in the prospect of resurrection

Your dead shall live; together with my dead body they shall arise. Awake and sing, you who dwell in dust; for your dew is like the dew of herbs, and the earth shall cast out the dead. —Isa. 26:19

READ ISAIAH 26:7–19

Isaiah began his famous word about peace of mind with a glorious promise: "You will keep him in perfect peace, whose mind is stayed on You, because he trusts in You" (Isa. 26:3). This peace (literally, *shalom shalom*/"peace peace") requires a process of active sanctification, in which our minds are "stayed on" the Lord, because we trust in him. Challenges buffet this peace, so if you are to "go in the strength of the Lord GOD," you will need to "put on the whole armor of God" (Ps. 71:16; Eph. 6:11). So, in verses 7–18, the prophet prays so as to root God's promise of peace in his power to save—and thus to encourage us to a confiding, peaceful spirit as we persevere in the faith once for all delivered to the saints (Jude 3).

God is the "*Most Upright*" (vv. 7–9). This calls us morally to commit to personal uprightness and spiritually to seek personal union and communion with the Lord. Practically, it implies that when God's "judgments are in the earth, the inhabitants of the world will learn righteousness" (v. 9). Are these not the desires of believing hearts?

God's judgments *awaken sinners* (vv. 10–11). Archbishop Cranmer once said, "There is no man…so blind as he who will not see, nor he so dull as he that will not understand." The unconverted are not naturally impressed by God's grace or his majesty, but some will "see and be ashamed…when the fire of [God's] enemies shall devour them" (v. 11). As the psalmist writes, "Before I was afflicted I went astray, but now I keep Your word" (Ps. 119:67). Present wrath argues fleeing the wrath to come.

God blesses his people out of his *free grace*, without any merit on our part (vv. 12–18). Our best efforts are like a pregnancy that "brought forth wind" instead of a baby! Isaiah confesses, "We have not accomplished any deliverance in the earth," whether for ourselves or others (v. 18). We

322

need the Lord for any real fruitfulness! How then shall we produce "the peaceable fruit of righteousness" (Heb. 12:11)? Isaiah urges two practical commitments to this end:

Rejoice in your coming resurrection! "Your dead shall live; together with my dead body they shall arise" (v. 19a). "If we believe the resurrection of the dead," writes Matthew Henry, "of our dead bodies at the last day, as Job did, and the prophet here, that will facilitate our belief of the promised restoration of the church's lustre and strength in this world. When God's time shall have come, how low soever she may be brought, they shall arise, even Jerusalem, the city of God, but now lying like a dead body, a carcase to which the eagles are gathered together." The key is in the resurrection of the then-future Messiah: as Paul says, "if Christ is not risen, your faith is futile; you are still in your sins!...But now Christ is risen from the dead, and has become the first-fruits of those who have fallen asleep" (1 Cor. 15:17, 20).

Sing for joy in your present and future eternal life! "Awake and sing, you who dwell in dust; for your dew is like the dew of herbs, and the earth shall cast out the dead" (v. 19b). "God enables his saints," writes Richard Alleine, "to maintain an equal, steady, fixed frame of mind, in all the changes of their outward condition....Both in his prosperity and in his patience, he possesses his soul. He still goes on in the service of God and in resistance against the devil. He is still traveling on heavenward and turns away from the world which lies in iniquity." Our peace of mind is too easily rattled in this fallen world. Let us go on in the service of our Savior who has given us new life.

PRAISE FOR EVERLASTING LIFE
Sing Psalm 49:1–15

THINGS I WILL PRAY FOR TODAY

June 10
Spread Your Trouble before the Lord

A prayer for a national crisis

Now therefore, O LORD our God, save us from his hand, that all the kingdoms of the earth may know that You are the LORD, You alone.
—Isa. 37:20

READ ISAIAH 37:14–20; 2 KINGS 18–20

Any kind of calamity is bound to be a challenge to our faith. Hezekiah has a very serious problem. As sole ruler of Judah from 716 BC, he rebels against Assyrian overlordship (2 Kings 18:7) and God prospers Judah. In 701 BC, however, the new Assyrian king, Sennacherib, descends upon Judah, takes city after city, and finally besieges Hezekiah in Jerusalem (2 Kings 18:13). Hezekiah attempts to buy him off, but this fails (2 Kings 18:15–16); he is called to surrender in terms that blasphemously mock God (Isa. 36). Hezekiah responds by going to God's house in sackcloth and also in asking Isaiah to "lift up...prayer for the remnant that is left" (Isa. 37:4). Isaiah assures him of Sennacherib's eventual flight and ultimately violent death in his own land (Isa. 37:6–7). As it turns out, a report of an Ethiopian invasion leads Sennacherib to try hastening Hezekiah's capitulation by sending a letter that once more mocks the promises of God: "Do not let your God in whom you trust deceive you, saying, 'Jerusalem shall not be given into the hand of the king of Assyria'" (Isa. 37:10).

What is Hezekiah to do? Once again, he turns to the God his enemies so contemptuously dismiss. He goes "up to the house of the Lord" (v. 14) and he does two things in particular toward solving the problem: he quite literally spreads the letter "before the Lord" (v. 14). He understands that the problem is basically theological. Assyria has its own gods and is saying "our gods are better than your God!" That is the Assyrian brand of atheism. It is also the common currency of all denials of the God of the Bible, from the serpent in Eden down to the anti-supernatural secularism of the present day. In one way or another, the "godless" all have their own "gods." Let God be the judge! He then prays systematically through the issues he faces, appealing to the only God who can save his people (vv. 15–20):

324

- ⟫ *Whereas*, the God of Israel, who dwells with his people, is "alone" the true God and the Creator of heaven and earth (v. 16);
- ⟫ *Whereas*, the living God hears every reproach against his holy name (v. 17); and
- ⟫ *Whereas*, the Assyrians have indeed defeated many nations and destroyed their idols of wood and stone (vv. 18–19);
- ⟫ "*Now therefore*, O LORD our God, save us from his hand, that all the kingdoms of the earth may know that You are the LORD, You alone" (37:20; italics added).

Notice that Hezekiah does not bargain with God. He does not say, "Save us, and we'll do better next time." He simply asks the Lord to vindicate himself against his enemies, which is something only he can do. He casts himself upon God in reliance upon his promises, most recently revealed through the prophet Isaiah (37:6–7).

What are we to do, when faced with seemingly insuperable problems? Will you spread it all before the Lord and trust Jesus with confiding faith? This is the test. When the sun is not shining, will you wait for the Son who is the Light of the World? Jesus honestly tells his disciples what to expect from the world: "In the world you will have tribulation; but be of good cheer, I have overcome the world" (John 16:33). God's promise stands: "But to you who fear My name the Sun of Righteousness shall arise with healing in His wings; and you shall go out and grow fat like stall-fed calves" (Mal. 4:2). Hezekiah spread his trouble before the Lord and the Lord turned back Sennacherib.

PRAISE TO THE GOD WHO OVERCOMES ENEMIES
Sing Psalm 108:7–13

THINGS I WILL PRAY FOR TODAY

_____

_____

_____

_____

_____

_____

June 11
His Face toward the Wall

A prayer in the prospect of death

*Then Hezekiah turned his face toward the wall, and prayed to the
Lord... —Isa. 38:2*

READ ISAIAH 38:1-8

Are you prone to worrying about the uncertainties of life? Jesus urges us, "Do not worry about tomorrow, for tomorrow will worry about its own things. Sufficient for the day is its own trouble" (Matt. 6:34). But would we be *less* tempted to worry if we had *certain* knowledge of everything, good and bad, that will happen to us in the future? Surely, knowing too much would trouble us even more! Today's trouble will be quite sufficient, as Jesus says.

Which of us wants to be told that he is terminally ill? Hezekiah was in his late thirties when he became "sick and near death." Furthermore, this was not a doctor's fallible diagnosis, but a prophecy from God through the prophet Isaiah! Small wonder then that Hezekiah "turned his face toward the wall, and prayed to the Lord" (v. 2). If a "normal" crisis can bring our life to a standstill, how much more will an imminent encounter with "the last enemy" stop us in our tracks, as it did him (1 Cor. 15:26)?

Let us be clear that "sickness" is not invariably a punishment for particular, personal sin. Hezekiah falls ill as we all do in this fallen world. Yes, the sin of Adam brought death upon us all, physically as well as spiritually. Sometimes, certain illnesses are the consequences of sinful behavior. Ananias's death was a divine judgment for specific sin, but we only know that because God reveals it to us (Acts 5:3). Job's comforters speculated that God was punishing Job for some secret sin, but they were wrong. Remember that Jesus went to Bethany because Lazarus's sisters told him, "Lord, behold, he whom You love is sick" (John 11:3). J. C. Ryle writes, "Lazarus was a good man, converted, believing, renewed, sanctified, a friend of Christ and an heir of glory. And yet Lazarus was sick. Thus sickness is no sign that God is displeased. Sickness is intended to be a blessing to us, and not a curse." Sickness, like every other human ailment, is something to be redeemed! Hezekiah would be given fifteen more years of life (v. 5).

Sickness is, however, always "the finger of God." In Exodus 8:19, God's plagues on Egypt are his "finger" pointing Pharaoh to let Israel go. In Luke 11:20, God's "finger" is emblematic of the power and authority by which Jesus heals sick people. For believers, Christ's love is in our sicknesses and is also in the overthrow of our death. Notice some practical lessons from Hezekiah's brush with sickness and death:

- Our first priority in sickness must be to *pray*: The young king faces the wall so that no distraction could interfere with his communion with God. When, so to speak, your back is to a wall, turn your face to that wall and cry out to the Lord. This is the place to start.
- Second, it is always right to pray for *healing*. Hezekiah did not want to die. His prayer records his testimony of faithfulness— it is not an argument that he deserves to live. It is the honest, heartfelt appeal of a believer intent on serving God with heart, soul, mind, and strength as long as he lives (Mark 11:20).
- Third, it is always good to *grieve*. We all know that death is an enemy and an outrage. It cuts all our links to this world, including our loved ones and our usefulness to the Lord and his people.
- Finally, remember that sickness will *bless* us if 1) it leads us to think seriously about death; 2) causes us to reflect on the claims of God and our eternal destiny; 3) softens and makes wise our hearts (Ps. 90:12); and 4) humbles us so that we turn in repentance and saving faith to Christ who is alone the Savior (Isa. 53:10–11).

PRAISE TO THE GOD WHO GUARANTEES OUR LIFE
Sing Psalm 31:19–24

THINGS I WILL PRAY FOR TODAY

_____

_____

_____

_____

June 12
Look Down from Heaven!

A prayer for revival (Part I)

Look down from heaven... —Isa. 63:15a

READ ISAIAH 63:15–19

he first place to go in all our prayers is to heaven and our Father-God. Jesus teaches us to pray to "our Father in heaven" (Matt. 6:9). Solomon dedicates the temple in a prayer, in which he calls on the Lord eight times in similar words to "hear in heaven Your dwelling place; and when You hear, forgive" (1 Kings 8:30–49). Isaiah's prayer is neither the quiet devotion of private worship, nor the uplifting worship of Israel in the flush of great blessing; instead, it is a pleading for the presence and power of God in a situation of desperate national declension. Isaiah's cry to "look down from heaven!" pleads for God's attention and intervention in a situation in which he appears to have abandoned his people to their own folly.

True prayer never comes out of a clear blue sky. You know this in your own experience. Dead recitation is not prayer. Real prayers always have a history with deep reasons rising in the soul. You don't go to the doctor to tell him you are so healthy you do not need him. "Those who are well," says Jesus, "have no need of a physician, but those who are sick" (Matt. 9:12). Isaiah knew the church of his day was sick. And God gave him prophecies of the coming Messiah and his future work of salvation (Isa. 61); of the rebuilding of Zion and the revival of the church (Isa. 62); and of a future day of salvation and judgment (Isa. 63:1–6). But these wonderful promises may have seemed too distant from fruition to be a practical solution for the immediate problems of the sixth century BC church. The gloom seemed unrelieved.

Prayer is about a real, living relationship with God. Down the centuries, God was good to Israel. They were his covenant people and he was their Savior. He was faithful to his covenant promises. He was compassionate toward them in their afflictions and in "His love and in His pity He redeemed them." Surely they felt this love. But they rebelled and

328

"grieved His Holy Spirit." Yet God mercifully led them, under Moses, through the wilderness to the Promised Land. In this, he blessed them and glorified his name (Isa. 63:7–14). So what went wrong?

Isaiah's prayer tells the story in a most affecting way. He asks God, "Where are your zeal...strength...yearning of Your heart and Your mercies toward me?" (v. 15). He isn't angry with God. He is just heartbroken because he cannot see him doing anything at that moment to turn around the wretched state of backslidden Judah. He appeals to God's covenant promises with Abraham and Jacob and affirms him as their Father and Redeemer (v. 16). Without blaming God, he asks why he let Israel "stray" from his ways and "harden" their hearts against any fear of God (v. 17ab). He then prays for the active, evident presence and power of God to revive his people (vv. 17cd–18). And then he grieves aloud for the deadly spiritual state of God's cause and people: "We have become like those of old, over whom you never ruled, those who were never called by Your name" (v. 19). The church had become the world and the "righteous" indistinguishable from the wicked! Christians! Pray for the pseudo-Christian churches and nations of our world!

The petition to "look down from heaven" also reveals something wonderful about prayer. It tells us that believing prayer is the bridge that connects our need with God's gracious provision. God sees. God hears. God is never actually absent from his believing people. And believing prayer has the promise of his answer and the prospect of his power to save being released afresh upon fields white for harvest. If our world seems as spiritually desolate and miserable as Judah's did to the prophet, then let us pray like the prophet—and believe God to be the Father and Redeemer that he is and for his Messiah, Jesus, to be whom he has sent to save sinners like us.

PRAYER CRYING TO GOD FROM THE DEPTHS
Sing Psalm 130

THINGS I WILL PRAY FOR TODAY

_____

_____

_____

_____

June 13
Oh...Rend the Heavens!

A prayer for revival (Part II)

Oh, that You would rend the heavens!—Isa. 64:1a

READ ISAIAH 64:1–12

saiah's prayer reflects the reality that revival must be preceded by repentance. He outlines the sorry state of the church and begs God to "look down from heaven" (63:15–19). He pleads, "O that You would rend the heavens!" meaning, "Don't just look down, come down! Answer the desperate need of your cause, kingdom, and people, and revive us again" (64:1–12). He appeals to "the Father of mercies and God of all comfort" (2 Cor. 1:3), arguing that the spiritual decline of the church cries out for the God who saves to revive her again! What looks ripe for judgment is also ripe for revival! Isaiah's importunity over Israel's declension is framed as an opportunity for God's redemption!

Isaiah's prayer is a model for our praying in distressing circumstances. A series of five petitions unfolds both the logic of grief and the plea for divine intervention, just the opposite sides of the one coin:

> ❧ The first petition pleads for God's *action*—visible, tangible intervention—to humble his adversaries and cause them to tremble at his presence. When the wicked seem to be having it all their own way, we are tempted to wonder if God is a *deus absconditus*—a hidden God. "Let things be put into a ferment," writes Matthew Henry, "in order to a glorious revolution in favour of the church: 'As the fire causes the waters to boil'" (vv. 1–2). Oh, Lord, "come down!"

> ❧ The second petition pleads God's *character*—his goodness and covenant faithfulness as shown to his people in the past (vv. 3–5). Why, even when his people were faithful, he bestowed blessings they neither looked for—nor deserved! Isaiah appeals to God as the one "who is able to do exceedingly abundantly above all that we ask or think" (Eph. 3:20). He acknowledges that God is justified in withdrawing his blessings: "You are indeed angry, for we have sinned." He admits, "In these ways we continue,"

and adds, most solemnly, "And shall we be saved?" (v. 5cd). God owes us nothing. Salvation is optional with God, and it is all of grace in Jesus Christ (Rom. 9:15ff.).

❧ The third petition lifts up our *desperate need*: "We have all become like one who is unclean, and all our righteous deeds are like a polluted garment." No wonder that God hid his face from us and "consumed us because of our iniquities" (vv. 6–7). Left to ourselves, we would perish eternally, and justly so! The prayer in effect begs the Lord not to abandon us and not to punish us as our iniquities deserve (Ps. 130:3; cf. Ezra 9:13).

❧ The fourth petition simply casts backslidden Israel on God's *free-grace mercy*: "But now, O LORD, You are our Father; we are the clay, and You our potter; and all we are the work of Your hand" (v. 8; cf. Rom. 9:20–21). No excuses, no blame-shifting, no protestations of innocence—just unconditional surrender appealing to God's mercy.

❧ The final petition seeks *forgiveness* of sin and the revival of the church (vv. 9–12). God's covenant faithfulness is the implicit basis of the appeal. Isaiah asks the Lord if, after all the ruin that the church has brought upon itself, he will still withhold his "peace, and afflict us very severely?" (v. 12). The prayer ends, as prayers do, with a question. But it is an appeal to the God who is love.

The answer soon follows: "Behold, My servants shall eat, but [the unrepentant and unbelieving] shall be hungry.…My servants shall sing for joy of heart" (Isa. 65:13ff.). How are they saved? By the "man of sorrows" who "was wounded for our transgressions" and "was bruised for our iniquities.…by His stripes we are healed" (Isa. 53:3–5). The same Savior, whose name is Jesus, calls you to himself: "Come to Me, all you who labor and are heavy laden, and I will give you rest" (Matt. 11:28).

PRAISE FROM A REVIVED SOUL
Sing Psalm 119:25–32

THINGS I WILL PRAY FOR TODAY

_____

_____

_____

June 14
I'm Too Young to...

A prayer to be excused from God's calling

Then I said, "Ah, Lord GOD! Behold, I do not know how to speak, for I am only a youth." —Jer. 1:6

READ JEREMIAH 1:4–10

Chronological age is a fertile source of excuses for not doing what we ought to do. You can certainly be too young to marry or too old to climb a mountain. Neither is it sin to doubt your competence for a specific task or to shrink from its challenges. The most poignant example of this is Jesus on the day of his death, when he prays, "O My Father, if it is possible, let this cup pass from Me; nevertheless, not as I will, but as You will" (Matt. 26:39). This is the sinless Son of God, in his true human nature, shrinking from the physical and spiritual trials he must face. It is not a sin for us, any more than it was for Jesus, to cry out for some relief in the face of the daunting pressures of our calling. When God tells Jeremiah he is to be a prophet, no wonder he trembles and prays to be excused.

God chose you for your calling(s). It is said, *Profeta nascitur, non fit*—"Prophets are born, not made." Perhaps all occupations have been similarly described. It is certainly true that God decreed, before Jeremiah was born, to ordain him "a prophet to the nations" (vv. 4–5). It is no less true of every child of God that he knew us "before [He] formed [us] in the womb" (v. 5). No one is merely an accident of biology, history, education, economics, or native wit! Furthermore, however humble your calling may seem to be, it is where God means to bless you and those around you. Jeremiah (655–586 BC) exercised a prominent ministry and was "famous" in his day, and because of the God-breathed Scriptures, his ministry still lives 2,600 years on. He "being dead still speaks" (Heb. 11:4). The other 99.99 percent of us are relatively obscure, and our service to the Lord may be quiet and unsung. Nevertheless, the God who chose us from eternity also delights in us as we witness a good confession of Christ in our allotted spheres of service, whatever they may be.

God will listen to your objections to your calling. Jeremiah begged off at first, citing his lack of speaking gifts on account of his youth (v. 6). We should not accuse him of sin for this. This is a very normal reaction of a humble saint to the challenges and prospects of a great work. Oh, that all the young were as humble and self-effacing! Far from Jeremiah taking, so to speak, a ship for Tarshish as did Jonah (Jonah 1:3), he is simply overwhelmed with a sense of being unqualified. This teaches us to take our questions to the Lord in prayer. He understands, "For He knows our frame; He remembers that we are dust" (Ps. 103:14).

God equips you for your calling. Negatively, Jeremiah is told not to despise his youth and not to fear the opposition. The ground for this is that God will give him the words to speak and will be with him to deliver him (vv. 7–8). Positively, the entail of Jeremiah's demurring prayer is sealed in God's dramatic bestowal upon him of speaking skills necessary to his office (v. 9), together with the assurance that he will be God's instrument to "root out and to pull down, to destroy and to throw down, to build and to plant" (v. 10). Jeremiah is uniquely gifted and tasked to be a prophet to both the Jews and the Gentiles. The miracle of transformed oratorical skill and the giving of revelatory messages not only enables him to think and speak as a prophet, but also to attest to the world that God has sent him and is revealing his will through him. We are not given either miraculous gifts or new revelation to speak, but the promises of God are the same to the extent that the Lord will enable us to serve him in all our callings, by deepening us in our soul, instructing us in our minds, and empowering us in our strength, even as we love the Lord with all our heart (Mark 12:30). We are never too young—or too old—to follow Jesus.

PRAISE THAT CALLS US TO SERVE THE LORD
Sing Psalm 100

THINGS I WILL PRAY FOR TODAY

June 15
The Only Way Home

The prayer of a repentant backslider

Indeed we do come to You, for You are the Lord our God. —Jer. 3:22

READ JEREMIAH 3:21–4:4

On a sodden Saturday long ago, I competed in the Scottish Universities Cross-country Championship. At one point in the two-lap, six-mile course, there was a short but steep section soon completely reduced to mud. The only way to keep your feet was to haul your way up by one of the fences on either side. A runner ahead of me decided to charge up the middle but he lost his footing, fell flat on his face, slid back down the slope, and rose at the bottom caked in mud from head to toe! That's how spiritual backsliding works. You go your own way in rebellion against God and you will discover that the mud of sin sticks not only from head to toe, but from heart to hand. "Backsliding" is an ugly word and the practice of backsliding has ugly consequences for those who choose that course.

Jeremiah cites the case of backslidden and defunct Israel. The kingdom of the ten tribes was destroyed in 722 BC by the Assyrians, as a direct judgment of God on its national depravity. Nearly one hundred years later, the prophet addresses Judah, calling her to repentance from similar backslidings. Israel's problem is solemnly summed up in the words of Jeremiah 3:21: "A voice was heard on the desolate heights, weeping and supplications of the children of Israel. For they have perverted their way; they have forgotten the LORD their God." The tragedy of this weeping is that it is not the voice of "godly sorrow" producing "repentance leading to salvation," but only "the sorrow of the world" that "produces death" (2 Cor. 7:10). The Israelites' weeping shares the attitude of the rich man in Jesus's parable, who asks Abraham to send Lazarus from heaven to cool him in his anguish in hell (Luke 16:24). If Judah is to escape just judgment, then she must learn from Israel's sad demise and "return" to the Lord, trusting him when he says, "I will heal your backslidings" (Jer. 3:21–22).

God calls his "backsliding children" to come home (see 3:12, 14, 22a; 4:1). The response God wants is summed up in verses 22c–25. Here is a model for the returning backslider—not the Israel that perished, but "the remnant according to the election of grace" that did and ever will return to the Lord (Rom. 11:5):

> ❧ The first step is to acknowledge *who God really is*: "Indeed we do come to You, for You are the LORD our God" (v. 22c). It's a fact!

> ❧ The second step is to admit that there is *no salvation in any other*: not "from the hills, and from the multitude of mountains"—the high places of pagan worship—but "truly, in the LORD our God is the salvation of Israel" (v. 23). This salvation is fulfilled in Jesus Christ, as Peter proclaims to the backslidden Jews of his day: "Nor is there salvation in any other, for there is no other name under heaven given among men by which we must be saved" (Acts 4:12).

> ❧ The third step is the *conviction and confession* of sin: "For shame has devoured the labor of our fathers from our youth.... We lie down in our shame....For we have sinned against the LORD our God, we and our fathers, from our youth even to this day, and have not obeyed the voice of the LORD our God" (vv. 24–25). We have truly blown it!

The homecoming prayer is one of true repentance. Like the prodigal son in "the far country," God's backslider must come to himself—realizing his true state and danger. He then must cry out, "I will arise and go to my father, and will say to him, 'Father, I have sinned against heaven and before you'" (Luke 15:18). And then do it! Return to the Lord and follow him! "Put away your abominations" and "break up your fallow ground"—that is, cultivate afresh your weed-filled hearts and renew your covenant with God with all your heart (4:1–4). This is the only way home to the Lord from all our backslidings.

PRAISE TO THE LORD WHO CALLS US HOME
Sing Psalm 60:1–5

THINGS I WILL PRAY FOR TODAY

_____

_____

_____

June 16
Has God Deceived Us?

A prayer asking God to recall backsliders

Then I said, "Ah, Lord GOD! Surely You have greatly deceived this people and Jerusalem, saying, 'You shall have peace,' whereas the sword reaches to the heart." —*Jer. 4:10*

READ JEREMIAH 4:5-10

On the face of it, this seems a strange prayer. It looks more like the accusation of a skeptic than the cry of a believing prophet. It surely cannot be Jeremiah's considered opinion. He knows God called him to prophesy judgment, and he knows it is false "prophets" who say God is promising peace for all and sundry. This is clear when the Lord tells him that "from the prophet even to the priest, everyone deals falsely. They have also healed the hurt of My people slightly, saying, 'Peace, peace!' when there is no peace" (Jer. 6:13–14). This is not news to Jeremiah. He already knows what the false prophets are saying; he is neither confused as to God's will, nor is he accusing God of lying to his people. His one sentence "arrow" prayer is flanked by God calling for Israel's repentance and promising that if they return to him, they "shall not be moved" (4:1)—and God's charge to Jerusalem: "wash your heart from wickedness, that you may be saved" (4:14). Not moved by what? Saved from what? Surely the judgments that God declares are coming on the land, if there is no repentance. It is the false prophets who are the Pollyannas of false peace!

How then is Jeremiah's prayer to be understood and applied? It is best to read what he says here, as Matthew Henry quaintly puts it, "with an interrogation." It is as if he asks God, "*Hast thou indeed thus deceived this people?* It is plain that they are greatly deceived, for they expect *peace*, whereas *the sword reaches unto the soul*; that is, it is a killing sword, abundance of lives are lost, and more likely to be." Jeremiah is speaking to the church people and the leaders who have promoted and/or persuaded themselves of the "Peace, peace" lie! What God thinks of it is obvious from the true prophecies that both precede and follow the prayer. So, asks Matthew Henry, "Was it God that deceived them? No,

336

he had often given them warning of judgments in general and of this in particular; but their own prophets deceive them, and cry peace to those to whom the God of heaven does not speak peace. It is a pitiable thing, and that which every good man greatly laments, to see people flattered into their own ruin, and promising themselves peace when war is at the door." All the hard sayings of Scripture are stating, in one way or another, "Wake up!" and "Return to the Lord in national and personal repentance and new obedience of faith!"

Why does God lay out so graphically the consequences of sin? One reason is that biblical sin is real. There is nothing artificial or abstract about it, and there is nothing arbitrary about God's righteous offense over it. Sin not only cocks a snook at God, but it also has frightful consequences for its victims and its perpetrators. A second reason is that biblical salvation is also real. While God will "by no means clear the guilty," he above all is determined to show "mercy to thousands, to those who love [Him] and keep [His] commandments" (Ex. 34:7; 20:6). He withholds judgment to extend salvation: "The LORD is merciful and gracious, slow to anger, and abounding in mercy" (Ps. 103:8; 145:8; cf. Nah. 1:3). And he sent his only begotten Son to be the Savior who bears the terrible cost of the sin of those who will believe on him. We are also given reason to hope in Jesus, however grim the times may be and however stern God's warnings. In a world where there is so much illusory "peace, peace" palmed off as if it were truth, the "God of hope" promises true "peace in believing" (Rom. 15:13)—"the peace of God, which surpasses all understanding, [that] will guard your hearts and minds through Christ Jesus" (Phil. 4:7). Jesus must be "our peace"…your *shalom* (Eph. 2:14).

PRAYER FOR GOD'S LIGHT AND TRUTH
Sing Psalm 43:3–5

THINGS I WILL PRAY FOR TODAY

_____

_____

_____

_____

_____

June 17
Faces Harder than Rock

A prayer mourning for the low state of the church

They have made their faces harder than rock; they have refused to return. —Jer. 5:3

READ JEREMIAH 5:1–9

Hard lives and hard times make for hard faces. On the positive side, the Lord sometimes makes his servants' faces like flint so as to stand up to opposition. He tells Ezekiel, "Like adamant stone, harder than flint, I have made your forehead; do not be afraid of them, nor be dismayed at their looks, though they are a rebellious house" (Ezek. 3:9). Isaiah contemplates how God will help his suffering Servant: "For the Lord GOD will help Me; therefore I will not be disgraced; therefore I have set My face like a flint, and I know that I will not be ashamed" (Isa. 50:7). We need a certain *godly* toughening if we are to be "steadfast, immovable, always abounding in the work of the Lord, knowing that [our] labor is not in vain in the Lord" (1 Cor. 15:58). Christians are to be neither hard-bitten moralists and controversialists, nor bleeding-hearted compromisers, but are to be firm and compassionate in faithfulness to the Word of God. And this involves a tough love from the Lord and toward the world.

The hard faces of Israel are the result of rejecting God. These are rebels against God and his truth—and it shows. The Lord tells Jeremiah to "run to and fro through the streets of Jerusalem" trying to find a man "who executes judgment, who seeks the truth" (v. 1). Like Diogenes who, some two centuries later, would wander the streets of Athens with a lamp supposedly looking for an honest man, Jeremiah's search is fruitless. Diogenes's antics were a stale philosophical joke, but with Jeremiah the destiny of Jerusalem and its inhabitants is at stake. When he prays, his focus is upon the rejection of God's revealed truth within the church: "O LORD, are not Your eyes on the truth?" God recalls his people to faithfulness, but they will have none of it: "You have stricken them, but they have not grieved; You have consumed them, but they have refused to receive correction. They have made their faces harder than rock; they have refused to return" (v. 3). Jeremiah lays this down to poverty and ignorance. So he goes to "the great men" (vv. 4–5c). But they are even more anti-God and anti-truth: "Their transgressions are many" and "their backslidings have increased" (vv. 5d–9). Philip Ryken notes that this is "much like the post-Christian West" in the twenty-first century. We see it in people's faces.

Jeremiah is crying to God for spiritual revival in the church. This is the silent subtext under his dismay at the hard faces of the godless. How will these hard faces be softened and determined sinners be transformed? For all the "jeremiad" gloom of God's impending judgments, there are also bright breaks in the clouds. These culminate in the promise of the coming Messiah and the "new covenant." Jesus is the "branch of righteousness" who is also called "the Lord our Righteousness" (Jer. 23:5–6). God promises, "I will put My law in their minds, and write it on their hearts; and I will be their God, and they shall be My people" (Jer. 31:33). Hard faces will melt in the love of Christ: "They looked to Him and were radiant, and their faces were not ashamed" (Ps. 34:5). And how marvelous is Jesus's promise to every believer: "Then the righteous will shine forth as the sun in the kingdom of their Father. He who has ears to hear, let him hear!" (Matt. 13:43). In his poem, "Jehovah Tsidkenu—The Lord our Righteousness," Robert Murray McCheyne (1813–43) recorded his own conversion to Christ:

> My terrors all vanished before the sweet name;
> My guilty fears vanished, with boldness I came
> To drink at the fountain, life-giving and free—
> Jehovah Tsidkenu is all things to me.

PRAISE FOR THE GOD WHO SAVED ME
Sing Psalm 34:1–10

THINGS I WILL PRAY FOR TODAY

_____

_____

_____

_____

_____

_____

June 18
Stop Praying for Them!?

A prayer prohibited by God

Therefore do not pray for this people, nor lift up a cry or prayer for them, nor make intercession to Me...—Jer. 7:16

READ JEREMIAH 7:16–27; CF. 11:14; 14:11

Christians are used to feeling they pray less than they should. But to hear God command the prophet not to pray—and for God's people at that—comes as a huge shock. Does Scripture not charge us to pray "without ceasing" and for those who "spitefully use...and persecute" us (1 Thess. 5:17; Matt. 5:44)? We understand that we should never pray for Satan and his legions, but we might expect to pray for lost people to be saved—and even for those we believe are "deceivers" and "antichrists" afflicted with "the spirit of Antichrist" (1 John 2:18, 22; 4:3; 2 John 1:7). We routinely pray for the overthrow of evil, while interceding that those in its grip be converted to Christ.

Why does God specifically prohibit intercession in this case? The answer is in the people's response to Jeremiah's great temple sermon (7:1–15). Basically they had, like much of the modern church in the West, introduced and excused certain pagan practices as a kind of religious progress acceptable to God. Hence the teaching of those who promoted their "lying words" as being "of the temple of the Lord" (7:4)! Then it was "only" burning incense to Baal—today it is "multi-faith worship." Thus does the church effectively become "the synagogue of Satan" (Rev. 2:9). They had crossed a line in their backslidings truly visible only to God! The consequences are that not only will God cast the apostates out of his sight (7:15), but he will also demonstrate his anger by removing the prophet's intercessory prayer from the picture. In saying to Jeremiah, "I will not hear you," God is telegraphing that, if he will not hear *his prophet's intercession* for them, how can they think for a moment that he will hear *them* if they pray? Now they hate Jeremiah, but in a strange way such folk want to believe he will pray for them and that God will forgive them anyway!

The modern manifestation of God's anger at being effectively put out of his church is that he withdraws himself and his faithful ministers and people. Within a half mile of my childhood home in Scotland, there were nine congregations of the Church of Scotland. Fifty years later, the only survivor is the one where the gospel is truly preached. The false teachers and their victims are gone, leaving a huge mission field for evangelism. Heresy kills, but the gospel brings life.

Is God telling us to stop praying for anyone? The answer to that must be no! What he does with Judah and Jeremiah is pull back the curtain to reveal something of his hitherto secret will for that specific situation. We can assume that today, in the present secrecy of his will, God is exercising his judgments upon apostasy and unbelief. But he is not revealing such secrets to us: "The secret things belong to the Lord our God, but those things which are revealed belong to us and to our children forever, that we may do all the words of this law" (Deut. 29:29). Not knowing his secret will, we may and must intercede for any and all while the world lasts.

We must also treasure sound ministry. Value the prayers of those who intercede for you. Don't be like the English "metalcore" band Asking Alexandria, whose 2013 hit "Don't Pray for Me" blasts out the determinedly hopeless nihilism of the reprobate mind. Listen to Christ, the Savior of sinners, revealed in Scripture and proclaimed by faithful ministers; as you intercede for others, know that he always lives to make intercession for you (Heb. 7:25).

PRAISE FOR THE GOD WHO REJOICES IN HIS PEOPLE
Sing Psalm 149

THINGS I WILL PRAY FOR TODAY

June 19
Who Is Really in Control?

A prayer for God to act with power

O Lord, I know that the way of man is not in himself; it is not in man who walks to direct his own steps. —Jer. 10:23

READ JEREMIAH 10:23–25

However low the spiritual state of the church, there is rarely any lack of outward show of religion. Whether in Jeremiah's Judah or in our twenty-first century world, such "show" invariably masks an effective denial of the God of the Bible (cf. Isa. 29:13–14). The "way of the Gentiles" (Jer. 10:2)—what Paul in 1 Corinthians 12:2 calls being "carried away to…dumb idols"—is a kind of practical atheism in which almost any "god" can be worshiped, provided it is not the one true God who "has in these last days spoken to us by His Son," the Lord Jesus Christ (Heb. 1:2). God's response to ancient Judah is to warn of coming judgment upon "the house of Israel" (Jer. 10:1–22; cf. 1 Peter 4:17). This is, however, no mere crack of doom, but a call to new life couched in a serious warning. The central focus is upon the character of the living God, who even in his righteous wrath reaches out in grace to his backsliding people.

Jeremiah closes his sermon with a prayer (10:23–25). This has a double effect: he both begs the Lord to intervene with grace and power in people's hearts, and he also implicitly appeals to the consciences of sinners to wake up to their danger and, instead of fighting God, turn to him as the "Savior and…Redeemer" he really is (Isa. 49:26)! He sets out three compelling arguments for such a course:

As to daily life, will you admit that "the way of man is not in himself"? You certainly can't control the providential agents of God's judgment—like the Assyrian armies! You cannot even "direct [your] own steps" (v. 23). Jeremiah knows this…and you don't!? Therefore, "do not boast about tomorrow, for you do not know what a day may bring forth" (Prov. 27:1). "Read all history," says William Jay. "See the consequences of Lot's choosing the vale of Sodom, 'because it was well watered [Gen. 13:10].'" As you review your own decision-making, successes and failures, and joys and sorrows, can you really say you are in control of your own life, on your own, apart from God?

As to your inner life—that of your soul and your eternal destiny—can you cure your guilt and sin and make yourself right with God, by your own best efforts? Jeremiah loves and serves the Lord, but he doubts himself precisely as he reverences the Lord: hence his prayer, "O LORD, correct me, but with justice; not in Your anger, lest You bring me to nothing" (v. 24). We need a Savior, for, as the psalmist says, "If You, LORD, should mark iniquities, O Lord, who could stand?" (Ps. 130:3). No one can be his own salvation.

As to your life in this fallen world—your comfort and even survival—left to yourself, are you able to secure your freedom from bullies, thieves, and assorted oppressors, far less the enemies of God? Jeremiah knows that the Jews cannot guarantee their national existence before the onslaught of the Assyrians. None of us is exempt from the need of the Lord and his upholding grace and power. The prophet therefore prays for God to deliver his people, employing in verse 25 the words of Psalm 79:6–7: "Pour out Your wrath on the nations that do not know You, and on the kingdoms that do not call on Your name. For they have devoured Jacob, and laid waste his dwelling place." You need a Savior—now and always.

This all points to Jesus Christ and his coming to save people from their sins (Isa. 59:20; Mal. 3:1; Matt. 1:21; Gal. 4:4). There is no "salvation in any other, for there is no other name under heaven given among men by which we must be saved" (Acts 4:12). Still, there is a sense in which you do have a hand in your destiny: you must, as Jesus puts it, "repent or perish" (Luke 13:1–5). Turn to him, trust in his death for sin and sinners, and so live forever!

PRAYER FOR DELIVERANCE FROM FORMER SINS
Sing Psalm 79:8–13

THINGS I WILL PRAY FOR TODAY

June 20
Can You Compete with Horses?

A prayer that needs some correction

If you have raced with men on foot, and they have wearied you, how will you compete with horses? —Jer. 12:5

READ JEREMIAH 11:18–12:6

There is too much loose talk about personal evangelism. Listening to some, you might conclude it to be the simplest, most user-friendly commitment in the Christian's life. Biblical truth and historical fact, however, reveal it to be one of the more discouraging, even dangerous, activities for God's people. Jesus reminds his disciples, "A prophet is not without honor except in his own country and in his own house" (Matt. 13:57). He tells us not to be afraid, "For He Himself has said, 'I will never leave you nor forsake you'" (Heb. 13:5). We may boldly say, "The LORD is my helper; I will not fear. What can man do to me?" (Heb. 13:6; cf. Jer. 1:8). It is not easy work, as Jeremiah discovered. It takes grit as well as grace, fortitude, and faith.

What perplexed Jeremiah was the question of why "the way of the wicked prosper[ed]" (12:1–2). This was very personal to him, because his own people back home in Anathoth threatened him: "Do not prophesy in the name of the Lord, lest you die by our hand" (11:19–21). Asaph, the writer of Psalm 73, saw the wicked getting away with murder (so to speak) and enjoying their rich and easy lives. Like Jeremiah, he cannot quite see past God's apparent outward goodness to the godless, as opposed to his own rather difficult circumstances in God's providence. Of course, it begs the question as to what God's "goodness" really is, as experienced respectively by the godly and the godless. Asaph finds his answer in the temple (Ps. 73:17–20). The material "goodness" in the lives of the wicked masks the fact that they are on "the slippery places" facing eternal destruction! The true goodness of God is in his saving grace and loving presence in believers' lives (Ps. 73:23–28). Evil in the world is always perplexing to us, but it is not the whole story, as Jeremiah needs to realize—and perhaps you also?

Jeremiah wants a simple answer to his distress. He already has his answer in mind—the instant and utter destruction of the wicked (12:3–4)!

344

How true to life this is! Our prayers often assume that our answer ought to be God's answer. We want God to say, "Amen to that!" After all, is it not obvious that evil must stop *now* if the Lord is really righteous and truly loves us? We don't expect God to say no.

God often counters our questions with questions. He asks, "If you have raced with men on foot, and they have wearied you, how will you compete with horses?" (v. 5; cf. Job 38:2–3). Why such a question? Surely it is because God wants us to think more deeply about what is troubling us. Jeremiah wants it all to end: threats to his life, prosperity for the wicked, and what he calls the mourning of the land (v. 4). As we might say, he has "had it up to here" and wants God to put an end to sin and misery. God's answer is basically saying, "You haven't seen anything yet! There is a lot more for you to do in your life and service to the Lord; compared to competing in a footrace with men, that will be more like running a race against horses! If you are ready to quit now in a relative 'land of peace,' then how will you cope with torrents of 'the floodplain of the Jordan?'" (v. 5). Yes, your enemies have turned out to be "those of [your] own household" (Matt. 10:36). But the men of little Anathoth are minnows beside the sharks he will face in Jerusalem, Egypt, and Babylon.

The point is that God is sovereign whatever new difficulties arise; it is by his grace that you will be given strength to keep pace and serve the Lord with gladness. Paul will later testify, "Therefore I take pleasure in infirmities, in reproaches, in needs, in persecutions, in distresses, for Christ's sake. For when I am weak, then I am strong" (2 Cor. 12:10). Christian! Look to Jesus and he will also enable you to "compete with horses"—and to prevail!

PRAISE ADMITTING OUR WEAKNESS
Sing Psalm 73:13–22

THINGS I WILL PRAY FOR TODAY

June 21
Never Stop Praying!

A prayer for deliverance from drought and sin

O the Hope of Israel...why should You be like a stranger in a strange land?—Jer. 14:8

READ JEREMIAH 14:7–9, 13, 19–22

Drought, to the urbanized people of the Western world, means limits on washing cars and watering lawns. But wherever food is grown, drought presages potential disaster. In Scripture, such events are always "the finger of God" and need to be taken seriously (cf. Ex. 8:19). This is not to say that bad weather must mean God is angry or that good weather must mean the converse. Judah's deep drought, however, is revealed to be a direct judgment of God upon the nation's sin (see Jer. 14:1–7). Jeremiah's response is to pray for God's mercy. And the more God says no, the more Jeremiah persists in prayer. Why? He knows that God is merciful and will reverse course, if people repent (Jer. 18:7–11). So never stop praying for the lost!

Prayer #1 sees Jeremiah acknowledge that God's judgments are fully justified (vv. 7–9). "Do it," he says, "for Your name's sake" (v. 7). God's name—Yahweh—is his *covenant* name, and it bears the fragrance of his eternal purpose of salvation by grace. Accordingly, Jeremiah latches on to God's character as "the Hope of Israel." Why should he "be like...a stranger [in His own land]...a traveler [merely passing through]," as if he were "a mighty one who cannot save?" Hence the strong plea, "O Lord...we are called by *Your name*; do not leave us!" (vv. 8–9). The point is that, while Jeremiah "could find no excuse for Israel, he could find a plea in the very character of God: and therefore he entreated Him to do, for *His own sake*, what he could not venture to ask *for theirs*." God's answer is no! (vv. 10–12). But this is intercessory prayer in its purest form: the seeking of God's grace for lost souls, who cannot save themselves, even if they wanted to!

Prayer #2 sees Jeremiah appeal to the fact that the people were badly taught by their "prophets," who tell them they will neither see

sword nor famine, but will have "assured peace in this place" (v. 13). As in too many churches today, the people are taught the opposite of God's Word! Again God says no and declares that the false prophets will die by sword and famine, and the people will perish in their wickedness (vv. 14–16). God is grieved about the inevitable consequences of unrepented sin. Sin has destroyed the community such that "both prophet and priest go about in a land they do not know" (vv. 17–18). The reality is a world away from the lying fantasies they put over on the people, which the people willingly imbibed!

Prayer #3 sees Jeremiah pleading with even greater fervor. He appeals for the healing that seems impossible (v. 19); he confesses Israel's sin, but the people will not (v. 20); and he begs God to keep his covenant, even if Israel broke hers (v. 21). In a crescendo of pleading, he affirms that God alone, in contrast to "the idols of the nations," can "cause rain"—that is, effect a genuine salvation. He importunes the Lord, "We will wait for You, since You have made all these"—these calamities that are his judgments (v. 22). God's reply is still an emphatic no! (15:1), but he promises Jeremiah, "I will deliver you from the hand of the wicked" (15:21). God will answer every believing prayer with his grace, but in his timing, even if it is too slow for us.

What are we to make of this? Just this: there is salvation in God, but not at the expense of his holiness and justice. There must be an acceptable atonement for sin. This could only come from the incarnate Son of God, the promised Messiah, Jesus Christ who was "delivered up for our trespasses and raised for our justification" (Rom. 4:25). And we must receive this salvation as we receive Christ as our Savior and Lord, in saving faith, simply, personally, and with all our heart.

PRAISE PLEADING FOR GOD TO REDEEM US
Sing Psalm 44:20–26

THINGS I WILL PRAY FOR TODAY

_____

_____

_____

_____

_____

June 22
Will My Pain Never End?

A prayer of deep discouragement with God

Why is my pain perpetual?—Jer. 15:18

READ JEREMIAH 15:1–21

pwards of 100 million Americans over the age of 20 are reportedly afflicted with some form of chronic pain—and that takes no account of the spiritual and psychological pain that afflicts millions more! Jeremiah's pain is not due to injury or illness, but arises from discouragement in his ministry. God had sent him "to root out and to pull down, to destroy and to throw down," but also "to build and to plant" (1:10). It seems to him, however, that God has left him with nothing but discouragements in the work. And so, like the psalmist, he offers up "A prayer of the afflicted, when he is overwhelmed and pours out his complaint before the Lord" (Ps. 102; cf. Ps. 55:2, 142:2). We should do the same, whenever we are similarly overwhelmed.

Complaint #1: God hasn't answered my *prayers* (vv. 1–14). He prayed for mercy for Judah (see 14:7–9,13,19–22). "It was," says Philip Ryken, "the best of prayers, offered from the purest of motives." God, however, does not relent, but explains that no intercession can be effectual (vv. 1–2), because their turning from him is resolutely final (vv. 3–9). In response, Jeremiah wishes he hadn't been born (v. 10), but God assures him a remnant will be saved (vv. 11–14). Notice in this that God's no is as much an answer to prayer as a yes. We just find his no harder to take than the yes for which we are praying. We need to "rest in the Lord, and wait patiently for Him" (Ps. 37:7). He is still our loving Savior, even if and when he denies what we ask of him.

Complaint #2: God hasn't relieved my *sufferings* (v. 15). "Lord, you know..." appeals to God's omniscience: "Know that for Your sake I have suffered rebuke" argues the injustice of the prophet's undeserved suffering under persecution; and his prayer for vengeance on his persecutors asks for the overthrow of his enemies, as God's enemies. This does not arise from self-pity or a spirit of revenge, but from a desire for the vindication of God's honor and a real fear for his own life. God told

Abraham, "I will bless those who bless you, and I will curse him who curses you" (Gen. 12:3). Jeremiah claims this promise, and so should we in our discouragements (Ps. 107:6, 13).

Complaint #3: God hasn't blessed my *faithfulness* (vv. 16–18). The prophet could say with the psalmist, "Judge me, O LORD; for I have walked in my integrity: I have also trusted in the LORD…" (Ps. 26:1). He devoured God's Word and it rejoiced his heart. God's name was on him as a believer and as God's prophet, and he "sat alone," apart from his detractors, because God has filled him with "indignation"—a holy zeal for the Lord (vv. 16–17). Battered from all sides, he feels his pain "perpetual" and wonders if his critics' charge that God will be to him "like an unreliable stream, as waters that fail" will stand (v. 18). He does not doubt God, but he wonders if his particular ministry will be all judgment and no revival.

Are you ever discouraged about God's work in your life? Jeremiah prophesies at a unique moment in history, in which the existence of the whole church is at stake (see 1:10a). But this very uniqueness instructs our ordinariness, points ahead to Jesus, and touches our everyday experience. Indeed, "to you it has been granted on behalf of Christ, not only to believe in Him, but also to suffer for His sake" (Phil. 1:29). But Jeremiah's pain will not be perpetual—he will be delivered (vv. 19–21)! Likewise, Christian, *in Jesus Christ* your pain will not be forever. And if your prayers seem at times to be "unanswered," remember that the Lord's no today does not cancel his promises of grace to those who will follow him. His yes stands, even if it seems to be long in coming. "Even so, come, Lord Jesus!" (Rev. 22:20).

PRAISE ANTICIPATING RELIEF FROM SORROWS
Sing Psalm 35:11–18

THINGS I WILL PRAY FOR TODAY

_____

_____

_____

_____

_____

_____

June 23
Will You Make "Gods"?

A prayer for an end to idolatry

Will a man make gods for himself, which are not gods? — *Jer. 16:20*

READ JEREMIAH 16:14–21

"Those who defy God turn to religion for justification," writes Derek Thomas, who adds, "Man's religions are his greatest crimes." In Jeremiah's Judah, church life is at a low ebb. Inside the outward shell of biblical forms, false religion rules, and, blind to their sin of idolatry, the putative "people of God" cannot fathom what they have done to deserve the disasters that are coming upon them. God pulls no punches: their fathers "walked after other gods and worshiped them, and have forsaken Me and not kept My law," but they are worse than their fathers, because each one has followed "the dictates of his own evil heart, so that no one listens to Me" (16:10–12). God will therefore scatter them to foreign lands, leave them to serve the idols of their hearts, and deprive them of His "favor" (16:13). Jeremiah would live to see the culminating fulfillment of these judgments of God in the Babylonian Exile of 586 BC.

Jeremiah is not to be dismissed as a mere "prophet of doom" — even if he often feels he is. All is not lost for either the people of God, or for the world as a whole. God turns in verses 14–15 to a remarkable promise that he will in a future time bring up "the children of Israel from the land of the north and from all the lands where He had driven them" and "will bring them back into their land which [He] gave to their fathers." There is "a mixture of mercy and judgment in these verses…and some seem to look as far forward as the times of the gospel." Jeremiah's response is to offer a short but glorious prayer in which he rejoices in the future worldwide advance of God's kingdom. The erstwhile "prophet of doom" has become, in a moment, a *prophet of grace*! Notice the three parts to this little gem of a prayer:

He *praises* the Lord for his *personal salvation* (v. 19ab). He *knows* the Lord as his "strength," his "fortress," and his "refuge in the day of affliction," and like the psalmist confesses God to be his "refuge and

350

strength, a very present help in trouble" (Ps. 46:1). How else will any true preacher of "righteousness and self-control and the coming judgment"—like Paul before Felix in Acts 24:25—persevere in a ministry that hazards his life? The Lord assures us in our weakness, "My grace is sufficient for you, for My strength is made perfect in weakness" (2 Cor. 12:9; cf. Ps. 107:1–2).

He *prophecies* a future *worldwide salvation* (v. 19c–f). Not only will a remnant of the Jews be restored to their land after their exile (v. 15), but, as Calvin says, "'The Gentiles' then 'shall come,' and the ignorance of their fathers shall not prevent them from confessing that they and their fathers were guilty before God." Gospel grace was on the way for Jew and Gentile, and every believer today is a fulfillment of this promise!

He *proclaims* the folly of *neglecting so great a salvation* (v. 20; cf. Heb. 2:3). The question "Will man make gods for himself, which are not gods?" certainly teaches that the idols we invent are not actual deities. But the prophet's thrust is subtler. Calvin convincingly argues that the reasoning is, "'Can he who is not God make a god?' that is, 'can he who is created be the creator?'" This distinction between the Creator and the creature is vital for your self-knowledge as a creature, for your personal relationship to the God who made you, and for your present and eternal blessedness. Notice that God answers Jeremiah's prayer by affirming his power both to judge and to save sinners (v. 21), thereby leaving a challenge at the door of your soul to "choose for yourself this day whom you will serve" (Josh. 24:15), whether the gods of human invention or the living God who sent his Son to be the Savior "of all who in every place call upon the name of the Lord Jesus Christ" (1 Cor. 1:2).

PRAISE FOR THE GOD WHO TRULY SAVES
Sing Psalm 96:1–8

THINGS I WILL PRAY FOR TODAY

June 24
Where Is the Word of the Lord?

A prayer for the confounding of his critics

Where is the Word of the Lord?—Jer. 17:15

READ JEREMIAH 17:14–18

"Physician, heal yourself" is a perennial challenge to all who claim to have solutions to problems. Physicians all die of something they cannot cure. If they don't practice what they preach, prophets and preachers will be charged with hypocrisy, which in turn gives "occasion to the enemies of the Lord to blaspheme" (2 Sam. 12:14). This same (false) perception moved those who mocked the dying Jesus: "He trusted in God; let Him deliver Him now if He will have Him; for He said, 'I am the Son of God'" (Matt. 27:43). People are always looking for visible proofs of invisible claims, or, as in the case of Jeremiah's Judah, they are looking for the absence of visible proofs as an excuse for their rejection of God's Word to them by his prophets.

Jeremiah's critics reject his ministry. He warns of God's coming judgments. Life is still pretty good in Judah, so they reply, in Calvin's words, "Many years have now elapsed since you have continually spoken of war, of famine, and of pestilence; but we still remain quiet, and God spares us; where then is the *word of Jehovah*, which you have announced?" This hostility wears on Jeremiah, but he will not give up. He tells God of their taunt: "Where is the word of the Lord? Let it come now!" (v. 15). He wants it to be over and done with. *Is this not so true to life?* Scripture tells of Jesus's coming. Time passes. Nothing happens. So the world mocks: "Where is the promise of His coming? For since the fathers fell asleep, all things continue as they were from the beginning of creation" (2 Peter 3:4–12). Christians are then, like Jeremiah, tempted to give up on account of a sense of defeat.

Jeremiah keenly feels his weariness but commits to faithfulness. He offers three evidences of faithfulness:

> ❧ He did not run away from his calling as a shepherd who follows the Lord (v. 16a);
> ❧ He had not "desired the woeful day" he was faithfully

proclaiming—this is God's message, not one of his own invention (v. 16b);

> He calls God as a witness to his faithful exercise of his ministry (v. 16c).

"Here are three characteristics of a true preacher and pastor," says Theodore Laetsch: "obedience to God's call and command, refraining from venting one's own spite, sincerity in doing the work of the ministry (1 Cor. 4:1–5; 2 Cor. 4:2–5; 1 Thess. 2:3–6)." They are also the principles that apply to every follower of Jesus, for we are all called to do whatever we do in life "as unto the Lord" (Col. 3:23), to do so lovingly, and to do so with integrity before God and man.

Jeremiah accepts that God is judging backslidden Judah (vv. 17–18). He knows and loves God as the One who is, by his free grace, "keeping mercy for thousands, forgiving iniquity and transgression and sin" even as he will "by no means" "clear the guilty" who reject him to their last breath (Ex. 34:7). Judah's great sins deserve a "double destruction," but God will not abandon his believing people, then or now. Isaiah, in that wonderful fortieth chapter of his prophecy, points to the future blessedness of God's people in the era of Jesus Messiah, when he joins a living hope to a double destruction: "'Comfort, yes, comfort My people!' says your God. 'Speak comfort to Jerusalem, and cry out to her, that her warfare is ended, that her iniquity is pardoned; for she has received from the Lord's hand double for all her sins'" (Isa. 40:1–2). Jeremiah rests in the Lord as his redeemer, defender, and vindicator. So also, in every generation, those who love the Lord can rest in their Savior, welcoming his "coming to judge the earth…with righteousness" (Ps. 98:9), knowing that their "labor is not in vain in the Lord" (1 Cor. 15:58).

PRAISE THAT URGENTLY SEEKS THE SAVIOR
Sing Psalm 40:10–17

THINGS I WILL PRAY FOR TODAY

_____

_____

_____

_____

June 25
Call It a Conspiracy

A prayer for the overthrow of evil counsel

Yet LORD, *You know all their counsel which is against me, to slay me....*
let them be overthrown before You. —*Jer. 18:23*

READ JEREMIAH 18:18–23

Conspiracies are endemic to human societies. Real or imagined, they engender an unhealthy alarmism in many minds—something terrorists in our day understand and exploit to their own ends. Some plots are serious, like the one that brings Jeremiah to this prayer. He discovers that his persecutors are scheming against him: "Come and let us devise plans against Jeremiah; for the law shall not perish from the priest, nor counsel from the wise, nor the word from the prophet. Come and let us attack him with the tongue, and let us not give heed to any of his words" (v. 18). Then and now, freedom *from* speech is the resort of those who cannot bear the freedom *of* speech that is exercised in the interest of God's revealed truth (cf. Acts 4:18–20; 5:29). The trigger of this conspiracy is the parable of the potter and the clay (vv. 1–11), in which God asserts His sovereignty in judgment and salvation: "Behold I am fashioning a disaster and devising a plan against you. Return now every one of you from his evil way, and make your ways and your doings good" (v. 11). Jeremiah's hearers will not accept this and respond by "fashioning a disaster and devising a plan" (v. 11) of their own against the prophet, as if killing the messenger will somehow kill his message! Jeremiah gets their drift and turns to the Lord in prayer.

Petition #1—He presents himself before the Lord: "Give heed to me, O Lord" (v. 19a). He *comes quickly* to "the throne of grace" for "grace to help in his time of need" (Heb. 4:16). We too often worry first and get to prayer later, maybe. The lesson for us is always to pray first, and as you "cast your burden on the Lord" you will discover that "He shall sustain you" whatever your trials (Ps. 55:22).

Petition #2—He asks God to listen to his enemies: "...listen to the voice of those who contend with me!" (v. 19b). If you would have

God's help, you must make an *honest appeal* to the evidence. But you also need to put your heart under the searchlight of the Word and Holy Spirit: "Search me, O God, and know my heart; try me, and know my anxieties; and see if there is any wicked way in me, and lead me in the way everlasting" (Ps. 139:23–24). We must always pray in this way.

Petition #3 — **He argues his case before the Lord:** "Shall evil be repaid for good?" (v. 20). Had he not interceded for God's apostate people, that he turn his wrath from them? Is he to be murdered for his faithful ministry? He rightly pleads for God to deliver him, and we likewise may pray to be delivered from our trials, even if we are called to suffer for Christ (Col. 1:24)!

Petition #4 — **He calls for God to judge his enemies** "in the time of [His] anger" (vv. 21–23). Some think Jeremiah here goes "beyond seeking vindication to being vindictive" and note that Jesus asked for forgiveness for his executioners (Luke 23:34). John Calvin believes it was "peculiar to the Prophet to know that they were reprobates" and that therefore he is "not to be condemned, nor...to be made an example of" in our prayers. *Loving* our enemies (Matt. 5:44), and *not knowing* their eternal destinies, should constrain us to seek their salvation — even as we ask for our deliverance from their evil intentions.

All the conspiracies in the world will, in any case, never thwart the Lord's purposes of grace and salvation, for "He who sits in the heavens shall laugh" and "hold them in derision" and will "dash them to pieces like a potter's vessel" (Ps. 2:4, 9). Meantime, we are called to be "praying always with all prayer and supplication in the Spirit" to the end that Jesus will save His people from their sins (Eph. 6:18).

PRAISE TO GOD WHO OVERTHROWS HIS ENEMIES
Sing Psalm 94:16–23

THINGS I WILL PRAY FOR TODAY

_____

_____

_____

_____

_____

June 26
Everyone Mocks Me

A prayer about being laughed at

I am in derision daily; everyone mocks me. —Jer. 20:7

READ JEREMIAH 20:7–13

The principal utility of Jeremiah's prayer is to show us both the sinfulness of sin and the sweetness of salvation in the experience of the believing child of God. The prayer itself arises from his deep despondency over opposition to his ministry. Here he was, sent by God to proclaim the word of God to the backslidden people of God, and his reward is outright hostility from every level of society. Sure, he was given to proclaim God's coming judgments, and prophets of doom can hardly expect to be popular. Truth is never palatable just because it is true. Unbelief always exchanges the truth of God for a lie (Rom. 1:25). Sinners will believe the lie and, rather than repent and return to the Lord, will cling to it like grim death. God's prophets, meanwhile, have to bear the twin discouragements of personal rejection and apparently fruitless ministry. Having just spent a period in the stocks and pronounced another judgment on the guilty (20:1–6), Jeremiah turns to the Lord in one of the most conflicted and confused prayers in Scripture. It is, however, far truer to real life than the smooth, measured, and unmoved performances of many Christian prayers.

The sinfulness of sin. Charles Simeon comments: "If we would see the corruption of human nature in its true light, we should look at it, not merely as existing in the worst of men, but as breaking forth even in the best. A more tender-hearted and pious man than Jeremiah did not perhaps exist on earth at his day: yet, under great provocation, he breaks forth into language most unseemly, both against God and man." The prophet opens with a torrent of bitterness: "O Lord, You induced me"—i.e., hoodwinked me!—and now I am "in derision daily" (vv. 7–8). So he decides to quit! No more speaking about God, or for God (v. 9ab)! God's message had become as painful to him as "a burning fire shut up in [his] bones" (v. 9cd). And people ridicule him, watch for him to stumble, and look for opportunities to take their revenge (v. 10). He might have asked where the promise of a

356

ministry "to build and to plant" had gone (cf. Jer. 1:10). He is not burning to preach, as much as he is just burning out! O how true to Christian experience this is! Here is a godly man of fragrant piety overwhelmed by the work, so that in the weakness of the flesh, he even accuses God of deceiving him. And "if the righteous is scarcely saved, what will become of the ungodly and the sinner?" (1 Peter 4:18).

The sweetness of salvation. This dark night of Jeremiah's soul is suddenly punctuated by a shaft of divine light: "But the Lord is with me as a mighty, awesome One" (v. 11). God's response to Jeremiah's anguished doubt is not to wag the finger at him, but to draw closer to strengthen his faith. The prophet is assured that the Lord is testing him, so as to see his "mind and heart." He knows he has been faithful thus far, and that he still trusts the Lord, even as frustration with the outcomes of his ministry brings great pain and even confusion. He understands that his persecutors are digging their own graves. He just longs for an end to his pain and a resolution of God's justice in the matter. In this he is able to rest in the Lord before whom he has "pleaded [his] cause" (v. 12). And he worships him with a whole heart: "Sing to the Lord! Praise the Lord! For He has delivered the life of the poor from the hand of evildoers" (v. 13). The sweetness amid the sourness of Jeremiah's suffering, and, Christian, your suffering also, is the same as that experienced by Paul centuries later: "For this reason I also suffer these things; nevertheless I am not ashamed, for I know whom I have believed and am persuaded that He is able to keep what I have committed to Him until that Day" (2 Tim. 1:12). May this be your testimony before those who mock you for your love of Jesus.

PRAISE FOR GOD'S HELP IN OUR WEAKNESS
Sing Psalm 6

THINGS I WILL PRAY FOR TODAY

June 27
Help Me Understand This!

A prayer of utter bewilderment

You have said to me, O Lord God, "Buy the field for money, and take witnesses"!—yet the city has been given into the hand of the Chaldeans.—Jer. 32:25

READ JEREMIAH 32:16–25

Would you buy a beach house in the middle of a hurricane? Wouldn't you wait for the storm to pass and see if the property is still there? Jeremiah has preached God's judgment for forty years and the Babylonians are at the gates of Jerusalem. He is in prison for the "crime" of offending King Zedekiah with his unhappy prophecies (32:1–5). Suddenly, God reveals that Jeremiah's cousin Hanamel will offer for sale a field in Anathoth and instructs him to buy it—which he does, for seventeen shekels of silver (32:6–14). This looks like lunacy, since Judah is on its last legs and the prospects for farming look pretty dim. But God has a reason for urging this unlikely purchase. He assures the prophet that "houses and fields and vineyards shall be possessed again in this land" (32:15). The purchase is an acted parable of better days to come.

To a hurting mind, however, such promises look suspiciously like "pie in the sky when you die," as in Joe Hill's angry parody of the hymn, "In the Sweet By-and-By":

You will eat bye and bye;
In that glorious land above the sky.
Work and pray, live on hay;
You'll get pie in the sky when you die.

Jeremiah's mind is not instantly settled, but his response is not disbelief or anger, but a resort to believing prayer (32:16–25). Bewilderment over God's promises and providences often touches the Christian's experience and challenges our faith (cf. Mark 9:24). When this is so, prayer is the place to go, that the Lord would give us understanding.

The prayer opens with a groan: "Ah, Lord God!" (v. 17a). Jeremiah elsewhere begins with a plaintive "Ah!" (1:6; 4:10; 14:13). Paul later explains such godly groans: "For we do not know what we should pray for as we ought, but the Spirit Himself makes intercession for us with groanings which cannot be uttered" (Rom. 8:26). We may lack the words, but the Holy Spirit brings our groans to words in the mind of our Father in heaven. Such groans are true prayer, when we lay our anxieties at the throne of God's grace.

The body of the prayer recounts the character, attributes, and actions of the living God (vv. 17b–22). He is the omnipotent Creator of all things (v. 17bc); he is the God of covenant love who saves sinners, but who is just in punishing the reprobate (vv. 18–19); and he is the God who reveals himself in human history in the redemption of his people (vv. 20–22). Notice that in this, the bulk of his prayer, Jeremiah is looking away from himself to God. There is no "Poor me" here—it is all about God. The more he thinks *theologically* about God, the more he is enabled *practically* to keep his balance as a servant of God and go forward with him in contented obedience.

The prayer closes with Jeremiah's revisiting his opening groan (vv. 23–25). His wordless "Ah" is now put into words. God's people came to the land, but fell away from his commandments, thereby causing "this calamity to come upon them" (v. 23). For more than a generation, through Jeremiah alone, God both warned and recalled them! With judgment in the form of Babylonian "siege mounds" staring them in the face, they simply deny reality. In the midst of this, Jeremiah says to the Lord, "You have said to me…'Buy the field for money, and take witnesses'!—yet the city has been given into the hand of the Chaldeans" (v. 24–25). His bewilderment is not so much answered as it is simply left with the Lord who does all things well. When we do not know the answers, we know for sure that God does. So, will you cast all your care upon him (1 Peter 5:7)? Jeremiah did. So should you.

PRAISE FOR GOD'S PRECIOUS PROMISES
Sing Psalm 119:153–160

THINGS I WILL PRAY FOR TODAY

_____

_____

_____

_____

June 28
Pray for Us

A hypocritical prayer request

Please, let our petition be acceptable to you, and pray for us...that the
Lord your God may show us the way in which we should walk and the
thing we should do. —Jer. 42:2–3

READ JEREMIAH 42:1–22

The Jewish state is destroyed for its sins, as God had warned them, and only a remnant remains in the land. Then a band led by Ishmael, a scion of Judaean royalty, attacks Mizpah, assassinates the governor Gedaliah (a Jew in the service of Babylon), murders many people and carries off the survivors, perhaps to sell them into slavery. Soldiers led by Johanan pursue them, free the captives, but allow Ishmael and most of his men to escape. Johanan and "the remnant of Judah" (40:11) are fearful of Babylonian reprisals and decide to flee to Egypt (41:1–18). They pause, however, and ask Jeremiah to pray to the Lord for them so that, as they put it, "the Lord your God may show us the way in which we should walk and the thing we should do" (42:2–3).

Jeremiah agrees to intercede for them and they solemnly promise to obey "everything" that the Lord tells them to do via the prophet (vv. 4–6). After forty years of rejection, Jeremiah may have doubted their sincerity, but he was very willing to pray for them—"like Samuel who said when he was slighted" by rebellious Israel centuries before, "far be it from me that I should sin against the Lord in ceasing to pray for you," but insisted, "I will teach you the good and the right way" (1 Sam. 12:23). Jeremiah duly prays and ten days later, God reveals his answer to his prophet (v. 7).

God's answer is to tell the Jews to stay in Judah (vv. 8–17). His promise is that they will be safe there: "I will build you and not pull you down...for I relent concerning the disaster I have brought on you" (v. 10). In Egypt, however, they will certainly "die by the sword, by famine and by pestilence"(v. 17). God's will is as clear as a bell! And then, a bombshell: Jeremiah reiterates God's will that they not go to Egypt, prophesying their hypocrisy in seeking God's will in the first place, and their death in Egypt for their apostasy from God (vv. 18–23)—and this before they register their response (see 43:1–7)! Clearly they wanted Jeremiah to confirm their prior desire to go to Egypt. Hence, they justify themselves by denouncing the prophet as a liar and accusing him of planning their deaths or exile to Babylon!

What are we to take from this sad story? Notice three things:

⮞ Seeking God's will is always the right thing to do: he calls "all men everywhere" to himself (Acts 17:30) and he faithfully "hears the prayer of the righteous" (Prov. 15:29). We have no promise of direct revelation through a prophet like Jeremiah. We have something even better: Jesus our Prophet, Priest, and King has given us the means of grace (the Word, sacraments and prayer, and the ministry of the Holy Spirit) to instruct our hearts and guide our actions.

⮞ We should never be afraid to ask for other believers to *pray for us*, but we should never do so hypocritically as did Johanan et al., who, says Calvin, sought God's will with a lie in their hearts and "doubled their crime" when they promised their obedience to him. Living faith in the Lord is of the essence: "Had there been a grain of faith in the Jews," says Calvin, they would have laid hold of God's promise of preservation in Judah. We should always be ready to pray for those who ask us to *pray for them*, even if—or should we perhaps say, especially if?—we have doubts of their sincerity. Remember then that "the effective, fervent prayer of a righteous man avails much" (James 5:16). As Jesus prayed, so are we called to pray. So, Christian, let the love of Christ, who "first loved us," constrain you to seek His blessings for yourself and those for whom you pray (1 John 4:19; 2 Cor. 5:14).

PRAISE FOR INTERVENING GRACE
Sing Psalm 106:24–31

THINGS I WILL PRAY FOR TODAY

_____

_____

_____

_____

June 29
My Heart Is Overturned

A prayer prompted by the consequences of sin

My heart is overturned within me, for I have been very rebellious.
—Lam. 1:20

LAMENTATIONS 1:12–22

Lamentations is one of the hidden treasures of Scripture—hidden only because it is largely neglected by Christians, both preachers and laymen. It consists of five laments over the demise of Judea in 587 BC. The Jewish state is no more, Jerusalem is destroyed, the people of God are mostly scattered to the four winds, leaving only a remnant in the land of promise. It seems, says Richard Brooks, "almost as if the covenant of God had been abolished." Calvin notes that, as dark as that day was, Jeremiah "understood that his teaching would not be without fruit" and "was thus induced to speak first of God's judgments; secondly, to exhort the people to repentance; thirdly, to encourage them to hope; and lastly, to open the door for prayer to God, so that the people in their extremities might venture to flee to God's mercy." All of the prayers in Lamentations should be viewed in this light.

A wrenching cry opens the prayer (1:20–22): "See, O Lord, that I am in distress; my soul is troubled; my heart is overturned within me" (v. 20). The writer speaks as Jerusalem personified. This is the "people of God," the church in the world, called in God's Word "the joy of all the earth, Mount Zion" (Ps. 48:2), reduced to desperate destitution. It echoes two earlier "arrow prayers": "O Lord, behold my affliction, for the enemy is exalted!" (v. 9) and, "See, O Lord, and consider, for I am scorned" (v. 11). It looks to her that God's enemies have won. But she is not an innocent victim; she has sinned away her blessings! Another prophet reassures God's people that if they "sow...righteousness" they will "reap in mercy." The fact is, alas: "You have plowed wickedness; you have reaped iniquity" (Hos. 10:12–13). She only has herself to blame. Is this not the way with all our sins? Jesus points out that what "defiles a man" is not what goes into him, but what comes "out of the heart" (Matt. 15:11, 19–20). This is what ought to cause us to weep. Sin is the self-inflicted wasting of lives and it is to be mourned before God's throne of grace (Heb. 4:16).

How should the fallen church deal with her distress? First realize that all of our afflictions—whether the oppressions of men or the judgments of God—call us to look to the Lord and his way of salvation, and stop merely circling the drain in anger or despair:

> ❧ Pray *confessing sin*: "I have been very rebellious" (v. 20). It is also vital that you accept that God is justified in visiting the consequences of your sin upon you: hence the words "the sword bereaves" and "home is like death." Even then, the Lord has "punished us less than our iniquities deserve" (Ezra 9:13). And he is calling us to repentance.

> ❧ Pray that God *glorify himself* in humbling those who "are glad" that God has brought you low for your sins (v. 21). It is never wrong to pray that God counter wickedness and more visibly establish his righteousness in this fallen world (Eph. 1:22; Rev. 6:9–11).

> ❧ Pray for God's *saving grace* for sinners in this world. To ask the Lord to "do to them as You have done to me" is not naked personal vindictiveness (v. 22). Jerusalem here prays in faith for deliverance from the evil fruit of her own sins and the depredations of her oppressors. But it is also *a word to the wise* to flee the wrath to come. The psalmist says, "Before I was afflicted I went astray, but now I keep Your word" (Ps. 119:67; cf. Heb. 12:5–6). The apostle reminds us that in Christ crucified we have a Savior, and in him "if we confess our sins, He is faithful and just to forgive us our sins and to cleanse us from all unrighteousness" (1 John 1:9).

PRAISE RISING FROM DESPAIR TO HOPE
Sing Psalm 42:6–11

THINGS I WILL PRAY FOR TODAY

_____

_____

_____

_____

_____

June 30
Why Is This Happening to Us?

Prayer of the grief-stricken

See, O Lord, and consider! To whom have You done this?—Lam. 2:20

LAMENTATIONS 2:17–22

"Why me?" is a common question of suffering people, a common implication being that their suffering is undeserved. Another tack is to say we are "lucky" if things go well and "unlucky" if things go badly. These are appeals, respectively, to either our innocence or our helplessness, and they can (and often do) carry a certain appearance of credibility. But they lead to anger, fear, and grief-stricken despair—even an overt hatred of God. Those who are "without God in the world" and have no personal saving interest in the Lord, are bound to be "strangers from the covenants of promise." They have "no hope," and deep down they know it (Eph. 2:12). Sooner or later, the chickens of a God-free life—however long and easy it may be materially—will come home to roost on the slippery slope to the undying despair of a lost eternity (cf. Ps. 73).

What is first needed is a sound grasp of God's role in your sufferings. This has to be set in the context of a believing and confiding relationship with the Lord. In verse 17, the buildup to the prayer proper (vv. 20–22), the key is found: "The Lord has done what He purposed; He has fulfilled His word which He commanded in days of old." The fact is that "His judgments are in all the earth" all the time (Ps. 105:7; Deut. 32:4). Sometimes he chastises his people and sometimes he punishes his enemies, but when "bad things" happen in this fallen world, the same thing, outwardly, "happens to the righteous and the wicked" (Eccl. 9:2). If our sufferings are merely the result of malicious people, we will, says Calvin, "probably become more hardened in [our] sorrow" and be consumed by anger and a desire for revenge. Bitterness solves nothing. "Our best remedy then," Calvin adds, "is not to have our thoughts fixed on the insolence of men, but to know what the Scripture often reminds us, that the wicked are the scourges of God by which he chastises us." Since the Lord loves those he disciplines, we have reason to humble ourselves and cause to rejoice in his grace toward us.

A prayer for the grief-stricken follows in verses 20–22. First, the prayer pleads that God remember his *covenant promises*: Yahweh/ LORD is the covenant name of God, while those "to whom" he has brought catastrophe are clearly the covenant people, the church of the day (v. 20). Second, the prayer recounts the *sufferings of the covenant people*, including starvation (and even cannibalism), the removal of the ministry of "the sanctuary of the Lord," and the slaughter of old and young alike (vv. 20–21). Third, the prayer acknowledges the *justice* of this "day of the Lord's anger" even though it is "enemies" who have wreaked such havoc (v. 22). Taken together, these petitions are a cry to God for mercy on the basis of his covenant grace, as if to say: "Remember Your covenant; look at our suffering with compassion; end our miseries in your love; remove Your anger; turn back our enemies!"

Remember that the hand of God is in your sufferings. Remember also that he is good and just in his judgments, for "we know that all things work together for good to those who love God, to those who are the called according to His purpose" (Rom. 8:28). This is not a "knock-down answer"—a psychological crutch for weak minds. It is a wonderful truth for sufferers—whether they love the Lord already, or will yet come in faith to love him. The key to coping with sorrows and sufferings of all kinds is knowing him and knowing that "your life is hidden with Christ in God" (Col. 3:3; cf. Rom. 8:18). The Lord promises us that he "shall regard the prayer of the destitute, and shall not despise their prayer" (Ps. 102:17). Amen.

PRAISE SEEKING TO BE RESTORED AGAIN
Sing Psalm 60:1–5

THINGS I WILL PRAY FOR TODAY

July 1
Faith Gets the Last Word

Prayer affirming the efficacy of prayer

You drew near on the day I called on You, and said, "Do not fear!"
—Lam. 3:57

READ LAMENTATIONS 3:55–66

The master-promise of God for his people is arguably that of Jesus to his apostles in the Great Commission: "And behold, I am with you always, to the end of the age" (Matt. 28:20, ESV). He is present with us—truly, actually, and supernaturally, by the Holy Spirit within us (Luke 11:13; 1 Cor. 6:19) and "always"—come rain or shine, joy or discouragement, through time and eternity (Ps. 121). This promise holds for every time and circumstance, however dark the day and desperate our feelings. Throughout Lamentations 3 the writer struggles "between sense and faith, fear and hope; he complains and then comforts himself, yet drops his comforts and returns again to his complaints." But then he turns to prayer and, writes Matthew Henry, "faith gets the last word and comes off a conqueror; for in these verses he concludes with some comfort." This prayer is made for discouraged Christians.

The first thing to notice about Jeremiah's prayer is that his "affliction drove him not *from* God, but *to* him." "I called on Your name, O LORD, from the lowest pit" (v. 55). Jonah likewise calls from the belly of the fish: "I have been cast out of Your sight; yet I will look again toward Your holy temple" (Jonah 2:4). This isn't the frantic last-resort prayer of those who "tried everything else" and now, in football parlance, are tossing up a "Hail Mary" pass in hope of a winning touchdown before the final whistle. The prophet's prayers arise from a living, personal faith in the Lord who saves! They could say with the psalmist: "I sought the LORD, and He heard me, and delivered me from all my fears." And in the end, "They looked to Him and were radiant, and their faces were not ashamed" (Ps. 34:4–5).

Five strands bind the prayer together (vv. 56–66). They recall the believers' past experiences of God's faithfulness in earlier troubles, and ask the Lord for fresh visitations of his grace, mercy, and peace in present discouragements and sufferings:

366

- God is the *Hearer* of prayer (v. 56). The prophet recalls God's past blessings and asks a hearing for his present "cry for help."
- God is the *Answerer* of prayer: he who earlier "drew near" and assured his servant, "Do not fear!" (v. 57). The promise stands: "Draw near to God and he will draw near to you" (James 4:8).
- God is the *Redeemer*: he who "pleaded the case" and "redeemed [his servant's] life" (v. 58). Expect blessing now and sing: "My lips shall greatly rejoice when I sing to You, and my soul, which You have redeemed" (Ps. 71:23).
- God is the omniscient *Judge*. He sees the persecution of his people (vv. 59–63). God is aware of the "schemes…reproach… whispering" and "taunting song" of his enemies. They all will certainly answer to God (2 Cor. 5:10).
- God is the omnipotent *Vindicator* of his kingdom and righteousness (vv. 64–66; cf. Jer. 51:36). This prayer is not about personal revenge, but rather seeks that God would vindicate his own honor and glory against those who deny him and, in the end, "crucified the Lord of glory" (1 Cor. 2:8).

Each petition builds upon those that precede it so as to raise us from "the lowest pit" (v. 55) all the way to the appropriation of the ultimate triumph of the Lord not only in our life, but also everywhere "under the heavens of the Lord" (v. 66). Let us then look to Christ our Savior that faith in him as Savior and Lord would not only "get the last word" in our troubles, but even be the first word we bring to the throne of his grace in our times of need (Heb. 4:16).

PRAISE FOR HOPE THAT OVERCOMES DISCOURAGEMENT
Sing Psalm 123

THINGS I WILL PRAY FOR TODAY

_____

_____

_____

_____

_____

July 2
From Sorrow to Hope

Prayer for spiritual revival

You, O LORD, remain forever; Your throne from generation to generation. — Lam. 5:19

READ LAMENTATIONS 5:1–22

he destruction of the Jewish state in the sixth century BC— with Jerusalem destroyed, temple worship discontinued, and the people of God scattered to the four winds—brings about a moment in history in which the work of God in the world seems to hang in the balance. This begs the question, "Is God still in charge? Can his church be revived?" This echoes in Christian experience, when troubles get us down and we wonder if there is any hope for us in the cauldron of our calamities. This fifth Lament is also a prayer, which speaks to its own time, but also applies to all the trials of our lives—personal, family, church, and community—by showing us how to respond effectively to them. The most basic lesson to grasp is from James, who exhorts us, "Is anyone among you suffering? Let him pray" (James 5:13). Notice how Jeremiah's prayer models most practically the way we should pray:

Call upon God as witness to your worries (v. 1). The "LORD" here is "Yahweh" the covenant-God, whose covenant of grace (Gen. 3:15) is ultimately revealed in his Son, Jesus, whose suffering for sin is salvation for all who believe in him. Believing prayer begins with "the God and Father of our Lord Jesus Christ, who according to His abundant mercy has begotten us again to a living hope through the resurrection of Jesus Christ from the dead" (1 Pet. 1:3; cf. John 3:16; Rom. 10:13). This is personal faith in action.

Communicate to him the details of your desperation (vv. 2–14). The church of approximately 2,600 years ago had virtually ceased to exist as a visible worshiping community. The Davidic kingdom was reduced to ruin. Imagine your hometown reduced to bombed-out buildings and your life subject to brutal exploitation and the constant threat of death. Whatever troubles you, large or small, take it to the Lord in prayer.

Confide in him the hankerings of your heart (vv. 15–18). The writer first confesses where the blame for their deep unhappiness lies:

"Woe to us, for we have sinned!" (v. 16). The oppressors are wicked, but God's people are not innocent. Notice also that the writer attributes their faint hearts and blind eyes to the desolation of "Mount Zion"—that is, to the removal of public worship and the means of grace as signified by the ministry of the temple (vv. 17–18). The visible church has vanished and that is a disaster, not just for the Jews, but for all peoples.

Cry earnestly to him for the renewal of his presence with, and his promises for, the church (vv. 19–22). How we seek the renewal of a dead church or a backslidden soul? By flying in faith to the God of grace—and expecting blessing:

> He is the *eternal* God who "remains forever" (v. 19a), with whom there is "no variableness, neither shadow of turning" (James 1:17).

> He is the *sovereign* God whose "throne" is over all things in his creation (v. 19b). His crown never slips (v. 16a) and therefore his kingdom will come and his will "be done on earth as it is in heaven" (Matt. 6:10).

> He is the *gracious* God who will not forsake his own (v. 20), even if, as, and when he chastises us for our good (Heb. 12:6–13).

> He is the *faithful* God who will restore and renew his church —sovereignly "turn us back" to himself (v. 21). This calls us to respond in repentance and faith: "If we confess our sins, He is faithful and just to forgive us our sins and to cleanse us from all unrighteousness" (1 John 1:9). Being "justified by faith, we have peace with God through our Lord Jesus Christ, through whom also we have access by faith into this grace in which we stand, and rejoice in hope of the glory of God" (Rom. 5:1–2) and discover afresh that in Christ, "His anger is but for a moment, His favor is for life" (Ps. 30:5).

PRAISE FOR THE SOVEREIGNTY OF GOD
Sing Psalm 103:19–22

THINGS I WILL PRAY FOR TODAY

_____

_____

_____

_____

July 3
Food, Famine, and Faith

Prayer seeking understanding

Ah, Lord GOD! Indeed I have never defiled myself from my youth till now; I have never eaten what died of itself or was torn by beasts, nor has abominable flesh come into my mouth. — Ezek. 4:14

READ EZEKIEL 4:9–17

zekiel is often described as a "crazy prophet" whose "antics" involved "weird stuff"—"bordering on madness." Compare the sober assessment of Charles Simeon (1759–1836), who observes that "Ezekiel is perhaps the most terrific writer of all the prophets: there is a force and energy in his denunciations which can find no parallel." Ezekiel is serious not only because God is serious about sin, *but also because God has a plan of salvation*, the promise of which is "essentially Messianic." God promises to renew Israel and Jerusalem, the essence of which is, in Ezekiel's closing words, "THE LORD IS THERE" (48:35). This statement reaches forward to Jesus, to the cross, to his church, as well as ultimately to that second coming which will answer the closing prayer of the Bible: "Even so, come, Lord Jesus!" (Rev. 22:20). This is the perspective that enlivens and illumines all of Ezekiel's recorded prayers.

Ezekiel's first prayer arises from an acted parable in which God tells him to make a little model of Jerusalem besieged by enemy circumvallation, battering rams, and a siege ramp. He is to set his face "against" the city, as "a sign to the house of Israel" of God's righteous anger at their rejecting him (vv. 1–3). Sometime each day for 390 + 40 days, he is to lie on his side. This fits with the 430 years of bondage in Egypt and/or the period of declension from Solomon's time to the exile(s) in Babylon, where Ezekiel is located. All the while he is to prophesy against Jerusalem (vv. 4–8). He is also to prepare and consume a half pound of "bread" and drink a half pint of water per day, to represent the famine inside Jerusalem (4:9–17)—the famine that is a picture of the self-inflicted *spiritual* famine in the hearts of the people.

The kicker to this parable is having to bake the bread over a fire fueled by dried *human* waste (v. 12). Ezekiel protests that he has never defiled himself with such a (ceremonially) "unclean thing" (v. 14; Deut. 23:12–14) and God responds by letting him use dried cow dung (v. 15). Some see God making this concession as weakening the parable. I rather think that God's allowing the prophet to remain ceremonially "clean" while still symbolically bearing the judgment for the iniquity of Israel and Judah (vv. 4, 6) *strengthens* the message. Why? By indicating to the Jews that outward ceremonial righteousness cannot save anyone. Sin is a matter of the heart and therefore requires a deep inward transformation by a work of God's grace in the inner being (Eph. 3:16).

Ezekiel's acted parable teaches us to take God very seriously. God is "a just judge, and is angry with the wicked every day" (Ps. 7:11)—and with the sins of sinners, saved or unsaved. Dear Christian, forgiveness of sin is not a free pass to flout God's revealed will for your holy life. A "faith" that has, as Paul says, "a form of godliness" but denies its power (2 Tim. 3:5) is a lie: "faith without works is dead" (James 2:20, 26). God is the God of grace; he means to save sinners. Ezekiel understood this and clearly enjoys the personal relationship of a redeemed believer to his Redeemer God, a loving son to his loving heavenly Father. How much richer this experience is now that the Messiah has come and Jesus is "exalted…to be Prince and Savior, to give repentance to Israel and forgiveness of sins" (Acts 5:31). Do you know Jesus as your Savior? Or does a famine gnaw at your soul? Will you then come to him, believing upon him as your Savior and Lord?

PRAISE FOR GOD'S CHASTISING GRACE
Sing Psalm 106:41–48

THINGS I WILL PRAY FOR TODAY

_____

_____

_____

_____

_____

_____

_____

_____

July 4
Is the Church to Disappear?

Prayer for the preservation of a remnant

*Ah, Lord GOD! Will You destroy all the remnant of Israel in pouring out
Your fury on Jerusalem?—Ezek. 9:8*

READ EZEKIEL 9:1–11

Churches die for all sorts of reasons, mostly sad. Local churches
come and go, but *the* church goes on. Ezekiel's prophecy of
Judah's destruction by *God's* "fury on Jerusalem" is not
about a local church closing. The Babylonian wars of 605
BC, 597 BC, and 586 BC saw the death of Judah, the dispersal of God's
people, and the destruction of the Jerusalem temple—the one place in the
world where God was to be worshiped and where sacrifices for sin were
to be offered. This catastrophe therefore portended the unthinkable—the
possible extinction of the entire *visible church* at that time!

Why was God so angry with his people? The answers are
astounding: they had adopted paganism—worshiping *idols* (8:1–6);
Satanism—worshiping *Satan* (8:7–12); and pantheism—worshiping *the
environment* (8:13–15). It had become a "synagogue of Satan" (Rev. 2:9;
3:9). This arose from two root sins: they *scorned* God (8:16) and they
trivialized his Word (8:17). This conspired to rob God of nothing less
than his glory: "I am the Lord, that is My name; and My glory I will not
give to another" (Isa. 42:8). We expect the "world" to trash God's name,
but the church!? So "Ichabod"—meaning "the glory has departed"—
was once more written large over Israel (1 Sam. 4:21–22). And judgment
must "begin at the house of God" (1 Peter 4:17), because it is the
"church" that is betraying God's honor and besmirching his glory.
God duly announces his judgments, appoints his agents, and addresses
his people's particular sins (9:1–2a). Matthew Henry comments: "Two
destroying angels were sent against Sodom, but six against Jerusalem:
for Jerusalem's doom in the judgment will be thrice as heavy as that of
Sodom." If human beings are to learn anything from all this, it surely
must be that "it is a fearful thing to fall into the hands of the living God"
(Heb. 10:31). For, says the psalmist, "God is a just judge, and God is

angry with the wicked every day" (Ps. 7:11); and if he "should mark iniquities...who could stand?" (Ps. 130:3).

Are these God's last words for the church and for sinners the world over? Ezekiel's vision reveals three answers from God:

- ⟡ God intervenes in his *sovereign grace* (vv. 2b–4). With the six destroying angels, God sends a seventh to mark with ink the foreheads of those who "sigh and cry over all the abominations" done in Jerusalem. Here is God's mediator sent to mark the elect remnant for salvation. "Even in wrath," God "remember[s] mercy" (Hab. 3:2).

- ⟡ God *hears believing prayer* for mercy (v. 8). Seeing the ruin of souls and judgment, Ezekiel cries out in prayer, pointedly using God's covenant name: "Ah, Lord GOD, will you destroy the remnant of Israel in pouring out your fury on Jerusalem?" Surely "no-one can preach judgement without praying for mercy. No-one can speak to people about God without also speaking to God about people."

- ⟡ God *bestows mercy* in answer to prayer (vv. 9–11). This has two aspects to it. The first is that *evil will be purged* (vv. 9–10), which includes both its *fruits* (moral decline, licentiousness, and repression) and its very *character* (the denying of God, despising of his Word, and dismissing both his warnings and his wooings; cf. Rev. 21:7). The second is that *the church will be preserved* (v. 11)—as Jesus explains his Father's will, "of all He has given Me, I should lose nothing, but should raise it up at the last day" (John 6:39).

No, Christ's church will never disappear! It is forever, and "whoever calls on the name of the LORD shall be saved" (Rom. 10:13). You, believer, and millions of others are proof of this promise!

A PRAYER FOR GOD'S MERCY
Sing Psalm 79:1–7

THINGS I WILL PRAY FOR TODAY

_____

_____

_____

July 5
A Little Sanctuary

Prayer for respite from continuing distress

See, O Lord, that I am in distress; My soul is troubled. — *Ezek. 11:13*

EZEKIEL 11:13-25

God's sure promises don't immediately abolish painful trials. The vision of the obliteration of the institutionalized church in Jerusalem—temple, priests, elders, and all— moves Ezekiel to beg the Lord to save at least a "remnant" of his people (9:8). As it happened, the Lord had already sent an angel to mark the foreheads of those who "sigh and cry over all the abominations done in [Jerusalem]" (9:4). These marked people will persevere in the faith and survive God's judgments upon the apostate church. This no doubt comforted the prophet, but it did not send him on his way rejoicing. His work was not done: he had more judgments of which to prophesy. The intensity of God's wrath was increasing and in Ezekiel's next vision (chapter 10), we have a graphic picture of the withdrawal of God's glory. After that, in another vision (Ezek. 11:1–12), the prophet meets with the Jewish church leaders, who turn out to be proud and self-confident, spiritually blind to their errors, oblivious to their danger, and clearly devoid of a true apprehension—a personal knowledge—of the Lord. Then the Spirit of God moves Ezekiel to pronounce their imminent demise. Before he is finished, a leader named Pelatiah drops dead (v. 13a), whereupon Ezekiel falls on his face and cries to God, asking if he intends to make "a complete end of the remnant of Israel" (v. 13b). We surely know the feeling in our distresses, and we cry out, "Is there no end to this problem? If it's not one thing, it's another!"

The glory of any prayer is in what the Lord does with it — in the lives of those who pray, and in the lives of those for whom the prayer is offered. The first principle here is that the church is renewed where it is seen to be meek and vulnerable, and where it is genuinely "humble[d]… under the mighty hand of God" (1 Peter 5:6). "God resists the proud, but gives grace to the humble" (James 4:6). God's answer to Ezekiel's prayer applies this truth along four lines of love for his people:

> *The Lord will be "a little sanctuary" for his scattered, apparently insignificant people wherever they are in this world (vv. 14–16).* As Paul later says, we can be assured that in the church's darkest times, there will always be "a remnant according to the election of grace" (Rom. 11:5). The Lord is our "hiding place" (Ps. 32:7).

> *The Lord will "gather [believers] from the peoples" (vv. 17–18).* This is partially fulfilled in the return from the Babylonian exile after 538 BC, but its ultimate fulfillment awaits the advent of Jesus and the gospel era—all the way from the cross to the "consummation" (Dan. 9:27), and "the glory that will be revealed"(1 Peter 5:1).

> *The Lord will "give [believers] a heart of flesh" (vv. 19–20),* later expanded upon in his promise: "I will give you a new heart and put a new spirit within you; I will take the heart of stone out of your flesh and give you a heart of flesh" (Ezek. 36:26). This is the "new covenant" that will come in Christ, of which God says, "I will put My law in their minds, and write it on their hearts; and I will be their God, and they shall be My people" (Jer. 31:33). This all comes to fruition in the intimate personal experience of God's grace in Christ.

> *The Lord will be with his elect people, however difficult their circumstances may be (vv. 24–25).* This is sealed by the Spirit of God, in the vision, by his transporting the prophet and his faithful ministry to the exiles in "Chaldea." God's judgments are real, but so is his free grace in Jesus Christ.

Because of this, in our troubles we can confess along with Paul: "Therefore I take pleasure in infirmities, in reproaches, in needs, in persecutions, in distresses, for Christ's sake." We will also bless the Lord with him, "For when I am weak, then I am strong" (2 Cor. 12:10). Is the Lord *your* "little sanctuary"?

PRAISE TO THE LORD, OUR "HIDING PLACE"
Sing Psalm 32:1–7

THINGS I WILL PRAY FOR TODAY

_____

_____

_____

July 6
A Secret Revealed

Prayer to God for answers

Then Daniel went to his house, and made the decision known to Hananiah, Mishael, and Azariah, his companions, that they might seek mercies from the God of heaven concerning this secret. — Dan. 2:17–18

READ DANIEL 2:17–23

There are times in life when no amount of thinking will give us the answers we seek. Will I get the job? Will that sweet girl marry me? Will I recover from this illness? Such a time dawned in teenage Daniel's life, and the question was a matter of life or death. There was no way he could think his way out of the problem. The problem was King Nebuchadnezzar's bad dreams, which caused "his spirit" to be "so troubled that his sleep left him" (2:1). He wanted to know what the dreams meant, but his "wise men" could not come up with an answer. This infuriated him and, like the Babylonian despot he was, he decided to kill off all his not-so-wise "wise men," which meant that his teenage Hebrew trainees—Daniel and his companions— also faced an untimely end. With this sentence of death hanging over them, Daniel went to Nebuchadnezzar, asked for time, and promised to "tell the King the interpretation" (vv. 14–16). What he did then provides us with practical principles to apply in all the crises of life, great and small, seemingly solvable or clearly insuperable.

Practical principle #1: Go to God for answers (2:17–19a). Daniel first called for a prayer meeting. It looks like he asked the king for time so that he and his fellow believers could go to their heavenly Father in *corporate* prayer. He evidently thought that meeting for prayer had priority over his own private prayer. Christians ought to feel that way about their church's prayer meetings: "The LORD loves the gates of Zion more than all the dwellings of Jacob" (Ps. 87:2). Much as the Lord loves to see us one by one in the secret place of prayer (Matt. 6:6) and delights in our praying as families (i.e., "the dwellings of Jacob"), he says he loves "more" our praying together as a church. Yet the "prayer meeting" is a Cinderella in most church's lives; if it exists at all, it is a faithful few that commit to it.

376

Daniel is calling us to view the prayer meeting as the furnace room of the church, where the "prayers of the saints" rise as a sweet incense before God (Rev. 8:4). And should we not be found praying together while the sun still shines, before dark days come? God answered the young men's prayer and revealed the meaning of Nebuchadnezzar's dreams. Will not God also answer our prayers when we come together to the throne of his grace (Heb. 4:16)?

Practical principle #2: Praise the Lord as you go (2:19b–23). Having received God's answer, "Daniel *blessed* the God of heaven" (v. 19b, emphasis added). He gives us a beautiful example of God's watchword for our trials: "Be still and know that I am God; I will be exalted among the nations, I will be exalted in the earth" (Ps. 46:10). These godly young men have a spiritual maturity that is manifestly lacking in many grown-up believers in our day. Daniel's prayer is imbued with a humble composure that rests in a holy confidence in the truth that God—and not the high and mighty king of Babylon—is sovereign in his "wisdom and might" (v. 20). He "removes...and raises up" the rulers, politicians (v. 21). He "reveals deep and secret things" and knows "what is in the darkness" as the One in whom "light dwells" (v. 22). If we will pray in Daniel's vein, we will also give thanks and praise to the Lord with Daniel's exaltation. Like Daniel, we still live in the age of Psalms 2 and 110, but we also live in the age of the risen and exalted Christ—the "Son" of Psalm 2:7 and 12 whom our rulers must "kiss" if they are not to perish, and David's "Lord" of Psalm 110:1 and 5 who will "execute kings" in the day of God's wrath. This ought to give us a certain peace as we view the political world around us. The "kings of the earth" can conspire all they like, but Christ will bring them down sooner or later—perhaps before our very eyes. Christians, take heart, and make the "prayer meeting" a priority in your church life.

PRAISE TO THE LORD
Sing Psalm 37:32–40

THINGS I WILL PRAY FOR TODAY

July 7
Prayer as Usual?

Prayer that is private, persevering, and prevailing

*In his upper room, with his windows open toward Jerusalem, he knelt
down on his knees three times that day, and prayed and gave thanks
before his God, as was his custom since early days.*—Dan. 6:10

READ DANIEL 6:1–17

"No good deed goes unpunished," quipped Oscar Wilde. Long
before, Solomon observed, "I saw that for all toil and every
skillful work a man is envied by his neighbor," and added,
"This also is vanity and grasping for the wind" (Eccl. 4:4).
"Vanity" is our basic human disposition with its sinful devices and desires.
Envy is the practical attitude that is never far from our transgression of
all the Ten Commandments (Ex. 20:1–17). Envy in high places put Daniel
into the lion's den. Now an old man, he was one of three governors,
responsible to oversee the 120 "satraps" who administered the provinces
of the Persian Empire. Daniel performed his duties with such integrity
and efficiency that the king was thinking of setting him over the whole
realm (6:1–3). Daniel's peers were envious and colluded successfully to
enact a law stating that anyone who petitioned "any god or man for thirty
days"—other than the King—"shall be cast into a den of lions" (vv. 4–9).
Daniel's known prayer life was obviously the focus.

Daniel prayed "as was his custom" (v. 10). He followed God's
word through Solomon, which taught exiles to pray toward Jerusalem
(1 Kings 8:46–51). He followed the psalmist's pattern of praying three
times daily, as in Psalm 55:17: "Evening and morning and at noon I will
pray, and cry aloud, and He shall hear my voice" (cf. Acts 2:2; 3:1; 10:9).
He was not going to suspend his praying for thirty days and so deny his
faithful Lord. He was engaged, of course, in private worship, but must
have expected some Peeping Toms to make every effort to expose his
time-honored devotional practice.

Daniel prayed in disregard for a wicked law (v. 11). It is
inconceivable that he, as a high official in the imperial administration,
did not know about the decree. Surely he knew he was being spied on.

Regardless, he prayed in his "upper room" and "on his knees." If they were able to see an old man on his knees, facing Jerusalem, the spies had to be higher than the second floor, or on a roof! Daniel knew very well he was sailing against the wind of the culture as well as the law of the land. But his hand was steady on the tiller of his living faith in the Lord. He knew that, humanly speaking, this would likely not end well. He knew he was being persecuted because he was faithful to the Lord he loved. He acted on principle even at hazard to his life because he knew the Lord loved him. He had no "martyr complex," but was simply resolved to be quietly faithful and trust his loving Savior for the consequences.

This recalls the witness of the Christian martyr and one-time student of the apostle John, Polycarp of Smyrna (AD 69–155). To save his life, he had only to say, "Caesar is Lord" (which meant "Caesar is God"). He replied instead, "Eighty-six years I have served Christ, and he never did me any wrong. How can I blaspheme my King who saved me?" He perished, burned at the stake; Daniel was delivered. But both men inherited "the crown of life" prepared for every believer in Jesus Christ (Rev. 2:10).

Here is a wonderful encouragement for us to be praying people—not for show like the Pharisee who prayed "to be seen by men" (Matt. 6:5), but to be humble believers who always ask a blessing even when there are visitors at your table, and who don't stay home from church when unbelieving relatives are visiting. Daniel is not a showy believer, but neither is he a secret believer. He lived as he was ready to die—a praying man who rejoiced in his Redeemer with all his heart.

PRAISE THAT PRAYS NOT TO BE FORSAKEN IN OLD AGE
Sing Psalm 71:9–15

THINGS I WILL PRAY FOR TODAY

July 8
Prayer That God Hears (Part 1)

Becoming close personally with God in prayer

Then I set my face toward the Lord God to make request by prayer and supplications, with fasting, sackcloth, and ashes. — Dan. 9:3

READ DANIEL 9:1-13

It is almost seventy years since Daniel came to Babylon. Now a high official in the government, he is reading Scripture one day and discovers in Jeremiah's prophecy that the Babylonian exile would last seventy years, after which God's people would "return to this place—Jerusalem" (25:8–11; 29:10–14). It dawns on him that God's promises are about to be fulfilled! With evident excitement, he turns to "prayer and supplications, with fasting, sackcloth, and ashes" (v. 3), and in the process he leaves to us one of *the* great prayers of recorded history. He prays to claim the promises of God, which can only be claimed in prayer, followed by obedient action. True prayer has five parts to it, two of which we consider today, and the other three tomorrow.

True prayer begins with an apprehending adoration of God (v. 4). Daniel expresses the privilege and pleasure of a believing relationship with God—who is "the Lord *my* God." He *apprehends* God personally. A. W. Tozer observes that to "most people God is an inference, not a reality. He is a deduction from evidence which they consider adequate; but he remained personally unknown to the individual." Daniel recognizes three particular facts in his opening address to God:

- Who God is in himself: the "great and awesome God," i.e., who is *sovereign* over all things and to be worshiped from the heart.
- Who God is to his people: he who "keeps his covenant and mercy," i.e., who acts in sovereign grace to those who love him.
- What God requires of us: that we "love Him, and keep his commandments," knowing that anything less is sheer hypocrisy.

When we pray, we are on holy ground, like Moses at the burning bush (Ex. 3:5), and, like Moses, we must enter God's presence reverently.

True prayer continues with confession of sin (vv. 5–13). Daniel emphasizes two essential elements of a sincere and genuine confession:

Daniel confesses sin in *specific* terms. There is nothing here of the easy, generalized "we all sin in thought, word, and deed" approach so popular today. This confesses nothing and is no better than a means of evading any real facing up to our particular personal sin. Undefined sin is unconfessed sin. And admitting "mistakes" is not repentance, nor is "moving on" reformation. Confession requires self-conviction.

Daniel confesses sin *corporately* for the whole people of God. This is inevitable when anyone leads a group in prayer, whether in a pulpit at a church meeting or at home in family worship. One person speaks audibly, but all participate: "*We* have sinned and committed iniquity" (v. 5). Daniel cites three main categories of the church's sin:

> Disobedience to God's specific known commands (vv. 5, 7–9).
> Disdain for God's messengers and their messages (vv. 6, 10–11).
> Denial of God's warnings and discipline (vv. 12–13).

Daniel is here justifying God's judgments upon his own people for their turning away from him. In Paul's words to the Galatians, this says to them and to the world, "God is not mocked" (Gal. 6:7).

This is "the sort of prayer that God hears," says Stuart Olyott. Daniel teaches us how to pray for ourselves and for our church. He teaches us that no one truly prays until he approaches the Lord in believing, heart-felt reverence. No one will truly confess their sin until they are convicted of it in their heart of hearts. Will you look your sins in the face, like Daniel? Cry to Christ, for he will receive you—it is his promise (see Matt. 11:28ff.). May we all pray with such transparent faith, heartfelt devotion, and godly discipleship!

PRAISE FOR GOD'S ABOUNDING LOVE
Sing Psalm 5

THINGS I WILL PRAY FOR TODAY

July 9
Prayer That God Hears (Part 2)

Continuing to become close personally with God in prayer

Now therefore, our God, hear the prayer of Your servant, and his supplications, and for the Lord's sake cause Your face to shine on Your sanctuary, which is desolate. —Dan. 9:17

READ DANIEL 9:14–19

aniel's prayer lifts off like a five-stage rocket to the Lord's throne of grace. The order of his prayer is this: 1) reverence for God; 2) confession of sin against God; 3) acknowledgment of God's righteous justice in our lives; 4) specific requests for God's mercy; and 5) an appeal to the glory of his name as the ultimate ground for his mercy and salvation. Yesterday we considered the first two of these; today we turn to the last three:

True prayer acknowledges God's unimpeachable righteousness (vv. 14–15). Daniel accepts that God is wholly justified when he "kept the disaster in mind, and brought it upon [Israel]" (v. 14). None of it was undeserved. They had been warned again and again (see Jer. 2–4), but brought thoroughly deserved judgment upon themselves (v. 15). If the Lord stops us with a "bang," we should thank him and return to him in faith and obedience without delay (Jer. 18:6ff.).

True prayer gives voice to God-honoring petitions (vv. 16–17). On this occasion, Daniel makes two specific prayer requests:

> *Mercy for the visible church*—*"Your city Jerusalem"* (v. 16). The reason for this plea is that God's (professed and so-called) people have become "a reproach to all those around [them]." The work of God's Word, church, and kingdom is put to shame before the watching world. God's people have "let the side down"—God's side—with disastrous results all round. The unspoken assumption behind this request is that if God cannot or will not save *his people*, then what substance can there be to any of his promises? And what hope can there be for sinners who are blinded and enslaved by sin, and utterly incapable of saving themselves?

382

⤳ *The restoration of God's presence with his people (v. 17).* Daniel begs God, "hear the prayer of your servant, and his supplications, and *for the Lord's sake* cause Your face to shine on Your sanctuary, which is desolate." The heart of this is the restoration of purity of worship among God's people so that he might exercise his sovereignty and his grace for the world to see and take notice. A godless pseudo-church is no witness to the living God who saves! Do you pray that God would manifest himself in his church (1 Tim. 3:15) and that the Lord Jesus Christ would "subdue all things to Himself" both in the overthrow of evil and the consummation of his plan of salvation (Phil. 3:21; 1 Cor. 15:28)?

True prayer appeals to the glory of God's name (vv. 18–19). You will have noticed that the recurring argument is not "save us for *our own sakes*," but, rather, save us for "*Your own sake*"—i.e., for God's righteousness, compassion, reputation, and glory! Our sins, sad to say, inevitably give "great occasion to the enemies of the LORD to blaspheme" (2 Sam. 12:14), whereas genuine godliness is a winsome witness to the world. This is why Jesus says to us: "Let your light so shine before men, that they may see your good works and glorify your Father in heaven" (Matt. 5:16). Ask yourself constantly whether your thoughts, words, and deeds will cause others to glorify your Savior God. Christians! You are God's ambassadors and your whole carriage and behavior will therefore either enhance or diminish the name of God before the world.

Daniel's prayer began with God's promises in Scripture (vv. 2–3). Daniel prays from the promises, seeking their fulfillment. Stuart Olyott notes that this "is the sort of prayer that God hears," and goes on to say, "If we would see God at work, we must find out what He has promised and pray for it like that." May the Lord so bless your prayers.

PRAISE FOR THE SURE PROMISES OF GOD
Sing Psalm 85:8–13

THINGS I WILL PRAY FOR TODAY

_____

_____

_____

July 10
Rewards of a Prayerful Life

Prayer as an experience of heaven on earth

*And suddenly, one having the likeness of the sons of men touched my lips;
then I opened my mouth and spoke...—Dan. 10:16*

READ DANIEL 10:10–19

aniel, now in his late eighties, is given a vision of an Angel by the river Tigris. This Angel is the pre-incarnate Jesus (compare 10:4–6 with Rev. 1:13–17). Like Paul on the road to Damascus, Daniel fell on his face, drained of energy (10:1–9). The same Lord reaches out to Daniel: "Suddenly, a hand touched me, which made me tremble on my knees." The Angel assures Daniel that he is a "man greatly beloved" and that he has come to give Daniel understanding of the vision (recorded in chapters 11–12). He enables Daniel to rise to his feet, and with the words "do not fear" embraces him with warm acceptance (vv. 10–12a). What follows is an extraordinary instance of communion with the Lord, in which believing prayer is revealed to be a real experience of heaven on earth.

The Lord assures Daniel that his prayer is being answered (vv. 12–14). That God steadfastly answers faithful prayers is a recurrent theme throughout Scripture, history, and teaching. What is special in this instance is that the veil is pulled back for a moment to reveal supernatural aspects of the way God answers prayer that are otherwise hidden from us. Notice three things in particular:

- God's answer to Daniel's prayer is *in the pipeline*—"from the first day" Daniel sets his heart to understand and humbles himself before God. Daniel's "words were heard" and the Lord came "because of [his] words" (v. 12). This is surely true of God's handling of all our prayers. His answering is contemporaneous with our praying—"from the first...."
- God's answer to Daniel is *delayed by warfare* in heavenly places, in this case by three weeks (v. 13). Here is a glimpse of the unseen enemy behind the visible evil in the world: "We do not wrestle against flesh and blood, but against principalities,

against powers, against the rulers, the darkness of this age, against spiritual hosts of wickedness in the heavenly places" (Eph. 6:12). Our prayers are all affected by this fact.

⮞ God's answer to Daniel will *reveal future events*—"what will happen to your people in the latter days" (v. 14). Again, though unique to Daniel, this revelation has a universality in its application to the normal experience of God's people in their uncertainties in life. The Lord has our future in his hands and we need fear it no more than did Daniel.

The Lord strengthens Daniel as God draws near to him (vv. 15–20). At first, however, Daniel is speechless, overwhelmed by sorrows (prayer sometimes can only be groanings [Rom. 8:26]). The Son of Man touches his lips and Daniel speaks, praying for strength and breath (vv. 15–18). The Lord answers this prayer by assuring Daniel of his love and bestowing upon him four particular rewards of a prayerful life, all of which are standing promises to believers to this day:

⮞ God's *peace* for our fears (v. 19a; cf. John 14:27; Phil. 4:7).

⮞ God's *strength* for our weakness (v. 19b; cf. Eph. 6:10).

⮞ Readiness to *hear and heed* God's words (v. 19c; cf. Ps. 85:8).

⮞ God's *light* for our present darkness (vv. 20–21; cf. Matt. 4:16). The "Scripture of Truth" is God's word as it will yet be revealed by the speaker, Jesus Christ. Meanwhile, the future Messiah strives with the nations, aided by the angel Michael.

In all of this, Daniel is given a vivid foretaste of the heavenly glory. "Where else, but in the place of prayer," asks Olyott, "can a weak, mortal, trembling sinner experience heaven on earth?" Do you have no personal knowledge of Christ's conquering in your own lives? Then pray earnestly, looking to Jesus, and as your heart is in the right place—in heaven with Jesus—you will find heaven is in your heart, multiplying the blessings of God's love in answer to your prayers.

PRAISE FROM ONE WHO FEELS HIS WEAKNESS
Sing Psalm 102:23–28

THINGS I WILL PRAY FOR TODAY

July 11
How Will Things End?

Prayer for more than we need to know

Although I heard, I did not understand. Then I said, "My lord, what shall be the end of these things?"—Dan. 12:8

READ DANIEL 12:8-13

Mention the end of the world and the last judgment, and you soon discover that many would rather not think about it. After all, it poses the most basic questions as to what we are living for, what our hopes are for this life, and where we will spend eternity. It confronts us with the claims of God and the state of our souls, and that does not sit well with those who are "without Christ…having no hope and without God in the world" (Eph. 2:12). On the other hand, God's people can become too interested in knowing about "the end of these things" and the world abounds with people almost obsessed with pinning down the date of Jesus's return—even when he has explicitly forbidden such speculation (Matt. 24:36; cf. Acts 1:11). Daniel had been given certain visions of "the end," including the last judgment and the glory of the saved (11:40–12:3). Then he was told to "seal the book until the end of time" (12:4), which indicates the finality of this word from God and implies careful attention to it as we patiently wait for fulfillment of the prophecies. Daniel's prayer—"what shall be the end of these things?" (v. 8)—is natural enough, but it turns out he is asking for more than God is willing to reveal. God's answer is richly practical for him and for all of us, as we seek to understand the opening of the seals of God's revelations regarding "the end" and the consummation of all things in Christ (Dan. 9:27; Rev. 5:1–2, 5, 9–6:1).

"**Go on living your life!**" is God's answer to Daniel's prayer—and also to our similar questions (12:9–12). The struggle with Antichrist is some way off, at "the time of the end" (v. 9)—just prior to Jesus's second coming. In other words, get on with your normal life and leave the end of the world to the Lord! This means:

Living a godly life (v. 10). The crossover structure of the verse (A1-B1-B2-A2) highlights how the Lord prepares his people for heaven, over against the corrupting consequences of being outside of Christ: A1—"many shall be purified"; B1—"the wicked shall do wickedly"; B2—"the wicked shall [not] understand"; A2—"the wise shall understand."

Trusting the Lord, who will shorten the time (v. 11). This seems to be the import of the numbers 1,290 (days) and 1,335 (days). The first number is literally three and a half years; the second is three and a half years plus one month. The gist of it seems to be "hang on an extra month and you will be through the worst of it." So put away your calculator and your date-setting speculations about "the end of…things" and trust the Lord!

Whenever you are anxious about the future, and begin to pray about it, you will be blessed in remembering three wonderful truths:

> ❧ God is doing a great work by the gospel of Christ. Your salvation is a supernatural work of the Holy Spirit. Paul may plant and Apollos water, but God gives the increase (1 Cor. 3:6). Salvation is by grace through faith, not of ourselves (Eph. 2:8).

> ❧ The gospel of Jesus Christ has a sharp edge. It is "sharper than any two-edged sword" (Heb. 4:12; Rev. 1:16). God's power to save runs parallel with his power to condemn. Come to Christ and inherit eternal life; do nothing and perish eternally (John 3:16-18)!

> ❧ The "time of the end" (v. 9) is not the end of time! That end is not the end, but a new beginning that will never end—the fullness and glory of heaven itself. When you ponder "the day of His coming" (Mal. 3:2), will you pray with earnest expectation, "Amen. Even so, come, Lord Jesus!" (Rev. 22:20), and wish it were today?

Meanwhile, the Lord says to all of his believing people, "But you, go your way until the end; for you shall rest, and will arise to your inheritance at the end of days" (v. 13). What inheritance? That "inheritance incorruptible and undefiled and that does not fade away, reserved in heaven for you, who are kept by the power of God through faith unto salvation ready to be revealed in the last time" (1 Peter 1:4–5).

PRAISE OF THE GLORIOUS GOD
Sing Psalm 57:5–11

THINGS I WILL PRAY FOR TODAY

July 12
Have You Rejected Us?

Prayer in an emergency

O LORD, to You I cry out; for fire has devoured the open pastures, and a flame has burned all the trees of the field. — Joel 1:19

READ JOEL 1:19-20

One man "falsely shouting fire in a crowded theater" and deliberately "causing a panic" is rightly regarded as dangerous. Many prophets have been dismissed as dangerous troublemakers. Joel is shouting "fire!" in a nation of drought-parched pastures and fire-consumed forests. Yet nobody is listening, far less turning to God. This is nothing new. God's warnings of judgment to come (the Law) and invitations to eternal life in Christ (the gospel) too often fall on dulled ears. There is a "fire" in the theater of humankind and the Lord holds out his hands in his grace to "a disobedient and contrary people" (Rom. 10:21), saying, "Hear, that your soul may live" (Isa. 55:3).

Judah was overtaken by unexpected calamities (vv. 2–12). Locusts galore and a whole lot more devastated the nation (vv. 2–4). Joel, with heavy irony, first tells the drunks to wake up and weep, for there's nothing to drink (v. 5). Things are so bad, the nation needs to "lament like a virgin" who has lost "the husband of her youth" (vv. 6–8); the "priests" should "mourn" for the lack of grain and drink offerings for God's house (vv. 9–10); and the "farmers" and "vinedressers" should be "ashamed" and "wail" over ruined crops — in sum, "surely joy has withered away from the sons of men" (vv. 11–12). But will church and nation turn to God with humbled hearts and a repentant spirit? That remains the question posed by all the calamities in human life.

These physical privations overlay spiritual problems (vv. 13–18). In Deuteronomy, notes Anthony Selvaggio, locusts (28:38–42) and drought (28:23–24) "are listed among the curses for disobeying God" (28:15). But is this recognized by even *God's* people? Joel calls for God's ministers to "lament" and "consecrate a fast, call a sacred assembly" and "gather the elders" and "all the inhabitants of the land" in God's house and "cry out to the Lord" (vv. 13–14). This apparently evokes no positive response and

388

Joel goes on to announce, "Alas for the day! For the day of the Lord is at hand" (vv. 15–18), which is to imply that without repentance toward God, they will only experience, as Calvin says, "something worse in future."

Did this cause people to turn to God? Sadly, only the prophet Joel appears to cry out to God: one man prays for the whole nation, he alone recognizing with urgency that the "fire" is not only real, but is God's judgment on the sin of the church (vv. 19–20)! To apply the Lord's call to us today, meditate on three great truths:

- For all God's words of judgment, remember that he has "no pleasure in the death of the wicked, but that the wicked turn from his way and live" (Ezek. 33:11). "No pleasure" really means *zero*! "It is holiness, not punishment of sin, which pleases God."

- Notice that the entire prophecy of Joel holds out the hope of pardon to sinners and even looks ahead to its wider fulfillment — which, as Peter proclaims in his sermon at Pentecost, quoting Joel, consists in the person and work of Jesus Christ and the pouring out of the Holy Spirit upon the church (Joel 3:20–21; cf. 2:28ff.; Acts 2:14–39).

- Understand that your personal ministry of intercessory prayer is not to be inhibited because nobody else is praying. A prayer meeting of one is infinitely more powerful than no prayer meeting at all. Be your church's prayer meeting until others join with you before the throne of grace (Heb. 4:16; Mal. 3:16).

A PRAISE-PRAYER FOR SPIRITUAL REVIVAL
Sing Psalm 60:1–5

THINGS I WILL PRAY FOR TODAY

July 13
Where Is Their God?

A prayer for pastors to pray

Why should they say among the peoples, "Where is their God?"
—Joel 2:17

JOEL 2:12-17

t is no accident that this second prayer of the book of Joel is surrounded by some of the most memorable Scripture verses with gospel connotations: on *repentance*, "So rend your heart, and not your garments; return to the Lord your God, for he is gracious and merciful, slow to anger, and of great kindness; and He relents from doing harm" (2:13); on *corporate worship and prayer*, "Consecrate a fast, call a sacred assembly...and cry out to the Lord" (2:15; cf. 1:14); on temporal and spiritual *restoration*, "I will restore to you the years that the swarming locust has eaten" (2:25); on *spiritual growth* in days to come, "I will pour out My Spirit on all flesh; your sons and your daughters shall prophesy," (2:28ff.; Acts 2:17–18); and on the ultimate *security* of God's people, "Beat your plowshares into swords and your pruning hooks into spears; let the weak say, 'I am strong'" (Joel 3:10; Isa. 2:4). This illustrates the wider truth, as Dr. Gareth Crossley observes, that "revelation of impending judgement is not intended to terrify the people, but to bring them back to God." Joel's prophecy begins with judgment from God by locusts and drought (1:1–2:11); moves to repentance toward God (2:12–27); and closes with the promise of the Holy Spirit poured upon the church in the coming age of the Messiah (2:28–3:21). The overarching vision, comments Dr. Theo Laetsch, is "the continuous, uninterrupted, unending dwelling of Jehovah in the midst of his Church Militant (Eph. 2:22) and Triumphant (Rev. 1:13)." Bearing this in mind, let us note what this present prayer is teaching us about the place of prayer in the life of God's people.

God is teaching his ministers to lead the church from the front: "Let the priests, who minister to the LORD, weep between the porch and the altar" (v. 17a). The "porch" is the entrance to the Holy Place, and the "altar" is the altar of burnt offering in front of the porch steps. If the shepherds of the church—teaching and ruling elders—will not lead the people in private and public prayer, nothing good can be expected from the sheep. Godly example is godly leadership. All else is ruin.

God is teaching us that our first prayer must be for mercy: "Let them say, 'Spare Your people, O LORD'" (v. 17b). Why mercy? As opposed, say, to prosperity, or gratitude, or healing, or opportunities to witness for the Lord, or confidence in daily living, or effective use of our gifts, or other people?—i.e., the things that so naturally populate our prayer requests? The answer is that it is always and daily a fact of Christian experience that it is "through the LORD's mercies we are not consumed, because His compassions fail not." In Christian experience, "they are new every morning: great is Thy faithfulness" (Lam. 3:22). Mercy in Christ is the first fruit of his love to us every morning when we wake up—and this is where prayer begins.

God is teaching us to prize and promote his honor before a watching world: "And do not give Your heritage to reproach, that the nations should rule over them. Why should they say among the peoples, 'Where is their God?'" (v. 17cd). The world will pounce on believers' failings in order to justify their denial of God's claims and their rejection of his offer of his saving grace in his Son. People can always find excuses to deny God himself and dismiss his people as hypocrites. Jesus was sinless, but was mocked on the cross in these very terms: "He saved others; Himself He cannot save. If He is the King of Israel, let Him now come down from the cross, and we will believe Him" (Matt. 27:42). If you know your Bible and you love your Lord, you know why he stayed put on his cross: It was love for sinners and atonement for their sins. But what an indictment of us, who say we love him, but like ancient Judah, proceed to sin away our witness and bring reproach upon the God who sent his Son to save the likes of us!

PRAISE CRYING TO GOD FOR HIS SAVING LOVE
Sing Psalm 44:20–26

THINGS I WILL PRAY FOR TODAY

_____

_____

_____

_____

July 14
Jacob Is So Small!

Prayer of intercession against God's judgments

Oh, that Jacob may stand, for he is small!—Amos 7:2

READ AMOS 7:1–6

N othing exposes human frailty like so-called "natural" disasters. Weather satellites can forewarn us and give us time to flee or hunker down, but we are helpless to calm the storms or turn them away. When God warns Amos of coming judgments—famine by locusts (vv. 1–2) and devastation by fire and drought (v. 4)—the prophet knows he is helpless to stop famines and firestorms. But he also knows he can intercede with God on Israel's behalf, even against God's declared intentions. In so doing, he models intercessory prayer for us and reminds us that God keeps mercy for all who flee to him in repentance and faith (Ex. 34:7; cf. Jer. 18:1–11).

Amos appeals for Israel's *pardon:* "O Lord God, *forgive*, I pray!" (vv. 2, 5). He doesn't say, "Please take away the locusts," as if the bugs are the real problem. What "fills him with fear," writes Herman Veldkamp, "is not the swarm of insects but the spiritual decay that had long ago robbed Israel of its purity. What Amos feared was sin!…Behind all the problems and plagues of our time is the guilt of the world and the church.…When will *we* ever learn that our sin is the cause of the world's problems?" Amos understands human sin and divine justice. His petition is therefore for forgiveness. Pesticide and good rainfall would solve nothing: Israel needs a Savior to revivify dead souls.

He addresses God by his *covenant name:* "O Lord GOD"— where the capitalized "GOD" translates the divine name, the Hebrew "Yahweh"—the God of the Covenant of Grace from Genesis 3:15 on. He is reminding God that he made a covenant to be the Redeemer of his people. He is appealing for covenant mercy, even for the covenant-breakers, whose national backsliding was so desperate. They are not worthy of being saved, but God is worthy to save them. And so Amos appeals to God's covenant promises to the generations of his people! Is he not the God of "an everlasting covenant" (Gen. 17:7)?

He claims Israel's *insignificance* as an argument for God's mercy: "Oh that Jacob may stand, for he is small!" (vv. 2, 5). Elsewhere, God promises, "'Fear not, you worm Jacob, you men of Israel! I will help you,' says the LORD and your Redeemer, the Holy One of Israel" (Isa. 41:14). The truth is, that they—and we—have no claim on God for what passes for righteousness in our lives (cf. Isa. 64:6; Rom. 3:10ff.). Our only resort must be to his covenant faithfulness and his provision of salvation in the gospel of his Son: "Nothing in my hand I bring, simply to the cross I cling." In other words, "small" = nothing!

The glorious thing here is that God relents because of Amos's intercession alone! Charles Simeon asks any "who are sinking under discouraging apprehensions" and asking, "How shall I arise, for I am small?" to see "how readily God interposed for Israel, at the cry of Amos; and *that* too for an obstinate and rebellious people: and will he not hear *your* cry, which is offered for yourselves? Moreover, you have a better intercessor than Amos: the Son of God himself 'ever lives' in heaven 'to make intercession for you' (Heb. 7:25). Put your cause into his hands... entirely to him....For HIM the Father hears always" (John 9:31). Do you feel small today? Then look to the One who is "greater than our heart, and knows all things" (1 John 3:20), for "if we confess *our* sins, He is faithful and just to forgive us our sins and to cleanse us from all unrighteousness" (1 John 1:9).

PRAISE TO THE GOD OF COVENANT MERCY
Sing Psalm 89:19-29

THINGS I WILL PRAY FOR TODAY

July 15
Fleeing or Found?

The first believing prayer of desperate men

We pray, O LORD, please do not let us perish for this man's life, and do not charge us with innocent blood; for You, O LORD, have done as it pleased You. —Jonah 1:14

READ JONAH 1:10-17

alled by God to go to Nineveh to prophesy against her wickedness, Jonah promptly takes a ship for Tarshish in modern Spain to get as far as possible "from the presence of the Lord" (vv. 1–3). God acts *in his grace* in two ways:

He pursues Jonah with a storm, which terrifies the pagan sailors who cry to their gods and toss the cargo over the side, but which finds the culprit fast asleep below deck (vv. 4–5). The captain wakens him and asks him at least to call upon his God, but Jonah says and does nothing. No explanation, no prayer, just guilty silence. The sailors cast lots and the Lord makes sure it *falls on Jonah* (cf. Prov. 16:33). When challenged, Jonah admits he is a Hebrew and adds, "I fear the God of heaven who made the sea and the dry land" (vv. 6–9). There is no confessing sin, but he must know "his sin" has "found [him] out" (Num. 32:23). Caught in the act, he is one of the "children of light" who chose the darkness and rejected God's known will. This is true of us Christians when we sin deliberately (1 Thess. 5:5–8)!

Jonah now owns up to fleeing from the presence of the Lord. The sailors are "exceedingly afraid," having put two and two together— i.e., the storm and the sovereign Creator God (v. 10). Since Jonah's God clearly is dealing with Jonah, it dawns on them that they are also accountable to God! God *in his grace* is at work in them in two ways:

> It is by his grace that the sailors discover in the storm that God is awakening them to their *eternal danger*—convicting them that "the fear of the Lord" is "the beginning of wisdom" (Prov. 1:7), and that "it is a fearful thing to fall into the hands of the living God" (Heb. 10:31).

> It is also by God's grace that the sailors learn that they cannot

save themselves by their own best efforts. Shrinking from simply heaving Jonah over the side, they row hard for the shore but without success (vv. 12–13). God is showing them that they *need a Savior*!

The sailors turn to God in prayer. The prophet Joel prophesies that "whoever calls on the name of the LORD shall be saved" (Joel 2:32). While this is prophetic of the fullness of the New Testament age in Jesus Christ (Acts 2:21; Rom. 10:13), it is a truth first established in the experience of Old Testament believers. These sailors, hitherto pagans and now made public executioners by the prophet's insistence, cry to the one and only living God for forgiveness for any spilling of "innocent blood" (v. 14). They throw Jonah "into the sea, and the sea ceased from its raging" (v. 15). That stilling of the waves is silent proof to God's answer to their prayer. But there is more, for these men affirm their faith in Jonah's God in three particulars: they reverence the Lord "exceedingly," they offer "a sacrifice to the Lord," and they take "vows." They confess God as their Savior and solemnly commit to him as his followers! Sinclair Ferguson notes that "Jonah's flight was not without spiritual fruit," and goes on to point out that this is "a very clear illustration of the principle that *the fruitfulness of our lives for God is not itself a guarantee of the closeness of our lives to his will.*...No matter what our gifts are, we may find ourselves in Jonah's position. God uses us for his glory, and yet our hearts are not in tune with his. Beware of mistaking usefulness to God for communion with God!" Jonah was still fleeing from God's presence—committed to the deep—given up for dead. The chapter ends with a note of hope: he is swallowed by the Lord's "great fish" to spend his next three days and nights within its belly (v. 17). Jonah was "found out"—by a gracious Savior whose love will not let him go: "I revealed myself to those who did not ask for me; I was found by those who did not seek me" (Isa. 65:1). Where are you?

PRAISE FOR DELIVERANCE FROM A STORMY SEA
Sing Psalm 107:23–32

THINGS I WILL PRAY FOR TODAY

_____

_____

_____

July 16
Salvation Is of the Lord

Prayer from the grave

Out of the belly of Sheol I cried, and You heard my voice. — *Jonah 2:2*

READ JONAH 2:1–10

hen Jonah was hurled into the sea, you might have said, "He doesn't have a prayer." He surely expected to drown. Yet God's hidden grace was at work, so that the man who "doesn't have a prayer"—and *would not pray* hitherto— would pray as never before and see that prayer from the grave answered in his "resurrection" from virtual "death" three days later (v. 10)! The heart of every true prayer is the faith that is "sure of what we hope for and certain of what we do not see" (Heb. 11:1). Jonah is given what the Puritan Thomas Goodwin calls "a new eye…that is as suited to behold spiritual things as the natural eye is to behold colours." True prayer is not mouthing the forms of words, but seeking and experiencing communion with God: "Draw near to God and He will draw near to you" (James 4:8a). This is the spirit in which Jonah prays "from the fish's belly" (v. 1). He prays in four steps:

Step #1 — *Call* upon the *sovereign* Lord (v. 2). Notice how Jonah's prayer unfolds, simply, logically, personally and effectually. First is his *action*: he "cried out" to the Lord to whom he is accountable. Second is his *reason*: the "affliction" that finds him in "the belly of Sheol" (i.e., the grave), under the justice of the Holy God. Third is his *heart's desire*: that God hear his voice and answer him, according to promise—"Then you shall call, and the LORD will answer; you shall cry, and He will say, 'Here I am'" (Isa. 58:9).

Step #2 — *Come* as to a throne of *grace* (vv. 3–4). Jonah grasps that God is dealing with him: "you cast me into the deep" (v. 3). It was not bad luck or somebody else's fault. He admits, "I have been cast out of your sight," and follows this up with a commitment: "I will look again toward Your holy temple" (v. 4). The temple is key, for there God manifested himself to his people (Ex. 37:1–9; 1 Sam. 4:4), and sacrifice was offered for forgiveness of sin. Jonah's looking to the temple means he is looking to God's covenant love and provision of salvation—exactly what looking to Jesus Christ as Savior means for the New Testament believer (see John 2:19–21; Rev. 21:3, 22).

Step #3—*Count* **the tokens of God's** *favor* **(vv. 5–7).** Deliverance dawns in the darkness (v. 5), for Jonah has a sense of his life being brought "from the pit," as thoughts upon the Lord stir his heart and earnest prayer rises from his lips (vv. 6–7). Christian, you have new life in your risen Savior, and the Holy Spirit testifies to your spirit that you are a child of God (Rom. 8:16). However dark this fallen world, "your life is hidden with Christ in God" (Col. 3:3; cf. Eph. 2:6).

Step #4—*Celebrate* **the Lord's** *salvation* **(vv. 8–9).** Instead of making an idol of looking inward to indulge his sinful selfishness, Jonah looks away from himself in three wonderful praises:

> ☙ He voices compassion for the plight of the lost who cling to "vain idols" and "forsake their hope of steadfast love" (v. 8, ESV).

> ☙ He renews commitment to the Lord. With the "voice of thanksgiving" he will offer the sacrifice of heartfelt praise and worship, and keep his vows of faith and obedience to "practice the truth" (v. 9ab; 1 John 1:6).

> ☙ He makes joyful confession of the sovereignty of God in salvation: "Salvation is of the Lord" (v. 9c). Like David before him, he discovers what it is to be restored to "the joy of [God's] salvation" (Ps. 51:12). Most profoundly of all, Jonah is given to be a sign of Jesus's resurrection (Matt. 12:38–42).

The Christian, like the prophet, is simultaneously surrounded by death and possessed of everlasting life in Christ, and therefore is able to rejoice in him "with joy inexpressible and full of glory, receiving the end of your faith—the salvation of your souls" (1 Peter 1:8–9). This is resurrection life in the risen Christ. Do you know this salvation in your heart? Then rejoice!

PRAISE OF ONE DELIVERED FROM DEATH
Sing Psalm 116

THINGS I WILL PRAY FOR TODAY

_____

_____

_____

July 17
Cry Mightily to God

Prayer in the face of divine judgment

Let man and beast be covered with sackcloth, and cry mightily to God...
—Jonah 3:8

READ JONAH 3:1–10

onah's mission to Nineveh looks like an evangelist's nightmare. This time, God's message is not simply against "their wickedness" (1:2), but is a death sentence: "Yet forty days, and Nineveh shall be overthrown" (3:1–4). The prophet gets to proclaim this over three days throughout the greatest city of the time. No hope is offered, no charge to "repent or perish"—as Jesus lays it out in Luke 13:1–5. There is, however, more than a wisp of gospel grace behind the prophecy of doom. The Ninevites would know Jonah's backstory: that he was thrown overboard to his "death" for his apostasy from his God; and was "resurrected" onto dry land after three days in the "belly of Sheol [i.e. the grave]." Might they too hope for life after three days of the prophet's "doom"? Were they also aware of the "forty days" theme in the Hebrew Scriptures—Noah at the flood (Gen. 7:4); Moses on the mount (Deut. 9:9); Goliath's challenge at Elah (1 Sam. 17:16)—all either tests of living faith or examples of the absence of a saving relationship with God? They surely knew that Israel had wandered "forty years in the wilderness" before admission to a new life in the promised land (Deut. 8:2; Josh. 5:6). Evangelism is more than words. Jonah's and Israel's experience of God's saving grace calls everyone everywhere to flee the wrath to come by turning to him in repentance and faith.

God's grace turns Nineveh into an evangelist's dream. The people of Nineveh "believed God, proclaimed a fast, and put on sackcloth, from the greatest to the least of them," and God relents and the city is not destroyed (4:5–10). Faced with imminent divine judgment—echoing the pagan sailors' *believing* prayer for God's mercy in the storm (1:14)—this hitherto pagan people, led by their king, prayed for deliverance. This has its application to every human being's personal relationship with the Lord, whether they are outright pagans like the Ninevites, or believers like Jonah indulging their backslidings. Notice five implications flowing from the Assyrian king's decree:

> Fasting is always an appropriate accompaniment to serious prayer (v. 7). Scripture does not require this for effectual prayer, whereas being fervent and righteous is essential (James 5:16). Fasting can concentrate the mind in a way that postprandial drowsiness never will.

> Literally being "covered with sackcloth" (v. 8a) is not required in Scripture either, but what it represents is essential: namely, having deep sorrow for sin and being "clothed with humility" (1 Peter 5:5). In this way we acknowledge God's holiness and our need of saving grace.

> "Cry mightily to God" (v. 8b) means crying in faith, for "without faith it is impossible to please Him, for he who comes to God must believe that He is, and that He is a rewarder of those who diligently seek Him" (Heb. 11:6). God delights to answer prayer (Ps. 86:7).

> Turning most sincerely from our "evil way" and "the violence" in our hands simply means coming in a repentant spirit, determined to commit to following the Lord's way, rather than our own (v. 8c).

> Finally, notice that when the king says "who can tell if God will turn and relent…so that we may not perish?" (v. 9c), he clearly understands that, notwithstanding the prophecy of destruction, all is not lost. God is not wrath; he "*is* love" (1 John 4:8).

God's toughest warnings come from love for the lost. He loves saving people—if you will repent, he will relent (Jer. 18:8–11). And Jonah points us to Jesus. God loves this lost, hell-bent world so much that he sent his Son to die in the place of sinners, to bear the penalty of their sin, that they might not perish but have everlasting life—if they will but repent toward him and believe upon the Lord Jesus Christ (John 3:16).

PRAISE OF ONE RAISED FROM THE DEPTHS
Sing Psalm 71:20–24

THINGS I WILL PRAY FOR TODAY

_____

_____

_____

July 18
Take My Life from Me!

The prayer of a man angry with God

Therefore now, O Lord, please take my life from me, for it is better for me to die than to live!—Jonah 4:3

READ JONAH 4:1–11; MATTHEW 12:39–41

You would think that any true prophet of God would be thrilled to see a great world-city "called out of darkness into [God's] marvelous light" (vv. 1–3; cf. 1 Peter 2:9). But when the Ninevites repented and God relented from his announced judgment (3:10), Jonah became angry *with God* (v. 1). He goes to God in a prayer that has two main intertwined threads. The first is *anger*: God is too forgiving for Jonah's taste, perhaps because he can't see past the Ninevites' enmity to God and his people. The second thread is *despair*: expressed in his insistence that he would rather be dead than see God extend the life of this "evil empire"! His thrice-repeated death wish (vv. 3, 8, 9) is aptly called "spiritual infantile regression" by Sinclair Ferguson, who reminds us that Jesus sees this as characteristic of the attitudes of people in his own day, especially in the Jewish leadership (Matt. 11:16–19). Jonah so despised the Assyrians that, even when they are evidently repentant, he has no room in his heart for the grace that God shows them.

God aims a vital question at Jonah's mind and conscience: "Is it right for you to be angry?" (vv. 4, 9). He drives this home by giving and taking away the plant that shades Jonah as he sits and sulks, still hoping for Nineveh's destruction. After the plant dies—and Jonah is furious about that—God compares the ground of the prophet's pity for the withered plant with the infinitely greater ground of God's pity for Nineveh. What Jonah did with this, we are not told, but it should not be too difficult to discern its practical application to ourselves. It is all about God's amazing, free and sovereign grace for pig-headed prophets and pagan peoples alike! His abiding message of salvation is for "all people everywhere" who need a Savior (Acts 17:30, ESV).

Have you ever been angry with God, for whatever reasons: personal, economic, social, medical, doctrinal, etc.? Will you, like Jonah, turn to believing *prayer* as your *first* resort (Heb. 11:6) and commit to believing *hearing* of what God says (Ps. 85:8)?

Ask yourself God's question: what makes you right to be angry? Might you, like Job, need to lay your hand on your mouth (Job 40:4; Prov. 30:32)? Jonah had a spiritual blockage that exposed his need for more love for God and grace in his heart for lost people. He was not prepared to love his enemies as much as he loved his plant!

Do you accept fully that you are a trophy of God's sovereign grace, not a product of self-generated faith and obedience? Jonah knew this when God set him on dry land, but he forgot it before his unrepentant prejudice against the Ninevites, and condemned God for being too gracious! How could God spare people like these pagans?

Apply this practically: ask yourself how diverse you want your church to be. Do you have room for some converted "Ninevites," or do you really only have a heart for people like yourself? The "poor man in shabby clothing" visiting the church too often exposes how easily we can behave as "judges with evil thoughts" and yet think ourselves unspotted disciples of Jesus (James 2:1–9).

Most important is the fact that one "greater than Jonah is here" (Matt. 12:39–41). Jesus died, rose the third day, and ascended to glory, securing everlasting life for a people who, like the Ninevites, "cannot discern between their right hand and their left" (Jonah 4:11). Jesus is the depth of the love, the measure of the grace, and the brightness of the glory of redemption. Without this written on your heart, all else is playing at religion. No, it is not better to die angry at God's grace for sinners, but rather to say with Jesus your Savior, "I shall not die, but live, and declare the works of the LORD" (Ps. 118:17).

PRAISE FOR NEW LIFE AND TESTIMONY
Sing Psalm 118:15–18

THINGS I WILL PRAY FOR TODAY

_____

_____

_____

_____

_____

July 19
O Lord, How Long?

Prayer for a world of wickedness and misery

You are of purer eyes than to behold evil, and cannot look on wickedness. Why do You look on those who deal treacherously?—Hab. 1:13

READ HABAKKUK 1:1–2:4

Nothing is more obvious than the fallenness of human nature. The psalmist's dictum is irrefutable: "On every side the wicked prowl, as vileness is exalted among the children of man" (Ps. 12:8). From the affairs of nations to the hidden motives of every human heart, there is "none righteous, no, not one" (Rom. 3:10; Ps. 14:1, 3), and, sad to say, its practical effects often bid to overwhelm us. Perhaps, like Habakkuk, you have cried to God with something of his desperation about his own time: "O Lord, how long shall I cry, and you will not hear? Even cry out to You 'Violence!' and You will not save" (v. 2). If so, you will identify with the two complaints in his exchange with God:

Complaint #1 is about the decline of the nation—which is also the church of the Old Testament. The prophet is moved by "the gross and growing evils which he is forced to see" *among God's people*. There is trouble, violence, and contention all around (vv. 1–3), and justice fails in church and state so that "the wicked surround the righteous" and "perverse judgment" is the norm (v. 4). We can ask in our day, "What is new?" Is the pseudo-Christian West less apostate than Judah was?

God's answer is to say, I hear you, but I have my own timing and I tell you that my righteous judgment is coming in the form of "the Chaldeans [i.e., the Babylonians], a bitter and hasty nation" (vv. 5–11). There is a reckoning for Judah's wickedness—and also for those churches and individuals throughout history who think they are right with God, when in fact they have broken covenant with God. In his earthly ministry, the Lord Jesus Christ pulls no punches with God's covenant (breaking) people, when he says, "unless you repent, you will all likewise perish" (Luke13:1–5). Judgment, says the apostle Peter, "must begin at the house of God; and if it begins with us first, what will be the end of those who do not obey the gospel of God?" (1 Peter 4:17). Habakkuk weeps for the fallen church—but cries for her revival and the salvation of a people who would serve the Lord with gladness.

Complaint #2 is about God's using an evil empire to scourge his own people for their sins (1:12–2:1). Habakkuk does four things here, giving us a model for our meditations and prayers in the face of similar circumstances: First, he acknowledges God to be the *"Holy One"* of Israel—a title applied to Jesus in both Testaments (v. 12; cf. Ps. 16:10; Isa. 48:16–17; Mark 1:24; Acts 2:27; 3:14; 13:35; 1 John 2:20), pointing to him as the Savior of sinners. Second, he affirms the *holiness of the God* who is "of purer eyes than to behold evil and cannot look upon wickedness" (v. 13ab). In this way, he implies that all God's judgments are perfectly just (Deut. 32:4; Zeph. 3:5; John 5:30). Third, he asks God *why he makes his people vulnerable*—"like fish of the sea"—to be caught in the nets of pagan despoilers who "continue to slay nations without pity" (vv. 14–17). Fourth, he stands *ready to be corrected* by, and to respond to, his Lord (2:1). Without this commitment, prayers are empty words.

God's answer is not to discuss the vexed question of "theodicy" —i.e., how a good God (*theos*) can be just (*dike*), when evil exists. He goes rather to the implication of that judgment for sinners—which is our need of the one Savior of sinners: "Though it [judgment] tarries…Behold the proud, his soul is not upright in him; but the just will live by faith" (2:2–4; cf. Rom. 1:17; Gal. 3:11; Heb. 10:28). Judgment will come to all unrepentant sinners, but there is deliverance for all who will believe upon Jesus Christ, who is the Holy One of Habakkuk's prophecy. When the miseries of sin in our world cause us to cry out, "O Lord, how long?" then let us turn to the God who is "of purer eyes than to behold evil." Look to his Son, Jesus, as the Savior the world so desperately needs, and commit to walking in his way henceforth.

PRAISE OUT OF THE SORROWS OF LOST BLESSINGS
Sing Psalm 89:46-52

THINGS I WILL PRAY FOR TODAY

_____

_____

_____

_____

July 20
O Lord, Revive Your Work!

Prayer for the revival of the church

O Lord, revive Your work in the midst of the years! In the midst of the years make it known; in wrath remember mercy. — Hab. 3:2

READ HABAKKUK 3:1–19

The great Reformer of Geneva says of Habakkuk's famous prayer that it is not the prophet's individual prayer, but a "form of prayer for his people, before they were led into exile," adding, "[And] so that they might not fall away from true religion, the Prophet sets before them the materials of faith, and stimulates them to prayer, and we know, that our faith cannot be supported in a better way than by the exercise of prayer." People, churches, and nations still turn their backs on God and his Word, and like Judah of old, are in urgent need of a complete reversal of the path they are on—the path to ruin: spiritually, culturally, politically, economically, and, not least, eternally. The prophet teaches us how to pray in dark days for just such a work of God's saving grace. The prayer itself is recorded in a single verse (v. 2). In a few simple words, it sets out the believer's affirmation of faith in the Lord, together with his consequent plea for God's reviving mercy. It will be a wonderful help to your praying, if you will but take it to your heart.

True and living prayer springs from a *personal faith* in "the God of my salvation" (v. 18; cf. Heb. 11:6). This is expressed along two lines:

"O Lord, I have heard your speech" (v. 2a). Believers listen seriously to God's words—the prophet to direct revelation, the modern Christian to the revealed Word, which is the Bible. What a glorious privilege it is to be able to say with the psalmist, "I will hear what God the Lord will speak, for he will speak peace to His people....Surely His salvation is near to those who fear him, that glory may dwell in our land" (Ps. 85:8–9).

"And [I] was afraid"—I was gripped by a spirit of awestruck reverence before the holy sovereign God (v. 2a). This is not some craven terror of judgment, but that loving "fear of God" that is "the beginning of wisdom" (Prov. 1:7), from which flows the believers' confidence of God's covenant faithfulness: "The secret of the LORD is with those who fear Him, and He will show them His covenant" (Ps. 25:14). How can we, if we know the Lord as our Savior, not tremble with joyous reverence in the appropriation of Jesus's assuring words, "I give them eternal life, and they shall never perish; neither shall anyone snatch them out of My hand" (John 10:28)? In Christ we are safe.

True and living prayer is exercised with a love for *God's glory* in his work of redemption of sinners. Three petitions are offered here:

> A prayer for *God's work* of revival in times of spiritual drought: "*Revive Your work* in the midst of the years" (v. 2b). And are there not enough discouragements in our experience to lead us to pray with the psalmist, "Will You not revive us again, that Your people may rejoice in You? Show us Your mercy, LORD, and grant us Your salvation" (Ps. 85:6–7). Can we ever have too much of the Lord's blessings?

> A prayer for the Lord to *open blind eyes* to his life-renewing work: "In the midst of the years *make it known*"—to every one (v. 2c, emphasis added). Habakkuk is reaching toward Christ, who, says another prophet, is given "as a covenant to the people, as a light to the Gentiles, to open blind eyes, to bring out…those who sit in darkness from the prison house" (Isa. 42:6–7).

> A prayer for the Lord to be *merciful to rebels* who, hitherto, have despised his overtures of grace: "In wrath *remember mercy*" (v. 2d, emphasis added). God's anger is just, and "His judgments are in all the earth" (1 Chron. 16:14). And sinners ought to tremble (vv. 3–16; cf. James 2:19)! We need God's mercy or we are lost. In Jesus, his Son, we have a Savior in whom, even in hard times, we will know a consoling joy and say, "Yet will I rejoice in the Lord" because he is "the God of my salvation" (vv. 17–18). Let us keep praying all our days: "O Lord, revive Your work" in the midst of our years, and "make it known; in wrath remember mercy."

PRAISE VOICING A DESIRE FOR REVIVAL
Sing Psalm 85:1–7

THINGS I WILL PRAY FOR TODAY

_____

_____

_____

July 21
I Have Loved You!

God is answered with petulant prayer

"Yet you say, 'In what way have You loved us?'"—*Mal. 1:2*

READ MALACHI 1:1–5

The last six prayers of the Old Testament have been called "prayer-protests," because in them God's people "answer back" to God by excusing themselves of their unworthy attitudes to his character, actions, claims, and promises. This demonstrates how people put up the shutters of the soul to keep out the light of God's Word and the grace of gospel salvation (Mal. 1:2, 6–7; 2:17; 3:7–8). These are all unbelieving prayers, but they are not always the prayers of unbelievers. Christians are only too capable of uttering such sentiments of anger, cynicism, and frustration. So believers and non-believers alike need to see how God answers our blind "anti-prayers" with both warnings of temporal and eternal danger and winsome words of love and salvation (cf. 3:16–18).

God opens the conversation by declaring his love for his people: "I have loved you" (v. 2a). God's intention is obvious: he is addressing the secret charge of Israel that he is unloving toward them. His declaration of love succeeds in winkling out their true attitude to him. Their reply, "In what way have You loved us?", tells it all (v. 2b). Behind this defensive question lies an attitude to God that they would rather not discuss, far less face honestly. Behind their outward religiosity there lies an inward lack of love for the Lord. The genie is out of the bottle and the truth is that "their heart was not steadfast with Him, nor were they faithful in His covenant"(Ps. 78:37). Even Christians who sincerely love the Lord can feel unloved by him. Crises in life, miseries in the world, and the like can tempt us to doubt his love. Personal failure with besetting sins can cause us to ask, "Why would God love the likes of me?" An unbeliever has real cause to wonder if, like Esau, he will turn out to be hated by God (vv. 2c–3; cf. Rom. 9:13). He also has real incentive and opportunity to turn to the Lord in repentance and saving faith. If you are a believer, however, your doubts that the Lord loves you are just self-doubt projected onto our

Savior. His declaration of love for you is to be believed—and on the basis of his solemn word, is not to be doubted. Consider this:

When God says to Israel, "I have loved you," he is speaking of divine love—"all loves excelling" (Charles Wesley). John Owen points out that "the love of God is like himself—equal, constant, not capable of augmentation or diminution; our love is like ourselves—unequal, increasing, waning, growing, declining. His, like the sun, always the same in its light, though a cloud may sometimes interpose; ours, as the moon, hath its enlargements and straightenings." To say "God is love" (1 John 4:8) is not to say his is the perfect version of our love and warmest feelings, but rather that his is the absolutely perfect love, of which ours is a derived image that, alas, is also marred by reason of sin. His is the divine attribute of love, which is communicable to our humanity, which we share by his saving grace, but only in a measure.

This love of God for his people is also his "willful, sovereign, and gracious love, the reason and motive for which is within God and not in what is loved." God loves us, not because we are so great or are better than others, but because, in his free grace, he chooses to love us (Deut. 7:7–8). Thomas Manton observes that "God could love nothing in Jacob above Esau but his own grace." His evidence for loving his people is his electing (vv. 2–3) and preserving them (vv. 4–5). Never be ashamed, then, of being chosen and blessed by the Lord. This is his gracious love applied to your soul, your earthly life and your eternal destiny: "To be loved by God is to be favored by grace." Marvel, then, at the love of God in Jesus Christ the Savior. Love him who first loved you (1 John 4:19), who brought you to faith and loves you still.

PRAISE FOR THE LORD'S ASTOUNDING LOVE
Sing Psalm 36:5–12

THINGS I WILL PRAY FOR TODAY

July 22
Where Is My Honor?

God is answered with a protesting prayer

In what way have we despised Your name?—Mal. 1:6

READ MALACHI 1:6–14

God reaffirmed his love for his covenant people verses 2–5, but do his people love him who first loved them? The fifth commandment—"Honor your father and your mother" (Ex. 20:12)—is not cited, but its practical teaching is directed to their consciences and ours: "A son honors his father, and a servant his master." So, God asks, "If then I am the Father, where is my honor? And if I am a Master, where is My reverence?" This is specifically put to the ordained church leaders—"priests," says God, "who despise My name" (v. 6). But it also extends to all of God's people and focuses on their irreverent worship. This sin was nothing new. Jeremiah had already noted that "the sin of Judah is written with a pen of iron; with the point of a diamond it is engraved on the tablet of their heart, and on the horns of your altars" (Jer. 17:1). Inwardly they despise God in their hearts: "these people draw near with their mouths and honor Me with their lips, but have removed their hearts far from Me, and their fear toward Me is taught by the commandment of men" (Isa. 29:13). God is not fooled by outward show, and we ought not forget, says Matthew Henry, that "the sin of sinners is never forgotten till it is forgiven." That requires genuine repentance and a living faith in the Savior of sinners.

God's professed people protest their innocence: "In what way have we despised Your name?" (v. 6). God's answer is uncompromising: their worship is a sham! Why? They offer the Lord what costs them little or nothing (vv. 7–8b; cf. 2 Sam. 24:24). They pay no attention to what God wants and treat their heavenly king with less carefulness and respect than their earthly superiors (vv. 8c–9). They profane God's name with their contempt for God and his revealed Word (vv. 10–13). Finally, they are exposed as hypocrites who are basically pretending to worship and serve the Lord. All the time they are deceiving themselves that they are right with God, who solemnly announces his sovereignty and the impending

408

judgment they so richly deserve (v. 14). Listen again to Jeremiah: "Thus says the LORD to this people: 'Thus they have loved to wander; they have not restrained their feet. Therefore the LORD does not accept them; He will remember their iniquity now, and punish their sins'" (Jer. 14:10). The modern church is not immune to these charges. Like Judah, much of the church has forgotten the greatness of God (vv. 11, 14; cf. Isa. 2:2–5), and many professed Christians treat the church as if it is theirs to do with as they please, and justify themselves in their disregard for God's holy and revealed Law (see vv. 6–7).

God's sternest warnings call us by his grace to honor him. When he says, "I am a great King...and My name is to be feared among the nations," he is directing us to honor him (v. 14). He long before promised his people, "Those who honor me, I will honor" (1 Sam. 2:30). This still stands. Even more significantly, it stands in Jesus Christ the Lord and King, to whom the prophets all pointed. It is in Christ that God's "name" is made "great among the Gentiles" (v. 11). And to this end, "all should honor the Son just as they honor the Father. He who does not honor the Son does not honor the Father who sent Him" (John 5:23). Charles Simeon reminds us that "if any service of ours" is ever to be "accepted of our God, it must be entirely through our Lord Jesus Christ." He alone is the perfect, acceptable sacrifice that we cannot offer for our sins and our salvation. God "made Him who knew no sin to be sin for us, that we might become the righteousness of God in Him" (2 Cor. 5:21). Thus reconciled to God through Jesus's blood and righteousness, your calling, Christian, is to honor and love him "with all your heart, with all your soul, with all your mind, and with all your strength" (Mark 12:30).

PRAISE REJOICING IN THE BEAUTY OF THE LORD
Sing Psalm 27:4–6

THINGS I WILL PRAY FOR TODAY

July 23
You Have Wearied Me!

God is answered with a self-justifying prayer

In what way have we wearied You? — Mal. 2:17

READ MALACHI 2:17–3:7

Aaccording to the *Shorter Catechism* 11, the works of God's providence are "his most holy, wise, and powerful preserving and governing all his creatures and all their actions" (cf. Ps. 145:17; 104:24; Isa. 28:29; Heb. 1:3; Ps. 103:19; Matt. 10:29–31). This rests on God's absolute sovereign decrees, "whereby, for his own glory, he has foreordained whatsoever comes to pass" (cf. Eph. 1:4, 11; Rom. 9:22–23). The whole world is in God's hands, whatever happens, good or bad. Hard providences do not prove God is angry with us, and happy providences do not prove he favors us. Scripture clearly teaches us that "all things come alike to all: one event happens to the righteous and the wicked; to the good, the clean, and the unclean" (Eccl. 9:2).

Malachi's audience takes a very different view: "They looked at the apparent prosperity of wicked nations and wicked individuals around them, then they looked at their own difficulties, and they were envious, and were bitter against God." This resulted in "the monstrous conclusion, that either God loved and rewarded the evil-doer, like the surrounding heathen; or if not, 'Where is the God of justice?'" It also seems that while they are so bitterly and self-righteously trashing God for not meeting their present needs and expectations, they seem to hope that when the promised Messiah comes—"the Messenger of the covenant, in whom [they] delight" (3:1)—all their present discontents will be redressed, the wicked will get their comeuppance, and they (God's people) will get their deserved rewards, presently unjustly withheld by God! God swiftly corrects their delusions (3:2–7): Christ will come, as they expect, but not to reward them, as they somehow imagine, but to "come near [them] for judgment" and scatter them across the nations! Nevertheless, the Lord graciously calls them to repent and to return to him.

God is not indifferent to sin, as Judah's backsliders charged, so

410

no wonder he is "wearied" by the blasphemous accusations that he is unjust—and from folk who seem to think themselves more upright than the God of the Bible. This is not unusual for any generation. People routinely and blatantly neglect the weightier matters of biblical faith and obedience, yet still expect that what passes for their religion or morality somehow entitles them to God's favor, a prosperous life, and a secure eternity! Do they love the Lord (1:2–5)? No! Is their worship sincere and what God commands of them (1:6ff.)? No! Do they follow faithful ministers (2:1–9)? No! Are they faithful husbands and fathers (2:10–16)? No! Do they tithe (i.e., at least ten percent) to the Lord's work (3:8–12)? No! And their view of God is manifestly unbiblical, and their motives for (allegedly) serving him are utterly warped (3:13–15)! Blind to their spiritual deadness and the sinfulness of their sin, they neither know nor wish to know God personally as their Savior and Lord, as revealed in Scripture. Is not much of today's church afflicted with such practice and attitudes?

A true knowledge of God and his providence will draw us closer to him. To be sure, God's providence can serve as a wake-up call for wandering or nonexistent faith, as the psalmist testifies: "Before I was afflicted I went astray, but now I keep Your word" (Ps. 119:67; cf. Luke 13:1–5). When bad things do happen, we need to trust the Lord all the more and watch as, in the long run, he makes them work together for good *to those who love the Lord* (Rom. 8:28). Jesus constantly loves his saints through the darkest clouds of life in this fallen world, so that by his grace we may say, "I have learned in whatever state I am, to be content" (Phil. 4:11). If you are "weary and heavy laden," come to Jesus, and his promise is, "I will give you rest" (Matt. 11:28).

PRAISE CONFESSING ENVY OF THE PROUD
Sing Psalm 73:1–12

THINGS I WILL PRAY FOR TODAY

July 24
You Have Rejected My Ordinances!

God is answered with a shameless prayer

In what way shall we return? — Mal. 3:7

READ MALACHI 3:6–7

od is routinely dismissed by those who will not have him in their lives, on the ground that a truly sovereign and just God would never allow gross evil in the world to exist. Seeing all the prosperity of the wicked nations around them, God's people in sixth century BC feel free to scoff at the Lord, saying, "Where is the God of justice?" (2:17). God first responds by asserting that his perfect justice is coming in the person and work of the "Messenger of the covenant," who will both revive the cause of God (3:1–4) and bring condign punishment upon the unrepentant apostates of God's people (3:5). They need not fear that revival is not coming for God's believing people, or that judgment is not coming upon the wicked. The question is, however, "Do they understand their own sin and danger?"

The prophet addresses the dismissal of God's justice along four doctrinal and practical lines:

> The fact that God does "not change" is the reason why sinners are "not consumed" (v. 6). He uses the *covenant* name of God—"the Lord" (Yahweh)—which indicates that he is sovereign, holy, just, and faithful and deals with people in terms of his covenants. Consequently, God neither favors the wicked covenant-breakers nor oppresses his covenant people. His every action is holy and faithful.

> The fact that God's people, for all their wickedness, are thus far "not consumed" proves that God is *merciful*: "gracious, slow to anger, and abounding in mercy" (Ps. 103:8; cf. Ezra 9:15).

> The fact that sinners are thus far "not consumed" implies that God is *giving time* for the salvation of lost people. This implies that we sinners waste no time turning to God. If we do so, he promises to return to us (v. 7). God's patience aims at saving more people, so that "as grace extends to more and

412

more people it may increase thanksgiving, to the glory of God" (2 Cor. 4:15, ESV; cf. Matt. 13:24–30). Where sin abounds, God intends grace much more to abound (Rom. 5:20).

> The fact of *specific personal sin* is laid on sinners' consciences: "You have gone away from My ordinances, and have not kept them" (v. 7). We tend to associate the word "ordinances" with the mechanics of church life—public worship, the sacraments, church government, office-bearers, and keeping the Lord's Day. In Scripture, however, "ordinances" encompass all of God's revealed statutes (e.g., Lev. 18:4; 1 Cor. 11:2). The obedience of faith is more than outward observance. It is inseparable from our inward *personal relationship* with the Lord. The vital question must always be: "Do I personally know and love Jesus Christ as my Savior and Lord, and thereby know and love God as my Father in heaven" (cf. John 14:15; Acts 20:21; 2 Pet. 1:11)?

People, alas, often do not react well to God's calls to return to him. In what Matthew Henry calls "a peevish answer" to a "gracious invitation," Malachi's hearers say to God, "In what way shall we return?" (v. 7e). Matthew Poole rightly assesses this as "a proud, shameless, and self-justifying question; 'Wherein, or what is the evil from which we should return to thee? What is our sin?'" This attitude is the otherwise "immovable wall" in human nature (1 Cor. 2:14), which, left to itself, always resists the "irresistible force" of the Holy Spirit in the application of gospel grace in Christ. The practical question for you, Christian friend, is: "How do you respond to God's Word when it puts its finger on some sin of yours?" With a protestation of deluded innocence, or with a humbled heart and a refreshed love for the Lord? Jesus, the crucified, risen, reigning, and returning Savior is still saying to the living in every generation, "Return to Me, and I will return to you."

PRAISE TO THE GOD WHO PLEADS WITH SOULS
Sing Psalm 81:8–16

THINGS I WILL PRAY FOR TODAY

413

July 25
You Have Robbed Me!

God answers a self-righteous prayer

In what way have we robbed You?—Mal. 3:8

READ MALACHI 3:8-12

From the Old Testament "tithes and offerings" to the New Testament injunctions "to give regularly (1 Cor. 16:2), cheerfully (2 Cor. 9:7), substantially, and freely (2 Cor. 8:3), the Bible has undeniably high standards for our giving to the Lord's work." A "tithe" is simply "one-tenth" of your "increase" (Deut. 14:22). Before you dismiss this as an outdated legalism, ponder Jesus's dictum that "unless your righteousness exceeds the righteousness of the scribes and Pharisees, you will by no means enter the kingdom of heaven" (Matt. 5:20). It is living faith, not legalism, to return to the Lord a portion of what he has given you in thanksgiving for salvation received. How seriously tithing is taken today may be gauged from a recent study that found that self-identified "Christians" in America on average give 2.3% of their income to the church—down from 3.3% in the 1930s' Great Depression Era!—and 33–50 percent of *church members* give nothing at all! This indicates that the commitment of most American Christians to anything like "tithing" is somewhere between minimal and negligible. Little has changed in 2,600 years, for this appears to be the case in Malachi's Judah. It is this neglect of tithing that occasions God's startling challenge.

"Will a man rob God? Yet you have robbed Me!" (3:8ab). The result is a howl of offended pride implicitly denying any wrongdoing. They respond, "In what way have we robbed You?" (v. 8c). The Lord defines their sin—the "whole nation" has defrauded God by withholding the required "tithes and offerings" (v. 8d)—and follows with an explanation of their sin and its consequences. He makes an appeal for renewed obedience, and promises good things to come. "All nations" will be moved to call them "blessed" for having been transformed into "a delightful land" (vv. 9–12). The flow of the passage as a whole makes clear that the fundamental issue here is not church finance and the support of her ministry, important as that is, but primarily the matter of the spiritual vitality of God's people. God does not need our money (Ps. 50:10), but he does delight in joining us to himself in the reconciled fellowship of a covenantal bond of love (Prov. 12:22; Isa. 61:8; Ezek. 16:8). God was being "robbed" of something vastly greater than the monetary value of the tithes and offerings themselves. He was being robbed of worship, robbed of joy, robbed of honor, and robbed of the thanksgiving of his people for blessings bestowed—which is the primary significance of returning the first-fruits of his provision and our labors. T. V. Moore points out that "we may try to defraud God, but in the end will only defraud ourselves... so men who retain God's money in their treasuries will find it a losing possession." Jesus's parable of the rich man and Lazarus wisely proves that point (Luke 16:19–31).

What we do with the Lord's money outwardly tells the story about who we really are inwardly. A historian researching the life of the Duke of Wellington (1769–1852), the victor of Waterloo, said, "When I saw how he spent his money, I knew the man." We see the love in the widow's "two mites" (Mark 12:42–43), but the earner's keeping back his tithe for himself is no evidence of giving from a loving soul. King David would not "offer burnt offerings to the LORD [his] God with that which [cost him] nothing" (2 Sam. 24:24). "In true, biblical, living religion," writes Michael Barrett, "everything keeps coming back to the heart." Where, then, is your heart? Are you a cheerful giver, a half-hearted semi-complier, or merely an uninterested non-contributor? Do you love the Lord who bought you on Calvary's cross? This is a gospel issue, because, as Jesus says, "where your treasure is, there your heart will be also" (Matt. 6:19–21).

PRAISE AS AN OFFERING OF THANKSGIVING
Sing Psalm 116:8–19

THINGS I WILL PRAY FOR TODAY

July 26
You Have Spoken against Me!

God is answered with a self-satisfied prayer

What have we spoken against You?—Mal. 3:13

READ MALACHI 3:13–18

he story is told of a farmer who hears a commotion in the chicken coop. He points his shotgun into the darkness and asks, "Who's in there?" only to hear the response, "Ain't nobody here but us chickens." Malachi's hearers are similarly unconvincing in their responses to God's challenging their various hypocrisies. They do no better than protest a bogus innocence in face of being caught in the act. The six prayers in Malachi's prophecy, which itself is aptly described by Michael Barrett as "Malachi's autopsy of dead religion," are the last recorded prayers in the Old Testament. They form a sad litany of unbelief for a church and covenant people who have lost their moorings in God's Word and are drifting on a Dead Sea of empty, nominal religion. In terms of the "big picture," they can be understood as an epitaph for the demise of theocratic Israel and the passing of the Old Testament order, as part of the preparation for the coming of the promised Messiah. In terms of the inner spiritual condition of the individual Jew, these prayers are markers of the decline of personal faith and godly behavior at the end of that age—not believing prayers, but a species of anti-prayer in which the suppliant pronounces judgment on God.

The sixth and final prayer puts the capstone on the five that precede it. God declares: "Your words have been harsh against Me." But they fob it off with a cold conversation-stopper: "What have we spoken against You?" (v. 13). They are indignant, and you can see the outline of their self-satisfied defense in the dismissive words they used about God: "It is useless to serve God: what profit is it that we have kept His ordinance, and that we have walked as mourners before the Lord of hosts?" (v. 14). They believe they have kept God's law and in the process have suffered long enough to justify the view that it was all useless. They are like those who pray for five minutes and, since no answer seems to be forthcoming, feel they might as well not bother praying at all. This takes us back to the first complaint that God doesn't love them (1:2) and their proof of this in God's favoring evildoers—i.e., the prosperous heathen nations around them (2:17). The root problem is that they neither love God nor see in him any love for them. The fruit of this practical unbelief is that they believe themselves deserving of better treatment than God has given them. On top of that, they are blind to their own hypocrisy in matters of faith and life. As Calvin observes, "hypocrites seem to themselves to be of all men the most perfect, though they have only the guise or mask of religion."They do not know God for who he is. They do not know themselves in light of God's Word. They have no personal heart-relationship with God.

Writing of church people in Puritan England, Richard Baxter (1615–91) said,

> One would think that a man who reads in scripture, and believes the everlasting glory offered, and the dreadful punishment threatened, and the necessity of holiness to salvation, and of a Saviour to deliver us from sin and hell…should have much ado to moderate and bear the sense of such overwhelming things. But most men so little regard or feel them, that they have neither time nor heart to think of them as their concern, but hear of them as of some foreign land, where they have no interest, and which they never think to see….Yea, one would think…they were asleep or in jest, when they confess that they must die…or did not believe that their turn is near.

Baxter pointedly reminds us that "God hath an awakening day for all, and he will make the most senseless soul to feel, by grace or punishment." Let us flee from all heartless empty religion and embrace the grace of God in the gospel of his "Sun of Righteousness," who is Jesus Christ, the Son of God and the Savior of sinners (4:2; 3:16–18).

PRAISE DECLARING LOVE FOR THE LORD
Sing Psalm 18:1–6

THINGS I WILL PRAY FOR TODAY

_____

_____

_____

_____

July 27
Leave Your Gift at the Altar

True reconciliation required for acceptable prayer

Therefore if you bring your gift to the altar, and there remember that your brother has something against you, leave your gift there before the altar, and go your way. First be reconciled to your brother, and then come and offer your gift. — Matt. 5:23–24

READ MATTHEW 5:21–26

You don't have to kill somebody to be a murderer. You only need, says Jesus, to be angry "without a cause" and hateful enough to dismiss him contemptuously as *raca* or *moré* (v. 22—*raka* is Aramaic for "empty-head," and *moré* is Greek for, well, "moron"). The Pharisees of Jesus's day taught that such thoughts and expressions were only minor faults, as long as they didn't involve violent acts and physical death. Furthermore, they taught that God would not judge anybody severely as long as—in modern terms—they went to church and put their money in the offering. In contrast, Jesus points out that breaking the sixth commandment—"You shall not murder" (Ex. 20:13)—is not confined to physical murder, but extends to attitudes of the heart. Call a man a moron, Jesus says, and you are "in danger of hellfire." "Whoever hates his brother is a murderer, and you know that no murderer has eternal life abiding in him" (1 John 3:15). What you think only differs in degree, not in kind, from what you actually do! More pointedly, your thought-life tells a story about your real relationship with the Lord.

In practice, too many people think that "good" deeds cancel out "bad" deeds. The trouble is that our "good" deeds are not so good and therefore cannot atone for outright sins (see Rom. 3:10–20). Self-atonement is an utter impossibility and is the most potent lie in Satan's repertoire. So, says Jesus, if you go to worship, turn to God in prayer and put your penny in the plate (i.e., "bring your gift to the altar"), and think that God is pleased with you and will overlook your hateful thoughts of others, you had better think again! Elsewhere Jesus notes, "You are those who justify yourselves before men, but God knows your hearts. For what is highly esteemed among men is an abomination in the sight of God" (Luke 16:15). You are like the "good" Boy Scout who is helping the old lady across the road, all the while cursing her in his heart for spoiling his beautiful day.

Jesus shows us, however, that there is a way out of this hypocrisy. Even if you are standing at "the altar" and you "remember that your brother has something against you" (v. 23), you can drop what you are doing, go to the brother, seek his forgiveness, and be reconciled (v. 24). Martyn Lloyd-Jones remarks that "we should, in a sense, keep God waiting rather than stay." The personal reconciliation has priority for the simple reason that "if I regard iniquity in my heart, the Lord will not hear" (Ps. 66:18). This may seem to you a hard teaching. It is easy to understand why God should put reprobates in hell, but we balk at the doctrine that the Lord will not accept the worship and the prayers of professing Christians in an unrepentant state over a particular issue, until and unless they confess their sin and mend their ways. But it is hypocrisy and God wants godliness, not pretention.

Jesus also stresses the urgency of swift obedience. Christian, if you have fences to mend, get to it! Why? Because unrepented sin is like cancer—you must kill it, or it will kill you. Jesus says, in verses 25 and 26, that you should settle out of court and save yourself the grief of unrepaired wrongs. If you are easy with your sins and won't deal with them, you are in great danger. An unrepentant spirit and, on the other side, an unforgiving spirit, evidence an unchanged heart and hazard a lost eternity. Has Jesus forgiven your sin? Then you will say daily with the apostle Paul, "the love of Christ compels us" (2 Cor. 5:14). If this is true of you, you will love your brothers and sisters in the faith with that love with which Jesus first loved you (1 John 4:19), and you will go and be reconciled to your brother or sister.

PRAISE OF A GODLY SOUL
Sing Psalm 66:8–20

THINGS I WILL PRAY FOR TODAY

July 28
When You Pray...

The right attitude for believing prayer

And when you pray, you shall not be like the hypocrites. — Matt. 6:5a

READ MATTHEW 6:5–8

The next best thing to a good example is a bad one. Jesus begins his teaching on prayer with the Pharisees—the most public hypocrites of the day. These fellows are great sticklers for religious duties of all sorts, and they want everyone to know how holy they are. The word "hypocrite" means "play-actor" and acting is not acting unless there is an audience to be dazzled by the performance. Jesus pinpoints three essential features of the prayers of such folk.

Hypocrites "love to pray" in synagogues and on street corners (v. 5ab). Jesus's point is that this is private, individual prayer in a public setting. If it is silent, all that is evident is that they may be praying—nobody else can know what is being prayed, or even if anything is being prayed. If it is aloud, it is a self-indulgent imposition upon those around them. It is by definition a species of showing off. Such is the sinfulness of sin, that prayer and good deeds, paraded before other people, can become the occasion of self-aggrandizement.

Hypocrites pray to "be seen by men" (v. 5cd). This is their motive for private prayer in a public place. It shows how subtle sin can be. Martyn Lloyd-Jones notes that "sin is something that follows us into the presence of God." Jesus tells us, "Let your light so shine before men, that they may see your good works and glorify your Father in heaven" (Matt. 5:16), but he also warns us, "Take heed that you do not do your charitable deeds before men, to be seen by them. Otherwise you have no reward from your Father in heaven" (Matt. 6:1). They may "have their reward," but it is not from God.

Hypocrites think God and men will be impressed "by their many words" (v. 7). Public prayer especially can be afflicted with the disease of high-flown verbiage. Just remember that it is with "groanings too deep for words"—our groaning conveyed to heaven by his groaning—that the Holy Spirit intercedes for us (Rom. 8:26). Such prayers are not

420

eloquent or wordy, but they speak to the heart and soul of true prayer as it addresses the true need of body and soul and a world in need of a Savior. Longer prayers do not command larger blessings.

The positive exercise of individual prayer is the exact opposite of the hypocrite's way. Jesus offers three essentials for believing prayer.

> The believer talks to God as his adoptive "Father" (v. 6). Personal, private prayer belongs in the "secret place" where, Jesus promises, your Father will be. Your heavenly Father is the only hearer you need and should desire. This keeps your focus where it needs to be, untrammeled by the temptation to look good in the sight of others. It is a great snare to parade one's piety for the public, whether in the church or in the world.

> The believer principally prays "in secret" (v. 6). "We may not pray with the Pharisees," says Thomas Manton, "merely to be seen by men, yet we may let our light shine before men, to draw them to duty, and give more glory to God." Public prayer has its place, but is for leading a group to the throne of grace. Private prayer is for the secret place. And it is no longer secret if you announce that between seven and eight a.m. you will be praying in your room. You have publicized your piety, when it is enough that God sees, hears, and knows—and blesses you.

> The believer understands that God knows what he needs before he asks. The Lord does not need polished words, or an exhaustive list of your needs and desires. He knows. He wants to hear from you. He knows you are weak and forgetful, but he means to do in you and for you "above all that [you] ask or think" (Eph. 3:20). And the reward? The hypocrite may be thrilled with himself, but you, beloved of Jesus, will be filled with the Holy Spirit and the deepest satisfaction of soul.

PRAISE OF A HUMBLED HEART
Sing Psalm 131

THINGS I WILL PRAY FOR TODAY

July 29
How Should You Pray?

The right attitude for believing prayer

In this manner, therefore, pray... — Matt. 6:9a

READ MATTHEW 6:5–13

he Lord's Prayer is surely the prime example of a pattern of prayer acceptable to God. Jesus gives both the matter and the method for ordering prayer, whether private or public. It can be repeated as a prayer in itself, but it can neither be reduced to *mere* repetition, nor be idolized as an *essential* part of every prayer. It is the prayer of prayers in that it contains not only the words to pray but the very *way* to approach the throne of grace (Heb. 4:16). It is a means of grace by which the Holy Spirit refreshes the soul. It is clear water from the Rock that is Jesus Christ (1 Cor. 10:4).

The Lord's Prayer is very simple in structure. It has a beginning, a middle, and an end, although it sounds more clever to call these the Invocation, the Petitions, and the Doxology.

The *Invocation,* "Our Father in heaven," calls upon God to hear us, even as we confess him to be the center of our worship and the focus of our love as the adopted children of our heavenly Father, saved by his free grace through faith in Jesus as Savior and Lord (v. 9b).

The *Petitions* address respectively God's purposes and our needs (vv. 9c–13b). The first three deal with what we owe God, while the second three focus on what God promises us. These are as follows:

> God's *glory*: "Hallowed be Your name."
> God's *goal*: "Your kingdom come."
> God's *present purposes*: "Your will be done."
> Our *physical needs*: "Give us this day our daily bread."
> Our *spiritual needs*: "And forgive us our debts."
> Our *deliverance* from temptation and evil: "And do not lead us into temptation, but deliver us from the evil one."

The *Doxology* entrusts us and our petitions to God: "For Yours is the kingdom and the power and the glory forever" (v. 13c).

422

The Lord's Prayer orders our prayers. In the first place, our prayers ought to be reverent in motive and expression. God is not our buddy in heaven, but our heavenly Father, through Jesus Christ his Son. He is Creator, Redeemer, and Judge. We are accountable to him, to serve him with "reverence and godly fear" (Heb. 12:28).

Our prayers also ought to be orderly. Think before you pray. Better five intelligible words than ten thousand in utter confusion (see 1 Cor. 14:19, 40). If we have to groan because we cannot find the words, the Holy Spirit will intercede and God will understand us. But for our sake, we should strive to know what we are praying and why.

Our prayers should be spiritually significant. Nowadays, Christians find it difficult to pray in a meeting unless they are spoon-fed "requests." But notice how half of the Lord's Prayer is taken up with meditating on God's attributes and actions. Do we know so little of our God that we have nothing to inspire us to praise him and his mighty acts? Are we only interested in his meeting our needs?

Our prayers should be, for want of a better expression, real— in the sense of arising with some spontaneity and relevance to the issues of life and a personal relationship with God. Sincere, godly repetition of Jesus's prayer cannot be wrong, nor should we ban written prayers. But it is clear that Jesus wants us to engage in lively communion with our Father, out of a heart and mind moved and directed by his Word and Holy Spirit. He wants to hear "the language of the soul" and bring heaven to our hearts in sweet communion with God in prayer. Let this be the air we delight to breathe through all our days, till his kingdom comes in all its fullness.

PRAISE FOR THE JOY OF COMMUNION WITH GOD
Sing Psalm 139:13–18

THINGS I WILL PRAY FOR TODAY

July 30
Our Father in Heaven

The believer's relationship to God

Our Father in heaven… — Matt. 6:9b

READ MATTHEW 6:9–13

The Lord's Prayer begins with a *personal* relationship with God. "Every man—the greatest sinner breathing," writes John Brown, "may, ought to, call God father, but he never really will call God father, till he believes the truth about him; and then he will not be able to refrain from calling him father."God is no impersonal deity, or vague power behind the universe. When Jesus is truly our Savior, God is truly and experientially *our* Father. Why? Because, says Jesus, "everyone who has heard and learned from the Father comes to Me" (John 6:45). Furthermore, every believer may then pray in "the Spirit of adoption" and so "cry out, 'Abba, Father'" (Rom. 8:15). "Our Father," as addressed to God, is no empty form of words.

God's fatherhood is *particular* in nature. It embraces all who come to know Jesus as their Savior. "All that the Father gives Me," says Jesus, "will come to Me, and the one who comes to Me I will by no means cast out" (John 6:37). In saving us, Jesus the Son brings us to his Father. To those who reject Jesus, but still claim God as their father, the Lord says, "If God were your Father, you would love Me, for I proceeded forth and came from God; nor have I come of Myself, but He sent Me." Consequently, he adds, "You are of your father the devil, and the desires of your father you want to do" (John 8:42, 44). The fatherhood of God is the fruit of the cross and a seal to your soul that you are indeed his. Unless you believe on the Lord Jesus Christ and are saved, you can and will only know him as Judge.

God's fatherhood is *heavenly* in its scope. The words "in heaven" tell us where blessings come from and how we are to draw near to God in seeking these blessings. "Every good gift and every perfect gift is from above" (James 1:17). Christians are blessed "with every spiritual blessing in the heavenly places in Christ" (Eph. 1:3). Every good thing we enjoy or could wish to enjoy is from the mind and disposition of God—even if we don't recognize it! When we pray, we must "lift our hearts and hands to God in heaven"(Lam. 3:41). He is the source of every grace and all blessings, great and small. This also teaches us that in our approaches to God we are "to be modest, humble, and cautious, in our conceptions of, and applications to him; as being a God of such inconceivable greatness, and glorious majesty, Eccl. 5:2—'Be not rash with thy mouth, and let not thine heart be hasty to utter anything before God; for God is in heaven, and thou upon earth, therefore let thy words be few.'"

God's fatherhood is *loving* in its intent and impact. He so loved us that he sent his Son to save his people from their sins and give them eternal life. As "the God and Father of our Lord Jesus Christ," who as "the firstborn among many brethren" (Rom. 8:29) secures the adoption of believers as children of God. Adoption is defined in *Shorter Catechism* 34 as "an act of God's free grace, whereby we are received into the number, and have the right to all the privileges of the sons of God" (1 John 3:1; John 1:12; Rom. 8:17). Knowing God, through Jesus, can only kindle love in our hearts to him who first loved us (1 John 4:19). "He sent from above, He took me; He drew me out of many waters. He delivered me from my strong enemy, from those who hated me, for they were too strong for me" (Ps. 18:16–17).

PRAISE FOR THE FATHER OF MERCIES
Sing Psalm103:1–13

THINGS I WILL PRAY FOR TODAY

July 31
Hallowed Be Your Name

The first petition of the Lord's Prayer

Hallowed be Your name. — Matt. 6:9c

READ MATTHEW 6:9–13

The word "hallowed" is not much used in our day. It is mostly seen in references to fields where men died in battle or prevailed in sports. Only the language of the King James Bible has preserved it from extinction in the church. Modern Bible translations mostly replace "hallowed" with "consecrated" or "holy." These words do catch the meaning, but sound strangely pedestrian by comparison with the beautiful rendering from the seventeenth century. The vital question is, of course, just what this first petition of the Lord's Prayer actually means. It cannot mean that we are asking God to become more holy than he is already. He is all-holy in his being and in all his attributes. It therefore has to do with how we human beings should respond to and interact with his holiness. When this petition issues from our hearts, it reveals something about what we desire God to do for the glory of his name and for the blessing of the human race.

We desire that God show forth his glory in the world. He says, "Among those who approach Me I will show Myself holy. In the sight of the people I will be honored" (Lev. 10:3). In other words, we pray that God would, by his Word and his works, add such luster to his name as to draw men and women to himself as the God who is to be worshiped. Malcolm Muggeridge, before he came to a Christian confession, was one day so gripped by the beauty of a view in his home county that he found himself saying aloud the words "Gloria in excelsis Deo!" in contradiction of his own unbelief. If scenery can so humble and disarm an agnostic, will we not pray that the grace of the gospel and the beauty of Jesus Christ (the Savior of sinners like you and me) will draw many to believe on him, to be saved, and so to see God glorifying his name before the watching world?

We desire that God be glorified in us. We want to know his blessing. We love his ordinances—the Word of God preached, the sacraments enjoyed, and prayer exercised day by day—and don't think of them as a burden or as mere options when "we feel like it." Jesus, speaking of his true disciples, says to the Father, "All Mine are Yours, and Yours are Mine, and I am glorified in them" (John 17:10). We glory in God's work of redemption. We feel it, we know it, we love it—and we glory in Christ who bought us with his own blood. We glory in the cross of Christ. His glory attends our thoughts, words, and deeds of faithfulness. We pray that we may glorify him, not let him down.

We desire that others may glorify him. *Fisher's Catechism* asks, "What do we mean when we pray that God would enable others to glorify Him, as well as ourselves?" and answers, "We thereby in effect pray, that *the earth* may *be full of the knowledge of the Lord, as the waters cover the sea*, Isa. xi. 9; that so *from the uttermost part of the earth* may *be heard songs, even glory to the Righteous*, chap. xxiv. 16." We pray for what God promises will take place: "Be still and know that I am God; I will be exalted among the nations, I will be exalted in the earth" (Ps. 46:10). This takes us to the heart of the gospel, for it is in Jesus Christ that God's name is hallowed—made holy—before the world and in heaven. Jesus gives voice to this in the night of his arrest: "Father, the hour has come. Glorify Your Son, that Your Son also may glorify You.…I have glorified You on the earth. I have finished the work which You have given Me to do. And now, O Father, glorify Me together with Yourself, with the glory which I had with You before the world was" (John 17:1, 4–5). When we pray "Hallowed be Your name," we simply pray for God's love in Jesus Christ to be lifted up in his world, in his people, and in his Son. His glory is our first request.

PRAISE FOR THE GLORIOUS GOD, OUR REDEEMER
Sing Psalm 46

THINGS I WILL PRAY FOR TODAY

_____

_____

_____

_____

_____

August 1
Your Kingdom Come

The second petition of the Lord's Prayer

Your kingdom come. — *Matt. 6:10a*

READ MATTHEW 6:9–13

The first three petitions of the Lord's Prayer are about God. They remind us that God and his glory ought to be our first concern even when we pray out of our need. Together, they give us a miniature summary of the biblical doctrine of God: there is his name (to be hallowed), his kingdom (to come), and his will (to be done). Each one builds on the other and unfolds the character and purpose of the living and loving God we have come to know in our life of faith.

What is the "kingdom" we are to pray will "come"? In common usage, such as "from here to kingdom come," these words merely refer to an indeterminate time off in the future. In Scripture, this "kingdom come" refers to the rule of God as exercised through his risen and glorified Son, Jesus Christ. It extends from here to the day of Christ's return. Christians are presently citizens of this kingdom, over which Jesus is "head over all things to the church" (Eph. 1:22). On that future day, "He delivers the kingdom to God the Father, when He puts an end to all rule and all authority and power" (1 Cor. 15:24). The kingdom is both "now" and "not yet," and so we pray, as *Shorter Catechism* 102 instructs us, "that Satan's kingdom may be destroyed and that the kingdom of grace may be advanced, ourselves and others brought into it and kept in it, and that the kingdom of glory may be hastened." It is "of *grace*" in connection with the gospel; "of *glory*" with respect to its final completion; and of *power* relative to the restraint and overthrow of evil (1 Cor. 4:20).

How are we to pray for this kingdom to come? The answer is that we should pray in the light of the threefold sovereign rule of our Lord — in grace, glory, and power — for the advancement of his kingdom in this needy world. His exercise of power serves his overarching purpose of saving sinners and transforming their world. We can set our sights too low, for instance, by praying only for the moral issues that beset our society (like abortion, drug abuse, and human trafficking). These are not unimportant matters, but they are essentially symptoms of what really needs to be cured—which is the state of people's souls and their relationship to God. What we need is more Christians living out a whole-life commitment and service to Jesus Christ. This takes a saving change in our hearts, and a growth in grace that strives to be holy as God is holy in all the relationships of life. Yes, we pray for God to restrain and overthrow wickedness and to convict and convert lost people; as we do, we look for the appearing of our Lord Jesus and "according to His promise, look for new heavens and a new earth in which righteousness dwells" (2 Peter 3:13).

How should God's kingdom impact your Christian experience? Let me suggest three ways. The first is that "Your kingdom come" is preeminently a *missionary* prayer. It is about the earth being "filled with the knowledge of the glory of the LORD, as the waters cover the sea" (Hab. 2:14). We pray and labor for the success of the gospel. The second is that it requires *personal* commitment to the Lordship of Jesus on your part—all of your thinking, your aspirations, and your actions— every thought captive to Christ (2 Cor. 10:4). Thirdly, it is an *affirmation* of the Christian hope for both our time and eternity. We pray expectantly for the blessing and the revival of the church and are encouraged to yearn for the coming of our Lord. We pray with a poet of a former day:

Thy Kingdom come, O God,
Thy rule, O Christ, begin;
Break with Thine iron rod
The tyrannies of sin.

PRAISE FOR GOD'S KINGDOM
Sing Psalm 22:27–31

THINGS I WILL PRAY FOR TODAY

_____

_____

_____

_____

_____

_____

_____

August 2
Your Will Be Done

The third petition of the Lord's Prayer

Your will be done on earth as it is in heaven. — *Matt. 6:10*

READ MATTHEW 6:9–13

The first three petitions of the Lord's Prayer are not about our immediate needs. They turn our hearts to who God is in himself (his "name"), to his plans for this world (his "kingdom"), and to the response he requires of all of us to his word for our lives (his "will"). The logic of verses 9–10 is clear: if we glory in who God is, and if we desire his reign in all things, it naturally follows that we want his will to be done "on earth as it is in heaven." This in turn forms the basis for both the requests we bring to him, and the confidence with which we await the outworking of his will.

What is God's "will"? It clearly covers more than we know. He has a *secret* will—a "will of purpose" from all eternity, unfolding as year succeeds to year (Isa. 46:10; Eccl. 3:11). God also has a *revealed* will—his "will of precept." This includes his *general* revelation in creation and providence, but preeminently consists in his *special* revelation in Scripture (see Rom. 1:18–32 and all of Ps. 19). Hence the focus of *Shorter Catechism* 103: "In the third petition...we pray that God, by his grace, would make us both able and willing to know, obey and submit to his will in all things, as the angels do in heaven." Thomas Watson notes that "knowledge is the eye that must direct the foot of obedience. Knowledge alone is like a winter–sun, which has no heat or influence. It [knowledge without obedience] does not warm the affections or purify the conscience. Judas was a great luminary, he knew God's will but he was a traitor." We are not truly doing God's will until we can say with the psalmist, "I delight to do Your will, O my God, and Your law is within my heart" (Ps. 40:8).

Why should *we* do God's will? Most obviously, it is because God commands our obedience, but most pointedly because it is the fruit and evidence of a saving relationship with God in Jesus Christ. "It is not all our golden words, if we could speak like angels," writes Watson, "but our works, our doing God's will which bears witness of our sincerity. We

430

judge not the health of a man's body by his high color, but by the pulse of his arm where the blood chiefly stirs; so a Christian's soundness is not to be judged by his profession, but by his obediential action, his doing the will of God."

"If you love me," says Jesus, "you will keep my commandments" (John 14:15, ESV). On the other hand, "Faith without works is dead"—that is, it is no true faith at all (James 2:20). Jesus saves us so we will go forward in obedience to him (Deut. 11:26–28). Wanting God's will to be done presupposes a solid commitment to practical godliness and a desire to see its growth in ourselves and in others. Doing God's will is not a spectator sport, but is the very fabric of faithfulness. It is the life of heaven applied to our life on this earth.

How shall we do God's will? Doing God's will is, in practice, the front line in the battle to advance the kingdom of God. Our obedience in the world of sinners rarely comes painlessly. Paul was so aware of the power of indwelling sin in the believer that he could cry, "O wretched man that I am! Who will deliver me from this body of death?" (Rom. 7:24). But he also knew the answer: "There is therefore now no condemnation to those who are in Christ Jesus, who do not walk according to the flesh, but according to the Spirit" (Rom. 8:1). He also knew the way ahead: "And He said to me, 'My grace is sufficient for you, for My strength is made perfect in weakness'" (2 Cor. 12:9). Not least, the final outcome of God doing his will: "But thanks be to God, who gives us the victory through our Lord Jesus Christ" (1 Cor. 15:57).

PRAISE FOR THE DELIGHT OF DOING GOD'S WILL
Sing Psalm 40:1–9

THINGS I WILL PRAY FOR TODAY

_____

_____

_____

_____

_____

_____

August 3
Our Daily Bread

The fourth petition of the Lord's Prayer

Give us this day our daily bread. — *Matt. 6:11*

READ MATTHEW 6:9–13

he second half of the Lord's Prayer also consists of three petitions. The first three focus on God and his plans for our lives, whereas the latter threesome addresses the most basic of human needs, the first of which is daily sustenance. It is a mistake to interpret this petition in a figurative way, as if it is about spiritual food. Of course, every aspect of human physical need and God's provision has a spiritual side to it. Jesus is the Bread of Life and the bread in the Lord's Supper is a symbol both of Jesus's body broken for us and of our feeding upon Christ for spiritual nourishment. These are figurative uses of the language. But the bread in the Lord's Prayer is referring to real bread and, by extension, other physical necessities of life.

"Our daily bread" is, however, more than just our food. *Shorter Catechism* 104 explains with masterful simplicity: "We pray, that of God's free gift, we may receive a competent portion of the good things of this life, and enjoy his blessing with them." The petition also places our physical needs in the context of a spiritual health in which we trust the Lord for his provision for both body and soul.

God also feeds believers and unbelievers alike, which means he also "puts bread in the mouths that are opened against him." This reminds us that God is so merciful—that it is "through the Lord's mercies we are not consumed, because His compassions fail not" (Lam. 3:22). God's provision of our basic necessities calls us all to "be thankful to Him and bless his name" (Ps. 100:4). Too many of the successful and self-reliant folk in our time are like the heathen fishermen in the ancient world who "sacrifice to their net, and burn incense to their dragnet; because by them their share is sumptuous and their food plentiful" (Hab. 1:16). It is so easy to worship the gift while ignoring the Giver, thereby exchanging "the truth of God for the lie" and so worshiping and serving "the creature rather than the Creator" (Rom. 1:25). We have wonderful blessings every

432

day and will thank and praise the Lord precisely as we know him and love him as the Giver of every good and perfect gift (James 1:17).

The petition for our "daily" bread emphasizes a constant believing dependence upon the Lord. When a "farmer's strike" was looming in the USA, a television reporter asked a young lad on a Pittsburgh street if he was worried about food supplies if the strike came off. "Naw!" he said. "We get our food from the supermarket." Who needs God or farmers when we can just go to the store?

"Why pray at all?" some might ask. Perhaps the pantry is full and you have half a cow in the freezer. Some people think we should have a *year's* supply stored away "just in case." Does such provision actually guarantee your future? Every hurricane season in the USA, whole communities are devastated by bad weather that has no respect for our best laid plans. Solomon wisely counsels us, "Do not boast about tomorrow, for you do not know what a day may bring forth" (Prov. 27:1). But you can trust God, not just in the sunshine, but under a hurricane. Self-sufficiency may seem to guarantee our needs and comforts much of the time, but it is best seen as a mirage, and is no substitute for a lively, daily confiding in our gracious Savior. The psalmist testifies, "I have been young, and now am old; yet I have not seen the righteous forsaken, nor his descendants begging bread" (Ps. 37:25). "Though the bread is in our hand," writes Thomas Watson, "yet the blessing is in God's hand, and it must be fetched out of his hand by prayer." Jesus said, "Ask and it shall be given to you" (Matt. 7:7).

PRAISE FOR GOD'S PROVISION OF DAILY BREAD
Sing Psalm 107:33–43

THINGS I WILL PRAY FOR TODAY

_____

_____

_____

_____

_____

_____

August 4
Forgive Us Our Debts

The fifth petition of the Lord's Prayer

And forgive us our debts, as we forgive our debtors. — *Matt. 6:12*

READ MATTHEW 6:9–13

I was told once that there was no need to keep confessing sin in the prayers in public worship. I asked why? and was informed that Jesus has forgiven all our sins and that is all we need to hear! If this is so, why does Jesus so clearly assume that Christians—whose sins are indeed forgiven—will daily need to seek forgiveness? Is Jesus not reminding us, tenderly yet emphatically, that we still sin and need to repent and seek forgiveness? We who know our own hearts know very well why Jesus enjoins us to pray, "Forgive us our debts." We surely know that "if we say that we have no sin, we deceive ourselves, and the truth is not in us" (1 John 1:8). We also know that this prayer is for our blessing. *Shorter Catechism* 105 succinctly states that here "we pray that God, for Christ's sake, would freely pardon all our sins; which we are rather encouraged to ask, because, by his grace, we are enabled from the heart to forgive others." The very experience of forgiving and being forgiven moves us to flee to and trust in Christ for forgiveness.

Why are sins called "debts"? The answer is that sin is primarily a debt we owe to God. We know this because where Matthew 6:12 uses the word "debt" (*opheilama*), Luke 11:4 uses the Greek word for "sin" (*hamartia*). As in the financial world, the debtor owes the creditor, so in God's world, we are in default of the perfect obedience the Lord requires when we sin. We are accountable to him, and so, like the man in Matthew 5:25–26, we are liable for "the last penny," spiritually, morally, and eternally. The problem of sin as debt is compounded by the facts that by nature we are *born* debtors, by behavior we are *chronic* debtors, and by attitude we are *bad* debtors (who don't like to be reminded of the facts). It is no surprise then that sinner-debtors by nature have little love for their Creator-Creditor. Worse still, we cannot work our way to reconciliation with God. We desperately need forgiveness and it has to come from another place, another Savior.

434

What is forgiveness of sin? Scripture illustrated this in terms of sin being "blotted out," "taken away," "covered," "cast into the depths of the sea," and "remembered no more." This teaches us that when God forgives, he forgets, and there is nothing that the Lord will not do to bless his believing children in reconciled fellowship with himself. What is vital is to realize that forgiveness is something that happens in the mind of God. We are too easily subjective about forgiveness, as if because we "feel forgiven" or "just know" we are "right with God," then we must actually be forgiven. What is essential is the objective reality of forgiveness (in the mind of God) and this we can *know,* whatever our feelings may be. Forgiveness is an act of God in his mind, which is given to everyone who repents of sin, believing Jesus as his Savior: "If we confess our sins, He is faithful and just to forgive us our sins and to cleanse us from all unrighteousness" (1 John 1:9). Jesus saves. Jesus forgives. And how wonderful this is to those whose sin is forgiven! Forgiving grace is forever amazing grace!

Why does Jesus add "as we forgive our debtors"? He is simply saying, in the words of David Brown, "To ask God for what we ourselves refuse to man, is to insult Him." The more we realize how much love there is in God for him to forgive us our sins, the more forgiving will be our attitude toward others. In Luke 7:41ff., Jesus says of the woman who washed his feet in the house of Simon the Pharisee, "She loved much," because "her sins, which are many, are forgiven." This is a promise to all who pray out of a forgiving spirit, who desire for others the same grace of the Lord Jesus Christ, the Savior of sinners.

PRAISE FOR GOD'S FORGIVENESS OF SIN
Sing Psalm 130

THINGS I WILL PRAY FOR TODAY

August 5
Lead Us Not into Temptation

The sixth petition of the Lord's Prayer

And do not lead us into temptation, but deliver us from evil.
— Matt. 6:13a

READ MATTHEW 6:9–13

emptation is always exciting. It has the thrill of the chase, the attraction of forbidden fruit, and, as long as we are *only* tempted, it has none of the obvious consequences of actual sin. Christians may even console themselves with the thought that Jesus "was in all points tempted as we are, yet without sin" (Heb. 4:15). We conveniently forget that, unlike Jesus, we are not sinless. The practical result of *our* mulling over any temptation to sin, is that we sin in the thought, even if we never do the deed! Temptation is like stepping onto a playground slide—dally with it, and pretty soon you are on the slide, even if you are still a long way from the bottom! *Shorter Catechism* 106 is helpful in describing what we are praying for in the sixth petition: it is "that God would either keep us from being tempted to sin, or support and deliver us when we are tempted." We need the Lord to break our fall.

Temptation is inevitable. In giving us this prayer, Jesus assumes this! But where does this "temptation" come from? The petition might seem to imply that it is God who leads us into temptation. But Scripture is clear that God does not tempt anyone to sin: "Let no one say when he is tempted, 'I am tempted by God'; for God cannot be tempted by evil, nor does He Himself tempt anyone" (James 1:13). There are Scripture passages in which God is said to "tempt" (KJV), but these are cases of testing rather than tempting, in which God tests people by withdrawing from them and leaving them to themselves for a while. One example is when he "moved" David to count the people. In 2 Samuel 24:1 we are told that God is angry with Israel, but in 1 Chronicles 21:1 we are told that the reason for this is that "Satan stood up against Israel, and moved David to number Israel." God is chastising his people, but Satan incites them to sin. A different example is recorded in Genesis 22:1 (KJV), where "God did tempt" Abraham by commanding him to sacrifice his son Isaac. This is, however, a test, not a temptation to sin (as is made clear in modern English translations). God meant to teach his servants vital lessons. If they were to sin, the problem was their own. And real temptation is all around us every day.

Temptation is beatable. The petition also assumes this. But we need to keep our eyes open: Jesus tells us to "Watch and pray, lest you enter into temptation." Why?—because "the spirit indeed is willing, but the flesh is weak" (Matt. 26:41). We are, day by day, in real danger!

Our own hearts are susceptible: "Each one is tempted when he is drawn away by his own desires and enticed" (James 1:14). Only by faithfully trusting in Christ will we "run against a troop" and by his enabling grace "leap over a wall" (Ps. 18:29). Jesus assures us that in all our tests, including outright temptation, "My grace is sufficient for you, for My strength is made perfect in weakness"—and all to the end that "the power of Christ may rest upon [us]" (2 Cor. 12:9).

Satan is active and powerful: "Be sober, be vigilant; because your adversary the devil walks about like a roaring lion, seeking whom he may devour" (1 Peter 5:8). Remember, however, he is not all-powerful, and in Christ we are promised, "Resist the devil and he will flee from you" (James 4:7). Thomas Watson writes, "If you ask what grace it is that Satan most strikes at, I answer, it is the grace of faith. He lays the train [gunpowder trail] of his temptation to blow up the fort of our faith." Watson goes on to point out that although Satan can never take away the *life* of true faith in the Christian, he can hinder its *growth* if we go along with him. If you struggle with temptation, then look to Jesus and pray the sixth petition till the matter is settled. He knows what temptation is and, even more importantly, he has borne your sin and will bring you through to victory and to glory.

PRAYER FOR DELIVERANCE
Sing Psalm 125

THINGS I WILL PRAY FOR TODAY

August 6
Deliver Us from Evil

The sixth petition of the Lord's Prayer

And do not lead us into temptation, but deliver us from evil.
— Matthew 6:13bc

READ MATTHEW 6:9–13

eliverance from evil presupposes our vulnerability to temptation. The problem is not temptation *as such*, but is our natural predisposition to succumb to, and even welcome, the blandishments of the world, the flesh, and the devil. "So the utterance should flow like this," says John Calvin, "'in order that we may not be led into temptation, deliver us from evil.' In brief, being conscious of our own weakness, we ask to be defended by God's protection, in order that we may have an impregnable position against all the devices of Satan." Temptations draw us to future defeat. Augustine's prayer applies to us all: "Deliver me, O Lord, from myself." That said, you know that there is more to this than our internal condition and struggles.

Deliverance by another is absolutely essential. There is a personal devil, who, with his legions of fallen angels, is at work in our world. Whether the Scripture text is rendered "deliver us from evil" or "deliver us from the evil one," the truth is the same: "We do not wrestle against flesh and blood, but against principalities, against powers, against the rulers of the darkness of this age, against spiritual hosts of wickedness in the heavenly places" (Eph. 6:12). There is a spiritual war for people's souls, and it involves powers outside ourselves that we cannot defeat by ourselves. Without a divine Savior we cannot win. Jesus tells us that without a living faith in him we are "condemned already" (John 3:18)!

Deliverance belongs to the Lord Jesus Christ. "Believe in the Lord Jesus Christ, and you will be saved," says Paul to the Philippian jailer (Acts 16:30). This salvation is more than dodging a few bullets along life's way and escaping the deserved consequences of our sins. It is deliverance *to*, as well as deliverance *from*. In Christ, we receive a new life: "If anyone is in Christ, he is a new creation; old things have passed away; behold, all things have become new" (2 Cor. 5:17). While we live in this fallen

438

world, however, indwelling sin remains part of our experience. We are responsible to "work out" our "own salvation with fear and trembling" (Phil. 2:12). And by God's enabling grace, we are indeed doing so.

Deliverance in Christ includes our continual obedience. God calls us: "Sanctify yourselves therefore, and be ye holy: for I am the LORD your God" (Lev. 20:7, KJV; cf. 1 Peter 1:15–18). There are four particular measures we must take toward gaining the victory.

> Remember that prayer itself is a means of grace by which God works in us "to will and to do for his good pleasure" (Phil. 2:13), and so secure our spiritual health and strength. Just as sin carries its own punishment, so prayer carries its own rewards—"In the day of my trouble I will call upon You, for You will answer me" (Ps. 86:7).

> Avoid situations that afford you opportunities to sin. Pinpoint your weaknesses and study to be holy. Jesus urges you, "If your right hand causes you to sin, cut it off and cast it from you; for it is more profitable for you that one of your members perish, than for your whole body to be cast into hell" (Matt. 5:30).

> Constantly remind yourself that the mark of righteousness is to do good rather than not to do evil: "do not grow weary in doing good" (2 Thess. 3:15; Gal. 6:9), and "pursue peace with all people, and holiness, without which no one will see the Lord" (Heb. 12:14).

> Look to the Lord of the Lord's Prayer. His is "the kingdom, and the power, and the glory forever." He has gained the victory *for* you, Christian, and you will share that as you grow in his grace. You will enjoy this victory in fullness when you shortly come to the glory of heaven.

A PRAYER FOR DELIVERANCE FROM EVIL
Sing Psalm 107:17–22

THINGS I WILL PRAY FOR TODAY

August 7
Ask, Seek, and Knock

Jesus's exhortation to expectantly earnest prayer

For everyone who asks receives, and he who seeks finds, and to him who knocks it will be opened. —Matt. 7:8

READ MATTHEW 7:7–11

"Remember you have a good Scots' tongue in your head" was my mother's advice whenever I went off on my own, whether for a day trip or a summer camp. In other words, don't be shy to ask for help. Speak up! Make your need known! This was a secular echo of the scriptural convictions that burned, and still burn, in many a Christian's heart. "Ask...seek...knock," says Jesus. Don't wait for someone else to do it for you. Don't expect God to solve your problems if you are unwilling to seek his help. For "you do not have, because you do not ask" (James 4:2). So ask, seek, and knock.

Prayer is essential. But what are we to ask, seek, and knock for? The parallel passage in Luke 11:13 says, "If you then, though you are evil, know how to give good gifts to your children, how much more will your Father in heaven give the Holy Spirit to those who ask him?" This tells us that it is our *need* of the gifts and graces of the Holy Spirit that our Lord has in view! We need the Holy Spirit every day to illumine our minds, strengthen our faith, and suppress sinful impulses and desires. Put simply, we need God's powerful influence upon our hearts, and we need to ask him for it, constantly, as of first importance. Many Christians, however, take for granted the presence and influence of the Holy Spirit in their day-to-day lives, and mostly ask, seek, and knock for *circumstances, events,* and *things* of the moment. Now, it is always proper to pray for particular needs and heart's desires, like a spouse, children, health, employment, housing, and a myriad of specific items and challenges. But, important as these are, the most fundamental need of the soul every day in life is the fresh influence of the Holy Spirit and the maintenance and cultivation of personal godliness. "Keep your heart with all diligence," says Solomon, "for out of it spring the issues of life" (Prov. 4:23).

Prayer must be earnest. The rising intensity of Jesus's triple exhortation calls for persistence in prayer. When someone says he is "beating the bushes" to find a job, we know how serious he is. Jesus tells us that we "always ought to pray and not lose heart" (Luke 18:1). Why? Because life is serious and we have many needs that only God can meet. If we are serious about our discipleship to Jesus we will need to be, as Paul says, "rejoicing in hope, patient in tribulation, [and] continuing steadfastly in prayer" (Rom. 12:12). Prayer *length* is not the point. There will be times for praying long and hard and moments for brief and pointed petitions, but "continuing steadfastly" must be the watchword for our prayer lives.

Prayer will be answered. He who prays faithfully, says Jesus, "receives…finds," and discovers doors "will be opened." This is a sure promise. It is not, however, *carte blanche* to expect from God anything we blurt out as a request. A "prayer of faith" (James 5:15) is one that makes requests for that which God has promised—actually promised—in his word. He has not promised us anything we want, but he has promised all the blessings of the Holy Spirit necessary to a life of Christ-honoring holiness. God's promises are sure and the proper objects of our prayers.

If we ask for something he has not promised—say, healing from a disease—then we must realize that he may say no and that will still be for our blessing. Prayer is rightly regarded as a means of grace. It is the believers' hotline to heaven, by which we may go "boldly to the throne of grace that we may obtain mercy and find grace to help in time of need" (Heb. 4:16). Jesus promises us explicitly, "And whatever things you ask in prayer, believing, you will receive" (Matt. 21:22). Expect blessing! Ask, seek, and knock!

A PRAYER IN EXPECTATION OF AN ANSWER
Sing Psalm 143

THINGS I WILL PRAY FOR TODAY

_____

_____

_____

_____

_____

_____

August 8
You Can Make Me Clean!

A prayer for healing from an incurable disease

And, behold, a leper came and worshiped Him, saying, "Lord, if you are willing, you can make me clean."—Matt. 8:2

READ MATTHEW 8:1–5

Skin diseases in general, and leprosy in particular, are often used in Scripture to symbolize the corruption of sin in our hearts. Under the law of Moses, those so afflicted were held to be ceremonially "unclean" and were to live in a kind of religious quarantine outside the community until such time as they could be healed and restored to society (Lev. 13:8). Leprosy, because it was incurable and slowly and irreversibly consumed its victims, served to illustrate the twin facts that sin kills and is, short of divine intervention, incurable (Rom. 3:23; Eph. 2:8). This sets the scene for the leper's plea that Jesus would heal him. In Mark's account, Jesus is "moved with compassion" by his appeal and does indeed restore him to health (Mark 1:41). Notice four vital points in connection with this miracle.

The leper comes to Jesus. The great assumption behind this was that only God could cure him (2 Kings 5:7). Nowadays the doctor would prescribe a cocktail of antibiotics and he would soon be cured. In those days, no physician could help him. It would take a miracle, quite literally! Therefore his coming to Jesus makes a powerful statement, for he had nowhere else to go. This in turn points to the only hope for man's most dangerous and humanly incurable condition—his condemnation under the righteous wrath of the living God. You will recall that, when some of Jesus's disciples were leaving him, the Lord asked Peter if he too would go. Peter answered, "Lord, to whom shall we go? You have the words of eternal life" (John 6:68). From condition to cure, the leper's healing paints a picture of the grace of God in the gospel. We also must flee to Christ if we are to be saved.

The leper worships Jesus. The word translated as "worshiped" can refer to any prostration before a superior, after the longstanding usages of the East. "He fell on his face," says Luke, "and implored Him"

442

(Luke 5:12). There is, in this case, every reason to believe that the leper was bowing to Jesus, not only as an instrument of God, but also as the promised divine Messiah. He understands that Jesus is no mere man, for he asks him to do what God alone can do.

The leper confesses faith in Jesus. He is somewhat tentative, for as Charles Simeon observes, he "believed our Lord's *ability* to heal him, but he knew not the marvelous extent of his compassion: hence he doubted his *willingness* to bestow so great a blessing. He submitted himself however to the will of this divine Physician, and with deepest humility implored his sovereign help." He simply trusted himself to Jesus, according to such light as he had been given.

The leper was healed by Jesus. In one breath, Jesus declares his willingness, reaches out and touches him, and effects a miraculous healing. We need to bear in mind that Jesus did not miraculously heal every illness brought to his attention. His miracles were signs and wonders attesting his authority as the Messiah. Had Jesus proclaimed his power to heal, touched the "unclean" leper, and then failed to heal him, he would have been exposed as a liar and been rendered "unclean" himself! But Jesus, in perfect compliance with God's law, directed this former leper to go to the priest before talking to anyone, so that he might give thanks to God and to be publicly confirmed as "clean" before God and the world (Lev. 14:3–7). This is all about the grace of God in the gospel, by which, when we receive Christ as Savior, we are assured that "the blood of Jesus Christ His Son cleanses us from all sin" (1 John 1:7).

A PRAYER FOR CLEANSING
Sing Psalm 79:8–13

THINGS I WILL PRAY FOR TODAY

_____

_____

_____

_____

_____

_____

August 9
Great Faith in Action

Interceding for a dying servant

Only speak a word and my servant will be healed. — Matt. 8:8

READ MATTHEW 8:5–13; LUKE 7:1–10

An atheist is a man who has no invisible means of support" wrote the famed Scottish novelist, fifteenth governor-general of Canada, and Presbyterian church elder John Buchan. This was his way of saying that those who deny the Lord have nowhere to go and no one to trust outside of this world and this life. The Roman officer who came to Christ was likely a pagan before he became a Jewish proselyte. But he had discovered that "all the gods of the peoples are idols, but the Lord made the heavens" (Ps. 96:5). He knows he has someone to go to—to the living God who really exists, who reveals himself in his Word, who is able to save sinners, who truly hears believing prayer, and who demonstrably keeps his promises! When his servant is ill and apparently dying, he pleads with Jesus to heal him. His appeal to Jesus stands as one of the most beautiful examples in Scripture of intercessory prayer.

The Roman officer acts out of love, faith, and hope. Luke tells us that the servant is "dear to him." The elders, who approached Jesus at his request, pointed out his love for the people of God, citing his building a meeting place for them (Luke 7:2, 4). He also demonstrates the reality of his faith and hope in Jesus as the one who is able to heal his servant. He says to Jesus, "Only speak a word, and my servant will be healed," and he seals his confidence with an illustration from his military experience: "I also am a man under authority, having soldiers under me. And I say to this one, 'Go,' and he goes; and to another, 'Come,' and he comes; and to my servant, 'Do this,' and he does it" (Matt. 8:8–9). "He believed," comments Charles Simeon, "that Jesus could effect whatsoever he pleased, by a word, and at a distance, without the intervention of any means." Is this not at the basis of *all* believing prayer? If God is who he is and Jesus is who he claims to be, then "all things are possible"—not, of course, for us, but in and with the Lord (Matt. 19:26; Mark 8:23). The Roman centurion accepted Jesus at face

444

value, and it gave him reason to hope that his prayer would be answered. This is true and believing prayer in action: "Without faith it is impossible to please Him, for he who comes to God must believe that He is, and that He is a rewarder of those who diligently seek Him" (Heb. 11:6).

The Roman officer is said by Jesus to have acted in "great faith." This soldier knew little about Jesus, but what he knew he held very firmly. It is inconceivable that he did not go on to trust Jesus, when in due course Jesus was revealed as the crucified and risen Messiah, the Savior of the world. This man loved Jesus from a distance, as surely as Jesus healed his servant from a distance (v. 13). Why can we be sure of this? For one thing, Jesus *compares him favorably* to those "sons of the kingdom" who will be "cast out into outer darkness" (v. 12). This Gentile is a believer, while too many in Israel are hypocrites. Notice also that Jesus points ahead to the many that will come to Christ "from East and West, and sit down with Abraham, Isaac, and Jacob in the kingdom of heaven" (v. 11).

For the Roman officer, *the evidence of the work of God's grace adorns his life:* he loves the people of God, he is committed to the church, he goes to Jesus with genuine humility of mind (v. 6), and places his full confidence in the authority and power of Jesus to give life to the sick and dying (vv. 7–8). His behavior anticipates the fuller confession of faith we find in Peter when he says to Jesus, "Lord, to whom shall we go? You have the words of eternal life" (John 6:68). In the faithful intercession of this Roman soldier for his beloved servant lies the most fragrant encouragement for our walk with the Lord each day. Oh, to hear Jesus say of ourselves, that we have "such great faith" (v. 10).

AN INTERCESSORY PRAYER FOR DISTRESSED BELIEVERS
Sing Psalm 20

THINGS I WILL PRAY FOR TODAY

_____

_____

_____

_____

_____

_____

August 10
Two Demoniacs Healed

Three wicked prayers answered

What have we to do with You, Jesus, You Son of God? Have You come here to torment us before the time?—Matt. 8:29

READ MATTHEW 8:28–34;
MARK 5:1–20; LUKE 8:26–37

esus does not only answer the prayers of believers. In the startling affair of the demoniacs and the Gadarene swine, Jesus answers the prayers of both demons and determined unbelievers! These are obviously *wicked* prayers. Still, they are real requests, directed to Jesus, as the Son of God, which is more than can be said of a lot of so-called prayer in our own day. Like all prayers, they reveal something of the character and commitments of those who utter them. Jesus's answers are even more instructive. They reveal the predicament of the lost, and also his compassion and determination to save people. Matthew records three prayers, and Jesus's response to each one.

Prayer #1, from the demons, asks Jesus to leave them alone. You don't need to be demon-possessed to respond this way to the uninvited attentions of enthusiastic evangelists. The unique thrust in this case is that these prayers of the demons are expressions of reprobate minds determined to resist God to the last (vv. 28–29). They know they are doomed. Not so millions of careless human beings who say they "believe in God." "You believe that there is one God," warns Jesus's brother, "You do well. Even the demons believe—and tremble!" (James 2:19). If you say, with the demons, "What have we to do with you, Jesus?", you are praying the most dangerous prayer of all. One day, God may take you at your word! Rather, ask Jesus *into* your life!

Prayer #2, also from the demons, begs Jesus to let them enter some nearby pigs. They know Jesus is determined to deliver the poor men they have so miserably oppressed. So they ask for a stay of execution (vv. 30–32). Even demons cannot face being locked up in hell forever! As Jesus speaks, and as you read this, the world is still before the *kairos*—the "appointed time" of the final judgment at the coming of the Lord (v. 29).

446

And so Jesus passes on their deferred judgment to the pigs, which were at that time visible symbols of the locals' flouting of the Jewish dietary laws (Deut. 14:8). The possessed pigs duly drown in the lake—a vivid emblem of the consequences of evil, and a powerful stimulus to their owners to take God seriously, repent, and turn to his Son, Jesus, for the salvation they need every bit as much as the poor demented souls from among the tombs. The demons are beyond saving, but lost people can be saved if they will only turn to Jesus and receive him as their Savior and Lord.

Prayer #3, from the farmers, is the most disturbing request of all. Why? Because it reveals the community's heart-resistance to Jesus: "Pigs and peace," writes John Legg, "were more important than the deliverance of the possessed men. This is the reaction of the world, both Jews and Gentiles, to the authority of Jesus Christ." The people of Gadara beg Jesus to get out of their lives (vv. 33–34). Jump ahead to the day of Jesus's crucifixion, when Pontius Pilate presents him to the mob with the words "Behold your King," and they roar back, "Crucify him" (John 19:13–15). The truth is that sinners by nature love their own sins and would rather not have the Savior disturb their lives!

But what a Savior is our Jesus! Don't forget, amid these deadly anti-prayers, that quietly overarching everything is Jesus's love and compassion for the poor men who could not even seek him if they had wanted to, but needed to be delivered by the free and sovereign grace of God, in Christ. Let us never ask Jesus to leave us alone, but rather let us walk ever closer to him and so constantly rejoice in his salvation.

PRAISE FOR THE LORD WHO SAVES
Sing Psalm 11

THINGS I WILL PRAY FOR TODAY

August 11
Lay Your Hand on Her

A father's prayer for his deceased daughter

My daughter has just died, but come and lay Your hand on her, and she will live. —Matt. 9:19

READ MATTHEW 9:19–26;
MARK 5:22–24; LUKE 8:40–42, 49–56

The death of a child is the most desolating of tragedies. Jairus, a ruler of the synagogue (Mark 5:22), knew his twelve-year-old daughter was dying when he left home and rushed to Jesus to seek his help. As he blurted out his desperate prayer, he knew for sure that the lass was dead (cf. Matt. 9:19; Mark 5:35; Luke 8:49). This is one of these tests of life from which we all hope to be spared. It is, however, all of God's grace that he prepares us for whatever trials may come our way by giving us a window, in his Word, into the darkest experiences in human life. While the sun is shining and there are no significant problems in our lives, it is easy to trust, or not to trust, in the Lord. Jairus's crisis teaches us about faith and faithfulness in both the sufferer and the Savior.

Faith is tested by trials. Sooner or later we will take some serious hits. When this happens, we will reveal to ourselves, and to those around us, in whom we are really trusting. The contrast between Jesus's decisive rejection on the east side of the Sea of Galilee, and his warmer reception on the western side, is hugely instructive. The Gergesenes (or Gadarenes) could not wait to get rid of Jesus. It cost them too much to accept him into their lives: they can no more face giving up their sins, than they can be happy to lose their pigs (Matt. 8:28–34). When troubles come, and the only response you can summon up is an *angry* "Why are you allowing this to happen to me, God?" you are already fleeing *from* the Lord when you should be fleeing *to* him!

Faith reaches past the trials to come to Jesus. When the test comes, Jairus runs to Jesus. Unlike the Gergesenes, Jairus believes Jesus can help. This surely illustrates the point that Jesus earlier made to his critics: "Those who are well have no need of a physician, but those who are

448

sick....For I did not come to call the righteous, but sinners, to repentance" (Matt. 9:12–13). Jesus is saying that those who remain content with their own "righteousness" will never really hear his call and come to him, because they are not convinced of their need of him as the Savior he has come to be. The self–satisfied "righteous" need to learn from the "tax collectors and sinners" who come to Jesus with apparent humility of mind and also learn what God means when he says "I desire mercy and not sacrifice" (Matt. 9:12–13 quoting Hos. 6:6).

Faith receives rewards from Jesus. As soon as news of the girl's death comes to Jesus's ears, he tells her father, "Do not be afraid: only believe and she will be made well" (Luke 8:50). When they arrive at Jairus's house, Jesus declares to the mourners, "Make room, for the girl is not dead, but sleeping." But the mourners "ridiculed Him" (v. 24). Jesus, together with the parents and some disciples, entered her room and Jesus "took her by the hand, and the girl arose." Charles Simeon's application is unsurpassed:

> Every man must expect trouble in this vale of tears...but let every trouble drive us to the compassionate Jesus, and every want be spread before him in prayer. We are not now indeed to expect *miraculous* interpositions; nor ought we to ask for *temporal* blessings in an unqualified manner. We should commit the concerns of this life to his all-wise disposal; but for *spiritual* blessings we cannot be too importunate, nor can our faith in his word be too strong.

What a Savior we have in Jesus! He who raised the little girl will raise you also, dear Christian, for he is, as Scripture affirms, the firstborn among many brethren (Rom. 8:29).

PRAISE FOR THE LORD WHO SAVES HIS PEOPLE
Sing Psalm 91:1–4

THINGS I WILL PRAY FOR TODAY

_____

_____

_____

_____

August 12
She Touched His Garment

The prayer of the woman with a flow of blood

She said to herself, "If only I may touch his garment…"—*Matt. 9:21*

READ MATTHEW 9:20–22;
MARK 5:25–34; LUKE 8:43–48

We are far too impressed by eloquent public prayers. A visitor to a prayer meeting in some corner of Scotland prayed fulsomely about this and that and everything, with not a comma out of place. Rising to a crescendo, he said, "What more can we say, O Lord?", only for a cracked old voice across the room to cry in a pleading tone, "Jist say a wee word aboot the Lord Jesus, son!" The woman in Matthew 9 who creeps up behind Jesus utters not a word, but she has a lot about Jesus on her mind. She speaks to herself, believing God hears. She touches the hem of his garment, believing Jesus can heal (v. 21). And between the two, God reads the agony of her soul and answers the simple prayer of her faith. Perhaps she has heard that Jesus had said, "And when you pray, do not use vain repetitions as the heathen do. For they think that they will be heard for their many words" (Matt. 6:7). The God of the love that gives his Son to save sinners sees the movements of our hearts and knows when we are crying to him, suffering but believing.

The woman secretly reaches out to Jesus. Jesus has just heard Jairus tell of his daughter's mortal illness and is on his way to heal her. "Suddenly," says Matthew, the woman "touched the hem of his garment" (Matt. 9:19–21). Luke says Jesus "perceived power going out" of him (Luke 8:46). This looks, at first glance, like magic—the kind of superstition that invests powers in material objects, like the "prayer cloths" of some so-called "faith-healers" today. But what is happening here? The woman with the "flow of blood for twelve years" is a medically hopeless case (Luke 8:43). However, she believes in Jesus, touches him, and is healed. Jesus is unaware of her thinking, her faith, and her prayer, but his God and Father knows these things and he effects a *secret* healing! There is no magic in Jesus's clothes. It is God revealing to the world that his incarnate Son has power to save sinners! Luke records that she emerged from the crowd, and "declared to Him in the presence of all the people the reason she had touched him and how she was healed immediately" (Luke 8:47). She confesses faith in Jesus and testifies that her otherwise incurable condition is miraculously healed.

Jesus pronounces a blessing that charts the future course of her life. There are four components to this blessing (v. 22):

> "Be of good cheer…" Here are words to encourage all suffering saints. The Lord even tells us to "count it all joy" when we fall into trials (James 1:2). "Why is trial an occasion of joy?" asks Octavius Winslow. "Because it is the triumph of the Holy Spirit in the soul." He adds, "It is not the believer himself who conquers; it is the divine Spirit within the believer."

> "Daughter…" emphasizes Jesus's love toward her. This reminds us also that the great consolation for suffering Christians is our adoption as the children of God through the atoning sacrifice of the crucified Jesus. In Christ, we have "received the Spirit of adoption by whom we cry out, 'Abba, Father'" (Rom. 8:15). We are never alone.

> "Your faith has made you well…" points beyond the physical healing, which is temporary—she will still die someday—to the greater healing, which is eternal. "Therefore, if anyone is in Christ, he is a new creation; old things have passed away; behold, all things have become new" (2 Cor. 5:17). Our salvation is both now and forever!

> "Go in peace" (Luke 8:48). She has peace in believing—that peace which passes understanding—and is sent on her way to live out of that peace every day. This is both her privilege and her duty—to live in the peace that is born of knowing Christ— "Christ in you the hope of glory" (Col. 1:27). We have no need to touch his garment, when he has touched our soul. Jesus heals both body and soul.

PRAISE FOR THE LORD WHO HEALS OUR DISEASES
Sing Psalm 103:1–5

THINGS I WILL PRAY FOR TODAY

_____

_____

_____

August 13
He Touched Their Eyes

The prayers of the two blind men

When Jesus departed from there, two blind men followed Him, crying out
and saying, "Son of David, have mercy on us!"—Matt. 9:27

READ MATTHEW 9:27–31

All of Jesus's healing miracles had temporary results. Every beneficiary subsequently died. Jesus did not heal all the sick people in all the regions where he ministered. The resurrected Lazarus lived to die another day. All the dead, except Jesus himself, await the Great Day of the resurrection of their bodies at Jesus's second coming. This reminds us that temporal blessings of all kinds are temporary. Whether miraculous or providential (as in our day), these bless us presently, while simultaneously calling us to look beyond this life: from the physical to the spiritual; from this world to the world to come; from earth to heaven; from the finite to infinite. All relate to our personal relationship with God in his Son, Jesus, "who was delivered up because of our offenses, and was raised because of our justification" (Rom. 4:25). The miracles of Jesus and the apostles are not to be reduced to ends in themselves, as if they are no more than symbols of Jesus's compassion and a vivid encouragement to Christian social work. Still less are they the building blocks in some self-promoting myth-making by Jesus's latter-day followers. No! These miracles are supernatural acts of God in history. They actually happened and were designed to be realtime testaments to God's power to save sinners like us by the mediation of his Son, the Lord Jesus Christ (1 Tim. 2:5). These miracles preach the gospel to an ever-needy world!

These two men were really blind. They knew they needed a true miracle if they were to see at all. They longed for normal sight and they cried to Jesus with desperate intensity. As Jesus was leaving the crowd, the blind men "followed Him, crying out and saying, 'Son of David, have mercy on us!'" (v. 27). Notice three components to their prayer:

    ➢ They *call upon the Lord* when he is near them: they "followed Him, crying out." They took the advice of the prophet when he

452

said, "Seek the LORD while He may be found, call upon Him while He is near" (Isa. 55:6). This is God's standing solution to all our distresses: "Draw near to God and He will draw near to you. Cleanse your hands, you sinners; and purify your hearts, you double-minded" (James 4:8). Your eyes may see, but does your soul not need light from the Lord who is the Light of the world (John 9:5)?

> They *acknowledge Jesus as the Messiah*. They address him as the "Son of David." Had they heard what the angel told Mary? "He will be great, and will be called the Son of the Highest; and the Lord God will give Him the throne of His father David" (Luke 1:32). At the very least, these men believe Jesus to be "made of the seed of David according to the flesh" (Rom. 1:3–4). And they come to him as to "the one Mediator between God and men, the man Christ Jesus" (1 Tim. 2:5).

> They *appeal to Jesus for mercy*, so affirming that they believe he is able to heal them. Thus Jesus does heal them, as he touches their eyes upon their positive response to his question, "Do you believe that I am able to do this?" (v. 28). They do believe and they are blessed according to their faith.

Jesus has in view a double blessing. The primary blessing is that "the eyes of your understanding" be "enlightened" (Eph. 1:18). Physical healing is actually a secondary blessing designed to confirm to us that the gospel of Jesus Christ is "the power of God to salvation to everyone who believes" (Rom. 1:16). Christ is the believer's light. Here is the greatest and most abiding miracle: to know from the heart and confess with the lips before the Lord: "For with You is the fountain of life; in Your light we see light" (Ps. 36:9). In Christ, God "has shone in our hearts to give the light of the knowledge of the glory of God in the face of Jesus Christ" (2 Cor. 4:6).

PRAYER THAT THE LORD WOULD OPEN OUR EYES
Sing Psalm 119:17–24

THINGS I WILL PRAY FOR TODAY

August 14
Marching Orders

A prayer request from Jesus

Therefore pray the Lord of the harvest to send out laborers into His harvest. — Matt. 9:38

READ MATTHEW 9:35–38; LUKE 10:1–12

This is arguably the most significant "prayer request" in recorded history. Together with Jesus's further instruction in Matthew 10:1–25, we are given, writes John Legg, "the marching orders of the church." Why? The vision behind Jesus's command to pray for laborers for his harvest is absolutely basic to the life and ministry of the church and every Christian. What are Christians for? Why does the church exist? Jesus tells us the answer so simply: "When He saw the multitudes, He was moved with compassion for them, because they were weary and scattered, like sheep having no shepherd" (v. 36). What is his solution to the problem? The answer is to send "shepherds" to these "sheep." But there is a problem: "The harvest truly is plentiful, but the laborers are few" (v. 37).

The world is like a farmer's field. There is sowing and reaping. The world is sown with lost sinners and must be reaped for any to be redeemed! When Jesus saw the villagers of Sychar stream out to see him, he said to the disciples, "Behold, lift up your eyes and look at the fields, for they are already white for harvest" (John 4:35). His point is that just as the farmer sees the corn maturing and must reap or it will rot, so the church sees each generation growing older and closer to eternity and must reap—by winning people to Christ—or they will perish forever in a lost eternity! Generations come and generations go. We often hear the term "lost generation" in describing a certain group of people who in some way suffered a common catastrophe in their lives. In his novel *The Sun Also Rises*, Ernest Hemingway applies it to the young men who came out of the trenches in the First World War. Others apply it to those who died and whose potential was never realized. For Jesus, *every* generation is already lost until and unless it is found and saved by the grace of God in the gospel. All of humanity is inching forward to eternity and the second

454

death, and the only hope of salvation is in Jesus Christ and him crucified (1 Cor. 2:2; cf. John 3:16–18).

There is work to be done. Workers are needed. They need to be "sent out"—and by God! It is true that every individual Christian has the duty of being a living advertisement for Jesus every day in life. You, Christian, are to "let your light so shine before men, that they may see your good works and glorify your Father in heaven" (Matt. 5:16). What Jesus has in view here, however, is the church—not merely as a collection of individuals, but as instituted by God in its congregations and with its officers and members—being the instrument of God, in *his* calling and sending out of men to preach the gospel to every creature (Mark 16:15; Matt. 28:18–20). Not everyone is "sent" to this ministry, but every Christian is called to "pray the Lord of the harvest to send out laborers into His harvest" (v. 38). This is to be your constant prayer, believer, for as long as this world lasts.

There is a promise to be realized. It is "His harvest," not ours. "So then neither he who plants is anything, nor he who waters, but God who gives the increase" (1 Cor. 3:7). Whether your planting and sowing is to pray for God's "laborers," or to be a laborer yourself in the work of preaching Christ, you have the promise of fruit from the Lord himself. So, says Paul, "He who sows sparingly will also reap sparingly, and he who sows bountifully will also reap bountifully" (2 Cor. 9:6). Therefore "let us not grow weary while doing good, for in due season we shall reap if we do not lose heart" (Gal. 6:9). Pray every day for the harvesters and the harvest.

PRAYER FOR GOD'S HARVEST OF REDEMPTION
Sing Psalm 72:16–19

THINGS I WILL PRAY FOR TODAY

_____

_____

_____

_____

_____

_____

_____

August 15
I Thank You, Father

Jesus's prayer of thanksgiving to his Father (Part 1)

I thank You, Father, Lord of heaven and earth. — Matt. 11:25

READ MATTHEW 11:25–27; LUKE 10:21–22

Only once in the Gospels is Jesus recorded as rejoicing. In his account of the prayer that Matthew records here, Luke says that "In that hour Jesus rejoiced in the Spirit" (Luke 10:21). On the other hand, Jesus is furious twice, weeps several times, and is always earnest and serious. But don't trust mere statistics, for he prays in his great high-priestly prayer that his disciples "may have My joy fulfilled in themselves" (John 17:13). There is a constant joy, a fountain of joy, even in the Man of Sorrows (Isa. 53:3). It is important to remember this, because it is on account of his joy that Jesus expresses thankfulness in this beautiful prayer. So we must ask what specifically causes Jesus to rejoice. His prayer reveals four distinct causes of the joy with which he gives thanks.

Jesus rejoices in the sovereignty of God in salvation. Jesus addresses God as his "Father, Lord of heaven and earth" (v. 25a). These wonderful words remind us that God *must* save us if we are to be saved; that God *can* save us since he alone has the power to save; and that God *will* save us "according to the good pleasure of His will" (Eph. 1:5).

Jesus rejoices in the wisdom of God in salvation. The gospel is "hidden...from the wise and the prudent" (v. 25b). The "wise and the prudent" are, in God's eyes, neither wise nor prudent. They are "wise in their own conceits" and are hardening their hearts against the light of God's truth (Rom. 11:25; 12:16, KJV). These cultured despisers of the gospel of Christ—the Pharisees and Sadducees and their modern descendants—are too clever to accept the gospel, and God is not going to reward them for their unwillingness to repent and believe in Jesus. The Pharisees are so confident that they cite the fact that *they* do not believe as a reason for *nobody* believing in Jesus (John 7:48)! God is wise in making sure that the lost will be seen to deserve to be lost. He is not a universalist. Unless you repent, you will perish (Luke 13:1–5)!

456

Jesus rejoices in the grace of God in salvation. His salvation is "revealed...to babes" (v. 25c). Jesus is surely thinking here of his disciples—both the twelve and the seventy (Matt. 10:1–15; Luke 10:1–20). They are spiritual babies! But they have believed in Jesus and they have taught others to believe in him. "For you see your calling, brethren, that not many wise according to the flesh, not many mighty, not many noble, are called," says Paul, "But God has chosen the foolish things of the world to put to shame the wise, and God has chosen the weak things of the world to put to shame the things which are mighty" (1 Cor. 1:26–27). This is all of God's free grace! It is the "foolish" and "weak" things—the most unlikely candidates for salvation in the world's eyes—that become glorious trophies of the unmerited grace of God in Christ.

Jesus rejoices in the goodness of God in salvation: "For so it seemed good in your sight" (v. 26). God might justly, at any time, destroy the whole human race, and still be good. He came close to destroying Israel after the golden calf incident, but relented in his goodness and mercy (Ex. 32:9–10). The truth is that it is always "through the Lord's mercies we are not consumed," and the reason for this is a goodness so great that "His compassions fail not" but "are new every morning." Great indeed is his faithfulness (Lam. 3:22–23)! Let us then rejoice and give thanks to God for his salvation and sing, "Oh, how great is Your goodness, which You have laid up for those who fear You" (Ps. 31:19).

PRAISE GOD FOR HIS GREAT GOODNESS
Sing Psalm 31:19–24

THINGS I WILL PRAY FOR TODAY

_____

_____

_____

_____

_____

_____

_____

_____

_____

August 16
Jesus and His Father

Jesus's prayer of thanksgiving to his Father (Part 2)

All things have been delivered to Me by My Father. — Matt. 11:27

READ MATTHEW 11:25–27; LUKE 10:21–22

esus first gave thanks to his Father out of joy over the salvation of sinners. No wonder! This work of God's grace through the sacrifice of his own Son is the greatest thing that ever happened in a world blighted by sin and darkness. Yesterday, in Matthew 11:25–26, Jesus rejoices in gospel success, i.e., his own *work of redemption*. In verse 27 he rejoices in the shared satisfaction, confidence, and fellowship that he enjoys with his Father, who sent him for this purpose. He rejoices and gives thanks on account of his *unique personal relationship* to God the Father. Three aspects of this unique relationship are revealed to us in this prayer of thanksgiving.

Jesus enjoys the perfect confidence of the Father: *"All things have been delivered to Me by My Father" (v. 27a).* "All things" simply means that nothing is outside Jesus's authority: "He shall have dominion from sea to sea" (Ps. 72:8). He says, "All authority has been given to me" (Matt. 28:18; cf. John 17:2; Eph. 1:10, 22). He has power to regenerate your helpless human nature; to transform your mind and thinking; to guide your circumstances; and to bring you to heaven! No wonder then, that Jesus rejoices in his relationship with the Father.

"Delivered" emphasizes that the Father has commissioned the Son to save sinners from their sins (Matt. 1:21). As the *eternal* Son, Jesus was already our Creator and Sustainer (Heb. 1:3), but as the *incarnate* Son, born of a woman, he is "the man Christ Jesus" sent to be "the one Mediator between God and men" (1 Tim. 2:5). His mediation on our behalf depends wholly on his sinless humanity making perfect atonement for our very human sin. Only in his true humanity is he able to be our Substitute and therefore our Savior.

Jesus enjoys an exclusive knowledge of the Father: "No one knows the Son except the Father. Nor does anyone know the Father except the Son" (Matt. 11:27). A unique knowledge and a pure fellowship

458

are shared between the Father and the Son. Paul touches on this in Colossians 2:9: "For in Him [Jesus] dwells all the fullness of the Godhead bodily." This tells us that God reveals himself *in Jesus*. God dwells in light inaccessible. He is incomprehensible. He is invisible. But Jesus is "the heir of all things," and "the brightness of his glory and the express image of his person" (Heb. 1:2–3). Jesus is the visible face of God.

Jesus as the mediator is the greatest gift of God to man. God's gift is to reveal himself in Jesus Christ. Jesus makes known the unknowable God. Hence Jesus says to Philip, "He who has seen Me has seen the Father" (John 14:9). Here is the great point of Matthew 11:27: no one truly knows the Father except the Son and "the one to whom the Son wills to reveal Him." How can any human being know God? Only by faith in Christ the Savior! It is only "by grace you have been saved through faith, and that not of yourselves; it is the gift of God" (Eph. 2:8). "The meaning therefore is," writes Calvin, "that life is exhibited to us in Christ himself, and that no man will partake of it who does not enter by the gate of faith."

This is pure gospel! Jesus rejoices in his Father's delight in him as the One given to be the Savior of the world. And so he turns to his hearers and warmly invites them to himself: "Come to me, all you who labor and are heavy laden, and I will give you rest" (Matt. 11:28–30). In Christ, we too come to know his Father as our Father in heaven, and so may rejoice with joy unspeakable and full of glory!

PRAISE FOR A SAVING KNOWLEDGE OF GOD
Sing Psalm 144:9–15

THINGS I WILL PRAY FOR TODAY

August 17
Asking the Blessing

Jesus gives thanks before eating

Looking up to heaven, He blessed and broke and gave the loaves to the disciples. — *Matt. 14:19*

READ MATTHEW 14:13–21;
MARK 6:30–44; JOHN 6:1–14

No category of prayer has been the subject of more ridicule and neglect than "saying grace" before a meal. It is perhaps the easiest exercise of prayer to dismiss or to lampoon. In the 1972 movie *The Wrath of God*, a gun-slinging "priest," played by the inimitable Robert Mitchum, is asked to say grace and complies with a mocking "Rub-a-dub-dub, thanks for the grub." Even the expression "say grace" suggests ritual observance rather than heartfelt devotion. It is therefore instructive to observe the Lord Jesus blessing a meal, because we are given a window into the motivation and conviction Jesus brings to this simple exercise of godly piety.

Jesus has retreated to "a deserted place by himself." He had recently learned of the murder of John the Baptist (v. 13). Prayer is not mentioned, but it had to be one purpose of his desire for solitude. J. C. Ryle notes, "Prayer is the main secret of success in spiritual business. It moves Him who can move heaven and earth." Mark records a more prosaic reason: "For there were many coming and going, and they did not even have time to eat" (Mark 6:31). There are times when we just need a break. We need to get away for a while. We need to breathe.

Jesus is filled with compassion for the people. The crowds follow him, and, moved by their needs, he ministers to them. His love of souls effectively cancels his vacation. He "healed their sick" (v. 14). When the hour grew late, he is unwilling to accept the disciples' suggestion that he "send the multitudes away" to "go into the village, and buy themselves food" (v. 15). He will feed them! And this he does in the feeding of the five thousand. The "five loaves and two fishes" are miraculously extended to fill them all and still leave "twelve baskets of the fragments that remained" left over (vv. 17–21)!

Jesus first asks a blessing before the meal. Why? On this occasion, he surely "gave thanks" (John 6:11) with "special reference to the multiplying of this food." In such miracles, God attests Jesus to be the promised Savior of the world. Jesus's miracles are his Father telling us "This is My beloved Son! Hear Him" (Mark 9:7).

Jesus also needs his daily bread. God the Son is truly human. He needs to eat, like all of us. Luke records Jesus's sharing an ordinary meal with two travelers in Emmaus. Jesus took the bread and "blessed and broke it, and gave it to them" (Luke 24:30). This jogged the men's memories, and they realized this was the crucified Jesus, arisen from the dead! So, what is the connection with us and for us?

Jesus is "the bread of life." He is "the bread of God...who comes down from heaven and gives life to the world" (see John 6:32ff.). If he gives thanks for his earthly bread, then we, who have received the heavenly bread of everlasting life in him, should do the same. But there is much more! In asking the blessing before our meals, we are not merely giving thanks for the food we will eat. We are consciously connecting our earthly bread with Christ our heavenly bread, who has given us eternal life. Asking the blessing bridges heaven and earth, for our earthly bread is from our heavenly bread, Jesus. We open our hearts in prayer to him in dependence upon his grace, and he fills our body and soul with all that we need for time and eternity: "He who comes to Me shall never hunger, and he who believes in Me shall never thirst" (John 6:35).

GIVING THANKS FOR DAILY BREAD
Sing Psalm 145:15–21

THINGS I WILL PRAY FOR TODAY

_____

_____

_____

_____

_____

_____

_____

August 18
Crumbs from the Masters' Table?

Persistent prayer in trying circumstances

Yes, Lord, yet even the little dogs eat the crumbs which fall from their masters' table. — Matt. 15:27

READ MATTHEW 15:21–28; MARK 7:24–30

esus's encounter with the "woman of Canaan" is both beautiful and shocking. She has a "severely demon-possessed" daughter and comes to Jesus for help. Jesus's first reaction is not to respond: "He answered her not a word." Does this look to you like callous indifference? In reality, it is "the silence of love." And this silence allows everybody to think. The disciples just want Jesus to get rid of this Gentile pagan (v. 23). For the woman, however, it is a test of her faith. The next step in that testing process is when Jesus tells her, "I was not sent except to the lost sheep of the house of Israel" (v. 24). What will she say to what looks like a rebuff? Will her faith in the "Lord, the Son of David" prove to be an ephemeral, empty thing, blown away by a little silence and a seemingly discouraging word?

Jesus is, in fact, drawing out the woman's faith by inviting her to persevere in prayer. And she prays more fervently! She "worshiped him, saying, 'Lord, help me!'" (v. 25). Jesus's response seems harsh: "It is not good to take the children's bread and throw it to the little dogs" (v. 26). "Dogs" in Scripture represent spiritual uncleanness, opposition to, and separation from the Lord (see Phil. 3:2; Rev. 22:15). The psalmist prophesies of the Messiah dying for our salvation: "For dogs have compassed me….[T]hey pierced my hands and my feet" (Ps. 22:16). Jesus reminds her of God's controversy with Gentile unbelief. Their exchange has an air of banter to it, because her riposte is almost an essay in good-natured humility: "Yes, Lord, yet even the little dogs eat the crumbs which fall from their masters' table." Jesus's final words, "O woman, great is your faith! Let it be to you as you desire" (v. 28), offer a glorious glimpse of the Lord's pleasure in the simple and steadfast faith of a believer. Her prayer is acceptable to God! What a wonderful contrast to the pretense and prattle that often passes for prayer in our world: "When men display to congregations wide, devotions every grace except the heart!" This "woman of Canaan" knows her Lord and Savior.

Jesus is answering believing prayer. The vital connection is between the woman's faith and her prayer. She *prays* because she believes in Jesus for who he really is (Heb. 11:6; cf. James 5:16). And she *persists* in praying because she still believes that, however negative his words, Jesus is able to heal her daughter if he is willing. She believes and *therefore* does not let go. She *humbles herself* because she grasps that Jesus can be assumed to regard her as an alien "from the commonwealth of Israel" (Eph. 2:12). Alien as she was, and humble as she was, she did not see herself beyond the saving touch of "the Lord, the Son of David" (v. 22). Only a true and living faith in Jesus could sustain such prayer and conversation. Her trust is in the Lord!

Jesus demonstrates the universality of the gospel. Kent Hughes rightly calls this event in general and the woman's faith in particular "a beautiful prophecy of that gospel which would soon capture much of the Gentile world." The Jew-Gentile "wall of partition" is coming down (Eph. 2:14)! No one is beyond the pale. The good news of the gospel is for the whole world. Jesus is saying to the world, "Incline your ear, and come to Me. Hear, and your soul shall live; and I will make an everlasting covenant with you—the sure mercies of David" (Isa. 55:3; John 6:37). And when *you* pray, do not give up until he answers you and blesses your soul!

PRAISE THAT GLORIES IN DELIVERANCE FROM DISTRESS
Sing Psalm 18:1–6

THINGS I WILL PRAY FOR TODAY

_____

_____

_____

_____

_____

_____

_____

_____

_____

_____

_____

August 19
If Two of You Agree

Jesus's promises for prayer meetings

If two of you agree on earth concerning anything that they ask, it will be done for them by My Father in heaven. — Matt. 18:19

READ MATTHEW 18:15–20

ome Scripture passages are easy to over-interpret and misapply. Matthew 18:19–20 is a case in point. Commentators variously take it to be primarily about prayer, or principally about the blessings of small-group prayer, and, less plausibly, that it defines the minimal size of a church— "Where three are there, there is a church." The context, however, indicates that this meeting of "two or three" is not the normal gathering of a congregation for worship, prayer, or church business. It is rather the "church" of verse 17, where "tell it to the church" refers to "those who bear rule in the Church" as they deal with a disciplinary case. In context, if "two of [the elders] agree on earth" concerning "anything that they ask" of God, Jesus promises, "it will be done for them by My Father in heaven" (v. 19)—i.e., he will ratify their decisions. The word "anything" translates the Greek *pragmatos*, which in 1 Corinthians 6:1 refers to a lawsuit. The primary focus, then, is decidedly judicial. In so far as prayer enters into the judicial process, it is prayer for grace, wisdom, and the ultimate effectiveness of that discipline for all involved.

There are, however, some universal principles embedded in this judicial focus. The elders are obviously not the whole church, and yet they are called "the church" (v. 17). Why? Because they are acting for the whole church as they exercise pastoral leadership. Jesus encourages them in this challenging task with a threefold promise, in which the key words are "gathered together," "in My name," and "in the midst of them" (v. 20). This same promise applies to all collective praying by Christians, from groups of two or three to much larger assemblies.

Jesus will particularly bless us when we are *"gathered together"* to pray. The fact that the elders are called to exercise discipline, and to pray about it, does not mean that the rest of the church is uninvolved.

464

The members of the church need to support their elders in prayer—and work themselves toward the restoration of those who are under discipline (Gal. 6:1). If anything, Jesus's promise conveys the sure prospect of a greater measure of God's grace when we unite together in prayer, as opposed to simply praying as individuals. God delights in our coming *together* to the throne of grace (Heb. 4:16) and will bless our prayer meetings—large and small, formal and informal—as he previously has and will for the meetings of the elders of the church.

Jesus requires us to gather *"in My name."* This means coming to him in prayer on the basis of a sincere "obedience to him as our Lord, and in deep dependence on him as our Savior." In other words, we come to him as our Mediator with his God and Father. Jesus tells us plainly, "I am the way, the truth, and the life. No one comes to the Father except through Me" (John 14:6). This calls for a conscious dedication to worship and serve the Lord in "the unity of the Spirit and the bond of peace" (Eph. 4:3). The size of the group does not determine our Lord's presence or absence. But the honor or dishonor we give to his name as we pray is absolutely crucial: "If I regard iniquity in my heart, the Lord will not hear" (Ps. 66:18).

Jesus assures us of his presence *"in the midst"* of all our gatherings in his name. His language emphasizes the intimacy and immediacy of his nearness to those whom he loves and who love him. And it anticipates the day when we will see him face to face: "For the Lamb who is in the midst of the throne will shepherd them and lead them to living fountains of waters. And God will wipe away every tear from their eyes" (Rev. 7:17). Let us often pray together.

A PRAYER THAT GOD WOULD VISIT HIS PEOPLE
Sing Psalm 80

THINGS I WILL PRAY FOR TODAY

_____

_____

_____

_____

_____

_____

August 20
You Don't Know What You Ask

A mother's misguided prayer

Grant that these two sons of mine may sit, one on Your right hand and the other on the left, in Your kingdom. — Matt. 20:21

READ MATTHEW 20:20–28; MARK 10:35–45

When Christians talk of "answered prayer," they invariably mean requests that God has apparently granted. "Answered prayer" equals granted prayer. There are, however, some things God will not give you. In other words, no can equally be an answer to prayer. In fact, God frequently says no to faultlessly *faithful* prayers! What makes the difference is God's perfect will. So, Paul prays for the removal of his thorn in the flesh, but God says no, and consoles him that divine grace will be sufficient to enable the apostle to bear his "thorn" (2 Cor. 12:9). Jesus prays that the "cup" of his death on the cross might "pass" from him, but is denied because of the divine will (Matt. 26:39). Remember then that all the prayers of God's people are "answered," whether with a yes or a no!

Jesus is approached by the mother of James and John (vv. 20–21). She has ambitions for her sons and they surely agree with her, for they also kneel before Jesus. Her request is breathtaking: "Grant that these two sons of mine may sit, one on Your right hand and the other on the left, in Your kingdom." This did not come out of a clear, blue sky! Jesus has already promised his disciples that "in the new world, when the Son of Man sits on the throne of His glory, you who have followed Me will also sit on twelve thrones, judging the twelve tribes of Israel" (Matt. 19:28). This apparently was not enough for Mama and her "Sons of Thunder" (Mark 3:17). Only thrones to Jesus's right and left will suffice for her boys!

Jesus gently disabuses them of their overweening aspirations (vv. 22–23). Where we, like the other ten disciples, would likely react with indignation (v. 24), Jesus gently remonstrates that they do not know what they are asking. And he tells them why: "Are you able to drink the cup that I am about to drink, and be baptized with the baptism that I am baptized with?" (v. 22bc). Jesus is asking if they (and we) are ready to suffer as he did. Glory, you see, comes at a price. And that price is a cross! Jesus has to bear all the weight of God's righteous judgment on all the sin of all the sinners he will save. That the intrepid brothers can say, "We are able," is a comment on how clueless they are about what Jesus has come to accomplish! No wonder they scattered when Jesus was arrested (John 16:32). There is only one suffering Savior, and the glory is all his. Even so, there is a sense in which all of Jesus's followers do share in Jesus's sufferings. His sufferings are the root and accomplishment of our salvation, while ours are the fruit and evidence of our salvation. The Christian is called to "know Him and the power of His resurrection, and the fellowship of His sufferings, being conformed to His death" (Phil. 3:10). First the cross, then the thrones.

Jesus calls us to be servants (vv. 25–28). Too many people want to be "famous for Jesus." Celebrity converts are routinely touted as being more influential for Jesus and as models for us all. This notion is, alas, as pernicious as it is attractive. Why? It is just the opposite of Jesus's teaching! Jesus is not influential because he became famous. He was despised and rejected by men—and still is! Christians also are regularly despised. The key to effective discipleship is not fame, or even leadership, as is endlessly trumpeted to Christian youth and students. It is lowliness, taking the last place, and following him faithfully. And so he says to us, "Whoever desires to be first...let him be your slave—just as the Son of Man did not come to be served, but to serve, and to give His life a ransom for many" (vv. 27–28). Let us pray, then, to be followers and servants, and lay worldly ambitions of fame and prominence in the dust before our Lord. Now you know what to ask for yourself!

PRAISE OF A HUMBLE HEART
Sing Psalm 131

THINGS I WILL PRAY FOR TODAY

August 21
Ask...Believing

The prayer of faith

And whatever things you ask in prayer, believing, you will receive.
—Matt. 21:22

READ MATTHEW 21:18–22; MARK 11:20–26

Years ago, I spied a shrub called a mock orange in someone's garden. It was covered with beautiful blooms. So I bought one for myself and planted it in the garden. It grew wonderfully in leafy splendor, but produced only one or two lonely blooms. It promised much but delivered little, and I was disappointed. Jesus's encounter with the fruitless fig tree tells a similar tale. Here was a tree that was green enough to promise some figs, but it turned out, upon closer inspection, to be barren. Jesus declares, "Let no fruit grow on you ever again," and the tree promptly withers (vv. 18–19). *Why* it happened is obvious enough—it is a judgment upon the offending tree. But *how* it happened is the great concern of Jesus's disciples. And what does it all mean for the rest of us? Jesus's answer is to apply this to the exercise of living faith. He does so along two distinct lines.

Jesus's first theme is the spiritual condition of the hypocrite—and the consequent necessity of a living faith (vv. 18–19). The disciples miss this—they are just "oohing and aahing" at the sudden death of the plant. But this is the first lesson and we certainly have no excuse for missing it. Jesus has just declared the temple to have been made—by the Jewish church leaders, no less—a "den of thieves" (Matt. 21:12–13). They are that fig tree—all leaves and no fruit—all show religion and no living faith, no godly practical fruit! J. C. Ryle writes, "Open sin, and avowed unbelief, no doubt slay their thousands. But profession without practice slays its tens of thousands." Jesus is writing the epitaph of the apostate church: "Let no fruit grow on you ever again." The words "ever again" translated from Greek literally read "unto the eon [i.e., age]." This indicates their judicial condemnation to future fruitlessness and ultimate death, the result of which would be the destruction of the temple in AD 70 and the end of its sacrifices. These are chilling words from Jesus's lips. And they warn churches and individuals today that, however flashy and successful they may look outwardly, with the absence of genuine inward and outward spiritual fruitfulness, they are spiritually dead. In fact, they are dicing with the eternal danger of hypocrisy before God and man. Read Matthew 23 for more of Jesus's light on this fearful state. If, then, you are a "leafy" Christian, are you also bearing fruit? That is the issue.

Jesus's second theme is the encouragement of living faith in his disciples. *How* Jesus blasted the barren fig tree was their question (vv. 20–22). Jesus's answer is, by faith! Soon, he will be gone and they will follow him in ministry in which they too will perform certain miracles. He will tell them, "Most assuredly, I say to you, he who believes in Me, the works that I do he will do also; and greater works than these he will do, because I go to My Father" (John 14:12). He had already said to them, "if you have faith as a mustard seed, you will say to this mountain, 'Move from here to there,' and it will move; and nothing will be impossible for you" (Matt. 17:20). James Boice rightly observes, "It is not a promise about moving mountains. It is a figure of speech meaning that seemingly impossible things are possible through the power of God, when the people of God take him at his word and pray in a believing way. It is an encouragement to pray often, well and rightly." The force of this is, "whatever things you ask in prayer, believing, you will receive" (v. 22).

"Believing" is not "feeling sure" about whatever you think you need or happen to want. It is trusting in the Lord for whatever is known to be consonant with his revealed will. Let us "ask...believing"—and expect his blessing.

A CONFIDENT BELIEVING PRAYER
Sing Psalm 119:153–160

THINGS I WILL PRAY FOR TODAY

_____

_____

_____

_____

_____

_____

August 22
Long Prayers

Jesus warns against pretentious prayers

Woe to you, scribes and Pharisees, hypocrites! For you…for a pretense make long prayers. — Matt. 23:14

READ MATTHEW 23:13–14;
MARK 12:40; LUKE 20:47

esus does not ban long prayers as such. Recorded biblical prayers range from the shortest (Peter's "Lord, save me!" in Matthew 14:30) to the longest (Solomon's prayer at the dedication of the temple in 1 Kings 8:26–53). Jesus often engaged in lengthy seasons of private prayer, for which purpose he would withdraw to remote places to be alone with his God and Father (Matt. 26:9; Mark 1:35). We may marvel at those who, like the English Puritan preacher Joseph Alleine (1634–68), rose at four a.m. and prayed for four hours before breakfast. But we should remember Jesus's instruction that our normal prayers be short and in secret (Matt. 6:5–6). The Lord's Prayer is the quintessential short but comprehensive prayer (Matt. 6:9–13). Jesus's watchword for all Christian prayer is surely, "When you pray, do not use vain repetitions as the heathen do. For they think that they will be heard for their many words" (Matt. 6:7).

Jesus decries long prayers that are made long "for a pretense." The context is Jesus's fearful but perfectly just "woes" against the church leaders of the time—the "scribes and the Pharisees" (23:1–39). Their hypocrisy is breathtaking, to say the least. Having detailed the enormity of their sins, Jesus passes sentence upon them: "Serpents, brood of vipers! How can you escape the condemnation of hell?" (23:33). Their so-called "ministry" is actually a ministry of death, because it can only "shut up the kingdom of heaven against men," and they can no more go in themselves than they can allow "those who are entering to go in" (v. 13). Their "long" prayers expose their deep hypocrisy. And their motives, which are to show off their religiosity and so garner the praise of men, condemn them. Calvin grieves about "how powerfully a foolish reverence for false teachers hinders simple people from getting clear of their erroneous views." Hypocrisy is not a victimless crime. Hence, Jesus says to them, "you will receive greater condemnation" (v. 14). "Our Lord's judgement," notes Kent Hughes, "was especially pronounced on those who persisted with their phony, proud, profit-making lifestyle." J. C. Ryle sums it up: "In one word, the hypocrite will have the lowest place in hell. These are awful things. But they are true."

Jesus calls us to frame our prayers with positive brevity and spiritual simplicity of expression. The believer's prayers need neither to be long, nor couched in flowery eloquence. If the Holy Spirit can intercede for us "with groanings that cannot be uttered" (Rom. 8:26), we can be assured that the simplest of sincere cries of a believing heart to the Lord will be heard and answered. Public prayers are especially susceptible to "putting on a show" just because others are there to hear them. Leading God's people in prayer may arguably be a particular gift of God, but even so, it can be abused by being too long. We should never be afraid of being "too short" or "not articulate enough." The Lord is interested in, in the words of Robert Burns, "the language of the soul." Furthermore, any breath of "show" and hypocrisy must be banished. Maurice Roberts notes that "when a truly spiritual soul is in prayer, we become conscious of the intimacy which he has with God....Those who are near to God and who are constant in prayer will turn a Prayer Meeting into a water-spring for God's thirsty people." Let us, then, always call upon the Lord with unaffected brevity and unadorned simplicity, praying with the Spirit and the understanding (1 Cor. 14:15). He will surely bless you.

A PRAYER THAT GOD WOULD HEAR OUR PRAYERS
Sing Psalm 17:1–7

THINGS I WILL PRAY FOR TODAY

_____

_____

_____

_____

_____

_____

_____

_____

August 23
Giving Account to God

Lord, you delivered to me five talents; look, I have gained five more talents besides them. — Matt. 25:20b

READ MATTHEW 25:14–30;
LUKE 19:12–27

We like to think that words are harmless. Hence the children's chant, "Sticks and stones may break my bones, but words will never hurt me." The first clause is true enough, but the second is a lie. What is more, *your own* words can hurt you: "For every idle word men may speak, they will give account of it in the day of judgment," says Jesus. "By your words you will be justified, and by your words you will be condemned" (Matt. 12:36–37). Scripture reminds us that "we shall all stand before the judgment seat of Christ" and "each of us shall give account of himself to God" (Rom. 14:10–12). Those who deny him altogether and persecute his people will not escape accountability either: "They will give an account to Him who is ready to judge the living and the dead" (1 Peter 4:5). Everyone will answer to God!

We are accountable to God in daily life. Do you not often pray "lead us not into temptation, but deliver us from evil" (Matt. 6:13)? You want to please God and bear fruit in your life for his glory. Of course, we need to be humble about the best of our service to the Lord. And Jesus is not a hard taskmaster. He encourages us with gentleness: "Take My yoke upon you and learn from Me, for I am gentle and lowly in heart, and you will find rest for your souls. For My yoke is easy and my burden is light" (Matt. 11:29–30). The calling to be Christlike in all things is the happy fruit of daily discipleship.

We have God-given responsibilities in our daily lives. In real life, the "talents" in Jesus's parable—five, two, and one—were significant amounts of money. In the story, they represent the different degrees of responsibility given to the Lord's servants "each according to his own ability" (v. 15). You know what happens: the five- and two-talent men follow through on their responsibilities and are rewarded, but the one-talent man does nothing, thereby proving he is no true servant of his master. The meaning and application is that the true servants of our Lord will work for the gospel wherever God places them. We are called to exercise our various responsibilities in the work of God's kingdom. The pseudo-believer will eventually show his true colors and confirm that his "faith" is "without works" and is "dead" (James 2:20). It is no faith at all! The challenge then is: Are you living for the Lord by taking seriously the responsibilities he has given to you?

The application to our prayer life is that we should pray accounting prayers. In Jesus's parable we have three examples of this. Those who tackled their (considerable) responsibilities were blessed in their service, were promoted to further service, and were given greater joy in the Lord (vv. 20–23). The man with the least challenging task does nothing and excuses himself by basically saying he was afraid of failure because he sees his master as "a hard man." But, of course, he loses all around. Money under the mattress shrinks, even if it only loses the interest it could have accrued at a bank. Likewise, the "do-nothing" Christian is not only a contradiction of terms and a wasting asset to himself, but he also ends up blaming God for his lack of faithfulness! Let your "accounting prayers" lead you to renewed faithfulness. Like the woman who was criticized for anointing Jesus's feet—"she has done what she could," says Jesus (Mark 14:8)—will you also do what you can out of love for Jesus? In this, you have the boundless privilege of living for him in happy expectation of him saying to you, "Well done, good and faithful servant!"

A PRAYER THAT GOD WOULD HONOR FAITHFULNESS
Sing Psalm 26

THINGS I WILL PRAY FOR TODAY

August 24
Not as I Will

A prayer of submission to God's will

O My Father, if it is possible, let this cup pass from Me; nevertheless not as I will, but as You will. — Matt. 26:39

READ MATTHEW 26:36–46;
MARK 14:32–42; LUKE 22:39–46

Prayer is for communion with God—if in the sunshine of God's blessings, then more so in the beclouded times of trials and testing. Jesus prepares for his death at the throne of grace. After the Passover meal, he and the eleven disciples sing Psalm 118 and go to the Mount of Olives to pray—"as He was accustomed" (Luke 22:39). Once there, Jesus withdraws "a little farther" to pray on his own. The disciples, whom he encourages to pray that they might "not enter into temptation," cannot stay awake. The contrast is most striking. While Jesus prays with unparalleled intensity—Luke says, "in agony...earnestly... with sweat...like great drops of blood"—his disciples fall asleep, helplessly, hopelessly, and prayerlessly depressed. This is the setting for Jesus's prayer, only the gist of which is recorded for us (vv. 39–42).

Prayer is for struggling souls. Jesus struggles with two aspects of his coming trial. One concerns the *will* of God, the other addresses the *cup* he must drink (v. 39). When Jesus says, as Luke records him saying, "if it is Your will," it looks as if he is challenging God's eternal decree. But Jesus was party to this plan of salvation "promised before time began" (Titus 1:2), knew what he was to do, loved the people he came to save, and had already fulfilled many messianic prophesies (see Ps. 18:4–5; 22:14–15; 55:4–5; 69:1–3). Why then his internal wrestling? Ambrose of Milan (AD 330–97) shows it was "necessary that he should experience grief, that he should overcome sorrow and not shut it out." Calvin notes that this "was not a pre-meditated prayer of Christ; but the strength and violence of grief suddenly drew this word from his mouth, to which he immediately added a correction." In other words, Jesus is truly human and cries out in the anticipation of extreme agony.

The "cup" Jesus must drink involves all he must go through to make atonement for sins not his own. He faces the death common to all human beings, which is of course "the wages of sin" (Rom. 6:23). He uniquely endures the spiritual and moral contradiction of his own perfect righteousness. God "made Him who knew no sin to be sin for us, that we might become the righteousness of God in Him" (2 Cor. 5:21). Also, uniquely, Jesus "had to deal with the judgment of God." God made "His soul an offering for sin" (Isa. 53:10). The sinless Son shrinks from being forsaken by his Father, God, to satisfy the penalty of sin for his people (Ps. 22:1).

Prayer is for submission to God's will. Jesus prays, "Nevertheless not as I will, but as You will" (v. 39). His single-minded submission is beautifully expressed in John 12:27–28: "Now My soul is troubled, and what shall I say? 'Father, save Me from this hour'? But for this purpose I came to this hour. Father, glorify Your name." Luke records that an angel appeared to him, "strengthening Him," and "being in agony, He prayed more earnestly" (Luke 22:43–44). Even his agony indicates his determination to go forward, for the word itself refers to intense painful striving. This is why the arena at ancient Olympia was called the *Agon*. Jesus is running the race set before *him*. "Nevertheless not as I will, but as You will" is the great coda to all faithful prayer. Jesus's obedience has made him "the author of eternal salvation to all who obey Him" (Heb. 5:7). Let us run *our* race, "looking unto Jesus, the author and finisher of *our* faith, who for the joy that was set before Him endured the cross, despising the shame, and has sat down at the right hand of the throne of God" (Heb. 12:1–2).

A SONG EXPRESSING DELIGHT TO DO GOD'S WILL
Sing Psalm 40:1–9

THINGS I WILL PRAY FOR TODAY

_____

_____

_____

_____

_____

_____

August 25
Let God Deliver Him!

Blasphemy masquerading as pious prayer

He trusted in God; let Him deliver Him now, if He will have Him; for He said, "I am the Son of God."—Matt. 27:43

READ MATTHEW 27:39–44

"All that glisters is not gold." So says William Shakespeare, who adds, for good measure, "Gilded tombs do worms enfold." The mocking by the "chief priests…scribes and elders" is an implicit prayer that assumes God will treat Jesus as the imposter they have painted him to be. Their appeal to God is, however, a "gilded tomb"—it is blasphemy hidden behind a curtain of pretended godliness. We know this simply because they condemn Jesus on two points: he cannot save himself, and therefore cannot save others (v. 42); and God will not save him, thereby exploding his claim to be the Son of God and the Messiah (v. 43). Their logic is as follows: Jesus is dying as a criminal; no true Son of God/Messiah would die as a criminal; therefore Jesus is no true Son of God/Messiah. In the name of God, they reject his Son.

Had the chief priests known *and believed* the Scriptures, they would have grasped the fallacy in their argument. God's Word is clear that the Messiah has to suffer, not only from wicked people, but also from God himself! A sound grasp of Psalms 16:10, 22:6–8, and Isaiah 53 explains that the Messiah must die as the substitutionary atonement for those he aims to save. The priests quote Psalm 22:8—"He trusted in the LORD, let Him rescue Him; Let Him deliver Him, since He delights in Him!"—and entirely miss its plain meaning. It prophecies how the *enemies* of the Messiah will mock him! The priests imagine they are speaking for God in discrediting the claims of a false messiah. In fact, they are exactly fulfilling David's prophecy in their enmity to Christ. Such is the nature of spiritual blindness. Meanwhile, the question for us is what this teaches about prayer and our relationship to Christ.

Without knowing Jesus as our Savior, our prayers can only miss the mark. The chief priests prayed to a God they did not know, whom they conceived of in terms that suited themselves—for "the natural man does not receive the things of the Spirit of God, for they are foolishness to him; nor can he know them, because they are spiritually discerned" (1 Cor. 2:14). They were students of Scripture and princes of the church, but they crucified the Lord of glory, while imagining they served the very God who both promised and sent his Son to be the Savior of sinners. Their abuse of God and of his Son, against all the evidence of Scripture and the ministry of Jesus among them, warns us against the deceitfulness of the human heart and calls us to draw close to the Lord Jesus Christ to cast all our cares upon him.

Without a crucified and risen Savior, we haven't a prayer! Jesus fully "trusted in God" and God did "deliver Him." God did "have Him" by accepting his sacrificial death as "the Lamb of God who takes away the sin of the world" (John 1:29). God confirms through the very death and resurrection of Jesus that he is indeed "His only begotten Son," given to us that "whoever believes in Him should not perish but have everlasting life" (John 3:16). The tragedy of the chief priests and their spiritual descendants in both the church and the world is that they can have all the forms and trappings of religion without the substance of a living faith. So, weep for the unconverted, pray for the salvation of the lost, and above all make sure that "you are Christ's," because "Christ is God's" (1 Cor. 3:23; cf. 2 Cor. 13:5).

MESSIAH'S PRAYER FOR DELIVERANCE FROM DEATH
Sing Psalm 16

THINGS I WILL PRAY FOR TODAY

_____

_____

_____

_____

_____

_____

_____

_____

_____

_____

August 26
Prayer on a Mountain

Jesus's practice of private prayer

And when He had sent them away, He departed to the mountain to pray.
— Mark 6:46

READ MARK 6:45–52

esus calls us to be people of prayer. Terms like "people of prayer" and "people of faith" are rather squishy nowadays. They allow people of undefined minimal and nominal "prayer" and "faith" to avoid facing the twin inconveniences of a bad conscience and the examination of their hypocrisies by others. Jesus wants prayer to be our oxygen and faith to be our fuel. His most basic emphasis is on *private* prayer alone with God: "But you, when you pray, go into your room, and when you have shut your door, pray to your Father who is in the secret place; and your Father who sees in secret will reward you openly" (Matt. 6:6). He specifically warns us against long and pretentious public prayers (Matt. 23:14; see August 22 entry). Such public show and vacuous verbosity is the death of genuine communion with God in prayer.

Jesus shows us the way. He is our perfect exemplar. Mark records that, after the feeding of the five thousand, "He departed to the mountain to pray" (v. 46). Earlier, he notes that Jesus, "having risen a long while before daylight...went out and departed to a solitary place; and there He prayed" (Mark 1:35). Luke notes that Jesus "would withdraw to desolate places and pray" (Luke 5:16). This emphasizes the twin practical themes of making prayer a *priority* and making *private prayer* the central conversation of our daily lives. Matthew Henry aptly observes that Jesus, "though he had so much preaching-work upon his hands, yet he was much in prayer; he prayed often, and prayed long." For Jesus, prayer is always a first-thought; for us, it is too often an afterthought. If you are too busy to pray, then you are just too busy and need to get some holy balance in your life! We all need time alone with God. "He went *alone*, to pray," adds the great Puritan, "though he needed not to retire for the avoiding either of distraction or of ostentation, yet, to set us an example, and to encourage us in our *secret* addresses to God, he prayed *alone*, and, for want of a closet, went up into a mountain, to pray. A good man is never less alone than when alone with God."

Jesus intercedes for us along the way. He is praying with us as we pray. Matthew Henry remarks that Jesus's prayer in the mountains and other solitary and desolate places is also "an encouragement to us to depend upon the intercession he is making for us at the right hand of the Father, that *continual* intercession." The gospel promise of salvation for all who come to Christ in faith is not applied and completed by our having come to him, but with his intercessory prayer throughout our lives: "Therefore He is also able to save to the uttermost those who come to God through Him, since He always lives to make intercession for them" (Heb. 7:25). He is our constant Mediator. Notice that while he is praying on the mountain, his disciples were in trouble "in the middle of the sea." He goes to them "walking on the sea" (vv. 47–48). Our experience of salvation runs parallel with Jesus's intercession. While we are sinking in the storms of life, Jesus is at God's right hand praying for us and with us. And so the constant discovery we make in believing prayer is that Jesus is the beginning, the middle, and the end of prayer, just as he is our salvation itself. What Jesus began in the solitude of the mountains of Judea continues "at the right hand of the throne of the Majesty in the heavens" where Jesus, our "High Priest," ministers in the heavenly sanctuary on behalf of all his people (Heb. 8:1). Let us then pray in the promise and prospect that we are never alone but constantly united to him as he intercedes for us at the throne of grace (Heb. 4:16).

PRAISE GOD WHO KEEPS US NOW AND EVERMORE
Sing Psalm 121

THINGS I WILL PRAY FOR TODAY

August 27
I Believe; Help My Unbelief!

A prayer of faith and for faith

Immediately the father of the child cried out and said with tears, "Lord, I believe; help my unbelief!" — Mark 9:24

READ MARK 9:1–29

esperate circumstances beget desperate prayers. The father was frantic for the healing of his profoundly afflicted child. But it would be a mistake to see his prayer as something altogether extraordinary. It is, says William Jay, "the common language of religious experience." As the Christian faces challenges great and small, he cannot escape the tension between what is seen and what is unseen. The trouble is seen with our own eyes—the boy has a spirit that makes him mute (v. 17) and is "convulsed" and "foaming at the mouth" (v. 20). But the power to heal him is unseen. No (seen) medicines, surgeries, or scientifically understood therapies afford any hope. As far as we can see, his condition is "incurable."

Faith, in contrast, looks into the unseen and "impossible"—and trusts and hopes in the Lord, understanding that a living faith in Christ "is the assurance of things hoped for, the conviction of things not seen" (Heb. 11:1, ESV).

The father's prayer illustrates four essential components of true prayer. If we really believe that nothing is impossible with the Lord, we will naturally turn to him for a cure of the otherwise incurable. Even so, living faith in the believer does not obliterate our succumbing to practical unbelief. This is exactly what we see in the father's prayer for his son. If we are honest, we see this disturbing tension in our own prayers, even in the ordinary stresses of the day, or the ordinary desires of the heart. Notice the four components of the father's prayer.

> First, he prays out of a *heart-felt faith*: "Lord, I believe…." Every believer has an awareness of God's work of grace in his life. The father knows Jesus to be God's sent Messiah. He has a living faith in him.

> Second, he prays confessing his *wavering faith*: "…help my

480

unbelief!" The father's faith is real, but imperfect. He hardly dares to believe. But he casts this also before the mercy of the Lord.

➢ Third, he prays with *sorrow* for his unbelief: he "said with tears...." His tears are no doubt for the boy, but surely also for his nagging fearfulness and doubt. Do you doubt the love, mercy, and power of Christ to save? Let us—of little faith—mourn our unbelief.

➢ Fourth, he cries *to Jesus* for help: he "cried out...Lord... help." The disciples elsewhere ask Jesus, "Increase our faith" (Luke 17:5). Jesus is the one Mediator reconciling sinners to God (1 Tim. 2:5)—the one alone by whom "we must be saved" (Acts 4:12).

The healing of the boy is a living parable of the fruit of Jesus's glory. The immediate context is Jesus's transfiguration, in which he gives Peter, James, and John a glimpse of his glory as it would be revealed in the future, after his death, resurrection, and ascension, and ultimately in his second coming (vv. 1–13). The boy's healing is a vivid picture of gospel salvation. The *need* is summed up in Jesus's words to his disciples: "O faithless generation, how long shall I be with you?" (v. 19). Jesus's answer is the *promise*, "all things are possible to him who believes" (v. 23). Our right *response* is, "Lord, I believe" (v. 24). And the power of God to deliver is received in "nothing but prayer and fasting" (v. 29). We are pointed to the *power* of resurrection faith in Christ, the prospect of our own resurrection (1 John 3:2), and the promise of Jesus's coming and our appearing with him in glory (Rev. 3:11–12; Col. 3:4). Believe, then, against all unbelief, and follow Jesus as your Savior from this day forth and forever.

A PRAYER FOR FAITH THAT OVERCOMES
Sing Psalm 31:9–16

THINGS I WILL PRAY FOR TODAY

_____

_____

_____

_____

August 28
Could You Not Watch One Hour?

Jesus wakes up the sleeping disciples

Simon, are you sleeping? Could you not watch one hour? Watch and pray, lest you enter into temptation. — Mark 14:37–38

READ MARK 14:32–42;
MATTHEW 26:36–46; LUKE 22:39–46

ost of us tend to lose sleep when we are faced with a personal crisis. There are those, however, who seem to find sleep in some way an antidote for anxiety. It was said of British Prime Minister Stanley Baldwin (1867–1947) that he would go to bed in a crisis. He must have slept a lot, because he presided over the Abdication Crisis of 1936, occasioned by the imminent marriage of King Edward VIII to the American divorcée Wallis Simpson, not to mention the many crises in the rise of Nazi Germany. The disciples seem to be of this ilk, for they know there is a crisis brewing with Jesus, but the closer Jesus comes to the death he keeps on predicting, the more confused and sleepy they become. Here we are in Gethsemane on the night Jesus is arrested and only hours from "the death of the cross" (Phil. 2:8). Jesus prays with such intensity that he sweats, as it were, "great drops of blood" (Luke 22:44). Meanwhile, the disciples are out for the count, such that it takes three tries to wake them up! The irony is that the only one who is awake is Judas Iscariot, the disciple who betrays him!

Jesus asks his disciples to "watch" with him (v. 37). The reason he gives them is that he is "exceedingly sorrowful even to death." A few days before, he had said to the people, "Now is My soul troubled" (John 12:27). His time—"this hour"—had come! James W. Alexander explains: "The genuine, though perfect, humanity of the Redeemer, having all the instinctive love of ease and hatred of pain which belongs to humanity, turns pale and shudders, and sinks and groans and dissolves in blood, before it drinks this cup: yet it drinks it!" He was made "to be sin for us" (2 Cor. 5:21) and, "being made a curse for us," he is able to redeem us from "the curse of the law" (Gal. 3:13). One writer comments, "He filled the silent night with his crying, and watered the cold earth with his

482

tears, more precious than the dew of Hermon; or any moisture next to his own blood, that ever fell on God's earth since the creation." It is so human to need sympathy, even if it is just the presence of friends. Fellow-feeling is the essential core of fellowship. Notice that it is not words—as with Job's comforters—that Jesus craves, but company that understands and sympathizes. Surely you know the feeling?

Jesus tells his disciples to watch "and pray" (v. 38). His reason, like a coin, has two sides to it. The obverse is "lest you enter into temptation," and the reverse is "the spirit indeed is willing, but the flesh is weak" (v. 38). Jesus knows all about temptation and is able to "sympathize with our weaknesses, but was in all points tempted as we are, yet without sin" (Heb. 4:15). If the sinless Son of Man could feel the pull of temptation, then we regular sinners of mankind will be hard put to offer serious resistance without outside help. The Lord knows that his followers will be in danger of falling away in the face of the testing time that is just around the corner. They will need all the help they can get. They could not watch out for him, but he forever watches out for *them*. They must seek his face and pray out of their weakness and need (Heb. 4:16)—not only in the secret place, but gathered together for prayer, for Jesus speaks in verse 38 in the second person *plural*. If your church has no meeting for prayer, why not begin a dedicated Mark 14:38 Prayer Meeting—and watch and pray with God's people for at least one hour each week?

A SONG OF COMMITMENT TO PERSISTENT PRAYER
Sing Psalm 123

THINGS I WILL PRAY FOR TODAY

August 29
Why Me?

Jesus's prayer of dereliction

My God, My God, why have You forsaken Me?—Mark 15:34

READ MARK 15:33–39;
MATTHEW 27:46; LUKE 23:44–49

Have you, in a personal crisis, ever asked, "Why me?" Jesus is saying something like this in the fourth of his Seven Words from the Cross. He already knows the answer: there is "no other good enough to pay the price of sin." He knows that, from the counsels of eternity, he, as the eternal Son of God, committed to his office as the incarnate Son, is the only Mediator between God and humanity (Zech. 6:13). To be forsaken by his God and Father concentrates upon him all the pains of hell deserved by all the sinners he will save. But it is much more than simply a voluntary submission to a finite punishment sufficient to save a particular number of people. It involves a breach in the fellowship of the Father and the Son. The Father never ceases to love the Son, but he separates from him when satisfying divine justice for the sin that the sinless Son undertakes to bear for his people. Earlier that week Jesus had prayed, "O My Father, if it is possible, let this cup pass from Me" (Matt. 26:39). The outcome is not in doubt—"nevertheless, not as I will, but as You will"—but the suffering is almost unimaginable. He must die if anyone is to be saved.

God forsakes his Son Jesus. Jesus cries out only the first four words of Psalm 22:1, "*Eli, Eli, lama sabachthani,*" but the full two verses express his agonizing sense of dereliction: "Why are You so far from helping Me, and from the words of My groaning? O My God, I cry in the daytime, but You do not hear; and in the night season, and am not silent" (22:1b–2). The cries of the psalmist are a prophecy of Jesus Messiah! They catch the sense we often experience in a crisis, namely that God is not listening. This is true for Jesus. On the cross he suffers an infinitely desolating abandonment by God as the righteous Judge. God withdraws from him and for the first and only time breaks the hitherto constant fellowship they have enjoyed through all eternity. Jesus, however, is faithful. He does not give up, unlike the pretend-Christian who prays for five minutes and complains God isn't there. Jesus was forsaken that we may be found and was faithful that we would be saved.

God will never forsake his children. The psalmist describes Jesus's affirmation of God's grace when he says to God, "Yet you are holy, enthroned on the praises of Israel. In you our fathers trusted; they trusted, and you delivered them" (Ps. 22:3–4). The fundamental truth here is that believers in Christ will not be forsaken because Christ was forsaken for them on Calvary's cross, where in his human nature he suffered the penalty of their sin. Because his payment of the penalty is accepted by God as satisfying his justice, everyone who believes truly in the Lord Jesus Christ will be saved. Jesus's forsakenness is overturned by his acceptance as the atonement for the sin of sinners. The resulting application to the Christian's experience of feeling forsaken is to see it more as a refining of faith than a punishment. The Lord does withdraw the blessings of his presence at times to chastise us and awaken us to our backslidings and his grace. If the heavens seem like iron and the earth like bronze (Lev. 26:19), then let us resolutely, earnestly, and confidently plead the promise of God that he will never leave us nor forsake us according to his promises (Heb. 13:5c; Deut. 31:6). The point is that, when we belong to Christ, we are *never* really forsaken. And even the sense of forsakenness is consistent with God's love, in that it is designed to draw us closer to the Lord so that we would all the more rest in his everlasting arms.

A PRAYER THAT CRIES TO GOD IN HOPE OF SALVATION
Sing Psalm 22:1–11

THINGS I WILL PRAY FOR TODAY

_____

_____

_____

_____

_____

_____

_____

August 30
Heaven Opened

Jesus prays at his baptism

While He prayed, the heaven was opened. — Luke 3:21

READ LUKE 3:21-22

Perhaps it sounds trite to say, "Prayer changes things." There is, however, no greater example of this truth in all of Scripture than that which happened at Jesus's baptism. John was baptizing repentant people in the Jordan, when Jesus attends his ministry. Then, "when all the people were baptized, it came to pass that Jesus also was baptized; and while He prayed, the heaven was opened" (Luke 3:21). Jesus prays, heaven opens, and God audibly declares Jesus to be his "beloved Son," in whom he is "well pleased"! The descent of the Holy Spirit in "bodily form like a dove" completes a quintessentially Trinitarian event in which the one God in three persons reveals the unique ministry of the Son and the dawning prospect of a new era in the history of redemption (v. 22).

Why did Jesus submit to baptism? He needed no baptism to symbolize the washing away of his sin, like John's converts, for he had no sin. Nevertheless, submission to baptism visibly declares two things: (1) Jesus's identification with sinners, and (2) his commitment to his mission as the Savior who pays the penalty of sin by his "baptism into death" on the cross and is "raised from the dead" that "we also should walk in newness of life" (Rom. 6:4). John Calvin notes that "Christ received baptism...that he might render full obedience to the Father," and also "that he might consecrate baptism in his own body, that we might have it in common with him."

Why did Jesus pray? After all, as the eternal Son of God, does he not have unhindered communion with God the Father? Yes, although he will be forsaken by the Father under the punishment of others' sin. As the incarnate Son, he is forsaken on the cross, and as the incarnate Son, Jesus bears our humanity and in it seeks communion with his God and Father. Jesus prays constantly, not merely as an example for us, but also for his own communion with God under his trials. Jesus's earthly ministry is full of his praying, as the prayer passages in the Gospels so clearly reveal. In Psalm 2:8, God the Father says to the Son of Man, "Ask of Me, and I will give You the nations for Your inheritance, and the ends of the earth for Your possession." Matthew Henry aptly observes, "What was promised to Christ, he must obtain by prayer." Again, his example applies to our becoming people of prayer: "Ask, and it will be given to you; seek, and you will find; knock and it will be opened to you" (Matt. 7:7). We can have no genuine union and communion with our Father in heaven unless we consciously and sincerely seek him with boldness at the throne of his grace in Jesus our Savior (Heb. 4:16). While our sin closes heaven, Jesus's mediation opens heaven, and his saving grace propels our prayers to the presence of his Father and ours.

God answers prayer on account of his beloved Son. While Jesus prays after being baptized, "heaven was opened." Then the Father declares of Jesus, "You are My beloved Son; in You I am well pleased." This echoes and fulfills Isaiah's prophecy of the Messiah, "Behold! My Servant whom I uphold, My Elect One in whom My soul delights! I have put My Spirit upon Him; He will bring forth justice to the Gentiles" (Isa. 42:1). When we pray out of a living faith in Jesus Christ our Lord, heaven is truly opened to us. It is not opened with the visible glory that will be revealed to us when we depart this world and meet Jesus face to face (1 Cor. 13:12). Heaven, however, is as open to us as the seal of God's acceptance and approval, without our seeing it with our eyes, as surely as it was, visibly, to Jesus on that day at the River Jordan. Our Father hears his adopted children and will answer.

PRAISE IN PROSPECT OF HEAVENLY GLORY
Sing Psalm 17:13–15

THINGS I WILL PRAY FOR TODAY

_____

_____

_____

_____

_____

_____

August 31
Far from the Madding Crowd

Making private space for secret prayer

So He Himself often withdrew into the wilderness and prayed.
—Luke 5:16

READ LUKE 5:12–16

We all have felt the need of "getting away from it all," escaping the hurly-burly of our lives for the unhurried quiet of some bucolic scene. The poet Thomas Gray (1716–71) expresses this in his famous *Elegy Written in a Country Churchyard*, when he says of the deceased villagers of Stoke Poges:

Far from the madding crowd's ignoble strife,
Their sober wishes never learn'd to stray;
Along the cool sequester'd vale of life
They kept the noiseless tenor of their way.
  (Lines 73–76)

This was a romantic reflection on the life of country folk. In fact, for all those moments under the "nodding beech" when "his listless length at noontide would he stretch, /And pore upon the brook that babbles by," (lines 101, 103–104) the peasant's life was one of hard work and meager returns.

When Jesus "withdrew into the wilderness" it was not to stretch his "listless length" under a rock and "pore upon" the scenery. He did so for several very important reasons. One is his burgeoning popularity—or perhaps we should say growing notoriety. His life is increasingly lived in a goldfish bowl. The upside of this is that more people are attending his ministry. The downside is that some in high places will soon want to silence him, but he has his own timetable for that. In the early days he declines to go up to Jerusalem because, he says, "my time is not yet come" (John 7:6, 8). The day does come eventually when he tells his disciples, "The hour has come that the Son of man should be glorified," and predicts his imminent death on the cross (John 12:23, 27ff.). Jesus's withdrawals have a unique purpose, and that is to time exactly the occasion of his arrest, death, burial, and resurrection (see Matt. 12:14; Mark 3:7).

488

The other reason is to get away from "the madding crowd" for the purpose of prayer. He is willing to heal those who come to him in genuine faith (vv. 12–13), but also needs private space for himself and his communion with his Father. In Mark 1:35, we read that "In the morning, having risen a long while before daylight, He went out and departed to a solitary place; and there He prayed." He made space for his personal praying and chose places and times when he would neither be observed nor disturbed. He warns us that it is "hypocrites" who "love to pray" where "they may be seen by men" (Matt. 6:5). Private prayer is for secret and intimate communion with the Lord, whose love has saved us and united us to him in personal faith and fellowship.

We therefore need to make private space for secret prayer. Jesus urges us, "But you, when you pray, go into your room, and when you have shut your door, pray to your Father who is in the secret place; and your Father who sees in secret will reward you openly" (Matt. 6:6). Matthew Henry observes, "Secret prayer must be made secretly. Those that have the most business in public, and of the best kind, must sometimes be *alone with God*; must retire into *solitude*, there to converse with God, and keep up communion with him." James and Joel Beeke have written, "He who does not pray privately is his own thief and murderer. He robs himself of the greatest blessings and kills his own spiritual life. Every newborn child cries for its mother: every spiritually newborn child of God calls out to Him. Can it be said of you as it was said of Saul at Damascus, 'Behold, he is praying'?" (Acts 9:11b).

PRAISE FOR SHELTER IN GOD'S "SECRET PLACE"
Sing Psalm 91

THINGS I WILL PRAY FOR TODAY

September 1
Up All Night

Prayer that cannot wait until tomorrow

He went out to the mountain to pray, and continued all night in prayer to God. — Luke 6:12

READ LUKE 6:12–16

Sleeplessness is not always a bad thing. Even if a personal crisis keeps us awake, we have opportunity to turn to the Lord in prayer. Are you upset with someone? Then, says the psalmist, "Be angry, and do not sin. Meditate within your heart on your bed, and be still" (Ps. 4:4). "I am weary with my groaning," he says. "All night I make my bed swim; I drench my couch with my tears" (Ps. 6:6). If it is just an active mind that keeps you up, then redeem the time by meditation on the things of God: "When I remember You on my bed, I meditate on You in the night watches" (Ps. 63:6). Some prayers cannot wait until tomorrow.

Jesus stays up all night to pray. Why should God the Son need to pray at all, never mind at such length (v. 12)? Was his communication with the Father not instantaneous, continuous, and complete? Surely, from eternity, he knew all the answers? Had he not, with the Father and the Holy Spirit, decreed the plan of salvation? The answer lies in his incarnation. As the Son who is "born of a woman, born under the law" (Gal. 4:4), Jesus is one person with two natures—a human and a divine. Jesus in his earthly ministry plays fair in his human nature as a man. He is truly God and truly man, but it is as a man that he exercises his earthly ministry in relation to the Father. He therefore prays in his human nature out of submission to the Father. As a man, he is "touched with the feeling of our infirmities" (Heb. 4:15, KJV). He prays as we are to pray—as a human being who is submissive to his Father, God, and striving to do his will.

Jesus prays all night because the matter is really important. He prays about the calling of his "apostles" (v. 13–16). The rule is, the greater the need, the longer the prayer. This is even true of hypocrites, who "for a pretense make long prayers" (Mark 12:40). Their reward is to impress people with their (false) piety. The efficacy of a prayer certainly is not in

490

either its length or its public visibility (see Matt. 6:5). However, when we have a lot to pray about, do we not tend to pray a lot about it? And should we not, as Ed Robson (an older pastor) counseled me as a young man, "pray till the matter is settled"? That is exactly what Jesus did. He is our great exemplar. He went to a secret place and talked to his heavenly Father until the matter was settled. The future leadership of the church was the issue and that exercised him tremendously. And when morning came he didn't go right to his bed to catch up on lost sleep, but called his disciples together and "chose twelve whom He also named apostles" (v. 13).

Jesus wants us all to be praying people. Here he gives us, says Matthew Henry, "an example of secret prayer, by which we must keep up our communion with God daily, and without which it is impossible that the soul should prosper." Secret prayer is basic to the Christian's life and spiritual growth. It is a means of God's grace to those who love him. In the words of Joseph Scriven (1819–60),

Blessed Saviour, You have promised
    You will all our burdens bear
May we ever, Lord, be bringing
    all to You in earnest prayer.
Soon in glory bright unclouded
    there will be no need for prayer
Rapture, praise and endless worship
    will be our sweet portion there.
—"What a Friend We Have in Jesus," stanza 4

PRAISE TO THE GOD WHO ANSWERS PRAYER
Sing Psalm 5

THINGS I WILL PRAY FOR TODAY

_____

_____

_____

_____

_____

_____

_____

491

September 2
Where Is Your Faith?

The believers' unbelieving prayer

Master, Master, we are perishing!—Luke 8:24b

READ LUKE 8:22–25;
MATTHEW 8:23–27; MARK 4:35–41

hy did the Savior cross the lake? Not just "to get to the other side"! Luke makes it clear that Jesus had business with both "the power of the air" and the "prince of the power of the air" (Eph. 2:2). He confronts the wind and the waves and also the demons that afflict the man from Gadara. In the storm he demonstrates his power over nature, and, with the demoniac, his power over evil. But there is something more here that is easily missed. As they cross the Sea of Galilee, a ferocious windstorm suddenly blows up. Jesus is asleep and has to be wakened by his frantic companions. Convinced the vessel is foundering, they cry out in a desperate half prayer, half epitaph, "Master, Master, we are perishing!" Jesus's reaction is to rebuke the "wind and the raging of the water," with the result that "they ceased and there was a calm" (v. 24). The disciples are amazed, but this immediately gives way to fear, when Jesus rebukes *them*, saying, "Where is your faith?" This question tells us some vital truths about prayer as it relates to the faith of the believer and to the grace of the Lord Jesus Christ whom we profess to believe.

The Scriptures tell us that "whatsoever is not of faith is sin" (Rom. 14:43). Jesus's rebuke indicates that it is possible to be a believer and yet come to the Lord with a prayer that is not a *believing* prayer. There is no evidence that the disciples really thought he could save them. It is clear that they did not expect Jesus to calm the storm, because when he did they "marveled" and asked, "Who can this be?" (v. 25). In other words, their idea of Jesus is still too small—as is their faith.

In stilling the storm, Jesus enlarges our view of who he really is. He is the Messiah come with power to save. Weather normally operates in a way that is intelligible in terms of measurable forces. Even so, the world is not a closed "under the sun" system. Scripture tells us that it is upheld by the word of Christ's power (Heb. 1:3). This is the fourth dimension of created reality. This is where "the finger of God" touches the natural world (Ex. 8:19).

Jesus answers the despairing half prayer of his disciples. He loves believers and answers their less-than-believing prayer by giving them more than they "ask, or think" (Eph. 3:20). This is just as well for them—and for us—because even our best prayers can miss the mark by asking for the wrong things or even the right things with the wrong motive. This tells us something wonderful about the grace of God. His answering of our prayers is propelled by free grace in him, rather than any perfection in our petitions. Jesus "knows our frame; He remembers that we are dust" (Ps. 103:14). Well do we pray in gratitude for his grace: "If You, Lord, should mark iniquities, O Lord, who could stand?" (Ps. 130:3). Even when our prayers are flawed, his grace answers with everlasting love.

Jesus teaches us to pray as much with his answers as with his precepts and example. He teaches the disciples, through the storm, to pray out of a real trust in God that expects blessing, as opposed to blurting out a desperate but essentially unbelieving and untrusting cry of despair. He understands why we are so often fearful, but he wants us to understand that despair is never the response of faith. He teaches us that there are no storms in life he cannot still and overthrow. Some he instantly subdues, as on the lake. Others, like Paul's "thorn in the flesh," may never go away, but he assures us, "My grace is sufficient for you" (2 Cor. 12:9). In every circumstance he calls us to "be still and know that I am God" (Ps. 46:10). God is still on the throne and he will remember his own.

PRAISE TO THE GOD WHO IS OUR REFUGE
Sing Psalm 46

THINGS I WILL PRAY FOR TODAY

_____

_____

_____

_____

_____

_____

_____

September 3
The Lord of Glory

Jesus prays and is transfigured

As He prayed, the appearance of His face was altered.—Luke 9:29

READ LUKE 9:28-36

Go back 2,000 years. You are one of Jesus's disciples. You saw him walk on water, feed the 5,000, heal the sick, and raise the dead. Then you saw his arrest, trial, and judicial murder on that awful cross! Would you have asked, "Where is the glory now?" Would you have been less devastated than Peter and the others, as you contemplated Jesus's death? But Jesus told you ahead of time about his imminent death. Three times, in fact, and with the assurance that he would rise on the third day, victorious over death and the grave, and therefore be the conqueror of sin and the guarantor of salvation. On one of these occasions—surely he saw your dejection?—he offered this comfort: "But I tell you truly, there are some standing here who shall not taste death till they see the kingdom of God" (Luke 9:27). Jesus will suffer death and the disciples will deny themselves and spend their lives for the Lord, but they will see something of God's kingdom in its power and glory with their eyes in this life! And how did this happen?

A week later, Jesus "took Peter, John and James up on the mountain to pray." There, in answer to his prayer, Jesus was transfigured: "As He prayed, the appearance of His face was altered, and his robe became white and glistening" (Luke 9:28–29; cf. Mark 9:2–3). Moses and Elijah also appeared and they conversed with Jesus about "His decease which He was about to accomplish at Jerusalem." Then a cloud enveloped the whole company, Moses and Elijah disappeared, and God's voice from the cloud declared, "This is My beloved Son. Hear Him!" Immediately, the cloud cleared and the three disciples found themselves alone with Jesus. The disciples were dumbfounded and "told no one in those days any of the things they had seen" (vv. 31–36). The question is: What were they—and what are we—to make of it all?

Jesus is transfigured, the disciples are thrilled but confused, and God speaks the Word. This transfiguration is a definite glimpse of the glory of the Lord Jesus Christ. There is a parallel with God's revelation of glory to Moses on the mountain and Moses's later "transfiguration" (Ex. 24:9ff.; 34:29–35). Jesus's transfiguration, however, shows him to be the fulfillment of both the covenant given through Moses and the restoration prophesied through Elijah. Jesus must go to the cross, but this will be glory for him and glory from God forever after.

That Jesus prays and is gloriously transfigured as he prays, affirms his office as the Messiah. His transfiguration assures us of his power to save. As the incarnate Son of God, he endures the ultimate humiliation of bearing the just judgment upon sin not his own, so that he saves his people from their sin (Matt. 1:21). J. C. Ryle notes that Jesus, in the context of the disciples' discouragement, "takes off the edge of his 'hard sayings', by promising a sight of that glory to some of those who heard him. And in the...transfiguration, which is here recorded, we see that promise fulfilled." Jesus's death will issue in greater glory for himself and for his Father, as well as issue in salvation for all who will trust in him as Savior and Lord. "My sheep hear My voice," Jesus declares, "and I know them, and they follow Me. And I give them eternal life, and they shall never perish; neither shall anyone snatch them out of My hand" (John 10:27–28). What the disciples saw was also a foretaste of the glory that will transfigure all of the redeemed on that day when Jesus returns at the end of the age. Will you pray for that day? That day when he will make known to you "what are the riches of the glory of this mystery among the Gentiles: which is Christ in you, the hope of glory" (Col. 1:27).

PRAISE TO THE EXALTED CHRIST
Sing Psalm 118:19–29

THINGS I WILL PRAY FOR TODAY

_____

_____

_____

_____

_____

_____

_____

_____

September 4
Lord, Teach Us to Pray

The model for prayer (again)

So He said to them, "When you pray, say..."—Luke 11:2a

READ LUKE 11:1–4

ost people assume prayer comes naturally. Who does not pray in a crisis? Does the Bible not say of God, "O You who hear prayer, to You all flesh will come" (Ps. 65:2)? Well, yes and no! Why? Because it begs the question as to what kind of prayer comes *naturally* to folk who think of praying, and of God, only when they are in trouble. For example, God doesn't accept the "vain repetitions" of "the heathen" as genuine prayer, because they merely "think they will be heard for their many words" (Matt. 6:7). He has no time for the showy, self-centered prayers of the hypocritical church people either (Matt. 6:5). Why so? The answer is that "without faith it is impossible to please Him, for he who comes to God must believe that He is, and that He is a rewarder of those who diligently seek Him" (Heb. 11:6). God tells us plainly the consequences of faithless prayer: "I will make your heavens like iron and your earth like bronze" (Lev. 26:18). The prayer that comes naturally does not make the grade *spiritually*. Sadly, so much "prayer" is just desperate noise sent into the void, with no more than a vague hope there is someone out there listening.

The only acceptable prayer is believing prayer. John Bunyan's definition of true prayer catches this beautifully and challengingly: "Prayer is a sincere, sensible, affectionate pouring out of the heart or soul to God, through Christ, in the strength and assistance of the Holy Spirit, for such things as God has promised, or according to his Word, for the good of the church, with submission in faith to the will of God." This was the kind of prayer the unnamed disciple heard as Jesus "was praying in a certain place." It led him to ask, "Lord, teach us to pray" (Luke 1:11). That disciple was a follower of Jesus and he clearly did not think prayer came naturally. He realized he needed to be taught how to pray. When he heard Jesus it dawned on him that prayer was not just a matter of reciting a form of words or blurting out a bunch of requests, no matter how sincere one felt them to be.

In response, Jesus gives the Lord's Prayer for a second time. Here is a model or pattern for our own prayers. It ought to be memorized and often repeated, but never rattled off by rote and thus made a ritual form of words. The Lord's Prayer teaches us priorities in prayer, to help us order our thoughts and concerns in proportion to their real weight. Paul tells us to be praying "with all *prayer* and *supplications*" (Eph. 6:18; italics added). The Lord's Prayer is in the former category—we might call it a "*prayer-*prayer," that is, a prayer that is formed around the basic framework of our relationship and walk with God. A "*supplication-*prayer" is more specific, circumstantial, urgent, and even unusual. Obviously, supplications may be spread on the Lord's Prayer, each one related to a theme in the outline (see tomorrow's meditation). But there needs to be a balance between the prayer proper and the supplications incorporated in it. We are not just consumers or complainers who only come to the Lord when we want him to give us something! "Prayer requests" are not *prayer itself as an exercise of the soul.* They are the practical fruit and focus of our communion with God. Following the form of the Lord's Prayer will help us to resist letting supplications (prayer requests) crowd out a prayer which is, after all, designed to be conscious conversation with our Father in heaven. This prayer does not come naturally, but by the teaching of the Lord. If it is not of faith, it is nothing at all.

PRAISE FOR THE HEARER OF PRAYER
Sing Psalm 65:1–4

THINGS I WILL PRAY FOR TODAY

September 5
The Shape of Living Prayer

The model for prayer (yet again)

So He said to them, "When you pray, say..."—Luke 11:2a

READ LUKE 11:2–4

he Lord's Prayer is surely the perfect pattern for our praying. Scripture abounds with prayers that teach us how to pray, but the Lord's Prayer is specifically given as a model outline for our prayers. It helps us think through our concerns and, most significantly, shows us how to approach the throne of grace with heartfelt reverence for the living God. Prayer is a thoroughly Trinitarian experience, for we come to God our heavenly Father through Jesus his Son and our Mediator, and by the ministrations of the Holy Spirit, our "Helper" in our hearts (John 14:26). You are never alone when you pray faithfully. The Lord assures you that "whatever things you ask in prayer, believing, you will receive" (Matt. 21:22). The outline is simple enough: there is an Invocation (v. 2b), followed by several Petitions (vv. 2c–4). (Matthew also records a doxology in his record of Jesus's first giving this prayer—see Matt. 6:13b).

The prayer begins with an *invocation*: "Our Father in heaven." These simple words call us to the reverent adoration of God and exhibit three distinct attitudes of heart:

- The first is *trust*, for God is "our" Father and we are his adopted children. This is personal, for in believing in Jesus our Savior we have peace with God and experience his fatherly care (Rom. 5:1; 8:15; Gal. 4:6; cf. Mark 14:36).
- The second is *adoration* for the divine Father who is "in heaven" and is the focus of our praise and worship in and through his Son, Jesus: "And the Word became flesh and dwelt among us, and we beheld His glory, the glory as of the only begotten of the Father, full of grace and truth" (John 1:14).
- Finally, he is therefore the One we *love* because he has first loved us and revealed his salvation to us in Christ: "Who is a God like You, pardoning iniquity and passing over the transgression

of the remnant of His heritage? He does not retain His anger forever, because He delights in mercy" (Mic. 7:18).

Specific petitions **comprise the body of the prayer.** These are in two groups, one focusing on God's *purposes*, the other on our *needs*.

God's purposes are expressed in three petitions: his glory, his goal, and his program for us (v. 2c–e). We pray "hallowed be Your name" and so lift up his glory in himself, in his perfect holiness. We pray "Your kingdom come," that his rule may be advanced through Jesus's victory in our personal lives and in the life of the church and world. We pray "Your will be done" because it is of first importance that his holy law and gospel grace be applied in this world and in our lives. Accordingly, we *adore* him, *affirm* his goals, and *agree* with his will being done "on earth as it is in heaven."

Our needs are likewise laid out in three petitions: our physical sustenance, our spiritual well-being, and our protection and perseverance in the faith (vv. 3–4). We pray for "our daily bread"—admitting our dependence on God's provision. We pray "forgive us our sins" with the testimony that we already acted to "forgive everyone who is indebted to us." We thereby confess our total indebtedness to Christ's free grace and everlasting mercy through his death on the cross. We plead that we not be led "into temptation" but be delivered from "the evil one." In other words, we ask for guidance to make the right decisions, and we need liberation from sin, in all its forms. In short, we admit we are *dependent* on the Lord, are *debtors* to his love and mercy, and need ongoing *deliverance* day by day from temptation and sin. Let us daily come to Jesus to "ask in faith, with no doubting" (James 1:6).

A BELIEVER'S PRAYER FOR DELIVERANCE
Sing Psalm 38:15–22

THINGS I WILL PRAY FOR TODAY

_____

_____

_____

_____

_____

_____

September 6
Pressing Onward

A parable of persistence in prayer

So I say to you, ask, and it will be given to you; seek, and you will find;
knock, and it will be opened to you. — Luke 11:9

READ LUKE 11:5-13

I t is often said that the squeaky wheel gets the grease. This is usually meant as criticism of complainers who whine and nag until they get what more noble, uncomplaining souls deserve but are denied by their suffering in silence. Fine, we get the message. But the other side to this is that rusty hinges do need lubrication and the answer to a real need may require repeated pleas for help. There is no particular virtue in not seeking help when you really need it.

Genuine need is, to be sure, the real issue. This is certainly the burden of Jesus's parable of the persistent friend in Luke 11:5–8. One man has a sudden emergency. A friend has just visited him and he has nothing in the house with which to feed him. It is midnight and the stores are closed; so, in desperation, he wakens his neighbor and asks for three loaves. The neighbor is not pleased and obviously thinks it can wait until morning. You notice that Jesus asks at the outset, "Which of you shall have a friend?" as if to say to all of us, "What would you do in this situation?" Whatever side of the door you were on, you would make a real effort to meet a friend's need. But the chances are that if you are the one dragged from your bed, it may take some persuasion to even help your friend then and there. What does Jesus say? He says, "I say to you, though he will not rise and give to him because he is his friend, yet because of his persistence he will rise and give him as many as he needs" (v. 8). Yes! The squeaky wheel will get the grease! Does Jesus criticize either the man with the need or the man who eventually helped him? No, Jesus makes practical application of the parable to prayer in the believer's life. He is teaching us *how* to pray (Luke 11:1).

Jesus's first application is that we must persist in our praying (vv. 9–10). We are to "ask...seek...knock." I once saw a church billboard that said, "Try prayer." Lots of people "try" prayer and never really get to asking, seeking, and knocking. Real prayer presses toward its goal. Pressing onward inevitably tests your faith. If your faith is true saving faith in Christ, you won't just "try" prayer. You will rather be like Jacob who, when he wrestled with the Angel, said, "I will not let You go unless You bless me" (Gen. 32:26). Why? You are committed to asking, seeking, and knocking, because you know God is committed to answering, albeit in his timing and his way. The persistent friend at midnight teaches us to pray and never give up. The sleepy neighbor assures us that God hears and will answer our prayers, whether it is only after asking, or following seasons of seeking and knocking. Merely "trying" prayer can only be trying to the Lord, because without faith it is impossible to please God (Heb. 11:6). Faith is first; prayer follows.

Jesus's second application is to affirm the promise of answers to persistent prayer. He argues from the lesser to the greater: we are not just talking about a friend-friend relationship, but that of a heavenly Father to his children. What do fathers—real fathers—do for their children in need? The answer is obvious (vv. 11-12). It follows that if you, "being evil"—that is, in a sinful, imperfect state—"know how to give good gifts to your children, how much more will your heavenly Father give the Holy Spirit to those who ask Him?"(v. 13). God *loves* his children more than we love ours. And God *gives* his children infinitely more than we can give ours. More than daily bread, he gives his Holy Spirit—the Spirit of adoption by which we cry "Abba, Father"—the Spirit who "bears witness with our spirit that we are the children of God" (Rom. 8:15–16). Let us then ask, seek, and knock in our praying, for we will surely find the Lord faithful to his promises.

A SONG OF COMMITMENT TO PRAYER
Sing Psalm 55:16–23

THINGS I WILL PRAY FOR TODAY

September 7
Father, I Have Sinned

The prayer of the lost son

And the son said to him, "Father, I have sinned against heaven and in your sight, and am no longer worthy to be called your son."—Luke 15:21

READ LUKE 15:11–21

 one of Jesus's parables is better known than that of the lost son. It so vividly portrays the desolation of a godless life, and the glory of the grace of God receiving his repentant child. The son leaving home is a picture of the way and the end of unbelief:

- He distances himself from his father, in "a far country" (v. 13).
- He wastes his personal assets and life-potential (v. 13).
- He suffers famine, both physical and spiritual (v. 14).
- He is in a dead end—he has to "feed swine" (v. 15).
- He wallows in intense frustration (v. 16a).
- He finds himself alone, in growing isolation (v. 16b).
- He is gripped by the feeling that his life is over (v. 17).

His dreams dashed, his life in ruins, he stares despairingly into eternity. He has discovered, the hard way, that the Lord "turns upside down" the "way of the wicked" (Ps. 146:9). Several things must happen for a lost soul to be found.

The young man "came to himself" (v. 17). This is God's sovereign grace at work—the "washing of regeneration and the renewing of the Holy Spirit" (Titus 3:5). The Lord "opened" his heart (Acts 16:14). "How many of my father's hired servants," he asks himself, "have bread enough and to spare, and I perish with hunger!" He looks squarely at the facts and sees himself as God—and others—see him. He comes to an end of himself and to the beginning of a new life redeemed from the ashes of the old. God has given him "a broken spirit, a broken and a contrite heart" (Ps. 51:17). The scales have fallen from his eyes—he who once was blind can now see.

He admits and confesses his sin: "I will arise and go to my father, and will say to him, 'Father, I have sinned against heaven and before you,'"

(v. 18). Genuine conviction of sin always sees it primarily as sin against God, and then secondarily as sin against those who have been wronged (Ps. 51:4). Why? God holds us to account for every sin of thought, word, and deed. His justice is as rigorous as it is righteous: "The Lord is the avenger of all such" (1 Thess. 4:16).

He casts himself on his father's mercy: "I am no longer worthy to be called your son. Make me like one of your hired servants" (v. 19). He makes no claim on his father. He had squandered his inheritance. His father owed him nothing. But he comes in *hope* of mercy. Why? He knows the character of his father. The God of the Bible reveals himself to be "the God of all grace" (1 Peter 5:10). Jesus still says to all who will hear him, "All that the Father gives Me will come to Me, and the one who comes to Me I will by no means cast out" (John 6:37). God is still "the Father of mercies" who calls "all men everywhere to repent" (2 Cor. 1:3; Acts 17:30).

He acts on his new faith; "he arose and came to his father" (vv. 19–20). Notice that long before he could confess his sin, his father "saw him and had compassion, and ran and fell on his neck and kissed him." Yes, he had "sinned against heaven" and is "no longer worthy to be called [a] son." But God, our Father in heaven, delights in mercy and rejoices to welcome all repentant and returning prodigals as his children: "But as many as received Him, to them He gave the right to become children of God, to those who believe in His name" (John 1:12). "Let the wicked forsake his way, and the unrighteous man his thoughts; let him return to the LORD, and He will have mercy on him; and to our God, for He will abundantly pardon" (Isa. 55:7). Then let us live as those who know him as our Father in heaven.

A SONG OF REPENTANCE AND NEW FAITH
Sing Psalm 51:9–19

THINGS I WILL PRAY FOR TODAY

_____

_____

_____

_____

_____

September 8
A Great Gulf Fixed

A "prayer" from hell

Then he cried and said, "Father Abraham, have mercy on me, and send Lazarus that he may dip the tip of his finger in water and cool my tongue; for I am tormented in this flame." — Luke 16:24

READ LUKE 16:22–31

The story of the rich man and Lazarus is unique in Scripture in that it describes the feelings of the lost after death. This is a parable, not a documentary movie of real people in eternity, but like all fictional stories it offers a window on something the author wants us to see. In this incomparable piece of divinely inspired Christian fiction, Jesus is facing us with the reality of hell, the plight of the lost, and the need of the gospel way of salvation. We should be careful not to over-interpret parables. There is no seeing into heaven from hell and there are no bodies in eternity until resurrection day (except for Jesus, Enoch, and Elijah). There are, however, lost people in hell and saved people in heaven, and we are here given insight into the reprobate mind via the person of the rich man.

The rich man prays from hell. Jesus sets this up as a conversation between hell and heaven, between the rich man and Abraham, in whose bosom the poor man rests. The point of this tableau is that both men are children of Abraham, of God's people, the Jews, but one is saved and the other is damned. Lazarus is saved by grace, not poverty, while the rich man is lost by unbelief, not his riches (his use of which only reveals his inner contempt for God and the poor man). There are three parts to the rich reprobate's prayer.

> *Petition one* — "Have mercy on me" (vv. 23–26). He wants mercy in his torment, but — surprise! surprise! — only *his* mercy! He is totally self-absorbed. There is no repentance for oppressing Lazarus or neglecting the things of God, and as there is no repentance in hell, there can be no so-called "second chance" and no possibility of redemption. There is a "great gulf fixed" between earth and eternity, heaven and earth.

504

- *Petition two* — "Send him to my father's house" (vv. 27–29). His thoughts now turn to his "five brothers." Let Lazarus warn them so they can escape hell. Abraham responds, "They have Moses and the prophets; let them hear them." That is, they have God's message of saving grace! The rich man knows nothing of gospel grace, but he knows his example has pointed his brothers to hell. And it won't be a happy reunion when they arrive! The truth is, the rich man is still just seeking relief for himself. He is miserably remorseful but totally unrepentant.

- *Petition three* — "They will repent" (vv. 30–31). "No they won't," says Abraham. If people will not listen to God's Word, even raising Lazarus from the dead will not convince them! Jesus gives the world exactly one sign, "the sign of Jonah" (Matt. 12:39–41), his own fully attested resurrection. Do all people turn to him as their Savior? No: "Jews seek signs, Greeks look for wisdom" (1 Cor. 1:22). The rich man neither believed God nor had that faith that is "being sure of what we hope for and certain of what we do not see" (Heb. 11:1).

Hell will be full of prayers but heaven full of praises. The irony is that the lost will pray self-serving prayers in eternity as they never prayed in this life. Those who prayed in this life, believing in Christ, will never pray in heaven for any need, except to praise the Lord for all his goodness in time and eternity and enjoy the perfect fruition of all the promises that are yes and amen in Jesus Christ our Lord.

A SONG THAT WARNS US ABOUT HELL
Sing Psalm 9:11–20

THINGS I WILL PRAY FOR TODAY

— To work out my salvation

September 9
Faith as a Mustard Seed

A prayer asking for more faith

And the apostles said to the Lord, "Increase our faith." —Luke 17:5

READ LUKE 17:1–6

Who does not want an increase of faith? More pointedly, who does not *need* a deeper faith? Jesus's disciples feel that need. Jesus abjures them to forgive people who have sinned against them and express repentance, even to seven times a day (vv. 1–4). Matthew records Jesus as saying "seventy times seven"—which means as often as it happens (Matt. 18:22). This blew their minds: Who is ever going to begin to be so forgiving? And how do we judge whether the repentance is sincere? Hence the question—actually a prayer with eyes wide open—"Increase our faith." After all, the most ordinary challenges—never mind those trials faced by believers like Abel, Noah, Abraham, Sarah, Isaac, Jacob, Joseph, Moses, and the others recounted in Hebrews 11—find us needing more faith, more solidity, in our trust in the Lord Jesus Christ. Our daily lives constantly confront us with the claims of faithfulness. And so do the doubts that lead us to cry out in the weakness of our faith, "Lord, I believe; help my unbelief!" (Mark 9:24). William Jay, the great preacher of Bath, observes, "an increase of faith is not only always desirable, but sometimes necessary." Jesus is asking his followers to live a real Christian life. He presents two main pointers as to how this must happen.

Turn your felt need into believing prayer (v. 5). The disciples feel weak and do two things: they turn to Jesus their "Lord" as the one who can supply their need; and they ask, literally, *"Add to us* faith." Joseph Scriven (1819–86) was twice engaged to be married. His first fiancée was drowned the day before their wedding, and the second also died before their wedding day. In his famous hymn, "What a Friend We Have in Jesus," he testifies to God's amazing grace in his life and catches the spirit of Luke 17:5.

> Are we weak and heavy laden,
> cumbered with a load of care?
> Precious Savior, still our refuge,

Take it to the Lord in prayer.
Do your friends despise, forsake you?
Take it to the Lord in prayer!
In His arms He'll take and shield you;
You will find a solace there.
    (stanza 3)

Realize that all you really need is "faith as a mustard seed" **(v. 6).** The mustard seed is tiny, as seeds go, but it is alive and has potential for tremendous growth. Jesus uses this as an illustration of the growth of the kingdom of God in this world (Mark 4:30–32). So the issue is not so much "How much faith?"—how impressive it may appear—but rather, "How *alive* is your faith in Jesus Christ?" Furthermore, remember that faith is always exercised *at a point*. In our passage the application of faith revolves around our response to the question, "Will I forgive this person, or will I still resent and accuse him? Whatever victories of faithfulness you have seen in the past are irrelevant, because *this* is the moment of testing now. Paul is saying that even a tiny dab of real faith in exercise will move that "mulberry tree" of wounded resentment and move it to the sea of forgetting forgiveness. The issue, as always, is the cross and your relationship to Jesus Christ as your Savior. Has he forgiven you? Then is a "forgiving spirit" not the air breathed by your forgiven soul? It ought to be, because it is the evidence of a saving interest in Christ. In Christ, who first loved you in your lostness, can you find no love for those who are his in their weakness? May the Lord increase your faith!

A SONG OF RESTING IN GOD FOR SALVATION
Sing Psalm 119:81–88

THINGS I WILL PRAY FOR TODAY

September 10
Where Are the Nine?

Gratitude is essential after answered prayer

So Jesus answered and said, "Were there not ten cleansed? but where are the nine?"—Luke 17:17

READ LUKE 17:11–19

ooner or later we will all experience serious health needs. But the ten lepers were already there. You feel their desperation. No doctor could help them, so they were doomed to be outcasts, separated to the undying misery of a living death. This is, of course, emblematic of the universal human problem with sin, death, and judgment to come: "the wages of sin is death" (Rom. 6:23). Sin is the leprosy of the soul. But as surely as the ten lepers called on Jesus to cure their illness, we sinners can call upon the Lord for salvation. The lepers needed a supernatural work of healing. We all need a supernatural work of redemption involving the regeneration of our very human nature (i.e., to be "born again") and our subsequent coming to saving faith in Christ (our conversion). The healing of the lepers points us to Jesus as the Savior of all those who call upon his name for salvation.

The ten lepers cried to Jesus and were healed. These men knew enough about Jesus to call on him by name as the "Master" who could "have mercy" upon them (v. 13b). They had enough faith to call on Jesus. Jesus responds by first sending them "to the priests," and only when they are on their way does the healing take place. Why the priests? Jesus was keeping God's Law, which prescribed that the priests certify that healing has occurred (Lev. 14:2–3). Why delayed healing? To ensure that the lepers acted on their faith in Jesus. In this way, the healings bore unimpeachable testimony to Jesus's power and deity (cf. Col. 2:9). Note two things:

> "Help meets men in the path of obedience," writes J. C. Ryle. We will never meet God halfway, but we can turn toward him, believing and praying. We will become close with Christ if we are his disciples.

> All ten men were healed, but only one, a Samaritan, came back to say thank-you to Jesus. He had a living faith in Jesus—his

faith had made him "whole" (see v. 19). What of the nine? They had a kind of faith, but it did not last. They were healed, but were they saved?

Will you be thankful for God's goodness to you? "The best of us," says J. C. Ryle, "are far too like the nine lepers." There is so much unthinking ingratitude in human hearts. So many blessings are received for what they are, yet never improved upon in terms of a right acknowledgment of God's grace. So many today, like the nine lepers, are healed of serious sickness but remain seriously lost! Will you pray for a thankful spirit? God says in his Word, "Be anxious for nothing, but in everything by prayer and supplication with thanksgiving, let your requests be known unto God" (Phil. 4:6). The Lord wants us to pray out of a sense of our need, but not without giving thanks. Listen to the psalmist: "O LORD my God, I cried out to You, and You healed me. O LORD, You brought my soul up from the grave; You have kept me alive, that I should not go down to the pit. Sing praise to the LORD, you saints of His, and give thanks at the remembrance of His holy name" (Ps. 30:2–4). The fact that he has heard our prayers in the past will surely move us to call upon him in the future. "Because He has inclined His ear to me," says the psalmist, "therefore I will call upon Him as long as I live" (Ps. 116:2).

The bottom line is that Jesus is full of grace. Jesus had passed through the same region a year earlier, and one village had rejected him. The disciples wanted him to call down fire from heaven (9:51ff.)! A year later, Jesus heals the ten lepers when they ask him. He came to seek and save the lost. Come to Christ and he will save you. And may it never be asked of you, "Where are the nine?"

A SOLEMN SONG OF OUR NEED OF A SAVIOR
Sing Psalm 88:9–18

THINGS I WILL PRAY FOR TODAY

- I will be thankful in ALL things
- I will sing praises & thanksgiving

September 11
Do Not Lose Heart!

An example of prevailing prayer

Then He spoke a parable to them, that men always ought to pray and not lose heart. —Luke 18:1

READ LUKE 18:1–8

In Jesus's parable of the unjust judge and the persistent widow, the widow nags the judge, who settles her case just to get her off his back. Jesus's application of this story to prayer is basically this: if a bad judge will listen to a complaining woman, how much more will "God avenge His own elect who cry out day and night to Him?" (v. 7a). The argument is from the lesser to the greater: If this world, with all its faults, is not without justice, how can you doubt the Lord and give up on his justice on behalf of those he loves and saves? Does God have to be nagged? Will he ever let us down? Does he not keep his covenant promises? Jesus brings out three basic applications to your prayer life.

Pray persistently "and do not lose heart." If a widow can persist with a lazy, uncaring judge in an unjust world, will you, Christian, not pray earnestly with believing perseverance for his grace in this world and the next? But what if the Lord "bears long" with us—i.e., takes his time answering? A long-serving pastor, already mentioned above (September 1) was asked how he coped with the terrible trials he faced over many years in his congregation. He answered quietly, "I prayed till the matter was settled." That's the challenge: to pray for as long as the reason for praying is still in place. It's a long way to Australia, but will you get off the plane before you arrive simply because you can't wait that long? James encourages us to "ask in faith, with no doubting, for he who doubts is like a wave of the sea driven and tossed by the wind" (James 1:6). If a widow's sheer doggedness can get satisfaction from an unrighteous judge, how much more will our dogged prayers obtain from *the* righteous Judge?

Expect blessing from your Father in heaven. Jesus offers certain incentives to praying people: *God will certainly answer.* Even if we have years to wait, he will answer "speedily" (Luke 18:8a; cf. Ps. 107:6). *God will also certainly execute justice in the earth*: "He is the Lord our God:

His judgments are in all the earth" (1 Chron. 16:14). Remember that "the Lord is not slow to fulfill his promise as some count slowness, but is patient toward you, not wishing that any should perish, but that all should reach repentance" (1 Peter 3:8–9). Paul reminds us that "God shall supply all your need according to His riches in glory by Christ Jesus" (Phil. 4:19). Furthermore, *God will certainly save his people.* Not one will be snatched from his hand (John 10:28). This further implies that *God's people will certainly persevere* in the faith once delivered to the saints. They will "pray without ceasing" (1 Thess. 5:17). Augustine, acknowledging that we cannot "bow the body, bend the knee and lift up the hands" all the time, points out this reality:

> There is another internal prayer without intermission, and that is the longing of your heart. Whatever else you may be doing, if you long for the Sabbath of God [i.e., heaven], you do not cease to pray. If you do not wish to cease to pray, see that you do not cease to desire; your continual desire is your continual voice. You will be silent if you leave off loving….The coldness of love is the silence of the heart; the fervency of love is the cry of the heart.

Persevering in the faith is Jesus's final challenge: "Nevertheless, when the Son of Man comes, will He really find faith on the earth?" (v. 8bc). There will be no shortage of unbelief, as at present. The question is personal: What will Jesus find *in each one of us* when he comes? Will he find you still praying day and night, or will you have given up? How does he find you today and every day?

A SONG OF PREVAILING PRAYER
Sing Psalm 5

THINGS I WILL PRAY FOR TODAY

_____

_____

_____

_____

_____

September 12
Two Men Went to Pray

Prayers can be dead or alive

I tell you, this man went down to his house justified rather than the other;
for everyone who exalts himself will be humbled, and he who humbles
himself will be exalted. — Luke 18:14

READ LUKE 18:9–14

"Most men will proclaim each his own goodness, but who can find a faithful man?" (Prov. 20:6). As J. C. Ryle comments, "We are all naturally self-righteous. It is the family disease of all the children of Adam." Like Willie Fisher, the real-life hypocrite of Robert Burns's scurrilous poem "Holy Willie's Prayer," we can tune our prayers to sing our praises and excuse our failings, all the while calling down fire from heaven on others less guilty than ourselves!

> But, Lord, remember me an' mine
> Wi' mercies temporal and divine,
> That I for grace an' gear may shine,
> Excell'd by nane,
> And a' the glory shall be Thine,
> Amen, Amen!
> (stanza 17)

In our passage, Jesus pinpoints the vital issue in his parable of two men, both committed to prayer yet an eternity apart.

The Pharisee prays about how good he is. As a member of an orthodox Jewish sect committed to the punctilious observance of rabbinical teaching, he carefully observed the appointed "hour[s] of prayer" (Luke 18:11–12; cf. Acts 3:1). But he prays what should be a private prayer where he can be "seen by men" (Matt. 6:5). Notice three things:

> ❧ He is a religious show-off. Jesus says he "prayed…with himself" (v. 11a). He, not God, is at the center of his prayer!
> ❧ He compares himself to others, giving thanks he is not like them (v. 11b). There is no sense of personal sin and God's saving grace, but there sure is a strong odor of self-congratulation.
> ❧ He reviews his accomplishments (v. 12). He fasts "twice a

512

week," when God only requires *once a year* (on Yom Kippur). He tithes of "all" he possesses, when God only commands a tithe of *earned* income. He is so pleased with himself (see Jesus's evaluation in Matt. 23:23).

The tax collector prays about how bad he is. He stands "afar off" in a quiet corner of the temple so as not to draw attention to himself. He humbles himself before God (v. 13). The irony is that he who cannot look up to heaven out of shame is the one fleeing to God! He cries "God be merciful to me *the* sinner." The Greek word translated "be merciful" means "be propitious"—he asks God to look on him with grace, rather than righteous, just anger. Here is true conviction of sin and the need of salvation, as in the words of Augustus M. Toplady in his hymn "Rock of Ages": "Not the labour of my hands / Can fulfill Thy laws demands / Could my zeal no respite know / Could my tears forever flow / All for sin would not atone / Thou must save and Thou alone. (stanza 2)

Saved or Lost? The tax collector "went down to his house justified" (v. 14). The other is left as a question mark, but the drift is obvious. Both prayed, but one was eternally alive, and the other was in eternal danger. Thomas Manton makes application to each one of us:

> Consider your misery by reason of sin. The Redeemer has no work to do in stupid and senseless souls. They that know not their misery regard not their remedy. The offers of the gospel are always made to the sensible [self-aware], the broken-hearted, the weary, the thirsty, the heavy-laden. Many are welcome to Christ that know not themselves penitent believers; but never any welcome that knew not themselves condemned sinners (Luke 18:13–14).

Jesus's punchline is directed at your heart and conscience: "Everyone who exalts himself will be abased, and he who humbles himself will be exalted." Are you a Pharisee? Or a tax-collector? Look to Jesus.

A SONG SEEKING THE MERCY OF GOD
Sing Psalm 57:1–4

THINGS I WILL PRAY FOR TODAY

September 13
Beggars Can Be Choosers!

Prayer that points to the Savior

Jesus, Son of David, have mercy on me. — Luke 18:38

READ LUKE 18:35–43;
MATTHEW 20:29–34; MARK 10:35–46

Whether healed by medicine or a miracle, it is the same in the end. Sooner or later you will die (Heb. 9:27). This proves that Jesus's healing miracles aimed higher than extending our lives. Miracles primarily tell us who Jesus is: "the very works that I do—bear witness of Me, that the Father has sent Me" (John 6:35; 20:31).

In the healing of the blind beggar episode, the main message is not that Jesus has compassion for our physical ills, but that he saves us from sin, death, and a lost eternity. It is not a coincidence that this comes after Jesus's third prediction of his death and resurrection (Luke 18:31–34). It is all about new life!

The blind beggar wants a new life. He is poor and blind and sits begging by the roadside (v. 35). He hears a commotion, asks what it is, and is told that "Jesus…was passing by" (vv. 36–37). He cries to Jesus for help (v. 38), and he persists in the face of discouragement (v. 39). "He felt his need," says J. C. Ryle, "and…was not to be stopped by the rebukes of people who knew nothing of the misery of blindness. His sense of wretchedness made him go on crying." The point we need to note is that what blind Bartimaeus (Mark 10:46) wanted and needed for his eyes is what we all ought to want for our souls. Having a blind soul is worse than having blind eyes. No one comes to Jesus, unless they are first convinced of their need of a new life, heart, and soul—and also believe Jesus is able to help them. The blind beggar points the way to Jesus as the Savior of spiritually blind people.

The blind beggar chooses to seek new life. When he cries "Jesus, Son of David, have mercy on me," he indicates his readiness to trust Jesus as the Messiah (vv. 38–41). When Jesus stops and asks him, "What do you want Me to do for you?", his prayer becomes a confession of faith in

514

Christ (vv. 40–41a). He doesn't pray to receive Jesus—he prays because he has already been received by Jesus!

His specific petition that his sight be restored is very matter of fact. But as Jesus makes clear in his response, this request was the fruit of a truly believing heart: "Receive your sight, your faith has made you well" (v. 41b). You can see the order of things here: his body is made well through Jesus's miracle of healing, because his soul was saved already through his faith in the Son of God. The heart of the matter is saving faith in Jesus Christ the Messiah. He does not pray at random, as if trying whatever might work. Like Abraham, he believed God and it was counted to him as righteousness (Rom. 4:3). With Jesus and the gospel call to saving faith in him, beggars can be choosers! This is all of the glorious grace of God, because we children of Adam are all beggars by nature. In Christ, however, we are made "more than conquerors through Him who loved us" (Rom. 8:37).

The blind beggar experiences new life. He follows Jesus right away and praises his God (v. 43). He discovers the glory of God, quite literally; this experience is captured in George Robinson's rhapsodic evocation of new faith and life in Jesus Christ.

> Heav'n above is softer blue,
> > Earth around is sweeter green!
> Something lives in every hue
> > Christless eyes have never seen;
> Birds with gladder songs o'erflow,
> > flowers with deeper beauties shine,
> Since I know, as now I know,
> > I am His, and He is mine.
> > —"I Am His, and He Is Mine," stanza 2

PRAISE FOR GOD'S WONDERFUL COMPASSION
Sing Psalm 145:8–14

THINGS I WILL PRAY FOR TODAY

_____

_____

_____

_____

_____

September 14
Sifted Like Wheat

A prayer of intercession

But I have prayed for you, that your faith should not fail. — *Luke 22:32a*

READ LUKE 22:31–32

When Jesus reveals to his disciples that Satan has asked to sift them, he does so to alert them to the clear and present danger of the work of the devil. Satan would just as well keep this a secret. He wants people to underestimate him, because, like any disease, he will make more progress when nobody is paying attention than he would if they understood what was happening to them. Evil spreads more effectively when it is not recognized for what it really is. Satan also has ploys to mask the seriousness of the damage he is doing. One is the illusion that "it can't happen to me" and another is the myth that there isn't a devil that can blind our minds and set us on the road to hell.

Jesus therefore wants us to be realistic about Satan. "Satan has asked for you," tells us that he means to do *us* harm (v. 31). The "you" in verse 31 is plural, and includes all the disciples, not just Peter. (By contrast, the "you" in verse 32 is a singular and clearly is directed at Peter in prospect of his denying Christ three times before dawn next morning.) To "sift…as wheat" means testing that sorts the real believers from the false, who are like chaff blown by the wind (Ps. 1:4). Satan intends "to prove them hypocrites, or make them apostates." He tried this with Job (1:9, 11; 2:5), and today he "walks about like a roaring lion, seeking whom he may devour" (1 Peter 5:8). Satan is a real and fearful enemy for every human being. He is, however, not a divine being but a finite fallen angel. He is neither all-powerful, all-knowing, all-seeing, nor is he omnipresent. He even has to ask the Lord's permission to sift the disciples, just as the demons at Gadara had to beg Jesus to let them into the pigs (Matt. 8:31). Our defeat is not inevitable.

Jesus calls us to trust in our true Deliverer. Satan is "the strong man" bound by Christ (Matt. 12:29). He assures Peter, "I have prayed for you, that your faith should not fail; and when you have returned to Me, strengthen your brethren" (v. 32). This assures all Christians that Jesus will bring them through their troubles to victory over Satan and the powers of evil. Jesus upholds us in his intercessory prayer as our advocate with the Father (Heb. 7:25; 1 John 2:1). It is his prayers for us and with us that give our prayers wings to come before the throne of God's grace. As we pray, the Father also hears the Son.

Jesus is the life of his disciples, sustaining in them a faith that will not fail. Bishop Ryle observes that "the continued existence of grace in a believer's heart is a standing miracle." Saving faith is "the gift of God" (Eph. 2:8), and will "not fail" because believers are "all sons of God through faith in Jesus Christ" (Gal. 3:26).

Jesus assures his disciples of future useful ministry. Peter will soon deny the Lord three times (see Luke 18:33–34), but he will return to Jesus, and be enabled to strengthen his fellow apostles. Your testing experiences will, by God's grace, likewise equip you to encourage others. Furthermore, when you resist the devil, *he* will flee from you (James 4:7)! When Jesus returns, God will "crush Satan under your feet" (Rom. 16:20), and "the saints will judge the world" (1 Cor. 6:2). We are sifted by Satan to serve our Savior. Peter later understands that believers "are kept by the power of God through faith for salvation ready to be revealed in the last time." He adds, "In this you greatly rejoice, though now for a little while, if need be, you have been grieved by various trials, that the genuineness of your faith, being much more precious than gold that perishes, though it is tested by fire, may be found to praise, honor, and glory at the revelation of Jesus Christ" (1 Peter 1:5–7).

A SONG REFLECTING ON TIMES OF TRIAL
Sing Psalm 118:1–9

THINGS I WILL PRAY FOR TODAY

September 15
Father, Forgive Them (Part 1)

Jesus prays for his murderers

Then Jesus said, "Father, forgive them…"—Luke 23:34a

READ LUKE 23:26–34

The first of Jesus's "seven words" on the cross is a prayer for the forgiveness of sinners who are party to his murder. "One would think," says Matthew Henry, "that he should have prayed, 'Father, consume them.'" That is what James and John wanted for certain Samaritans who were inhospitable to Jesus (Luke 9:54). Peter literally stabbed at something similar when he cut off Malchus's ear in Gethsemane (Luke 22:50). Getting even and more comes naturally to the human heart. Doing good to "those who spitefully use you" (Matt. 5:44) defines a true forgiving spirit. Jesus exemplifies this on the cross toward his murderers. This is a work of God's grace we all need in our hearts. Let us learn from the suffering Savior. Notice in verse 34a how, in just three words, Jesus shows us who we should be praying for and how we should pray for them.

Jesus prays for people who are accountable to God. To whom does he go? He goes to his "Father" and asks that he "forgive them." This presupposes what Jesus has already taught us, namely that all who are *not* presently forgiven are "condemned already" (John 3:18), and that his Father is the one who does the condemning. Jesus's Father is our judge. Every one of us is by nature accountable to God. Scripture makes this clear. The biblical definition of a "fool" is one who "says in his heart 'There is no God'" (Ps. 14:1)—that is, rejects his accountability to his Creator God. The most basic fact of life is that "we must all appear before the judgment seat of God that each one may receive the things done in the body" (2 Cor. 5:10). And if you are tempted to think that a bare recognition of the existence of God clears you with him, he reminds us all: "There is none who does good" (Ps. 14:1).

Jesus prays for guilty people. His immediate focus is "them"—those who are killing him. They are sinners caught in the act of sinning. Their rejection of Jesus is proof that they cannot know his Father-God.

518

The universal truth is that we are all accountable, our best efforts at goodness are not sinless, and we are lost and condemned already. Our lives prove it. We need a saving change. This is where Jesus comes in: "God did not send His Son into the world to condemn the world, but that the world through Him might be saved" (John 3:17).

Jesus prays for his enemies. The "them" he prays for are his persecutors who, whether they know it or not—they don't!—are crucifying the Lord of glory (1 Cor. 2:8). The problem of sin is not that we make a "mistake" here and there. We are not sinners because we sin: we sin because we are sinners. And that involves nothing less than a preexistent disposition of heart and soul to be at "enmity against God" (Rom. 8:7; James 4:4). Jesus says, "Greater love has no man than this, than to lay down his life for his friends" (John 15:13). But Jesus lays down his life for his *enemies*! There is the greatest love of all!

Jesus prays for the salvation of lost, guilty enemies. Just to utter the word "forgive," and to do so while dying on a cross, is surely an act of pure grace. It is not just a pious hope in a form of words. Jesus can actually save! How? He knows that his death is an atonement for sin, and he is asking that their murdering him be the very means of their salvation. This is the gospel, to be believed and received through repentance toward God and faith in the Lord Jesus Christ (Acts 20:21). We who were not there at Calvary consenting to his death are as guilty as those who were. And everyone today who has turned to Jesus and trusted in him as Savior and Lord has heard him pray "Father, forgive" as surely as those who heard him audibly at the cross and believed and were saved. Hallelujah! What a Savior!

A SONG OF THE BLESSING OF FORGIVENESS
Sing Psalm 32:1–7

THINGS I WILL PRAY FOR TODAY

_____

_____

_____

_____

_____

September 16
Father, Forgive Them (Part 2)

Jesus prays for his murderers

"...for they do not know what they do." — Luke 23:34b

READ LUKE 23:26–34

aving asked God to forgive his murderers, Jesus offers a reason: "they do not know what they do." God uses the same argument when he challenges Jonah's lack of compassion for Nineveh: "And should I not pity Nineveh, that great city, in which are more than one hundred and twenty thousand persons who cannot discern between their right hand and their left?" (Jonah 4:11). You will hear of people latching on to these two statements to the effect that the Bible teaches that "ignorance" is an excuse for forgiving sin and overlooking mistakes. One of the spokes in the great wheel of entitlement-thinking in the twenty-first century is the notion that my ignorance excuses me from the consequences of my actions. Children in school will plead ignorance to roll back a bad grade. Someone stopped by the police for speeding will offer the excuse that they didn't know the speed limit. So what does Jesus mean when he says "they do not know what they do"? Is ignorance a good excuse?

Ignorance is not an excuse for sin and spiritual deadness. Jesus excuses no one merely for rejecting him in ignorance. Ignorance is a malady, not a free pass to heaven. Scripture makes plain that however ignorant we may be of Christ and the gospel message of salvation, we are "without excuse" (Rom. 1:20). There is "none righteous, no not one" (Rom. 3:10). The basic human problem is not ignorance *in itself*, but unrighteousness. When the psalmist asks, "If You, Lord, should mark iniquities, O Lord, who could stand?" (Ps. 130:3), the answer is nobody. We need a Savior, not an excuse. What ignorance does do is extenuate our guilt. A good example is the apostle Paul, who says of himself, "Although I was formerly a blasphemer, a persecutor and an insolent man...I obtained mercy because I did it ignorantly in unbelief" (1 Tim. 1:13; cf. Luke 12:47–48). Sinning in ignorance excites, but does not earn, mercy.

Ignorance is a problem Jesus came to overturn. Ignorance is more than simply not knowing certain facts. It is the same as spiritual blindness. Furthermore, most of the people had been taught ignorance by their unsound and willfully reprobate teachers—hence Jesus's trenchant denunciation of the church of the scribes and Pharisees (Matt. 23). They taught people, for example, to believe that rejecting Jesus was "offering a service to God" (John 16:2). Every false doctrine on the lips of a modern cleric is planting a commensurate ignorance in the hearers' minds. The decline of the churches in the Western world is the fruit of top-down dissemination of studied ignorance. *But this is exactly the problem Jesus died in order to change!* Jesus is "the Light of the world" precisely to dispel the darkness in human souls (John 8:12). Ignorance, as the multi-faceted condition of lost sinners, is the pitiable condition that calls forth the application of redeeming love in Jesus Christ.

Can you be ignorant in unbelief and not know it? Paul certainly never saw his true condition until his conversion on the Damascus road. Ignorance—spiritual blindness—will keep us from Christ. So, like Paul, we need the scales to fall from our eyes by God's grace and so come to Christ in faith (Acts 9:18). Are you personally convinced and encouraged that Jesus is a great Savior? That he is "the fountain of living waters" (Jer. 17:13) to "cleanse…from sin and uncleanness" (Zech. 13:1)? Then never despair of his forgiveness. Just look to him. Believe him and follow him. His example is our calling: "Christ also suffered for us, leaving us an example, that you should follow in his steps" (1 Peter 2:21). The unconverted really "do not know what they do" and are in the greatest danger under heaven. The love in your heart will pray to the end for their salvation.

A SONG OF LOVE TOWARD ENEMIES
Sing Psalm 35:11–18

THINGS I WILL PRAY FOR TODAY

September 17
Lord, Remember Me

The prayer of a dying man

Then he said to Jesus, "Lord, remember me when You come into Your kingdom."—Luke 23:42

READ LUKE 23:39–43

he essence and simplicity of the gospel is nowhere more clearly set out than in the story of the repentant thief. "These verses," says J. C. Ryle, "deserve to be printed in letters of gold." Why? Here is a man with a lost soul and a wasted life, on the very lip of hell, brought by God's free grace to saving faith in Jesus Christ and to the door of heaven. This breathes gospel hope, for it shows that all that separates a sinner from eternal life is coming to Jesus, who will "save to the uttermost those who come to God through Him" (Heb. 7:25).

Notice how the thief is saved.

He is gripped by an appropriate fear of God. When the other thief mocks Jesus—"If You are the Christ, save Yourself and us" (v. 39)—the repentant one asks, "Do you not even fear God, seeing you are under the same condemnation?" (v. 40). Here is where the experience of salvation has to begin. He grasps that God is "of purer eyes than to behold evil, and cannot look on wickedness" (Hab. 1:13), and that this is a death sentence for the unrepentant and unbelieving.

He is convicted of his personal sin against God. Both thieves are "justly" condemned (v. 41ab). They have no excuse. He humbly accepts the *dicta* of Psalm 14:2–3: "The Lord looks down from heaven upon the children of men, to see if there are any who understand, who seek God. They have all turned aside, they have together become corrupt; *there* is none who does good, no, not one." He is, as an old American evangelist used to say, "jes' plumb lost"—and he knows, if it depends on him, he is lost for all eternity.

He acknowledges the perfect righteousness of Jesus. In contrast to them, Jesus "has done nothing wrong" (v. 41c). If Jesus is a sinner, he cannot be a Savior. But he is "without sin" and so, "if anyone sins, we have an Advocate with the Father, Jesus Christ the righteous" (1 John 2:1). Come to Jesus. He can and will save you (Matt. 11:28).

He confesses Jesus as "Lord" (v. 42a). Charles Simeon comments that the thief "beheld him upon the cross as though he had seen him upon his throne." Paul emphasizes that "no one speaking by the Spirit of God calls Jesus accursed, and no one can say that Jesus is Lord except by the Holy Spirit" (1 Cor. 12:3). This man has surrendered to Jesus as Savior and Lord of his life.

He applies to Jesus for salvation. He only asks that Jesus "remember" him. He does not "pray to receive Jesus." He prays for Jesus to receive him! He offers no good works to earn salvation; no protestations of being a decent chap to demand salvation; and no plea of past religiosity to presume salvation. He believes Jesus has "the words of eternal life" (John 6:68), and he believes on Jesus and is saved (Acts 16:31)…and Jesus assures him, "Today you will be with Me in Paradise" (v. 43). The thief can sing from Augustus M. Toplady's hymn:

Nothing in my hand I bring,
Simply to Thy Cross I cling;
Naked, come to Thee for dress;
Helpless, look to Thee for grace;
Foul, I to the fountain fly;
Wash me, Saviour, or I die.
—"Rock of Ages," stanza 3

A SONG ASKING GOD TO REMEMBER US WITH FAVOR
Sing Psalm 106:1–5

THINGS I WILL PRAY FOR TODAY

_____

_____

_____

_____

_____

_____

_____

September 18
Father, into Your Hands

Jesus's prayer committing himself to the Father

"Father, into Your hands I commit My spirit." Having said this, He
breathed His last. *— Luke 23:46*

READ LUKE 23:44–49

"Famous last words!" is usually a sardonic comment on
someone's silly remark. Real last words can vary from
depressing to uplifting, and they can be very revealing.
Robert Bruce, King of Scots, dying in 1328, said, "Now
God be with you, my dear children. I have breakfasted with you and
shall sup with my Lord Jesus Christ." U. S. President Lincoln's assassin,
John Wilkes Booth, said, "Tell mother I died for my country…useless…
useless." And some last words were not intended to be "last." Union
General John Sedgwick, at the battle of the Wilderness in 1864, observing
the Confederate fire, said, "They couldn't hit an elephant at this dist—"
and died from a sniper's bullet. Jesus's last words from the cross are, of
course, deliberate. He dies with Scripture on his lips: David's words in
Psalm 31:5, *"Into Your hands I commit my spirit; You have redeemed me,
O Lord God of truth."* These words proclaim the good news of the Savior
who really saves sinners through his death and resurrection. They are
designed to lead us to trust the Lord. Notice three things in this brief
prayer.

He expresses his abiding love for the Father. Earlier, in his
forsakenness under God's wrath against others' sin (2 Cor. 5:21), he cries
words from Psalm 22:1: "My God, My God…" (Matt. 27:46). Why the
change from "My God" to "Father"? Remember that he had just uttered
the words, "It is finished" (John 19:30), indicating that, in Matthew Henry's
words, "the dreadful agony of his soul was now over." Even through the
experience of crucifixion, Jesus never wavers in his love for the Father. He
knows "the Father loves the Son, and has given all things into His hand"
(John 3:35). He declares, "I and the Father are one" (John 10:30).

He submits himself completely to his Father's will. He says, "Into
Your hands," accepting the Father's holy justice against sin. He presents

himself as the substitute for sinners. He "who knew no sin" becomes the embodiment of sin (2 Cor. 5:21), in order to atone for others: "It pleased the Lord to bruise Him; He has put Him to grief. When You make His soul an offering for sin, He shall see His seed, He shall prolong His days, and the pleasure of the Lord shall prosper in His hand" (Isa. 53:10). He "did not come to be served, but to serve and give His life a ransom for many" (Matt. 20:28). Jesus submits to the "hell" due to those he comes to save and so reconcile to his Father and theirs. His trust is absolute.

He anticipates his Father's favor: "I commit My spirit." He says "spirit" because his body is destined for the grave (until his resurrection on the third day), while his spirit flies to heaven. His committal is made in hope of the resurrection that will seal his victory over sin and death. "It was not in reference to Himself alone that Christ committed His soul to the Father," writes John Calvin, "but He included…in one bundle all the souls of those who believe in Him, that they may be preserved along with his own [soul]." His sacrifice offered, he "breathed his last."

How should you respond to this wonderful prayer of the dying Jesus? The centurion believes, the crowd is gripped by confusion and regret, and Jesus's acquaintances wonder what it all means (vv. 47–49). You know more than all of them. Christ is risen. And so "how much more shall the blood of Christ, who through the eternal Spirit offered Himself without spot to God, cleanse your conscience from dead works to serve the living God?" (Heb. 9:14). He died: you live.

PRAISE TO GOD FOR LIFE FROM THE DEAD
Sing Psalm 118:15–18

THINGS I WILL PRAY FOR TODAY

_____

_____

_____

_____

_____

_____

_____

_____

_____

September 19
A Parting Blessing

The risen Jesus blesses his disciples

He lifted up His hands and blessed them. — Luke 24:50

READ LUKE 24:50–53

esus's parting blessing is the benediction of benedictions. More than just another closing prayer, it uniquely marks the ascension of the crucified and risen Christ—the last moment of his bodily presence in our world, until the day he comes again with the voice of the archangel and the trumpet of God. He here fulfills his own prophecy: "I came forth from the Father and have come into the world. Again, I leave the world and go to the Father" (John 16:28). Ten days later, at Pentecost, he fulfills another promise—that of the coming of the Holy Spirit once and forever upon the church. This great benediction—of which words he spoke we have no record—is that of our Great High Priest, Messiah Jesus, authoritatively bestowing his blessing as it flows from his victory over sin and death on Calvary's cross.

Jesus ascends in plain sight for good reasons. It is to leave a public witness for all time and to impress some wonderful truths upon our hearts and minds.

- Christ's sacrifice was a sacrifice to God. His visible ascension emphasizes the sufficiency of his atonement for sin. He is visibly received into glory to reign in *his* glory as the mediatorial King.
- Christ ascends to heaven to continue his ministry as Prophet, Priest, and King on behalf of those he has saved, is saving, and will yet save. He is not inactive. He is *preparing* a place for believers (John 14:1–3); he is *providing* continuing blessings for believers (John 17:20–26); he is *praying* as the intercessor for his people (Isa. 53:12; Heb. 7:25); and he is *presiding* over his creation as Head over all things to the church (Eph. 1:20–23; 1 Peter 3:22).
- Christ's ascension is both a prophecy and a promise that all believers will ascend to heaven in like manner to be with him. God has "made us alive together with Christ (by grace you have been saved), and raised us up together, and made us sit

526

together in the heavenly places in Christ Jesus" (Eph. 2:5b–6). This is the heritage of everyone who believes on Jesus as Savior and Lord. What was true for the "Eleven" in these matters is also true for modern believers.

Jesus's ascension transforms his disciples. Whereas before they could not imagine Jesus leaving them, now they respond with rejoicing and worship! Why so? There are two basic reasons. For one thing, this parting is not the end of seeing Jesus or of enjoying fellowship with him. Surely we would weep if the parting were forever! Furthermore, this parting is to the glory of Jesus and the benefit of his people. Surely we would weep if the parting meant irreversible and unrelieved loss and misery! But the fruit of his ascension is not loss, but gain.

The key is that the disciples at last understand Jesus and his mission; why he died on the cross; why he rose the third day; why he ascended before their very eyes; and why he is coming again for sure! They could not but delight in the Lord's ascension! Therefore they "worshiped him" and "returned to Jerusalem with great joy" (v. 51). They gave themselves "continually" to serve the Lord, while they waited for "power from on high" (Luke 24:52–53; cf. v. 49; Acts 1:4–5).

They also grasped that Jesus's ascension is the guarantee of their own entrance into glory. And this great hope touched their lives most powerfully. The Puritan Samuel Willard says, "That man is out of reach of harm in this life, who is sure of processing heaven in the next." John Cennick (1717–55) catches this blessing so beautifully:

Jesus, my all, to heaven is gone,
He whom I fix my hopes upon;
His track I see, and I'll pursue
The narrow way, till him I view.
— "Jesus, My All, to Heaven Is Gone," stanza 1

GOD'S BENEDICTION ON HIS PEOPLE
Sing Psalm 128

THINGS I WILL PRAY FOR TODAY

_____

_____

_____

September 20
Looks, Walks, and Quacks?

A "prayer" that is not a prayer

Sir, give me this water, that I may not thirst, nor come here to draw.
—John 4:15

READ JOHN 4:1–26

t is said that if something looks, walks, and quacks like a duck, it must be a duck. If we apply this criterion to prayer, however, the fact that some utterance "looks, walks, and quacks" like a prayer does not prove it is a real prayer. The Samaritan woman's request of Jesus, taken in isolation from the story around it, looks quite like a prayer. But no verse in Scripture is "an island, entire of itself," and one look at what leads to her seeming petition reveals that there is more to it than meets the eye. Not only is it not a sincere prayer, it is merely a brush-off in the form of a mock prayer.

She is intrigued by Jesus. She is at the well to draw water when Jesus asks her for a drink (v. 7). Realizing he is a Jew and noting that "Jews have no dealings with Samaritans," she marvels that he asks this favor of her (v. 9). Jesus resists any discussion of "denominational" differences between the Jews and the Samaritans, and immediately turns the conversation to spiritual matters and the central issue of gospel salvation. So Jesus answers her by saying, "If you knew the gift of God, and who it is who says to you, 'Give Me a drink,' you would have asked Him, and He would have given you living water" (v. 10). The "gift of God" that Jesus tells her she does not know is Christ himself, the Savior of sinners. The gift that he can give is "living water"—not the static water in the well, but the water of new life that flows for believers from Christ, who is the fountain of everlasting life (John 7:38–39; cf. Zech. 13:1). The woman needs this gift and Jesus is the one who alone can—and soon does—give it to her.

She is dismissive of Jesus. She immediately becomes defensive and talks as if she understands Jesus to be speaking about physical water—perhaps the "living" source (i.e., the spring) feeding the still waters of Jacob's well (vv. 11–12). "She understands quite well," says John Calvin, "that Christ is speaking figuratively" and fobs him off by proceeding to "charge him with arrogance in exalting himself above the holy patriarch Jacob." Jesus doesn't let her off the hook—he makes it absolutely clear that he is speaking about personal salvation right out of the Scriptures that proclaimed the Messiah to be the "fountain of living waters" (Jer. 2:13). Her back is to the wall. She gets the point. She knows he is aiming for her soul and calling her to believe in him as her Savior. But all she can bring herself to do is stall Jesus with an absurd attempt at a conversation stopper: "Sir, give me this water, that I may not thirst, nor come here to draw" (v. 15). She cannot face his obvious meaning and his challenge to her conscience! She wants to escape, so she mumbles her way to the exit!

She is found by Jesus. If there is such a thing as an answer to a non-prayer, this is a wonderful example. The Lord knows we cannot truly pray before we are truly converted. That doesn't stop some Christians asking people to "pray to receive Jesus" when what they need is to receive Jesus so they can pray. The conversation goes on for a while and Jesus never lets the woman get away with her evasive tactics. If her salvation had depended on her honest response and free will, she would be in hell right now. But Jesus loves her and never lets her go. And he never stoops to a gospel sales pitch sealed by a commitment in a form of words fed to her to be repeated back as evidence of a saving change. Her coyness in pointing her fellow Samaritans to Jesus, however, tells us she is truly converted to Christ: "Come see a man who told me all things that I ever did. Could this be the Christ?" (John 4:29). She knows Jesus is the Christ and knows him as her Savior and Lord.

A SONG OF RESTING IN GOD FOR SALVATION
Sing Psalm 62:1–8

THINGS I WILL PRAY FOR TODAY

_____

_____

_____

_____

_____

_____

_____

_____

September 21
That You Might Believe

Purpose, prayer, and power

Father, I thank You that You have heard Me. And I know that You always hear Me, but because of the people who are standing by I said this, that they may believe that You sent Me. —John 11:41–42

READ JOHN 11:38–44

I t is no mere accident that the raising of Lazarus immediately precedes Jesus's own death and resurrection. It is all about Jesus's defeating death. Lazarus's temporary resurrection is a foretaste of the permanent resurrection of Jesus and of all whom he will save. John's account highlights three remarkable features of this amazing event, namely, Jesus's purpose, prayer, and power in the raising of Lazarus.

Jesus's *purpose* in raising Lazarus is to glorify God. When Lazarus is sick, Jesus tells Mary and Martha, "This sickness is not unto death, but for the glory of God, that the Son of God may be glorified through it" (John 11:4). We now know what Jesus already knew, that Lazarus was dying but would be raised to life. Jesus hints at this several times (John 11:11, 14b–15, 23, 25–26). Martha believes Jesus can heal a sick Lazarus, but not one who was four days dead (John 11:21, 24, 32, 39). So when Jesus orders that the tomb be opened, clearly to raise Lazarus, she objects that the body will be decomposed (v. 39). Jesus reminds her, "Did I not say to you that if you would believe you would see the glory of God?" (v. 40). Believe what? The answer: believe that Jesus is indeed "the resurrection and the life" and that "whoever lives and believes" in him "shall never die" (John 11:25–26). God glorifies himself in this, in that by his Son he gives everlasting life both here and hereafter to people who are dead in trespasses and sins and incapable of resurrecting themselves from death to life! Do you believe this (John 11:26)?

Jesus's *prayer* at the tomb aims to reveal him as the life-giving Mediator between God and man. After the tomb is opened, Jesus prays publicly (v. 41). Why? After all, he already knew the outcome and knew it was planned from before the foundation of the world (Eph. 1:4)! He tells us himself: "I know that You always hear Me, but because of the people who are standing by I said this, that they may believe that You sent Me" (v. 42). By predicting this resurrection, opening the tomb, and calling on God, Jesus put his claims to a public test! George Hutcheson notes that "as God, he is a principal efficient [i.e., has power to act], as man, he is the instrument of the Godhead, and as Mediator, he acts as the father's servant." His prayer is a public testimony to his being the true Son of God.

Jesus's *power* in raising Lazarus attests him as the true Messiah and Savior of sinners. Jesus commands, "Lazarus, come forth!" and "he who had died came out bound hand and foot with graveclothes, and his face was wrapped with a cloth" (vv. 43–44). Lazarus is a mess, but a live one! His resurrection day points to two great days yet future: Jesus's resurrection (John 20:1) and that of the great day when he comes again (Acts 17:31; 1 Cor. 15:52). Had Lazarus not come forth, Jesus's claims would have collapsed and the authorities would have had no Lazarus to persecute (John 12:10). They would hardly have wasted time arresting, trying, and crucifying Jesus had he been a charlatan and an imposter! Purpose, prayer, and power come together uniquely in Jesus's raising of Lazarus. This is a one-off moment in redemptive history. But all believing prayer with purpose will have power: "The effective, fervent prayer of a righteous man avails much" (James 5:16). On the other hand, prayer without purpose will always be powerless. If you would pray powerfully, you must pray purposefully that Christ would be exalted, his kingdom extended, and his heavenly Father and ours glorified.

PRAISE FOR NEW LIFE
Sing Psalm 118:15–18

THINGS I WILL PRAY FOR TODAY

September 22
My Soul Is Troubled

Jesus prays for himself (Part 1)

Now My soul is troubled, and what shall I say?—John 12:27

READ JOHN 12:20–33

It was not easy for Christ to die for the likes of us. Jesus has been approached by some Greek converts to Judaism, and they apparently want to know more about him and his mission. Jesus responds with three somber and challenging predictions about what was about to happen:

- "The hour has come that the Son of Man should be glorified" (v. 23)—his time is *now*, he is the promised Messiah, and his destiny is to be glorified in his work of redemption. In a moment Jesus will predict his death, repeating his words to Nicodemus: "And as Moses lifted up the serpent in the wilderness, even so must the Son of Man be lifted up" (vv. 30–33; 3:14).

- "Unless a grain of wheat dies" emphasizes *the necessity of his death* as the atonement for sin (v. 24). Jesus is the "Seed" through whom and in whom all who believe become his seed—the fruit of his giving his life as "a ransom for many" (Gal. 3:16; Mark 10:45).

- "If anyone serves Me, let him follow Me" (vv. 25–26) reveals that Jesus's *disciples will also bear fruit*. They will not die *for* their sins, but will in Christ die *to* their sins and live forever in the honor of God. They will, in Jesus, have a right attitude toward life (v. 25), follow a right pattern of life (v. 26a), and look for the right satisfaction in life (v. 26b).

All that Jesus says here depends upon the death he is to die. That is why he prays as he does. For his followers to follow him, he has to lead from the front. That means delivering on the death that he says is eternal life and salvation for all who believe on him. He knows what he must do—it was settled "from the foundation of the world" that "the Lamb" who "takes away the sin of the world" would be "slain" (Rev. 13:8;

John 1:29). Jesus's true humanity, however, shrinks from death, as we all do instinctively, and most pointedly of all, is troubled by the horror of paying the wages of sin. The heart of the incarnate Son of God trembles at the prospect of suffering his Father's just wrath against sin not his own. This is a foretaste of his sufferings in Gethsemane (Mark 14:36).

Jesus first ponders a potential prayer suggested by his troubled soul—"What shall I say? 'Father, save Me from this hour'?"—but reminds himself that "for this purpose I came to this hour" (v. 27). He never rebels against his readiness to be obedient to the death of the cross (see Phil. 2:6–8). In this way, he demonstrates to all those around him his unswerving commitment to his saving work and seals it with the positive prayer: "Father, glorify Your name" (v. 28a). Jesus bites the bullet and faces down any temptation to recoil from his mission. The Father then responds audibly with the voice of his affirmation: "Then a voice came from heaven, saying, 'I have both glorified it and will glorify it again'" (v. 28b). It is love in both the Father and the Son that leads to Calvary and thereby accomplishes the salvation of the world.

Jesus's example points the way for us. The cost of discipleship is never cheap, but the rewards are glorious. Thomas Manton notes, "A love to our private interests hinders us from seeking the glory of God: Rom. 15:3, 'For even Christ pleased not himself'; John 12:27–28, 'For this cause I came to this hour: Father glorify thy name.' Every Christian should be thus affected: let Christ dispose of him and his interests as it seemeth good to him." In other words, we are called in following Jesus to lay aside, as he did, "the innocent inclinations of…human nature" and seek above all the glory of his Father and ours. To God be the glory!

PRAYER TO PERSEVERE
Sing Psalm 34:11–22

THINGS I WILL PRAY FOR TODAY

_____

_____

_____

_____

_____

_____

September 23
The Hour Has Come

Jesus prays for himself (Part 2)

Father, the hour has come. — *John 17:1*

READ JOHN 17:1–5

Jesus is only hours from his death by crucifixion. He and his disciples have left their Last Supper (John 14:31) and are somewhere on the path to crossing the Kidron brook (John 18:1) and entering the garden of Gethsemane, where Christ will be arrested (18:12). They pause on the way for Jesus to instruct them at some length (John 15:1–16:33), and to engage in that prayer of prayers, the aptly named "Great High-Priestly Prayer" (17:1–26). Jesus prays, says Charles Ross, as "the great High-Priest of the Church, offering up to God himself and all his people, both present and future; while at the same time, it is obvious that this prayer brings down upon them the blessing of God. For what Jesus here asks, Jesus *obtains*." Furthermore, "this prayer was answered, is being answered still, and will continue to be answered, until the last vessel of mercy is gathered home to glory (verse 24)."

Jesus's first words breathe the spirit of messianic intercession. Even his posture is that of the "one mediator between God and men, the man Christ Jesus" (1 Tim. 2:5): "he lifted up His eyes to heaven, and said…" (John 17:1a). Here is God the Son *incarnate* come to "save His people from their sins" (Matt. 1:21). As the God-man, he submits without reservation to his work as the Mediator who must die in the place of sinners. His uplifted eyes acknowledge both sovereignty and the sufficiency of his Father God, while his prayer presupposes accountability to and dependence upon God. He gives himself up to the will and to the mercies of God in the full knowledge of the trial he is facing.

Jesus submits to his heavenly Father and ours. His first word is "Father." He looks *away* from himself. How different the attitude of modern man, who is often told, "Reach inside of yourself," or "Believe in yourself," in order to find resources with which to face down the challenges life brings. As Jesus cries to the Father, he shows us the soul of prayer—our prayers too—and seals his willingness to do the Father's will and be obedient to the point of death, all the while depending upon his sovereign grace.

Jesus also submits to God's appointed hour. Our English "hour" is borrowed straight from the Greek New Testament *hora*, but it does not here mean "sixty minutes." This "hour" encompasses Jesus's arrest, trial, death, burial, resurrection, and glorification. Up to now, this had "not yet come" (John 2:4; 7:6, 8, 30; 8:20), but now "has come" (John 12:23–31; 13:1, 31). This hour is not merely the moment of personal crisis for Jesus, but it is the very hinge of history, for with the cross a door swings open on a new era: "the old has passed away" and "the new has come" and each believer is made a "new creation" in Christ.

Jesus submits to his personal destiny. D. A. Carson notes that, when Jesus asks the Father to "glorify Your Son," he is asking him to "reverse the self-emptying entailed in his incarnation and to restore him to the splendor he shared with the Father before the world began." But not just that glory of the *eternal* Son, because Jesus takes his human body to heaven and so fulfills his destiny as the conqueror of sin and death. He is exalted as a Prince and a Savior (Acts 5:31) and is glorified as the firstborn among many brothers (Rom. 8:29). This is the destiny of all who believe and are saved. Then pray, and live, out of that "inheritance incorruptible and undefiled and that does not fade away, reserved in heaven for you" (1 Peter 1:4).

PRAYER IN FACING A DIFFICULT TIME
Sing Psalm 119:113–120

THINGS I WILL PRAY FOR TODAY

_____

_____

_____

_____

_____

_____

_____

_____

September 24
To Give Eternal Life

Jesus prays for himself (Part 3)

...that He should give eternal life to as many as You have given Him.
—John 17:2

READ JOHN 17:1–5

he word "doctrine" is not popular these days. It is more often than not used in a negative way. "Doctrine divides and service unites" was adopted as the motto of the ecumenical movement in Stockholm, Sweden, as long ago as 1925. This codified for modernist churches a retreat from orthodox biblical faith into liberal social and political activism that continues to this day. By the 1960s, many evangelicals echoed this by opposing "doctrine" and "life" and linking the words "dead" and "orthodoxy" in describing churches and people that seemed to have "a form of godliness but denying its power" (2 Tim. 3:5). Experience, feelings, and practicality were allegedly being stifled by doctrine's deadly embrace. In the twenty-first century, the fruit of these movements is painfully obvious: the anti-biblical, politically correct message of the declining mainline churches; the drift to entertainment-as-worship; and the increasing biblical illiteracy among the evangelicals! But how does this relate to Jesus's prayer? The answer is that Jesus prays doctrine all the time! Specifically, when he states the reasons for praying in John 17:2, he sets out the doctrines that give life to his prayer! For Jesus, doctrine *is* life and doctrine *is* service! Far from being opposing categories, these are inseparable, with sound life and service flowing from sound teaching (which is simply what "doctrine" is). Why should God glorify his Son and any glory accrue to the Father? Jesus answers with three great doctrines that are writ large in God's Word and should be prominent in the life of the soul.

First is the doctrine of the mediatorial kingship of Christ. The Father has "given Him authority over all flesh" (v. 2a). The verb indicates completed action. In eternity past, the Father invested the Son with a mediatorial authority over humanity. As the Son made flesh, Jesus is Mediator between God and man and has "authority"—is King—in virtue of his saving work. As Mediator-Priest he dies to accomplish salvation, and as Mediator-King he lives to apply that salvation by converting sinners to himself (1 Peter 3:18–22). As mediatorial King he is "head over all things to the church" (Eph. 1:22). No priesthood would mean no redemption accomplished. No kingship would mean no redemption applied. This doctrine is our life!

Second is the doctrine of substitutionary atonement. Christ has authority so that he "should give eternal life" (v. 2b). A kingdom without citizens is no kingdom at all. Jesus atones for sin, to give new life to all who will believe on him as Savior and Lord (Rom. 6:23; Eph. 2:8–9; 1 Peter 3:7). Eternal life populates Christ's kingdom both here and hereafter in heaven. This doctrine is our very life!

Third is the doctrine of divine election. The scope of Jesus's atonement and the saving reach of his authority is simply "as many as" the Father has "given Him" (v. 2c). The *intent* of the atonement determines its *extent*. Election, whether by God or men, is a choice in the gift of the elector. We choose a politician; God chooses a people. What he intends, however, he perfectly accomplishes. God, in his mercy, saves "as many as" he gives to Jesus. They are a reward for his faithfulness (Isa. 53:10); they come willingly (John 6:37–40); he knows them all (2 Tim. 2:19); he cares for them and keeps them (John 10:3); and he will present them to the Father on the last day with joy (Luke 12:8; Jude 24). This doctrine too is our life!

Far from being irrelevant, sound doctrine feeds the soul. It also moves all true Christian life and service. Life flows from and depends upon every word that proceeds from the mouth of God—and these are the doctrines the Lord wants us to believe and practice every day.

PRAYER REJOICING IN SOUND DOCTRINE
Sing Psalm 119:33–40

THINGS I WILL PRAY FOR TODAY

September 25
The Path of Glory

And now, O Father, glorify Me together with Yourself, with the glory which I had with You before the world was. —John 17:5

READ JOHN 17:3-5

esus prays as one who is on the road to glory! His goal in saving sinners is the glory of both himself and his Father-God (John 17:1). His reasons for pursuing this path rest upon three great truths: his mediatorial kingship, his substitutionary atonement for human sin, and God's election of those he will save (John 17:2). These respectively declare his power to save sinners, his authority to pay the price of their sin, and his reliance on God's eternal purpose to redeem a people "according to the election of grace" (Rom. 11:5). Jesus now prays about three things vital to accomplishing his purposes (John 17:3–5).

Jesus prays about eternal life for those he came to save (v. 3). Eternal life is not merely endless life. The lost in hell have endless life of a kind, but Scripture calls it "the second death" (Rev. 2:11; 20:6, 14; 21:8). Eternal life is the life of heaven come to earth in a new spiritual condition that consists in a personal knowledge of and union with God made possible in and through Christ. We must do three things:

- We must know the "only true God," who is "the God and Father of our Lord Jesus Christ" (Eph. 1:4). He is only truly known in and through his Son, who is "the express image of His person" (Heb. 1:3). All other gods are false and nonexistent.
- We must also know "Jesus Christ." Joining these names for the first time, Jesus is saying, "I am the promised Messiah." "Jesus" means "God saves" (Matt. 1:21) and "Christ" means "Messiah" (John 1:41). No mere teacher or visionary, Jesus is both God and man.
- We must know Jesus as the one "sent" by God to purchase the church with his blood (John 1:18; 10:36; Gal. 4:4; Acts 20:28). Saving faith believes in this God and this Jesus: "Nor is there

salvation in any other, for there is no other name under heaven given among men by which we must be saved" (Acts 4:12).

Jesus prays about the completion of the work of redemption. Although he is still to be crucified, he declares, "I have finished the work which You have given Me to do" (v. 4). He anticipates the final crisis of the cross the very next day with perfect determination and the implicit prayer that God's will be done. This has its echoes in every Christian's life. It teaches us the *what, where,* and *how* of our discipleship to Jesus. The *what* of our calling is to glorify God with everything we've got. The *where* is here and now, in this life, every day. The *how* is the obedience of faith in which we serve God, doing his will, by his grace, in Jesus Christ our Savior and Lord.

Jesus prays about his glory as the exalted Savior. Filled with a sense of the impending success of his death and resurrection, Jesus expresses his desire to return to the Father's presence, resuming that preincarnate glory he had "before the world was" (v. 5). His glory will be different from now on, however, because by his bodily resurrection and subsequent ascension, he will take his human body with him to heaven to reign as "head over all things to the church" at "the right hand of the Majesty on high" (Eph. 1:22; Heb. 1:3). Jesus's glorification in his body is forever a testimony to his death for sinners and is also a pledge of the resurrection and glorification of all for whom he died.

Jesus's followers will follow him to glory. This is the believer's calling in this life and for the life to come. "Dear brethren," Charles Simeon exhorted his flock in Cambridge, "only follow your Saviour in the exercise of faith and love; and his glory shall be your glory, his kingdom your kingdom, forever and ever."

PRAISE ANTICIPATING GLORY FROM GOD
Sing Psalm 85:8–13

THINGS I WILL PRAY FOR TODAY

_____

_____

_____

_____

_____

September 26
The Men You Have Given

Jesus prays for his disciples (Part 1)

You gave them to Me. —John 17:6

READ JOHN 17:6–8

esus, having prayed for himself, prays for his disciples. Where we might pray for the future of the movement, Jesus prays for "the men" he personally knows and loves. Jesus is vitally committed to adding "to the church daily" those who will be saved (Acts 2:47). But there is nothing abstract or coldly institutional about his goals and his prayers. The most basic and ongoing need is faithful disciples who will be the agents of spreading the gospel and making new disciples. He therefore begins to pray for them by setting out the most essential characteristics of a true disciple. In this way, he affirms his faithful followers and, by way of contrast, prepares them for the apostasy of Judas Iscariot, the backsliding of Peter, and the scattering of the rest. Jesus emphasizes the special relationship they bear to him, and he to them, and that they and he bear to God the Father. To be personally "hidden with Christ in God" is the life and hope for their mission to the world, and for ours today (Col. 3:3).

Jesus calls his disciples out of this world. Jesus says, "I have manifested Your name to the men whom You have given Me out of the world" (v. 6a). The revelation of God's *name* is vastly more than some formal identification of God. It is nothing less than God's self-disclosure to his people. As such, it implies an ever-growing insight into his character, promises, and purposes. It also involves, through the ministry of the Son, a personal, experiential grasp of God's fatherhood. Jesus assures Philip, "He who has seen Me has seen the Father." This is not some cold unfelt proposition, but rather the experience of a heart that knows what it is to be reconciled to a heavenly Father. The communication of God's transforming grace through the Lord Jesus Christ, as he is believed upon and followed in faith, guarantees the future for every disciple and for the church as a whole. God is the one who has sovereignly and freely given a people to Jesus for him to save from their sins and sanctify in their walk with him.

540

Jesus's disciples come to him by the work of God's grace: "they were Yours, You gave them to Me" (v. 6b). "Christ declares," says John Calvin, "that the elect always belonged to God. God therefore distinguishes them from the reprobate, not by faith, or by any merit, but by pure grace; for while they are alienated from him to the utmost, still he reckons them as his own in his secret purpose." God loves sinners from eternity and saves them in time. The evidence and proof of a saving work of God's grace is very practical: "And they have kept Your word." This does not gloss over their (and our) weaknesses, but it does say that they have the root of the matter: a saving knowledge of Christ. They believe the Word of God and love the Son of God.

Jesus's disciples know him as the Savior sent by God. True disciples grasp two great truths: that everything Jesus said and did was given by God, and that Jesus himself had been sent by God (vv. 7–8). They still did not understand or accept what Jesus said about his death, but they believed in him as the divine Messiah promised in Scripture. For all their perplexities, the disciples are simply and genuinely united to Jesus in living faith. They are God's men and nothing will pluck them from Jesus's hand: not their failings, not the world, and not the devil. "They shall be Mine," God says, "on the day that I make them My jewels" (Mal. 3:17). This applies not merely to Jesus's immediate disciples, but to everyone who truly believes in Christ. The word "disciple" simply means "witness." It applies to each and every true Christian. And that, disciples of Jesus, means you too!

PRAISE OF A GENUINE DISCIPLE
Sing Psalm 119:129–136

THINGS I WILL PRAY FOR TODAY

_____

_____

_____

_____

_____

_____

_____

September 27
I Pray for Them

Jesus prays for his disciples (Part 2)

I pray for them…for they are You. —John 17:9

READ JOHN 17:9-10

Interceding for those we love is the most natural thing in the world. Jesus is unique, of course, because of who he is and what he means to accomplish. His immediate focus is on the eleven disciples, although, by his own extension, it applies also to those who will believe in him in the future (17:20). He says, "I pray for them" because he loves them as their Savior and Mediator "by means of death" (1 Tim. 2:5; Heb. 9:15). He emphasizes this with the startling contrast, "I do not pray for the world but for those whom You have given me, for they are Yours" (v. 9). The "world" here must refer to the world of unrelentingly unrepentant people, as opposed to the world of unbelievers, created by God, fallen in Adam, and set to be redeemed through Christ (John 3:16; 4:42). Elsewhere Jesus prays for the world that needs the gospel when, from the cross, he prays, "Father, forgive them, for they do not know what they do" (Luke 23:34).

This reminds us that salvation is not universal. There are different worlds in play in Scripture. One is the world God loves enough to send his Son as its Savior. This includes the creation as a whole and the lost who will believe and be saved. It is comprehensively redeemed (Rev. 21:1). The other is the world of the reprobate lost, who choose to reject Jesus to their last breath. Jesus intercedes for those God has given him—from "before the foundation of the world" (Eph. 1:4)—but not for the rest. Thomas Manton observes,

> Universal redemption is disproved, for those for whom Christ prayed not, for them he died not. These two offices of the priesthood [i.e., atonement and intercession] must not be severed. Christ doth not only profess to pray for these, but denieth to pray for the world. His intercession is of the same latitude with his redemption; they are acts of the same office, and of the same extent and latitude. All men were not intended in his passion and intercession.

542

When Jesus prays for his persecutors and we pray for our world, we pray as those who take no pleasure in the death of the wicked and long for people to be saved, while knowing there will be those who refuse to believe and remain lost.

Why does Jesus intercede for his own disciples? His reasons reach even deeper than the motives of love and service to others that are foundational to all acts of human kindness. Even when he speaks of his power to save, his love for the lost and his promise of eternal life roots everything in the God of the Scriptures. It is because those he came to save belong first to God that he interceded for them. To say "all mine are Yours" is to define his mission as the Servant of the Lord (v. 10a). To add "Yours are Mine" is to assert his messiahship as the God-man. Jesus serves the Father in terms of a union that reaches from eternity into time and issues in his dying for the ungodly whom God has given to him to save from their sins (Rom. 5:6; Eph. 5:25).

The rest is glory. As Jesus says, "I am glorified in them" (v. 10c). Of course! Every father knows how to glory in the accomplishments of his child. Of course there is "joy in the presence of the angels of God over one sinner who repents" (Luke 15:10). Of course the God and Father of our Lord Jesus Christ rejoices before his angels! He rejoices in the glory of saving sinners and in the beloved Son in whom he is well pleased (Matt. 3:17). What a privilege to have Jesus as *our* intercessor. We may say with inner joy and confidence, "His eye is on the sparrow, and I know he watches me."

PRAYER FOR INTERCESSION
Sing Psalm 122 (see v. 6)

THINGS I WILL PRAY FOR TODAY

_____

_____

_____

_____

_____

_____

_____

September 28
Keep Them from the Evil One

Jesus prays for his disciples (Part 3)

I do not pray that You should take them out of the world, but that You should keep them from the evil one. —John 17:15

READ JOHN 17:11–16

Many a movement has collapsed on the death of a strong leader. Jesus knew how fragile his disciples' morale really was. If they could not face the predictions of his death, how would they handle the real thing? Jesus tells them, "All of you will be made to stumble because of Me this night, for it is written: 'I will strike the Shepherd, And the sheep of the flock will be scattered'" (Zech. 13:7). He also predicts his resurrection, their later finding him in Galilee, and Peter's threefold denial (Matt. 26:31–34). He therefore prays that God would protect and strengthen the disciples as they go through these trials.

Christ prays for four specific blessings:

Coherent unity. Jesus's first petition is in two parts. He prays for the *protection* of his disciples. He speaks as one effectively "no longer in the world" but vitally concerned for those still "in the world." He asks his "Holy Father" to "keep them in [his] name"—that is, in the *place* of faithfulness, which is walking with God as a disciple (v. 11, ESV). He also prays for *unity* among them as they must face the world—"that they may be one as We are." The unity of believers is to mirror the unity of the Father and the Son. This in turn enables them to live together as those who "have obtained like precious faith…by the righteousness of our God and Savior Jesus Christ" (2 Peter 1:1).

Committed faith. Jesus had hitherto preserved all of his disciples, he says, except for "the son of perdition" (v. 12). His implicit prayer is that in the future they will all persevere in the faith of Christ and his good news of salvation. Judas did not fall away because Jesus could not "keep" him, but to fulfill the prophecy of Psalm 41:9 (see John 13:18). Jesus assures us, "All that the Father gives Me will come to Me, and the one who comes to Me I will by no means cast out" (John 6:37).

Confident joy. Jesus prays "in the world" — that is, in their hearing — that his disciples might have his "joy" (v. 13). Jesus's joy is to keep his Father's commandments and abide in his love (John 15:9–11). He prays that his joy will be "fulfilled" in them! How so? As Jesus rejoices while facing his death for sinners, so the disciples will be enabled to rejoice in him, even when all the circumstances appear to be against them. This promise is for every believer. By his grace, we will "rejoice in the Lord always" (Phil. 4:2).

Conquering power. Clearly, the unity, faith, and joy that Jesus's requests for his people are the things that will sustain and strengthen believers in the face of a hard world (vv. 14–16). Jesus is utterly realistic. The world hates the people of the Word because neither Jesus nor his followers are "of the world" (v. 14). The opposition of "the evil one" is inevitable, but Jesus wants us in the world, not "out" of it, and fully engaged in the war for people's souls. His Father and ours will "keep [us] from the evil one." Christians are therefore called to be radically different — in the world, but not of it (v. 16): "Therefore, if anyone is in Christ, he is a new creation; old things have passed away; behold, all things have become new" (2 Cor. 5:17). Our separation from the world, while being fully engaged in it, is "evidence of [our] conformity to Christ and a sure pledge that God will keep us from the evil of the world" so that "we will not lose those good things which grace has begun in us" (Phil. 1:6).

PRAISE TO THE LORD WHO PRESERVES HIS PEOPLE
Sing Psalm 66

THINGS I WILL PRAY FOR TODAY

_____

_____

_____

_____

_____

_____

_____

September 29
Sanctify Them

Jesus prays for his disciples (Part 4)

Sanctify them by Your truth. Your word is truth. —*John 17:17*

READ JOHN 17:17–19

The logic of Jesus's prayer for the disciples unfolds in three steps. He first shows that the basis for his intercession is his ownership of his disciples (John 17:6–10). He then addresses their need for protection from the evil in the world (John 17:11–16). Then he concludes with the positive prescription for their spiritual growth, namely, their perseverance and progressive sanctification (vv. 17–19). The word "sanctify" simply means "make holy." God says, "You shall be holy, for I the LORD your God am holy" (Lev. 19:2). Thomas Manton notes that believers are "set apart by God and by themselves" (Eph. 1:4; Rom. 12:1), "purged by degrees and made free from sin" (1 Cor. 6:11), and "adorned with grace" (2 Tim. 2:12). Jesus unfolds how this happens in three simple but profound petitions.

Jesus's disciples are sanctified by truth. Not just any truth, mind you, but the truth of God (v. 17). The definition that follows—"Your word is truth"—removes any potential for subjectivism and ambiguity: it is the truth that is the Word of God, given "in time past to the fathers by the prophets," and "in these last days spoken to us by His Son" (Heb. 1:1–2). Jesus, as the divine Logos/Word (John 1:1), is the embodiment and message of truth, and the Scriptures are the tangible abiding and sufficient residuum of all God's special revelation to man. If we are to be sanctified, it is to the Word we must go (Isa. 8:20; 2 Tim. 3:16). We will otherwise inevitably wither on the vine.

Jesus's disciples are sanctified to be sent into the world. He says to the Father: "As You sent Me into the world, I also have sent them into the world" (v. 18). He saves to send. We are saved to serve. The world, which will be the source of so much trouble and opposition, is, after all, to be won for God! He is sending them "into" the world for the same basic reason that the Father sent him into the same world. He came to proclaim salvation; they must go to proclaim that same salvation. The redemption

546

that Jesus alone accomplishes in his death and resurrection will be applied through the faithful preaching of the apostles and succeeding generations of faithful gospel ministers.

Jesus's disciples are sanctified by the Savior himself. He says, "For their sakes I sanctify Myself, that they also may be sanctified by the truth" (v. 19). But how could sinless Jesus sanctify himself? He is the Lamb without blemish (1 Peter 1:19). True, but he took our human nature and did "sanctify" himself in the sense that he "learned obedience by the things which he suffered" (Heb. 5:8), and "humbled Himself and became obedient to the point of death, even the death of the cross" (Phil. 2:8). As the God-man—the Savior of sinners—he consecrated himself to his redemptive work, inch by agonizing inch. He did this for "their sakes"— the eleven disciples—and, by extension, for the world he had come to save. His self-sanctification secures their sanctification. This is the source of the power that will transform all who follow Jesus. When Paul was troubled by his weakness, the Lord assured him, "My grace is sufficient for you, for My strength is made perfect in weakness." This led the apostle to exult in the transforming power of Jesus in his own life. He can praise the Lord: "For when I am weak, then I am strong" (2 Cor. 12:9–10). This is a phrase for every Christian, for, as Paul reminds Titus, Jesus "gave Himself for us, that He might redeem us from every lawless deed and purify for Himself His own special people, zealous for good works" (Titus 2:14). United to Christ by faith, we are sanctified to be holy as he is holy.

PRAISE FOR PROGRESSIVE SANCTIFICATION
Sing Psalm 18:30–36

THINGS I WILL PRAY FOR TODAY

_____

_____

_____

_____

_____

_____

_____

September 30
Dwelling Together in Unity

Jesus prays for the future Church (Part 1)

I do not ask for these only, but also for those who will believe in Me through their word. —John 17:20

READ JOHN 17:20–23

Behold, how good and how pleasant it is," says the psalmist, "for brethren to dwell together in unity!" (Ps. 133:1). Disunity is not good, often unpleasant, and always an easy excuse for people to brush off the claims of Christ. It can be no surprise to find Jesus, having prayed for himself and his immediate disciples, now interceding for the unity of the church he intends to build in this world: "I do not pray for these alone"—the eleven disciples (17:6–19)—"but also for those who will believe in Me through their word" (v. 20). "The eye of Jesus scans the centuries," writes William Hendriksen, "and presses to his loving heart *all* his true followers *as if they had all been saved at this very moment.*"

The heart of true church unity is personal union with Christ. There was a visible, organizational unity to the apostolic church, and that remains as a reproach, a model, and a goal for the fractious denominations of our day. Jesus's prayer, however, is more concerned with "the unity of the Spirit in the bond of peace" (Eph. 4:3). The *scope* of this unity is defined by Jesus's desire that believers "all may be one" (v. 21a). The focus is on inward unity that binds believers together in heart and soul, whatever may presently divide them outwardly. The *source* of this unity is the unity of the Father and the Son. Jesus wants us to be united, he says, "as You, Father, are in Me, and I in You" (v. 21b). The *substance* of this unity consists in shared union with Jesus and the Father. Hence Jesus's prayer "that they also may be one in Us" (v. 21c). This is a "supernatural unity," says Bruce Milne, in which "the life we share as Christians is therefore nothing less than a participation in the life of the Godhead!" Christ saves us to be one people. Our life "is hidden with Christ in God" (Col. 3:3).

The fruit of true church unity is a credible witness for Christ. The goal is "that the world may believe that You sent Me. And the glory which You gave Me I have given them, that they may be one just as We are one" (vv. 21d–22). Party spirit in the church divides the indivisible Christ (1 Cor. 1:12–13). The world does not see this as either credible or desirable. Who will be attracted to a "salvation" proclaimed by people who are clearly unloving toward each other? What makes the witness of true unity compelling is the "glory" of Christ reflected in Christlike love for one another.

The goal of true church unity is that people would love God. Jesus's prayer rises to a glorious crescendo: "I in them, and You in Me; that they may be made perfect in one, and that the world may know that You have sent Me, and have loved them as You have loved Me" (v. 23). Jesus first prays that believers will grow in the love that binds them to the Father through him as their Savior. He then prays for the unbelieving world, that this sincere, visible love in the church will persuade many that Christ is the real Savior by whom they can be reconciled to the living God. The practical point is that a loving church witnesses to a loving Savior! If, in contrast, we are like the church in Corinth, blighted with a party-spirited lovelessness, we are in danger of making "the cross of Christ...of no effect" (1 Cor. 1:10–17). Let us respond to Jesus's love for us by living out our calling to love one another as he loves us and as the Father loves him. Then we will shine as lights in this dark world and be a living community of faith that invites and embraces people in Christ's name (Phil. 2:15).

PRAISE CELEBRATING TRUE UNITY
Sing Psalm 133

THINGS I WILL PRAY FOR TODAY

_____

_____

_____

_____

_____

_____

_____

_____

October 1
Eternal Glory

Jesus prays for the future church (Part 2)

Father, I desire that they also whom You gave Me may be with Me where I am, that they may behold My glory which You have given Me; for You loved Me before the foundation of the world. —John 17:24

READ JOHN 17:20–24

esus's focus now shifts. From the believers' present participation in his glory he turns to what is yet future and eternal. His opening address—"Father"—heralds his climactic conclusion. Manton notes, beautifully, that "Christ is now suing for a child's portion for all his members, and therefore he saith 'Father.' God is Christ's father by eternal generation, and ours by gracious adoption, whence our title to heaven ariseth." His forthright "I desire" tells how passionate he is that all who follow him will share his future glory in heaven (cf. Col. 3:24).

Who will receive this eternal glory? Jesus prays for "[them] also whom You gave Me" (v. 24a). Every single person God intends to save will come to saving faith and go on to glory! God does not plan, nor does Jesus secure, only the *possibility* of salvation. He chooses, he gives, and he saves. All that the Father gives will come to him (John 6:37). None of these will perish. None will be plucked from his hand (John 10:28–29; cf. Matt. 25:4; Eph. 1:4). The end is not in doubt.

Why does Jesus want believers to enjoy eternal glory? We all naturally want to share the joyous moments of our lives with our loved ones. If we win a race, gain a promotion, receive an honor for service to our country, graduate with a degree, get married, have a baby, or observe an anniversary, we want others to enjoy our enjoyment. Jesus is no exception: he asks the Father that his loved ones "may be with Me where I am, that they may behold My glory which You have given Me" (v. 24b). The triumph of the great day when Jesus comes to judge the living and the dead will occasion a celebration like no other. Jesus wants his people to be there, not least because they were the reason he gave himself to his sufferings and death. His "heart is not satisfied till we be in like condition

550

with himself," says Manton. He wants us to eat and drink at his table in his kingdom (Luke 22:20) and to sit upon his throne (Rev. 3:21).

What is the reason for this gift of eternal glory? It is, as Jesus tells his Father, because "You loved Me before the foundation of the world" (v. 24c). The gift of future eternal glory comes from the past *eternal* love of the Giver. Your personal salvation turns upon God's *eternal* purpose of love in his only begotten Son. Paul's famous "golden chain" reflects this movement from the eternal plan, through its outworking in history, to its future eternal fruition: "For whom He foreknew, He also predestined to be conformed to the image of His Son, that He might be the firstborn among many brethren. Moreover whom He predestined, these He also called; whom He called, these He also justified; and whom He justified, these He also glorified" (Rom. 8:29–30). Jesus desires that the saints "behold" the glory of their Savior, seeing him "face to face" and "as He is" (1 Cor. 13:12a; 1 John 3:2; cf. Job 19:26–27). Our knowledge of God will no longer be "in part," but will have a fullness of the order of God's knowledge of us (1 Cor. 13:12b). "We go to heaven," says Manton, "to study divinity in the Lamb's face." The psalmist rejoices in this wonderful prospect: "Nevertheless I am continually with You; You hold me by my right hand. You will guide me with Your counsel, and afterward receive me to glory" (Ps. 73:23–24).

PRAISE IN PROSPECT OF HEAVENLY GLORY
Sing Psalm 73:23–27

THINGS I WILL PRAY FOR TODAY

October 2
The Bonds of Love

I have declared to them Your name, and will declare it, that the love with which You loved Me may be in them, and I in them. —John 17:26

READ JOHN 17:25–26

esus's crowning petition appeals to God as his "righteous Father!" Here is grace for sinners because God's righteous fatherhood guarantees the application of redemption to all those for whom Christ died. They will come to glory because the Father stands by his love for the Son who became sin for them (2 Cor. 5:21) and is not willing that any of them should perish (2 Peter 3:9). When we confess our sins, "He is faithful and just to forgive us our sins and to cleanse us from all unrighteousness" (1 John 1:9), because he has accepted Christ's sacrifice as the ground of our salvation. God is always just, but to those who trust in Jesus he is a heavenly Father. Consequently, God's children are distinguished from the world by three great realities in their experience: the knowledge of God, the love of God, and union with God in Christ. It is with these blessings of salvation that Jesus closes his great prayer.

The knowledge of God. God's work of redemption has to beat against the wind of fallen human nature. Sin in the heart issues in a willful denial that God has any claims upon us, assuming there is a God. We have no excuse, for we chose to believe the lie (Rom. 1:18–25; John 15:24). Eventually, "the wicked shall be turned into [a] hell" they do not believe they deserve, by the God whose authority and power they discounted (Ps. 9:17). So how can anyone come to know God? Jesus provides the answer: "The world has not known You," says Jesus, "but I have known You; and these have known that You sent Me. And I have declared to them Your name" (vv. 25b–26a). Jesus knows God, believers know that God sent him, and they know him because he reveals God to them. By grace and through faith they came to Jesus, acknowledging him as their Mediator, and so came to know the Father (see John 1:18; 5:23; 14:6; Matt. 11:27; 1 John 5:20).

The love of God. The true knowledge of God is bound up with the love of God. This means, says Jesus, "that the love with which You loved Me may be in them" (v. 26bc). The glue that affixes them to future blessing is God's love in their hearts. This is the grace of all graces. "We are loved into holiness, loved into pardon, loved into grace," says Manton. The disciples' faith is weak, but real, and so they can expect to know more of God more richly in the future because of God's personal abiding love for his own people. "Observe, for your comfort," says Manton, "that Christ...prayed not only for grace, but for assurance, that we may feel ourselves beloved by the Father. The Lord delighteth not only to love us, but to assure us of his love."

Union with Christ. The key words are "I in them" (v. 26d). The love of God is always bound up with the love of Christ. Union with Christ is entered into by believing in him as alone able to save us from our sins. Jesus's prayer brings us to the very promise of his gospel and commands our response: "To as many as received Him, to them He gave the right to become children of God, to those who believe in His name: who were born, not of blood, nor of the will of the flesh, nor of the will of man, but of God" (John 1:12–13). While God is the fountain of mercy, Christ is the opening of the fountain to cleanse those who trust themselves to him (Zech. 13:1). Christ *in you* is "the hope of glory" itself (Col. 1:27).

PRAISE FOR GOD'S LOVE FOR HIS CHURCH
Sing Psalm 85:8–13

THINGS I WILL PRAY FOR TODAY

October 3
With One Accord

The Upper Room prayer meeting

These all continued with one accord in prayer and supplication. — Acts 1:14

READ ACTS 1:1-14

his has been called the first prayer meeting of the church. This distinction, however, rightly belongs to Adam and his extended family in the distant day when "men began to call on the name of the Lord" (Gen. 4:26). The church is not the exclusive creation of the New Testament, but the assembly of the people of God in every age. What is distinctive about this prayer meeting in Acts is that it finds the church suspended between the past and the future, waiting for the Lord to fulfill his specific promise of the coming of the Holy Spirit in power. This is not an ordinary prayer meeting, but one that is uniquely a milepost in the unfolding of God's redemptive plan in history. As such, it stands in relation to the emerging New Testament era as the prayer meeting of Genesis 4 marks the first appearing of the church after Adam's fall and subsequent redemption.

It is also a thoroughly Trinitarian event. God reveals himself here explicitly in terms of the distinct ministries of the Father, the Son, and the Holy Spirit. This brilliantly contrasts the veiled promise of the gospel as revealed in Genesis 3:15 and sought in prayer in Genesis 4:26 with the clarity of gospel fulfillment in Jesus Christ:

- The crucified and risen Son secures *salvation* for sinners (vv. 1–3). How? By taking our human nature, giving himself to death on a cross as the atoning sacrifice for sin, and rising triumphant over sin and the grave for our justification (Rom. 4:25). Because he lives, all who accept him as Savior gain eternal life (Acts 16:25). He died, but lives forever — "the firstborn among many brethren" (Rom. 8:29). His post-resurrection ministry proves his ability to save sinners.

- The promise of the Father secures the *hope* of the Christian with respect to the future (v. 4). The disciples are at a unique, unrepeatable crossroad both in their personal experience and

554

the very history of the world. God has spoken, Christ has died and is alive, but they are to wait for the decisive coming of the Holy Spirit upon the church. Within just a few days, their ministry will begin in earnest.

> The baptism of the Holy Spirit secures the *power* by which the church becomes an effective witness to Christ even to "the end of the earth" (vv. 5–8). This is a decisive moment in history—not a reference to a subjective, inward experience repeated in certain individual Christians in all the centuries to come. Yes, the Spirit lives in every believer from his conversion to Christ. But that is a reality that flows from the sending of the Spirit at the first Pentecost of the present New Testament era. Promised by Jesus before his crucifixion (John 14:15–18; 15:26; 16:13–14), the Holy Spirit is explicitly revealed to the church before the world—never to leave it.

The infant New Testament church—in the persons of the eleven disciples—"continued with one accord in prayer and supplication" for the outpouring of the Spirit (vv. 12–14). Present also were "the women and Mary the mother of Jesus, and…his brothers"—and perhaps all of the 120 mentioned in verse 15ff. The promise of the Spirit is not the same as the presence of the Spirit. The fruition of God's promises may and must always be prayed for with earnest faith. We will need to pray all the way to heaven. The words "with one accord" underline the role of *corporate* prayer in the life of the church. Prayer meetings are not optional extras for the few that feel the need. The church waits upon the Lord *together*, in harmonious, united prayer. You could have chosen to stay home and pray in "the secret place" (Matt. 6:6). But the church is a body united in love for God in Christ, and is ultimately the Christian's true and eternal home. Let us love to pray with one accord in the assemblies of the people of God.

A PRAYER FOR THE HOLY SPIRIT
Sing Psalm 143:7–12

THINGS I WILL PRAY FOR TODAY

October 4
Rebuilding the Leadership

Praying for the man of God's choosing

And they prayed and said, "You, O Lord, who know the hearts of all,
show which of these two You have chosen." — Acts 1:24

READ ACTS 1:15–26

Losing leaders can be hard on any community. When Judas Iscariot betrayed Jesus, it was a knife in the heart of the church that precipitated Jesus's death and the subsequent scattering of the other eleven disciples. This was God's means of securing our salvation, but it was a moment of great peril and confusion for Jesus's disciples. Judas's defection also opened a breach in the church's leadership. It did not, however, come out of a clear blue sky. It fulfilled ancient prophecies of both his removal and his replacement (Ps. 69:25; 109:8). Accordingly, the first gathering of the apostolic church after Jesus's ascension addresses the matter of restoring the leadership to "the Twelve"—the number of completeness as representing the twelve tribes of Israel.

Looking for leaders may be very challenging. This is, of course, a unique and unrepeatable occasion in the life of the church—a one–off event. We need to be careful when applying it to our time. We are not called to appoint new apostles and have no warrant to cast lots for our ministers, elders, and deacons today. In finding an apostle for the Twelve, aside from the assumption that he must be a godly man, the preconditions were that he had accompanied the other eleven apostles "*all the time* that the Lord Jesus went in and out amongst us" and was a *witness with them* of the resurrection of Jesus (v. 21–22, emphasis added). All agreed that this narrowed the field to Barsabas and Matthias (v. 23).

The next step was to pray, asking that the Lord who knows "the hearts of all" would show which of the two he had chosen (v. 24). This is of universal application to all issues and outcomes in life: "in everything by prayer and supplication, with thanksgiving, let your requests be made known to God" (Phil. 4:6).

Rather than vote, which would surely have compromised unanimity, they drew lots, and the lot fell on Matthias (v. 26). This instance of an ancient practice in Scripture was taken to reveal the Lord's will impartially: "The lot is cast into the lap, but its every decision is from the LORD" (Prov. 16:33). Subsequent choosing of deacons and elders in the New Testament is by a process of nomination and appointment by the members of the church (Acts 6:3; 14:23; Titus 1:5).

Lessons for choosing leadership must be taken to heart and applied faithfully by God's people. Obedience to God's will has far-reaching consequences for those who choose, as well as those who are chosen. The existing elders have a vital role in guiding the process, the potential leaders, and the people of God:

> First, recognize that our call is to be *God's* call. We are looking for God's choice. "If a man desires the position of a bishop, he desires a good work" (1 Tim. 3:1), but such a desire is not proof a man is called. An inward call is not conclusive.

> Second, exercising spiritual discernment of character and gifts is vital to discovering God's choice — "Do not lay hands on anyone hastily" (1 Tim. 5:22). The great "qualification" passages need to be taken very seriously (1 Tim. 3:1–13; Titus 1:5–16). Is there a heart-commitment to Christ and evidence of the imitation of Christ (1 Cor. 4:16)? Is there a zeal to serve, as opposed to merely exercising rule (Luke 22:25–26)?

> Third, pray, as did the apostles, that God would choose out those who will pastor and serve his people, kingdom, and cause to the everlasting joy of his people and the eternal glory of his name. Pray today for tomorrow's leaders. Pray constantly for those who lead today, that God will bless their service to Christ with joy and not with grief, for that would be unprofitable for you (Heb. 13:17).

PRAISE FOR GOD'S CHOSEN LEADER
Sing Psalm 78:65–72

THINGS I WILL PRAY FOR TODAY

October 5
Prayer and the Church

And they continued steadfastly in the apostles' doctrine and fellowship, in the breaking of bread, and in prayers. — Acts 2:42

READ ACTS 2:42–47

he key word here is "church." It is used only three times before this in the New Testament, all by Jesus (Matt. 16:16; 18:17). In Acts 2, the New Testament church that Jesus promised was coming is unveiled. The "church" in Acts is not a *place* where people go for a worship service or a wedding, nor is it an abstract *notion* of worldwide Christianity. It is a real, on-the-ground *body* where believers join in living out their lives together in worship, fellowship, communion, and prayer with the Lord.

The church is God's institution. In recent decades, the "institutional" church has taken a back seat to the "small group" and the individual's "quiet time." Modern "fellowships" will say, "We don't do church," and downplay the place of preaching and the sacraments. The church in Acts 2, however, is not about small groups, one-on-one mentoring, or individual "quiet times." It shows the apostolic *church* in action, as instituted by God with members and elders. In one day it grows from 120 members to over 3,000 men (plus women and children). These are received and baptized by God's ministers (v. 41), and they "continued steadfastly" in the "means of grace" as ministered by the church—the Word, prayer, and sacraments (vv. 42–43).

> The apostles' "doctrine" is better rendered "teaching," as it encompasses not only what the believers *believe*, but what the apostles are *doing*. The "sound preaching and conscionable hearing of the Word" come together in the life of the church Jesus is building.

> "Fellowship" indicates that they were so drawn together (Heb. 10:25; Mal. 3:16) that—"wherever you saw one disciple, you would see more, like birds of feather."

> The "breaking of bread" refers to the frequent celebration of

558

the Lord's Supper, which is too often an afterthought of church life today.

> ✧ "Prayers" refers not to individual habits of personal private prayer, but to corporate prayer in meetings of the church dedicated for the purpose. The ordained leadership leads in all of these functions.

The church is the family of God. A praying church is a caring and sharing church. Believers delight to have "all things in common," to join together in worship and around the table, and to do so with "gladness and simplicity of heart" (vv. 44–46). Notice how all of life is involved. There is no reduction of the church either to an in-and-out worship service once a week, or to a social club devoid of the devotion of the heart. Here is the model of a true church where believers are "members one of another" (Rom. 12:5), practicing the unity of the Spirit in the bond of peace (Eph. 4:3).

The church's focus for prayer is the salvation of people (v. 47). Notice that the church to which God adds those being saved has a *good witness* ("praising God") and *goodwill* in the community ("favour with all the people"). And they pray together. We are good at praying for our needs and comforts, but we are first called to pray—together as congregations of the church—for God to glorify himself through conversions to Christ. This is a great standing work of faithfulness. Are you personally committed to such corporate prayer? When the church meets to pray, are you there, continually steadfast in seeking that God would "add to the church daily those who [are] being saved"?

PRAISE FOR GROWING IN THE HOUSE OF GOD
Sing Psalm 52:8–9

THINGS I WILL PRAY FOR TODAY

October 6
Sweet Hour of Prayer

The regular observance of prayer

*Now Peter and John went up together to the temple at the hour of prayer,
the ninth hour. — Acts 3:1*

READ ACTS 3:1–10

Godly Jews prayed three times a day, whether at the temple in
Jerusalem or, if at a distance, "toward" it (Ps. 5:7; Dan. 6:10).
These "hours of prayer" were equivalent to our 9:00 a.m.,
12:00 noon, and 3:00 p.m. Although widely observed, they
were never required by the law of Moses. There are no stated hours of
prayer *commanded* in Scripture. But prayer is a means of grace and to
be observed in the church, the family, and in private (Matt. 6:6), even if
the timing of such prayers is a matter of circumstance, convenience, and
conscience. The psalmist frames his days with prayer (Ps. 88:13; 6:6) and
cries out in moments of immediate crisis (Ps. 59:1). The church has always
had its stated times for prayer. Each Lord's Day worship service is in a real
sense an "hour of prayer"—one which God does require us all to attend
(Heb. 10:25). The modern descendants of the temple's "hour[s] of prayer"
are those stated prayer meetings of the church that afford opportunity for
corporate prayer at other times. Likewise, Daniel's individual devotions
are today represented in the private prayer of believers in what Jesus calls
"the secret place," rather than in a place calculated to be seen by others
(Matt. 23:5). There do need to be times of prayer in our lives, and, although
the times may vary as to both occasion and duration, they need to be a
regular feature of our Christian experience. Prayerlessness is neither good
for the soul, nor pleasing to God.

The "hour of prayer" puts us in the way of usefulness. Peter
and John made time for the "hour of prayer," but they were waylaid by a
beggar and never made it to the meeting! The Lord heals the beggar, attracts
a crowd, and Peter preaches the gospel of Christ, only to be arrested and
dragged before the Jewish leaders! Peter could have passed by the beggar
"on the other side" (Luke 10:31). But what is the goal of prayer but love
to God and man? You can be sure Peter and John were praying while they

dealt with the beggar and the Jewish leaders. God diverted them from piety to practicality and preaching, not because prayer is unimportant, but because pointing people to Jesus is a matter of life or death for those who are lost and in need of a Savior. Prayer impels us to serve the Lord in practical ways.

The "hour of prayer" puts us in the way of God's blessing. Prayer is for our own growth in grace. As the blind English preacher William Walford (1773–1850) expresses in his famous poem, the desire to pray is both an evidence and an engine of sanctification:

> Sweet hour of prayer! Sweet hour of prayer!
> That calls me from a world of care,
> And bids me at my Father's throne
> Make all my wants and wishes known.
> In seasons of distress and grief,
> My soul has often found relief,
> And oft escaped the tempter's snare,
> By thy return, sweet hour of prayer!
> —"Sweet Hour of Prayer," stanza 1

The "hour of prayer" nurtures our communion with Christ. Prayer deepens our desire for more of his presence and power:

> Sweet hour of prayer! Sweet hour of prayer!
> Thy wings shall my petition bear
> To Him whose truth and faithfulness
> Engage the waiting soul to bless.
> And since He bids me seek His face,
> Believe His Word and trust His grace,
> I'll cast on Him my every care,
> And wait for thee, sweet hour of prayer!
> (stanza 3)

A PRAYER OF TRUST IN THE LORD
Sing Psalm 38:15–22

THINGS I WILL PRAY FOR TODAY

_____

_____

_____

October 7
Stand Up for Jesus

A prayer for boldness to speak God's Word

Now, Lord, look on their threats, and grant to Your servants that with all boldness they may speak Your word. — Acts 4:29

READ ACTS 4:23–31

ave you ever "chickened out" in standing up for Jesus? There are probably no exceptions in all of Christian history. It costs to follow Jesus and that often gives us pause to speak out about Christ. There are many reasons for a lack of boldness. It may be temperament, as with Timothy (1 Tim. 4:12; 2 Tim. 1:6–8; 2:15); or fear allied to weak faith, as with Peter (Luke 22:54ff.); or a sense of a lack of gifts, as with Moses (Ex. 3:11); or just being too young, as with Jeremiah (1:6). We may be bold today and timid tomorrow, as was Peter at certain crisis points in life (Matt. 14:29–30; Luke 22:23). After Jesus's death the first Christians were in total disarray (Matt. 26:31). Yet, two months after Jesus's resurrection, even the Jewish leaders marveled at their newfound boldness, and, significantly, they "realized that they had been with Jesus" (Acts 4:13). The Lord wants you, Christian, to stand up for Jesus and "always be ready to give a defense to everyone who asks you a reason for the hope that is in you, with meekness and fear" (1 Peter 3:15). In the face of this calling, God assures us that we are not left to our own resources in this matter. "For by You," says the psalmist, "I can run against a troop, by my God I can leap over a wall" (Ps. 18:29). The apostles accordingly gathered to pray for holy boldness (vv. 23–24a).

Why do we need holy boldness (vv. 24b–28)? The apostles had already shown great boldness before they prayed about it. Having healed the beggar at the Beautiful Gate, Peter went on to preach Christ in the temple (Acts 3). This led to his arrest and trial before the Jewish leaders, who charged the Christians not to "speak at all nor teach in the name of Jesus" (Acts 4:18). Peter and John resolutely defied the gag order and were released unharmed "because of the people" (v. 21). Even in the Roman Empire, public opinion had some weight! The apostles, however, knew that their freedom was the work of God and knew that Christians are free, however much their lives are under outward restrictions and threats. They also know that past boldness does not guarantee boldness in the future. So they prayed that the Lord would continually embolden them. "Therefore let him who thinks he stands take heed lest he fall" (1 Cor. 10:12). They note two essential truths, the first being that *opposition to Jesus* belongs to the territory of this world (vv. 24–26). They recall Psalm 2:1–2, noting that God's creatures rebel against their Creator and therefore rise up against his Son. The second and countervailing truth is that this perennial opposition is always encompassed within *God's plan* (vv. 27–28). That is, God has a *redemptive* purpose that is worked out even through Psalm 2 opposition! These realities require bold witness for Jesus Christ, if the gospel is to spread and lives are to be transformed.

How do we acquire holy boldness (vv. 29–31)? The apostles never rested on past success. They show us the way in praying that the Lord would (1) deal with threats from enemies of the gospel (v. 29a); (2) empower his servants (vv. 29b–30a); and (3) exalt his "holy Servant Jesus" (v. 30b). This is a prayer for every day the world lasts. And it is a prayer that will be answered while the world lasts. The apostles discover that, when God fills them with the Holy Spirit, they speak the Word of God with boldness (v. 31). In that "great power," they "witness to the resurrection of the Lord Jesus," and they experience "great grace" coming upon them all (v. 33). Their "lives were in full harmony with their lips." Prayer, boldness, and blessing are the means by which you will stand up for Jesus as a true soldier of the cross.

A PRAYER FOR COURAGE
Sing Psalm 27:9–14

THINGS I WILL PRAY FOR TODAY

_____

_____

_____

_____

_____

_____

_____

October 8
Given to Prayer and the Word

Prayer and ministry

We will give ourselves continually to prayer and to the ministry of the word. —Acts 6:4

READ ACTS 6:1-7

Prayer so easily disappears into the cracks between the regular duties and interests of daily life. In the account of the appointment of the church's first deacons, prayer is mentioned almost in passing, but is no less important for that. The church had grown by thousands since the first Pentecost (Acts 2:41; 4:4). The leadership was, however, still the same twelve apostles. The work was fast overwhelming them. The practical needs of certain widows were being neglected (v. 1). Their solution was to delegate the work of what they call "tables" to seven men who would be chosen by the church as a whole and ordained to their service by the apostles (vv. 2–3). This is the beginning of a distinct office of deacon (*diakonos* simply means "servant") and the formal organization of what is often called today "the ministry of mercy." Three priorities for the church's ministry come into focus.

The ministry of mercy is to be led and promoted by deacons (vv. 1–2). The Lord's institution of an office of deacon underscores that the church is *a covenant community* in which God's people are to "bear one another's burdens" (Gal. 6:2). A distinct calling is created for effective leadership in meeting practical needs of believers suffering peculiar trials. This is both spiritual and physical in its scope and application. Deacons are set apart to focus on social welfare within the church. This is far broader—and more challenging—than the standard and shriveled idea that diaconal duty is only about looking after the church property. The case of the widows shows us the way. John Stott comments, "Assuming that they were unable to earn their own living, and had no relatives to support them [see 1 Tim. 5:3–16], the church had accepted the responsibility, and a daily distribution of food was made to them." God's people are to care for God's people.

The ministry of prayer and the word is to be faithfully exercised by God's pastors (vv. 3–6). "There is no hint whatever that the apostles regarded social work as inferior to pastoral work or beneath their dignity," writes Stott. "It was entirely a question of calling. They had no liberty to be distracted from their priority task." Hence their proposal to set apart seven men for the work while they gave themselves "continually to prayer and to the ministry of the word." The latter refers to the preaching and teaching of God's Word. The explicit connection of "prayer" to this ministry emphasizes the importance of both public and personal prayer in their ministry. Experiential personal piety is foundational to fruitful public ministry in both prayer and proclamation. Being "given to prayer" takes time—in this case, time that is freed up by deacons taking charge over practical temporal needs.

The whole church is involved in the ministries of the church (v. 7). When the ministries of word and prayer and mercy are faithful, fruit follows. The Word of God spreads and lives are changed. But what of those who are neither pastors nor deacons? The first answer is that all Christians are called to uphold all the church's ministries with their *ministry of intercession.* "Pray without ceasing" is every believer's calling (1 Thess. 5:17)! Furthermore, all are also called to a *ministry of support* that facilitates the work of the gospel. Where did the funds come from for the support of needy Christians (Acts 4:37)? How many hours do you want your pastor to have free to pray and to minister God's Word, or elders to serve the local church? Let us all be so given to prayer and ministry that all of God's servants may have real help to be fruitful in the exercise of their gifts and callings.

A PRAYER FOR THE CHURCH'S MINISTRIES
Sing Psalm 122

THINGS I WILL PRAY FOR TODAY

October 9
Heaven Opened

A martyr prayer

Lord, do not charge them with this sin. — *Acts 7:60*

READ ACTS 7:55–60

No prayers reveal the state of the soul like those uttered in the face of death. Thomas Bilney (1495–1531), perishing in the flames of persecution in England, was heard to say repeatedly, *"Credo"*—"I believe." Stephen was a gifted young man with every prospect of a long and fruitful life and ministry. This was all nipped in the bud by the hatred of fellow Jews outraged by his preaching of Jesus as the Messiah. They "were cut to the heart" and "gnashed at him with their teeth" and "stoned" him even "as he was calling on God" (Acts 7:54, 59). This should remind Christians today that "a disciple is not above his teacher, nor a servant above his master" (Matt. 10:24). Jesus tells us, "If the world hates you, you know that it hated Me before it hated you" (John 15:18). His own sufferings at the hands of wicked men were predicted long before: "Many bulls have surrounded Me; strong bulls of Bashan have encircled Me" (Ps. 22:12). Similarly, Stephen is engulfed in his assailants' frenzy of hatred. Yet in the middle of this horrific scene, he offers three petitions that stand forever as a model of prayer in the face of an unjust death.

He testifies to the glory of the Lord Jesus Christ. Stephen, the proto-martyr of the New Testament era, is given a vision of heaven in which God reveals himself as being with him and already welcoming him into glory. As at Jesus's baptism, "heaven was opened" (Luke 3:21). In his case, Stephen is granted a glorious view of the triune God: "he, being full of the Holy Spirit, gazed into heaven and saw the glory of God and Jesus standing at the right hand of God" (v. 55). No wonder he responds with a prayer of praise to the glory of his Savior: "Look! I see the heavens opened and the Son of Man standing at the right hand of God!" (v. 56). What Stephen sees before his death, all believers will see instantly after they depart this life.

He casts himself upon the Lord Jesus Christ. Echoing Jesus's final word from the cross—"Father, into Your hands I commit My spirit"

(Luke 23:46)—Stephen cries out, "Lord Jesus, receive my spirit" (v. 59). He expresses a personal and unreserved trust in Jesus his Savior. There is instant recognition of the Lord—whether he had seen Jesus in the flesh, we do not know. You recall that Jesus said to Thomas, "Because you have seen Me, you have believed," but then added, "Blessed are those who have not seen and yet have believed" (John 20:29). Since Jesus's ascension, no one in this life has seen Jesus in the flesh. But, for the Christian, believing is seeing. Indeed, more than merely seeing—it is confiding in him and enjoying his presence on account of knowing him personally and being united to him by faith.

He asks for mercy for his murderers. Like Jesus his Savior, he takes time even in his dying to intercede for his persecutors (cf. Luke 23:34). He says, "Lord, do not charge them with this sin" (v. 60). He wants heaven to be open for them, knowing that without the free and sovereign grace of God—and their responding in repentance and faith—they will surely perish forever in endless punishment (Luke 13:5). This is perhaps the ultimate application of the fifth petition of the Lord's Prayer (Matt. 6:12), for as Stephen enters into the eternal experience of forgiveness of sin and salvation in Christ, he shows he has the forgiving spirit of a man who knows the meaning of God's free and sovereign grace. But for that grace, he would be as lost and hell-deserving as his murderers; he desires their salvation every bit as much as he blesses the Lord for his own. The one murderer that we know for sure was saved in answer to Stephen's prayer is the one at whose feet "the witnesses laid down their clothes"—"a young man named Saul." And with that prayer, Stephen's spirit returned to God who made him.

A PRAYER CONCERNING ENEMIES
Sing Psalm 35:11–18

THINGS I WILL PRAY FOR TODAY

October 10
Do You "Have a Prayer"?

Why believing prayer is a must

Then Simon answered and said, "Pray to the Lord for me, that none of the things which you have spoken may come upon me."—Acts 8:24

READ ACTS 8:4-25

To say someone doesn't "have a prayer" is to say he is a lost cause. Usually this refers to things like applying for an impossible job or seeking election to Parliament for the Monster Raving Loony Party! But rarely is it applied to a sinner's prospects of making it to heaven. Prayer is the great last resort that is assumed to be always available. For many, prayer is like a magic bottle—just rub it and out pops a genie to grant your wishes! The God of the Bible, however, is not a genie, and prayer is not a magic spell. God is not callous and uncaring: he does "hear prayer" (Ps. 65:1), but insists upon *believing* prayer (Heb. 11:6). He is not impressed by mere forms of words, however desperate they may be.

The fact is that the Lord will not hear certain prayers! He tells us that if we won't listen to him, we had better not expect him to hang on our every word: "I will break the pride of your power; I will make your heavens like iron and your earth like bronze" (Lev. 26:19; Deut. 28:23). The foolish girls in Jesus's parable found this out the hard way. They didn't have oil in their lamps and so could not go out to meet the bridegroom. They asked—"prayed"—for oil from the wise girls but were told they had to get their own oil. But it was too late. The door was shut to them (Matt. 25:1–13). The oil is salvation, the bridegroom is Christ, the feast is heaven, and the door is the last day. The wise girls could not give salvation to the foolish ones. The foolish girls needed to go to the Lord themselves and "buy wine and milk without money and without price" (Isa. 55:1). They "prayed"—but it was not saving, confiding faith. They were sad at being caught out, but the point is that they never really were committed to the Bridegroom.

Simon the magician had apparently become a Christian. His life had seemingly changed quite radically. But when he saw the effects

568

of the apostles laying hands on believers, he offered to buy their power. This indicated a serious lack of understanding of the work of the Spirit and even of the grace of God in the gospel of Christ. Peter rebukes him roundly and calls for repentance (vv. 20–23). Simon's response is to ask Peter to pray for him that he might escape God's judgment (v. 24). He gives no indication of repentance or personal faith in Christ. He seems only to be concerned with escaping the consequences of his actions. He appears unready to pray for himself as Peter exhorts him to do (v. 22).

Does Simon's request for prayer seem pious to you? James Boice comments that when Simon says "Pray for me," he was "not being pious at all but rather disobedient....He was refusing to do what he had been told he should do and was passing the buck to Peter." Boice goes on to apply this to you and me: "If *you* are sinning, *you* are the one who must repent of the sin. If prayer is needed, *you* are the one who must pray." If you won't pray for yourself, you really don't have a prayer! That's the lesson of Simon. People can pray for you, and should. But nobody can repent or believe for you and save you from the sins you won't confess. If you will not call on the name of the Lord, you "won't have a prayer" on judgment day either. Jesus promises you, however, "All that the Father gives Me will come to Me, and the one who comes to Me I will by no means cast out" (John 6:37). Simon is a call to get right with the Lord in the Lord's way. In personal union with Jesus Christ through saving faith, you not only have a prayer, you have a heavenly intercessor praying for you and with you at the throne of grace. God calls us all: "I desire therefore that the men pray everywhere, lifting up holy hands, without wrath and doubting" (1 Tim. 2:8).

A VERY PERSONAL PRAYER
Sing Psalm 102:1–12

THINGS I WILL PRAY FOR TODAY

October 11
Surprised by the Savior

The prayer of a man in shock

And he said, "Who are You, Lord?"—Acts 9:5

READ ACTS 9:1–11

"The saddest road to hell," says Brownlow North, "is that which runs under the pulpit, past the Bible and through the midst of warnings and invitations." This could have been said of the apostle Paul had he not been converted to Christ. He had "according to the strictest sect of our religion…lived a Pharisee" (Acts 26:5). He was not just what we call a "churchgoer." He was zealous, believed he was right with God, and was sure God wanted him to eradicate the followers of the late Jesus of Nazareth (Acts 9:1–2; 26:4–11). He had impressive religious credentials, but he hated Jesus and was really "not of God" (1 John 4:3). He was on the road to hell, but he was in for a great surprise!

The road to heaven always begins with the Lord. We must be spiritually "born again"—but as with physical birth, no one can bear himself again (John 3:3–8). The first regenerating breath of the Holy Spirit is always unanticipated and uninvited. It is essentially subconscious, even if it immediately begins to break into a conscious conversion to Christ. This can be dramatic and sudden, as with Paul on the road to Damascus, or muted and almost leisurely, as with the Ethiopian official on the road to Gaza (Acts 8:26–40). Regeneration (being "born again") is a subconscious work of God's initiative, while conversion (coming to Christ in saving faith) is our conscious response to and interaction with the Holy Spirit speaking in the Scriptures.

The road to heaven always has spiritual speed bumps. Paul's conversion begins when the Lord arrests him on his journey to Damascus to arrest Christians. A light from heaven shines around him, he falls to the ground, and he hears a voice ask, "Why are you persecuting Me?" (vv. 3–4). "Me"—not just "them"—this is the voice of the Lord. Paul knows it and it stops him in his tracks.

His first response is *consternation*: he says, "Who are You, Lord?"

570

(v. 5). The reply shakes him to the core: "I am Jesus, whom you are persecuting. It is hard for you to kick against the goads." The "late Jesus of Nazareth" is the very much alive risen Christ! This will be the first discovery of the lost on the day of judgment when they see Jesus "sitting at the right hand of the Power and coming on the clouds of heaven" (Matt. 26:64)—but by then it will be too late to repent!

His second response is one of *conviction* (vv. 6–7). No wonder he is shaking like a leaf: "So he, trembling and astonished, said, 'Lord, what do You want me to do?'" This is a response of faith! He bows to Christ, surrenders to his will, and seeks his instruction. Then the Lord said to him, "Arise and go into the city, and you will be told what you must do." He must wait on the Lord and be ready to trust and obey him. He goes to Damascus, deprived of his sight, and fasts for three days (vv. 8–9).

The road to heaven is always a highway of God's grace. Paul's third response is *commitment* (v. 11). While he waits, the Lord sends Ananias to him with the information that he will find him praying. What is Paul praying about? He gives an insight in his testimony before King Agrippa years later when he recounts God's words to him at his conversion: "I will deliver you from the Jewish people, as well as from the Gentiles, to whom I now send you, to open their eyes, in order to turn them from darkness to light, and from the power of Satan to God, that they may receive forgiveness of sins and an inheritance among those who are sanctified by faith in Me" (Acts 26:17–18). This is his calling as a disciple of Jesus and the apostle to the nations. For every believer, personal commitment to Christ is always a surprise and always an entrance into the wonderful ways of his grace.

A PRAYER FOR MORE OF GOD'S GRACE
Sing Psalm 119:33–40

THINGS I WILL PRAY FOR TODAY

October 12
Tabitha, Arise!

Prayer for the resurrection of a dead woman

And turning to the body, he said, "Tabitha, arise." And she opened her eyes. — Acts 9:40

READ ACTS 9:36–43

Praying for healing is commonplace in Christian experience. Indeed, we would love for God to eliminate all diseases. We share the sentiment of the first century AD pagan Roman writer Juvenal, who famously bids us pray for a sound mind in a sound body—*mens sana in corpora sano*. If we could work miracles, we would raise the dead to life. That is why we hope doctors will work wonders. It is why sick and hurting people will always be vulnerable to snake-oil peddlers and faith healers. We are always warranted to pray that God would restore the ill to good health and grant long life. John writes to his friend Gaius, "Beloved, I pray that you may prosper in all things and be in health, just as your soul prospers" (3 John 1). He knows that a spiritually healthy mind does not confer bodily health, but only desires that Gaius would enjoy physical health as full and as blessed as the healthy maturity of his soul in his personal relationship with the Lord.

Praying for a resurrection is something else again. We have never seen anyone we know rising from the dead—whatever tales are told of lights in tunnels and so-called "near-death experiences." Life is a one-way street and death happens to all. God's Word does not lead us to expect any resurrections until the great day when Jesus returns, and land and sea give up their dead for the last judgment (Rev. 20:13). Even so, resurrections have happened and particular instances are recorded in Scripture for our encouragement and comfort, especially with respect to the Christian's hope of heaven. Peter is called to the house where Tabitha, having fallen ill and died, is laid out ready for burial (vv. 36–38). When Peter arrives, the mourners are "weeping" and recalling the life and work of this excellent lady. He promptly puts them out of the room, kneels down, and prays. He then turns to the corpse and says, "Tabitha, arise," whereupon she opens her eyes, sits up, and is presented alive to her grieving friends (vv. 39–41)!

Now, why did God lead Peter to pray for Tabitha in this way and make him the agent of her resurrection? There are two pointers in the text to the answer:

> ❧ The first is in the lady's name. "Tabitha" is of Syrian origin. Here is a Gentile believer, not a Jew like Lazarus or Jairus's daughter (cf. John 11:43; Mark 5:41). The gospel of Jesus Christ is sealed as a message of new life for all the peoples of the world, not just the Jews.

> ❧ The second is in the fact that "many believed on the Lord"— that is, came to Christ in saving faith. The miracle points to Jesus and marks out Peter and his ministry as the proclamation of life in the risen Savior! Even his language may have made that connection in many minds: Jesus had said, *"Talitha koumi"* ("Little girl, arise"), and Peter had said, *"Tabitha anastethi"* ("Tabitha, arise"). Jesus is the true giver of life from the dead.

Praying for salvation is our constant task. It would be a mistake were we to conclude that the absence of miracles among us somehow deprives us of benefits we might otherwise have. The God who healed at that time by these extraordinary means still heals today through ordinary means. The miracles in Scripture tell us that God has a "Word of Life" for the world (1 John 1:1–2). Salvation is the resurrection of a dead soul. The dead cannot raise themselves to life. But the God who heals the sick and raises the dead in a split second is able to save someone like you and bring you to eternal life through his Son, Jesus Christ! He makes his people willing in the day of his power (Ps. 110:3). Meanwhile, our constant ministry must be to pray that this new life—and the resurrection that goes with it—may be experienced by millions who presently do not know him, by their personally embracing Jesus as their Savior.

PRAISE FOR THE PROMISE OF ETERNAL LIFE
Sing Psalm 17:13–15

THINGS I WILL PRAY FOR TODAY

_____

_____

_____

_____

October 13
An Unexpected Answer

The prayer of a Roman soldier

Cornelius, your prayer has been heard, and your alms are remembered in the sight of God. — *Acts 10:31*

READ ACTS 10

Dramatic answers to prayer are always a surprise. When Cornelius has his regular prayer time that day, he surely does not expect a vision from God (vv. 1–8). Little does he know that this will place him at the center of one of the turning points of history. Jesus long before told his (Jewish) disciples, "Other sheep I have which are not of this fold; them also I must bring, and they will hear My voice; and there will be one flock and one shepherd" (John 10:16). The "other sheep" are "the Gentiles"—the non-Jewish peoples of the world. Jesus promises the worldwide spread of the gospel. So, for four amazing days, Cornelius finds himself witnessing the unveiling of a new era.

Day One: Cornelius is told to send for Peter (vv. 1–8). The Roman soldier is an Old Testament believer—not a Jew, but a "proselyte" or foreign convert. He is a praying man, noted for his kindness to others and his devotion to God (v. 2). No doubt he regularly prayed for the first coming of the promised Messiah, just as we should pray for Jesus's second coming. Suddenly, God tells him in a vision to send for Peter, who is not far away, in Joppa. He duly sends off his messengers and waits. Now he knows that something wonderful is about to happen.

Day Two: Peter is given a vision of all sorts of animals (vv. 9–23). In the vision the apostle is told three times to kill and eat these beasts. Peter objects since these are declared unclean in the law of Moses. But God declares them "cleansed" (v. 15). As Peter ponders this, Cornelius's messengers appear. In the meantime, the Holy Spirit directly reveals to the apostle that he should go with the men. Day Three is spent traveling to Caesarea for the meeting with Cornelius (v. 23).

Day Four: the Gentile Pentecost (vv. 24–48). The meeting between Peter and Cornelius was earth shaking for the relations between Jew and Gentile. Things would never be the same again. A new era dawned.

Peter says of his vision of the animals, "God has shown me that I should not call any man common or unclean" (v. 28). There would be no more separation between Jew and Gentile.

Cornelius tells of his vision and concludes, "We are all present before God to hear all the things commanded you by God" (v. 33). There would be no more separation of Gentiles from the faith once delivered to the (Jewish) saints (Jude 3).

Peter then preaches the gospel of Jesus Christ to the Roman officer and his household, emphasizing "whoever believes in Him will receive remission of sins"—both Jew and Gentile (v. 43).

The Holy Spirit then "fell upon all those who heard the word," thus astonishing the Jews present and persuading them that "the gift of the Holy Spirit had been poured out upon the Gentiles also" (vv. 44–45). Christian baptism is administered to the new (Gentile) members of the covenant community (v. 48). This is the Gentile Pentecost, which attests that the original Pentecost is not just for the Jews.

Let us continue to pray for the fruit of God's answer to Cornelius's prayers. Pray for the Lord to save more and more people until his glory covers the earth as the waters cover the sea. Cornelius prayed for conversions against the dark background of a world in the grip of the Evil One. Shall we do less when we know the strong man is bound? And pray for the appearing of our Lord Jesus and the completion of his work of redemption. Gentile proselytes prayed for many centuries before the Gentile Pentecost. We may pray for many centuries before the second coming of our Lord. Cornelius's prayer for our day is surely, "Amen. Even so, come, Lord Jesus!" (Rev. 22:20).

A PRAYER FOR JESUS'S TRIUMPHANT RETURN
Sing Psalm 98

THINGS I WILL PRAY FOR TODAY

October 14
A Day of Trouble

The church prays for Peter

Peter was therefore kept in prison, but constant prayer was offered to God for him by the church.—Acts 12:5

READ ACTS 12:1–19

eter is in prison, closely guarded by four squads of soldiers. Herod Agrippa I has recently executed James, the brother of John, and intends the same fate for Peter in a few days—"after Passover" (vv. 1–4). The church has neither the physical power nor the legal recourse to secure his freedom and save his life. But the Lord promises us, "Call upon Me in the day of trouble; I will deliver you, and you shall glorify Me" (Ps. 50:15). This was certainly a "day of trouble" for Peter and the church, and, therefore, a moment to embrace God's gracious promise. But what is the use of praying? How does prayer work? Is it just that praying comforts us, distracting us from the hurt and misery of something we can do nothing about—like our crying out and rolling about in agony when struck by some sharp physical pain? Is praying merely a psychological crutch? Or does it key into real objective power that resolves otherwise insoluble problems?

The ultimate question is, of course, "What is the use of God?" How does the invisible God materially affect our visible troubles? The answer lies in the biblical teaching that Jesus Christ is King. The risen Savior is also a Prince: "Him God has exalted to His right hand to be Prince and Savior, to give repentance to Israel and forgiveness of sins" (Acts 5:31). Because Jesus took our humanity, died in atoning for sin, and rose again to life eternal, "He [God the Father] put all things under His feet, and gave Him to be head over all things to the church" (Eph. 1:22). The point is that Jesus is the divinely appointed Sovereign ("Prince and Savior") over "all things." That is, he saves all who believe on him as Savior, *and* he rules everything and everybody else in the interest of those who are his ("the church")! How does he do this? The answer is that in every detail his power is applied supernaturally to accomplish his will. His kingdom has two sides to it:

576

> The *Kingdom of Grace* is his rule for and of his people: his bringing them to himself, growing them in his grace, keeping them in the palm of his hand, and bringing them to heaven (John 10:28–29).

> His *Kingdom of Power* is his authority over all creatures, all things, and all the powers of evil (Ps. 2:6ff; Matt. 28:18; Phil. 2:9–11). "He does according to His will in the army of heaven and among the inhabitants of the earth. No one can restrain His hand or say to Him, 'What have You done?'" (Dan. 4:35). How? By the projection of absolute divine power, silently, invisibly, directly, and through means—"The king's heart is in the hand of the LORD, like the rivers of water; He turns it wherever He wishes" (Prov. 21:1). He wills and things happen (Gen. 1:3). The Lord is at work constantly (John 5:17).

This points us to both the necessity and value of praying. We might fatalistically leave all to God and see how it all turns out. William Jay, the great preacher of Bath, notes that "it is one of the designs of affliction to excite us to pray more frequently, and more earnestly: and God, who knows the importance of the exercise, and what will conduce to it, says, 'I will go and return to my place, till they acknowledge their offence, and seek my face: in their affliction they will seek me early' [Hosea 5:15]." Here there is no offense on Peter's part, but there certainly is affliction. And the response of the church is to "come boldly to the throne of grace" that she might "obtain mercy and find grace to help in time of need" (Heb. 4:16). God deals with us personally and dynamically. The church prays—together, for they met for prayer—and Peter is miraculously delivered! If we do not pray, why would we expect any positive answers from God?

A PRAYER FOR DIVINE DELIVERANCE
Sing Psalm 50:7–15

THINGS I WILL PRAY FOR TODAY

October 15
Prayer and Fasting

Prayer at vital moments in the church's mission

Then, having fasted and prayed, and laid hands on them, they sent them away.—*Acts 13:3*

READ ACTS 13:1–3; 14:23

"Prayer and fasting" has a familiar, and not uncomfortable, ring to it. But whereas praying is ubiquitous in church life, fasting has all but vanished from Christian practice. "Fasting" is a secular word in our day—it is something we do before blood tests or surgery, or is a by-product of stress or sickness. Christian fasting, in contrast, is always about faith rather than health. It is about the soul rather than the body, or, better, it is where our body is enlisted to help our soul. Daniel, for example, intercedes for God's people in their desperate need: "Then I set my face toward the Lord God to make request by prayer and supplications, with fasting, sackcloth, and ashes" (Dan. 9:3). His fasting and outward self-abasement concentrated his mind and heart for the matter of intercessory prayer. It is only an intensification of the intended effect of withdrawing to a quiet corner and/or closing your eyes for the purpose of prayer. Fasting is nothing in itself. Its sole utility is to lay aside normal activities to focus on prayer in a special way.

In Scripture, fasting is reserved for particularly testing times. Our forefathers were much more keenly attuned to this than we are today. The historic 1645 *Westminster Directory for the Publick Worship of God*, written when Europe was racked with wars and persecutions, states that special days of fasting are appropriate for times "when some great and notable judgments are either inflicted upon a people, or apparently imminent, or by some extraordinary provocations notoriously deserved," but also for those happy occasions "when some special blessing is to be sought and obtained." Barnabas and Paul are sent out by the church as missionaries to the nations (Acts 13:1–3). The Mediterranean world could hardly suspect what the apostles knew: this mission was the evangelistic Rubicon for the gospel of Jesus Christ, and Paul was God's appointed minister for this marvelous mission (Gal. 2:7–9; Acts 9:15; 22:21)—or that what was then a Jewish church with Gentile converts was on its way to becoming a multiracial church with Jewish origins. Elders are ordained in local congregations established through this mission (Acts 14:23). This fasting is not out of fear of the future or about repentance for sin, but arises from excitement at what God is doing in evangelizing the unconverted world. This is prayer with glorious desires and expectations of blessing! Who stops to eat when he is breathless with anticipation of God's wonderful work in his world and his own life?

Fasting should often be a joyous exercise. Jesus, of course, warned against making both fasting and prayer into an outward and joyless show: "When you fast, do not be like the hypocrites...for they disfigure their faces that they may appear to men to be fasting. Assuredly, I say to you, they have their reward. But you, when you fast, anoint your head and wash your face, so that you do not appear to men to be fasting, but to your Father who is in the secret place; and your Father who sees in secret will reward you openly" (Matt. 6:16). Some people prided themselves on fasting twice a week, even though God *commanded* fasting only once a year, on the Day of Atonement (Lev. 16:29; Luke 18:12). The same folk made a point of praying where people could see them—that is, could see how holy they thought themselves to be (Matt. 6:5). We have no command in the New Testament to fast on a specific day, but we do have the *warrant* of our Lord and the apostles to engage in fasting together with prayer at those times when we stand at the threshold of new service for him. The stomach may be empty of food, but the heart is all the more full of grace and love for Jesus and his plan to reach and save a lost world to himself and fill our earth with the knowledge of the Lord.

A PRAYER FOR A TIME OF TESTING
Sing Psalm 109:22–31

THINGS I WILL PRAY FOR TODAY

_____

_____

_____

_____

_____

_____

October 16
Come and Help Us!

A women's open-air prayer meeting

And on the Sabbath day we went out of the city to the riverside, where prayer was customarily made. — Acts 16:13

READ ACTS 16:6–16

The D-day invasion of France in 1944 did not happen on a whim, the way we will wake up on a sunny summer day and say, "Let's all go to the beach!" There was a plan, and the order to "Go!" went down to the wire as the planners assessed every circumstance. The timing had to be right. A solid bridgehead had to be secured. Then the liberation of Europe could proceed. The same can be said about the invasion of the New Testament church from Asia to Europe. God had a plan and he already had his people working here and there behind the lines. It begins with women meeting for prayer. These Old Testament believers were waiting for "the Hope of Israel" to be revealed (Jer. 14:8; Acts 28:20). Their faithfulness was about to be rewarded. The vision given to Paul reveals as much. The "man of Macedonia" surely represents real believers, on the ground, praying and waiting for the Messiah. It is at this point that we are given a lovely picture of how God's prior planning impacts and blesses our present praying.

Prayer flows from the plan of God (vv. 6–12). God is always ahead of us—he always has something in the works for his people. And here is how it works: the first step is the *leading of the Holy Spirit* (vv. 6–8). They are "forbidden" by the Holy Spirit from preaching in Asia Minor—whether by direct revelation, inward conviction, or outward circumstances, we are not told. They end up at Troas wondering what to do. Doors close, others don't open. Uncertainty grows. This is common in life.

Then comes the *revelation of God's will* and they sail to Europe (vv. 9–10). Here it is a vision on top of whatever circumstances have already set them on their new course. God interprets his own actions and makes plain his will in one way or another. If one job doesn't work out, he wants you somewhere else.

The final step is simply *active obedience* that heeds God's call

(vv. 11–12). They set sail for Neapolis and from there travel inland to Philippi. Each step of the way is surely salted with earnest prayer; it points us to the beauty and privilege of every Christian in every waking hour, so we may "pray without ceasing" (1 Thess. 5:17). He who watches over us "shall neither slumber nor sleep" (Ps. 121:4).

Prayer prepares for the work of God (vv. 13–15). Philippi was a Roman colony and there seems not to have been a synagogue there. All the apostles found was a group of women meeting for prayer (v. 13), but this would prove to be the beginning of the church in Europe. God's "fifth columnists" were already preparing the ground for Christ to build his church (Matt. 16:18). From this comes the first fruit of Paul's ministry in Europe, and she turns out not to be a European woman, but one from Asia named Lydia! "The Lord opened her heart to heed the things spoken by Paul," (v. 14). God's powerful initiative of saving grace—with people of his choosing, in the place of his appointment, and in his timing—establishes a bridgehead for the gospel to spread throughout a whole continent!

With the baptism of Lydia and her household, the church as a covenant community begins to take shape in Philippi (v. 15). You will notice that her baptism, and not her professing faith, marks that moment. Why? Because without baptism, her mere words of testimony would have been hollow and indecisive. She believes and is baptized. God's minister applies the sign and seal of the covenant (that means of grace that only the church may administer). Prayer at the riverside led to a solid bridgehead in Europe for the church and her ministry, or the Word and the sacraments.

PRAISE FOR GOSPEL FRUIT ON UNPROMISING SOIL
Sing Psalm 72:16–19

THINGS I WILL PRAY FOR TODAY

_____

_____

_____

_____

_____

_____

_____

October 17
Light in the Darkness

Praying in prison

But at midnight Paul and Silas were praying and singing. — Acts 16:25

READ ACTS 16:25-34

Before gas and electricity, nights were very dark. A nocturnal flyover of much of our world today unfolds a vast map etched in a trillion points of light. In past times, however, even a moon-bright night would have revealed a world devoid of manmade light. Streets were dark and dangerous. Doors were closed and windows shuttered. Only the flickering flames of oil lamps penetrated the gloom of darkened dwellings. When Paul and Silas were singing and praying at midnight in their Philippian "inner prison," it was very likely pitch black. Their prospects, on the face of it, also must have seemed dark indeed. They had been severely beaten, their feet were fastened in the stocks, and they had no reason to expect a more lenient judgment on the morrow.

Darkness is emblematic of the reality of sin in our fallen world: "And this is the condemnation, that the light has come into the world, and men loved darkness rather than light, because their deeds were evil" (John 3:19). Jesus says the good news of his gospel is to be preached to the world "to open their eyes, in order to turn them from darkness to light, and from the power of Satan to God, that they may receive forgiveness of sins and an inheritance among those who are sanctified by faith in Me" (Acts 26:18). As light penetrates darkness, so Jesus is the light of the world: "I am the light of the world. He who follows Me shall not walk in darkness, but have the light of life" (John 6:12). As his disciples, we, who are his church in the world, are likewise called to be salt and light (Matt. 5:14).

Spiritual light is always resisted by spiritual darkness. With the coming of Jesus, "light shines in the darkness, and the darkness did not comprehend it" (John 1:5). Christianity is not a boutique religion you can take or leave without serious consequences. God commands all people everywhere to repent. Jesus means to save sinners, and the gospel is about repenting or perishing. But no unbeliever is by nature inclined to repent of sin and accept Jesus as Savior and Lord! When gospel light came to

Philippi, some people were converted to Christ. But where people pray, the devil will play. He sends a demon-possessed girl against the missionaries. When she is converted to Christ, her masters rouse the rabble against these "Jews" who "exceedingly trouble our city" (Acts 16:20). Paul and Silas are duly arrested, beaten, and thrown in jail. The darkness always works to blot out the light of Christ!

The true light is never extinguished. On that dark night it shone in (1) Paul and Silas's witness to God's saving grace, (2) God's overthrowing of spiritual darkness in the shattering of the jail, thereby overthrowing the powers that be, and (3) most importantly, the conversion of the jailor! "Sirs, what must I do to be saved?" is followed with the immortal injunction full of promise: "Believe on the Lord Jesus Christ, and you will be saved, you and your household" (vv. 30–31). And he believed and was saved! The darkness of a dead soul was wakened to new life by the effectual calling of the very light of Christ. "For it is the God who commanded light to shine out of darkness, who has shone in our hearts to give the light of the knowledge of the glory of God in the face of Jesus Christ" (2 Cor. 4:6). This is why Jesus came: "I have come as a light into the world, that whoever believes in Me should not abide in darkness" (John 12:46). Consequently, Christians, "you are a chosen generation, a royal priesthood, a holy nation, His own special people, that you may proclaim the praises of Him who called you out of darkness into His marvelous light" (1 Peter 2:9). You "were once darkness, but now you are light in the Lord." Therefore, "walk as children of light" (Eph. 5:8). Will you then pray and sing praise in your midnights?

JOYFUL PRAISE AND PRAYER IN TROUBLED TIMES
Sing Psalm 63

THINGS I WILL PRAY FOR TODAY

_____

_____

_____

_____

_____

October 18
Sweet Sorrow

Prayer on parting with beloved brethren

And when he had said these things, he knelt down and prayed with them all. — Acts 20:36

READ ACTS 20:17–38

arting is such sweet sorrow." So says Juliet to Romeo in the famous balcony scene from Shakespeare's play. "Sweet" today means something amazing, enjoyable, and welcome, but in the Bard's day its meaning was far more subtle—more like "not offensive." The lovers' parting is not an amazing, fabulous romantic moment, but rather an experience of sadness made less offensive by the prospect of a future reunion that will be all the more glorious. That, I think, catches something of the mood in Miletus as Paul leaves his brother-elders to travel on to Jerusalem and future trials. No one enjoyed this parting for they, Paul says, "will see my face no more" (v. 25). But the sorrow thus occasioned is tempered by other considerations and richer prospects that will render it "sweet" rather than tragic and irretrievable.

The parting of Paul and the elders was permanent, but not eternal. Not surprisingly, their brief reunion rehearses what God has done, is doing, and will yet do in their lives.

Paul first reviews the *past blessings* they shared together (vv. 18–21). He reminds them that his ministry had been selfless, earnest, faithful, and manifestly blessed by the Lord. Many were converted to Christ. He had faithfully proclaimed to Jew and Greek alike, "Repentance toward God and faith toward our Lord Jesus Christ" (v. 21). The gospel had truly been "good news" among them.

He then turns to *future challenges* they will surely face (vv. 22–31). He will not be there for them. They will see him no more. But he had shown them the way to follow: he was "innocent of the blood of all men" because he "had not shunned" to declare "the whole counsel of God" (vv. 26–27). The point is that this is their calling also—let them get to work and proclaim the same gospel! Another challenge is that, as Paul goes out, "wolves" come in. Therefore they must "shepherd the church of God"

(vv. 28–29). Furthermore, heretics will come from among them—they will need to be vigilant and, as Paul did for three years, "warn everyone night and day with tears" (vv. 30–31). Paul is saying, "Imitate me, just as I also imitate Christ" (1 Cor. 11:1).

When it comes to *present prospects*, Paul commends the elders to God and "the word of His grace" (vv. 32–35). God is the source who alone can supply every need. The "word of His grace" is the means by which God communicates his enabling grace to his people. This "word" is Scripture (1 Peter 2:2; Matt. 4:4) and the "grace" is that of Jesus the living Word revealed in Scripture. He will build them up in their faith and establish them in their eternal inheritance with all the saints in glory (v. 32). Paul recalls a saying of Jesus's—recorded nowhere else in Scripture—in which he said, "It is better to give than to receive" (v. 35). This is to remind them—and all of us—that Jesus gave himself as a ransom for many (Matt. 20:28), and this is the perfect example of personal godliness for all of us to emulate in our life and service to the Lord.

Prayer is a "means of grace" tailor-made for farewells between Christians. As Paul prays "with them all," they weep and make their farewells (vv. 36–38). What did they pray for? The answer is, "All of the above!" That is, all that flows from the intersection of personal experience and the promises of God. Paul, the apostle who was father in the faith for these Ephesians, is being taken from them, but God will never leave them nor forsake them (Heb. 13:5). Furthermore, our earthly partings may be "permanent" here, but will give way to the eternal reunion of heaven. No one can separate believers from the love of Christ (Rom. 8:35). The believers' every earthly sorrow will be made more than sweet in the fulfillment of God's gracious purposes.

A PRAYER FOR GOD'S SUSTAINING GRACE
Sing Psalm 20

THINGS I WILL PRAY FOR TODAY

October 19
All at Sea?

An answer to prayer

For there stood by me this night an angel of the God to whom I belong.
—Acts 27:23

READ ACTS 27:13–44

There is no record of Paul praying in the storm that shipwrecked him on Malta. That does not, of course, imply that he did not pray throughout that desperate voyage. Much unrecorded prayer is also secret prayer, and as such is nobody else's business but the suppliant's. It is, like all silent prayer, between him and the Lord. Jesus states the basic principle and its faithful practice in the Sermon on the Mount: "But you, when you pray, go into your room, and when you have shut your door, pray to your Father who is in the secret place; and your Father who sees in secret will reward you openly" (Matt. 6:6). This makes plain that the other side of secret prayer is an open answer. Believing prayers are always sooner or later acknowledged by God's answers. On the other hand, the absence of believing prayer will usually be attended by the silence of heaven: "Surely God will not listen to empty talk, nor will the Almighty regard it" (Job 35:13).

There is, however, a record of God answering the needs of his servant Paul. This came, Paul tells everyone, in the form of a visitation from "an angel of the God to whom I belong and whom I serve" (v. 23). In this way, the Lord revealed that he was determined to get Paul to Rome to be "brought before Caesar," and that none of the 276 people on board would perish, as God had "granted" them to Paul (v. 24)! The natural conclusion to draw from this supernatural intervention of God is surely that Paul had prayed that their lives all be spared. God granted Paul's prayers, both for his own future ministry in Rome and also for the deliverance of his shipmates. The explanation is that "the prayer of a righteous person has great power as it is working" (James 5:16, ESV). The glorious encouragement for us is that this is as true for every Christian's believing prayer in the pursuit of a quiet life as it was for Paul on that perilous voyage. Sometimes, in less dramatic circumstances, we may

586

have even forgotten what we prayed for by the time the Lord gives us his answer. Do we not frequently pray to be delivered from storms we fear are coming our way, even though they have not come upon us as yet? Do we as readily acknowledge that, when nothing happens, this is as much an answer to prayer as any deliverance in the middle of crisis? When God's people pray, the Lord always answers. Jesus tells us to "ask… seek…knock" and assures us that he will "give," we will "find," and "it will be opened" to us (Matt. 7:7). There is no "secret" to this. All we need do is "pray without ceasing," looking to "Jesus, the author and finisher of our faith, who for the joy that was set before Him endured the cross, despising the shame, and has sat down at the right hand of the throne of God" (Heb. 12:2). Why? The answer is that "He is also able to save to the uttermost those who come to God through Him, since He always lives to make intercession for them" (Heb. 7:25).

There is a wonderful pattern of faithfulness in the example of the apostle Paul. Contrast Paul with Jonah. Both found themselves on ships traversing the Mediterranean in heavy weather. But while Paul is heading to Rome to continue his mission as apostle to the nations, Jonah is fleeing to Tarshish (Spain) to get as far away as he can from God's will that he preach to Nineveh. Paul "stood in the midst of them" on the deck of the ship when "all hope" had been given up by all but him (vv. 20–21). Jonah, whose name means "dove," remains below deck, no doubt having wished for "the wings like a dove" that he might "fly away and be at rest" (Ps. 55:6). Paul prays. Jonah sleeps. God is gracious. By his free grace he answers Paul's faithful prayers, and he overthrows Jonah's faithless backslidings. But don't wait until you are in the belly of the fish before you cry to the Lord….

A PRAYER FOR DELIVERANCE
Sing Psalm 6

THINGS I WILL PRAY FOR TODAY

_____

_____

_____

_____

_____

October 20
When Sickness Strikes

Praying for the healing of a sick man

Paul went in to him and prayed. —Acts 28:6

READ ACTS 28:1–10

We all want to be well. When we fall ill, we expect the doctor to prescribe a cure. If we are Christians we will already be praying for healing and may have asked others to intercede for us before "the throne of grace" (Heb. 4:16). We know that there is more to healing than the most effective pills and doctors—and much more needed healing than merely letting nature take its course. Paul and his shipmates understood there was more to their deliverance from storm and shipwreck than luck or skill. They knew at least what Paul had told them God had said to him before it happened, and they knew that the apostle saw it as a miracle of God's grace (Acts 27:21–26). Then, having been saved from the sea, they witnessed Paul being bitten by a poisonous snake. They conclude, in their superstitious way, that he must be a murderer being punished for his sins, but then when he suffers no harm "they changed their minds and said he was a god" (vv. 3–6). This leaves Paul with a serious problem and sets the context for the events that follow.

A physician who seems able to heal himself will never lack for patients. The leading citizen of Malta is a man named Publius. His father is seriously ill, and this illness gives occasion for Paul to clarify the meaning of the miracles of deliverance that everyone had just witnessed. Paul goes to the old man's bedside, prays, and lays hands on him—and he is healed. News gets around. Others come and they too are healed (vv. 7–9). But after this no one is calling him a god. Why?

Paul first "prayed." He knew he did not have the power to heal, but he did know the God who can heal. He prays for the very same reason we pray for healing (and everything else). He no more has it in him to make people well than we have it in ourselves! Prayer presupposes powerlessness in the one who prays.

Paul then "laid his hands" on the sick man. Far from proving that he has the power in his hands to perform the healing, this rather indicates the role he has as the minister of the God whose power actually restores the man's health. Both Paul's praying and laying on of hands point *away* from himself to the Lord. Furthermore, the muted language describing how many others "also came and were healed" if anything takes the focus away from Paul and quietly points to God who is the true source of the desired healing.

Neither Jesus nor Paul healed merely for the sake of healing. All those healed by them were only temporarily healed. None of them walks the earth today. They all died. Jesus did not miraculously heal all the sick people in Palestine during his earthly ministry. Paul left Trophimus, "who was ill," in Miletus and made no effort to heal him (2 Tim. 4:20, ESV). Jesus raised Lazarus from the dead, but he only lived a little longer. These healings had a purpose, but it was not the mere conquest of disease. They were rather attestations of the message and messengers of the gospel of Christ, who has secured everlasting life for all who believe on him. Miracles were tokens, in time, of what the God "who forgives all your iniquities, who heals all your diseases" is doing more fundamentally for all eternity (Ps. 103:3). Physical sickness and death are the proofs of our need of comprehensive salvation through the Savior who has come to seek and save those who are lost. Jesus, in his death and resurrection, is both the ground and the proof that he can heal *all* our diseases and save us, body and soul, both now and for all eternity. We may and must always pray for the healing of the sick, but remember that such healing is only for a moment, for "it is appointed for men to die once, but after this the judgment" (Heb. 9:27). It is trusting in Jesus — "the Sun of Righteousness" who has arisen "with healing in His wings" (Mal. 4:2) — that will heal all that ails us now and forevermore.

PRAISE TO THE LORD WHO HEALS
Sing Psalm 103:1–5

THINGS I WILL PRAY FOR TODAY

_____

_____

_____

_____

_____

October 21
Making Mention of You All

Fellowship in prayer

Without ceasing I make mention of you always in my prayers.
—Romans 1:9

READ ROMANS 1:8–12

"There must be fellowship in prayer." So writes that giant of the Reformation, Martin Luther. "Christian prayer," he adds, "is complete only when we intercede for the common good of all and not merely for ourselves." Prayer is not so much about what you and I need or want for ourselves, but more about what God wants for all of us who are or will yet be his people. Paul cares about God's flock—specifically, the believers "in Rome, beloved of God, called to be saints" (Rom. 1:7). If I *know* the grace of God in Jesus Christ *my Savior*, then I want that same grace for others, with no ifs, buts, or maybes. Grace in my heart ought always to put grace on my lips and grow me in the fellowship of prayer. And then with Paul, I will "without ceasing...make mention...always" of others in my prayers (v. 9). We are all challenged here as to how much we care about people—and how much this is reflected in our prayer life.

Paul's praying is driven by two inextricably intertwined motives. The first is thankfulness to the Lord and the second is goodwill toward others.

Are you not constantly *thankful* for God's grace in saving otherwise lost people—including yourself—and so giving you brothers and sisters in Christ? Notice how Paul is thankful *to* God *through* Jesus *for* all fellow-believers (v. 8a). This is where intercessory prayer starts. It is the most basic impulse of the heart of every true Christian in relation to other Christians. Even if you have justifiable complaints or concerns about certain brothers in Christ, these should be distantly secondary to a profound thankfulness to God through Jesus for them. Surely a simple thanks for the work of the gospel in their hearts and for their witness to Christ before the church and the world (v. 8b) must warm our souls and bind us to them in fellowship?

Are you not then moved to pray for God's *future blessing* of his people? Notice how the apostle outlines his commitment to such prayer.

His *personal starting point* is an open-hearted honesty before the Lord: "For God is my witness" (v. 9a). Without God, our best intentions will die in the air. Too often these are no more than show and a form of words anyway. Real blessing begins with the God who is able to answer our sincere goodwill in prayer with gracious providence in others' lives. God is the starting point, always, invariably, and without exception. Apart from him there are only passing feelings and illusory expectations, however pious-sounding.

His *personal history* is one of wholehearted service to the Lord's goals for his people. He prays for people because he serves God "with [his] spirit in the gospel of His Son" (v. 9bc). The word "serve" is translated "worship" elsewhere in Scripture (cf. Matt. 4:10; Heb. 8:5). He is saying, "Lord, you know I am most sincere and consistent day by day in this." This is single-minded Christian devotion in action—that "sincere love of the brethren" in which believers "love one another fervently with a pure heart" (1 Peter 1:22). Oh, what a privilege to love one another in Jesus our Savior!

His *personal desire* is expressed in a large-hearted intercession for the Roman Christians that includes a request that he might "find a way in the will of God" to fellowship with them in person, and both minister to them and be ministered to by them in their "mutual faith" (vv. 10–12). Here is a three-point program for your practice of loving the Lord's people. Care about God's flock and be open-hearted, wholehearted, and large-hearted in the gospel of his Son, the Savior who died on earth, that you might have everlasting life both on earth and in heaven. Let us make mention of each other every day!

A PRAYER FOR GOD'S PEOPLE
Sing Psalm 122

THINGS I WILL PRAY FOR TODAY

October 22
Abba, Father

Praying as children adopted by God

For you did not receive the spirit of bondage again to fear, but you received the Spirit of adoption by whom we cry out, "Abba, Father."
—*Romans 8:15*

READ ROMANS 8:15, 23, 26–27

he glory of these verses is that God never leaves his believing people to their own resources. Prayer is too often looked upon not only as a last resort, but also as a human resource that we can always fall back on in a tight spot. Such notions turn God into someone we only need when we run out of options. Like the lifeguard you don't need until you're drowning, he is someone with whom you have no personal relationship. He is about as personal as a welfare check, in which all that matters is that your name is on it and it will clear the bank! Paul makes plain that the Christian's God is not a social service one may need someday. He must be our personal "Father in heaven" (Matt. 6:9). As he loves us and ministers his grace to us, we must love him back as those who have a saving relationship with him in and through his Son, the Lord Jesus Christ.

Christians know themselves to be the *adopted* children of God. They know this as a truth to be believed, and they also know it in their Christian experience. The psalmist affirms that "when my father and my mother forsake me, then the LORD will take care of me" (Ps. 27:10). This first impacts us in terms of the contrast between "the spirit of bondage… to fear" and the "the Spirit of adoption by whom we cry out, 'Abba, Father'" (v. 15). The "spirit of bondage" is where we were before we were converted to Christ. This is that work of the Holy Spirit by which Jesus, having come into our world, proceeds to "convict the world of sin, and of righteousness, and of judgment" (John 16:8). It is a Holy Spirit–imposed bondage "to fear," because insofar as it affects godless consciences it offers only the dreadful prospect of having to face a just God with nothing better than the "filthy rags" of our own "righteousnesses" (Isa. 64:6)! It is simultaneously a judgment and a wake-up call to the lost. Paul's point is that when we are saved by God's grace through faith in Christ, we receive the Holy Spirit "of adoption" and so relate to God as "Abba, Father." "Abba" is just Aramaic for the familiar "Dad." Unconverted, we were children of Adam alienated from God. Once converted, we are the adopted children of a heavenly Father and are delivered from that fear that binds the Christless sinner to the prospect of judgment to come. The Holy Spirit binds us in love to our Abba-Father.

Christians therefore eagerly welcome the coming fullness of their adoption: "Not only that, but we also who have the first-fruits of the Spirit, even we ourselves groan within ourselves, eagerly waiting for the adoption, the redemption of our body" (v. 23). As we "groan" under the burdens of this life, we find that our "Abba" has already sent us help for our weakness, namely, the indwelling Holy Spirit: "Likewise the Spirit also helps in our weaknesses. For we do not know what we should pray for as we ought, but the Spirit Himself makes intercession for us with groanings which cannot be uttered" (v. 26). His intercession and our groaning meet with God's approval, because our Abba-Father, who "searches the hearts," also "knows what the mind of the Spirit is," and the Spirit "makes intercession for the saints according to the will of God" (v. 27). As his adopted children we are never left to ourselves, especially when we are praying alone. For as we pray, the Spirit intercedes for us, and our loving Father hears and answers according to his perfect will. In the words of James Montgomery (1771–1854)

> Nor prayer is made by man alone
> The Holy Spirit pleads,
> And Jesus, on th' eternal throne,
> For sinners intercedes.
> —"Prayer Is the Soul's Sincere Desire," stanza 7

A PRAYER TO OUR FATHER IN HEAVEN
Sing Psalm 27:7–10

THINGS I WILL PRAY FOR TODAY

_____

_____

_____

_____

_____

October 23
Your Heart's Desire and Prayer

Praying for your bitterest enemies

Brethren, my heart's desire and prayer to God for Israel is that they may be saved. — Rom. 10:1

READ ROMANS 10:1–13

I t's easy to pray for friends and loved ones. It is easier still to want "to command fire to come down from heaven" on our enemies (Luke 9:54)! Jesus, of course, tells us to do the difficult thing: "Love your enemies...and pray for those who spitefully use you and persecute you" (Matt. 5:44). The real test and evidence of a true "spirit of grace and of supplications" (Zech. 12:10) is praying for your enemies' salvation from the very bottom of your heart! We are to love both friends and enemies and seek God's best for them.

Love calls us to pray for the conversion of our persecutors. Paul tells his "brethren"—converted Jews—about his desire and prayer for the salvation of "Israel"—unconverted Jews (v. 1). "We see here," comments Robert Haldane, "the love of a Christian to his bitterest enemies. Paul was abused, reviled and persecuted by his countrymen, yet he not only forgave them, but constantly prayed for their conversion." Paul's "heart's desire and prayer" is best understood in this light, because, to the Jewish establishment, he is a traitor and an enemy. Indeed, some bore such enmity toward him that they took an oath not to eat or drink until they had killed him (Acts 23:11)! We hopefully will be spared such toxic hostility, but surely we realize that the Christian message is bound to offend those who are not open to its challenges. Jesus warns us that in the world we will have troubles (John 16:33). He also tells us to take heart because he overcomes the world—which includes converting sinners to himself.

Love is moved by the plight of the lost. They are in bondage to the hopeless, hell-bent task of justifying themselves before God and man.

They have a misplaced sincerity: "a zeal for God, but not according to knowledge" (v. 2). When tested by knowledge—the truth of God's Word—this sincerity is found wanting. The tragedy of billions of sincere people is their commitment to dangerous errors. False zeal is fatal blindness. Mere sincerity does not save sinners.

Their righteousness is also illusory (v. 3). At best, it is "filthy rags" (Isa. 64:6). Paul unfolds the anatomy of this delusion: they are "ignorant" of God's righteousness, are "seeking" to establish their own righteousness, and so have "not submitted" to the righteousness of God. In contrast, Paul testifies, "I…count all things loss for the excellence of the knowledge of Christ Jesus my Lord…that I may gain Christ and be found in Him, *not having my own righteousness*…but that which is through faith in Christ, the righteousness which is from God by faith" (Phil. 3:8–9). They need to grasp that Christ's righteousness *alone* can be the basis of their salvation.

Love is shown in sharing the gospel of Christ. Christ is the "end of the law for righteousness to everyone who believes" (v. 4). The "end" of the Old Testament law is its "goal" (*telos*), not its disappearance. This goal still stands and it is Jesus dying to save sinners. We can't keep God's law—so it kills us! (Rom. 7:10)—but Jesus kept it perfectly (Rom. 8:3–4) and bore its penalty in our place (John 17:4; 19:30). Faith alone in Christ alone is the only way to be saved: "So then it is not of him who wills, nor of him who runs, but of God who shows mercy" (Rom. 9:16). This is what Paul shares with his enemies in the verses that follow, culminating in the invitation to believe and be saved, "For 'whoever calls on the name of the LORD shall be saved'" (Rom. 10:5–13, quoting Joel 2:32). Love calls us to pray for lost people, out of compassion for their plight, and impels us to reach out to invite them to come to Jesus and be saved.

A PRAYER FOR ISRAEL'S SALVATION
Sing Psalm 80

THINGS I WILL PRAY FOR TODAY

October 24
Steadfast in Prayer

Prayer as continuing ministry

...continuing steadfastly in prayer... — Rom. 12:12

READ ROMANS 12:9–13

Martin Luther called prayer *bombarda Christianorum*—the Christian's artillery. When Paul exhorts us to be "continuing steadfastly in prayer," or to "pray without ceasing" (1 Thess. 5:17), he means for us to bombard heaven with our petitions. This, of course, cannot mean continuously engaging in the formal words and posture of prayer. Nowhere in Scripture does God call on anyone to pray all day and be supported by other people for that purpose. We have work to do and people to see. But it does mean keeping a prayerful attitude at all times and focusing on prayer in an intentional and devoted way. We are good at reminding ourselves that Jesus condemned the church leaders of his day who "for a pretense make long prayers" (Mark 12:40). This does not, however, prove that short prayers are pleasing to God because they are short. We may not make short prayers "for a pretense," but maybe we are short because we can't be bothered and are content to be perfunctory in personal devotion. When cannons fire just to shoot off their ammunition, the targets are irrelevant and the battle already lost. The Christian's artillery must be both timed and targeted so the battles are won. Make all our words count!

"Continuing steadfastly" requires focused commitment. The two words in English translate a single Greek word that means "to stick to the task in hand with devotion and energy." It carries the idea of always applying strength. It is used in four other places in the New Testament with reference, among other things, to the exercise of prayer:

> Acts 1:14—"These all *continued* with one accord in prayer and supplication, with the women and Mary the mother of Jesus, and with His brothers."

> Acts 2:42—"And they *continued steadfastly* in the apostles' doctrine and fellowship, and in breaking of bread, and in prayers.

- Acts 6:4 — "But we will give ourselves *continually* to prayer and to the ministry of the word."
- Colossians 4:2 — "*Continue earnestly* in prayer, being vigilant in it with thanksgiving."

Thomas Brooks (1608–80) claims the metaphor is taken from hunting dogs chasing down their quarry. Thomas Watson (1620–86), commenting on the application of Matthew 11:12 to prayer — "And from the days of John the Baptist until now the kingdom of heaven suffers violence, and the violent take it by force" — observes, "Prayer without fervency and violence is no prayer, it is *speaking*, not *praying*. Lifeless prayer is no more prayer than the picture of a man is a man. To say a prayer is not to pray."

Jesus teaches us what this means practically. He tells us to "ask...seek...and knock" when we pray. Each action requires continuing steadfastness. To "knock" takes effort and importunity. Shouting more loudly is not the point, of course. We must come pleading Christ's merits and laying aside any of our self-justifying protestations of innocence. Plenty of unbelieving prayers are fiery and insistent. But, "if I regard iniquity in my heart, the Lord will not hear" (Ps. 66:18). Believing prayer comes to God in Christ by the Holy Spirit, committed to his will and looking for his blessing, and expecting blessing in terms of the promise of Christ's covenant faithfulness.

C. H. Spurgeon tells of watching a baby bird alone on a branch calling out for its mother, clearly expecting to be fed. Why expecting? Because it had been fed before! Let us be "steadfast in prayer." The Lord will answer.

A PERSISTANT PRAYER OF TRUST IN THE LORD
Sing Psalm 13

THINGS I WILL PRAY FOR TODAY

_____

_____

_____

_____

_____

October 25
One Mind and One Mouth

A prayer breathed in passing

With one mind and one mouth glorify the God and Father of our Lord Jesus Christ. —Rom. 15:6

READ ROMANS 15:5–7

ordy prayers are usually windy ones." Jesus has no time for verbosity, whether in prayer or anything else, and makes this plain by both his teaching and example (Matt. 6:7). Length, as such, is not the issue. Some Bible prayers are quite long—one thinks of Solomon's prayer at the dedication of the temple, and some of the Psalms. But most are short. In Romans 15:6, Paul exemplifies sanctified succinctness when he breathes a prayer in the middle of a practical exhortation. In so doing, he (1) reminds us that weightiness can live in a very few words and (2) teaches us that every good wish for others ought to be accompanied by a prayer that God will bless that desire. The preacher who doesn't pray as he preaches is not serious about his work. The first lesson in the apostle's prayer is that if we really care, we will really pray. And we will be doing this as we live life from hour to hour and day to day. This is one practical, everyday application of Paul's injunction to "pray without ceasing" (1 Thess. 5:17).

Paul's prayer is that we "glorify the God and Father of our Lord Jesus Christ." What prompted this prayer in the first place was the fact that some Christians in Rome were critical of other believers for views and practices that were actually a matter of Christian liberty. The "strong" were despising the weak and the weak judging the strong (Rom. 14:1–3). And this was just meat eaters *versus* vegetarians—nothing to do with the substance of the gospel or the requirements of God's Word! By their own reckoning they were all glorifying God, but they were at each other's throats over their various differences. They were all making these differences into badges of superiority. In this way they were holding things against each other, and this, Jesus says, is inimical to worship: "Therefore if you bring your gift to the altar, and there remember that your brother has something against you, leave your gift there before the altar, and go

598

your way. First be reconciled to your brother, and then come and offer your gift" (Matt. 5:23–24). God is not interested in the worship of people who think they can nurse their animosities and prejudices toward other Christians and imagine this is fine with him! The psalmist understands that God will not hear the prayers of folk who are intent on clinging to their sinful attitudes and actions: "If I regard iniquity in my heart, the Lord will not hear" (Ps 66:18). If you have a sense that God is not answering your prayers or blessing you through the worship of his people, then you need to examine yourself—and not cast around for others to blame.

Our unchanging calling is to glorify God with "one mind and one mouth." It should be obvious that if you are to "let this mind be in you which was also in Christ Jesus" (Phil. 2:5), then it cannot be glorifying to God to squabble and backbite over our disagreements. "Do not destroy the work of God for the sake of food," says Paul (Rom. 14:20). This is, sad to say, the level at which fellowship is breached and churches split: arguments over whether children should be schooled at home, in a Christian school, or in the public school; whether this or that design should be used for a building program; who should teach Sunday school; who was or was not elected an elder, etc. The list is endless and the Scriptural basis is obscure to nonexistent. What the Lord wants, expects, and blesses is "the unity of the Spirit in the bond of peace" (Eph. 4:3). We are free to be divided on our dietary views or the color of the walls and flooring in the church building. On a myriad of matters from the minor to the incidental we may differ. But we must be of "one mind and one mouth" in the matter of loving the Lord and loving his people.

A PRAYER FOR UNITY IN THE FELLOWSHIP
Sing Psalm 133

THINGS I WILL PRAY FOR TODAY

_____

_____

_____

_____

_____

_____

October 26
Abounding in Hope

A prayer for peace in believing

Now may the God of hope fill you with all joy and peace in believing,
that you may abound in hope by the power of the Holy Spirit.
—Romans 15:13

READ ROMANS 15:8-13

What use should we make of the Bible's prophecies? A. W. Pink suggests we "turn them into believing prayer, requesting God to make them good." His point being that God's prophecies, promises, and precepts all imply practical prayer requests! They also all look to the future in *hope*. Paul's prayer that Christians "abound in hope" arises from the assurance that God has long promised to bring the Gentile peoples into the church hitherto reserved for the Jews. "Jesus Christ was a minister of the circumcision for the truth of God, to confirm the promises made unto the fathers" (v. 8), which promises Paul cites from Psalm 18:49, Deuteronomy 32:43, Psalm 117:1, and Isaiah 11:1, 10. Jesus is "the root of Jesse" in whom "the Gentiles shall hope"—which is to say that they will be saved by God's grace through faith in Christ in fulfillment of this cosmic messianic promise (vv. 9–12).

The origin of our hope is "the God of hope." Remember that the problem for the Gentiles was that they were "without Christ, being aliens from the commonwealth of Israel and strangers from the covenants of promise, having *no hope* and *without God* in the world" (Eph. 2:12). The answer to that is that God has revealed his hope, "that we through the patience and comfort of the Scriptures might have hope" (Rom. 15:4). God's Word promises hope for all the peoples of the world. God is the sovereign source of this hope, which of course is the hope of salvation both here and now and for all eternity—through his Son, believed upon, and followed after.

The engine of our hope is "joy and peace in believing." This is surely the first, last, and perennial prayer request for those not yet converted to Christ and those who are converted and are seeking to follow him faithfully. We all need hope—in Christ. There is no hope outside of

600

a saving knowledge of Christ. And those who have hope because they already know Christ as their Savior are in constant need of their hope being sustained and encouraged. It is the filling of the believer's heart with "all joy and peace in believing [in Jesus Christ]" that stirs up a refreshed and deepening hope. The more warmly we look to Jesus in faith—"believing"—the more we will experience "joy and peace," and find ourselves possessed of an expanding hope. This hope "does not disappoint, because the love of God has been poured out in our hearts by the Holy Spirit who was given to us" (Rom. 5:5). As we "rejoice in the Lord always," "rest in the Lord," and "wait patiently for Him" (Phil. 4:4; Psalm 37:7), we will not be hopeless and cast down, however difficult the challenges we face. Peace in believing is the engine of a living, growing hope.

The goal of our hope is to "abound" in hope. Paul has us looking ahead here. We don't need hope for what we already see and have (Rom. 8:24–25). His prayer is that abounding in hope be the normal, ongoing condition of our hearts and minds. Needless to say, if our hope depends on our feelings, or favorable circumstances, we will—as they used to say—"go up and down like a yo-yo"! We have, however, the prospect of "the power of the Holy Spirit" to help us. We are accountable to the Lord to actively hope in him, but we are also dependent upon him to overcome our frailty, for "the Spirit also helps in our weaknesses. For we do not know what we should pray for as we ought, but the Spirit Himself makes intercession for us with groanings which cannot be uttered" (Rom. 8:26). In this blessedness, we will grow by the grace of our Lord Jesus Christ, so as to abound in hope.

PRAISE FOR AN ENLARGING HOPE
Sing Psalm 71

THINGS I WILL PRAY FOR TODAY

October 27
Pray for Me!

Praying together for the peace of God

Now I beg you, brethren, through the Lord Jesus Christ, and through the love of the Spirit, that you strive together with me in prayers to God for me... —Rom. 15:30

READ ROMANS 15:30–33

I doubt if I could go on, if I did not know that people were praying for me," said James Philip, the late revered minister of Holyrood Abbey Church in Edinburgh, one Lord's Day over forty years ago. At the time, to my young mind, this seemed so weak and unbecoming a great man of God, as I believed Mr. Philip to be. Surely he would "go on," I reasoned, even if he were the last minister of God standing. Did he not believe the Lord would sustain him, even if no one prayed for him at all? I had forgotten about Elijah (1 Kings 19:10). Youthful confidence owes more to pride than to spiritual discernment and the awareness of personal frailties! Such are the bold, untested, and ill-informed opinions of the spiritually immature. Forty years on and an ocean away, one of the sustaining encouragements in my ministry is knowing that certain people regularly meet before the worship services to pray for the blessing of the pastors and the people.

We all need prayer because we all have personal limitations. The African-American spiritual "It's Me, O Lord," captures this beautifully,

It's me, It's me, O Lord—Standin' in the need of prayer...
Not my mother (not my father), but it's me oh Lord...
Not the preacher (not the sinner), but it's me oh Lord—
Standin' in the need of prayer.

In our prayer meetings we are perhaps so used to praying for others in notable urgent needs that we lose sight of the fact that we need prayer for ourselves in our service to the Lord. This is what Paul is putting to us in our passage for today: "Now I *beg you*, brethren, through the Lord Jesus Christ, and through the love of the Spirit, that you strive together with me in prayers to God *for me*" (v. 30, emphasis added). Do we imagine that God's great men "have it all"? The reality is that they too have clay feet and apart from the Lord they can do nothing (John 15:5; cf. Dan. 2:33–42). Paul's plea for their prayers is the echo of his own prayer. Notice its Trinitarian character: he appeals to Jesus as his Mediator, the Holy Spirit as the loving Helper, and the Father as the source of the answer and blessing he seeks. In the economy of the triunity of God, we are helped to form prayer in terms of the dynamics of salvation—planned by the Father who loves us, accomplished by the Son who dies in our place, and applied by the Spirit who sanctifies us. These great doctrines tell us why we need prayer—and why prayer will be answered for sure.

We all need prayer because our challenges are always bigger than we are. Paul anticipated opposition from the enemy and suspicion from the saints. So he asks that they pray (1) that he "may be delivered from those in Judea who do not believe," (2) that his "service for Jerusalem may be acceptable to the saints," (3) that he may be reunited with them "with joy by the will of God," and (4) that they be "refreshed together" (vv. 31–32). He analyzes the various challenges and sketches the perfect outcome. Why pray for less? God is bigger than the challenges that are bigger than we are.

We all need prayer because we all need the peace of God. Paul's concluding blessing—like all benedictions—is a prayer request presented as a sure promise: "Now the God of peace be with you all. Amen" (v. 33). The gifts of God are his essential attributes applied to our ever–present needs. God is peace in himself. He sends his Son so that by the cross, he may be our peace in believing in Christ and receiving him as our Savior (Rom. 15:13). Every need is a *dis*peace to our hearts, and so, whatever the specific requests, we may pray. The universal desire for ourselves is that "the Lord of peace Himself give [us] peace always in every way" (1 Thess. 3:16).

PRAISE FOR GOD'S ENDURING MERCY
Sing Psalm 138

THINGS I WILL PRAY FOR TODAY

October 28
To God Be the Glory

A benediction for our establishment in Christ

To God, alone wise, be glory through Jesus Christ forever. Amen.
—Rom. 16:27

READ ROMANS 16:25–27

The closing prayer of Paul's letter to the Romans is a benediction—the formal proclamation of a blessing from God. Thanks to the modern Christian obsession with "prayer requests"—those spiritual grocery lists of detailed needs and wants—we hardly recognize such beautiful blessings as prayers at all! This is only to our loss, since benedictions are arguably prayer in its highest form. In one long sentence, the apostle bridges earth and heaven, time and eternity, saint and Savior, and gives the glory to God "through Jesus Christ"—all due to God because of his marvelous grace in providing a Savior for sinners. His people share this glory as they are established in the gospel of Christ. There are no conventional "prayer requests" here, just the pure exalted adoration of God. Yet, in asking for nothing, Paul asks for everything, because he asks that heaven be in our hearts and in our daily lives here and now and forever.

God's glory through Jesus is the great cause of our praise. Paul's "thesis statement" forms the bookends of the benediction as a whole: "Now to Him who is able to establish you" (v. 25a) and "to God, alone wise, be glory through Jesus Christ forever. Amen" (v. 27). The key words in verse 25a are "able" and "establish." The potential of a promise depends on the power of the promise maker to keep his promise. Men are only too good at promising what they cannot deliver. God is able to keep his promises: "The Lord is faithful, who will establish you and guard you from the evil one" (2 Thess. 3:3). Notice, too, that the glory accrues to God "through Jesus Christ." Jesus is the jewel in God's crown, in that he is "exalted...a Prince and a Savior, to give repentance to Israel and forgiveness of sin" (Acts 5:31). He actually secures the salvation promised in the gospel.

God establishes his people through specific means. These are set

604

out in the middle of his "thesis statement" and flagged by the thrice-used formula "according to…" (vv. 25b–26).

Concerning Jesus Christ, a *new message* of "good news" has come to our world. Believers are established, says Paul, "according to my gospel and the preaching of Jesus Christ"—that is, the gospel as preached by Paul and as proclaimed by Jesus in his earthly ministry and subsequently recorded in Scripture. "Ministers are the ambassadors, and the gospel is their embassy," says Matthew Henry. The *preaching* of God's Word is the first and foremost means of grace. Good preaching is a wonderful gift of God's grace and we should, as Isaiah says, "fly like a cloud, and like doves to their roosts" (Isa. 60:8) to receive the word of the truth of the gospel.

Through Jesus Christ *a new era* has dawned upon the world. This was "kept secret since the world began" (v. 25). "It was eternally in God's mind, and later revealed in time." The world has never been the same, and never more blessed with the transforming light of God, than since Jesus, the Light of the World, was "made manifest, and by the prophetic Scriptures has been made known to all nations" (v. 26).

The reason for this is that in Jesus Christ *new life* is given to all who believe in him as their Savior and subsequently follow him as his disciples. "All the glory that will redound to God through the ages of eternity, from the salvation of sinners," writes Robert Haldane, "proceeds through Jesus Christ….It is through Jesus Christ that we ought to ascribe to God the glory." Hence Paul closes, "to God, alone wise, be glory through Jesus Christ forever. Amen."

A PRAYER THAT GOD BE GLORIFIED
Sing Psalm 102:11–17

THINGS I WILL PRAY FOR TODAY

_____

_____

_____

_____

_____

_____

_____

October 29
Growing Together

Prayer for growing fellowship in Christ

God is faithful, by whom you were called into the fellowship of His Son, Jesus Christ our Lord. — 1 Cor. 1:9

READ 1 CORINTHIANS 1:1–9

All Bible doctrines are truths to be believed. Some are wonderfully warm—one thinks of "God is love" (1 John 4:8). Others, like "the wages of sin is death," are less enthralling (Rom. 6:23). Some can just seem puzzling. One such is what I call "the doctrine of the imperfection of the church." This sounds more like an affliction than a doctrine. It inspires no enthusiasm and sets no lofty goals, but it actually pervades Scripture and frequently confronts us in church life. But what are we to do with this "doctrine"? Beyond describing reality, what positive practical import does it have for the way we think about the church and the way we conduct ourselves within her fellowship?

All Christian churches are less than perfect. Many observe this with glee, cry "Hypocrites!" and excuse themselves from listening to the gospel message. Does the imperfection of the church unchurch the church? Does it fatally discredit her mission, her message, and her Master? Paul's handling of the situation in Corinth points us to God's answer to these questions. Notice first of all that he sets the imperfection of the Corinthian church squarely in the context of God's saving grace! He doesn't dismiss the believers as not being children of Christ because there is evidence of backsliding in their lives. Before ever addressing specific problems, he points out that they are "called to be saints"—which means they are in fact, inconsistencies and all, "sanctified in Christ Jesus" (v. 2). And he repeatedly underlines this with the plural "you"—it is the body as a whole, the fellowship as a group, the church *qua* church that has experienced God's grace in Jesus Christ. It is a place for sinners to grow and also go out to fight the good fight of faith as trophies of God's grace. The very imperfection of the church invites people to Christ and proves we are saved by grace and not any unspotted righteousness of our own.

All true Christians have received God's grace, know it, and

606

are called to act on it. Paul's first word is not to rebuke the backsliders, but to assure them—the "you" is plural—that he always prays for them, giving thanks for "the grace of God" given to them "by Christ Jesus" (v. 4). Encouragement, not guilt, is his starting point. He mentions four blessings in particular that call them to spiritual renewal:

> The first blessing is the *grace* that the church has received from God through Christ Jesus (v. 4). The believers know in their hearts that they have a Savior who has indeed saved them by bearing their sins in his body on the cross and brought them by his grace through faith to trust in him (2 Cor. 5:21; Eph. 2:8–9).

> Another blessing is *growth* in Jesus (vv. 5–6). Believers see— and those who observe them can bear witness to this reality— that their lives are being transformed by God's grace. They are "enriched" and "established" in ways that clearly confirm Christ's "testimony"—the claims of the gospel—in them. The church body has a life in which people are evidently growing in their love for the Lord.

> Yet another blessing is that the church has *gifts* from Jesus (vv. 7–8). The "you" is still plural. The body as a whole "comes short in no gift." No individual has every spiritual gift. We are meant to need one another as we serve our Savior.

> Finally, there is the blessing of *God* himself, who is faithful (v. 9). This is the bedrock of our hope and of the "fellowship of His Son" into which he has called us. We are not alone and left to ourselves. In addressing the church as a body, the apostle is pointedly challenging each individual. God has given *the church* grace, growth, gifts, and himself. Christians are *personally* possessed of these benefits and joyfully united to Christ in their hearts. Are *you* exercising a personal faith that is growing in the happy fellowship of the Lord's redeemed?

PRAISE FOR THE FELLOWSHIP OF THE CHURCH
Sing Psalm 133

THINGS I WILL PRAY FOR TODAY

October 30
The Spirit and the Understanding

On being clear in prayer

I will pray with the spirit and I will pray with the understanding...
—1 Cor. 14:15

READ 1 CORINTHIANS 14:14–17

"barbarian" in our language is someone uncivilized and cruel. This was not its meaning in Bible times. The Greek *barbaroi*, some suggest, came from the way "civilized people"—Greeks and Romans—heard foreigners speaking in their own tongues (see Rom. 1:4). You know yourself that if you have no knowledge of a foreign language, and you are listening to a native speaker, it is difficult to distinguish words and sentences. They all seem to merge together in one unintelligible stream. To the Greeks, the speech of foreigners sounded like "brr...brr," and so, the theory goes, *barbaros* became the term for a foreigner. The point of mentioning this is to underscore that, until and unless a language is understandable to a hearer, there will be little or no understanding. Even when both parties speak the same language, the speaker's words need to be chosen so that the hearers understand his message clearly.

There was serious disorder in public worship in Corinth. Some people were speaking in tongues that people could not understand. Some, Paul included, had the extraordinary gift of tongues (1 Cor. 14:1–5). We need not discuss whether such charismatic gifts continue today, although Paul indicates they eventually "will cease" (1 Cor. 13:8). In apostolic times they had not ceased, but even such a spiritual gift can only be unhelpful if nobody understands the words (1 Cor. 14:9). So Paul says that, while it is good to "excel" in spiritual gifts, the focus has to be on "edification." If you must speak in tongues, he concludes, you must also seek the gift of interpretation (1 Cor. 14:12–13). People need to understand what you are saying. If you were just speaking privately to God—the primary purpose of "tongues" (14:2)—interpretation would not matter, as God knows all languages. This would be true in private prayer, as Matthew Henry notes, citing Moses and Hannah (Ex. 14:15; 1 Sam. 1:13): "There may be praying in the Spirit where there is not a word spoken." At times our prayers "are so confused, the soul is in such a hurry with temptations and troubles, we know not what to say, nor how to express ourselves." But in public worship there needs to be clarity, for without it, all will be gibberish and confusion.

Paul offers a practical solution. He notes, "If I pray in a tongue, my spirit prays, but my understanding is unfruitful" (v. 14). He means that, even if he exercises a charismatic gift of the Holy Spirit but there is no clear communication, all he understands will help no one. He needs to have regard for the content of the prayer and the comprehension of the hearers. So whether he prays, sings, or blesses from his spirit, if it is not in understandable words, no one will be able to say "Amen" (vv. 15–16). And however well you "give thanks," the "other is not edified" (v. 17). What then is the general lesson and the godly application? It is to bring spirit and understanding together! "I will pray with the spirit and…with the understanding" is just to say that I will use whatever gifts I may have to build up everyone who is present. "Public worship," says Matthew Henry, "should be performed so as to be understood." God will understand all your "groanings which cannot be uttered" (Rom. 8:26), but if you want to lead any human being in prayer, you must express yourself clearly and pointedly! Paul spoke in "tongues" more than anyone, but in *public* worship he was committed to "five words with my understanding, that I may teach others also, than ten thousand words in a tongue" (Rom. 14:19). Five words is a very short prayer, but if they are understood they will be vastly more fruitful than gales of an unknown foreign language that only sounds like "brr…brr" to untutored ears.

A PRAYER FOR CLEAR SPIRITUAL UNDERSTANDING
Sing Psalm 119:73–80

THINGS I WILL PRAY FOR TODAY

_____

_____

_____

_____

_____

October 31
Victory through Jesus Christ

The great cause for thanksgiving

But thanks be to God, who gives us the victory through our Lord Jesus Christ.—1 Cor. 15:57

READ 1 CORINTHIANS 15:50–58

"We have a lot to be thankful for" is not only universally true, but is also frequently heard from almost everyone's lips. There is, however, thankfulness and then there is thankfulness. In his famous poem "Invictus," W. E. Henley (1849–1903) thanks "whatever gods may be" for his "unconquerable soul." If this is thanks, it is at best confused and at worst contemptuous, for it is clear that the source of his soul, the living God, is "in none of his thoughts" (Ps. 10:4). Godless people are often sincerely thankful, but, "they sacrifice to their net, and burn incense to their dragnet; because by them their share is sumptuous and their food plentiful" (Hab. 1:16). They are thankful because they are successful, or talented, or even just "lucky." But this robs God by praising the gifts while denying their Giver. The great corrective is to know *whom* to be thankful to and *why*. When Paul exclaims, "But thanks be to God," he speaks to both issues. God, in Christ, is the *who* of every cause for thanksgiving, for "every good gift and every perfect gift is from above, and comes down from the Father of lights, with whom there is no variation or shadow of turning" (James 1:17). The *why* is explained in terms of three absolutely basic doctrines of God's revealed truth.

Christians give thanks because we have "the victory." It is "the victory over death and the grave." This is both a present reality and a future prospect. We have eternal life, now and forever. Even the grave will be defeated, for "death is swallowed up in victory" (vv. 54–55). All that is truly "life" in our experience rests on the defeat of death, spiritual and physical, in time and for eternity. All good things flow from this victory—it is "through the Lord's mercies we are not consumed, because His compassions fail not" (Lam. 3:22). This victory is "now" for believers, even if it is "not yet" completed as in its future, permanent perfection in heaven.

Christians give thanks because this victory is through "our Lord Jesus Christ." Jesus alone delivers us from the power of death—and all its various echoes in our daily lives in this wicked world. He satisfied the demands of God's righteousness and justice. He took our flesh and blood "that through death He might destroy him who had the power of death, that is, the devil, and release those who through fear of death were all their lifetime subject to bondage" (Heb. 2:14). Not only does Jesus wash away sin and its penalty, but he restores the broken image of God in us, so as to "transform our lowly body that it may be conformed to His glorious body, according to the working by which He is able even to subdue all things to Himself" (Phil. 3:21). He died his death as the substitute for all the sinners he will save. The "word of the truth of the gospel" is "written that you may believe that Jesus is the Christ, the Son of God, and that believing you may have life in His name" (Col. 1:5; John 20:31).

Christians give thanks because God "gives" us this victory. God gives the victory because he accepts the once-for-all sacrifice of his beloved Son. Jesus saves us *from God*—that is, from his perfect justice—so that God's perfect love could be fulfilled in the salvation of otherwise hopelessly and helplessly lost people. The Christian's new life and destiny is a gift of grace. It is grace in God that drew the plan of salvation and it is grace in Christ that took him to the cross: "For He [God] made Him who knew no sin [Jesus] to be sin for us, that we might become the righteousness of God in Him" (2 Cor. 5:21). Here is where true thankfulness begins, grows, and abides—in Jesus embraced and followed as Savior and Lord. Let us give thanks!

A PRAYER OF THANKSGIVING
Sing Psalm 34:1–10

THINGS I WILL PRAY FOR TODAY

_____

_____

_____

_____

_____

_____

November 1
Consolation through Christ

A prayer of praise for comfort through Jesus Christ

For as the sufferings of Christ abound in us, so our consolation also abounds through Christ. — 2 Cor. 1:5

READ 2 CORINTHIANS 1:3–7

When Jesus was dying on the cross, he was ridiculed as an imposter. Suffering, of course, never looks like victory. It doesn't feel like it either. It is distressing. "He saved others," they taunted, "let Him save Himself if He is the Christ, the chosen of God….if You are the King of the Jews, save Yourself" (Luke 23:35–36). In other words, you are just another loser—messiahs are not meant to die shameful deaths! Jesus's followers have shared in this experience down the centuries. Paul was beaten from pillar to post in his ministry (2 Cor. 11:22–28). His character also came under fire. He is variously accused of being worldly, physically unimpressive, lacking spiritual gifts, financially crooked as well as being a poor speaker (2 Cor. 10:2, 20; 11:5–6; 12:12, 17)! All this is, of course, designed to persuade people he is not worth giving a hearing. This is why Paul explains his sufferings. He means to establish the validity of his apostolic ministry, but he also intends to encourage the Lord's people in their trials and in their testimony to the Lord Jesus Christ. He begins with basic truths to be believed and follows up by showing how this truth applied will be powerful in our lives (vv. 5–7).

The truth to be believed is about what God is to his people. Paul's introductory praise, "Blessed is…," gives God all the glory for his abounding grace (v. 3; cf. Ps. 68:19). Three titles reveal *who God is*: he is "the God and Father of our Lord Jesus Christ," the "Father of mercies," and "the God of all comfort." The logic of these titles points to the promise of deliverance from troubles. Over all is the fatherhood of God. He is the Father of the Savior, and the Father of mercy—free-grace redemption in Christ—and therefore is the Giver of comfort. His very names tell us that "God is love" (1 John 4:8).

We are also told about what God does for his people. He comforts us in our troubles, so that we may comfort others "with the comfort with which we ourselves are comforted by God" (v. 4). Today, we think of comfort as a consumer product. It is warm and cuddly. Our English word is from the Latin *con* and *fortis*, meaning "with strength." It has warmth, but it also has muscles. This is biblical comfort. In Psalm 119:49–50, the psalmist testifies that "hope" is his "comfort in my affliction," and ascribes the reason for this: "for Your word has given me life." Since he has new life, he has real hope, and this clothes him with a comprehensive comfort that arms him against his trials, for "hope does not put us to shame" (Rom. 5:5).

This truth applied is powerful in believers' lives. It is *powerful in Jesus Christ*, because, as we share in his sufferings, we also experience his consolation (v. 5). It is not that we invite suffering, still less inflict it upon ourselves like superstitious medieval flagellants. Rather, it is our experience of union with Christ by faith coming into its own; Paul's goal is "that I may know Him and the power of His resurrection, and the fellowship of His sufferings, being conformed to His death, if, by any means, I may attain to the resurrection from the dead" (Phil. 3:10). Jesus ministers new life to us in our need.

This truth is also *powerful through ministry*. As Paul suffers in his service to Christ, others are blessed. He is comforted, because his ministry is used to their "consolation and salvation" (v. 6)

It is also *powerful in hope*, for it comes from seeing the trials of believers overthrown by consolation (v. 7). In Christ, sufferings and comfort are linked to bring spiritual growth and fruit in the Christian life. This in turn calls us all the more to trust the Lord (2 Cor. 1:8–9), expect his blessings (2 Cor. 1:10), and share in prayer and thanksgiving with all the saints for God's good gifts to us in Christ (2 Cor. 1:11).

A PRAYER FOR CONSOLATION
Sing Psalm 20

THINGS I WILL PRAY FOR TODAY

_____

_____

_____

_____

_____

November 2
Thorn in the Flesh

Praying under pain

And He said to me, "My grace is sufficient for you..." — *2 Cor. 12:9*

READ 2 CORINTHIANS 12:7–10

Suppose God takes you on a day trip to heaven. Might you not be tempted to feel a little proud and perhaps think yourself a little better than others? Fourteen years before writing, Paul had been "caught up to the third heaven"—to God's heaven. He could not say if it was "in the body or out of the body" (2 Cor. 12:1–6). Like his encounter with Jesus on the Damascus road, these unique "visions and revelations" certified his calling as an apostle and his equality with the Twelve. They answered the critics who denounced him as a false or inferior apostle. But they could also have turned his head, as great gifts often do. This is where the "thorn in the flesh" comes in. Also, fourteen years before, Paul was afflicted with this "thorn"—and it kept his feet squarely planted on *terra firma*.

Any "thorn in the flesh" is meant to humble us (v. 7). Paul's "thorn" was probably a chronic physical condition, although it might well have been some recurring temptation. Whatever it was, Paul saw it as a targeted providence from the Lord, "lest," as he says, "I should be exalted above measure by the abundance of the revelations." That neither makes the "thorn" a good thing in itself, nor does it imply that suffering is desirable and virtuous. Paul says it was a "messenger of Satan" to "buffet" him! God's purpose is that he not be "exalted above measure" in his own mind. It was designed to keep him down to earth. Unhealed illness surely reminds us we are human. It dents our pride and self-sufficiency. Are we willing to be humbled and ready to depend on the Lord? Or will we resent being confronted with serious limitations? "Before I was afflicted I went astray," says the psalmist, "but now I keep Your word" (Ps. 119:67). How about you?

Any "thorn" is, however, meant to enrich our experience of God's grace. Paul pleads for its removal, and prays just "three times" before God answers him, to tell him that the "thorn" is for keeps, and

God's grace will be sufficient for him! He will cope, says God, "because My strength is made perfect in weakness" (vv. 8–9a). Our twenty-first century entitlement mentality—cradle-to-the-grave health and social security on the public purse—makes God seem cruel, compared to the promises of the compassionate "nanny state" welfare system. Would a good God who loves us perfectly not remove all our "thorns" when we ask him? And do we not tend to define the goodness of God toward us exclusively in terms of happy experiences and remarkable, preferably instant, deliverances from potential dangers? We can't imagine a good God allowing us to suffer long-term troubles—unless, of course, we are *very* wicked. (This was the attitude of Job's not very comforting "comforters.") People easily reproach God for not curing cancer, not stopping wars, and not diverting natural disasters from populated areas. We feel owed a good life with minimal trouble.

In stark contrast to modern social expectations, the Christian discerns the wisdom and grace of God in his troubles. He declares, "I will rather boast in my infirmities, that the power of Christ may rest upon me....For when I am weak, then I am strong" (vv. 9b–10). Jesus's free, enabling grace is far more evident in the overcoming of manifest weakness and disability than in the full flush of great strength and remarkable gifts. The latter more often tends to pride in those so gifted and to resentment in those who are not so advantaged. "It's easy for you!" complain the latter. The gospel of Christ is, however, not about Jesus helping us a little—that is, self-reliance with a "leg up" from God. The gospel is all of Christ, his atonement for our sin, his light for our darkness, his life for our deadness, and his strength for our weakness...thorns and all, to his glory now and forevermore.

A PRAYER FOR RELIEF
Sing Psalm 119:169–176

THINGS I WILL PRAY FOR TODAY

November 3
The Trinitarian Benediction

Praying the witness of the covenant-God

The grace of the Lord Jesus Christ, and the love of God, and the communion of the Holy Spirit be with you all. Amen. —*2 Cor. 13:14*

READ 2 CORINTHIANS 13:11–14

I once heard a pastor say, "I don't care what doctrine people believe, as long as they love Jesus." Does it really matter what you believe? Can we love Jesus without believing the Bible's teaching about Jesus? Jesus certainly never drives a wedge between love for him and knowing and believing his doctrine, as revealed in all of Scripture (Luke 4:27; John 10:35b). Jesus is "the Truth" (John 14:6), and we are "taught by Him, as the truth is in Jesus" (Eph. 4:21). Jesus says, "If you love me, you will keep my commandments" (John 14:15, ESV).

This is wonderfully exhibited to us in the apostolic benediction, or blessing. This flows entirely from the truth of the doctrine of the trinity of God—believed, understood, and applied. This benediction "plainly proves the doctrine of the gospel, and is an acknowledgment that Father, Son, and Spirit, are three distinct persons, yet but one God; and herein the same, that they are the fountain of all blessings to men." To love the real Jesus, we must grasp the essential Christian doctrines, not only of God, but also of man, salvation, the church, and the last things. And without a sound doctrine of Scripture in the first place, we will never begin to know Jesus! A faith without doctrinal content is no more real, alive, believable, and life-changing than a "faith without works" (James 2:20).

The benediction encapsulates the practical application of the doctrine of the Trinity. God is not some "man in the sky," or some formless entity "up there." Nor is he a vague mystical feeling inside us. He is the one living God in three Persons, as revealed in the Bible. He relates to us and our salvation in distinct ways relative to each Person. In his dealings with us as his creatures, the Father is the source (John 5:17, 19), the Son is the wisdom and mediator in dealing with us (John 1:3; Heb. 1:2), while the Holy Spirit is the one who effects his operations within our heart, mind, and life (Gen. 1:2; 1 Cor. 12:11). Note three things:

- ☙ "The *grace* of the Lord Jesus Christ" takes us to the cross—to the way we come to have a blessing in the first place. It is the grace of Christ as the Redeemer, dying on the cross to bear the penalty of sin in our place, that saves us (Eph. 2:8; cf. Phil. 2:8).
- ☙ "The *love* of God" takes us to eternity, and the decree of God to save sinners, chosen in Christ, "from before the foundation of the world" (Eph. 1:4). It is God's love that sends Christ to be the Redeemer—a love all the more amazing because it is love for the unlovable, such a love that proves itself in God's willingness to sacrifice his own Son (John 3:16).
- ☙ "The *communion* of the Holy Spirit" is the means by which we enjoy the grace of Christ and the love of God in the experience of personal redemption. He guides us into all truth (John 16:13). He is the Spirit of adoption by whom we cry "Abba, Father" (Rom. 8:15).

God teaches us in the benediction, writes Matthew Henry, "to have an eye by faith to Father, Son, and Holy Ghost—to live in a continual regard to the three persons in the Trinity, into whose name we were baptized, and in whose name we are blessed." He concludes that "we can desire no more to make us happy than the grace of Christ, the love of God, and the communion of the Holy Ghost."

A PRAYER PROCLAIMING GOD'S BLESSING
Sing Psalm 59:9–17

THINGS I WILL PRAY FOR TODAY

November 4
Enlightened Eyes

Prayer for our knowledge of Christ's person

...the eyes of your understanding being enlightened.—*Eph. 1:18a*

READ EPHESIANS 1:15–18A

Paul's letter to the Ephesians begins with excited and exalted praise for God's work of salvation (1:1–14). The Father's sovereign election of those who are saved (vv. 3–6), the Son's atoning sacrifice for their sins (vv. 7–10), and the Holy Spirit's sealing of believers in the promise of their inheritance (vv. 11–14), shows how the triune God plans and effects the salvation of his people. And it is all grace, undeserved, unmerited, and unearned: grace from eternity in God's predestination of his elect; grace in history in Jesus's coming to be the Savior of sinners; and grace from here to heaven in the application of redemption in the lives of believers by the Holy Spirit. This is how God—Father, Son, and Holy Spirit—prepares us for "our inheritance" in heaven. No wonder Paul praises the Lord so earnestly! And no wonder he turns to prayer for God's people, praying that they would flourish day by day in their lives in fellowship with God. His first prayer is that we might grow in our understanding of gospel grace, specifically with respect to the person of Jesus Christ.

"Open my eyes," prays the psalmist, "that I may see wondrous things from Your law" (Ps. 119:18). His assumption is that, if the Lord doesn't open the psalmist's eyes, he is not going to see these "wondrous things" in the way he needs to. Such spiritual discernment of the work of God is lacking in the unbeliever (1 Cor. 2:14), but it is not automatic in the believer. It is a progressive work of the Spirit. "With You is the fountain of life," says the psalmist. "In Your light we see light" (Ps. 36:9). Paul's prayer for Christians is that they know this supernatural illumination in their experience (v. 17).

First, he prays for God to act in terms of his triune character. He calls upon "the Father" who is glorious—"the God of our Lord Jesus Christ"—to continue to act in his sovereign grace, by giving every believer "the Spirit of wisdom and revelation," so that they will grow "in the knowledge of Him"—Jesus Christ, his Son. Knowing and growing in Jesus is a Trinitarian experience. The Father directs, the Spirit illumines, and the Son rules in our hearts in love as we increase in a personal understanding of who he is.

It is important to grasp that the "spirit of wisdom and revelation" is not our human spirit or state of mind, but is none other than the Holy Spirit who ministers within us to our hearts and minds! In several places, the Holy Spirit is referred to simply as "the Spirit" (John 15:25; Gal. 4:6; Rom. 8:15; 15:30). When Paul speaks of the "wisdom of God" in 1 Corinthians 2:6–10, he emphasizes that God has "revealed" this to us "through His Spirit. For the Spirit searches all things, yes, the deep things of God."

This suggests some things about the knowledge of Christ, which Paul prays God will give us. Clearly it is not mere information, even if they are the words of the Bible in black and white. Knowing the facts is one thing, but discerning them as Christians is something else again. Neither does Paul mean for the Ephesians to be divinely "inspired" as he was in certain of his utterances and writings. His prayer is that they be taught and so be enabled to grasp the meaning of that which God has revealed in his Word. What the Holy Spirit does is to enlighten "the eyes of your understanding" (v. 18a). We all know what switching on the light does for a dark or dim room. It extends our vision into territory otherwise hidden to us. Or, to change the image, remove a blindfold and suddenly light floods our eyes! In neither case do we generate the light. The light is from an external source. Our eyes are not lamps, but the Holy Spirit, accompanying God's Word, brings light—the light of the personal, intimate, and saving knowledge of Jesus Christ (2 Cor. 4:6). For "the entrance of Your Word brings light" (Ps. 119:130).

A PRAYER FOR LIGHT
Sing Psalm 43

THINGS I WILL PRAY FOR TODAY

_____

_____

_____

_____

_____

November 5
Calling, Inheritance, and Power

Prayer for our knowledge of Christ's work

…what is the exceeding greatness of His power toward us who believe…—Eph. 1:19a

READ EPHESIANS 1:18–19A

n Ephesians 1:17, Paul prays that we might more fully know God. That means more than having a bare outline of who he is. It must also mean knowing what he has done in us and for us, and will yet do. Consequently, the apostle continues in his prayer, at verse 18, to explain just how the triune God works in our lives. He focuses on three things in particular.

First, we are given to know "the hope of His calling" (v. 18b). God the Father is in view here, for he calls sinners to new life, having decreed from eternity to seek and to save them (Eph. 1:3–4). Christians are "beloved of God, called to be saints" (Rom. 1:7). Therefore they "press toward the goal for the prize of the upward call of God in Christ Jesus" (Phil. 3:14). This call is revealed in Scripture, made effectual by the Holy Spirit, and received by faith. As we know, understand, and apply the promise of the gospel, we reach forward to its fruition in "hope." Hope, in Scripture, is not an optimistic feeling arising from what today is often called "the human spirit." It is an actual work of God as his Word is "poured out in our hearts by the Holy Spirit who was given to us." It will not put us to shame (Rom. 5:5).

Second, we are given to know "the riches of the glory of His inheritance in the saints" (v. 18c). God the Son is in view here. Notice that it is not simply that *believers* ("saints") have an inheritance on account of Christ's securing salvation by his death on the cross. This is gloriously true—there is an "inheritance of the saints in light" (Col. 1:12). Here Paul speaks of *God's* inheritance in those he saves! These are riches of glory indeed that he should count us such a catch, such a prize, and such a pleasure! Jesus has not only secured a glorious inheritance for us, but also one for his Father and himself—and that is those who are saved and sealed as the saints of the Lord!

620

Third, we are given to know "the exceeding greatness of His power toward us who believe" (v. 19a). Here, God the Holy Spirit is in view. This is both promise and accomplishment, because the Word declares the gospel to be "the power of God unto salvation," and the experience of faith and faithfulness confirms that the Lord, by the Spirit, makes perfect his strength in our weakness (Rom. 1:16; 2 Cor. 12:9).

All of this reminds us that we cannot know the real Jesus without knowing what Jesus has done and is doing. Many believe that Jesus was a great teacher, an example of self-sacrifice, and a good, caring individual. The "good news" is actually none of these, because Jesus did not come to "inspire" us to be better people and get right with God through trying to do better. Faith in a Jesus who is no more than good, self-giving, and a great example is not saving faith. The real Jesus came to save sinners by bearing the real penalty for their sins in their place and by living the perfectly sinless life they could not live. Our sins, then, are reckoned by God to be his, and his perfect righteousness is reckoned by God to be ours. God accepts Jesus's real atonement and cancels the sin of all who will believe on him. God also imputes his perfect righteousness to believers so that they are righteous in his sight on account of Christ. Jesus's person and work are inseparable in the matter of truly believing upon Christ as the Savior and Lord of our life. This is the good news: Jesus "was delivered up because of our offenses and was raised for our justification" (Rom. 4:25; cf. Eph. 2:8). In Christ we have a real calling, are a real inheritance, and know the power of God to our salvation.

PRAISE FOR GOD'S POWER IN HIS SAINTS
Sing Psalm 111:6–10

THINGS I WILL PRAY FOR TODAY

November 6
Exalted Prince and Savior

Prayer for our knowledge of Christ's exaltation

...which He worked in Christ when He raised Him from the dead...
—Eph. 1:20

READ EPHESIANS 1:19B–21

The power that saves a soul is the same power that raised Jesus from death. Paul's reasoning is as follows: in order to understand the "exceeding greatness of His power toward us who believe," we must also grasp that it flows from the power God exercises in the exaltation of the crucified Jesus—which includes his resurrection, ascension, and heavenly rule. Notice how Paul heaps up the most pointed words for power to drive this home. This power (*dunamis*) toward us who believe, is the same as that working (*energeia*) of His mighty (*ischous*) power (*kratos*) in raising Jesus (v. 19). We all realize that Jesus's resurrection was a miracle of God's supernatural power, but we routinely underestimate what it takes to save a sinner. Being saved is often reduced to little more than an intellectual, or even emotional, decision on our part. We have a crisis, we "believe," God's hand is in it in some indistinct way, and we are "saved." God helped, but we do not think of it as a miraculous work of the Holy Spirit that changes the unchangeable and awakens the dead! But what is salvation but a spiritual resurrection requiring the same divine power necessary for a bodily resurrection?

This power raised Christ from the dead (v. 20a). It is surely no stretch to believe that the God who created all things out of nothing can breathe life into a dead body. The fact is that, without the resurrection, there is no hope. Paul honestly admits that "if Christ is not risen, your faith is futile; you are still in your sins!" (1 Cor. 15:17). An *unrisen* Jesus—crucified and still dead—cannot save anyone. He was *raised* for our justification (Rom. 4:25). No resurrection means no forgiveness, no salvation, no eternal life, and therefore no hope! Those who are trusting a Jesus who did not really atone for sin and did not really rise from the dead are still in their sins. They can know nothing of the power of God that raised him from the dead and will raise all those who believe on Christ as their Savior. Christ's resurrection is a pledge guaranteeing the believers' resurrection (1 Cor. 6:14; 15:20–23).

This power exalted Christ as a Prince and a Savior (v. 20b): "Him God has exalted to His right hand to be Prince and Savior, to give repentance to Israel and forgiveness of sins" (Acts 5:31). He who was the Son from all eternity is now enthroned as the God-man and in virtue of the victory of the cross. Jesus, in his body, sits at God's "right hand in the heavenly places." Psalm 110 is fulfilled: "The Lord said to my Lord, 'Sit at My right hand, till I make Your enemies My footstool.'"

This power is comprehensive and universal in its extent (v. 21). Once exalted, Jesus is not passive. His heavenly session (sitting) is intensely active and involves the exercise of his absolute authority over everything in creation for all time. The power that raised Jesus and exalted him will forever secure the purposes of God against all opposition (see Col. 1:16; 2:25). Paul's great point here is that the Lord pulls out all the stops for saving his people. There is nothing of our (illusory) power in our own salvation. It is all of God's wonderful love and grace and power in and through his Son. He makes us willing by his power. The very power that raised Jesus saves us, takes us from spiritual death to eternal life, and will reunite body and soul in the resurrection of the great day. The gospel is "the power of God to salvation for everyone who believes" (Rom. 1:16). The exalted Christ is our Surety and nothing whatsoever "shall be able to separate us from the love of God which is in Christ Jesus our Lord" (Rom. 8:39). This armed Paul against all the privation and persecution that came his way, and he could testify that "in all these things we are more than conquerors through Him who loved us" (Rom. 8:37).

PRAISE FOR THE RISEN AND RULING CHRIST
Sing Psalm 110

THINGS I WILL PRAY FOR TODAY

November 7
Head over All Things

A prayer for the knowledge of Christ's rule

He put all things under his feet and made Him head over all things to the church... — Eph. 1:22

READ EPHESIANS 1:15–23

e have already seen, in this wonderful prayer, that the power God exercises in the lives of believers (v. 19) is the same power that raises Jesus from the dead, exalts him a Prince and a Savior, and is comprehensive and universal in its scope (vv. 20–21). In verses 22–23, Paul takes us a step further and shows us that the risen Jesus is not only exalted above all things created, but actually is given dominion over them. He opens up the biblical doctrine of the mediatorial kingship of Christ. God has "put all things under His feet" (v. 22). This recalls Psalm 8:6: "You have made him to have dominion over the works of Your hands; You have put all things under his feet." This is quoted as referring to Christ in 1 Corinthians 15:27 and Hebrews 2:8. Psalm 8 talks about man in general being exalted over creation, but the New Testament shows that this is actually realized in the man Christ Jesus—and thus in those who are united to him by faith and are part of his kingdom. Christ's kingship as the risen, victorious Mediator is crucial to the fulfillment of Psalm 8, which is about us, but about us in Christ!

Christ is given as "head over all things to the church" (v. 22b). This explains how and for what purpose "all things" come to be "under His feet." His power over all things is not the whole story. It is "to the church." He has a particular relationship to the church (Eph. 4:15–16; 5:23, 29). It is in terms of this special relationship that he rules all things. To the church, Christ is "the head of the body, the church, who is the beginning, the firstborn from the dead, that in all things He may have the preeminence" (Col. 1:18). But he is also the head of everything else in the interest of, and for the benefit of, the church! This is the power that adds "to the church daily those...being saved," that surrounds God's people "with favor" like "a shield," and in every detail of history does his will among "the army of heaven and among the inhabitants of the earth" (Acts 2:47; Ps. 5:12; Dan. 4:35). As the Mediator between God and man, Jesus is King and Head over all things to build his church: "Then comes the end, when He delivers the kingdom to God the Father, when He puts an end to all rule and all authority and power" (1 Cor. 15:24).

Christ's church is "His body" (v. 23a). Like the human body, the church is a unity, whatever its diversity: "For as the body is one and has many members, but all the members of that one body, being many, are one body, so also is Christ" (1 Cor. 12:12); "For as we have many members in one body, but all the members do not have the same function, so we, being many, are one body in Christ, and individually members of one another" (Rom. 12:4–5). Therefore, "above all…put on love, which is the bond of perfection. And let the peace of God rule in your hearts, to which also you were called in one body; and be thankful" (Col. 3:14–15). We are called to unity with all God's people.

Christ's church is "the fullness of Him who fills all in all" (v. 23b). The key to unity in the body is union with Christ. The church is filled with Christ, or else it is not the church. How will we be blessed, be a blessing, and give glory to God in our witness to the world if we have no desire or thirst for Christ, either in our own hearts or in our shared fellowship in the church? Nothing on earth can be the "fullness" of Christ but the church, the body of the Lord's redeemed. This happens when he "fills" everything that we are with himself, in every way. "Beloved, now we are children of God," writes John, "and it has not yet been revealed what we shall be, but we know that when He is revealed, we shall be like Him, for we shall see Him as He is" (1 John 3:2).

PRAISE FOR THE RULE OF CHRIST AS KING
Sing Psalm 8

THINGS I WILL PRAY FOR TODAY

_____

_____

_____

_____

_____

November 8
Might in the Inner Man

Prayer for the strengthening of faith

For this reason I bow my knees to the Father of our Lord Jesus Christ...
—Eph. 3:14

READ EPHESIANS 3:14–17A

he apostle Paul practiced what he preached. He urges us all to "pray without ceasing" (1 Thess. 5:17) and he gives us a wonderful example of what this means in his letter to the Ephesians. He first praises God for their salvation (1:1–14). Then he seamlessly transitions into prayer for the deepening of their knowledge of the Lord (1:15–23). In the second chapter, he turns to the doctrine of salvation by grace through faith in Christ. In the third chapter, he is about to turn to prayer, but pauses to speak of his ministry to Jews and Gentiles (3:1–13), only to break out into a rhapsodic prayer that believers would "be strengthened with might...in the inner man" (3:14–21). This is "prayer without ceasing" in action! Praying and living are integral and inseparable in Christian experience. His faith is practical and his practice is faithful, and so his doctrine is prayerful and his prayer is doctrinal.

Every true prayer begins and ends with faith. Faith is not mentioned in Paul's prayer until verse 17a, but it is the "elephant in the room" from the start. Paul is speaking to those who have a personal relationship with God through faith in the Lord Jesus Christ. To those who have no such personal faith, it is an invitation to receive and rest in Jesus Christ as he is offered in the gospel! Notice four things in this first part of the prayer (vv. 14–17a):

> ☞ Prayer does not come out of a clear blue sky. Paul had his reasons for praying. He says, "For this reason" (v. 14). What is this reason? Any or all of the things he had written about so far could be excellent reasons for praying. The simplest answer may be that, as he thought about their potential discouragement over his sufferings in the gospel ministry (Eph. 3:13), he was moved to cry out to the Lord that he would encourage them. The dynamic of real need, keenly felt, takes him quite

626

literally to his knees! Prayer is not a ritual performance, or a form of words repeated like some mantra, but a fruit of godly interaction with real circumstances in the church, in the world and in our own hearts and inner life.

> Prayer also does not go *into* a clear blue sky. It is directed to the "Father of the Lord Jesus Christ," to whom he "bows his knees" in ready submission as one who belongs to God's "whole family in heaven and earth" (vv. 14–15). This echoes the words of the Lord's Prayer, "Our Father in heaven" (Matt. 6:9).

> Prayer seeks nothing less than the enabling power of God (v. 16). Our faith will be strengthened, not by our coming up with inner resources of our own, but by nothing less than power from God through the work of the Holy Spirit, who strengthens us in the "inner man." The "might" of which he speaks is—literally—the *dynamic* of a closer relationship with the Lord wrought by the indwelling Spirit.

> Prayer seeks specific results (v. 17a). In this instance it is that "Christ may dwell" within our hearts. Jesus makes a promise to those who love him and keep his word, that he and the Father will make their "home" with them. This happens "through faith." This is a work of the Father, Son, and Holy Spirit: "Paul seeks the Father's glorious riches, the Spirit's strengthening power, and the Son's abiding presence." God is a Trinity and union with him by faith is Trinitarian and therefore supernatural. Living faith is not a merely intellectual transaction, and godliness is not merely the product of a determined commitment on our part. The Christian's "inner man" is where the triune God makes his home and where, by the literal presence of his Holy Spirit, he pursues his work of love and free grace in us till he brings us to heaven.

PRAISE FOR WALKING BY FAITH
Sing Psalm 1

THINGS I WILL PRAY FOR TODAY

November 9
Love That Passes Knowledge

Prayer for the strengthening of love

...that you, being rooted and grounded in love... — Eph. 3:17b

READ EPHESIANS 3:17B–19

God's Word makes it clear that a mere external form of religion is a dangerous illusion. Empty rituals are not evidence of living faith, but rather a form of magic. The same can be said of "faith" as many seem to think of it. James emphasizes that "faith *without works* is dead" (James 2:26). He points out that "even the demons believe—and tremble!" (v. 19). Only "faith working *through love*" avails anything, says Paul (Gal. 5:6). The Lord warns the church in Sardis, "I know your works, that you have a name that you are alive, but you are dead" (Rev. 3:1). Saving faith in Christ is alive and active, and as Paul now shows us, is about being "rooted and grounded in love"—which includes both love *toward* Christ (v. 17b) and the knowledge of the love *of* Christ (vv. 18–19).

Christians are rooted and grounded in love (v. 17b). Every enthusiastic supporter of a football team knows what it is to be gripped by love for his side. So, having believed upon Christ as your Savior, do you love him such that he is always on your mind?

When Paul says, "that you, being rooted," he means that, when someone believes in Christ truly, they are in a basic condition of love toward God in Christ. "Love is the fundamental grace," says John Eadie. "It is the root and foundation of Christian character." Christ dwells in the believer's heart by faith. We are like trees with roots and buildings with foundations—in love for Christ. "We love Him, because He first loved us" (1 John 4:19), and this is the "living basis" of your discipleship to him.

Christians grow in the knowledge of the love of Christ (vv. 18–19). Love is a "step on the staircase of Paul's prayer." It is also a vital stairway to personal discipleship. The prayer is that we might grow in our knowledge of Jesus's love for us in four ways:

❧ We are made "able to comprehend" Christ's love. That is, we gain a solid conviction that it was love, and nothing else, that took Jesus to the cross to bear the penalty of sin.

❧ We grow in our understanding "with all the saints"—not in isolation, but in the worship and fellowship of the church, which is Christ's body (Rom. 12:5).

❧ We will gain an ever more complete grasp of Jesus's love. The mathematical metaphor—"width and length and depth and height"—just means that, any way you look at your salvation, you will see his love for you in ever brighter colors of glory.

❧ We will accordingly never exhaustively know Christ's love, because it "surpasses knowledge." We might say it "boggles the mind." We will grow *forever*! While we live in this world, and even throughout all eternity, the Lord will expand our heart knowledge of his love for us. We will never be tired of it, never be bored by it, never cease to delight in it: "The steadfast love of the LORD never ceases; his mercies never come to an end; they are new every morning; great is your faithfulness" (Lam. 3:22–23, ESV). Christians will be "filled with all the fullness of God" (v. 19b) all along the way. Paul Bayne asks, "Why should we think that God loves us less when we are old friends, than he did when we were new? No, he that has shall have more, as Christ said to Nathanael, John 1:50, 'Do you believe because I saw you under the fig tree? You shall see greater things than these.'"

A SONG OF LOVE TO THE LORD
Sing Psalm 18:1–6

THINGS I WILL PRAY FOR TODAY

November 10
A Ladder to Heaven

A prayer of rising hope

Now to Him who is able to do exceedingly abundantly above all that we ask or think… —Eph. 3:20

READ EPHESIANS 3:20–21

Every believing prayer is a ladder to heaven. Psalm 130 is a wonderful example of this. The psalmist cries "out of the depths" (v. 1), realizes afresh that there is forgiveness with the Lord (v. 4), and rises to "hope in the Lord," who "shall redeem Israel from all his iniquities" (vv. 7–8). Paul's prayer in Ephesians 3:14–21 follows a similar trajectory, except that his steps are his beloved "triad of Christian virtues": faith (vv. 14–17a), love (vv. 17b–19), and now hope (vv. 19–20; see 1 Cor. 13:13).The strengthening of faith and love can only issue in hope—the kind of hope he expresses here.

There is a lot of talk about "hope" in our world. Much of it, however, has no more substance than the notion that—as Charles Dickens's Mr. Micawber put it—"something will turn up." It is true, as Solomon says, that "for him who is joined to all the living there is hope, for a living dog is better than a dead lion" (Eccl. 9:4). While there's life, there's hope. But merely living is not the same thing as having an abiding hope if that hope is only a feeling that something better will turn up. The expression "hoping against hope" is often seen as the triumph of subjective optimistic sentiment against the more or less relentless hopelessness of the facts of present circumstances. When Paul says of Abraham that "in hope he believed against hope, that he should become the father of many nations," it was not because the patriarch just somehow felt positive about the future. It was because "he had been told, 'So shall your offspring be'"(Rom. 4:18). It was the fruit of a living faith in the God who loved him and had revealed his promises to him. The facts of God's revealed will, embraced in faith and love for God, issues in a hope founded solidly on the sure mercies and promises of God.

"This hope," says Scripture, "we have as an anchor of the soul, both sure and steadfast" (Heb. 6:19). Why is the Christian's hope more than notion, more than feeling, more than wishful thinking? Paul gives four reasons:

> ⸖ God is the *source* of this hope. He is the One "who is able" (v. 20a). This is not an unfelt hope, but a hope built upon the experience of God's power to save and to sustain. Past and present experiences of his gracious dealings feed into our persuasion of the happy fruition of his promises for us in the future.

> ⸖ God will surely bless us *above and beyond* our largest imaginings of his goodness to us, "exceedingly abundantly above all that we ask or think" (v. 20b). Has sober reflection on God's answers to your prayers not powerfully proved this to be the rule rather than the exception?

> ⸖ God's power is *already* at work within us (v. 20c). Paul appeals again to the explicit promise of God, on the one hand, and, on the other hand, our experience of his workmanship in us in the dynamic of our faithful walk with him (Eph. 2:10).

> ⸖ God's purpose is the demonstration and application of his glory "in the church by Christ Jesus" (v. 21). Hope in Christ blesses the people of God and lifts up the Lord as the amazing Redeemer of his people throughout history and in all eternity! The church is the central repository of hope in this world, because Jesus is the Savior who saves "to the uttermost those who come to God through Him" (Heb. 7:25).

"Blessed be the God and Father of our Lord Jesus Christ, who according to His abundant mercy has begotten us again to a living hope through the resurrection of Jesus Christ from the dead" (1 Peter 1:3).

A CELEBRATION OF HOPE IN THE LORD
Sing Psalm 131

THINGS I WILL PRAY FOR TODAY

_____

_____

_____

_____

_____

November 11
Singing to the Lord

Making thankfulness our song of prayer

...and making melody in your heart to the Lord... — Eph. 5:19

READ EPHESIANS 5:15–21

Becoming a Christian is a work of the Holy Spirit. He makes the call of the gospel effectual, subconsciously regenerating our otherwise dead soul (that is, giving us a *new birth*), so that we consciously turn to Jesus in repentance and faith (that is, we are *converted* to Christ). Thereafter, the Holy Spirit lives in the Christian's heart. We really need his presence and sanctifying influence, because we still have to deal with sin's powerful influences, which, as Paul says of his own experience, are "warring against the law of my mind, and bringing me into captivity to the law of sin which is in my members" (Rom. 7:23). And because we are "in Christ" and the Holy Spirit is in us, we are exhorted to be "filled with the Spirit" (Eph. 5:18). Of course, that does not mean we determine the presence or absence of the Holy Spirit, or the degree of his influences upon us. He is *God* the Holy Spirit and does his will as he wishes. But it does mean that we bend ourselves to make the Spirit the measure of our satisfaction, and the controller of our desires, hopes, ambitions, plans, thinking, and prayers, for the present time and the eternity to come. The fruit of this exercise of faithfulness is described in Ephesians 5:19–20.

First comes *speaking* to one another out of the fullness of the Spirit. The content of this is, following the order of the Greek text, the use of "psalms, hymns and songs—spiritual" (v. 19a). "Spiritual" in this context has reference to the same Holy Spirit, whose filling of our hearts we are to earnestly desire and nurture. These properly refer to songs of Scripture given to the church by divine inspiration, most obviously in the "Book of Praises"—the Bible's title for what we call the Psalms, but what is in fact God's collection of inspired psalms, hymns, and songs. And mere recitation is not in view, but, as the parallel passage in Colossians 3:16 shows, the way this is to be done is through "teaching and admonishing one another" in terms of these rich passages of God's Word. In his classic

632

commentary, John Eadie notes that this involves "giving expression…to your joyous emotions in 'psalms and hymns, and spiritual songs.'" In this use of God's songs, we progressively bring "every thought into captivity to the obedience of Christ" (2 Cor. 10:5).

Second comes our *singing* to the Lord within ourselves. Praise is just one kind of prayer. In this case, the expression of God's goodness through the medium of Scripture's songs issues in overwhelming thankfulness to our Father in heaven (v. 20). This arises from your "making melody in your heart to the Lord" (v. 19b) as you ponder and rejoice in his matchless grace. You "were once darkness, but now you are light in the Lord" (v. 8). The "fruit of the Spirit"—which is in "all goodness, righteousness and truth"—is our joy and therefore our song. Everything God's songs teach us about God gives a happiness that issues in song. If we sing a song of God's love toward us in Christ—Psalm 22 comes to mind—or a song of God's gracious deliverance from our sins and miseries, as in Psalm 40, how can we be sad? Even songs of God's judgments at the coming of his Son, as in Psalm 110, remind us that, notwithstanding his righteous anger against wickedness, the overwhelming motive and purpose of the Lord is to save us from that very wickedness. God's songs all lead us, by one path or another, to the cross of the Messiah he sent to save his people from their sins. There will be no weeping in the great day among the redeemed of the Lord: "Let us be glad and rejoice and give Him glory, for the marriage of the Lamb has come, and His wife has made herself ready" (Rev. 19:7). And until then, "Rejoice in the Lord always, and again I say, rejoice!" (Phil. 4:4).

THE MELODY OF AN OVERFLOWING HEART
Sing Psalm 45

THINGS I WILL PRAY FOR TODAY

November 12
All Kinds of Prayer

Prayer's first principles (Part 1)

With all prayer and petition... — *Eph. 6:18 (NASB)*

READ EPHESIANS 6:10–20

rayer too often plays second fiddle to the myriad of other calls upon our time. The busyness of our lives crowds out the business of our prayers. No single verse in Scripture serves as an antidote to our deficiencies in prayer like Ephesians 6:18. It contains five distinct practical principles of prayer. The first—as stated in the Greek text, if not in your English translation—is that we may pray "with all prayer and petition"—that is, with *all kinds* of prayer. It is not an accident that this word comes after Paul's description of the Christian's armor. "It is not arms or weapons which make the warrior," writes Charles Hodge. "There must be courage and strength; and even then he often needs help." This is why "the apostle urges the duty of prayer."

There are many kinds of prayer. We tend to treat public prayer as the standard, but this is a great mistake because it tends to promote a formalistic attitude to prayer itself. Even that irreverent skeptic Robert Burns, Scotland's national poet, understood this much. In his poem "The Cotter's Saturday Night," he contrasts the simple family worship in a cottager's home with "the pomp of method and of art" in what we would call "high church" practice. He then opines, "The Power incens'd, the pageant will desert, / The pompous strain, the sacerdotal stole: / But haply, in some cottage far apart, / May hear, well-pleased, the language of the soul, / And in his Book of Life the inmates poor enroll" (stanza 17). Neither vain repetition nor profane and idle babblings are models for believing prayer. What then are the various kinds of prayer?

> *Public prayer.* Acts 20:36: "And when he [Paul] had said these things, he knelt down and prayed with them all." (See also the prayers of Solomon in 1 Kings 8:22–53, and Ezra in Ezra 9:5–15.)
> *Private prayer in a group setting.* Acts 16:13: "And on the Sabbath day we went out of the city to the riverside, where prayer was customarily made."

- *Secret prayer.* Matthew 6:6: "But you, when you pray, go into your room, and when you have shut your door, pray to your Father who is in the secret place; and your Father who sees in secret will reward you openly."
- *Mental prayer.* 1 Samuel 1:13: "Now Hannah spoke in her heart, only her lips moved, but her voice was not heard." Nehemiah 2:4: "Then the King said to me, 'What do you request?' So I prayed to the God of heaven and I said to the king...."
- *Occasional prayers.* 1 Chronicles 5:20: "And the Hagrites were delivered into their hand, and all who were with them, for they cried out to God in the battle. He heard their prayer for they put their trust in Him." (These last two categories used to be called "arrow" prayers.)

The assumption behind all of this is that we constantly stand in the need of prayer. Prayer is never needed so that God can be informed about what's happening, or so that he can change his eternal mind. He declares the end from the beginning (Isa. 46:10). Still, prayer does change things. It is needed to change us, and since God deals with us in *our* changeableness, prayer is one means by which he tracks our ups and downs and ministers to us in all our circumstances. God ordains the means as much as the ends, so he integrates his unchanging will with his changing providence. Hence "you do not have because you do not ask" (James 4:2). Pray and he will answer. Prayer is integral to a living faith and essential to communion with God—in all situations. Therefore speak to him with all kinds of prayers.

A PRAYER COMMITTING TO ALL PRAYER AND PETITION
Sing Psalm 27:5-9

THINGS I WILL PRAY FOR TODAY

_____

_____

_____

_____

_____

November 13
At All Times

Prayer's first principles (Part 2)

...pray at all times... — Eph. 6:18 (NASB)

READ EPHESIANS 6:10–20

Not only may we pray in all sorts of ways—"with all prayer and petition"—but we may "pray at all times." The meaning of this is that believers will pray on all kinds of occasions. Charles Hodge's rendering—"on every emergency"—is too restrictive and, in any case, is unnecessary. Few need special encouragement to pray in an emergency. Jesus teaches us that "men ought always to pray and not lose heart" (Luke 18:1). Paul says elsewhere, "Rejoice always, pray without ceasing, in everything give thanks; for this is the will of God in Christ Jesus for you" (1 Thess. 5:16–18). This obviously cannot mean that we are to pray continuously through our waking hours. God has given us all sorts of other things to do. Even so, there is plenty of time for praying, even in the course of an otherwise busy day.

If you prayed even a fraction of the time you nurse your coffee and look out the window, would it increase your praying substantially? Of course, it is important that there are times for recreation and rest in daily life. Paul's point is that prayer in all its forms is to be made so much a part of the Christian's life that it can be said almost literally that the Christian prays "without ceasing." He prays on and off all through his normal day, even if there are set times when, as Jesus instructs us, he goes into his room, shuts the door, and prays to his Father in secret (Matt. 6:6). The Christian is constantly conversing with his Lord God. He does not merely "say" prayers, he talks to his Father in heaven.

Why does this happen quite normally in the Christian life? There are at least three main reasons. First, it is because of *who the Lord is to us.* He is our heavenly Father through his Son, Jesus, whom he sent to be our Savior. This comes first because Jesus in his person and work is our preeminent motive for prayer. Even if it often takes personal needs to bring us to pray, adoration and thanksgiving must be uppermost in our minds. In our selfish way, we too often use prayer as a need-driven tool to secure some favor from God. But what he has already given us in Jesus Christ is both the cause and the ground of confidence for praying without ceasing—and that is nothing other than salvation itself and peace in believing (Rom. 15:13).

Also, we have need of *constant fellowship with God*. This is not solely because we have sins to confess and forgiveness to seek, or problems to air and requests to make. It is because we are the finite creature-children of the infinite uncreated Father-God who loves us. Hence the Christian cries to him in the familiar and endearing language of a child to a beloved father, "Abba, Father!" (Rom. 8:15; Gal. 4:6).

Finally, it is only through prayerfulness that we will *grow spiritually in the way God desires*. Without prayer "at all times" the other means of grace will not profit us as they could. The preaching of the Word will not be understood as it might be; Scripture itself will not grip us; truth will be resisted; prayers will be hindered; hearts will be cold; and we will not enjoy sweet fellowship with the Lord and with his people as God intends for us. If this is true in your experience, you will only have yourself to blame, for "you have not because you ask not" (James 4:2).

So let us pray as we go! At any time and at all times and occasions we may turn to the Lord in prayer. Driving to work, waiting in a line, between meetings and in quiet moments, we may indeed "pray without ceasing." This is a gift of God's grace. It is the oxygen of the soul. His throne of grace is near us wherever we are (Heb. 4:16). Prayer opens the gate of heaven (Gen. 28:17) "at all times."

A SONG OF UNCEASING ADORATION OF GOD
Sing Psalm 34

THINGS I WILL PRAY FOR TODAY

_____

_____

_____

_____

_____

_____

November 14
In the Holy Spirit

Prayer's first principles (Part 3)

Pray...in the Spirit—Eph. 6:18 (NASB)

READ EPHESIANS 6:10–20

Prayer is a gift to us. We need to pray. It is the particular means God uses to involve us consciously and intentionally in the outworking of his will in our world. It draws us into his plans, embraces us in his fellowship, and grows us in the understanding and living out of our faith. It is our lifeline to the very throne of God (Heb. 4:16). This is the "why" of prayer. The "how" of prayer is what Paul addresses in the five parts of Ephesians 6:18. We have seen (see November 12 and 13) that the first of these practical principles is that we can pray all kinds of prayers—public, private, secret, mental, and occasional. The second is that we should be praying at all sorts of times along the course of each day's happenings.

The third practical principle is praying "in the Spirit." The text simply says, in Greek, *en pneumati* (literally, "in spirit"), but it is not simply a reference to the human spirit. This is always translated as referring to the Holy Spirit. It parallels Jude 20, which says *"en pneumati hagio"* (literally, "in Spirit Holy"). Consequently, John Eadie very firmly asserts that "it is surely an unhallowed and perverse opinion, which gives these words the meaning...'out of the heart, or sincerely.'" It rather means "in or by the power of the Holy Spirit." Here, says Harry Uprichard, Paul "notes the Spirit's enabling grace in prayer, as he does in Romans 8:26–27....God's Spirit, not our spirit, is in control and orders our groanings in line with God's will. It is divinely controlled through humanly ordered prayer." The "spirit" is God the Holy Spirit and the prayer enjoined is prayer influenced by the Holy Spirit at work within the believer. He teaches us how to pray and "makes intercession for us with groanings which cannot be uttered" (Rom. 8:26). Believing Christian prayer is more than our best intentioned and most concerned thoughts sent skyward; it is the outpouring of Spirit-assisted contemplation of everything from apprehension to desperation, and from adoration to thanksgiving.

Prayer influenced by the Holy Spirit has to be from the depth of our being, because it is an inward and spiritual transaction. Christian prayer has, as it were, a supernaturally assisted takeoff! This has powerful implications for the attitude we bring to prayer. We must take care to root out selfish and worldly motives. Jesus says, "Take heed that you do not do your charitable deeds before men, to be seen by them. Otherwise you have no reward from your Father in heaven" (Matt. 6:1). What is true of good deeds in general is true also of prayer. Paul Bayne (1573–1617) offers us two practical applications:

> Negatively, he says that prayers that do not come from the heart, and are not informed by the Spirit, "are nothing but vain babbling…as with many, the mind is running on twenty things, while the body boweth to prayer."

> Positively, he says we should be "crying to Him that is the quickening Spirit, not being quiet until we get some warmth into our spirits; and these be the winged prayers that fly beyond all the visible heavens, these be the prayers of smoke in which the church ascendeth to God, out of this world, a barren wilderness."

Needless to say, prayer that is only a form of words or a show to impress either God or other people can expect no hearing from the Lord. What is of vital importance is not that others can hear you praying, or even know you are praying, but that you are praying under the leading of the Holy Spirit for all that is pleasing to God.

A PRAYER FOR THE LEADING OF THE HOLY SPIRIT
Sing Psalm 143:7–12

THINGS I WILL PRAY FOR TODAY

November 15
On the Alert

...being watchful to this end with all perseverance and supplication...
—Eph. 6:18

READ EPHESIANS 6:10–20

If we are to "pray in the Spirit," we must be on the alert. Prayer, like sentry duty, is killed by distraction and sleepiness. Obviously, we will need to be on the alert if we are to be both consistent and persistent in our prayers. Scripture frequently associates mental alertness with effectiveness in prayer. Here are three examples:

> Matthew 26:41: "Keep watching and praying, that you may not enter into temptation."
> Colossians 4:2: "Devote yourselves to prayer, keeping alert in it with an attitude of thanksgiving."
> 1 Peter 4:7: "The end of all things is at hand, therefore be of sound judgment and sober spirit for the purpose of prayer."

You cannot pray in your sleep. Neither is prayer an afterthought. Nor is it to be a desperate shot in the dark. Prayer is meant to be the most thoughtful thing we do in daily life. It is the medium of the Christian's union and communion with God. Being "watchful" is essential to living the Christian life successfully (1 Cor. 16:13; 1 Peter 5:8).

This spiritual discipline and mental vigilance is emphasized for at least four reasons:

> We need to be alert to the Holy Spirit speaking in the Scriptures. He leads us into the truth of God's Word (John 16:13). Prayer "in the Spirit" will be alert to God's Word and his promises.
> We need to be alert in order to be effective in prayer; we also need to be alert to God's concerns, to people's needs, to the state of our own souls, to the condition of the world, and to the advance of God's kingdom.
> We need to be alert to keep ourselves from sin: "Let everyone who names the name of the Lord abstain from wickedness"

(2 Tim. 2:19). Long ago, Paul Bayne illustrated the difficulty of praying after a day of sinning: "If one should eat codlings, gooseberries, pease, would you wonder at night he were wrung in his belly? Would you not bid him mend his diet if he meant to see it otherwise? So when we let our hearts loose all day, feed upon earthly vanity, how should they be heavenly minded on a sudden, when bed-time calleth us to prayer?"

> We will be alert when we set aside time for prayer. How can we be alert for prayer—either when to pray or for what to pray—if we make no firm plans to pray and never make it part of each day's life? The psalmist organized himself to pray at "evening, morning and at noon" (Ps. 55:17). Jesus "departed to a mountain" to pray (John 6:15). He told us to go into our room, "shut the door," and pray in secret (Matt. 6:6). The options are many.

The fruit of spiritual alertness in prayer is always "all perseverance and supplication." This is a way of describing prevailing prayer: prayer that will not give up. The same language is used in Romans 12:12, which urges us to "continue steadfastly in prayer." Faithful response will say, like Jacob wrestling with God at Bethel, "I will not let you go unless you bless me" (Gen. 32:26). When Jesus illustrates perseverance in prayer, his subjects—the friend at midnight (Luke 11:5–8) and the persistent widow (Luke 18:2–5)—both persuade reluctant helpers to assist them. How much more can we be encouraged to keep pleading with the Lord, who delights in answering our prayers! Let us be alert to pray steadfastly every day in life.

A PRAYER OF EXPECTANTLY WAITING ON THE LORD
Sing Psalm 40:1–9

THINGS I WILL PRAY FOR TODAY

November 16
For All the Saints

Prayer's first principles (Part 5)

With all prayer and petition for all the saints...—Eph. 6:18a (NASB)

READ EPHESIANS 6:10–20

ome of the first practical principles of prayer—five in number—are set out in Ephesians 6:18. The first four of these have been the subject of our most recent meditations as follows:

> *Pray all kinds* of prayers: public, private, secret, mental, and occasional. Don't put your prayer in a box of mere formality: like an oft-repeated "grace" rattled off before a meal, or the reading of set prayers by a clergyman in a church, or the "saying" of form prayer for yourself.

> *Pray at all times*: not only "in church" or in personal and family worship, but also on the street, at work, at rest, and in a crisis. You don't need closed eyes, folded hands, and a bowed head to be praying most seriously! Don't limit prayer to church services and "quiet times." Observe these, certainly, but remember that the Lord can hear you at any time and in any place.

> *Pray in the (Holy) Spirit*: as he speaks in the Scriptures. Sincerity without obedience to God's Word is self-deceit and a lie. If I regard iniquity in my heart, the Lord will not hear me (Ps. 66:18). God's revealed will in Scripture must guide and inform our praying.

> *Pray with alertness, persistence, and focus*: "without ceasing" (1 Thess. 5:17). Know what to pray for and don't give up until the Lord gives his answer.

Reading this list, you might be forgiven for thinking that prayer is largely an individual matter: just you and God. Perhaps the very personal character of prayer conveys the impression that we really are on our own, and that prayer is a kind of survival technique for embattled souls. Indeed, many people associate prayer with the challenges

642

of loneliness and despair and the need to cope with life's problems. Paul adds his fifth principle of prayer with the words "all the saints," reminding us in three little words that we are *never alone* but part of an assembly of believers. The poet John Donne said, "No man is an island, entire of itself." We can add to that by saying that no man is a church and no one is called to be a secret Christian, unconnected to the body of Christ. "There is not a moment in our life," writes John Calvin,

> at which our wants ought not to urge us to prayer. But there is another reason for praying without ceasing—that the necessities of our brethren ought to touch us. And when is it when some members of the church are not in distress, and needing our assistance? If at any time we are cold in prayer or more negligent than we ought to be, because we do not feel the pressure of immediate necessity, let us instantly reflect how many of our brethren are worn out by varied and heavy afflictions, are weighed down by deep anxiety; or are reduced to the worst distress.

Prayer must lead away from ourselves, precisely because we are in the same boat with all of God's children. Whatever our woes may be, others of "the saints" face troubles too. Whatever blessings may lead us to thank the Lord, other believers also have reasons to rejoice. We share weeping and rejoicing alike in the ministry of prayer: we cannot but "rejoice with those who rejoice, and weep with those who weep" (Rom. 12:15). Why? The saints fill up the ranks of the *church*. They are heirs of the *covenant* of God's grace, and they have been purchased by *Christ* in his death as their sin-bearer and substitute. Bound together by the blood of the everlasting covenant in Jesus our Savior, we who are his people will always love one another and pray for all the saints.

A PRAYER FOR GOD'S PEOPLE
Sing Psalm 67

THINGS I WILL PRAY FOR TODAY

November 17
Smart Love

Prayer for spiritually discerning love

...that your love may abound still more and more in knowledge and all discernment. —Phil. 1:9

READ PHILIPPIANS 1:8–11

Nowadays, the military has "smart" bombs that find their way to the target. The old "dumb" bombs just fall out of the aircraft and often miss. Love can also be smart or dumb. A Buddy Holly (1936–59) song goes this way:

You think true love has come at last
But by and by you're gonna find—
crazy love has made you blind.
When you're feeling sad and blue
you know love's made a fool of you.
—"Love's Made a Fool of You"

"Love" that isn't smart gets people into trouble. Others might call it different names: infatuation, obsession, or just plain lust. The Roman poet Virgil has said, "Love conquers all; let us all yield to love," but what "love"? Does passion make it smart love? Paul lays three qualities of genuine love and shows us that the truly smart love is that which flows from the love of God and the knowledge of God's will for our love of him, our fellow men, and our world.

Answer #1—Genuine love "abounds" (v. 9). First of all, it abounds "in knowledge." This includes both a personal saving knowledge *of* God in Christ (John 17:3; 2 Cor. 4:6) and a knowledge instructed in righteousness *from* God (2 Tim. 3:16). Love *requires* knowledge. Passions that are "not according to knowledge" produce problems (Rom. 10:2). "All You Need Is Love" is a fantasy, not a solution. To be fruitful, lasting, and satisfying, love must be shaped by knowledge.

Second, love is to abound in "all discernment." Love must be judicious. That is the result of experience and spiritual growth (1 Cor. 2:9–14). Such love is not blind. It sees through the mists of mere sentiment and the murk of unhallowed desire. It looks realities in the face and loves with understanding and wisdom. It is capable of what we call "tough love."

Answer #2 — Genuine love approves what is "excellent" (v. 10a). Positively, "do not be conformed to this world, but be transformed by the renewing of your mind, that you may prove what is that good and acceptable and perfect will of God" (Rom. 12:2; Phil. 4:8–9). "Prove" and "approve" are the same Greek word. The more we set our hearts and minds on the things of God, the more we will "acquire the capacity to *prove* for ourselves the excellence of his will." We are to "test all things; hold fast what is good" (1 Thess. 5:21).

Answer #3 — Genuine love is "sincere and without offense" (v. 10b). The word "sincere" is rendered "pure" in in 2 Peter 3:1: "I stir up your pure minds." In 2 Corinthians 1:12, we have "godly sincerity." Arthur W. Pink is correct to say, "Godly sincerity is the sincerity of God." This is the standard of "excellence" applied: are you sincere according to the Lord, or a dissembler and a hypocrite? To be "without offense" is to be careful to have a "conscience without offense toward God" (Acts 24:16), together with a pattern of behavior that walks in the light as God is in the light and does not offend against godly principles (1 John 1:7), and takes pain not to cause other believers to stumble into sin (1 Cor. 10:32), even to "the day of Christ."

These are the tests of the love of Christ in the believer's life: Does this love abound, approve what is excellent, and bear witness to a sincerity that consistently carries itself without offense? Smart love abides "more and more."

A SONG OF GOD'S LOVINGKINDNESS
Sing Psalm 89:1–5

THINGS I WILL PRAY FOR TODAY

_____

_____

_____

_____

_____

_____

645

November 18
Good Fruit

Prayer for the fruits of righteousness

...being filled with the fruits of righteousness, which are by Jesus Christ, to the glory and praise of God. —Phil. 1:11

READ PHILIPPIANS 1:8–11

ohn Keats described the autumn as the "season of mists and mellow fruitfulness." The psalmist says of the harvest, in praise to his God, "You crown the year with Your goodness, and Your paths drip with abundance" (Ps. 65:11). In Scripture this theme is used to illustrate growth in grace and spiritual maturity in those who love the Lord. If a year without a harvest is a natural disaster, a life without spiritual fruit in Jesus Christ is a calamity with eternal consequences. "A farmer only keeps a fruit tree," observes Michael Bentley, "if it gives him a good crop." Like the farmer, God expects to see a good return from his people. Jesus speaks to this in the parable of the barren fig tree. The gospel is to people as fertilizer is to the fruit tree. The day will come, if there is no fruit, when the fruitless will be cut down (Luke 13:6–9). The Lord is looking for good fruit in all of us.

Fruitfulness is Paul's desire for every Christian. The three preceding requests were that love might abound in believers' lives (v. 9), that they would value what is excellent (v. 10a), and that they might be sincere and without offense even until Christ comes again (v. 10b). Wonderful as these goals are, however, they are not everything. There is still more to be achieved in us and by us. Not bearing bad fruit is not the same as actually being fruitful! It seems too obvious to say, but good fruit is the only evidence of fruitfulness! Jean Daillé has written, "It is not enough, believing soul, to give no offence, you must edify; it is not enough to abstain from evil, you must do good." We are "being filled with the fruits of righteousness" (v. 11a).

What are the "fruits of righteousness?" Solomon says, "The fruit of the righteous is a tree of life" (Prov. 11:30). He alludes to the "tree of life" in the garden of Eden, from which Adam was excluded by an angel with a flaming sword. This symbolized the sinner's forfeiture of

646

eternal life and fellowship with God because of his sin (Gen. 3:22–24). The tree itself symbolizes the completeness of salvation in Christ. Christians, saved by grace through faith in Jesus Christ, are themselves made trees of life even in this life. Their lives are adorned with "the fruit of the Spirit" which is "love, joy, peace, longsuffering, kindness, goodness, faithfulness, gentleness, self-control" (Gal. 5:22). Like fruit from a tree, practical godliness blesses and nourishes others: "Now the fruit of righteousness is sown in peace by those who make peace" (James 3:18).

How are these "fruits" attained? The answer is, "by Jesus Christ" (v. 11b). For "Christ is now to us the tree of life (Rev. 2:7; 22:2) and the bread of life (John 6:48, 53)." When we are in a right personal saving relationship with him, his chastening of us brings the "peaceable fruit of righteousness to those who have been trained by it" (Heb. 12:11).

To what goal are these "fruits" directed? Paul answers, "To the glory and praise of God" (v. 11c). This is the motive that alone defines the character of true fruits of righteousness. "Therefore, whether you eat or drink, or whatever you do, do all to the glory of God" (1 Cor. 10:31). Christ is our seed, our growth, our fruit, and our harvest. "He who glories, let him glory in the Lord" (2 Cor. 10:17).

A PRAYER FOR SPIRITUAL FRUITFULNESS
Sing Psalm 92:9–15

THINGS I WILL PRAY FOR TODAY

November 19
The Answer to Anxiety

Prayer and peace of mind

Be anxious for nothing.—Phil. 4:9

READ PHILIPPIANS 4:4–9, 19–20

There is always plenty to be anxious about. Making ends meet, maintaining good health, keeping or finding a job, and a myriad of concerns bid to rob us of peace. The quest for peace of mind has spawned a plethora of counselors and treatments, while unresolved anxiety has driven many to the bottle and not a few to the grave. Against the depressing realities of human anxiety, Paul's counsel may seem a bit too spare, even facile, to many ears: "Be anxious for nothing." But he is not dismissing anxiety as if it is an illusion invented by an overwrought psyche. He points us away from the real, or imagined, causes of our distress, toward the God who hears prayer and gives his "peace" in hearts and minds "through Jesus Christ."

Paul does not talk about the things our world likes to believe will give peace of mind. Things like good health, job security, and the right medication may indeed relieve anxiety. But we need real solutions, not temporary palliatives. He echoes Jesus's teaching in Matthew 6:8–9 that we turn to the God who knows the things we need before we ask him. Anxiety is often well founded. There are all sorts of nasty and uncertain events in life. Even so, anxiety inevitably rests more on doubt about God than on certainty about future woes. Whatever our circumstances—good or bad—Paul's counsel is to "rejoice in the Lord *always*" (v. 4, emphasis added). His powerfully practical theological reason is that "the Lord is at hand" (v. 5). Anxiety is understandable enough, but at its root it is atheism. *Rejoicing* in the Lord is faith in action, looking to the Lord who is there and who loves his people.

In Christian experience true prayer is the breath of the soul set free by Christ. For many, prayer appears to be a last desperate resort when all else fails. Love for the Lord and personal saving knowledge of Jesus doesn't enter into it. Just say the prayer or ask someone to do it for you. In a genuine believer, whose heart is reborn by the Holy Spirit and whose affections are set on Christ who first loved him, "one of the blessed results of prayer is the flooding of the soul with a habitual peace and confidence even in the midst of danger and difficult duty." Believing prayer not only cries to the Lord in trouble but also communes with the Lord as he ministers his truth to bring us to "be still" and know that he is God (Ps. 46:10). We need to stand on Christ the solid rock, for "all other ground is sinking sand."

As you bring your requests to the Lord, trusting him means committing to three things. First, be anxious about nothing, "casting all your care upon Him, for He cares for you" (1 Peter 5:7). Second, be prayerful in everything, "praying always with all prayer and supplication in the Spirit, being watchful to this end with all perseverance and supplication for all the saints" (Eph. 6:18). Third, be thankful for everything, for "whoever offers praise glorifies Me; and to him who orders his conduct aright I will show the salvation of God" (Ps. 50:23). To this, God adds two promises:

> The "peace of God" will guard your hearts and minds "through Christ Jesus" (v. 7). As you trust Christ, God-given peace stills your heart even in the face of the worst troubles. No wonder that it "surpasses all understanding."

> The "God of peace" will be with you as you meditate on things true, noble, just, pure, lovely, and of good report, and follow the apostolic teaching and example (vv. 8–9). The Lord will supply your needs (vv. 19–20)—answering the very things that engendered anxiety to begin with. "Rejoice in the Lord always…and be anxious for nothing."

A PRAYER FOR PEACE IN HEART, MIND, AND DAILY LIFE
Sing Psalm 4

THINGS I WILL PRAY FOR TODAY

November 20
Motives for Prayer

Prayer out of faith, love, and hope

We give thanks...since we heard of your faith in Christ Jesus and of your love for all the saints... — Col. 1:3–4

READ COLOSSIANS 1:3–8

"I have no greater joy than to hear that my children walk in truth." So writes the apostle John in 3 John 4. In writing to "the elect lady," he says, "I rejoiced greatly that I found some of your children walking in truth" (2 John 1, 4). How parents and pastors long to see this. There is no greater encouragement than watching the transforming grace of God at work in the hearts of the children of the church. Paul expresses the same joy over his Colossian flock. In one glorious sentence (vv. 3–8), he prays with enthusiastic praise for the faithfulness of the "saints and faithful brethren in Christ who are in Colossae" (v. 2); he also manages to survey what he knows about their lives in Christ, past, present, and future! Excitement leaps from his pen! Notice, too, how faith, love, and hope unite Christ and Christian lives: "And now abide faith, hope, love, these three; but the greatest of them is love" (1 Cor. 13:13).

The present: living by faith and living out love (v. 4). This is all cause for joy and encouragement for Paul. In an echo of Jesus's word about the two great commandments of God's law (Matt. 22:36–40), the apostle notes the Colossians' love for the Lord and also for their neighbor. Their faith is "faith in Christ Jesus," and the proof of it is their "love for all the saints."

Faith is more than a generic nod toward the existence of God. It is a personal relationship with the God and Father of the Lord Jesus Christ through "repentance toward God and faith toward our Lord Jesus Christ" (Acts 20:21). "Apart from this faith," writes Kent Hughes, "there is no Christian experience."

Love for fellow believers is the acid test of living faith: "For in Christ Jesus neither circumcision nor uncircumcision avails anything, but faith working through love" (Gal. 5:6). This affords personal assurance: "We know that we have passed from death to life, because we love the brethren. He who does not love his brother abides in death" (1 John 3:14). And it is essential for our evangelistic witness in the world: "A new commandment I give to you, that you love one another; as I have loved you, that you also love one another. By this all will know that you are My disciples, if you have love for one another" (John 13:34). Epaphras could observe their "love in the Spirit" (v. 7).

The past: hope of heaven (v. 5). They believed "the word of the truth of the gospel" and had assurance of their heavenly inheritance (1 Peter 1:4). This "hope of heaven" is not a subjective feeling of hope in their minds, but the object of hope appropriated by faith. They believed God's promise and are possessed of eternal life in Christ.

In the future: bringing forth fruit (v. 6). Spiritual fruit continued to flow in them and from them since the day they "heard and knew the grace of God in truth." This would continue into the future, "for of His fullness we have all received, and grace upon grace" (John 1:16). "And God is able to make all grace abound toward you, that you, always having all sufficiency in all things, may have an abundance for every good work" (2 Cor. 9:8). You see what glorious motives caused Paul to pray "always" for these Christians and to "give thanks" for them? Similar motives ought to move us, surely! Think often of the godly children of God's people. Give thanks for every evidence of saving grace in people's lives. Pray always—endlessly—for the Lord's hand to be upon us all for blessing: "As for the saints in the land, they are the excellent ones, in whom is all my delight" (Ps. 16:3, ESV).

A PRAYER REJOICING IN GODLINESS AND THE GODLY
Sing Psalm 16

THINGS I WILL PRAY FOR TODAY

November 21
Walking Worthy of Christ

Prayer for wisdom and spiritual understanding

...that you may be filled with the knowledge of His will... — Col. 1:9

READ COLOSSIANS 1:9–10

Knowledge is often regarded as an affliction. Scripture warns that "knowledge puffs up" (1 Cor. 8:1). The proverb asks, "Do you see a man wise in his own eyes? There is more hope for a fool than for him" (Prov. 26:12). Knowledge, when perverted or misapplied, has its dangers. Lack of knowledge, however, is regarded in Scripture as a problem and a curse. "For like the crackling of thorns under a pot, so is the laughter of the fool," says Solomon (Eccl. 7:6). Ignorance is no way to build a life, either for time or eternity. Then again, the wrong kind of knowledge is no more of an advantage. Error, however erudite, always ends up in ruin. Paul found this problem in Colossae. Some people were promoting a certain brand of knowledge (the Greek *gnosis*—pronounced "no-sis") as being necessary to *really* knowing God. This was mystical, speculative, and not from Scripture. Therefore it could not give a right view of God or foster a truly Christian discipleship.

Paul's first petition is that we be "filled" with knowledge (v. 9). Paul calls this knowledge *epignosis* to distinguish it from the mystical *gnosis* of the false teachers who were leading the church astray. This is the knowledge of God's revealed will as opposed to mystical speculation (2 Tim. 3:16). It is knowledge from above rather than knowledge from within. This knowledge will bear fruit in the Christian along two lines.

The first is that it imparts "all wisdom"—the wisdom of God as opposed to the wisdom of the world: "And my speech and my preaching were not with persuasive words of human wisdom, but in demonstration of the Spirit and of power, that your faith should not be in the wisdom of men but in the power of God. However, we speak wisdom among those who are mature, yet not the wisdom of this age, nor of the rulers of this age, who are coming to nothing" (1 Cor. 2:4–6). The Holy Spirit guides the believer into all truth—to grasp God's truth as it is to be understood (John 16:13). It is

God who adds wisdom to the bare reading of his words, "Open my eyes, that I may see wondrous things from Your law" (Ps. 119:18).

The second fruit of truly knowing God's will is "spiritual understanding." This is discernment that sifts the true from the false and makes sound assessments, even on the basis of incomplete knowledge. Paul prays that the Lord would give Timothy "understanding in all things" (2 Tim. 2:7). There is something uncanny about discernment that seems to see, almost instantly, right through a problem—or a person! We need to be spiritually streetwise, discerning good and evil, and discerning the times in which we live (Heb. 5:14; 1 Chron. 12:32).

The second petition is that we act on this knowledge so as to "walk worthy" of Christ (v. 10). Knowledge without fruit is willful ignorance. The Bible describes how the Christian behaves day by day as a "walk." Behavior that is "worthy" of Christ, says Paul, will have three practical results. Our conscious aims are to be "pleasing" the Lord, to be "fruitful" in choices and actions, and, thereby, to be "increasing in the knowledge of God." These are also the fruit of God's work in our sanctification, that "work of God's free grace, whereby we are renewed in the whole man after the image of God, and are enabled more and more to die unto sin, and live unto righteousness." Resolved to follow our Savior more closely, we will be rewarded to know his God and Father ever more intimately. Let us walk worthy of our Lord.

A PRAYER FOR DEEPENING KNOWLEDGE OF GOD
Sing Psalm 86:11–16

THINGS I WILL PRAY FOR TODAY

November 22
Strengthened with Might

A prayer for longsuffering

...strengthened with all might... — Col. 1:11a

READ COLOSSIANS 1:9–11

Even the best of things have "side effects." Ice cream adds to your waist. Medication helps one condition and produces another. Becoming a Christian also has some predictable "side effects." Jesus tells his disciples up front, "In the world you will have tribulation" (John 16:33). Paul warns Timothy that "all who desire to live godly in Christ Jesus will suffer persecution" (2 Tim. 3:12). His first two petitions for the Colossians (1:9–10) are that they might know the Lord's will and also "walk worthy" of him, "fully pleasing Him." But he also knows that many in this world don't appreciate Christians being Christians in deed. That is why Paul's third petition is that Christians be "strengthened with might" (v. 11). You, Christian, need strengthening by the Lord, because, as Arthur Pink has noted, "the closer you walk with Christ the more you will be persecuted."

The *need* of our souls: to be "strengthened with all might." This is, of course, a prayer for what God will do in us. The flow of Paul's thought shows that we are not passive spectators in the process. As we "walk worthy" of Jesus, we actively give ourselves to be both "fruitful" in every good work and "increasing" in our knowledge of God (v. 10). This doesn't happen *to* us, as much as it happens *in* us! This in turn is the context in which we are strengthened. The more we live as God wants us to, the more fruitful we become; the more we work at doing good, the more we experientially learn from and commune with our Lord; and the more that is true, the stronger we become with power from above. The Lord is the invisible enabler and provider, but our faithful obedience is the visible means through which he deepens our faith and strengthens our obedience. If we are merely passive, we will never grow. We are called to *act* on our faith. "Faith without works is dead" — that is, is no true saving faith in Christ at all (James 2:26)!

The *source* and *measure* of this strength: "according to His glorious power." That is just to say that, however diligently faithful we are, we will need an extra measure of God's grace at every turn. It is true that "to each one of us grace was given according to the measure of Christ's gift" (Eph. 4:7). We who are Christians have gifts—although these are a variety of gifts, given in differing measures. Grace never confers all the resources we need without having to depend continuously upon the Lord. If our experience teaches us anything, it is surely that, whatever our gifts, self-reliance is a broken cistern that holds no water (Jer. 2:13). From beginning to end, it is God who must be "our refuge and our strength" and "a very present help in trouble" (Ps. 46:1).

The *purpose* of this enabling: "for all patience and longsuffering with joy." The idea is that we come to each challenge with Philippians 4:13—"I can do all things through Christ who strengthens me"—and we leave it with Psalm 126:3—"The Lord has done great things for us, and we are glad." And between these two reference points we have patience, longsuffering, and joy. Patience is a meek and gentle spirit that is actively applied to the frustrations of the problem we face. Longsuffering is just the determined extension of patience for as long as it all takes. Joy is the attitude of heart that rejoices in the Lord even while going through trial and tribulation and the weariness of the flesh. James writes, "My brethren, count it all joy when you fall into various trials, knowing that the testing of your faith produces patience" (James 1:2–3). Notice how this closes the circle. From patience to longsuffering—and that mixed with joy—we come to more patience. And so go on to victory through every trial, thus "strengthened with all might."

PRAISE FOR GOD'S PROVISION OF HIS STRENGTH
Sing Psalm 46

THINGS I WILL PRAY FOR TODAY

November 23
Light, Love, and Liberty

Prayer for a thankful walk

…giving thanks to the Father who has qualified us to be partakers of the inheritance of the saints in the light.—Col. 1:12

READ COLOSSIANS 1:9–14

n the Boy Scouts, we learned to use Ordinance Survey maps. This was so as to get to our desired destination, avoid trouble along the way, and derive the maximum pleasure and profit from the journey. Living life from here to eternity also works that way. It is easy to get lost. Sinners are lost by nature. But God reveals himself in his Word and in his Son. He finds lost people, even when they don't feel lost (Isa. 65:1). And, once found, they freely confess with the psalmist in Psalm 40:2, "He also brought me up from the fearful pit, out of the miry clay, and set my feet upon a rock, and established my steps." Jesus Christ, believed upon for salvation, is that Rock (1 Cor. 10:4). When Jesus saves us, he puts us on solid ground, shows us the way we should go, and guides our steps to "press toward the goal for the prize of the upward call of God in [Him]" (Phil. 3:14).

To "walk worthy" of Jesus Christ is the central goal of Paul's prayer for the Colossian Christians (v. 10). And how will we "walk worthy" of Christ? In three ways, says Paul: by being filled with the right "knowledge of his will in all wisdom and spiritual understanding" (v. 9); by being "strengthened with all might" by God's power for "patience and longsuffering with joy" (v. 11); and by "giving thanks to the Father" as our very way of life. You surely see the inextricable way in which these are bound up together in real Christian experience: in living faith we will know God's will and strive accordingly, know God's enabling grace and grow accordingly, and as we follow after the Lord, thankfulness will be both the sustaining and the rejoicing of our hearts. We will be different people with a new life to live, walking in the light of our Lord (1 John 5:7).

To that end, Paul gives us three motives to encourage us. All of them are to do with what our Father-God has done for us in Christ—not, you will notice, what we have done for him, or promised to do for him. It is, as Matthew Henry has said, "a summary of the doctrine of the gospel."

> The *first motive* is that "the Father has qualified us to be partakers of the inheritance of the saints in the light" (v. 12). The tense of the verb "qualified" (the Greek *aorist*) indicates an already accomplished and continuing reality in the present experience of the believer. This inheritance is not just something in the future. Believers are *in* "His marvelous light" (1 Peter 2:9). It shines "in our hearts" (2 Cor. 4:6). And so we are by God's grace "sons of light and sons of the day" (1 Thess. 5:5). How pitiable the ungrateful complaining of so many professed Christians! We only have reason to rejoice in his light!

> The *second motive* is that the Father has "delivered us from the power of darkness and conveyed us into the kingdom of the Son of his love" (v. 13). For all the darkness around us in the world we once reveled in, believers know they are now under a rule of love. God loves us, undertakes for us, and will bring us home. Meantime, he surrounds us with the tokens of an everlasting love. He will never forsake us. Why then would we live as if Christ is not the King and his kingdom is far away and into the future?

> The *third motive* is that in the Son "we have redemption through His blood, the forgiveness of sins" (v. 14). He bought us. He was the price of our liberty from sin, death, and hell. We are free even in an otherwise enslaved world! Jesus's truth has set us free.

Light, love, and liberty—these are the reasons and motives for a thankful walk in the Christian. Christ is our thankfulness: therefore, says the psalmist, "I will bless the Lord at all times; His praise shall be continually in my mouth" (Ps. 34:1).

PRAISE FOR A THANKFUL WALK WITH GOD
Sing Psalm 40:10–17

THINGS I WILL PRAY FOR TODAY

_____

_____

_____

November 24
Interconnected Prayer

The fellowship of prayer

Continue earnestly in prayer. — Col. 4:2

READ COLOSSIANS 4:2-4

here is something intensely private about prayer. In fact, Jesus's primary instruction about prayer is that it be done behind closed doors. "But you, when you pray, go into your room, and when you have shut your door, pray to your Father who is in the secret place; and your Father who sees in secret will reward you openly" (Matt. 6:6). There are, of course, a multitude of examples of public and corporate prayer in the Bible, and that is reflected in gatherings of the church for worship, prayer, and Bible study, and in family worship. Clearly, in public settings, the prayers of the saints are making connections with God's people. Public prayer is interconnected prayer. Indeed, this is its very purpose. Every time someone leads in public prayer, all the hearers become participants and may follow the psalmist's injunction in Psalm 106:48, when he says, "And let all the people say, 'Amen!'" This is not meant to be some perfunctory liturgical recitation, but an expression of the heart that is engaged with the content of the prayer and adding the personal endorsement that "amen" actually conveys (i.e., "So be it!").

Curiously, perhaps, prayer does not need to be heard in public to be interconnected. The prayer Paul mentions in Colossians 4:2–4 and 11 very likely encompassed both the private and public prayers of the Christians involved, but there is wide geographical separation between the places where they are uttered and the subjects to whose welfare they are directed. Even if they were all prayed in the secret place by individual believers, they are still interconnected in the sense that the God, who is the hearer of prayer (Ps. 65:2), is at work in the hearts of his people as he ministers to each one in terms of his promises to answer and make effectual the prayer of righteousness (James 5:16).

Appropriately, the apostle demonstrates this interconnectedness of prayer in a seamless way. He offers three closely related exhortations:

‹ First, be praying people, each one of you: "Continue earnestly in prayer, being vigilant in it with thanksgiving" (v. 2). In this verse there are only eight words in the Greek text, and four of them are major exhortations to our hearts! These are "continue," (don't give up); "earnestly," (with utmost sincerity of heart); "vigilant," (being alert to the issues of life); and "thanksgiving" (doing this out of gratitude to the Lord for all his goodness and grace in your life and in his promises).

‹ Second, pray for the ministry of God's Word (vv. 3–4). Paul asks for three things here: prayer for Paul and his team ("also for us," v. 3a); prayer for an open "door for the word," meaning with places, people, and souls (v. 3b); and prayer for clarity in proclaiming "the mystery of Christ" in just the right words (vv. 3c–4). The "mystery" is just the gospel itself in all its simplicity and profundity.

‹ Third, pray for others and be assured others are praying for you. Epaphras, the original church planter in his home town (Col. 1:7), sends his greetings and "has a great zeal" to intercede for his brothers and sisters in Christ, that they would be "complete in all the will of God" (Col. 4:12–13). How many Christians today think of this as the great practical goal of their lives—completeness in personal discipleship to the Lord? This is what we all need and what the church as a whole needs.

Under this rubric, there is plenty to pray for, night and day (1 Tim. 5:5). And what goes around comes around. From your faithfulness, ministry spreads out. Intercession from others returns. And so on, until Jesus comes! Be encouraged, then, to pray and to reach out in prayer for others, for these are interconnected in the work of God in us and among us. You are not alone and never forgotten—even by man, but especially by the Lord!

A PRAYER FOR THE BLESSING OF GOD'S PEOPLE
Sing Psalm 67

THINGS I WILL PRAY FOR TODAY

_____

_____

_____

November 25
We Thank God for All of You

A prayer for fellow believers

…remembering without ceasing… — *1 Thess. 1:3*

READ 1 THESSALONIANS 1:1–10

It is so easy to be absentminded when it comes to our prayers. We do usually remember to pray for those nearest and dearest to us, whether children, parents, or longstanding friends. It is astonishing—and a huge rebuke to forgetful and uncaring attitudes—that we discover Paul, one day in the year AD 50, praying passionately for a church that was perhaps three months old, and for people among whom he had ministered for only three consecutive (Jewish) Sabbath days. The members were all new believers, and they had been bullied and badgered from day one! But what a solid, committed group of Christians they were in so short a time. They were living proof of what God can do almost overnight, when he brings people to saving faith in Jesus Christ. No wonder, then, that Paul's first words were to tell them how thankful he was to God for all of them!

There are two aspects to Paul's thankfulness. The first is that his prayer is *ongoing*. The other is that it is *focused on people*.

Paul gives thanks *"always."* Not every second, but constantly. He doesn't forget them. He is always bringing them to mind. He also wants us to follow his example: "Rejoice always, pray without ceasing, in everything give thanks; for this is the will of God in Christ Jesus for you" (1 Thess. 5:16–18). He will tell the Corinthians how he is willing to go through hardships so that the grace of Christ may spread to many people and so "cause thanksgiving to abound to the glory of God" (2 Cor. 4:15).

Paul was also always *"making mention"* of *them*—no doubt by name—in his *"prayers."* He was not just saying this. He loved these new converts to Christ. He prayed specifically, thoughtfully, and long and hard. His thanks for what God was doing in their lives in the present soon turned to prayer for good things to happen to them in the future.

This ought to help our praying today in practical ways. Giving thanks always, not endlessly complaining, ought to dominate our thoughts about fellow believers. We need to develop an eye for what God is doing. It is too easy to slip into finding fault and get to mumping and moaning about what we think is wrong in the church and the world. Look at what God has done! And what he will yet do! We need this reminder every day. Our prayers for the church must have at least four goals:

- ❧ Spend *time at the throne of grace* (Heb. 4:16). Not just two minutes to read off some words someone else has written in a "quiet time" booklet, but real time with some exercise of the heart and soul before the Lord. Take time to cry to God. No fancy words are needed, just a sincere soul. Even silent waiting on the Lord will bless you (Ps. 62:1).
- ❧ Focus on *individuals and their needs*. Not everybody in the world. Start with folks you know and real situations that concern them and have touched your soul with sympathy and given you a heart to pray for them.
- ❧ Love those you pray for and seek *God's highest blessings* for them. Praise the Lord. Claim his promises. Glory in the cross of Jesus (Gal. 6:14). Intercede for friends, neighbors, and loved ones.
- ❧ Come together in *corporate prayer* as God's people. Sharing prayer concerns is natural for Christians. This is what some women did every (Jewish) Sabbath by the riverbank in Philippi, even before Paul came to Macedonia and evangelized them. How much more should we love to pray with God's people?

A PRAYER OF THANKSGIVING FOR GOD'S PEOPLE
Sing Psalm 92:1–8

THINGS I WILL PRAY FOR TODAY

November 26
Reasons for Thanksgiving

More prayer for fellow believers

...remembering without ceasing your work of faith, labor of love, and patience of hope in our Lord Jesus Christ.—1 Thess. 1:3

READ 1 THESSALONIANS 1:1–10

Americans celebrate Thanksgiving on the fourth Thursday in November. More people travel around this holiday than even at Christmas. It traditionally looks back to the first harvest of the Puritan colonists in Massachusetts in 1621, but the word "harvest" is from the Anglo-Saxon word for August—*haerfest*—and Christian thanksgivings were observed for at least a thousand years before Plymouth Rock. Their original focus, of course, was upon thanking God for temporal provisions. It is a sign of the secularization of our time that it is increasingly called "Turkey Day." Like the godless fishermen of Judah, "they sacrifice to their net, and burn incense to their dragnet; because by them their share is sumptuous and their food plentiful" (Hab. 1:16). They thank everything but the living God—their skill, their tools, their lucky stars, and, ultimately, themselves.

Paul gives thanks to God for the believers in Thessalonika. He gives three reasons for doing so: their "work of faith," their "labor of love," and their "patience of hope." These three fruits of faith, love, and hope are exercised, he notes, "in the Lord Jesus Christ in the sight of our God and Father." People will talk about things like faith, love, and hope in the abstract, as if they can be pleasing to God apart from knowing God through living faith in Jesus Christ. Paul wants us to be clear that these are empty passing illusions of godliness and blessedness if they are not *in* Jesus Christ as the only Savior, believed and loved from the heart:

> The "work" in "work of faith" is the Greek *ergos*, from which we get our words energy, synergy, and ergonomics. This focuses on simple effort at practical obedience. Paul says elsewhere, "whatever you do in word and deed, do all in the name of the Lord Jesus, giving thanks to God the Father through Him" (Col. 3:17).

662

> The "labor" in "labor of love" is a different Greek word, *kopos*. While *ergos*-work is about effort, *kopos*-work includes the cost of the effort. The love that labors for God accepts the cost of faithfulness. God's "labor of love" was very costly (John 3:16). God's love *for* us motivates us to serious discipleship to advance his kingdom in our world. Christ's love *in* us redeems the blood, toil, tears, and sweat of the costly labors of faith. Our love *toward* God, in Christ, does not run away when pain and trouble comes along: "Beloved, if God so loved us, we also ought to love one another" (1 John 4:11).

> Patience without hope is only resignation. We need some promise of success in order to be hopeful. This "patience of hope" is that "stick-to-it-iveness" that presses on to a definite goal and prize, with hope and expectation "looking unto Jesus, the author and finisher of our faith." Jesus persevered, "endured the cross, despising the shame" and he did it "for the joy that was set before Him" (Heb. 12:2). So should we, because we can live in anticipation of the certain blessings of victory in Christ, both here and in the glory to come in heaven.

Too often, appreciating our fellow Christians takes second place to criticizing and complaining about them. Paul's thankfulness calls us to look for the work of God in other people's lives. He sees the good things first, dwells on them, talks about them, and encourages his readers and then later ministers any counsel and correction he may have for them. If we are united to Christ by faith and rejoice every day in his full and free salvation, we will enjoy overflowing gratitude for all that God has done, especially for those he has saved. Then we will be filled with encouragement, and go forward in happy service to our wonderful Savior, thankful in his saving grace and love.

PRAISING GOD WITH WHOLEHEARTED THANKS
Sing Psalm 9:1–10

THINGS I WILL PRAY FOR TODAY

_____

_____

_____

November 27
We'll Meet Again!

A prayer for a return visit and more

Now may our God and Father Himself, and our Lord Jesus Christ, direct our way to you. — 1 Thess. 3:11

READ 1 THESSALONIANS 3:1–13

The more time and distance separate us from friends and loved ones, the more we wish to see them again. Years may have fled since last meeting, but then some event lends an immediacy and urgency that spurs us to action. Paul had not been long separated from the Christians in Thessalonika. It was only a few months before that Paul and Silas had ministered to them, and then for a mere three consecutive Sabbaths. This ministry was richly blessed, however, for "some of them were persuaded, and a great multitude of the devout Greeks, and not a few of the leading women, joined Paul and Silas" (Acts 17:4). Not everyone was pleased, however, and such was the ferocity of the opposition, that "the brethren" sent Paul and Silas "by night to Berea" (Acts 17:10). Many had been converted to Christ, to be sure, but the church was very young and the apostle was deeply concerned for their steadfastness, spiritual growth, and safety. Accordingly, he had sent Timothy to see how they were doing (v. 6).

There is nothing better than hearing some good news from afar to move us to plan a reunion with old friends. Even in our day of instant messaging and webcam conversations, there is still no substitute for a shared meal and a warm embrace. People are vastly more than images on a screen and words on a piece of paper. Timothy's report was a huge encouragement to Paul: It reinforces his desire to visit the church in Thessalonika (v. 6). It comforts him in his affliction and distress over their situation (v. 7). It invigorates him with a refreshed liveliness to hear they are standing fast in their faith (v. 8). It moves him to exultant thanksgiving because of the joy with which he rejoices for their sake before God (v. 9). All of this builds his prayers for them "night and day," that he might see them in the flesh and instruct them further in the faith in their hearts and minds (v. 10). You can feel the excitement in Paul's words—how he wants to be with them and share fellowship with them face to face.

Paul prays for three things in verses 11–13. Notice, by the way, the balance between the narrow concern of a specific prayer request with the wider abiding themes of our continuing walk with the Lord. Too often prayer requests are lists of detailed needs, and the latter—the actual state of our souls—is entirely neglected.

> The first petition is for Paul's return visit. You will notice his emphasis on direction by God the Father and the Lord Jesus Christ (v. 11). "God willing" ought to be a serious attachment to all our plans (see James 4:15). The application is: get together with Christian friends when you can, God willing.

> The second petition is for love among the Christians (v. 12). Paul offers himself—in all humility—as an example to follow (1 Cor. 11:1; Gal. 4:12). The application is: exercise brotherly love all the time.

> The third petition is for perseverance in personal godliness, in anticipation of "the coming of the Lord Jesus Christ with all His saints" (v. 13). The application here is: live in the light of eternity. Persevere in your faith both in the prospect of Christ's coming and in the certainty of your going soon to be with him.

One of the best-loved songs of the World War II years was Vera Lynn's "We'll Meet Again." It reflected the uncertainties of war—"Don't know where, don't know when"—but answered them with a kind of vapid mysticism—"But I know we'll meet again some sunny day." In truth, there is no solid hope in such godless sentiments. Our happy reunions in this life need to be set in the context of our union and communion with Christ and the hope of that heavenly reunion with him, which is the promise for all who believe upon him as their Savior and Lord.

IN PRAISE OF THE FELLOWSHIP OF BELIEVERS
Sing Psalm 133

THINGS I WILL PRAY FOR TODAY

November 28
The Soul's Oxygen

Prayer-nuggets from Paul (Part 1)

...pray without ceasing. — *1 Thess. 5:17*

READ 1 THESSALONIANS 5:16–24

My grandfather was a bit of an adventurer. Before he married and settled down as a pig farmer, he went off to see the world. In 1899, he went over the Chilcoot Pass in Alaska at the time of the famous Gold Rush. He didn't strike it rich, but I have a piece of rock he brought back. In it there is a tiny gold nugget sparkling amid the otherwise quite beautiful but more prosaic quartz. Scripture can be like that. The end of 1 Thessalonians certainly is: there are so many "prayer-nuggets," as Herbert Lockyer has called them, that the standard form for ending a letter vanishes in a blaze of divine jewels. Still, you have to mine for them, and as you do, they reveal to you their value and weight. They assay *you* and test your mettle and give you something to take home with you. We will look at the first three today. These focus on the inner life of the believer in Christ.

Prayer-nugget #1: "Pray without ceasing" (v. 17). Matthew Henry notes that "the meaning is not that we should do nothing but pray, but that nothing else we do should hinder prayer in its proper season." Notice also how this connects with the command in verse 16 to "rejoice always." How can we rejoice, especially in disheartening circumstances? The answer is to pray. We will never rejoice in the Lord if we never pray to the Lord. The equation is: "Rejoice more? Pray more!" You will truly rejoice as much as you truly pray. Jesus put it very simply in the parable of the persistent widow: we "ought always to pray and not lose heart" (Luke 18:1). If the answer is slower in coming, then let your prayers be more frequent in going.

Prayer-nugget #2: "In everything give thanks" (v. 18). You will notice that the chain is from the charge to "rejoice always," to the exercise of "prayer without ceasing," and onto giving "thanks" in "everything." These three steps are inseparably related to one another in "the will of God in Christ Jesus" for believers. When we commune with the Lord in prayer, giving thanks for his goodness to us in saving us and keeping us, we are likely to fill up with gratitude. Paul realizes this when he says, "But we are bound to give thanks to God always for you, brethren beloved by the Lord, because God from the beginning chose you for salvation through sanctification by the Spirit and belief in the truth" (2 Thess. 2:13). He is bound by love for the Savior who loved him first (2 Cor. 5:14). Compelled by love, only gratitude can fill his soul—and ours.

Prayer-nugget #3: "May the God of peace sanctify you completely" (v. 23). What is prayer about, in the last analysis, but the holiness of God's people and their knowing "the peace of God, which surpasses all understanding" (Phil. 4:7)? Believers desire to have more of Christ. Believing prayer is about having more of Christ. What is certain is that we discover that

> Prayer is the Christian's vital breath,
> The Christian's native air;
> His watchword at the gates of death;
> He enters heaven with prayer.

A PRAYER FOR WHOLEHEARTED DEVOTION
Sing Psalm 86:11–17

THINGS I WILL PRAY FOR TODAY

November 29
Pray for God's Ministers

Prayer-nuggets from Paul (Part 2)

Brethren, pray for us. — *1 Thess. 5:25*

READ 1 THESSALONIANS 5:25–28

As we have already seen, this passage of Scripture is laced with what Herbert Lockyer calls "prayer-nuggets." As with gold nuggets, these do not have to be large to be lustrous and impressive. As the Scots say, "There's guid gear in sma' bulk." What may seem almost to be passing pious pleasantries turn out to be, on careful examination, profound pointers to the marvelous blessing of believing prayer. There are five of these "nuggets" that reflect upon prayer. The first three, which we looked at yesterday, focused on the inner life of the believer. The last two focus on the body-life of the church. This reminds us that we are not to be individualistic islands. We are never called to be "Lone Rangers" for Jesus. Monasticism, ancient and modern, has no support in Scripture. The church is the body of Christ. It is meant to be a real fellowship, locality by locality. Alas, the monastic cell approach lives on in modern times in the plethora of blogs on the internet launched by people who cannot find a church good enough for them to attend. "Fellowship" in cyberspace is as real as "worship" in the same medium would be, but it obviates any necessity to get on with real people. That is why Paul does not leave off his counsel with words on personal piety and the inner life, but instead extends his scope to the wider covenantal character of God's people and the believers' responsibility to be involved with the real local church.

Prayer-nugget #4: "Brethren, pray for us" (v. 25). This is a plea for prayer support for God's ministers. Pray for your pastor. He tends to hear the complaints, and would be blessed hearing that you pray for him. Paul is not a "prince of the church" that cannot call his spiritual children "brethren" and mean it from the heart. Neither is he above standing in the need of prayer. Congregations that never pray for their pastors, elders, deacons, and missionaries can only wither on the vine, as God removes the leadership and ministry they have no heart to support. But if you

668

want God to do your pastor some good, and be blessed yourselves in the process, than apply this injunction every day in the secret place of your prayers.

Prayer-nugget #5: "The grace of our Lord Jesus Christ be with you" (v. 28). Having asked the people to pray for him, the pastor now prays for the people. This is the great desire of the apostle for the church—and it should be the very thing that gives us happiness for the Lord's people. How easy it is to be unhappy about the church and her members—and for reasons quite removed from her real mission. The people can't sing.... the preacher is not very exciting....the people could be friendlier....there is no great youth program....and so on, almost ad infinitum! You would think that complaining was a mark of grace, the way that Christians so righteously engage in it. It would be better to ask: Is "the grace of our Lord" evident among us? Is it held out in the preaching? Is it proclaimed in the Lord's Supper? Is it poured out in prayer? Is it evidenced in people's lives, in their conversation and in their response to trials? Does it impact their expressions of concern for one another, their personal witness, and their kindness and compassion? Will more and "better" programs guarantee that we will be filled with the peaceable fruit of righteousness? If the grace of our Lord Jesus is with us, what should we be like? Should we not at least pray for the church, instead of complaining about it? And for each other and the glory of Christ in us and among us? We have the promise of God: "I will also clothe her priests with salvation, and her saints shall shout aloud for joy" (Ps. 132:16). Amen to that!

PRAISE GOD FOR THE CHURCH AND HER MINISTERS
Sing Psalm 132:11–18

THINGS I WILL PRAY FOR TODAY

_____

_____

_____

_____

_____

_____

_____

November 30
Worthy of Your Calling

Prayer for persevering grace

...that our God would count you worthy of this calling...
—2 Thess. 1:11–12

READ 2 THESSALONIANS 1:1–12

When you have faced some challenge, you may have asked yourself if you could see it through to a happy ending. When I took up post-graduate study in Philadelphia, I was parked temporarily in a room with an incoming first-year student. Every day he came back from classes more discouraged than ever and after four days he disappeared. It was all too much for him. He had packed his bags and gone home. Such things happen in life because daunting tasks are testing and are not for the fainthearted. Sometimes we are overwhelmed by them.

Even at the best of times, prior success does not guarantee an easy passage in the future. Many of us have discovered this to our cost. You can be promoted to the level of your incompetence in your day job. You can find a defeated temptation suddenly roar back into your life in a moment of carelessness or fear. The Christians in Thessalonika had been through the fires of persecution (v. 4). They had also grown in faith and love (v. 3). They had evidently persevered quite effectively. But, as Paul implies in verses 7–10, there was still some time to go until Christ's return and their final victorious vindication. They are not yet home and dry! There was still plenty of scope for future failure, notwithstanding the successful faithfulness of the past and the present.

The apostle Paul does not stop with encouraging words about eternal outcomes when Jesus returns (v. 10). No one can charge Paul with preaching a "pie in the sky by and by" message. There is no "opium of the people" in his religion. He prays that the Thessalonians will actively persevere in the faith and, to that end, he prays for four things in particular:

> He first prays for Christians to be worthy of their calling from God. God's grace to us in Christ has given us something to live up to (v. 11a). This emphasis upon God's gracious *provision* of

salvation underscores that the evidence of a living faith in Christ is a lively obedience to God's will.

- Second, he prays for Christians to fulfill the "good pleasure of His goodness" (v. 11b). This emphasizes God's gracious *intention* in calling us. He means to do good to us, so that we would be "always abounding in the work of the Lord" (1 Cor. 15:58).

- Third, he prays that God would seal his "work of faith with power" in Christians (v. 11c). This emphasizes God's *enabling* in our lives. God has the power to impart to us that which will make his strength known to us even in our weakness.

- Finally, he prays that the "name of our Lord Jesus Christ may be glorified" in Christians, that they in turn would be glorified in the Lord—and all according to the grace of the Father and the Son (v. 12). This emphasizes God's marvelous *grace* in the gospel of his Son. It is worth reminding ourselves that everything in God's dealings with us serves his aim to bring glory to Jesus. Let us expect blessing!

What then is required for Christians to persevere in their faith? The answer is, in a nutshell, "Christ in you, the hope of glory" (Col. 1:27). And in Christ, God's calling applied, his goodness applied, his power applied, and his free grace applied! In case we are tempted to say that this is too good to be true, Paul reminds us in another place that "so then it is not of him who wills, nor of him who runs, but of God who shows mercy" (Rom. 9:16). We will never be worthy of our calling if it depends on us and our own resources. As far as our performance is concerned, we are at best "unprofitable servants" (Luke 17:10). But in Christ are "more than conquerors through Him who has loved us" (Rom. 8:37).

PRAISE FOR GOD'S ENABLING GRACE
Sing Psalm 26

THINGS I WILL PRAY FOR TODAY

_____

_____

_____

_____

_____

December 1
Stand Fast

A prayer for comfort and stability

Now may our Lord Jesus Christ Himself, and God our Father…comfort your hearts and establish you in every good word and work.
—*2 Thess. 2:16–17*

READ 2 THESSALONIANS 2:13–17

Prayer does not happen in a vacuum. There is always something that presses us to pray. In this instance, Paul's prayer for the Thessalonians arises from the assurance that God has wonderfully saved them, and the concern that they continue to "stand fast" in the sound doctrine they had been taught (v. 15). Notice the flow of his thought, as he goes from doctrine to life and then to the prayer that God would enable their faithfulness:

- First, he glories in the sovereign grace of God that chose them and by the Holy Spirit brought them to saving faith, through the preaching of the gospel and all to the goal of obtaining the glory of Christ (vv. 13–14).
- Second, he applies this to their lives. They are to "stand fast" and "hold to the teachings." What "distinguishes Christians from non-Christians," says Arthur Pink, "is their surrender to the authority of Christ." Then he is ready to pray that they will remain faithful to the Lord and so encourage them to give themselves to "every good word and work."

How will this actually happen? Paul prays that their Lord and Father would do two things: encourage their hearts and strengthen them in their actions. What makes all the difference here is who is doing the encouraging and the strengthening. We encourage people all the time. "You can do it," we say to our college-student daughter as she faces her biochemistry exams, even though we have neither any knowledge of her subject nor actual power to concentrate her mind. Jesus and our Father-God, however, can actually help us powerfully and effectually. We know this because they have demonstrated it in our lives already! Jesus and his

672

Father have "loved us" and "by grace" have given us precious gifts of grace—namely, "everlasting consolation" and good hope" (v. 16). Paul knew what the Lord had done for him in saving him and sending him out to preach Christ to the world. This was more than the encouraging words of a friend, however warm and sincere. This was "power from on high" (Luke 24:29). This was the invisible hand of the power of God bursting into the context of need and relative weakness that is always the point from which believing prayer arises: "Lord, I believe; help my unbelief!" (Mark 9:24).

The "everlasting consolation" of knowing that the Lord has loved us out of sheer grace translates into comforting our hearts day by day. It will last forever in our experience of his care for us. And the "good hope" that we have in Christ our Savior is again and again imparted to our souls to move us to "every good deed and word" (v. 17). It is a "good" hope that motivates us to "good" actions, because in Jesus we have a sinless Savior who bore our sins away and clothed us with his righteousness. That is why a real Christian wants to present his body as "a living sacrifice, holy, acceptable to God." It is simply our "reasonable service" as it flows from what Christ has done in saving us (Rom. 12:1).

Stand fast, then, and covenant with God as the psalmist did when he said, "I will go in the strength of the Lord GOD; I will make mention of Your righteousness, of Yours only" (Ps. 71:16). In another place the apostle charges us with a beautiful and profound simplicity: "As you have therefore received Christ Jesus the Lord, so walk in Him" (Col. 2:6).

PRAISE FOR COMFORT FROM GOD
Sing Psalm 85

THINGS I WILL PRAY FOR TODAY

December 2
An Answering Love

A prayer for love toward God

Now may the Lord direct your hearts into the love of God...
—2 Thess. 3:5

READ 2 THESSALONIANS 3:1–5

ime was when we all had hobbies. Today, we are all just "into" things. What once were pastimes are now consuming passions. This can be good and it can be bad. Getting "into" the wrong things can do us a lot of damage. Paul's prayer is for us to get "into" good things, the first of which is the "love of God." Whereas in 2 Thessalonians 2:16–17 the apostle prays for *God's* love to comfort our hearts, here he prays for *our* love to increase toward God. We are to get "into" loving God. Leon Morris calls this an "answering love"—the love that responds to God's goodness toward us. God blesses us long before we are either able or even willing to bless him. So now it is our turn!

Our coming to love God, then, does not start with us. "We love Him because He first loved us" (1 John 4:19). The starting point for the Christian is never within himself. Our world is always telling us to look within ourselves and to believe in ourselves and to love ourselves. Some think we find the love of God for us in this way. We never come up with God's love first within ourselves. It begins in our God and Savior reaching out to us and into our hearts by his Word and Holy Spirit. This is simply because it is *who God is* that alone can make it happen in us! It is in his character as our Redeemer God that we find both the beginning of our salvation and the strength, stability, and security with which to live in faith before him and the world. He loved us from before the foundation of the world, so much so that he sent his only begotten Son to bear our sins in his own body on the cross (Eph. 1:4; John 3:16; 1 Peter 2:24). His eternal love sets in motion the way of salvation that brings us into fellowship with him.

God's faithfulness means that he will continue what he has begun. Elsewhere, Paul says he is "confident of this very thing, that He who has begun a good work in you will complete it until the day of Jesus Christ" (Phil. 1:6). Here, he mentions two things God will do for us. He will "establish" us—the word refers to putting up a buttress to support a wall. And he will "guard" us—from Satan, no less (v. 3)! Confidence that the Lord will do this in turn issues in confidence that God's people will continue to be faithful day by day—namely, "both that you do and will do the things we command you" (v. 4). What you are already doing, you will continue to do. The Lord will help you and see it through to glorious completion. Of this, you may be certain.

The petition "now may the Lord direct your hearts into the love of God" takes us back to the most basic response of a believing heart, namely, love toward God! "However lofty our words of devotion may rise," writes Arthur Pink, "they are empty without our active obedience, the proof of our love." "Keep yourselves in the love of God," says Jude (v. 21). "Keep your heart with all diligence," says Solomon, "for out of it spring the issues of life" (Prov. 4:23). Pink observes:

> All religion is in effect love. Faith is thankful acceptance, and thankfulness is an expression of love. Repentance is love mourning. Yearning for holiness is love seeking. Obedience is love pleasing.…When our love for God decreases, the love of the world grows.…"God is love" (1 John 4:8) and therefore His love is infinite, incomprehensible, adorable. We may feed on it now, and it shall be our endless delight in heaven.

PRAISE WITH LOVE TOWARD GOD
Sing Psalm 18

THINGS I WILL PRAY FOR TODAY

December 3
Waiting for God's Time

A prayer for patience

Now may the Lord direct your hearts into the love of God and into the patience of Christ. —2 Thess. 3:5

READ 2 THESSALONIANS 3:1–5, 16

Patience does not come easily to most of us. Are you patient in *working*—to stick at the job when it seems to be getting nowhere? Are you patient in *suffering*—bearing provocation from someone uncomplainingly or coping with ongoing illness? Are you patient in *waiting* for someone to do something or for the Lord to fulfill a promise in his Word? Are you patient to *pray*—"without ceasing" (1 Thess. 5:17)—for some matter that never seems to come to a happy conclusion? Are you patient with *failings in others*? Are you patient for *God's will* to be done in his time? Or is God *always* too slow for your liking? Patience is an elusive virtue, because what we want is not patience, but our own way—and an end to the waiting that tries our patience so painfully and exposes how impatient we are.

Impatience among Paul's readers was about the coming of Christ. Some were afraid he had already come and they had missed out on his promises (2 Thess. 2:1–2). We know that elsewhere others were afraid he was never going to come (2 Peter 3:3–4). Paul's first answer is for them to "stand fast" in the truth they had been taught (2 Thess. 2:15). Then they needed the patience to wait—and to live normal, faithful lives while they waited—however long it took for Jesus to return (2 Thess. 3:12–13). Easily said, you might say. Uncertainties, doubts, confusion about the facts, crises in the world, contradictory teachers, and fearful thoughts all conspire to steal away our peace. How shall we ever keep an even keel in such a shaky world? Jesus says, "By your patience possess your souls" (Luke 21:19). Impatience causes us to lose possession of our souls. Arthur Pink puts it this way: "Whatever *title* we have to our souls, we have no *possession* of them without patience. As faith puts us in possession of Christ, so patience gives us possession of our souls. The soul of an impatient person is dispossessed, for he no longer acts as a rational creature."

676

This is where the connection with the love of God is vital. It is that love that "will reduce the distance between our hope and its realization and enable us to 'wait patiently' for Him." The prayer for direction into "the patience of Christ" strengthens this point.

We need the same patience—better rendered "endurance"—that was in Jesus. He finished the work the Father gave him to do (John 17:4). He was oppressed and afflicted and led like a lamb to the slaughter but "He opened not His mouth" (Isa. 53:7). "When he suffered He did not threaten, but committed Himself to Him who judges righteously" (1 Peter 2:23). At every point in his earthly ministry, Jesus waited with perfect patience. Who among us has ever come close to this?

How will we grow in such patient waiting? The Lord tells you that the "testing of your faith produces patience" (James 1:3). And the Lord can direct your heart into the patience that Jesus exemplified and taught. Let us pray for the patience of our Savior, and say to the Lord with a humbled David, "Let Him do to me as seems good to Him" (2 Sam. 15:26).

PRAYER TO REST IN THE LORD
Sing Psalm 37

THINGS I WILL PRAY FOR TODAY

677

December 4
Overwhelmed with God's Glory

Prayer as worship

Now to the King eternal, immortal, invisible, to God who alone is wise,
be honor and glory forever and ever, Amen. — 1 Tim. 1:17

READ 1 TIMOTHY 1:12–17; 6:15–16

"Many of our petitions begin and end with self," writes Arthur Pink, "and therefore in no way honor God." There is no petitionary prayer recorded in 1 Timothy. That is, there are no "prayer requests" for the particular needs of specific individuals. What is prayed in the two doxologies (1:17; 6:15–16), and said about prayer elsewhere, is simply and wonderfully occupied with the glory of God. The pattern is: here is how God has blessed me, and here is God's glory praised for what it is! Check out other doxology prayers, such as Romans 1:25; 9:5; 11:36; Galatians 1:5; Philippians 4:20; Jude 24–25; and Revelation 1:5b–6. Notice how each one begins with the goodness of God to us and then goes on to praise the glorious God of our salvation. This is most appropriate, for the highest expression of prayer is surely the praise and adoration of God. Hearts filled with God's grace will always empty their praises into heaven.

Why is the apostle overwhelmed by God's glory? Paul here gives praise to the Lord for two amazing gifts that changed his life forever:

> - The first is the *new life* Jesus has given him (1:12–14). He used to be "a blasphemer, a persecutor, and an insolent man." He was drowning in unbelief, ignorant of his deadness and danger. Nevertheless, the Lord was merciful, his grace was "exceedingly abundant," and he brought Paul to faith and love in Christ.
> - The second is the *life-giving Savior* Jesus is (1:15–16). Paul didn't forge his new life for himself. It was the work of "Christ Jesus," who "came into the world to save sinners." Paul adds that he regards himself as the "chief" of sinners, the point being that his sense of the gracious condescension of Christ—to love him enough to save a sinner like him—just blows his mind. As Charles Wesley expresses it,

And can it be that I should gain
    an interest in the Saviour's love?
Died He for me, who caused his pain?
    For me, who him to death pursued?
Amazing love! How can it be
    that thou, my God, shouldst die for me?
    —"Amazing Love," stanza 1

Who is this God whose glory so overwhelms us? He is none other than the triune God of the Bible—Father, Son, and Holy Spirit—who saves lost people from their sins. Paul gives the praise to our God:

> He is "the king eternal"—"the blessed and only Potentate, the King of kings and Lord of Lords" (6:15)—who is sovereign over all and cares for us.

> He is the "immortal, invisible" God, whose purpose of grace from all eternity "has now been revealed by the appearing of our Savior, Jesus Christ, who has abolished death and brought life and immortality to light through the gospel" (2 Tim. 1:10).

> He is the "God who alone is wise"—the omniscient God who "declares the end from the beginning" (Isa. 46:10). "O the depth of the riches both of the wisdom and knowledge of God!" (Rom. 11:33).

Therefore, the only response of a believing heart is to say, to him be "honor and glory forever. Amen."

PRAISE TO THE LORD OF GLORY
Sing Psalm 107

THINGS I WILL PRAY FOR TODAY

_____

_____

_____

_____

_____

_____

_____

_____

December 5
The Scope of Public Prayer

Prayer in public worship (Part 1)

Therefore I exhort first of all that supplications, prayers, intercessions and giving of thanks be made for all men... —1 Tim. 2:1

READ 1 TIMOTHY 2:1–2

Prayer is a priority in public worship. Paul tells Timothy, "I write so that you may know how you ought to conduct yourself in the house of God, which is the church of the living God, the pillar and ground of the truth" (1 Tim. 3:15). Paul urges him to "wage the good warfare" (1:18). To that end—"therefore"—he exhorts the church "first of all" to pray "for all men" (2:1). For most speakers, political or religious, it's the last point that is usually the most important and the most powerfully delivered. Here, "first of all" means "as of first importance." If God's people are to fight the good fight, they will need help and focus. Prayer is where this starts. Public worship is where we must collectively seek the Lord and his enabling grace and power if we are to share in the victory of Christ. A prayerless church is a powerless church. The public prayer of the church is a key indicator of its spiritual condition and is therefore a priority for public worship.

Prayer is comprehensive in scope. Paul uses four Greek words to open this up. "Supplications" (*deeseis*) are petitions related to *our* specific needs, whether as a church body or as individuals; "prayers" (*proseuche*) are about the experience of *communion with God*, that he would draw near to us and deepen our knowledge of and our walk with him. Here we would adore the Lord and confess our sin and need of Christ our Savior; "intercessions" (*enteuchis*) are requests for *others*, that God would help them in particular ways; and "giving of thanks" (*eucharistia*) encompasses *praise-prayer* for blessings received or anticipated—for everything from life and breath, to gospel grace, Christ's coming again, and heaven itself. This may remind you of the mnemonic "ACTS" that is often used to encourage structure in our personal prayers. Adoration, Confession, Thanksgiving, and Supplication are all here, albeit in a slightly different format.

Prayer is meant to cover the whole world. "All men" is no doubt more about attitude than numbers. No one can pray for everyone, one by one. The Bible often uses the term "all men" in a less than literal way (see Mark 1:37; 5:20; 11:32; Luke 3:15). It is often best understood as referring to all types and conditions of people. With that in mind, we surely can pray for all kinds of people, without distinction. We can certainly pray for those we know personally. We can care about our world and express that in prayer.

Prayer for the world includes "kings and all who are in authority," says Paul. Why this special mention of political leaders? Could it be because they are often regarded as "the enemy" and so are more criticized, reviled, and prayed against, than they are prayed for with any sympathy or beneficial intention?

Prayer in public worship, then, should range from the lowest to the highest, the closest to the furthest away, the most familiar to the least known, and from our friends to our foes! Why? Because the gospel is directed to the whole world and the church is the only body that is sent by God to intercede for the world and to evangelize it with the good news of Jesus Christ. For this reason, we must let our prayers reach as far as the Lordship of Jesus Christ extends—"from sea to sea…and to the ends of the earth" (Ps. 72:8) with "supplications, prayers, intercessions and giving of thanks…for all men."

A PRAYER FOR ALL PEOPLE
Sing Psalm 67

THINGS I WILL PRAY FOR TODAY

December 6
The Heart of Prayer

Prayer in public worship (Part 2)

For there is one God and one Mediator between God and men, the Man Christ Jesus. — 1 *Tim. 2:5*

READ 1 TIMOTHY 2:2-7

Prayer has a practical purpose (v. 2). Public prayer is not psychobabble meant to cheer us up with the mere illusion of doing something substantial. We are to pray for "all men," not just friends and relatives (1 Tim. 2:1), and we should also pray for our politicians (v. 2a)—sometimes even against them! The practical reason for this is "that we may live a quiet and peaceable life in all godliness and reverence" (v. 2b). When you think about it, civil government is bound to be a key factor in outward well-being. But it is also relevant to our inward exercise of personal godliness. We don't want to be poor and oppressed in our society, but neither do we want to be persecuted and distressed in our hearts! We want a government that is a minister of God for good and a terror to evildoers—in short, one that maintains our freedom to live as the people of God without hindrance (Rom. 13:3–4).

Prayer pleases God and furthers his plan of salvation (vv. 3–4). Faithful public prayer accomplishes two tremendous blessings. The first of these is that such prayer is pleasing to God. God is described as "God our Savior," which is to say that God delights in seeing in us the fruit of his saving grace in our lives (v. 3).

The second is that prayer furthers the spread of the gospel. When it is said that God desires "all men" to be saved, we must again remember this expression does not mean every single person that ever lived. People are lost (Rom. 5:18; 9:14ff.; 1 Cor. 15:22; Titus 2:11). Mercy is optional with God, and his desire and his will are never in conflict. All kinds of people, however, will be saved. "There is neither Jew nor Greek…slave nor free…male nor female; for you are all one in Christ Jesus" (Gal. 3:28). And every single soul the Father gives to the Son, says Jesus, "will come to Me, and the one who comes to Me I will by no means cast out" (John 6:37).

682

Prayer is made effective by the atoning sacrifice of Jesus Christ (vv. 5–7). Why are we able to pray with confidence? Paul gives us four solid reasons:

> There is "one God" (v. 5a). There are no others besides him and he is absolutely sovereign over all things. He is therefore able to hear and to answer: "O You who hear prayer, to You all flesh will come" (Ps. 65:2).

> There is "one Mediator between God and men, the Man Christ Jesus" (v. 5b). And Jesus prays for us and with us: "Therefore He is also able to save to the uttermost those who come to God through Him, since He always lives to make intercession for them" (Heb. 7:25).

> Jesus Christ "gave Himself to "ransom" all who will be saved (v. 6a). As mentioned before, "All that the Father gives Me will come to Me, and the one who comes to Me I will by no means cast out" (John 6:37).

> This gospel message of the Christ crucified was preached to all by the apostle "in faith and truth" (v. 6b–7). Why must we pray in our churches for "all men"? Surely because we love to see lost people saved by the Savior who first loved us when we were lost! To that end, we pray fervently that the Word of God would have free course and be glorified (2 Thess. 3:1).

CALLING ALL PEOPLE TO PRAISE GOD
Sing Psalm 117

THINGS I WILL PRAY FOR TODAY

_____

_____

_____

_____

_____

_____

_____

_____

December 7
Leading Prayer in Public Worship

Praying in public worship (Part 3)

Therefore I desire that men pray everywhere....Let a woman learn in silence with all submission. — 1 Tim. 2:8, 11

READ 1 TIMOTHY 2:8–15

There must have been some disorder in the church in Ephesus for Paul to tell Timothy how they "ought to conduct [themselves] in the house of God" (1 Tim. 3:15). One aspect of disorder appears to have involved men and women not acting responsibly in leading and quietly supporting, respectively, the people of God in worship. Men were not leading and women were not silent, as they "ought." All this is about the reversal of the role relationship of men and women as God purposes it for our blessing, as well as that of the church and its ordinances. This is not arbitrary. It is not a matter of inherent superiority versus inferiority. It is about the order in the family, church, and society, in which God matches gender roles to patterns of mutual support, well-being, and spiritual growth. The disorder Paul seeks to counter is so well established today in homes and churches that we have no lack of evidence for the wisdom of God, if we have eyes to see!

Men are to exercise responsibility in leadership (v. 8). In public prayer in public worship — this is the context — they are to lead. "Everywhere" reads literally, "in every place." This expression is also used in 1 Corinthians 1:2, 2 Corinthians 2:14, and 1 Thessalonians 1:8 — all likely referring to public worship. How are men to lead? By godly actions and godly motives. "Lifting up holy hands" is more about intentional holiness in approaching God, than a mere physical posture. We need "clean hands and a pure heart" (Ps. 24:4). This needs to be "without wrath and doubting." The latter word is better rendered "disputing." The Greek *dialogismos* — from whence our English "dialogue" comes — is about being double-minded and hypocritical. In other words, talking out of both sides of the mouth (cf. Matt. 11:25; 18:21–35). Men are to lead in the church — spearheaded by the elders of 1 Timothy 5:17.

Women are called to exercise responsibility in being led through quiet and modest submission (2:9–15). This is exercised a number of ways:

- ⤷ Modesty in dress and deportment (v. 9).
- ⤷ Godliness through the spiritual adornment of "good works" (v. 10).
- ⤷ Willingness to learn in a quiet and submissive spirit (vv. 11–12).
- ⤷ Seeking fulfillment in covenant living—being faithful mothers in "faith, love, and holiness with self-control" (vv. 13–15).

Women are also to focus on building up the covenant community—the church—almost from "behind the scenes" and yet with transparent public godliness. In the case of wives and mothers, this will even roll back something of the curse upon childbearing intimated at the fall of our first parents (Gen. 3:16).

This is not to be dismissed as Paul's peculiar opinion and desire (v. 8)! Neither is it to be seen as a cultural thing, long rendered obsolete by the advance of what is called "progress." These are as much the words of divine inspiration as all the other writings of the New Testament (2 Tim. 3:16). The key to understanding this and applying it correctly is the Christ the apostle proclaims in his every breath. It is in Christ we discover our true manhood and womanhood. In Christ we fulfill our true callings as men and women. In Christ we call the world, through our godly witness to gospel grace, to Christ as the one and only Savior, and to a new life as it can be blessed by the Lord in his free grace.

PRAISE THE LORD OF GLORY!
Sing Psalm 141:1–2

THINGS I WILL PRAY FOR TODAY

_____

_____

_____

_____

_____

_____

_____

_____

December 8
Asking the Blessing

Prayer's sanctifying influence

For every creature of God is good, and nothing is to be refused if it is received with thanksgiving; for it is sanctified by the word of God and prayer. —1 Tim. 4:4–5

READ 1 TIMOTHY 4:1–5

There have always been people in the church who want to make rules for the Christian life that God never gave in his Word. The two examples Paul cites concern forbidding marriage (enforced celibacy) and abstaining from certain foods. These both impinge upon basic God-given freedoms. God created both marriage and food. While we are obliged neither to marry nor to eat every conceivable form of food, we are in fact free to do both these things. They are to be "received with thanksgiving by those who believe and know the truth" (v. 3). Such views that would curtail our Christian freedom in these areas are not to be regarded as somewhat mistaken or slightly over-zealous. They are serious errors and to be rejected as infringements on true Christian liberty.

God's Word has hard words for these teachings. They are the result of "giving heed to deceiving spirits and doctrines of demons" and they involve hypocritical lies and the searing of the conscience (vv. 1–2).

Why does God express such tough criticism? The answer is that these folk are denying that "every creature of God is good." They are presuming to be wiser and more righteous than God, precisely because they declare that some of his gifts are not gifts to be enjoyed, but curses to be rejected.

Furthermore, all false teaching arises from the influences of "deceiving spirits." That is why we must constantly pray, "Lead us not into temptation, but deliver us from the evil one" (Matt. 6:13). It is the work of the devil that erodes the plain teaching and the glorious freedom of God's Word.

This kind of unbiblical self-denial is bound to be a breeding ground for self-righteousness. We imagine that these extra-scriptural rules we make up give us a clearer testimony, as if it shows who the real believers are. Real Christians don't eat this or drink that, don't wear these clothing styles, don't dance and go to movies, and so on. Now, there are principles in Scripture that apply to every area of life, but there is no such thing as a biblical diet, and celibacy is not taught in Scripture.

God's answer is to remind us of three simple themes:

 ⟡ Everything God created is *good* (v. 4a). Believe it! And think about why God made it all in the first place. Why did God give us plants and animals, and minerals and fossil fuels? Surely to be husbanded and harvested for our widest benefit.

 ⟡ These are all to be received with *thanksgiving* (v. 4b). They are not rejected as unclean or unchristian. The resources of God's creation are a gift of God's common grace to mankind. Praise the Lord for them!

 ⟡ They are to be *sanctified* in their use by the Word of God and prayer (v. 5). That means they are to be separated to God in our conscious use of them as his provision for our lives. The Word points us to a godly use of these things, while prayer prepares us to praise God and give the glory to him.

Christians often use the expression "Say grace" to describe prayer before a meal. That smacks of ritual repetition of a form of words. Let us rather "ask a blessing" or "give thanks" and so maintain both the lively expression of heartfelt love for the Lord, and the earnest desire of a believing, trusting heart for God to bless us in our enjoyment of his benefits.

PRAYER BEFORE A MEAL
Sing Psalm 145:15–16

THINGS I WILL PRAY FOR TODAY

December 9
The Christian Widow's Prayer

Prayer night and day

Now she who is really a widow, and left alone, trusts in God and continues in supplications and prayer night and day.—1 Tim. 5:5

READ 1 TIMOTHY 5:3–16

P raying Christian widows are the most underestimated force in the work of God's kingdom. In his days as a student, G. N. M. Collins, later principal of the Free Church College, Edinburgh, supplied a pulpit on the island of Arran. He stayed with a family that included a widowed matriarch who was stone deaf and who, being bedridden, could not attend the services. After he had walked over to the church, Collins discovered that he had left his sermon notes by his bedside, so he raced back to retrieve them. As he entered the house, he heard a loud voice. It was the old lady, praying for the young preacher; she was praying that the Lord would bless his ministry among God's people that morning! Over fifty years later, he told me that he never experienced more "liberty" in preaching God's Word as he did that morning: "The prayer of a righteous person has great power as it is working" (James 5:16, ESV).

The Christian community is to care for its widows (vv. 3–8). The prayers of Christian widows and their care in the church come together in verses 3–16, while the wider context gives practical instruction as to how the church is to be a caring community—that "the name of God and His doctrine are not blasphemed" (1 Tim. 5:1–6:2). Those who are "really widows"—literally, "widows indeed" (5:3)—are to be cared for by the church, with certain qualifications. Notice that God's welfare rolls are both means-tested and faith-tested. The essential material criterion is having no resources at all. "The Merry Widow" of Franz Lehar's same-titled operetta need not apply! The spiritual criteria to be applied are a credible personal faith and evidence of particular devotion to prayer (v. 5). Widows who live for themselves are also ineligible—"she who lives in pleasure is dead while she lives" (v. 6). This standard is to be commanded "that they may be blameless" (v. 7). The first responsibility for a "widow

688

indeed" does not, however, fall to the church but to her children and grandchildren (vv. 3–4). Abdication of this God-required duty of love and compassion is to deny the faith and behave in a manner "worse than an unbeliever" (v. 8). Why worse? Because it is not only a sin against known duty, but against the light of God's Word and the love of Jesus Christ. That over half of Americans admit no such obligation to an aged parent is proof positive of that nation's turning from the God of the Bible.

Widows are to care about serving Jesus Christ (vv. 9–16). We must pass by the various rules and regulations as to which widows are to be supported and which not, except to note what the Lord is looking for in a godly widow. She is to have been a faithful wife to her late husband and to be "well reported for good works," whether in raising children, showing hospitality to strangers, washing the saints' feet (see Luke 7:44), relieving the afflicted, or "diligently following every good work" (vv. 9–10). What a glorious prescription for usefulness in the work of God's kingdom! And what a contrast with the way in which these women are so often discounted in the church, when in fact God means them to be both soul and spine of the ministry of compassion within the body. Pray for widows who will give themselves to prayer and to those other facets of church life where their experience of God's grace so beautifully equips them to minister to others. Herbert Lockyer never spoke more discerningly than when he said, "We will never know what the church owes to its lonely, godly, praying widows."

PRAISE FOR THE LORD WHO CARES ABOUT
THE HURTING AND THE NEEDY
Sing Psalm 146

THINGS I WILL PRAY FOR TODAY

December 10
Without Ceasing

Prayer for a beloved son

…without ceasing I remember you in my prayers night and day.
—2 Tim. 1:3

READ 2 TIMOTHY 1:3–7

Paul is an old man, imprisoned in Rome, when he writes to Timothy, telling him that he prays for him "without ceasing." Timothy is a younger man (1 Tim. 4:22), who is often sick (1 Tim. 5:23) and sometimes timid in the face of the challenges of his work as a minister of the gospel (1 Cor. 16:10). Here is a beautiful example of an older minister counseling one who is younger and less experienced in pastoral work. It stands as a universal call to seasoned Christians to minister to and pray for the next generation of Jesus's followers. Paul shows older Christians how to pray for their younger co-laborers, and he shows the younger believers what to be working on in their hearts and lives.

Paul shows us how we are to pray for one another (vv. 3–5). Notice that he addresses Timothy, not as a minister of the gospel, but as "a beloved son" (2 Tim. 1:2). Timothy is never far from Paul's prayers because he is lodged deeply in Paul's heart. Add the young man's trials in the ministry and the older man is even more exercised to go to the throne of grace on his behalf. How ought we to pray for others? A few notes:

- First, be praying "without ceasing…day and night" (v. 3). This neither means that Paul actually and formally prayed through all his waking hours, nor suggests that this literally be made a regular practice by anyone. God gave us six days each week in which to work. The Sabbath is our God-given rest from work and is certainly given for the mandated pieties of worship, of which prayer is only a portion. Prayer does, however, run parallel to our daily responsibilities and surely punctuates them. So praying "without ceasing" is not measured by a timer, but it happens all the same. Paul is a prisoner and he takes the time he has to pray for his young friend. His mind is focused upon God—"whom I serve with a clear conscience" (v. 3, ESV). Yours can be, too.

> Second, be sharing others' burdens—"mindful of [their] tears" (v. 4). Paul mentions his desire to see his friend in person again—to renew fellowship. And he so wants to "be filled with joy"—obviously, as the prayer is answered in the lifting of the cause of his tears (see Gal. 6:2).

> Third, encourage and reaffirm "genuine faith" wherever you find it (v. 5). Paul rejoices in Timothy's faith and recalls the faithfulness of his mother and grandmother. God was faithful in the line of the generations of his people. But notice his personal persuasion of Timothy's faith, for "God has no grandchildren." Children can and do reject their parents faith. Each of us must directly and personally be a child of God through faith in Christ.

Paul has two stated goals for Timothy (vv. 6–7). As surely as he would have prayed for them, he now exhorts Timothy to live them out with intentional effort. The first is that he "stir up the gift of God which is in you"—in this case with respect to his ordination to the ministry (v. 6). For all believers it is a matter of stirring up the gift of the Holy Spirit, and the cultivation of particular gifts he has given us for our calling in life. The second goal is that Timothy would realize the full fruit of "the spirit of power and of love and of a sound mind" (v. 7). If we have "a spirit of fear," it did not come from the Lord. Fear of this kind is not a grace, but a denial of grace and of Christ. We are weak, of course, but as Paul says elsewhere, when he entrusts himself to the Lord, he discovers, "When I am weak, then I am strong" (2 Cor. 12:10). Let us pray—without ceasing.

A SONG OF CONTINUING, CONFIDENT PRAYER
Sing Psalm 27:5–9

THINGS I WILL PRAY FOR TODAY

December 11
He Often Refreshed Me

Prayer in remembrance of kindness received

The Lord grant mercy to the household of Onesiphoros, for he often refreshed me…—2 Tim. 1:16

READ 2 TIMOTHY 1:16–18

O ne who brings profit" is the literal meaning of the name of Onesiphoros. He originally hailed from Ephesus and may well have been converted under Paul's ministry in that place. He seems to have traveled to Rome quite frequently, because Paul, who was under house arrest there, mentions that Onesiphoros "often refreshed" him and was not "ashamed" of his "chain." It seems that—like Ebedmelech who visited Jeremiah in King Zedekiah's dungeon—Onesiphoros had a steadfast resolve to minister to one of God's suffering ministers so as to lift both his burden and his spirit (cf. Jer. 38:7–13). The Scottish preacher A. A. Bonar rightly calls him the Ebedmelech of the New Testament. Paul was deeply touched by Onesiphoros's kindness and fellowship. As he writes to Timothy, who is in Ephesus, he remembers his good friend and expresses his prayers for his "household" (v. 16) and for Onesiphoros himself (v. 18).

This is a somewhat controversial passage, because it is claimed as an example of a prayer for the dead—the only one that comes even close in all of Scripture. The arguments for this, however, are rather flimsy. It is claimed that Onesiphoros is dead because Paul speaks of him in the past tense, mentions him apart from his household, and doesn't mention him at all in 2 Timothy 4:19. The fact is that, aside from this speculation, there is no concrete evidence that the man was dead. The past tense only proves he is not in Rome and mention of him separate from his household only proves he was not in Ephesus at the time. Besides, there is no evidence in Scripture that prayers for the dead are either warranted or effective. Prayer is for the living, here in this present life.

Paul prays for the fruition of God's mercy for Onesiphoros and his family: "The Lord grant to him that he may find mercy from the Lord in that Day"—the great day of Christ's coming to judge the living and the

692

dead (v. 18). Notice that the apostle remarks in the same breath on "how many ways" Onesiphoros ministered to him in Ephesus, before either of them met up in Rome. Paul is rejoicing in his perseverance in the practice of his faith. When he prays for mercy in the great day, he is praying for the reward of his faith in glorious measure. On that day, the people of God will be acknowledged before heaven and earth with the Lord's "well done, good and faithful servant....Enter into the joy of your Lord" (Matt. 25:21).

There is tremendous encouragement here for us to pray for God's best for believers and their families:

- Strive to *refresh* one another spiritually—especially when troubles cast their long shadows over people's hearts and circumstances: "Yes, brother, let me have joy from you in the Lord; refresh my heart in the Lord" (Philem. 20).
- Don't *wait* until someone else steps forward—as A. A. Bonar counsels, "Work yourself and let others follow." Your faithfulness may seed the clouds that eventually pour out the faithfulness of many others.
- Live *in the Holy Spirit* and walk in the light of eternity—rejoicing every day in Jesus Christ and the hope of heaven.
- Look *forward* to that day when you will appear with all the saints in heaven itself—forever with the Lord in the fruition of his grace.

PRAYER FOR THE MERCIES OF GOD
Sing Psalm 119:41–48

THINGS I WILL PRAY FOR TODAY

_____

_____

_____

_____

_____

_____

_____

_____

_____

_____

December 12
When People Let You Down

Praying for false friends

May it not be charged against them. — *2 Tim. 4:16*

READ 2 TIMOTHY 4:9–18

You have no doubt heard it said of some, "With friends like these, who needs enemies?" Among other things, this is a reminder that it really hurts when friends fail us. Paul understood personal betrayal and, more than that, saw the horror of it when it involved someone also betraying Christ by falling away from the faith. As he winds up his second letter to Timothy, you can feel both his irritation and his need of encouragement and reinforcements:

- Demas has "forsaken" him, "having loved this present world" (v. 9).
- Crescens and Titus had left to minister further afield (v. 10c).
- Tychicus had been sent by Paul to Ephesus (v. 12).

The apostolic mission team is reduced to Luke and Paul and the continuing pressure of the work of the gospel compels Paul to ask that Timothy and Mark join him, bringing his cloak and his books (v. 11, 13). While the defection of erstwhile friends strikes a blow at the very work of the gospel, the sending out of three men and the claims of ongoing ministry are the problems of growth, and Paul surely sees these as a blessing.

There are two great threats to our spiritual stability in all of this. The first is, of course, *discouragement.* Alexander did Paul "much harm" and "greatly resisted" Paul's ministry and counsel (vv. 14–15). The second threat arises from a sense of *isolation.* In a matter-of-fact tone, Paul records, "all forsook me" (v. 16). There is a slight echo here of Elijah's more depressive refrain, "Even I only, am left" (1 Kings 19:10, 14). The prophet almost gave up. While Paul shows no sign of quitting, betrayal and isolation tend in that direction. "What's the use," we will ask, "if even our friends turn away from us?" The unspoken implication is that the Lord is also forsaking us.

694

Paul's response is as simple as it is resolute: he prays and he stands firm in dependence upon the Lord. His prayers run the gamut from judgment to mercy. In the case of Alexander, he prays for condign punishment: "May the Lord repay him according to his works" (v. 14). There is no more personal vindictiveness here than there was in Jesus's call for judgment on the Pharisees in Matthew 23. In any case, Paul is not asking for Alexander's eternal damnation, but just that he not escape the consequences of his actions. There is a place for such prayer. Should we not pray for the Lord to defend his suffering people by bringing down their oppressors?

On the other hand, the apostle seeks mercy for the brethren who forsook him. "May it not be charged against them" (v. 16). They were faithful but fearful. They were believers who cut and ran when the enemy attacked. The disciples scattered after Jesus was arrested. Jesus knew this would happen when he prayed that God "should keep them from the evil one" (John 17:15). Should the weaknesses of well-meaning souls not lead us to cry out in sympathy for the Lord to restore and to strengthen them?

When others fled, Paul stood firm under attack. The key is that, as he prayerfully held his ground, the Lord stood with him and strengthened him. He was delivered "out of the mouth of the lion"—that is, from serious threats to life and limb. He was delivered to preach the gospel more fully and effectively, and he was filled with a certain hope of deliverance and of eternal glory (vv. 17–18). This promise is also for us, and it is God's promise that "we shall reap if we do not lose heart" (Gal. 6:9).

PRAISE THE LORD WHO STANDS BY US
Sing Psalm 146:1–5

THINGS I WILL PRAY FOR TODAY

December 13
A Throne of Grace

Confident prayer in time of need

Let us therefore come boldly to the throne of grace, that we may obtain mercy and grace to help in time of need. —Heb. 4:16

READ HEBREWS 4:14–16

Too many people imagine that God has "call waiting" and will grab the phone whenever they deign to call him. People assume that God will hear any prayer from anybody, any time. Contrary to such assumptions, there is no inherent human right to come to God in prayer. The reason for this is that "without faith it is impossible to please Him, for he who comes to God must believe that He is, and that He is a rewarder of those who diligently seek Him" (Heb. 11:6). Billions of people "pray," but God is not listening. Oh, he hears, but he is offended. But short of a saving knowledge of Jesus Christ—for "no one comes to the Father except through Him" (John 14:6)—we humans are by nature out of fellowship with God (Rom. 8:7). What God requires first is repentance toward him and faith in the Lord Jesus Christ. Until then "the heavens which are over your head shall be bronze" (Deut. 28:23).

Believing prayer only happens in praying believers. Only believers have the promise of answered prayer. Even then, it was a believer who said, "If I regard iniquity in my heart, the Lord will not hear" (Ps. 66:18). So, you rightly ask, how can any of us get a hearing with God? How can his unapproachable throne of righteousness become accessible to us?

The Bible's answer is that Jesus is the reason there is a "throne of grace" for believers. He is the great High Priest, because, unlike all other Old Testament priests, he is the "Son of God" who "passed through the heavens," who is able to "sympathize with our weaknesses" (vv. 14–15), and who is "the author of eternal salvation" (Heb. 5:9).

Union with Christ by faith brings us, not to God's just judgment of us, but to his free grace to us in Christ. John Owen says that "the throne of grace...is unto us, God as gracious in Christ, as exalted in the

696

way of exercising grace and mercy toward them that through the Lord Jesus believe in Him and come unto Him." When believers pray, they come to God's loving smile. The heavens are not "bronze," but open and welcoming, because he is our Father in heaven on account of Christ's atonement for our sins.

We may approach this throne "boldly" because Jesus is our Savior. The Lord welcomes our prayers and urges us to a holy confidence in prayer (v. 16a). Theodore Beza, the sixteenth century French Reformer, translates this to "with liberty of speech." We are free in Jesus our Savior to come right into God's presence! We have, says Paul, "boldness and access with confidence through faith in Him" (Eph. 3:12). Of course, Jesus assures us we can "ask…seek…and knock" with happy expectation of receiving, finding, and entering into all that we bring to the Lord in prayer (Matt. 7:7). We are free to share our most honest thoughts and heartfelt needs with the Lord: "If any of you lacks wisdom, let him ask of God, who gives to all liberally and without reproach, and it will be given to him" (James 1:5).

We must approach this throne "boldly" in times of need. The Lord has "grace to help" when troubles arise (v. 16b). Do we have needs? Do we ever *not* have needs? Do we ever not have need of God's grace to help us? Then let us grasp the urgency of this encouragement and call upon him when any need rushes in upon our hearts and minds. The door is open. The promise stands: "O You who hear prayer, to You all flesh will come" (Ps. 65:2).

A PRAYER IN A TIME OF NEED
Sing Psalm 5

THINGS I WILL PRAY FOR TODAY

December 14
Jesus's Daily Prayers

The intercession of the ascended Savior

He always lives to make intercession for them. — Heb. 7:25

READ HEBREWS 5:7–8; 7:24–25; 9:24

ave you ever asked yourself why Jesus prays? After all, he is the Son of God, truly God though also truly human, and so co-equal with the Father and the Holy Spirit. Does his oneness with the Father not render prayer totally unnecessary? Is Jesus not the one to whom and through whom we are to pray? We surely need to pray, but why would he need to pray at all?

The most basic answer to this question is that Jesus is truly human. In his human nature he is fully "touched with the feeling of our infirmities" (Heb. 4:15). This is not just a mental transaction. Still less is it merely a warm sentiment. The reality is that Jesus bears our nature and our flesh, albeit without our sin. He therefore shares our humanity in every way except sin itself — and it is as a man that he turns to God in prayer.

Jesus prays for himself during his earthly ministry. In "the days of His flesh, when He had offered up prayers and supplications... though He was a Son, yet He learned obedience by the things which He suffered, and having been perfected, he became the author of salvation" (Heb. 5:7–8). When Jesus prays in the garden before his arrest, it is with the intensity of a man who is facing terrible trial and death as the bearer of others' sin and condemnation (Matt. 26:39). Jesus prays from the perspective of his humanity — a humanity that is accountable to God who judges righteously: "For He made Him who knew no sin to be sin for us, that we might become the righteousness of God in Him" (2 Cor. 5:21). In his humanity, Jesus cries to God for sustaining grace as he faces his death on the cross.

Jesus prays for his people during his heavenly ministry. "But He, because He continues forever, has an unchangeable priesthood. Therefore He is also able to save to the uttermost those who come to God through Him, since He always lives to make intercession for them" (Heb. 7:24–25). He is the heavenly intercessor for those who are his and will be his in the future and forever. He never ceases to be the "one mediator between God and man" (1 Tim. 2:5; cf. Heb. 8:6; 9:15; 12:24). Notice that our continuing experience of salvation ("to the uttermost") flows from Jesus's continuing intercession on our behalf. Our Lord never leaves us to our own devices. Our salvation, accomplished at the cross, is applied to us in our time through the continuing priestly mediation of our Intercessor in heaven.

Jesus bears us into the presence of God. When "he had by himself purged our sins," he "sat down on the right hand of the Majesty on high" (Heb. 1:3). "For Christ has not entered the holy places made with hands, which are copies of the true, but into heaven itself, now to appear in the presence of God for us" (Heb. 9:24). As believers we are united to Jesus in his death and his acceptable sacrifice. We are united to him in his entrance into the presence of God, because his acceptance as the Mediator is the acceptance of all for whom he died and rose as Mediator.

Furthermore, Jesus's once and final sacrifice "to bear the sins of many" carries the promise of his coming again, "a second time, apart from sin, for [our] salvation" (Heb. 9:28). When we pray faithfully, so Jesus intercedes for us along with us: "I have declared to them Your name, and will declare it, that the love with which You loved Me may be in them, and I in them" (John 17:26). And so we are assured that in prayer we too are borne into the presence of his Father, and ours, in heaven.

PRAISE FOR GOD'S INTERCESSION FOR US
PSALM 115:9–18

THINGS I WILL PRAY FOR TODAY

_____

_____

_____

_____

_____

_____

_____

_____

_____

December 15
To Whom Do You Pray?

Praying to the God of peace

Now may the God of peace who brought up our Lord Jesus from the dead, that great Shepherd of the sheep, through the blood of the everlasting covenant... —Heb. 13:20

READ HEBREWS 13:20–21

he closing prayer of Hebrews is one of the most glorious intercessory prayers in Scripture. No doubt this is why it is often used as a benediction at the end of a worship service. The writer has already asked that his readers pray for him (vv. 18–19), but now he shows them how to do this by praying for them! In this way, he leaves us all a beautiful model for our own prayers for others. Notice that he prays to "the God of peace." He knows the God he is addressing. There is a personal dimension to his relationship with God through Jesus Christ his Savior. He is inviting us to share in this relationship.

Who is this "God of peace," to whom we are to pray? The expression is found throughout the New Testament. He is with believers (Rom. 15:33; Phil. 4:9). He crushes Satan under our feet (Rom. 16:20). He sanctifies us (1 Thess. 5:23). He gives us peace "always in every way" (2 Thess. 3:16). He establishes peace and communicates this to those he saves. This is not the peace of brotherly love—peace between people. Neither is it "peace of mind," as people often think of internal tranquility of heart, mind, and conscience. It is, rather, the condition of peace between the believer and his God, on account of Jesus's atonement for sin. It pleased God "to reconcile all things to Himself, by Him, whether things on earth or things in heaven, having made peace through the blood of His cross" (Col. 1:20). This will in turn bear fruit in our Christian experience, because "the peace of God, which surpasses all understanding, will guard your hearts and minds through Christ Jesus" (Phil. 4:7).

What has God done to bring about this peace? He has raised Jesus from the dead and has made him to be "the great Shepherd of the sheep." We do not make peace with God by *our* believing in Jesus. God makes the peace through sending his Son to die for our sin and by raising him for our justification (Rom. 4:25). Jesus gave his life for his sheep. They hear his voice and follow him. He saves them so no one can pluck them from his hand (John 10:11–18, 27–30). He feeds his sheep forever (Isa. 40:11). The establishment of peace is the work of God in us, and we enter into it as we believe in Jesus Christ and are saved.

Why did God make this peace between himself and his people? It arose from his "everlasting covenant"—a "covenant of peace" made in eternity (Ezek. 37:26). In this, the Father and the Son covenanted that the Son would be the "lamb slain from the foundation of the world" (Rev. 13:8). Through his sufferings and death, he bears the penalty of sin and secures the believers' reconciliation with God. God seals his covenant in the "blood" of Jesus Christ.

This is the Father-God to whom the believer turns in prayer. This is the God he has come to know personally through faith in Christ and to fellowship with intimately in the person of his Son (John 14:9). "For it is the God who commanded light to shine out of darkness, who has shone in our hearts to give the light of the knowledge of the glory of God in the face of Jesus Christ" (2 Cor. 4:6). We know the God of peace. We know the Savior who is our peace (Eph. 2:14). Knowing his "peace in believing" in our hearts (Rom. 15:13), we pray for others with the large expectation that he will answer with rich blessings and bring them to rejoice in the Lord as we have come to do by his grace.

PRAISE TO THE LORD MY GOD
Sing Psalm 38:15–22

THINGS I WILL PRAY FOR TODAY

December 16
To Do His Will

A prayer for maturity

... make you complete in every good work to do His will, working in you what is well pleasing in His sight, through Jesus Christ... —Heb. 13:21

READ HEBREWS 13:20-21

We often console ourselves that "nobody is perfect." It ought not to be so, because, true as the proposition is, this is the easiest way to accept moral failure and spiritual defeat. For one thing, God wants us to be holy because he is holy. So we should never accept anything less as our goal in life. Certainly, God knows us inside out and "remembers we are dust" (Ps. 103:14). And there is forgiveness with him that he may be feared (Ps. 130:4). God is gracious to "forgive us our sins," but also to "cleanse us from all unrighteousness" (1 John 1:9). He means to make us "complete" and that means doing his wonderful will in every department of thinking and living. Not being perfect is neither an excuse for staying that way, nor a ground of forgiveness for habitual failings. It is a call to completeness.

The scope of this completeness does not leave much wiggle room. We know from Scripture that we will never be perfect in holiness on this side of eternity. All the same, that is what we are striving for in the Christian life. The text drives this home by holding out, not some fantasy of achieving the impossible, but the prospect of an ongoing work of God in our lives that applies victory to our faithfully following his paths:

> There is God's work *in us*. The prayer is "that He would make you complete." He and he alone can turn this impossibility into a reality. Do you believe Matthew 19:26—that "with God all things are possible"? We can pray for God to cure cancer, knowing we can't lift a finger to help. Why do we find it so forbidding to pray to overcome our own sins, when we can actually choose to throw our whole being, body, and soul into the fight with God's assurance of blessing?

> There is God's promise *for us*. We can, by his grace, be progressively completed "in every good work." It can be done,

even if it isn't going to happen in our strength alone. It is not impossible, therefore don't accept defeat—ever!

⪼ There is God's will to *direct us*. We are "to do His will." We are not left to grope in the dark. The way is mapped out in his Word and prompted by the Holy Spirit. And it isn't some onerous infliction upon us, but it can be a "delight," as the psalmist testified (Ps. 40:8). It is a matter of commitment: "I will delight myself in Your commandments, which I love" (Ps. 119:47).

⪼ There is God's pleasure to *warm us*. He assures us it is "pleasing in His sight." Godliness has his approval; he never fails to stir believing hearts in their exercising godliness in faith and life. There is a delight in doing his will. Only a legalist or a libertine will grudge doing what God wants us to do. We feel the Lord's pleasure when we delight in being faithful.

The means of this completeness is Jesus Christ. He is God's means to enable us. Completion in every good work happens "through Jesus Christ." As Paul says, "we are His workmanship, created in Christ Jesus for good works, which God prepared beforehand that we should walk in them" (Eph. 2:10). "Therefore, my beloved," writes Paul, "as you have always obeyed, not as in my presence only, but now much more in my absence, work out your own salvation with fear and trembling; for it is God who works in you both to will and to do for His good pleasure" (Phil. 2:12–13). Let us pray for one another, that our "every thought" will be brought into "captivity to the obedience of Christ" (2 Cor. 10:5). He assures us, "My grace is sufficient for you, for My strength is made perfect in weakness" (2 Cor. 12:9). He is full of grace, and he will have us holy.

PRAISE FOR A WORK OF GRACE IN MY HEART
Sing Psalm 4

THINGS I WILL PRAY FOR TODAY

December 17
Glory Forever and Ever

Praying to see Christ's glory

… through Jesus Christ, to whom be glory forever and ever. Amen.
—Heb. 13:21

READ HEBREWS 13:20–21

The conclusion of this great prayer is the ultimate goal of all true prayer. The words "through Jesus Christ" tell us that he is the "one Mediator between God and men" (1 Tim. 2:5). It is through him "who was delivered up because of our offenses, and was raised because of our justification" (Rom. 4:25), that believers are made "complete in every good work to do His will" (Heb. 13:21). Without God sending his Son to die on the cross and accepting his Son's sacrifice as the satisfaction of his justice against sinners, there could be no "good news" for this world of ours and no salvation for a single soul! And there would be no glory in heaven from the lips of grace-saved and blood-bought sinners. Hell would be filled with Satan and his demons, the fallen angels, together with Adam and his progeny—all lost forever in the endless consciousness of separation from all that is of God except his righteous wrath.

Scripture makes plain from the start that this prospect was never going to happen. The "seed" of the woman was to come and "bruise" the head of the serpent (Gen. 3:15). The rest of God's Word progressively unfolds this plan of redemption. This is clear in the prophetic announcements of the Messiah and the foreshadowing of his person and work in the ceremonies, sacrifices, and infrastructure of the Old Testament worship. It also comes out in Christ's manifestation of himself in divine miracles and his appearances as the Angel of the Lord. From Genesis to Revelation, Jesus is the Savior, through whom all the saved are saved and God is magnified in glory!

Because of Jesus, glory belongs to him forever and ever. That is why believers consciously pray through Jesus Christ. The words at the end of a prayer, "for Jesus's sake, Amen," are not a mere form. I confess Jesus as *my* Savior, personally and profoundly. One commentator has rightly said, "It is only because of Jesus that prayer can take place." Calling on "God" without consciously going to him "through Jesus" is not Christian prayer. Jesus *is* our prayer, because he is our Mediator (John 3:17; 20:21; 1 John 4:9). He alone is our Savior.

Our prayer is also for Christ's glory to be magnified both now and for all eternity. God's glory is complete and unsurpassable as to his essence. But as to his standing with the human race, his glory may indeed be enhanced. In saving sinners and making them complete, his reputation is magnified before the world and the angels. Our inconsistencies and failings cast a shadow on the Lord. We let him down. We can even give "great occasion for the enemies of the Lord to blaspheme" (2 Sam. 12:14).

When we live godly lives, do good deeds, and observably grow in grace, then the opposite is true. We actually create the conditions, as Peter puts it, for people to "glorify God in the day of visitation" (1 Peter 2:12). Instead of hardening the hearts of unbelievers, we put them in the way in which God may call them to himself in his time. This has a powerful implication for our prayers and our prayer meetings. As J. Philip Arthur has written: "We need to repent of the self-centredness of much of our praying and focus instead on crying to God to magnify the name of his Son. The Lord Christ is supremely worthy of it."

A PRAYER FOR GOD TO GLORIFY HIS NAME
Sing Psalm 79:9–13

THINGS I WILL PRAY FOR TODAY

December 18
Are You Suffering?

Prayer is for times of trouble

Is anyone among you suffering? Let him pray. —*James 5:13*

READ JAMES 5:13

O nly once did I hear my father swear. He hit his finger with a hammer while driving in a nail. Out came one of the mildest of oaths, for which he was instantly apologetic. On the other hand, I have known many people who would turn the air blue for any reason, or no reason at all. Sad to say, most people's common reaction to trouble or distress is to answer it with profanity or blasphemy, openly and without shame. Just watch television and listen to people. For millions, it is a way of life.

What is your reflex response to trouble? Many turn every way but to God in search of relief. Some curse and complain and object angrily that such things should ever happen to them. Others retreat into brooding silence. Still others escape into drunkenness, or crash-dive into depression and even suicide. Our troubles, small as well as great, have the potential to do us great damage. If we embrace them, they will fester like a cancer in the soul and eventually overwhelm us.

James teaches us that our first reaction to trouble ought to be to pray. Sufferings and difficulties ought to move us to call on God in prayer. "Would it not be better, if God places a heavy burden upon our back," asks Earl Kelly, "for us to pray for a strong back, rather than to curse the load?" "Yes," someone says, "I know all that, but when I'm troubled I get so upset I just can't pray. I start to pray, but in no time my mind wanders and my prayer is crowded out by frustration, sadness, and anger."

This is, of course, a self-fulfilling prophecy. You ensure your defeat whenever you excuse yourself from making a real fight of it. Every trouble can be "a messenger of Satan" (2 Cor. 12:7). Troubles pummel you and tempt you to turn away from God—which you will do if you will not turn to Him. When Paul was so buffeted, he "pleaded with the Lord three times" (2 Cor. 12:7). He tells us to pray without ceasing (1 Thess. 5:17). Satan doesn't want us to do this. He wants us to pity ourselves, not look

706

to Christ in faith and ask him for his help. Andrew Gray (1634–56) says, "Faith is the grace that goes up to the Captain of salvation and lays hold upon His strength; prayer is the grace that goes to Christ and says to Him, 'Pity me, pity me, lest I fall and become a prey.'"

If we find it hard to pray when we are hurting, then we need to cry out all the more persistently. We need to pray into the wee hours. We need to pray like the people of God in Psalm 107:6, 13, 19, and 28 who "cried out to the Lord in their trouble" until "he delivered them out of their distresses." Perhaps we are too used to prayers without passion and tears in the church, in the family, and in private. So much of the praying we hear and utter is little more than an exercise in sentence construction or the reading back of a prearranged list of "prayer requests." Distressed believers *cry* to the Lord in their troubles. A sense of urgency and real need will do that. To be sure, prayer is for happy things too, but notice that James sees prayer as responding to pain and praise as responding to pleasure: "Is anyone cheerful? Let him sing psalms" (v. 13b). When we are suffering, troubled, or even just concerned, our first resort must be to turn to the Savior who "always lives to make intercession" for us (Heb. 7:25). Jesus knows what we are going through. He is already interceding. So if we are troubled, let us pray.

A PRAYER OF THE SUFFERING CHRIST
Sing Psalm 22:11–19

THINGS I WILL PRAY FOR TODAY

_____

_____

_____

_____

_____

_____

_____

_____

_____

_____

_____

December 19
Sharing Your Burdens

The fellowship of prayer

Confess your trespasses to one another, and pray for one another, that you may be healed. —James 5:16a

READ JAMES 5:13–18

Praying for healing from whatever ails us is surely the most common form of prayer in the world. All but the most committed atheists, irrespective of their religion (or the lack of it), pray to somebody or something in the face of illness. The sick usually want to be cured. On top of that, there is nothing like the fear of death to convince people of their need of a power greater than their own proven helplessness. Modern medicine has not given us eternal life. This does not mean, however, that all such prayer is evidence of a living faith in the God and Father of our Lord Jesus Christ. Just hoping there is someone out there that can help is not the same as knowing Christ as one's own Savior and Lord. Desperate application to any old god, or even to the Bible's God and the Bible's Jesus—just hoping someone up there is listening, whoever he, she, or it may be—is not the same thing as believing prayer according to God's Word (see Heb. 11:6; Lev. 26:14–19).

James's linking of confession of sin with prayer and healing offers a timely corrective to abstract notions of "prayer" offered in the name of equally abstract notions of "God." He makes this connection in verses 14–15, where the sick person is enjoined to call for the elders of the church to "pray over him." The promise is that "the prayer of faith will heal the sick and the Lord will raise him up." This "prayer of faith" is not some special category of prayer that will guarantee healing. It is just faithful prayer that claims the general promise of God (cf. Mark 11:24), and trusts God for his sovereign disposition of the outcome. Our responsibility is fervent prayer that looks expectantly to God, without any assumption of instant and automatic healing. Prayer is not a magic spell. It is how the believer talks to God.

James casts the net even wider when he adds, "And if he has committed sins he will be forgiven." It is not that we are to conclude that we are ill because of some unforgiven sin. It is just that any prayer of "faith" cannot leave sin unconfessed, even if its specific focus is illness. How can we not desire comprehensive healing—spiritual as well as physical—when we seek the Lord's blessing? Therefore, let us make a time of bodily healing also the occasion of the healing of the soul.

James now extends confession into the fellowship of sharing: "Confess your trespasses to one another, and pray for one another, that you may be healed" (v. 16a). The focus is upon dealing with obstacles to fellowship and developing mutual support between the believers. Not least, there is the need to ensure that our prayers are not hindered by unrepented sin (Matt. 5:23–24). This reminds us that our prayers—even the most private—always have a bit of the plural in them. Why is this so? It is surely because we come to our Father-God through the mediation of the Son and in the motivating guidance of the Holy Spirit, and we do so as part of the church in the world.

This is why prayer in the church, prayer meeting, family, and small group should be in the third person plural, not the first person singular, as is fashionable today. We begin to pray, "We pray…" and not "I pray…," because we are not praying for ourselves but for all present listening to us. There is a fellowship in prayer in the simple and constant reality that it is about sharing both your burdens and the burdens of other in the body of Christ.

BLESS THE LORD WHO BLESSES YOU
Sing Psalm 103:1–5

THINGS I WILL PRAY FOR TODAY

December 20
Powerful Prayer

The prayers of serious godliness

The effectual fervent prayer of a righteous man avails much.
—James 5:16b

READ JAMES 5:13–18

Prayer is not whistling in the dark. Believing prayer, says James, "avails much." The New King James Version rendering is no better than a truism—of course "effectual" prayer will be effective! The English Standard Version Bible is both accurate and intelligible, if a little flatly expressed: "The prayer of a righteous person has great power *as it is working.*" The idea is that, when believing prayer is actively and energetically crying out to God, it is blessed with availing usefulness and power even in the act of praying.

The Psalms are replete with examples of this phenomenon. In Psalm 130, for example, the psalmist begins to pray "out of the depths" of a sense of sin and of helplessness, and ends with "hope in the Lord… mercy and…abundant redemption." His believing prayer becomes its own reward, as he prays with effectual fervor. This is not a merely subjective effect, after the fashion of modern secular assertions that if you feel better about yourself things will go well for you.

The reality in "effectual" prayer is that God actually and objectively rewards it in the inner life of the one who prays, as he prays! The two great characteristics of this prayer, then, are the godliness in the one who prays and the effectual nature of faithful prayer as it goes forth to the Lord. Elijah is a perfect example of what James is talking about. He "prayed earnestly"—literally, "prayed with prayer"—and the Lord answered with mighty demonstrations of his sovereign power (vv. 17–18). First he sent drought, then he sent rain (1 Kings 17:1; 18:1). Remarkable as this was, it was the ministry of "a man with a nature like ours." Elijah was no superhuman with magical powers at his fingertips. He was a normal human being like the rest of us. But he "prayed with prayer" and God heard him and answered. As Thomas Manton wrote:

Prayers rightly managed cannot want effect. This is the means which God has consecrated for receiving the highest blessings. Prayer is the key by which those mighty ones of God could lock heaven, and open it at their pleasure.... It is wonderful to consider what the Scripture ascribes to faith and prayer: prayer sues out blessings in the court of grace, and faith receives them....Well, then, pray with this encouragement, God has said in an open place, that is solemnly avowed before the world, that none shall seek his face in vain (Isaiah 45:19). In that verse, the Lord says, "I have not spoken in secret, in a dark place of the earth; I did not say to the seed of Jacob, 'Seek Me in vain'; I, the LORD, speak righteousness, I declare things that are right."

James begins with the place of prayer and confession in the life of the fellowship of God's people, and ends with a ringing affirmation of the power of true prayer. The Lord who could open and shut the heavens for Elijah has promised to do great things for us today when we pray in the way James lays it out in Hebrews 4:14–16:

Seeing then that we have a great High Priest who has passed through the heavens, Jesus the Son of God, let us hold fast our confession. For we do not have a High Priest who cannot sympathize with our weaknesses, but was in all points tempted as we are, yet without sin. Let us therefore come boldly to the throne of grace, that we may obtain mercy and find grace to help in time of need.

In this way, we will surely "come to the unity of the faith and of the knowledge of the Son of God, to a perfect man, to the measure of the stature of the fullness of Christ" (Eph. 4:13).

PRAISE FOR GOD'S BLESSING WHILE PRAYING
Sing Psalm 3:1–4

THINGS I WILL PRAY FOR TODAY

_____

_____

_____

_____

711

December 21
Reserved in Heaven for You

Thanksgiving for an inheritance

...an inheritance incorruptible and undefiled and that does not fade away... — 1 Peter 1:4

READ 1 PETER 1:3–5

ust to say in faith, "Blessed be the God and Father of our Lord Jesus," is an act of coming before the Lord in the attitude of prayer. Even though Peter is writing a letter to instruct the Christians in Asia Minor, these particular verses (3–5) are a prayer to God set within his teaching for them. This reminds us that any invocation of the name of God is to call upon him and enter into his presence. This is even true of the casual curses of the street and the outright blasphemies of defiant unbelief. God hears these as surely as he hears the faithful prayers of his dear saints. He takes them all very seriously. He loves to hear his people bless him, but he is not deaf to the abuse that is showered on him daily in our world, and, short of repentance and faith, there will be a reckoning some day soon for all who take his name in vain (Ex. 20:7).

Why does the apostle bless God with such obvious passion? The answer is found in what the Lord does in saving sinners. Peter gives a thumbnail sketch of the doctrine of our salvation, not as a set of formal theological truths, but as a prayer of gratitude and rejoicing for what God does in his free grace for those who come to Christ in faith. He answers three crucial questions about the believer's life and destiny:

> How do people come to be saved by Jesus Christ? He has "begotten us again" by his free, unmerited grace (v. 3a). The image of birth is apt, for not only is it emblematic of passing from death to life, but also of the transformation from being "children of wrath" to "children of light" (Eph. 2:3; 5:8). Becoming a believer means first being born again, or regenerated by a sovereign work of the Holy Spirit (John 3:3). We don't bear ourselves again spiritually, any more than we bear ourselves physically. It is God's gracious initiative. Then we believe in Christ and are saved.

712

> ◇ What is this doing for our lives right now? We have a "living hope" through Jesus's resurrection from the dead (v. 3b). Christ was delivered for our offenses and was raised again for our justification (Rom. 4:25). He is the way, the truth, and *the life* (John 14:6). Living hope is resurrection hope—in the risen Savior, Jesus.

> ◇ Where are we going now and forever? "An inheritance incorruptible…reserved in heaven…ready to be revealed in the last time" (vv. 4–5). Believers are "kept by the power of God" all the way to heaven (John 10:28; Rom. 8:35). "Death," says Robert Leighton (1611–84), "which cuts the sinews of all other hopes, and turns men out of all other inheritances, alone fulfills this hope and ends it in fruition; as a messenger sent to bring the children of God home to the possession of their inheritance."

Christian thankfulness, like Christian prayer, too often dwells on temporal mercies. Prayer requests tend to be dominated by urgent needs, and so are largely focused on immediate health and welfare issues, physical, spiritual, and political. Peter here teaches us to reach deeper and higher, and from here to eternity. We have an inheritance, which is coextensive with Christ's kingdom—"of His kingdom there will be no end" (Luke 1:33). Second Corinthians 5:1 says, "For we know that if our earthly house, this tent, is destroyed, we have a building from God, a house not made with hands, eternal in the heavens."

PRAISE TO THE LORD FOR OUR INHERITANCE
Sing Psalm 33:12–19

THINGS I WILL PRAY FOR TODAY

713

December 22
Seriously Watchful

A plea for solid prayer

...be serious and watchful in your prayers. — 1 Peter 4:7

READ 1 PETER 4:7-11

This is not a prayer, but a plea for weightiness in prayer. Peter knew very well that prayer, like every good thing, can easily become shallow and trivial and so be reduced to a parody of what God designs it to be. It can end up as an empty form of words: more prattle than petition, more chatter than communion with God. Prayer can easily become an offense to God and an illusion of communion with God. There is a right way to approach the Lord and many wrong ways. Peter therefore wants us to come *carefully*, as well as boldly, to the throne of grace (Heb. 4:16). He assumes that we Christians will pray. His concern is that we pray effectively and in a way that blesses both God and man.

It is vitally important that we be intentional in our practice of prayer. "Serious" translates the Greek *sophronein*, which means "to keep a cool head"—to be clear-minded as opposed to overly excitable or manic. Paul counsels, "I say to every man among you not to think of himself more highly than he ought to think; but to think so as to have *sound judgment*, as God has allotted to each a measure of faith" (Rom. 12:3, NASB). He also instructs Titus to "urge the younger men to be *self-controlled*" (Titus 2:6, ESV). Peter is saying we need to be possessed of a quiet spirit and good judgment by being spiritually discerning.

The charge to be "watchful" in prayer carries this idea still further into our heart and manner of life. "Watchful" translates the Greek *nephein*. This is often rendered "sober," because it has its roots in the sin of drunkenness. In the New Testament, while it can include application to this specific failing, the primary focus is a broad application to the whole of life, body, and soul. Just as the drunk is oblivious to reality and hardly knows what he is doing, so the Christian whose prayer is not "sober" is out of touch with the seriousness of our Father in heaven. Biblical sobriety is a lifestyle. It extends beyond the physical state of the mind to the spiritual

714

and moral state of the heart, and its attendant outworking in living a life that honors God. Peter earlier says, "Gird up the loins of your mind," to the end that you "be sober," *nepho* (1 Peter 1:13). It is about that inward spiritual quality, a sober "heart" remodeled by the Holy Spirit, that issues in a life of practical discipleship to Jesus Christ. About four centuries ago, Robert Leighton observed that "the heart of the real Christian is really taken off from the world, and set heavenwards." Nevertheless, he added, "There is still in this flesh so much of the flesh hanging to it, as will readily poise all downwards, unless it be often wound up and put in remembrance of those things that will raise it still to further spirituality."

It is a natural extension of a serious and watchful practice of prayer to cultivate all the deepest graces of the believing heart and life. Hence Peter goes on to urge us to exercise "fervent love for one another," to be "hospitable...without grumbling," and to share God's gifts in ministry to others that "God may be glorified through Jesus Christ" (vv. 8–11). Serious prayer is essential to successful living for Christ. If God is not glorified in the secret place of prayer, you will not glorify him in the public places of your life and witness. Therefore, Christian, "continue earnestly in prayer, being vigilant in it with thanksgiving" (Col. 4:2).

A SERIOUS PRAYER FROM THE PSALMS
Sing Psalm 6:6–9

THINGS I WILL PRAY FOR TODAY

December 23
Established in Christ Jesus

Prayer for a steady faith

But may the God of all grace, who called us to His eternal glory by Christ Jesus, after you have suffered a while, perfect, establish, strengthen and settle you... —1 Peter 5:10–11

READ 1 PETER 5:5–11

Jesus was not born into this world to provide slogans and stage-props for the annual social and commercial extravaganza we now know as "Christmas." He came to save his people from their sins (Matt. 1:21). He came to be delivered for our offenses and raised for our justification (Rom. 4:25). The glory of his advent is ultimately the cross, because it is in his death that he accomplished the redemption that was implicit in his birth. An incarnation that reaches no further than warm thoughts about the baby Jesus and hearty renderings of "Joy to the World" simply misses the point; it only serves to bury the gospel under the superficial glitter of the modern Christmas season.

Life is a serious business. Peter exhorts younger people to humble themselves "under the mighty hand of God" (vv. 5–9). The pride and self-confidence of youth remain to be challenged by the realities of middle life. There are avenues that offer a faster track to maturity. We should cast our cares on the Lord, be "clothed with humility," and follow the counsel of our elders. If we remember that "our adversary the devil" is a real threat to our well-being, then we can actively "resist him, steadfast in the faith" and be blessed in knowing that we share in the "same sufferings" experienced by our Christian brothers and sisters across the world.

Life needs a godly stability. Perhaps you have noticed, however, that Peter does not pray that Christians will try harder, be more thoughtful, or become more sensitive. He doesn't pray that we will read our Bibles and pray more regularly. He has already exhorted us as to our duty throughout the whole of 1 Peter to this point. His prayer is rather for a work of God in our lives.

Peter first calls upon God and reminds his readers *who* God is. He

716

is "the God of all grace," and is so called because he has "called us to his eternal glory by Christ Jesus." This establishes God's intention to do good to his people now, and bring them to heaven later.

Peter also offers specific requests that we will be blessed with a steady and established faith in the Lord—even though we may experience sufferings in the short term ("a while"). Four terms are used describe this deepening assurance:

> "Perfect" is the Greek *katartizei* from which comes the English "artisan." The idea is that of a reworking so as to equip and outfit us for our life and witness for the Lord.

> "Establish" is the Greek *sterizei*, which emphasizes a firming of belief and resolve—being "steadfast in the faith," as in verse 9.

> "Strengthen" translates from a word found nowhere else in Scripture, but with its antecedent in classical Greek. The idea here is of a strength that is willing to stand alone and never waver.

> "Settle" renders *themeliosei,* which means "will found," as in laying a solid footing for a building.

Is this not exactly what we desire for ourselves and for others when we bring our requests to God's throne of grace (Heb. 4:16)? Surely every prayer, however specifically focused, carries the general desire for the people for whom we intercede to be established in the faith? Steadfastness in the faith is the general spiritual condition for all seasons and types of testing. Let us pray and work to be solid and sober in the secret place of prayer.

PRAISE THE LORD OUR ROCK
Sing Psalm 144:1–2

THINGS I WILL PRAY FOR TODAY

_____

_____

_____

_____

_____

December 24
Glory to God Our Savior

A prayer for God's eternal glory

To God our Savior, who alone is wise, be glory and majesty, dominion and power, both now and forever, Amen. —Jude 25

READ JUDE

Jude's letter is about the basic mission of every Christian to "contend earnestly for the faith once delivered to the saints" (v. 3). How is this to be achieved? Most of the letter warns us to look out for false teachers inside the church (vv. 5–19). Jude then has us look in and apply to ourselves no fewer than seven basic components of a solid life of faith (vv. 20–23). We are, says Jude, always to be building, praying, keeping, looking, caring, saving, and hating in our daily living of the Christian life:

> **Building** is about adding to, and not declining from, personal holiness (2 Peter 1:5; 3:18).

> **Praying** is about constant and quality communion with God in the fellowship of the indwelling Holy Spirit (1 Thess. 5:17; Phil. 4:4, 7).

> **Keeping** is about loving the Lord and being loved by God, surely by devoting ourselves to him with all our heart, soul, and strength (Deut. 6:4–5).

> **Looking** is about actively anticipating the mercy of God and eternal life in Christ—that is, claiming the promises of our covenant God (Titus 2:13).

> **Caring** is about compassion that discerns needs in others—"making a distinction"—and reaches out in practical ways (Matt. 25:36; James 2:15–17).

> **Saving** "with fear, pulling them out of the fire" is about caring enough about certain people in trouble to intervene in their lives, facing all the risks that can be involved (Acts 13:46–47).

> **Hating** "even the garment defiled by the flesh" means simply hating sin in all its forms (Ps. 97:10; 101:3; 119:104; 139:21).

718

Not surprisingly, this takes Jude to prayer (vv. 24–25). His purpose is that Christians would "not walk after the flesh, but after the Spirit" (Rom. 8:1, 4; Gal. 5:16), and his seven-part challenge surely proves we will never meet it in our own strength. In a prayer that is also a benediction, he does two things:

> First of all, he asks for *God's enabling power*. God is "able." What do all of us need most? Surely, on the one hand, to be kept from "stumbling" in this life, and, on the other hand, to enter the presence of God's glory "faultless" and full of "joy" (v. 25a)? The seventeenth century Scottish preacher Alexander Peden, in his old age, put it this way to twenty-three-year-old James Renwick: "Go on, in single dependence upon the Lord, and you will win honestly through and get cleanly off the stage." Two years later, Renwick perished on the scaffold, the last of the Covenanter martyrs of Scotland.

> Second, Jude asks for *God's eternal glory* to be revealed in all the fullness of his wisdom and saving grace. If God glorifies himself in these, then his believing people will also come to glory through his Son who died for them on that awful cross. To pray for his glory is to pray for his enabling grace and, with his answer, to receive the assurance that we will be kept from stumbling and brought holy so as to glory in his presence. In the modern Christian obsession with prayer requests—that too often are concerned with our comfort—we too easily forget that the highest prayer of all is for God to glorify his own name. We forget that his glory is the guarantee of our own. His glory is in fact our highest goal. It ought therefore to be our greatest joy and the very center of our every prayer.

PRAISE GOD OUR SAVIOR
Sing Psalm 18:16, 17, 19

THINGS I WILL PRAY FOR TODAY

_____

_____

_____

_____

_____

December 25
Bowls Full of Incense

The prayers of the saints

Now when He had taken the scroll, the four living creatures and the twenty-four elders fell down before the Lamb, each having a harp, and golden bowls full of incense, which are the prayers of the saints. —Rev. 5:8

READ REVELATION 5:1–10

The prayers in this passage are not recorded in words, but represented by the image of incense rising from a censer, as in the temple worship of the Old Testament. The passage draws a picture of the church's praise in heaven at the time of the second advent of Christ. The vision of the four living creatures and the twenty-four elders falling down before the Lord Jesus Christ celebrates the fact that the redeemed creation and the completed company of God's elect will praise the Lord in glorious harmony. The redeemed of the Lord have both harps and censers. The former is symbolic of praise and the latter of prayer.

The use of incense was commanded in God's word to Israel. God told Aaron, "I make an altar to burn incense on; you shall make it of acacia wood" (Ex. 30:1). God's people understood this was connected to prayer. When John's birth was announced at Herod's temple, 1,500 years later, "the whole multitude of the people was praying outside at the hour of incense" (Luke 1:10). David understands this when he asks God, "Let my prayer be set before You as incense" (Ps. 141:2). Incense was fragrant and costly in those days. The priest dispensed it from a "golden bowl," which was emblematic of the heart that turns to God. God promises his people, when they were exiles in Babylon, "I will accept you as a sweet aroma when I bring you out from the peoples and gather you out of the countries where you have been scattered; and I will be hallowed in you before the Gentiles" (Ezek. 20:41). The prayers of the godly are "a sweet aroma," because the Lord is "hallowed" in their hearts. Paul takes that up in 2 Corinthians 2:15–16: "For we are unto God a sweet savour of Christ, in them that are saved, and in them that perish: To the one we are the savour of death unto death; and to the other the savour of life unto life" (KJV). When your life is "hid with God in Christ," even—perhaps especially—your most difficult prayers will be sweet to the Lord.

The incense of believing prayer can be costly to us. It is sometimes very hard to pray. Sorrow makes it a painful exercise. So does a deep sense of need, or helplessness, or sinful shortcomings. But the true cost has already fallen upon Christ who, in his death upon the cross, first "loved us and gave himself up for us, a fragrant offering and sacrifice to God" (Eph. 5:2). In Revelation 8:3, an "angel, having a golden censer, came and stood at the altar. He was given much incense, that he should offer it with the prayers of all the saints upon the golden altar which was before the throne." Surely this is Christ mediating for his people. Why was he born to Mary? Why did he pay the penalty of sin? It was to win the costly incense of hearts saved by grace through his shed blood. His "incense" is that intercessory prayer that accompanies the prayers of "all the saints" right now.

As we pray, Christ's fragrance will suffuse our prayer and carry it to heaven. Octavius Winslow once said,

> Prayer will soothe you, prayer will calm you, prayer will unburden your heart, prayer will remove or mitigate your pain, prayer will heal your sickness, or make your sickness pleasant to bear, prayer will expel the temper, prayer will bring Jesus sensibly near to your soul, prayer will lift your heart to heaven, and will bring heaven down into your heart.

May he so bless you today.

PRAYER THAT OUR PRAYERS MAY RISE TO GOD
Sing Psalm 141:1–2

THINGS I WILL PRAY FOR TODAY

_____

_____

_____

_____

_____

_____

_____

December 26
A New Song

A prayer of praise for salvation

And they sang a new song... — Rev. 5:9

READ REVELATION 5:9–10

This "new song" is a prayer meant to be as "new every morning" as the Lord's "compassions" that "fail not" (Lam. 3:22–23). This song is always new and can never grow old. Why? Because its newness does not lie in any novelty it might have on our first acquaintance with it, but in its eternal freshness as praise to the Lord for our personal salvation by his sovereign grace. If all it is to you is "the same old message"—as so many justify their lack of interest in many parts of God's Word—then it is to be wondered if you know the Lord of whom and to whom it offers prayerful praise. The exercise of saving faith never ages, it only matures, for, as the psalmist says, "They still bear fruit in old age; they are ever full of sap and green" (Ps. 92:14, ESV). The aged believer is never tired of Christ, however much the weariness of the flesh hangs heavy around his soul.

This is the praise of the church triumphant in which the saints look back to the death of Christ from the vantage of his glorious coming as the risen Savior at the end of the age. If this is the new song, what was the old one? The old song is the one where the thrice-holy Creator God is praised in heaven (Rev. 4:8, 11). John then looks for someone to open the scroll with the seven seals—signifying the completion of redemption—and, seeing "no one worthy to open and read the scroll," he began to weep profusely (5:4). Then one of the elders tells him to stop weeping. There is such a worthy man to do that task. He is "the Lion of the tribe of Judah, the Root of David," who is none other than Jesus, "the Lamb of God who takes away the sin of the world" (John 1:29). This is the basis of the "new song"—salvation for sinners and a new creation! For "if anyone is in Christ, he is a new creation; old things have passed away, behold, all things have become new" (2 Cor. 5:17).

Why is Jesus worthy to take the scroll? This prayer-song essentially celebrates the gospel. Jesus was "slain" and redeemed a people to God by his "blood" out of every "tribe and tongue and people and nation" (v. 9). Christians are a blood-bought people. He died, "the just for the unjust, that he might bring us to God" (1 Peter 3:18). This is the grateful acknowledgment of his work as the "one Mediator between God and men" (1 Tim. 2:5). Christ himself is the first and preeminent cause of our thanksgiving, because he is our life. The saints dwell upon their Savior and the glory of his saving grace.

A second cause of thanksgiving wells up in the believers' hearts. It is that the power of the gospel applied to believers makes us "kings and priests" to God, so that "we shall reign on the earth" (v. 10). Peter writes, "You are a chosen generation, a royal priesthood, a holy nation, His own special people, that you may proclaim the praises of Him who called you out of darkness into His marvelous light" (1 Peter 2:9). Whatever the world may think, however powerless you may feel in a hostile world, this is what you are, Christian, in the sight of God. This is your story, this is your (new) song, in your Savior, Jesus Christ. And this new song is your witness now, as you wait for that great day when Jesus comes in which you will certainly reign with him in the new heavens and the new earth (Rev. 20:6).

How is this a prayer most suitable for us today? Simply put, it is our salvation even now and our destiny hereafter. Our salvation in Christ is also our praise to Christ, and our prayer to our Father in heaven through Christ. Psalm 40:3 says, "He has put a new song in my mouth—praise to our God; many will see it and fear, and will trust in the LORD."

AN OLD SONG THAT IS ALWAYS NEW
Sing Psalm 96

THINGS I WILL PRAY FOR TODAY

December 27
Wait a Little Longer

The prayer of the martyrs

How long, O Lord, holy and true, until You judge and avenge our blood on those who dwell on the earth?—Rev. 6:10

READ REVELATION 6:9–11

he breaking of the seven seals unfolds pictures of the coming of God's judgments upon this world. They are not in chronological order, and do not represent periods of history or specific judgments. They are like the breakers of an angry sea marching up the beach toward a mighty high tide that will sweep away all the filth and flotsam, and then recede to leave a sparkling and pristine shore that will never be sullied or polluted in any way for all eternity. They are windows on the contemporary experience of the church in the world as the Lord marches through history to the consummation of his kingdom.

These visions encourage us to be steadfast in the faith. The fifth seal is especially poignant. Here are the martyrs of past generations—who suffered and died because of their witness for Christ and the gospel—crying out to God for the end of martyrdom and the just punishment of the persecutors of the church. This is, of course, a vision and not a video. We are not hearing the literal prayer of the martyrs in heaven awaiting the great day, but rather the figurative appeal of murdered blood crying from the ground, like the blood of the very first martyr, Abel (Gen. 4:10; Matt. 23:35; Heb. 11:4). The martyrs are to "rest a while longer, until both the number of their fellow servants and their brethren, who would be killed as they were, were completed" (Rev. 6:10).

There will be martyrs as long as there is hatred for God in the world. Jesus has said it: "In the world you will have tribulation" (John 16:33). He does not promise us a rose garden. Discipleship costs. Lives are lost. But victory is at hand:

> *Martyrs are a witness to the power of the gospel.* "The oftener we are mowed down," writes Tertullian to the persecuting Roman Empire, "the thicker do we spring up again. The blood of the Christians is the seed of the church....Therefore we give

thanks for your sentence, knowing that the judgments of men do not agree with those of God; for when we are condemned by you, we are absolved by Him."

❧ *Martyrs follow Jesus in the fellowship of his sufferings and count it all grace.* Samuel Rutherford, exiled though never put to death, wrote to James Guthrie, who was martyred in Edinburgh on June 1, 1661. "As for me," he wrote, "when I think of God's dispensations, he might justly have brought to the Market Cross and to the light my unseen and secret abominations, which would have been no small reproach to the holy name and precious truths of Christ. But in mercy he hath covered all these and shapen and carved out more honorable causes of suffering of which we are unworthy."

❧ *Martyrs are blessed with the hope of heaven.* On the eve of his martyr's death in AD 107, Ignatius of Antioch testified, "Now I begin to be a disciple, desiring nothing of things seen or unseen, that so I may gain Christ. Let fire, cross, droves of ravenous beasts, wounds and convulsions come upon me, so only that I may enjoy Jesus Christ." Stephen, the first New Testament martyr, was given to see "heaven opened" before he passed into the presence of God. That same heaven is opened for every believer, and Christ will surely bring us home.

Even as we pray for an end to persecution in our world, let us wait with patience, remembering that God's plan of salvation will be accomplished in his good time. There will be justice in the earth in finality and fullness in that great day when Christ returns (1 Thess. 4:16). *Ora et labora*! Pray and work!

PRAISE THE LORD WHO SAVES!
Sing Psalm 17:6–7

THINGS I WILL PRAY FOR TODAY

_____

_____

_____

_____

_____

December 28
The Amen Chorus

The prayer of the angelic host

Amen! Blessing and glory and wisdom, thanksgiving and honor and power and might, be to our God forever and ever, Amen!—*Rev. 7:12*

READ REVELATION 7:9–12

"Amen" is the best known Hebrew word in the English language. Handel's oratorio *Messiah* closes majestically with the famous "Amen Chorus." When people say it, you know they approve. "Amen" means, in effect, "May it be," or even, "Make it so!" Accordingly, a prayer beginning and ending in "amen" is bound to be especially enthusiastic. So it is with the prayer of the angels as they fall on their faces before the throne of God and praise him for the "sealing" of the "one hundred and forty-four thousand of all the tribes of the children of Israel" (Rev. 7:4).

They have good reason to be enthusiastic. The context is the Lord's setting his seal on his people in connection with the last judgment. In Revelation 6, a series of visions record the breaking open of six seals, each of which sets out something of the impact of God's wrath upon this world of sinners and their sin. In Revelation 7, the scene changes and we are given a vision that seems to be a flashback to a moment before the opening of these seals. An angel calls out to the avenging angels not to "harm the earth, the sea, or the trees till we have sealed the servants of our God on their foreheads" (7:3). First God's elect are sealed; then God's judgments are unsealed. When the last sinner has been saved, the judgment of the reprobate lost begins!

The completed assembly of the redeemed is represented both by specific symbolic numbers and also by an innumerable multitude. These are one and the same body, namely the body of Christ in its fullness on the day of judgment. John first hears the number 144,000, which comprises 12,000 from each tribe of Israel (7:4–8). Then he sees "a great multitude which no one could number." These were from "all nations, tribes, peoples, and tongues, standing before the throne and before the Lamb, clothed with white robes, with palm branches in their hands, and crying out with

726

a loud voice, saying, 'Salvation belongs to our God who sits on the throne, and to the Lamb'" (vv. 9–10). But why does he *hear* the number and *see* the innumerable? Surely it is because he *heard* God's perspective and *saw* man's perspective. Both "Israel" and the number 144,000 are symbolic rather than literal. "Israel" here is spiritual Israel, which is the church, the "Israel of God" (Gal. 6:16). This comprises 12×12 (for the Old and the New Testament churches—the twenty-four elders), multiplied by 10×10×10 representing completeness, to give 144,000 as the symbolic number of the elect of God. The number 12 also has significance, for it is 3×4, where 3 is the triune God and 4 is the creation he has made—"the four living creatures" of Ezekiel 1:5. What is envisioned, as if it had already happened, is the finished work of salvation on the very threshold of heaven at the end of history as we now know it.

The angels' prayer centers entirely on the glory of God in his work of creation and redemption. There are no prayer requests, no cries for mercy, and no pleadings for forgiveness of sin or for increase in faith, love, and godliness. There is no intercession for the conversion of the lost. There is one swelling call for God to be glorified in all the "blessing and glory and wisdom, thanksgiving and honor and power and might" that is due to him "forever and ever." The viewpoint of the prayer is the accomplishment of the work of redemption in its finality and fullness: Christ is the glory of the saints. This too can even now be our perspective in prayer every day as we await this great day when Christ comes and gathers all his people to himself into the glory yet to be revealed (1 Peter 5:1). To this coming consummation we may say, "Amen" and "Amen."

PRAISE FOR THE KING OF GLORY
Sing Psalm 24:7–10

THINGS I WILL PRAY FOR TODAY

_____

_____

_____

_____

_____

_____

December 29
Giving Thanks for Judgment Day

The prayer of the twenty-four elders

Your wrath has come and the time of the dead, that they should be judged... —Rev. 11:18

READ REVELATION 11:15–19

The very idea of a "day of judgment" sends shivers down the spine. Like the day of death—which is everybody's preliminary day of judgment—it tends to be pushed to the back of the mind. People don't want to be judged by anybody, far less by God. Many just stick their heads in the proverbial sand and try not to think about it! Scripture never indulges such a lack of realism. God means to alert us to the judgment to come. The Bible is full of such warnings. The book of Revelation is virtually a reprise of the Old Testament prophecies about "the Day of the Lord" (e.g., Isa. 2:12; Ezek. 30:3; Zech. 14:1; Amos 5:18; Mal. 4:5). The apocalyptic visions of Revelation lead us to the final day of world history. But they have a crucial "update" on the Old Testament prophecies, and his name is Jesus, who comes in that day to be the Judge of the living and the dead (Acts 10:42). Who could possibly welcome such a day?

The seventh trumpet heralds "the great and terrible day of the Lord." Loud voices in heaven declare, "The kingdoms of this world have become the kingdoms of our Lord and of His Christ, and He shall reign forever and ever" (Rev. 11:15; Joel 2:31). The day has dawned! The last soul for whom Christ died has come to salvation through faith in him! Every promise and purpose of God for this world has been accomplished. This is 1 Corinthians 15:24–26 fulfilled: "Then comes the end, when He [Jesus] delivers the kingdom to God the Father, when He puts an end to all rule and all authority and power. For He must reign until He has put all enemies under His feet. The last enemy that will be destroyed is death."

The twenty-four elders represent the whole glorified church in heaven—the twelve Old Testament tribes plus the twelve New Testament apostles. No wonder the church prays with exalted praise, giving thanks for the final victory that has now been revealed before their eyes. "Every eye shall see Him" is suddenly a reality (Rev. 1:7)! Their prayer is comprised of three parts:

> > The church thanks the Lord for *who he is*: "The One who is and who was and who is to come." He has "taken His great power and reigned" (v. 17). He has revealed himself in his absolute sovereignty. All prayer needs to begin with the glorious attributes of the God of all grace.

> > The church thanks the Lord for *the just judgment of the "angry" nations and the "dead" (v. 18)*. Since His "wrath" is in view, this must refer to the last judgment upon the world of unbelief and, of course, all of its institutionalized opposition to Christ. "The wicked shall be turned into hell," says Psalm 9:17, "and all the nations that forget God."

> > The church prays for the Lord to *reward his "servants the prophets"* and his *"saints,"* even while he would "destroy those who destroy the earth" (v. 18). The point is a double one. Both the elect (see Rev. 6:9) and the earth (see Rom. 8:19) have hitherto suffered persecution and depredation because of human wickedness. Now their redemption is to be consummated in perfection.

The day of the Lord is the most welcome day in the future for all who hope in Christ. It is not a fearful prospect for the Lord's people. And the prayer of the twenty-four elders provides us with an outline for our own prayers. What do we pray for day by day? Surely we bless the Lord who saves us, ask for his hand to restrain and overthrow evil, and seek his good blessings for our lives as we wait for that great day when Jesus comes at the end of history.

PRAISE FOR THE LORD WHO IS COMING!
Sing Psalm 50:4–5

THINGS I WILL PRAY FOR TODAY

_____

_____

_____

_____

December 30
The Four Alleluias

The prayers of the glorified saints

…give Him glory, for the marriage of the Lamb has come…
—Rev. 19:7

READ REVELATION 19:1–10

The praise of the glorified saints in heaven must also be pure prayer. This is because it is praise for fully answered prayer, unsullied by the mixed motives, uncertainties, and doubts that are inherent in the best petitions in this world. In heaven, the redeemed no longer pray for things they cannot see, or for hopes that have not been realized, or for promises still beyond their reach. They pray for the glory of God, out of a salvation that is not only fully accomplished but also perfectly applied. All their prayers are praise and all their praise is prayer. The use of the word "Alleluia" is a window on this glorious prospect.

"Alleluia" means "Praise the Lord!"—in an exultant tone. It is the transliteration of the Hebrew word that combines *"hallel"* (praise) with *"Jah"* (God). It is generally held to be the most joyous word for praise in the English language. Not surprisingly, it is used in psalms that became associated with the temple worship. Some of these begin and/or end with "Alleluia" (Psalms 106; 111; 113; 117; 135; 146–150). Psalm 150 ends God's praise-book with an "Alleluia" in every verse! Psalms 113–118 are called the "Hallel," because they were sung at the great Feasts of Tabernacles and Weeks, and the Passover, and at the "New Moons" every first of the month (Col. 2:16). This connects to the New Testament most pointedly in Hebrews 8, where the earthly temple is seen as a model of the heavenly "true tabernacle" (Heb. 8:2). The pattern of temple worship anticipates to the perfect worship of the "great multitude in heaven," a mighty chorus that four times sends out swelling waves of praise around the throne of God (Rev. 19:1, 3, 4, 6).

The four "Alleluias" are prayers in praise that focus upon the complete victory of God as the Redeemer of his people and his creation.

⮞ *The first Alleluia* declares "Salvation and glory and honor and power belong to the Lord our God!" (v. 1). He is, in himself and in his works, worthy to be praised.

> *The second Alleluia* celebrates the utter destruction of the evil and the avenging of the martyrs slaughtered by "the great harlot," whose "smoke rises up forever" (vv. 2–3). He has gained the victory over sin and death.

> *The third Alleluia* comes from the "twenty-four elders and the four living creatures," representing the church and the creation (v. 4). He has given life to his redeemed people and his renovated world.

> *The fourth Alleluia* is the climactic response of all the servants of God, human and angelic, to the command "from the throne" to praise God: "Alleluia! For the Lord God Omnipotent reigns!" (v. 6). He is the Sovereign God over all.

This is followed by the announcement of "the marriage supper of the Lamb" (vv. 7–10) and the glorious revelation of Christ as "King of kings and Lord of lords" as he casts Satan into the lake of fire (Rev. 19:11–21). The point for us—as we still await this victory and consummation—is that, what the glorified saints in heaven give praise for in its fulfillment, is that which the church on earth prays for in its promises! Things to come are unfolded so as to give us a road map to our destiny. Heaven is opened to show us that for which we pray. Even as we march toward eternity, we who belong to Jesus live out of eternity into time. Therefore, as the angel told John, "Worship God! For the testimony of Jesus is the spirit of prophecy" (v. 10).

ALLELUIA!

JUST PRAISE THE LORD!
Sing Psalm 150

THINGS I WILL PRAY FOR TODAY

_____

_____

_____

_____

_____

December 31
Come, Lord Jesus!

The last prayers in the Bible

Even so, come, Lord Jesus.—Rev. 22:20

READ REVELATION 22:6–20

he last promise of Jesus to the church is "I am coming quickly" (vv. 7, 12, 20). It was, however, not all that long after Jesus ascended to glory that the critics of the gospel were suggesting that "quickly" was going to be "never"—that, in fact, the whole thing was a hoax. Peter warns the first-generation Christians that "scoffers will come in the last days, walking after their own lusts, and saying, 'Where is the promise of His coming? For since the fathers fell asleep, all things continue as they were from the beginning of creation'" (2 Peter 3:3–4). Two thousand years after Peter's day, even those who most sincerely look for the Lord's return might be forgiven for wondering how quick "quickly" is supposed to be! The apostle goes on, however, to remind us that "with the Lord, one day is as a thousand years, and a thousand years as one day." He goes on to assure us that "the Lord is not slack concerning His promise, as some count slackness, but is longsuffering toward us, not willing that any should perish but that all should come to repentance" (2 Peter 3:8–9). Jesus has a plan, from before the foundation of the world (Eph. 1:4), to save people from every generation in human history. That accomplished, he will come again—"quickly" enough to save his elect, so that not one is lost of all that the Father gives him (John 6:37)!

The last prayer in Scripture responds affirmatively to Jesus's promise, calling upon him to "come." It is offered twice: first by "the Spirit and the bride" (v. 17a) and then by the apostle John (v. 20):

> The first is the only recorded prayer of the Holy Spirit in Scripture. He is earlier recorded as interceding for us, but with "groanings that cannot be uttered" (Rom. 8:26). He joins with the church—the "bride" of Christ (Rev. 22:2, 9)—calling for the Lord to fulfill his promise. There is a wonderful symmetry to this, for this is the same Holy Spirit whose first outpouring marked the inauguration of the New Testament church. This

prayer of the Holy Spirit marks in anticipation the entrance of the church into the era of her eternal destiny in heaven. From Pentecost to the *parousia*, the heavenly Comforter ministers to the people of God and his final word, as it were, becomes the church's ultimate prayer—that her Savior would "come" and carry her to glory. It is not an accident that John calls all who "hear" to second this prayer, and all who "thirst" to "take of the water of life freely" (v. 17). Now is the time to close with Christ, to believe and be saved. Now is the day of salvation (2 Cor. 6:2).

➢ The second utterance of this prayer is—literally—John's "amen" (v. 20). It reads "Amen, come Lord Jesus!" Most old people look back to past glories that are now only memories. The aged apostle looks forward to being forever with the Lord. "Surely I am coming quickly," says Jesus. "Amen to that," says John. "It will never be too quick for me." And that's the way it ought to be for every Christian.

If Jesus is coming soon, how soon is "soon"? Will it be this year, or in thousands of years? No one knows, and the Lord told us not to speculate (Mark 13:32). The bottom line is: you need to know Jesus as your Savior before your short life is over, for if you do not, there will only be a fearful waiting for the final judgment that will consume the enemies of God (Heb. 10:27). For all who love the Lord, the prospect of his coming is the glorious consummation of that bliss that will be entered at the moment of our passage from this life. We pray with the Holy Spirit, the whole church, and the apostle, "Amen, come Lord Jesus!" because we desire to be with the Lord and also to see his glory on the great day.

THE BEST IS YET TO COME!
Sing Psalm 98

THINGS I WILL PRAY FOR TODAY

_____

_____

_____

_____

_____

Reading Plan for Prayers of the Bible

JANUARY

DAY	TITLE	SCRIPTURE	PSALM
1	The First Meeting for Prayer	Genesis 4:1–26	42
2	Praying for Children	Genesis 15:1–6	128
3	Big Problem: Brief Prayer	Matthew 14:22–33	54
4	An Encouragement to Pray	Isaiah 65:17–25	143
5	Let Your Word Come True	1 Kings 8:22–26	130
6	Will God Dwell on the Earth?	1 Kings 8:27–30	139:7–12
7	Fearing God and Enjoying Life	1 Kings 8:31–40	34:11–22
8	Separated to be God's Inheritance	1 Kings 8:41–53	16
9	Wrong Prayer: Right Answer	Genesis 17:17–22	23
10	The First Intercessory Prayer	Genesis 18:22–33	117
11	Praying Against God's Will	Genesis 18:18–22	73:23–27
12	Praying for Guidance	Genesis 24:1–14	25:1–7
13	An Anxious Prayer	Genesis 32:9–12	64
14	Wrestling in Prayer	Genesis 32:24–32	35:1–6
15	I'm Not Up to This Job!	Exodus 4:10–17	34:1–10
16	Trouble in the Church	Exodus 17:4–7	120
17	The Boldest of Prayers	Exodus 32:11–14	51:14–15
18	Punish Me Instead of Them	Exodus 32:30–35	67
19	Face to Face with God	Exodus 33:12–23	102:11–17
20	Whose People Are These?	Exodus 34:1–9	44:20–26
21	Prayer as Benediction	Numbers 6:22–26	4
22	Framing Each Day with Prayer	Numbers 10:33–36	68:1–6
23	Please End It All!	Numbers 11:11–15	55:1–8
24	Please Heal Her!	Numbers 12:1–13	103:1–4
25	God's Accountability to Himself	Numbers 14:11–19	136
26	Praying Against Our Enemies	Numbers 16	43:1–3
27	Praying for New Leadership	Numbers 27:15–17	126
28	"No" Is an Answer	Deut. 3:23–29	91:14–16
29	Praying for Unsolved Murder	Deut. 21:1–9	26:9–12
30	Giving God the "First Fruits"	Deut. 26:5–15	9:1–2
31	Praying with an Ear to Hear	Joshua 5:13–15	119:9–16

FEBRUARY

DAY	TITLE	SCRIPTURE	PSALM
1	Prayer after a Setback	Joshua 7:6–15	107:4–7
2	Asking the Impossible	Joshua 10:1–15	68:34–35
3	From Puzzled to Persuaded	Judges 6:11–24	86:11–13
4	Seeking a Sign?	Judges 6:36–40	119:33–35
5	Practical Change	Judges 10:10–16	69:1–3
6	Come to Us Again	Judges 13:1–9	91:1–2,14–16

24	Let Us Reason Together	Job 23:2–7	119:17–24
25	God Breaks His Silence	Job 38:1–7; 40:1–7	85:8–13
26	Now I Get It!	Job 42:1–6	131
27	A Ministry of Intercession	Job 42:7–10	20
28	The One Who Lifts Up My Head	Psalm 3	3
29	Stressed Out?	Psalm 4	4
30	The Shield of God's Favor	Psalm 5	5
31	Weary with Groaning	Psalm 6	6

APRIL

DAY	TITLE	SCRIPTURE	PSALM
1	But I Am Innocent!	Psalm 7	7:8–13
2	What Is Man?	Psalm 8	8
3	The Third Side to Every Story	Psalm 9	9
4	The Godly Man Ceases!	Psalm 12	12
5	The True Worshiper	Psalm 15	84
6	Pleasures Forevermore	Psalm 16	16:5–11
7	I Shall Be Satisfied	Psalm 17	17:13–15
8	Before the Battle	Psalm 20	20
9	Forsaken?	Psalm 22:1–5	69:14–21
10	I Am a Worm	Psalm 22:6–8	18:16–24
11	You Have Answered Me	Psalm 22:9–21	118:1–9
12	The Wings of Hope	Psalm 22:22–31	22:27–31
13	The Secret of the Lord	Psalm 25	25:8–15
14	Standing in an Even Place	Psalm 26	26
15	Confidence in the Lord	Psalm 27	27
16	Our Strength and Shield	Psalm 28	28
17	God's Goodness to Believers	Psalm 31	31:19–24
18	The Fruit of Forgiveness	Psalm 32	32:1–7
19	Hated Without a Cause	Psalm 35	35:19–23
20	Make Me to Know My End	Psalm 39	39:7–13
21	Sickness and Salvation	Psalm 41	41:7–13
22	I Will Remember You	Psalm 42	42:6–11
23	Hope for the Dejected Soul	Psalm 43	43
24	Why Do You Sleep, O Lord?	Psalm 44	44:20–26
25	The Sacrifices of God	Psalm 51	51
26	Do You Need Help?	Psalm 54	54
27	O for the Wings of a Dove!	Psalm 55	55:16–23
28	Fears, Tears, and Cheers	Psalm 56	56:8–13
29	God's Glory Exalted!	Psalm 57	57:5–11
30	Backs to the Wall?	Psalm 59	59:13–15

MAY

DAY	TITLE	SCRIPTURE	PSALM
1	Defeat into Victory	Psalm 60	60:1–5
2	Our Only Rock and Shelter	Psalm 61	61
3	My Soul, Wait Silently…	Psalm 62	62:1–8

JULY

DAY	TITLE	SCRIPTURE	PSALM
1	Your Kingdom Come	Matthew 6:10a	22:27–31
2	Your Will Be Done	Matthew 6:10b	40:1–9
3	Our Daily Bread	Matthew 6:11	107:33–43
4	Forgive Us Our Debts	Matthew 6:12	130
5	Lead Us Not into Temptation	Matthew 6:13a	125
6	Deliver Us from Evil	Matthew 6:13b	107:17–22
7	Ask, Seek, and Knock	Matthew 7:7–11	143
8	You Can Make Me Clean!	Matthew 8:2–4	79:8–13
9	Great Faith in Action	Matthew 8:5–13	20
10	Two Demoniacs Healed	Matthew 8:28–34	11
11	Lay Your Hand on Her	Matthew 9:18–26	91:1–4
12	She Touched His Garment	Matthew 9:20–22	103:1–5
13	He Touched Their Eyes	Matthew 9:27–31	119:17–24
14	Marching Orders	Matthew 9:35–38	72:16–19
15	I Thank You, Father	Matthew 11:25–26	31:19–24
16	Jesus and His Father	Matthew 11:27	144:9–15
17	Asking the Blessing	Matthew 14:19	145:15–21
18	Crumbs from the Master's Table?	Matthew 15:21–28	18:1–6
19	If Two of You Agree	Matthew 18:19–20	80
20	You Don't Know What You Ask	Matthew 20:20–28	131
21	Ask...Believing	Matthew 21:18–22	119:153–160
22	Long Prayers	Matthew 23:14	17:1–7
23	Giving Account to God	Matthew 25:20–24	26
24	Not as I Will	Matthew 26:36–46	40:1–9
25	Let God Deliver Him!	Matthew 27:39–44	16
26	Prayer on a Mountain	Mark 6:46	121
27	I Believe; Help My Unbelief!	Mark 9:14–29	31:9–16
28	Could You Not Watch One Hour?	Mark 14:32–42	123
29	Why Me?	Mark 15:34	22:1–11
30	Heaven Opened	Luke 3:21–22	17:13–15
31	Far from the Madding Crowd	Luke 5:12–16	91

SEPTEMBER

DAY	TITLE	SCRIPTURE	PSALM
1	Up All Night	Luke 6:12	5
2	Where Is Your Faith?	Luke 8:22–25	46
3	The Lord of Glory	Luke 9:29	118:19–29
4	Lord, Teach Us to Pray	Luke 11:1–4	65:1–4
5	The Shape of Living Prayer	Luke 11:1–4	38:15–22
6	Pressing Onward	Luke 11:5–13	55:16–23
7	Father, I Have Sinned	Luke 15:11–21	51
8	A Great Gulf Fixed	Luke 16:24	9:11–20
9	Faith as a Mustard Seed	Luke 17:5–6	119:81–88
10	Where Are the Nine?	Luke 17:11–19	88:9–18

11	Do Not Lose Heart!	Luke 18:1–8	5
12	Two Men Went to Pray	Luke 18:9–14	57:1–4
13	Beggars Can Be Choosers!	Luke 18:35–43	145:8–14
14	Sifted Like Wheat	Luke 22:31–32	118:1–9
15	Father, Forgive Them (Part 1)	Luke 23:34a	32:1–7
16	Father, Forgive Them (Part 2)	Luke 23:34b	35:11–18
17	Lord, Remember Me	Luke 23:42–43	106:1–5
18	Father, into Your Hands	Luke 23:46	118:13–15
19	A Parting Blessing	Luke 24:50–53	128
20	Looks, Walks, and Quacks?	John 4:15	62:1–8
21	That You Might Believe	John 11:41–42	118:15–18
22	My Soul Is Troubled	John 12:27–28	34:11–22
23	The Hour Has Come	John 17:1	119:113–120
24	To Give Eternal Life	John 17:2	119:33–40
25	The Path of Glory	John 17:3–5	85:8–13
26	The Men You Have Given	John 17:6–8	119:129–136
27	I Pray for Them	John 17:9–10	122(see v. 6)
28	Keep Them from the Evil One	John 17:11–16	66
29	Sanctify Them	John 17:17–19	18:30–36
30	Dwelling Together in Unity	John 17:20–23	133

OCTOBER

DAY	TITLE	SCRIPTURE	PSALM
1	Eternal Glory	John 17:24	73:23–27
2	The Bonds of Love	John 17:25–26	85:8–13
3	With One Accord	Acts 1:1–14	143:7–12
4	Rebuilding the Leadership	Acts 1:15–26	78:65–72
5	Prayer and the Church	Acts 2:42–47	52:8–9
6	Sweet Hour of Prayer	Acts 3:1	38:15–22
7	Stand Up for Jesus	Acts 4:23–31	27:9–14
8	Given to Prayer and the Word	Acts 6:1–7	122
9	Heaven Opened	Acts 7:55–60	35:11–18
10	Do You "Have a Prayer"?	Acts 8:14–25	102:1–12
11	Surprised by the Savior	Acts 9:1–9	119:33–40
12	Tabitha, Arise!	Acts 9:36–43	17:13–15
13	An Unexpected Answer	Acts 10:1–9, 31	98
14	A Day of Trouble	Acts 12:5–19	50:7–19
15	Prayer and Fasting	Acts 13:1–3 ; 14:23	109:22–31
16	Come and Help Us!	Acts 16:11–24	72:16–19
17	Light in the Darkness	Acts 16:25–34	63
18	Sweet Sorrow	Acts 20:17–38	20
19	All at Sea?	Acts 27:23–26	6
20	When Sickness Strikes	Acts 28:7–10	103:1–5
21	Making Mention of You All	Romans 1:8–12	122
22	Abba, Father	Romans 8:15–27	27:7–10
23	Your Heart's Desire and Prayer	Romans 10:1–12	61
24	Steadfast in Prayer	Romans 12:12	13
25	One Mind and One Mouth	Romans 15:5–7	133
26	Abounding in Hope	Romans 15:13	71

27	Pray for Me!	Romans 15:30–33	138
28	To God Be the Glory	Romans 16:25–27	102:11–17
29	Growing Together	1 Cor. 1:4–9	133
30	The Spirit and the Understanding	1 Cor. 14:14–17	119:73–80
31	Victory through Jesus Christ	1 Cor. 15:50–58	34:1–10

NOVEMBER

DAY	TITLE	SCRIPTURE	PSALM
1	Consolation through Christ	2 Cor. 1:3–7	20
2	Thorn in the Flesh	2 Cor. 12:7–10	119:169–176
3	The Trinitarian Benediction	2 Cor. 13:11–14	59:9–17
4	Enlightened Eyes	Eph. 1:15–18a	43
5	Calling, Inheritance, and Power	Eph. 1:18–19a	111:6–10
6	Exalted Prince and Savior	Eph. 1:19b–21	110
7	Head over All Things	Eph. 1:15–23	8
8	Might in the Inner Man	Eph. 4:14–17a	1
9	Love That Passes Knowledge	Eph. 3:17b–19	18:1–6
10	A Ladder to Heaven	Eph. 3:20–21	131
11	Singing to the Lord	Eph. 5:15–21	45
12	All Kinds of Prayer	Eph. 6:10–20	27:5–9
13	At All Times	Eph. 6:10–20	34
14	In the Holy Spirit	Eph. 6:10–20	143:7–12
15	On the Alert	Eph. 6:10–20	40:1–9
16	For All the Saints	Eph. 6:10–20	67
17	Smart Love	Phil. 1:8–11	89:1–5
18	Good Fruit	Phil. 1:8–11	92:9–15
19	The Answer to Anxiety	Phil. 4:4–9, 19–20	4
20	Motives for Prayer	Col. 1:3–8	16
21	Walking Worthy of Christ	Col. 1:9–10	86:11–16
22	Strengthened with Might	Col. 1:9–11	46
23	Light, Love, and Liberty	Col. 1:9–14	40:10–17
24	Interconnected Prayer	Col. 4:2–4	67
25	We Thank God for All of You	1 Thess. 1:1–10	92:1–8
26	Reasons for Thanksgiving	1 Thess. 1:1–10	9:1–10
27	We'll Meet Again!	1 Thess. 3:1–13	133
28	The Soul's Oxygen	1 Thess. 5:16–24	86:11–17
29	Pray for God's Ministers	1 Thess. 5:25–28	132:11–18
30	Worthy of Your Calling?	2 Thess. 1:1–12	26

DECEMBER

DAY	TITLE	SCRIPTURE	PSALM
1	Stand Fast	2 Thess. 2:13–17	85:8–13
2	An Answering Love	2 Thess. 3:1–5	18:1–7
3	Waiting for God's Time	2 Thess. 3:1–5, 16	37:7–15
4	Overwhelmed with God's Glory	2 Thess. 2:13–17	107:23–32
5	The Scope of Public Prayer	1 Tim. 2:1–2	67

Endnotes

viii. *"And so, as..."* John Bunyan, *Pilgrim's Progress* (London: James Nisbet, nd), 1.
xi. *"Or, as Bunyan said..."* Ibid., 7.

January

3. *"In his Christmas day..."* Minnie Haskin, *The Desert* (London: privately printed, 1912).
16. *"There is grace for..."* Jerry Bridges, *Transforming Grace: Living Confidently in God's Unfailing Love* (Colorado Springs: NavPress, 2008), 82. This is a wonderful treatment of the nature of God's saving grace.
17. *"He delivered them..."* The record of Solomon's prayer in 2 Chronicles 6 closes with a quotation of Psalm 132:8–10 that is not found in the version in 1 Kings 8. See the meditation on Psalm 132 in the entry for May 27.
37. *"But, wonderful as their..."* From her famous hymn, "There Is a Green Hill Far Away."
42. *"Bible scholar Gordon Wenham..."* Gordon J. Wenham, *Numbers* (Downers Grove, IL: International Varsity Press, 1981), 90.
54. *"Sometimes it is because..."* From his poem "To a Mouse," in which Burns says of the harvest mouse, whose home his plow destroyed:

> But Mousie, thou art no thy-lane,
> In proving foresights may be vain:
> The best laid schemes of Mice an' Men
> Gang aft agley,
> An' lea'e us nought but grief an' pain,
> For promis'd joy!
>
> Still, thou art blest, compar'd wi' me!
> The present only toucheth thee:
> But Och! I backward cast my e'e,
> On prospects drear!
> An' forward tho' I canna see,
> I guess an' fear!

February

77. *"We can and must..."* Matthew Henry, *Commentary on the Whole Bible* (Iowa Falls, IA: World Bible Publishers, nd), 2:217.
78. *"So it was with..."* Ibid., 2:224.
79. *"'I want nothing but..."* Samuel Rutherford, *Religious Letters* (London: The Religious Tract Society, nd), 389.
104. *"His 'kindest visits are..."* Henry, *Commentary*, 2:594.
106. *"We may resort to..."* Charles Simeon, *Expository Sermon Outlines on the Whole Bible* (Grand Rapids, MI: Zondervan, 1956), 3:347.

122. *"He assures us that..."* Bruce Wilkinson, *The Prayer of Jabez: Breaking Through to the Blessed Life* (Colorado Springs: Multnomah, 2000), 87.

122. *"Jesus is not essential..."* Ibid., 91–92.

123. *"In his wistful evocation..."* Robert Burns, "The Cotter's Saturday Night," in *Poems and Songs of Robert Burns,* James Bark, ed. (Glasgow: Collins, 1969), 105–10.

123. *"Charles Spurgeon, the great..."* Charles H. Spurgeon, "An Encouraging Lesson from Paul's Conversion," Sermon No. 994, in *The Metropolitan Tabernacle Pulpit,* vol. 16 (London: Passmore & Alabaster, 1870).

132. *"The temple 'had been...'"* Andrew Stewart, *2 Chronicles: A House of Prayer* (Faverdale, UK: Evangelical Press, 2001), 340–41.

133. *"Now is the day..."* Ibid., 371–72.

134. *"He dabbled with witchcraft..."* John Milton, *Paradise Lost,* book 1, lines 392–96.

139. *"It is true, of..."* Henry, *Commentary,* 2:1056.

144. *"Nehemiah's short prayer has..."* Augustine, "Letters," Letter No. 130, in *Nicene and Post-Nicene Fathers* (1886; repr., Peabody, MA: Hendricksen, 1999), 1:465.

145. *"He who prays without..."* Spurgeon, *The Metropolitan Tabernacle Pulpit* (London: Passmore & Alabaster, 1870), 18:138.

154. *"When faced with..."* John Calvin, *Sermons on Job* (Grand Rapids, MI: Baker, 1979), 21.

156. *"'It is as ill...'"* Henry, *Commentary,* 3:338.

157. *"'In our repentance,' says"* Ibid., 3:47.

157. *"My soul answered, 'Yes..."* Thomas Boston, *Memoirs* (Edinburgh: Banner of Truth, 1988), 61.

163. *"He needs someone who..."* Derek Thomas, *The Storm Breaks: Job Simply Explained* (Faverdale, UK: Evangelical Press, 2004), 110.

165. *"'Christ has brought life..."* Herbert Lockyer, *All the Prayers of the Bible* (Grand Rapids, MI: Zondervan, 1959), 99.

168. *"He wants to dialogue..."* In his libretto for Felix Mendelssohn's oratorio *Elijah,* the Lutheran pastor Julius Schubring puts Job 23:3 together with Deuteronomy 4:29 to craft the glorious tenor aria in which backsliding Israel is called to seek the Lord: "'If with all your hearts ye truly seek Me, ye shall ever surely find Me.' Thus saith our God. Oh! that I knew where I might find Him, that I might even come before His presence!" This puts a more positive cast on Job's words than they have as uttered by Job.

173. *"Green adds, 'The faith..."* W. H. Green, *The Argument of the Book of Job Unfolded* (New York: Robert Carter and Brothers, 1874), 309.

177. *"comfort in all calamity..."* David Dickson, *A Commentary on the Psalms* (1653–55; repr., London: Banner of Truth Trust, 1965), 1:11.

177. *"He must have victory..."* Eric Lane, *Psalms 1–89: The Lord Saves* (Fearn, UK: Christian Focus, 2006), 35.

178. *"Then Psalm 4:1 came..."* *The Book of Psalms for Worship* (Pittsburgh, PA: Crown & Covenant, 2009), selection 4B.

178. *"David Dickson wrote 'Faith…"* Dickson, *Commentary,* 1:15.

179. *"'The most satisfactory revenge…"* Ibid., 1:16.

179. *"Here is, as Andrew…"* Andrew A. Bonar, *Christ and His Church in the Book of Psalms* (New York: Robert Carter & Brothers, 1860), 13.

180. *"David prays about his…"* Dickson, *Commentary,* 1:19.

181. *"There is no vindictive…"* Psalm 5 is one of the "imprecatory" psalms (Ps. 5, 10, 17, 35, 58, 59, 69, 70, 79, 83, 109, 129, 137, and 140), so-called because they call for God to judge the wicked rebels against him (v. 10). The focus of these imprecations is never mere personal revenge, but always Gods vindicating his own righteousness and justice, and the removal of the immediate injustice being laid upon the Lord's faithful servant(s).

181. *"As David Dickson said…"* Dickson, 1:24.

183. *"Notice that 'though sense…"* Ibid., 1:25.

April

197. *"This has to do…"* James G. Murphy, *The Book of Psalms,* 138.

197. *"'The soul that loves…"* John Howe (1630–1705), quoted in C. H. Spurgeon, *The Treasury of David* (London: Passmore & Alabaster, 1870), 1:260.

198. *"The army followed and…"* Count de Montalembert, *The Monks of the West* (London, 1896), 6:58. The abbot chanted the Latin, *Hi in curribus et hi in equis: nos autem in nomine Domini.*

198. *"'Zion' refers to the…"* J. A. Alexander, *The Psalms Translated and Explained* (1873; repr., Grand Rapids, MI: Baker, 1975), 92.

199. *"The plural 'we'…"* Allan M. Harman, *Psalms* (Fearn, UK: Mentor, 1998), 116.

199. *"Although David is immediately…"* Bonar, *Christ and His Church,* 69.

202. *"miracle in language…"* C. H. Spurgeon, *The Treasury of David* (1870; repr., Grand Rapids, MI: Guardian Press, 1976) 1:367.

202. *"What a contrast…"* Ibid.

206. *"'The supplicant now rises…'"* Murphy, *Book of Psalms,* 177.

206. *"Noting the messianic character…"* Dickson, *Commentary,* 1:116.

207. *"The psalmist's words proclaim…"* Bonar, *Christ and His Church,* 79.

209. *"Read in this blessed…"* Bella Bathhurst, *The Lighthouse Stevenses* (New York: Harper Collins, 1999), 198.

210. *"Even getting there by…"* "The Lord of the Isles," Canto 3, verse 14, in *The Poetical Works of Sir Walter Scott* (Boston: Crosby and Ainsworth, 1880), 263. The easy way to get there is by a boat ride followed by a short ramble along the River Scavaig.

210. *"Here 'the context suggests…'"* Harman, *Psalms,* 131.

211. *"He 'entered into the…'"* Simeon, *Expository Sermon Outlines,* 5:175–6.

211. *"On Christ, the solid…"* "My Hope is Built on Nothing Less," by Edward Mote (1797–1874).

212. *"Hearing this name, however…"* Matthew Arnold, "Sohrab and Rustum," 1853; *Poetry Foundation.* www.poetryfoundation.org/poem/172860. In the end, Sohrab is killed by Rustum, who discovers he has unwittingly killed his son!

214. *"The 'pit'—like the…"* en.wikipedia.org/wiki/St_Andrews_Castle

215. *"'Every stream,' notes A. A. Bonar…"* Bonar, *Christ and His Church*, 98.

216. *"Calvin notes that David…"* John Calvin, *Commentary upon the Book of Psalms* (Grand Rapids, MI: Baker, 1979), 4:498–9.

217. *"'The people of God…"* Murdoch Campbell, *From Grace to Glory: Meditations on the Book of Psalms* (Edinburgh: Banner of Truth, 1970), 60.

218. *"Read Psalm 32…"* Psalm 32 is a "penitential" psalm—see March 31 entry on Psalm 6.

218. *"He understands, as Charles…"* Simeon, *Expository Sermon Outlines*, 5:222.

219. *"Personal instruction is imparted…"* Calvin, *Commentary upon the Book of Psalms*, 5:534.

220. *"This 'imprecatory' psalm…"* See endnote 27 in March. "Imprecation" is from the Latin *precari*, meaning "pray".

220. *"This 'imprecatory' psalm…"* See Michael LeFebvre, *Singing the Songs of Jesus* (Fearn, UK: Christian Focus, 2010), 113–31, for an excellent treatment of imprecation in the Psalms.

220. *"A. A. Bonar invites us…"* Bonar, *Christ and His Church*, 119.

221. *"It would thus be…"* Wilhelmus a' Brakel, *The Christian's Reasonable Service* (Orlando, FL: Soli Deo Gloria, 1994), 3:445–6.

223. *"The brevity of our…"* Andrew Gray, *Loving Christ and Fleeing Temptation* (Grand Rapids, MI: Reformation Heritage, 2007), 110. Andrew Gray died of a fever on February 8, 1656, after 27 months in the ministry, aged only twenty-two! He rested from very short labors, but his works have followed him in the printed word to the blessing of many for most of four centuries!

224. *"'The occasion of this psalm…"* Matthew Poole, *A Commentary on the Whole Bible* (1685; repr., London: Banner of Truth, 1962), 2:66.

224. *"'Poor' here is not…"* Alexander, *The Psalms*, 183.

225. *"'What was true of…"* Harman, *Psalms*, 178.

225. *"He concludes by trusting…"* Note that verse 13 is a doxology closing out the entire Book I of Psalms (1–41).

225. *"But those whom God…"* Campbell, *From Grace to Glory*, 77.

226. *"'Blessed are they that…"* George Horne, *A Commentary on the Psalms* (1771; repr., Audubon, NJ: Old Paths, 1997), 189.

227. *"He is saying, in effect…"* Alexander, *The Psalms*, 192.

228. *"'It has pleased God…'"* Simeon, *Expository Sermon Outlines*, 5:335. Simeon (1759–1836) faced protracted opposition in a ministry that still bears fruit to this day. See Handley Moule, *Charles Simeon: Pastor of a Generation* (1892; repr., Fearn, UK: Christian Focus, 1997).

229. *"He adds, 'We should…"* Simeon, *Expository Sermon Outlines*, 338.

230. *"When the 'slings and…"* William Shakespeare, *Hamlet*, act 3, scene 1.

231. *"He is grieved, but…"* Dickson, *A Commentary*, 1:253.

231. *"Through the dismay and…"* The same Hebrew term as in Psalm 23:4, "Yea, though I walk through the valley of the shadow of death, I will fear no evil…"

232. *"The sin of David…"* Henry, *Commentary*, 3:29. He quotes 1 Corinthians 10:12.
232. *"Only a brilliant ploy…"* Psalm 51 is one of the seven "penitential" psalms (Ps. 6, 32, 38, 51, 102, 130, and 143).
232. *"'But,' notes Bishop Horne…"* Horne, *A Commentary*, 222.
233. *"the account between God…"* Ibid.
233. *"For one thing, says…"* Henry, *Commentary*, 3:435.
234. *"To pray or hope…"* Alexander, *The Psalms*, 238 (commenting on Ps. 52:11: "I will praise You forever, because You have done it; and in the presence of Your saints I will wait on your name, for it is good").
235. *"When we invoke his…"* Ibid., 241.
235. *"David Dickson, no stranger…"* Dickson, *A Commentary*, 1:324.
236. *"One day in April…"* "O for the Wings of a Dove" is the final section of Mendelssohn's anthem based on Psalm 55:1–8, "Hear My Prayer."
236. *"And this anticipates…"* Horne, *Psalms*, 231.
236. *"Andrew Bonar aptly observes…"* Bonar, *Christ and His Church*, 169.
238. *"Shakespeare's Julius Caesar declares…"* *Julius Caesar*, act 2, scene 2.
238. *"'You see the magnitude…"* Quoted in Bonar, *Christ and His Church*, 171.
238. *"Andrew Bonar answers…"* Ibid., 172.
239. *"It is an interesting figure…"* Robert Hawker, *Poor Man's Commentary*, 4:289. (See www.monergism.com.)
240. *"As he writes Psalm 57…"* See the psalm's title: "the cave" is probably the Cave of Adullam (1 Sam. 22:1).
242. *"British commander Douglas Haig…"* www.firstworldwar.com/source/backstothewall.htm
243. *"He affirms his conviction…"* Harman, *Psalms*, 220.

May

244. *"One of the great memoirs…"* W. Slim, *Defeat into Victory* (1956; repr., New York: Cooper Square Press, 2000), 616.
244. *"How Israel prays when…"* Bonar, *Christ and His Church*, 238.
244. *"Three kingdoms…"* Mesopotamia, Syria of Zobah, and Edom (see the psalm's title).
245. *"If Israel is…"* Winston Churchill in his speech "This Was Their Finest Hour" (June 18, 1940), from *Never Give In!: The Best of Winston Churchill's Speeches* (New York: Hyperion, 2003), 229.
246. *"My favorite since childhood…"* See www.historicenvironment.scot/visit-a-place/places/tantallon-castle
246. *"'The best expedient for…"* Dickson, *A Commentary*, 13:61.
247. *"In this, David is led…"* Simeon, *Expository Sermon Outlines*, 5:447.
247. *"This fallen world is…"* The expression "vale of tears" arises from the Valley of Baca [lit. "weeping"] in Psalm 84:6—"As they pass through the Valley of Baca, they make it a spring; the rain also covers it with pools." Thus the Lord relieves believers from their trials and blesses their hearts with his grace.

248. *"The assumption is that..."* Timothy J. Keller, *The Songs of Jesus* (New York: Viking, 2015), 131.

249. *"Let this therefore..."* Campbell, *From Grace to Glory,* 10.

250. *"This can only begin..."* Poole, *A Commentary,* 2:97 (For further reference, see 2 Sam. 15:23, 28; 16:2, 14; 17:16; cf. 19:9).

250. *"The wilderness..."* The title of the psalm reveals David to be in "the wilderness of Judah."

251. *"Because of going over..."* Dickson, *A Commentary,* 1:373.

251. *"'What encouragement,' say Charles..."* Simeon, *Expository Sermon Outlines,* 5:455–6.

252. *"The psalmist takes us..."* Notice the chiastic (crossover) arrangement of the two pairs of parallel thoughts (A1-B1-B2-A2) rising from the enemies' initial threat to the Lord's final deliverance.

253. *"Character assassination is their..."* Lane, *Psalms 1–89,* 284.

253. *"Fierce may be the..."* From "Who is on the Lord's Side?" by Francis Ridley Havergal (1836–79.)

254. *"This most exalted of prayers..."* Alec Motyer, *Psalms by the Day* (Fearn, UK: Christian Focus, 2016), 174.

254. *"The very elegance of..."* Dickson, *A Commentary,* 1:392.

256. *"The Psalms have been..."* See LeFebvre, *Singing the Songs of Jesus.*

256. *"The Psalms have been..."* The so-called "messianic" psalms.

256. *"While it records something..."* Campbell, *From Grace to Glory,* 116.

258. *"Princeton theologian Addison Alexander..."* Alexander, *The Psalms,* 297 (cf. the preceding and following meditations in this month).

259. *"Sometimes he does answer..."* See March 29—the mediation on Psalm 4— for a true instance of this.

260. *"The prayer unfolds..."* Harman, *Psalms,* 248–51. He persuasively proposes this division of the text.

262. *"The state of the church..."* This "Asaph" was likely one of the school of Asaph, writing in the aftermath of the destruction of the temple by the Babylonians in 586 BC.

263. *"On November 28, 1666..."* Psalm 74 (Scottish Metrical Version); see also T. Campbell, *Standing Witnesses* (Edinburgh: 1996), 164–5; and R. E. Prothero, *The Psalms in Human Life* (London: 1903), 206.

264. *"His thoughts rush desperately..."* W. Shakespeare, *Macbeth,* act 5, scene 3.

264. *"For Asaph, this is..."* Simeon, *Expository Sermon Outlines,* 6:32.

266. *"In a sermon entitled..."* Gray, *Loving Christ,* 178 (cf. entry April 20, note on Psalm 39).

266. *"This, says Andrew Bonar..."* Bonar, *Christ and His Church,* 238.

269. *"Andrew Bonar notes that..."* Ibid., 241.

270. *"He begins, 'Do not..."* Harman, *Psalms,* 286.

272. *"The idea in verse 1 is..."* Ibid., 288.

272. *"Its holiness, loveliness, and..."* Henry, *Commentary,* 3:557.

272. *"He is far from..."* "On an instrument of Gath" (Hebrew *Al Gittith*) in the heading may indicate his location.

273. *"Afterwards he said..."* Thomas Halyburton, *Halyburton's Works* (Aberdeen: James Begg Society, 2005), 4:245.

276. *"Blackness Castle is a..."* en.wikipedia.org/wiki/Blackness_Castle

277. *"This reminds us of Job..."* Bonar, *Christ and His Church*, 264.

277. *"'We hear in this psalm..."* Horne, *Psalms*, 379.

278. *"This is the gnawing..."* The psalmist here is not David but Ethan the Ezrahite, one of Solomon's wise men (1 Kings 4:31), now an old man (Ps. 89:47), writing during Israel's decline after Solomon's death.

279. *"It is 'the covenant..."* Brakel, *The Christian's Reasonable Service*, 1:253.

279. *"the 'counsel of peace..."* This is the Covenant of Redemption in eternity, from which flow, in time, the Covenant of Works and the Covenant of Grace.

279. *"Blessed be the Lord..."* Verse 52 is a benediction for Book III of Psalms (73–89).

280. *"As long as the wicked..."* Henry, *Commentary*, 3:597.

280. *"'God is hidden from..."* Eric Lane, *Psalms 90–150: The Lord Reigns* (Fearn, UK: Christian Focus, 2006), 23.

282. *"The New Testament, however..."* Murphy, *Psalms*, 530–1.

282. *"Alec Motyer aptly states..."* Motyer, *Psalms*, note 11, p. 283.

282. *"A. A. Bonar sees here..."* Bonar, *Christ and His Church*, 304.

283. *"The psalmist's prayer looks..."* "Eschaton" just means "the last" and so "eschatology" is the theology of the "last things"—the goal and end in God's purposes for humankind as unfolded in time and consummated in eternity.

283. *"This our prayers and..."* Harman, *Psalms*, 335.

284. *"Motyer calls this 'an..."* Motyer, *Psalms*, 310.

286. *"While this states the..."* Harman, *Psalms*, 372.

286. *"Now he is at..."* Lane, *Psalms 90–150*, 116.

288. *"Before John Bunyan coined..."* From the opening sentence in John Bunyan's *The Pilgrim's Progress*.

288. *"Psalm 120 is the..."* Harman, *Psalms*, 401.

290. *"Matthew Poole notes that..."* Poole, *Commentary*, 2:193.

291. *"princes decree judgement..."* Bonar, *Christ and His Church*, 386.

291. *"'This lovely psalm..."* Campbell, *From Grace to Glory*, 175, 177. He references Hebrews 11:16, "But now they desire a better, that is, a heavenly country. Therefore God is not ashamed to be called their God, for He has prepared a city for them."

292. *"But, as Alan Harman observes..."* Harman, *Psalms*, 406 (cf. the comments on Psalm 120 in May 23).

293. *"Matthew Henry points out..."* Henry, *Commentary*, 3:729.

293. *"Prayer is the burden..."* By James Montgomery, (1771–1854).

294. *"This short prayer is..."* Psalm 130 is the sixth of the penitential prayers (Ps. 6, 32, 38, 51, 102, 130 and 143). See the masterly 325-page exposition by John Owen (1616–83) in his *Works*, 6:323–648.

295. *"But, as Allan Harman has noted..."* Harman, *Psalms*, 415.

295. *"This exalted spirit is..."* Alexander, *Psalms*, 522.

296. *"In a cartoon entitled..."* Reformed Presbyterian pastor, missionary, and cartoonist.

296. *"In a cartoon entitled..."* Covenanter Witness, vol. 73, 1964, 144.

296. *"He does not stop..."* Psalms 47, 68, 96, and 98 celebrate this time of revival.

297. *"The temple and the..."* Bishop Horne notes that this is the reason the Church of England appointed Psalm 132 to be used on Christmas Day (Horne, *Psalms*, 596).

298. *"Their prayer here consists..."* Psalm 137 is another instance of a so-called imprecatory psalm. These psalms look for divine justice upon the enemies of God (Ps. 5, 10, 17, 35, 58, 59, 69, 70, 79, 83, 109, 129, 137, and 140).

298. *"This deep sadness tends..."* See the meditation on May 21 (Psalm 109) and particularly the quoted comments of the Anglican scholar Alec Motyer, who describes this as "an unthinking reaction."

300. *"So intimate and personal..."* Poole, *Commentary*, 2:203.

301. *"Bonar concludes, 'Thus we..."* Bonar, *Christ and His Church*, 425.

302. *"'Terrorism has gripped the world..."* September 11, 2001, when 2,996 people perished in terrorist attacks on the USA (2,335 were killed at Pearl Harbor on December 7, 1941).

302. *"The English philosopher Francis Bacon..."* Bacon modified a saying of the French philosopher Michel de Montaigne (1533–92): "The thing of which I have most fear is fear (1580). Franklin D. Roosevelt applied this idea to the Great Depression in his inaugural address as US president in 1933, saying that "the only thing we have to fear is fear itself."

302. *"He assures us, as David..."* Dickson, *A Commentary*, 2:483.

302. *"Such people 'exist in..."* Horne, *Psalms*, 623.

302. *"The believer can say..."* The Day of Judgement, at Jesus's Second Advent.

303. *"But the Lord will..."* Horne, *Psalms*, 624.

304. *"'Auld Sandy' said to him..."* Maurice Grant, *Preacher to the Remnant*, (Edinburgh: Scottish Reformation Society, 2009), 130.

304. *"generations yet unborn shall..."* Scottish Metrical Psalter, 1650; Ps. 102:18.

305. *"David 'wants his prayer..."* Harman, *Psalms*, 436.

305. *"With 'The Wayfaring Stranger..."* See www.youtube.com/watch?v=3wTZ_-Lr7Xg for a marvelous rendering of this song by the late great American bass-baritone Norman Treigle.

JUNE

306. *"David is in such..."* Lane, *Psalms 90–150*, 209. Lane aptly entitles his comments on Psalm 142 "David's Tight Corner".

306. *"While David's men saw..."* Ibid.

306. *"This psalm is entitled..."* Motyer, *Psalms*, 80.

306. *"let us follow the..."* Horne, *Psalms*, 629–30.

307. *"Andrew Bonar sees this..."* Bonar, *Christ and His Church*, 431.

308. *"This psalm-prayer is one..."* Psalms 35, 64, 36, 12, 59, 140, 143, and 141 (in chronological order) come from that time. See Lane, *Psalms 90–150*, 255–7.

308. *"This rich prayer unfolds..."* Here I follow the marvelous exposition of David Dickson in *A Commentary on the Psalms*, 2:497–502.

309. *"Bishop Horne observes that..."* Horne, *Psalms,* 2:497–502.

310. *"These happy clauses..."* Alexander, *The Psalms,* 553.

310. *"God's people rejoice because..."* James G. Murphy, *Psalms,* (1876; repr., Minneapolis: James, 1977), 680.

311. *"It is a prospect that awaits..."* Bonar, *Christ and His Church,* 437.

311. *"Then, without fear of contradiction..."* Simeon, *Expository Outlines,* 6:484.

312. *"It is 'a good duty..."* James Ussher, *Eighteen Sermons Preached in Oxford 1640,* 69.

312. *"On the other hand..."* Simeon, *Expository Sermon Outlines,* 7:156.

313. *"His desire to seek..."* Charles Bridges, *Proverbs* (Darlington, UK: Evangelical Press, 1991), 202.

314. *"God is not to be..."* Derek Thomas, *God Delivers* (Darlington, UK: Evangelical Press, 1993), 61.

314. *"Charles Simeon observes that..."* Simeon, *Expository Sermon Outlines,* 7:505.

317. *"God's promises revealed, ratified..."* Henry, *Commentary,* 4:78.

320. *"This double shalom denotes..."* John Calvin, *Commentary on the Prophet Isaiah,* in vol. 7 of 22 vol. reprint of Calvin Translation Society edition (Grand Rapids, MI: Baker, 1979), 1:214.

321. *"in relation to everything..."* Simeon, *Expository Sermon Outlines,* 7:619–20.

322. *"Archbishop Cranmer once said..."* Thomas Cranmer, "Answer unto... Stephen Gardiner" [1551], in *Cranmer's Remains* [1833], 3:97.

323. *"When God's time shall have come..."* Henry, *Commentary,* 4:142.

323. *"He is still traveling on..."* Richard Alleine, *The World Conquered by the Faithful Christian* (Morgan, PA: Soli Deo Gloria, 1997), 91.

324. *"As sole ruler of Judah..."* Hezekiah (born c. 739 BC) was co-regent with his father, Ahaz (729–716 BC), and reigned a further 29 years (died 687 BC). Sargon II destroyed the northern kingdom of Israel in 722 BC, enslaved the population, and exiled them across the Assyrian Empire.

326. *"Hezekiah was in his..."* Hezekiah was born c. 739 and fell ill c. 703 BC. Isaiah 38 is a flashback to an event that preceded the Assyrian siege of Jerusalem recorded in Isaiah 36–37.

326. *"Sickness is intended to be..."* J. C. Ryle, *Sickness* (Grand Rapids, MI: Inheritance Publishers, nd), series 35, no. 3, p. 5.

330. *"As the fire causes..."* Henry, *Commentary,* 4:375.

337. *"It is a pitiable thing..."* Ibid., 4:428.

339. *"Philip Ryken notes that..."* Philip Ryken, *Jeremiah & Lamentations* (Wheaton, IL: Crossway, 2001), 88.

341. *"Not knowing his secret..."* Matthew Henry comments, "God here forbids the prophet to pray for them (v. 16): 'The decree has gone forth, their ruin is resolved on, therefore pray not thou for this people, that is, pray not for the preventing of this judgement threatened; they have sinned unto death, and therefore pray not for their life, but for the life of their souls.' 1 John 5:16."

342. *"because it was well watered..."* William Jay, *Morning and Evening Exercises* (New York: Harper, 1858), 2:397.

346. *"The point is that..."* Simeon, *Expository Sermon Outlines,* 9:122.

348. *"Upwards of 100 million…"* paindoctor.com/resources/chronic-pain-statistics

348. *"He prayed for mercy…"* See entry for June 21: "Never Stop Praying!"

348. *"the best of prayers, offered…"* Ryken, *Jeremiah & Lamentations*, 254.

350. *"Man's religions are his…"* Thomas, *God Delivers*, 135.

350. *"There is 'a mixture…"* Henry, *Commentary*, 4:514.

351. *"Not only will a remnant…"* John Calvin, *Commentaries on the Book of the Prophet Jeremiah and the Lamentations*, in vol. 9 of 22 vol. reprint of Calvin Translation Society edition (Grand Rapids, MI: Baker, 1979), 2:332.

351. *"Calvin convincingly argues that…"* Ibid., 2:333.

352. *"Many years have now…"* Ibid., 2:368.

353. *"'Here are three characteristics…"* Theodore Laetsch, *Jeremiah* (St. Louis, MO: Concordia, 1965), 165–6.

354. *"Return now every one…"* Paul defends God's sovereignty in salvation with the same parable in Romans 9:21 (see also Gen. 3:19: Isa. 29:16).

355. *"Prophet to know that…"* Jesus rebukes James and John for asking to call down fire from heaven on certain folk: "You do not know what manner of spirit you are of" (Luke 9:54–55).

356. *"A most tender-hearted and pious…"* Simeon, *Expository Sermon Outlines*, 9:162.

358. *"You will eat bye and bye…"* *The Little Red Songbook*, 4th ed. (1911).

360. *"After forty years of rejection…"* Henry, *Commentary*, 4:656.

361. *"We should never be afraid…"* John Calvin, *Commentaries on Jeremiah*, 4:484.

361. *"Had there been a grain of faith…"* Ibid., 4:491.

362. *"It consists of five laments…"* This event foreshadows the destruction of Jerusalem in AD 70, and so reminds us of Jesus's lament for Jerusalem in Matthew 23:37–39.

362. *"almost as if the covenant…"* Richard Brooks, *Great is Your Faithfulness* (Darlington, UK: Evangelical Press, 1989), 11.

362. *"was thus induced to speak…"* Calvin, *Commentaries on Jeremiah*, 5:300.

364. *"Prayer of the grief stricken…"* Walter C. Kaiser, *Grief & Pain in the Plan of God* (Fearn, UK: Christian Focus, 2004), 74.

364. *"Our best remedy then…"* Calvin, *Commentaries on Jeremiah*, 5:376.

JULY

366. *"But then he turns to prayer…"* Henry, *Commentary*, 4:735.

366. *"The first thing to notice…"* Simeon, *Expository Sermon Outlines*, 9:337.

370. *"Ezekiel is perhaps…"* Ibid., 9:343. Note that "terrific," referring to the content of the writing, means "terrifying"—not "great!" as in modern usage.

370. *"Ezekiel is serious…"* E. W. Hengstenberg, *Ezekiel* (Edinburgh: T & T Clark, 1869), 102.

372. *"This catastrophe therefore…"* Other occasions when the church's existence is on the line include the flood (Gen. 6–8), the golden calf (Ex. 32:10), Haman's attempted "final solution" of the Jews (Est. 3–9), and the scattering of Jesus's disciples at his crucifixion (Matt. 26:31).

372. *"Matthew Henry comments..."* Henry, *Commentary,* 4:375.

373. *"No-one can speak to..."* R. Clements, *Practising Faith in a Pagan World* (Downers Grove, IL: IVP, 1997), 47.

374. *"The intensity of God's..."* Derek Thomas observes that "God's greatest judgement is to leave people to the consequences of their sin," and solemnly notes, "When God departs, hell begins" (*God Strengthens: Ezekiel Simply Explained* [Darlington, UK: Evangelical Press, 1993], 81). Tell God long enough that you don't want him in your life and you may discover one day — to your eternal sorrow — that he has answered your prayers! (See Isaiah 65:1–7.)

379. *"He had no 'martyr..."* The proper definition of a "martyr" is simply a "witness" who suffers injustice. The suicide bombers of our time are not martyrs — they are just plain murderers.

380. *"He is a deduction..."* A. W. Tozer, *The Pursuit of God* (Harrisburg, PA: Christian Publications, 1948), 49.

381. *"This is 'the sort..."* Stuart Olyott, *Dare to Stand Alone* (Darlington, UK: Evangelical Press, 1982), 122.

383. *"Stuart Olyott notes that..."* Ibid.

384. *"This angel is the..."* Ibid., 132.

384. *"What follows is an..."* See Ephesians 1:16–21.

385. *"The Lord has our future..."* See 1 John 4:18.

385. *"Where else, but in..."* Olyott, *Dare to Stand Alone,* 139.

388. *"One man 'falsely shouting..."* Justice Oliver Wendell Holmes Jr. used this as an illustration of a US Supreme Court decision in 1919 (*Schenk v. United States*), in asserting that the defendant's speech opposing the draft in the Great War was not protected free speech under the US Constitution.

388. *"In Deuteronomy, notes Anthony..."* Anthony Selvaggio, *The Prophets Speak of Him* (Darlington, UK: Evangelical Press, 2006), 30.

389. *"For the day of the..."* John Calvin, *The Twelve Minor Prophets* (Grand Rapids, MI: Baker, 1979), 2:36.

389. *"It is holiness..."* James Phillip, *The Glory of the Cross* (Peabody, MA: Hendriksen Publishers LLC, 2016), 32.

390. *"This illustrates the wider truth..."* G. Crossley, *The Old Testament Explained and Applied* (Darlington, UK: Evangelical Press, 2002), 647.

390. *"The overarching vision..."* Laetsch, *The Minor Prophets* (St. Louis, MO: Concordia, 1956), 135.

392. *"When will we ever learn..."* Herman Veldkamp, *Farmer from Tekoa: On the Book of Amos* (St. Catharines, ON: Paideia, 1977), 201.

393. *"Our only resort must..."* Stanza 3 from "Rock of Ages" by A. M. Toplady (1740–78).

393. *"Charles Simeon asks any..."* Simeon, *Expository Sermon Outlines,* 10:234.

394. *"Called by God to..."* Capital of the Neo-Assyrian Empire, the eighth century BC superpower.

394. *"It is by his grace..."* The motto of my alma mater the University of Aberdeen since 1495 — *initium sapientiae timor domini* — is now comprehensively dismissed in the life of that institution.

395. *"Beware of mistaking…"* Sinclair B. Ferguson, *Man Overboard!* (London and Glasgow: Pickering & Inglis, 1981), 29–30.

396. *"Jonah is given what…"* Thomas Goodwin, *The Object and Acts of Justifying Faith* (Marshallton, DE: N.F.C.E., 1958), in *Goodwin's Works,* 8:260.

398. *"The prophet gets to…"* At 2.7 square miles (1,730 acres) and with approximately 120,000 little children (Jonah 3:3, 4:11), Nineveh was the largest city in the world at its height.

398. *"The people of Nineveh…"* Nineveh was destroyed some 160+ years later, in 612 BC, in fulfillment of the prophecy of Nahum. All traces of it vanished until rediscovered in 1847 by British archaeologist Austin Layard. Mosul (in modern Iraq) developed much later and now encroaches somewhat on the site.

400. *"The first is anger…"* Around 60 years later (in 723 BC), they would destroy the northern kingdom of Israel (cf. 2 Kings 18:29–35, 19:21–28).

400. *"The second thread is…"* Some 180 years later (in 612 BC), Assyria would be destroyed, according to God's judgment as proclaimed by the prophet Nahum. You remember how President Reagan called the USSR the "evil empire" of the twentieth century.

400. *"His thrice-repeated death wish…"* Ferguson, *Man Overboard!,* 88–9.

402. *"The prophet is moved by…"* G. C. M. Douglas, *The Six Intermediate Minor Prophets* (Edinburgh: T&T Clark: nd), 113.

403. *"He goes rather to the…"* See John Currid's crystal clear treatment of the New Testament use of Habakkuk 2:4 in *The Expectant Prophet: Habakkuk Simply Explained* (Darlington, UK: Evangelical Press009), 81–4.

404. *"The great Reformer of Geneva…"* Calvin, *Commentaries* (Grand Rapids, MI: Baker, 1979), 15:132–3.

406. *"The last six prayers…"* Lockyer, *All the Prayers of the Bible,* 167.

407. *"His, like the sun…"* John Owen, *Works* (1850–3; repr., London: Banner of Truth, 1966), 2:29–30.

407. *"This love of God…"* Michael P. V. Barrett, *The Next to Last Word* (Grand Rapids, MI: Reformation Heritage Books, 2015), 216.

407. *"Thomas Manton observes that…"* Thomas Manton, *The Complete Works* (Worthington, PA: Maranatha, 1975), 4:468.

407. *"To be loved by God…"* Ibid.

408. *"God is not fooled by…"* Henry, *Commentary* (on Jer. 17:1), 4:517.

409. *"Like Judah, much of…"* John Benton, *Losing Touch with the Living God* (Darlington, UK: Evangelical Press, 1985), 33.

409. *"Charles Simeon reminds us…"* Simeon, *Expository Sermon Outlines,* 10:591.

410. *"This rests on God's absolute…"* *Shorter Catechism 7:* What are the decrees of God?

410. *"Malachi's audience takes…"* Benton, *Losing Touch,* 89.

410. *"This resulted in…"* T. V. Moore, *Haggai & Malachi* (1856; repr., London: Banner of Truth, 1960), 142.

411. *"A true knowledge of God…"* See Psalm 73 for how the psalmist Asaph wrestles with adverse providences.

413. *"In what Matthew Henry…"* Henry, *Commentary,* 4:1495.

413. *"Matthew Poole rightly assesses..."* Poole, *A Commentary*, 2:1026.

414. *"From the old testament..."* Selvaggio, *The Prophets Speak of Him*, 183.

414. *"A 'tithe' is simply..."* See Moore, *Haggai & Malachi*, p. 159, for a list of the various tithes.

414. *"How seriously tithing is..."* churchm.ag/giving-statistics-every-church-should-know.

415. *"T. V. Moore points out..."* Moore, *Haggai & Malachi*, 162.

415. *"A historian researching..."* Quoted by J. Benton, *Losing Touch with the Living God*, 104.

415. *"In true, biblical, living..."* Barrett, *The Next to Last Word*, 225.

416. *"The six prayers in..."* Ibid.

417. *"As Calvin observes..."* Calvin, *Commentaries*, 15:598.

417. *"Baxter pointedly reminds us..."* Richard Baxter, *Sermon XI* (on 2 Cor. 2:7), in Samuel Annesley (ed.) *Puritan Sermons 1659–1689* (1682; repr., Wheaton, IL: Richard Owen Roberts Publishers, 1981), 3:254.

419. *"We should, in a sense..."* Martyn Lloyd-Jones, *Studies on the Sermon on the Mount* (Grand Rapids, MI: Eerdmans, 1971), 1:228.

420. *"These fellows are great..."* Manton, *Works*, 1:4.

420. *"Martyn Lloyd Jones notes..."* Lloyd-Jones, *Sermon on the Mount*, 2:23.

421. *"We may not pray..."* Manton, *Works*, 1:5.

422. *"The Lord's prayer is..."* See also Jesus in Gethsemane (John 17).

422. *"For yours is the kingdom..."* The *Textus Receptus* behind KJV/NKJV includes this in verse 13, whereas the "Critical" Nestle text underlying many modern translations omits it as a late gloss inserted in certain older manuscripts.

424. *"Every man—the greatest sinner..."* John Brown, *Discourses and Sayings of Our Lord*, 1:240.

424. *"Furthermore, every believer..."* *Abba* is not a child's "Daddy" as opposed to a more adult "Father." It is simply the Aramaic equivalent of the Greek *pater.* Paul is saying that the believer in Jesus, whether Jew or Gentile, is an adopted child of God and so knows God as his heavenly Father both intimately and personally.

425. *"Be not rash with..."* Fisher's Catechism, 2:172, Q. 23.

427. *"Fisher's Catechism asks..."* Ibid., 2:174, Q. 20.

AUGUST

429. *"Thy Kingdom come..."* Leighton Hayne, 1836–83, "Thy Kingdom Come, O God!", stanza 1.

430. *"Judas was a great..."* Thomas Watson, *The Lord's Prayer* (Carlisle, PA: Banner of Truth, 1993), 152.

431. *"We judge not the health..."* Ibid., 153.

432. *"God also feeds believers..."* Ibid., 197.

433. *"Though the bread is..."* Ibid., 200.

435. *"He is simply saying..."* David Brown, *The Four Gospels*, 41.

437. *"He lays the train..."* Thomas Watson, *A Body of Practical Divinity* (Glasgow: John Johnston, 1797), 551.

438. *"In brief, being conscious…"* John Calvin, *Commentary on a Harmony of the Evangelists, Matthew, Mark, and Luke,* in vol. 16 of 22 vol. reprint of Calvin Translation Society edition (Grand Rapids, MI: Baker, 1979), 1:327.

443. *"He submitted himself…"* Simeon, *Expository Sermon Outlines,* 12:6.

444. *"'He believed,' comments…"* Ibid., 12:355.

447. *"This is the reaction of…"* John Legg, *The King and His Kingdom* (Faverdale, UK: Evangelical Press, 2004), 160.

449. *"Every man must…"* Simeon, *Expository Sermon Outlines,* 12:380.

451. *"Be of good cheer…"* Octavius Winslow, *Evening Thoughts* (Grand Rapids, MI: Reformation Heritage Books, 2005), 148–9.

454. *"Together with Jesus's further…"* John Legg, *The King and His Kingdom,* 175.

459. *"The meaning therefore is…"* Calvin, *Harmony,* 2:40.

460. *"It moves Him who…"* Ryle, *Expository Thoughts on Mark,* 123.

461. *"On this occasion, he…"* Henry, *Commentary,* 5:202.

462. *"In reality, it is…"* R. Kent Hughes, *Mark: Jesus, Servant and Savior* (Wheaton, IL: Crossway, 1989), 1:173.

463. *"to congregations wide, devotions…"* From Robert Burns's poem, "The Cotter's Saturday Night."

463. *"Kent Hughes rightly calls…"* Hughes, *Mark,* 172.

464. *"Where three are there…"* As quoted by Herbert Lockyer (no source provided) in his book, *All the Prayers of the Bible,* 200.

464. *"It is rather the…"* Simeon, *Expository Sermon Outlines,* 11:478.

465. *"This means coming to…"* Ibid.

468. *"J. C. Ryle writes…"* Ryle, *Expository Thoughts on the Gospels: Luke,* 1:195.

468. *"The words ever again…"* εἰς τὸν αἰῶνα

469. *"It is not a promise…"* J. M. Boice, *The Gospel of Matthew,* 453.

470. *"how powerfully a foolish…"* John Calvin, *Harmony,* 3:82.

471. *"Our Lord's judgement…"* Hughes, *Mark,* 2:126.

471. *"But they are…"* Ryle, *Expository Thoughts on the Gospels: Luke,* 1:195.

471. *"Those who are near to God…"* *Free Church Witness,* 2003.

472. *"In the story, they…"* The "talents" are neither spiritual gifts nor personal abilities. See my exposition of the parable in Gordon J. Keddie, *He Spoke in Parables* (Faverdale, UK: Evangelical Press, 1994), 237–47.

474. *"Calvin notes that this…"* Calvin, *Harmony,* 3:227.

475. *"Also, uniquely, Jesus…"* Ibid., 3:229.

476. *"Gilded tombs do worms…"* W. Shakespeare, *The Merchant of Venice,* act 2, scene 7, lines 1054, 1058.

476. *"Their logic is as follows…"* This is an example (no kidding!) of the "No true Scotsman" logical fallacy, which goes as follows: Angus puts sugar on his porridge; no (true) Scotsman puts sugar on his porridge; therefore Angus is not a (true) Scotsman. Therefore, Angus is not a counter-example to the claim that no Scotsman puts sugar on his porridge. By this fallacious reasoning, Jesus dying on a cross cannot be used as a counter-example to the claim that no Messiah could die as a criminal.

478. *"But you, when you..."* See the readings for July 28–August 6.

478. *"Such public show and..."* See August 28 for the application to intercessory prayer in Mark 14:37.

478. *"Matthew Henry aptly observes..."* Henry, *Commentary,* 5:491.

479. *"A good man is never..."* Ibid.

479. *He is praying with us..."* Ibid.

480. *"It is, says William Jay..."* Jay, *Morning and Evening,* 2:305.

480. *"Notice the four components..."* I can do no better than follow the outline of William Jay (1769–1853), the great English Congregationalist preacher who ministered at Argyle Chapel in Bath for sixty years.

482. *"The genuine, though perfect..."* James W. Alexander, *Consolation* (New York: Charles Scribner, 1853), 247.

482. *"He filled the silent..."* Robert Traill, *Works* (1810; repr., London: Banner of Truth, 1975), 2:11.

484. *"Jesus is saying something..."* These are found in Luke 23:34; 23:43; John 19:26; Mark 15:34; John 19:28; 1930; and Luke 23:46.

484. *"He already knows the answer..."* From "There Is a Green Hill Far Away," by Cecil Frances Alexander (1847), stanza 3.

486. *"John Calvin notes that..."* Calvin, *Harmony,* 1:203.

487. *"Matthew Henry aptly observes..."* Henry, *Commentary,* 5:617.

489. *"Matthew Henry observes..."* Matthew Henry, commenting on Mark 1:35.

489. *"Can it be said of you..."* James W. and Joel R. Beeke, *Developing a Healthy Prayer Life* (Grand Rapids, MI: Reformation Heritage Books, 2010), 12.

September

491. *"Here he gives us..."* Matthew Henry, commenting on Luke 6:16.

495. *"And in the..."* Ryle, *Expository Thoughts on the Gospels: Mark,* 174.

496. *"Prayer is a sincere..."* John Bunyan, *Prayer* (1662; repr., London: Banner of Truth Trust, 1965), 13.

497. *"In response, Jesus gives..."* For the first time, see Matthew 6:5–13 and the meditations earlier in this volume (July 31–August 9).

504. *"The story of the rich..."* Ryle, *Expository Thoughts on the Gospels: Luke,* 2:212.

504. *"In this incomparable piece..."* Trace back through Jesus's teaching in his previous parables in Luke: 16:13; 15:32; 15:10; 14:33.

506. *"William Jay, the great..."* Jay, *Morning and Evening,* 2:26.

508. *"Help meets men in..."* Ryle, *Expository Thoughts on the Gospels: Luke,* 2:233.

509. *"The best of us..."* Ibid., 234.

511. *"The coldness of love..."* Augustine, commenting on Psalm 37:10.

512. *"It is the family disease..."* Ryle, *Expository Thoughts on the Gospels: Luke,* 2:259.

512. *"But Lord, remember me..."* Robert Burns, "Holy Willie's Prayer," in *Poems and Songs of Robert Burns,* James Barke ed. (Glasgow: Collins, 1969), 222–5.

513. *"God be merciful to..."* The Greek has the definite article.

513. *"Many are welcome to..."* Manton, *Works,* 22:59.

514. *"His sense of wretchedness…"* Ryle, *Expository Thoughts on the Gospels: Luke*, 2:285.

517. *"Bishop Ryle observes that…"* Ryle, *Expository Thoughts on the Gospels: Luke*, 2:411.

518. *"One would think…"* Henry, *Commentary*, 5:826.

522. *"'These verses,' says…"* Ryle, *Expository Thoughts on the Gospels: Luke*, 2:470.

522. *"Here is where the…"* But not the work of the Holy Spirit in salvation, which is to regenerate our nature so that we do experience being converted to Christ.

523. *"Charles Simeon comments that…"* Simeon, *Expository Sermon Outlines*, 13:150.

524. *"It is finished…"* Henry, 5:830.

525. *"It was not in reference…"* Calvin, *Harmony*, 3:322.

527. *"The Puritan, Samuel Willard…"* Samuel Willard, *A Compleat Body of Divinity*, Sermon 110, July 6, 1697.

529. *"charge him with arrogance…"* John Calvin, *Commentary on John*, in vol. 17 of 22 vol. reprint of Calvin Translation society edition (Grand Rapids, MI: Baker, 1979), 1:150.

531. *"George Hutcheson notes that…"* George Hutcheson, *An Exposition of the Gospel According to John* (Grand Rapids, MI: Sovereign Grace Publishers, 1971), 235.

533. *"In other words, we…"* Manton, *Works*, 21:12.

534. *"Furthermore, 'this prayer was…"* Charles Ross, *The Inner Sanctuary: An Exposition of John 13–17* (London: Banner of Truth Trust, 1967), 201.

535. *"D. A. Carson notes that…"* D. A. Carson, *The Gospel According to John* (Leicester, UK: Apollos, 1991), 555.

539. *"'Dear brethren,' Charles Simeon…"* Simeon, *Expository Sermon Outlines*, 14:120.

541. *"God therefore distinguishes them…"* Calvin, *Commentary on John*, 2:170.

542. *"All men were not…"* Manton, *Exposition of John 17*, 146.

544. *"He asks his 'Holy Father…"* "Holy Father" occurs this once in Scripture, and, of course, refers to the Fatherhood of God. It is routinely and entirely inappropriately used as a title of the Pope of Rome.

544. *"Jesus had hitherto preserved…"* The term "son of perdition" is used in 2 Thessalonians 2:3, where it applies to the "man of sin" who is to be revealed at the end of the present age.

545. *"Our separation from the world…"* Hutcheson, *Exposition of John*, 36.

546. *"Thomas Manton notes that…"* Manton, *Exposition of John 17*, 290.

548. *"The eye of Jesus…"* William Hendriksen, *Commentary on John* (London: Banner of Truth, 1964), 2:363.

548. *"This is a 'supernatural…"* Bruce Milne, *The Message of John* (Leicester, UK: InterVarsity Press, 1993).

OCTOBER

550. *"God is Christ's father…"* Manton, *Exposition of John 17*, 403.

551. *"with himself,' says Manton…"* Ibid., 411.

551. *"We go to heaven..."* Ibid., 418.

553. *"We are loved into..."* Ibid., 444.

553. *"The Lord delighteth not..."* Ibid., 448 (see Rom. 8:35).

558. *"The key word here..."* The first undisputed usage of *ecclesia* in Acts is foundf in 5:11. Since it only appears in the *Textus Receptus*/Western variant of the Greek texts in Acts 2:47, many scholars regard it as a scribal gloss, added to make the (obvious) meaning clearer.

558. *"These are received and..."* Westminster Confession of Faith, 21:5.

558. *"The 'sound preaching and..."* Ibid.

558. *"wherever you saw one..."* Henry, *Commentary,* 6:28.

563. *"Their 'lives were in..."* Lockyer, *All the Prayers,* 231.

564. *"John Stott comments..."* John Stott, *The Spirit, the Church and the World* (Downers Grove, IL: InterVarsity Press, 1990), 120.

569. *"not being pious at all..."* James Montgomery Boice, *Acts* (Grand Rapids, MI: Baker, 1997), 138.

565. *"They had no liberty..."* Ibid., 121.

570. *"The saddest road to..."* Brownlow North, *A Great Gulf Fixed: Sermons on the Rich Man and Lazarus* (London: Banner of Truth Trust, 1999), 124.

577. *"William Jay, the great..."* Jay, *Morning and Evening,* 2:330.

590. *"There must be fellowship..."* Martin Luther, *Romans* (Grand Rapids, MI: Zondervan, 1954), 22.

594. *"Paul was abused, reviled..."* Robert Haldane, *An Exposition of the Epistle to the Romans* (Lakeland, FL: MacDonald Publishing Company, nd), 500.

597. *"To say a prayer..."* Thomas Watson, *Heaven Taken by Storm* (1669; repr., Morgan, PA: Soli Deo Gloria, 1997), 20.

598. *"Wordy prayers are usually..."* A. W. Pink, *Gleanings from Paul* (Edinburgh: Banner of Truth, 2006), 7.

600. *"A. W. Pink suggests we..."* Ibid., 37.

605. *"It was eternally in..."* Stuart Olyott, *The Gospel as It Really Is* (Darlington, UK: Evangelical Press: 1979), 163.

605. *"It is through Jesus Christ..."* Haldane, *Romans,* 652.

605. *"Minister are ambassadors..."* Henry, Commentary, 6:503.

609. *"At times our prayers..."* Henry, *Commentary,* 6:579.

609. *"Public worship,' says Matthew Henry..."* Ibid.

610. *"It is 'the victory..."* Charles Hodge, *1 Corinthians* (1857; repr., London: Banner of Truth, 1958).

November

616. *"This benediction 'plainly proves..."* Henry, *Commentary,* 6:646.

616. *"In his dealings with..."* James Ussher, *A Body of Divinity* (Birmingham, AL: Solid Ground, 2007), 77.

617. *"He concludes that 'we..."* Henry, *Commentary,* 6:647.

627. *"This is a work..."* Harry Upichard, *A Study Commentary on Ephesians* (Darlington, UK: Banner of Truth, 2004), 183.

628. *"It is the root..."* John Eadie, *Ephesians* (Edinburgh: T & T Clark, 1883), 257.

628. *"Love is a..."* Uprichard, *Ephesians*, 186.

629. *"You shall see greater..."* Paul Bayne, *Ephesians* (1618; repr., Edinburgh: James Nichol, 1866), 200.

630. *"Paul's prayer in Ephesians..."* Uprichard, *Ephesians*, 190.

633. *"John Eadie notes that..."* Eadie, *Ephesians*, 399.

634. *"This is why..."* Charles Hodge, *Ephesians* (New York: Robert Carter and Bros., 1878), 389–90.

636. *"Charles Hodge's rendering..."* Hodge, *Ephesians*, 391.

638. *"Consequently, John Eadie very..."* Eadie, *Ephesians*, 475.

638. *"It is divinely controlled..."* Uprichard, *Ephesians*, 373.

639. *"Positively, he says we..."* Bayne, *Ephesians*, 405.

641. *"So when we let..."* Ibid., 406.

643. *"If at any time..."* John Calvin, *Commentaries on the Epistle of Paul to the Galatians and Ephesians* (Edinburgh: Calvin Translation Society, 1854), 341.

644. *"All You Need Is Love..."* The title of the Beatles's 1965 hit song by John Lennon and Paul McCartney.

645. *"The more we set..."* Pink, *Gleanings from Paul*, 281.

645. *"Arthur W. Pink is correct..."* Ibid., 287.

646. *"A farmer only keeps..."* Michael Bentley, *Shining in the Darkness* (Darlington, UK: Evangelical Press, 1997), 35.

646. *"Jean Daillé has written..."* Jean Daillé, *Philippians* (Lakeland, FL: Tyndale Bible Society, nd), 26.

647. *"Christ is now to us..."* Henry, *Commentary*, 1:16 (See also 6:1125, 1186ff.)

649. *"one of the blesses results..."* Lockyer, *All the Prayers of the Bible*, 251.

650. *"Apart from this faith..."* Kent Hughes, *Colossians* (Westchester, IL: Crossway, 1989), 17.

653. *"These are also the..."* *Shorter Catechism* 35.

654. *"You, Christian, need strengthening..."* Pink, *Gleanings from Paul*, 336.

657. *"a summary of the doctrine..."* Henry, *Commentary*, 6:752.

666. *"My grandfather was a..."* James Dunn Keddie (1877–1950) was not finished with adventures after the Gold Rush. In 1917, as a private in the Royal Scots, he went "over the top" at the Third Battle of Arras. At some point he was wounded and captured by the Germans. He spent the rest of the Great War in a POW camp. He lived to take me, in the last year of his life, on a memorable walk along the Union Canal in Edinburgh—the only concrete memory I have of "Grandpa Keddie."

666. *"The end of 1 Thessalonians..."* Lockyer, *All the Prayers*, 255.

666. *"the meaning is not..."* Henry, *Commentary*, 6:790.

667. *"Prayer is the Christian's..."* James Montgomery (1771–1854) in his famous poem "What Is Prayer?"

668. *"As we have already seen..."* Lockyer, *All the Prayers*, 255.

DECEMBER

672. *"What 'distinguishes* Christians *from..."* Pink, *Gleanings from Paul*, 426.

674. *"We are to get..."* Leon Morris, *1 & 2 Thessalonians* (Grand Rapids, MI: Eerdmans, 1959), 250.
675. *"However lofty our words..."* Pink, *Gleanings from Paul,* 447.
675. *"We may feed on it..."* Ibid., 453–4.
676. *"whatever* title *we have..."* Ibid., 460.
677. *"It is that love..."* Ibid., 468.
678. *"Many of our petitions..."* Ibid., 474.
684. *"This expression is also..."* See J. N. D. Kelly, *A Commentary of the Pastoral Epistles* (Grand Rapids, MI: Baker, 1963), 65.
689. *"We will never know..."* Lockyer, *All the Prayers,* 258.
691. *"But notice his personal..."* Gary W. Demarest, *The Communicator's Commentary: 1, 2 Thessalonians; 1, 2 Timothy; Titus* (Waco, TX: Word Books, 1984), 241.
692. *"A. A. Bonar rightly calls..."* Bonar, *Christ and His Church*, 136.
693. *"Don't* wait *until someone..."* Andrew A. Bonar, "Onesiphorus: the New Testament Ebedmelech," a sermon transcribed from Marjory Bonar, *Reminiscences of Andrew A. Bonar D. D.* (London: Hodder & Stoughton, 1895) by Jane Newble, available online at bible.prayerrequest.com/4765-anthology-of-3000-classic-sermons/213.
697. *"way of existing grace..."* John Owen, *Works,* 20:432.
705. *"The Lord Christ is..."* J. Phillip Arthur, *No Turning Back: An Exposition of the Epistle to the Hebrews* (London: Grace Publications, 2003), 234.
706. *"Would it not be better..."* Earl Kelly, *James: A Primer for Christian Living* (Nutley, NJ: Craig Press, 1969), 233.
711. *"In that verse, the Lord says..."* Manton, *Works,* 4:465.
713. *"Death,' says Robert Leighton..."* Robert Leighton, *First Peter* (Grand Rapids, MI: Kregel, 1972), 31.
715. *"Nevertheless, he added..."* Ibid., 411.
719. *"The seventeenth-century Scottish preacher..."* Maurice Grant, *Preacher to the Remnant* (Edinburgh: Blue Banner Productions, 2009), 130.
721. *"Prayer will soothe you..."* Octavius Winslow, *Midnight Harmonies* (New York: Robert Carter, 1853).
725. *"'As for me..."* Samuel Rutherford, *Religious Letters* (London: Religious Tract Society, nd), 383–4.